D0430576

Kenya

a Lonely Planet travel survival kit

**Hugh Finlay
Geoff Crowther**

Kenya

3rd edition

Published by
Lonely Planet Publications
Head Office: PO Box 617, Hawthorn, Vic 3122, Australia
Branches: 150 Linden St, Oakland, CA 94607, USA
               10a Spring Place, London NW5 3BH, UK
               71 bis rue du Cardinal Lemoine, 75005 Paris, France

Printed by
Colorcraft Ltd, Hong Kong

Photographs by

Geoff Crowther	Dawn Delaney	Greg Elms
David Else	Hugh Finlay	Greg Herriman
Roger Jones	Mark Savage	Debra Tan
David Wall	Tony Wheeler	

Front Cover: Lake Nakuru's spectacular flamingos (David Wall)
Safari Guide title page: David Wall
Tribal Groups & Cultures title graphic: Steve Barnes

First Published
February 1991

This Edition
April 1997

**Although the authors and publisher have tried to make the information as
accurate as possible, they accept no responsibility for any loss, injury or
inconvenience sustained by any person using this book.**

National Library of Australia Cataloguing-in-Publication Data

Crowther, Geoff, 1944-
Kenya.

3rd ed.
Includes index.
ISBN 0 86442 460 4.

1. Kenya – Guidebooks. I. Finlay, Hugh. II. Finlay, Hugh. Kenya,
travel survival kit. III. Title. IV. Title: Kenya, travel survival kit.
(Series: Lonely Planet travel survival kit).

916.762044

text © Hugh Finlay (as trustee for Araluen Trust) 1997
maps © Lonely Planet 1997
photos © photographers as indicated 1997

All rights reserved. No part of this publication may be reproduced, stored in a retrieval system or transmitted
in any form by any means, electronic, mechanical, photocopying, recording or otherwise, except brief extracts
for the purpose of review, without the written permission of the publisher and copyright owner.

Hugh Finlay

After deciding there must be more to life than civil engineering, Hugh took off around Australia in the mid-70s, working at everything from spray painting to diamond prospecting, before hitting the overland trail. He joined Lonely Planet in 1985 and has written *Jordan & Syria*, co-authored *Morocco, Algeria & Tunisia* and *Nepal* and has contributed to other LP guides including *Africa*, *India* and *Australia*. He lives in central Victoria, Australia, with his partner Linda and his daughters Ella and Vera.

Geoff Crowther

Born in Yorkshire, England, Geoff took to his heels early on in search of the miraculous, taking a break from a degree in biochemistry. The lure of the unknown took him to Kabul, Kathmandu and Lamu in the days before the overland companies began digging up the dirt along the tracks of Africa.

In 1977, he wrote his first guide for Lonely Planet – *Africa on the cheap*. He has also written *South America on a shoestring*, and guides to *Korea, Taiwan* and *East Africa*, and has co-authored guides to *India, Malaysia, Singapore & Brunei* and *Morocco, Algeria & Tunisia*.

From the Authors As always, many people lent assistance in many ways. Among them Hugh would especially like to thank: Graeme Thomson, Phillip Jackson and Alistair Brown (Flight Centres), Malcolm Gascoigne (Yare Safaris), Hans-Peter Erismann, Rulan Desai (Kilimanjaro Safari Club), Ian Vincent (Kilimanjaro Buffalo Lodge), Jane & Julia Barnley (Sirikwa Safaris), Raj Shah (Naiberi River Camp Site) and Max Cheli (Tortilis Camp). Thanks also to fellow Lonely Planet author David Else for his assistance with trekking information.

In addition to many of the above, Geoff would also like to thank Alice Jane Njoki Chege, Kris Zachrisson (Tour Africa Safaris), 'Sonny' Pinto, Jim Shaner and Kim Baker.

This Book

Hugh Finlay and Geoff Crowther researched and wrote the first two editions. Hugh updated this edition, with assistance from Geoff.

From the Publisher

Cathy Lanigan edited this book with assistance from Miriam Cannell, Janet Austin, Liz Filleul, Chris Wyness, Lindsay Brown, Jane Rawson and Anne Mulvaney. Chris Klep was responsible for cartography and design. Thanks to Sally Gerdan for the initial layout and Indra Kilfoyle for miscellaneous bromiding and design work. Thanks also to Matt King for the Safari Guide illustrations. Other illustrations were provided by Margaret Jung, Valerie Tellini and Miriam Cannell. David Kemp designed the cover and Adam McCrow was responsible for the back cover cartography. Sharon Wertheim did the indexing.

Thanks

Thanks to the following travellers who found the time and energy to write us to us from all over the world with their suggestions and comments:

Kim Adam-Peters, Susan Arnason, Tom & Robin Baird, Magali Barre, Mark Benford, John Bennett, Paul Bennett, David Blanchard, Marie Louise Bole, Adrian Booth, J Breitweiser, Debbie Byrne, Rob Chatwin, Matt Chester, David Chianda, M Cooper, Bram Cordemans, Barrie Cosford, John & Elisabeth Cox, Greg & Mary-Lou Diete, Lucy Dixon, Janet Dott, David Dovalina, Annemeike Dreuth, W Ebbens, David Ellison, A M Epstein, Gareth Evans, Roland Evans, Neal Finch, Tom Finnegan, Patrick Finney, H Fung, Janet Gibb, Elias Goncalo, Joey Goodings, Albert Gopin, Joanne Grindlay, L A S Grumbley, Antonde Haan, Roger Harris, Zul Hasham, Erika Herrnsdorf, N Horner, Cissie Hultberg, Hennik Jensen, Andrew Joncus, John Kalaitzis, Sabine Knodlstorfer, Devi Krishnamoni, Tony Lam, Alison Lloyd, Wolfgang Loew, Yvonne van der Loo, Bernt Magnusson, Rachel Matut, Rhoda McKenzie, Theo Molenaar, John & Sallie Morris, Josh Morris, Bob Muirhead, Sylvia Nagel, James Njau, Michael Nkaduda, Nigel Odin, Paula Parke, Joseph Petrzilka, Werner Pfaff, Jeanine Phillips, Tracy Polowich, Stephen Potter, Wayne Rasmus, Tony & Gill Reeves, Dave Reid, Malcolm Reid, Nicolas Rigaudiere, C Robinson, Hugo Rodger-Brown, Steve Rourke, Robert Royal, William Rubel, Balwant Singh, Kasom Skultab, Jill Sockett, Jo Spackman, Rod Spackman, Michael Sullivan, Tina Suomalainen, P & S Sweeney, Gary Sze, George Taylor, Reto Toggwiler, Frances Valdes, D Versteeg, Tamsin Wade, Albert Peter Walsweer, Phil White, S Wilber, T L de Winne and Maria Witz.

Warning & Request

Things change – prices go up, schedules change, good places go bad and bad places go bankrupt – nothing stays the same. So, if you find things better or worse, recently opened or long since closed, please tell us and help make the next edition even more accurate and useful.

We value all of the feedback we receive from travellers. Julie Young coordinates a small team who read and acknowledge every letter, postcard and e-mail, and ensure that every morsel of information finds its way to the appropriate authors, editors and publishers.

Everyone who writes to us will find their name in the next edition of the appropriate guide and will also receive a free subscription to our quarterly newsletter, *Planet Talk*. The very best contributions will be rewarded with a free Lonely Planet guide.

Excerpts from your correspondence may appear in updates (which we add to the end pages of reprints); new editions of this guide; in our newsletter, *Planet Talk*; or the Postcards section of our Web site – so please let us know if you don't want your letter published or your name acknowledged.

Contents

Map Legend

BOUNDARIES

—·—·—·—·—·—·— .... International Boundary

—··—··—··—··— .... Regional Boundary

ROUTES

——————————— .... Freeway

——————————— .... Highway

——————————— .... Major Road

——————————— .... Minor Road

— — — — — — — .... Vehicle Track

——————————— .... City Road

——————————— .... City Street

+++++++++++++++++ .... Railway

▬▬▬▬▬▬▬ .... Tram

— — — — — — ·— .... Walking Track

•••••••••••••••••••••••• .... Walking Tour

— — — — — — — — .... Ferry Route

–H–H–H–H–H–H–H–H– .... Cable Car or Chairlift

AREA FEATURES

.... Parks

.... Built-Up Area

.... Pedestrian Mall

.... Market

+ + + + + + ... Cemetery

.... Reef

.... Beach or Desert

.... Rocks

HYDROGRAPHIC FEATURES

.... Coastline

.... River, Creek

.... Intermittent River or Creek

.... Rapids, Waterfalls

.... Lake, Intermittent Lake

.... Canal

.... Swamp

SYMBOLS

✪ CAPITAL	.... National Capital	
◉ Capital	.... Regional Capital	
🏙 CITY	.... Major City	
● City	.... City	
● Town	.... Town	
● Village	.... Village	
■ ▼	.... Place to Stay, Place to Eat	
⚲ ▯	.... Cafe, Pub or Bar	
✉ ☎	.... Post Office, Telephone	
❶ ❸	.... Tourist Information, Bank	
◔ Ⓟ	.... Transport, Parking	
🏛 ⌂	.... Museum, Youth Hostel	
⚏ Ⓧ	Caravan Park, Camping Ground	
⛪ ✚	.... Church, Cathedral	
☪ ✡	.... Mosque, Synagogue	
卐 ❶	.... Temple, Toilet	
✛ ★	.... Hospital, Police Station	

✈	⛽	.... Embassy, Petrol Station
✈	✚	.... Airport, Airfield
♿	✿	.... Bicycle Hire, Gardens
❖	🐘	.... Shopping Centre, Zoo
⚜	⌐	...Winery or Vineyard, Picnic Site
←	A25	One Way Street, Route Number
🏛	⚑	.... Stately Home, Monument
♜	▣	.... Castle, Tomb
⌒	⌂	.... Cave, Hut or Lodge
▲	🏞	.... Mountain or Hill, Lookout
⚱	⚓	.... Lighthouse, Shipwreck
)(	◎	.... Pass, Spring
🏊	⚡	.... Beach, Surf Beach
	∴	...... Archaeological Site or Ruins

▬■▬■▬■▬■▬ .... Ancient or City Wall

〰〰⟹ ⟸ .... Cliff or Escarpment, Tunnel

+++■■■+++ .... Railway Station

Note: not all symbols displayed above appear in this book

Introduction

In past centuries, the main visitors to Kenya were the Arab traders who plied their dhows along the eastern coast of Africa. These days it's tourists and adventurers who come to Kenya in large numbers – currently around one million annually – and little wonder as it has an amazing variety of attractions.

For many people Kenya means wildlife and in this field alone it is one of the best places in Africa. Millions of wildebeest on their annual migration, and equally large numbers of pink flamingos massing on the shores of the Rift Valley soda lakes are breathtaking sights. For sheer majesty it's hard to beat the sight of a herd of elephants crossing the plains with Africa's most famous mountain, the evocative snowcapped Kilimanjaro, rising in the background. Kenya is the heart of safari country and a trip

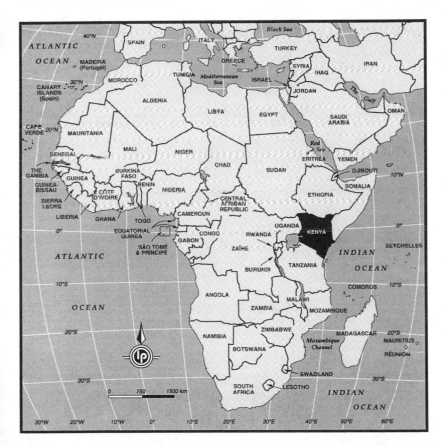

through a few of Kenya's spectacular reserves is a memorable experience.

If relaxation is on your mind then head for the coast. Mombasa is a town with a history, and from here any of the superb picture-postcard beaches are easily accessible. But without doubt the highlight of the coast is the island of Lamu, where the Arab influence is evident and the pace of life definitely a few steps behind the rest of the country – the perfect place to unwind for a week, or two...

Those people seeking more energetic pursuits will find no shortage of challenges – Kenya has some excellent mountains to climb, especially the popular Mt Kenya with its unusual alpine flora, and the much less visited Mt Elgon in the west on the Ugandan border. Organised camel treks through Kenya's semidesert north also attract a steady stream of hardy souls.

The heart of this relatively prosperous country is the bustling capital, Nairobi. It is a modern and efficient city where things work and business can be taken care of in a snap – a far cry from so many other African countries where even simple things like a telephone call can be a major exercise. Added to this is the fact that Kenya has excellent air connections with Europe, Asia and elsewhere in Africa, making it the ideal place for a short visit, or the starting or finishing point for a longer sojourn in Africa. Either way it's a great place – don't miss it.

Facts about the Country

HISTORY
The Birthplace of Humanity
Thanks to the Leakey family's now famous digs in Olduvai Gorge (Tanzania) and around Lake Turkana (Kenya), the Rift Valley which runs through the centre of Kenya has been established as the 'cradle of humanity'. The Leakeys' discoveries of several hominoid skulls, one of which is estimated to be 2½ million years old, have radically altered the accepted theories on the origin of humans.

Before the East African digs, the generally accepted theory was that the ancestors of modern humans were of two different species: ape-like *Australopithecus africanus* and *Australopithecus robustus*. It was believed that one of these species died out while the other gave rise to *Homo sapiens*. The Leakey discoveries suggested that there was a third contemporary species, *Homo habilis*, and that it was this one which gave rise to modern humans while both the Australopithecus species died out, leaving no descendants. The dust has yet to settle on this anthropological issue.

Early Settlement
This area of Africa has people from all over the country – Kenya is home to almost every major language in Africa. Even Khoisan, the 'click' language spoken by the Bushmen and Hottentots in southern Africa, has its representatives, although these days they are only a tiny community close to the Tana River near the coast. This diversity is clear evidence that Kenya has been a major migratory pathway over the centuries.

The first wave of immigrants were the tall, nomadic, Cushitic-speaking people from Ethiopia who began to move south around 2000 BC. They were pastoralists and depended on good grazing land for their cattle and goats, so when the climate began to change and the area around Lake Turkana became more arid, they were forced to resume their migration south. They got as far as central Tanzania.

A second group of pastoralists, the Eastern Cushitics, followed them in around 1000 BC and occupied much of central Kenya. The rest of the ancestors of the country's medley of tribes arrived from all over Africa between 500 BC and 500 AD, though there was still much movement and rivalry for land right up to the beginning of the 20th century. Even today it hasn't ended completely: the Bantu-speaking people (such as the Gusii, Kikuyu, Akamba and Meru) arrived from West Africa, while the Nilotic speakers (such as the Maasai, Luo, Samburu and Turkana) came from the Nile Valley in southern Sudan.

Arab & Persian Traders
While migrations were going on in the interior, Muslims from the Arabian peninsula and Shirazis from Persia (now Iran) began to visit the East African coast from the 8th century AD onwards. They came to trade, convert and settle, rather than conquer as they had done in North Africa and Spain. Their dhows would head down on the northeast monsoon bringing glassware, ironware, textiles, wheat and wine, and return with ivory, slaves, tortoiseshell and rhino horn.

This trade soon extended right across the Indian Ocean to India and beyond. (Even China entered the fray at one point early in the 15th century, with a fleet of 62 ships and an escort of some 37,000 men, after the king of Malindi had sent the Chinese emperor a gift of a giraffe!) Many of the traders stayed to settle and intermarry with the Africans. As a result, a string of relatively affluent and Islamic-influenced coastal towns sprang up along the East African coast from Somalia to Mozambique, acting as entrepôts for the cross-Indian Ocean trade. Though there was naturally rivalry between these towns from time to time, up until the 16th century life was relatively peaceful. All this was to be rudely shattered with the arrival of the Portuguese.

Portuguese Invaders

While the Spanish Crown was busy backing expeditions to the Americas, the Portuguese were determined to break the Ottoman Turks' grip on trade with the Far East, particularly the trade in spices – worth more than their weight in gold in Europe. Throughout the 15th century, the Portuguese had been exploring further and further down the western coast of Africa until, in 1498, they finally rounded the Cape of Good Hope and headed up the east coast under the command of Vasco da Gama.

They were given a hostile reception both at Sofala on the Mozambique coast and at Mombasa, but were lucky to find a friendly sultan at Malindi who provided them with a pilot who knew the route to India. Da Gama was back again with another expedition in 1502, after selling the first expedition's cargo of spices in Portugal and reaping a small fortune.

The main Portuguese onslaught began with Dom Francisco de Almeida's armada of 23 ships and some 1500 men in 1505. Sofala was looted and burned to the ground, Kilwa was occupied and garrisoned, and Mombasa was taken after a naval bombardment and fierce street fighting. Mombasa was sacked again by Nuña da Cunha in 1528. Despite attempts by the Ottoman Turks to wrest control back from the Portuguese in 1585 and 1589, the Arab monopoly of Indian Ocean trade had been broken.

After the original onslaught, there followed two centuries of harsh colonial rule. Tribute was demanded and levies were imposed on all non-Portuguese ships visiting the coastal towns. Severe retribution was the punishment for the slightest offence. Economic exploitation came hand in hand with a drive to convert the local population to Catholicism, but the Portuguese never had much success at this, and whenever an outpost was abandoned, those who had been 'converted' reverted to Islam. Mombasa came to be the principle Portuguese outpost following the construction of Fort Jesus there in 1593.

The Portuguese made their task easier by playing one sultan off against another, but their grip over the East African coast was always tenuous as their outposts had to be supplied from Goa in India, where the viceroy had his headquarters. Delays were inevitable. The colonial bureaucracy also became moribund because offices were sold to the highest bidder. And, in the final analysis, Portugal was too small a country and lacked sufficient resources to effectively hold on to a worldwide empire.

The beginning of the end came in 1698 when Fort Jesus fell to the Arabs after a siege lasting 33 months. By 1720, the Portuguese had packed up and left the Kenyan coast for good.

Omani Dynasties

The Arabs remained in control of the East African coast until the arrival of the British and Germans in the late 19th century. The depredations of the Portuguese period, however, had exacted a heavy price and the constant quarrelling among the Arab governors who succeeded them led to a decline in the trade and prosperity which the East African coast had once enjoyed. Political and economic recovery had to wait until the beginning of the 19th century.

Throughout the 18th century, Omani dynasties from the Persian Gulf entrenched themselves along the East African coast. They were nominally under the control of the Sultan of Oman, but this control was largely ineffective until Seyyid Said came to the Omani throne in 1805.

The Omanis had built up a relatively powerful navy during the latter part of the 18th century, and Seyyid Said used it to bring the East African dynasties into line. In 1822 he sent an army to subdue Mombasa, Paté and Pemba, which were then ruled by the Mazrui clan.

The Mazruis appealed to Britain for help, which it provided the following year in the form of two warships on a survey mission. The commander of one of these ships, Captain Owen, decided to act first and ask questions later, so the British flag was raised over Fort Jesus and a protectorate was declared. A small garrison was left in charge, but three years later the British government repudiated the protectorate and the flag was hauled down. Seyyid Said reasserted his control the following year, garrisoned Fort Jesus and began to lay out clove plantations on Zanzibar. In 1832 he moved his court to Zanzibar.

19th Century Colonialism

By the mid-19th century, several European nations were showing an interest in the East African coast, including the British and the Germans. The British were interested in the suppression of the slave trade, and when Seyyid Said moved to Zanzibar they set up a consulate on the island. Later an agreement was reached between the British and the Germans as to their spheres of interest in East Africa. Part of the deal was that the Sultan of Zanzibar would be allowed to retain a 16-km-wide strip of the Kenyan coastline under a British protectorate. The agreement remained in place right up until independence, when the last Sultan of Zanzibar, Seyyid Khalifa, ceded the territory to the new government.

The Kenyan interior, particularly the Rift Valley and the Aberdare highlands, remained impregnable to outsiders until the 1880s because it was occupied by Maasai pastoralists. Their reputation as a proud warrior tribe had been sufficient to deter Arab slavers and traders and European missionaries and explorers up to that date. But with the rest of Africa being combed by European explorers, Kenya's turn was soon to follow.

Notable early explorers who lived to tell the tale were Gustav Fischer (a German whose party was virtually annihilated by Maasai at Hell's Gate on Lake Naivasha in 1882), Joseph Thomson (a Scot who reached Lake Victoria via the Rift Valley lakes and the Aberdares in 1883) and Count Teleki von Szek (an Austrian who explored the Lake Turkana region and Mt Kenya in 1887). James Hannington, an Anglican bishop who set out in 1885 to set up a diocese in Uganda, wasn't quite so fortunate. He discovered Lake Bogoria (known as Lake Hannington during colonial days) but was killed when he reached the Nile.

By the late 19th century, the Maasai were considerably weakened and their numbers reduced by years of civil war between two opposing factions, the Ilmaasai and the Iloikop. The dispute was about which of the two were the true descendants of Olmasinta, the legendary founder of the tribe. Rinderpest (a cattle disease), cholera, smallpox and famine had also taken their toll between 1880 and 1892. Because of this, the British were able to negotiate a treaty with Olonana (known as Lenana today), the *laibon* ('chief' or 'spiritual leader') of the Maasai. Armed with this treaty, the British were able to construct the Mombasa-Uganda railway through the heart of the Maasai grazing lands. The approximate halfway point of this railway is where Nairobi stands today.

White Settlement

With the railway completed and the headquarters of the colonial administration moved from Mombasa to Nairobi, white settlers began to move into the fertile highlands north of Nairobi in search of farming lands. Their interests clashed with those of the Maasai, prompting the colonial authorities to pressure Olonana into restricting the Maasai to two reserves, one on either side of the new railway. Though this was a blow to Maasai independence, worse was to follow – the white settlers soon wanted the northern reserve as well. In 1910 and 11, those Maasai who lived there were forced to trek south, despite Olonana's objections.

Though it's probably true that it was the Maasai who had the greatest amount of land taken from them by the white settlers, the Kikuyu, a Bantu agricultural tribe which occupied the highlands around the western side of Mt Kenya and the Aberdares, also suffered. The Kikuyu came to nurse a particular grievance about the alienation of land by white settlers later on in the 20th century (see African Nationalism later in this section). Many of the numerically larger tribes such as the Luo and Luyha and the tribes of the north-east were hardly affected, if at all.

White settlement in the early years of the 20th century was led by Lord Delamere, a pugnacious gentleman-farmer from Cheshire, England. Since he was not familiar with the land, its pests and its wildlife, his first ventures – into sheep farming and, later, wheat growing – were disastrous. By 1912, however, following the move to the highlands, Delamere and his followers had put the colony onto a more realistic economic footing by establishing mixed agricultural farms. Other European settlers established coffee plantations about the same time, including Karen Blixen and her hunter husband, Bror. Her memoirs are to be found in the book *Out of Africa*, which has been made into a very successful film starring Meryl Streep and Robert Redford.

White settlement of Kenya was interrupted by WWI, during which some two-thirds of the 3000 white settlers formed impromptu cavalry units and went off in search of Germans in neighbouring Tanganyika, leaving their wives behind to manage the farms. The soldiers were not entirely successful but they did eventually manage to drive the German forces into Central Africa with some able assistance from Jan Smut's South African units. However, General von Lettow-Vorbeck's intrepid unit of 155 Germans and 3000 Africans remained undefeated when the armistice was signed in November 1918. It was during a skirmish between the two armies in January 1917 that Captain Frederick Selous (after whom the national park in Tanzania was named) was killed. Under the Treaty of Versailles, Germany lost Tanganyika and the British were given a mandate by the League of Nations to administer the territory.

Settlement of Kenya resumed after the war under a scheme where veterans of the European campaign were offered land in the highlands, either at rock-bottom prices or on long-term loans. The effect of this was to raise the white settler population to around 9000 by 1920. By the 1950s it had reached 80,000.

African Nationalism

While all this was going on, more and more Kikuyu were migrating to Nairobi or being drawn into the colonial economy in one way or another. They weren't at all happy about the alienation of their land and this led to the formation of a number of associations whose principle concern was the return of land to the Kikuyu.

One of the early leaders of the Kikuyu political associations was Harry Thuku. Shortly after he was arrested for his activities by the colonial authorities in March 1922, a crowd of Africans gathered outside the Nairobi Central Police Station where he was being held. Reports differ as to what happened next, but by the time the police had stopped shooting, between 21 and 100 people had been killed.

Thuku was eventually exiled to Kisimayo and was only finally released from jail in 1930 after he had agreed to cooperate with the colonial authorities. His cooperation cost him his leadership of the Kikuyu movement since he was thenceforth regarded as a collaborator. This early Sharpeville led to the politicisation of the Kikuyu and was the start of a sustained campaign for political, social and economic rights. (Sharpeville refers to the notorious massacre by police of unarmed black demonstrators in 1960 in the town of the same name in South Africa. It signalled the beginning of the armed struggle by the African National Congress (ANC) against the apartheid regime.)

While Harry Thuku's star was on the wane, that of another member of the tribe was on the rise. His name was Johnstone Kamau, later changed to Jomo Kenyatta, and he was to become independent Kenya's first president. Kenyatta was born in 1892 in the highlands north of Nairobi, the son of a peasant farmer. He spent the early years of his life as a shepherd tending his father's flocks. When he was in his teens he ran away to a nearby Church of Scotland mission school where he picked up an education.

At the age of 29 he moved to Nairobi. He worked there as a court interpreter and water-meter reader but his real skills lay elsewhere

– as an orator. He soon became the secretary for propaganda of the East Africa Association, which had been set up to campaign for land reform, better wages, education and medical facilities for Africans. At this time, Africans were barred from hotels and restaurants and were only considered for the most menial jobs within the colonial administration.

Although it was official British government policy to favour African interests over those of the settlers in the event of conflicts, this was often ignored in practice because of the dominance of Lord Delamere's lobby in the whites-only legislative council. Recognising this, Kenyatta soon moved to join the more outspoken Kikuyu Central Association as its secretary-general.

Shortly afterwards, in 1929, with money supplied by Indians with communist connections, he sailed for London to plead the Kikuyu case with the British colonial secretary. Though the colonial secretary declined to meet him, Kenyatta teamed up with a group called the League Against Imperialism which took him to Moscow and Berlin and then back to Nairobi. He returned to London the following year and remained there for the next 15 years. He spent his time perfecting his oratory with Trafalgar Square crowds, studying revolutionary tactics in Moscow, visiting cooperative farms in Scandinavia and building up the Pan-African Federation with Hastings Banda (who later became the president of Malawi) and Kwame Nkrumah (who later became the president of Ghana). By the time he returned to Kenya in 1946, he was the recognised leader of the Kenyan liberation movement.

During WWII, the Belgian, British, French and Italian governments all recruited African troops to fight. The overall effect on Africans (as well as soldiers from other colonised peoples) was a realisation that the Europeans were not omnipotent. They could be defeated or, at the least, forced to come to terms with African aspirations for the same benefits and opportunities as their European overlords. Africans had also been trained in the use of arms. When the war ended, therefore, the returning soldiers were in no mood to accept the status quo and began to actively campaign for change.

The main African political organisation involved in the confrontation with the colonial authorities was the Kenya African Union (KAU), first headed by Harry Thuku and then by James Gichuru who himself stood down in favour of Kenyatta on the latter's return from Britain. The Kikuyu Central Association had been banned in 1940 along with many other similar organisations.

Mau Mau Rebellion

As the demands of the KAU became more and more strident and the colonial authorities less and less willing to make concessions, oath-taking ceremonies began to spread among various tribes like the Kikuyu, Maasai and Luo. Some of these secret oaths bound the participants to kill Europeans and their African collaborators. The Mau Mau was one such secret political society which bonded its members, willingly or otherwise, to the organisation via oath-taking ceremonies. Formed in 1952, it consisted mainly of Kikuyu tribespeople, and its aim was to drive white settlers out of Kenya.

The first blow was struck early in 1953 with the killing of a white farmer's entire herd of cattle. This was followed, a few weeks later, by the massacre of 21 Kikuyu loyal to the colonial government. The Mau Mau rebellion had started. The government declared an emergency and began to gather the tribespeople into 'protected villages', surrounded by barbed wire and booby-trapped trenches, which they were forbidden to leave during the hours of darkness. Some 20,000 Kikuyu 'home guards' were recruited to assist British army units brought in to put down the rebellion and to help police the 'protected villages'. By the time the rebellion came to an end in 1956 with the defeat of the Mau Mau, the death toll stood at over 13,500 Africans – Mau Mau guerrillas, civilians and troops – and just over 100 Europeans, 37 of whom were settlers. In the process, an additional 20,000 Kikuyu had been thrown into detention camps where many died of disease or exposure.

Only a month after the rebellion started, Kenyatta and several other KAU leaders were arrested and put on trial as the alleged leaders of the Mau Mau. It's very doubtful that Kenyatta had any influence over the Mau Mau commanders, let alone that he was one of their leaders, but he was, nevertheless, sentenced to seven years jail in the remote Turkana region after a trial lasting five months. He was released in 1959 but was immediately sent to Lodwar under house arrest.

The rebellion shook the settlers to the roots and gave rise to a number of white political parties with opposing demands, ranging from partition of the country between blacks and whites to the transfer of power to a democratically elected African government. It should have been obvious to anyone with eyes to see that the latter view would have to prevail in the end, but it wasn't adopted as official policy until the Lancaster House Conference in London in 1960. The rebellion did lead, however, to an exodus of white settlers who packed their bags and headed off to Rhodesia, South Africa and Australia. At the conference, independence was scheduled for December 1963 and the British government agreed to provide the new Kenyan government with US$100 million in grants and loans so that it would be able to buy out European farmers in the highlands and restore the land to the tribes from whom it had been taken.

In the meantime a division occurred in the ranks of the KAU between those who wanted a unitary form of government with firm centralised control in Nairobi and those who favoured a federal setup in order to avoid Kikuyu domination. The former renamed their party the Kenya African National Union (KANU) and the latter split off under the leadership of Ronald Ngala to become the Kenya African Democratic Union (KADU). Many of the white settlers, who had come to accept the inevitable, supported the KADU.

Kenyatta was released from house arrest

in mid-1961 and assumed the presidency of the KANU. Despite his long period of incarceration by the colonial authorities, he appeared to harbour no resentment against the whites and indeed set out to reassure the settlers that they would have a future in the country when independence came. At a packed meeting of settlers in Nakuru Town Hall in August 1963, he asked them to stay, saying that the country needed experience and that he didn't care where it came from. He assured them of the encouragement and protection of the new government and appealed for harmony, saying that he wanted to show the rest of the world that different racial groups were capable of living and working together. It did the trick. Kenyatta's speech transformed him, in the eyes of the settlers, from the feared and reviled spiritual leader of the Mau Mau into the venerable *mzee* ('respected elder') of the post-independence years.

Most of the white settler farms have been bought out by the government over the subsequent years and the land divided up into small subsistence plots which support 15 to 20 people. This may well have appeased the pressure for land redistribution in a country with one of the world's highest birth rates, but it has led to a serious decline in agricultural production (and therefore a diminishing tax base for the government) and has threatened to damage the region's delicate ecology. By 1980, Kenya was forced to import half the grain it needed, whereas in 1975 it was self-sufficient. The government is keen to halt the break-up of the settler farms which remain, but the prospects of being able to do this in a land-hungry nation are not good. In any case, many of the vast properties held by former white settlers were snapped up by prominent Kikuyu politicians in the years following independence. Many black radicals in Kenya regarded this as a betrayal of the independence struggle and the stand-off continues to this day.

Independence
The two parties, KANU and KADU, formed a coalition government in 1962, but after the

DAWN DELANEY

DAVID ELSE

DAWN DELANEY

GREG ELMS

Most people who visit Kenya go to the Masai Mara National Reserve. As well as finding that essential room with a view, you'll see plenty of game, including lions. Some travellers experience the traditional land of the Maasai tribe by cruising across the plains in a hot air balloon.

MARK SAVAGE

TONY WHEELER

Top: Adrenaline-pumping rafting on the Athi River.
Bottom: It's snack time as the bus pulls into Voi.

May 1963 elections, KANU and Kenyatta came to power. Independence came on 12 December 1963 with Kenyatta as the first president. He ruled Kenya until his death in 1978. Under Kenyatta's presidency, Kenya developed into one of Africa's most stable and prosperous nations. Unlike many other newly independent countries, there was no long string of coups and counter-coups, military holocausts, power-crazy dictators and secessionist movements. It wasn't all plain sailing, but Kenyatta left the country in a much better state than he found it and, although there were excesses, they were minor by African standards. By the time he died, there were enough Kenyans with a stake in their country's continued progress to ensure a relatively smooth succession to the presidency – violence and instability would have benefited few people. Kenyatta's main failings were that he was excessively biased in favour of his own tribe and that he often regarded honest criticism as tantamount to treason. Opponents of his regime who became too vocal for comfort frequently 'disappeared'.

Control of the government and large sectors of the economy still remain in the hands of the Kikuyu, to the social and financial detriment of other ethnic groups. Corruption in high places remains a problem and once prompted JM Kariuki, a former Mau Mau fighter and later an assistant minister in the government, to remark that Kenya had become a nation of '10 millionaires and 10 million beggars'. There are indeed great disparities in wealth. Many destitute squatters and unemployed people, especially in Nairobi, have little hope of ever finding employment – but this is hardly a problem peculiar to Kenya. The accumulation of wealth and land by a handful of top politicians and their business associates and the concurrent dispossession and impoverishment of tens of thousands of their fellow countrymen is a theme frequently addressed by the more politically aware of Kenya's novelists and, in some cases, has led to their exile.

In 1964, Kenya effectively became a one-party state following the voluntary dissolution of the opposition KADU party. With it died the party's policy of federalism, and the two chamber legislature became the single chamber legislative assembly. However, when Oginga Odinga, a Luo, was purged from the KANU hierarchy in 1966, due to allegations that he was plotting against the government, he formed his own opposition party, the Kenya People's Union. The party was later banned and Odinga was jailed. He was released when he agreed to rejoin KANU, but was imprisoned again in 1969 on spurious charges. After his release in 1971 he was banned from running for public office until 1977.

Tom Mboya, an intelligent young Luo who was widely regarded as future presidential material, was murdered by a Kikuyu gunman in 1969. The ambitious Mboya was

Jomo Kenyatta became independent Kenya's first president in 1963. He led the country until his death in 1978.

feared by influential Kikuyu, who felt that he had designs on succeeding Kenyatta as president. JM Kariuki, a very popular Kikuyu who spoke out stridently and often about the new black elite and their corrupt practices, met a similar fate: he was assassinated in 1975. Other politicians who opposed Kenyatta – however mildly – found themselves arrested and held for long periods, often without trial.

The 1980s

Kenyatta was succeeded by Daniel arap Moi, Kenyatta's Vice President. A member of the Tugen tribe, Moi was regarded by Kikuyu power brokers as a suitable front man for their interests. He lacked the charisma and cult following of Kenyatta, and so was even less willing to brook criticism of his regime. The early years of his regime were marked by the arrest of dissidents, the disbanding of tribal societies and the closure of universities. There were allegations of conspiracies to overthrow the government, the details of which were often so labyrinthine that they could have come straight out of a spy novel. Whether these conspiracies were real or just a convenient façade to justify Moi's consolidation of power is hard to tell, since names and details were rarely released.

What certainly *was* real was the attempted coup by the Kenyan air force in August 1982. It was put down by forces loyal to the government, but by the time it was over about 120 people were dead and there had been widespread looting of the major shopping areas. Twelve ringleaders were subsequently sentenced to death and 900 others received jail sentences. The entire Kenyan air force was disbanded and replaced by a new unit.

Since then, other alleged conspiracies have come to light but, again, the details are rarely made known. The most publicised of these clandestine opposition groups was Mwakenya, which supposedly centred around a number of lecturers at Nairobi University along with the exiled novelist and playwright Ngugi wa Thiong'o. Certainly Ngugi has made his opposition to the Kenyan government quite plain, but there is little evidence to support the claim that he was a leading light of the movement.

President Moi was re-elected in March 1987 in an election which was most notable for the controversial voting system it employed. Candidates could only run in the secret ballot election after gaining a set percentage of the vote in a preliminary election whereby voters queued behind the candidate of their choice. If the candidate gained more than 70% of the queue vote, they were automatically elected and did not have to take part in the secret ballot election. The outcome was that at least 45 constituencies had no secret ballot as the candidate who had received over 70% of the turnout in the queue vote was automatically elected (it didn't matter that in one case the turnout was less than 9% of registered voters). In other constituencies, the number of candidates was significantly reduced because the nominees failed to win sufficient support at the preliminary election.

After the election, Moi expanded his cabinet to 33 ministers – many on the basis of political patronage – and, as a result, the government's (and therefore Moi's) position seemed totally secure. With the fall of a couple of outspoken politicians in the 1987 elections (amid allegations of vote rigging) it seemed unlikely that parliamentary opposition to Moi on major issues in the immediate future would be anything more than a whisper. Perhaps more significantly, changes to the constitution were rushed through parliament unopposed in late 1987, giving Moi increased presidential powers, including the right to dismiss senior judges and public servants without redress. The independence of the judiciary had been a much-admired cornerstone of the Kenyan political system ever since independence and the changes were viewed with alarm by many sections of society.

From this point on there ceased to be any effective political opposition within the parliamentary system and the party further strengthened its hold by augmenting the ranks of the KANU Youth Wing, who essentially served as pro-government vigilantes.

They were frequently unleashed to disrupt demonstrations, harass opposition figures and maintain a climate of intimidation among those who might have similar sympathies. Many opposition political leaders were detained without trial during this period, including Mwai Kibaki and Kenneth Matiba.

Yet the government was unable to silence various leaders of the Christian churches (especially the bishops of the Anglican church), who increasingly turned their sermons into political speeches. They were supported by an outspoken critic of government nepotism, Professor Wangui Mathai, the leader of the Green Movement. All of these people were vilified by both the president and various ministers and there were calls for their removal and even arrest on charges of sedition. Mathai probably suffered most, as she was thrown out of her modest offices on University Way and forced to endure a public character assassination blitz, whose script could have been put together from the trash scrawled on toilet walls.

But times were changing. Multiparty politics was sweeping Africa and Kenya was not to escape.

The 1990s

With the collapse of Communism in Eastern Europe and the break up of the Soviet Union, the west's attention was abruptly refocused. It was no longer necessary to prop up corrupt African regimes in the name of containing Communism.

The Kenyan government quickly found itself under intense pressure from the donor countries to introduce a multiparty system and to name a date for elections if it wanted aid to be maintained. Though it prevaricated, the government – faced with a foreign debt of some US$9 billion, a downturn in the economy and determined grass-roots opposition in the form of FORD (Forum for the Restoration of Democracy) – was forced to capitulate. To drive the point home, aid was suspended by virtually all Western countries in early 1992.

Suddenly, everyone was talking politics everywhere and anywhere and there emerged a clear consensus that FORD would sweep to victory in any election, assuming it could get its act together and that the elections were reasonably free and fair. Unfortunately, the opposition shot itself in the foot in the lead-up to the elections. The principle players were Oginga Odinga, Kenneth Matiba and Mwai Kibaki. Originally all members of FORD, but unable to stomach the idea of anyone but themselves being the new president, they split the party into three – FORD-Kenya (Oginga Odinga), FORD-Asili (Kenneth Matiba) and the Democratic Party or DP (Mwai Kibaki). From that point on, they had no chance.

In the meantime, Moi, according to the IMF/World Bank, authorised the printing of KSh 9 billion bank notes (over US$250 million), unsupported by foreign currency or gold reserves. He used these to line the pockets of his supporters and blatantly buy votes for the ruling party (KANU). In the lead-up to the elections, the newspapers were full of pictures and stories of *wananchi* ('peasants and workers') lining up to collect their KSh 500 and KANU-emblazoned T-shirt and cap. Moi knew that full stomachs would buy votes even if the economy collapsed shortly after the elections – which it virtually did.

He also played the tribal card for all it was worth in his home area, allowing the Kalenjin to wreak havoc among Kikuyu settlers in the area. Hundreds were killed and injured in these tribal clashes and thousands left homeless and destitute. Hardly anything has been done since to rehabilitate these people, and violence continues to simmer. The violence succeeded in driving Kikuyu (who were clearly not going to vote for KANU) from Kalenjin areas (Moi's home ground).

Another blatant ploy was to postpone the election until the final week of December and to ensure that it fell on a normal working day. Had it not finally been declared a public holiday about a week in advance, tens of thousands of registered voters, particularly in Nairobi and other major towns, would have been unable to travel back to the place where they were registered in order to vote. Moi was aware that he had little support in the Nairobi area and among the Kikuyu, as the election results were to show. His support among the Luo was also tenuous.

To curry the favour of the donor nations, international observers were brought in to monitor a cross section of the polling stations and to decide whether the elections had been free and fair. As far as the voting itself went, the elections were fair to a greater rather than a lesser degree, though the various opposition parties, predictably, denied this. The trouble was, the observers were flown in only days before the election and, by then, the dirty deeds had been done. Moi and KANU swept to victory, but with only one-third of the total vote. Clearly, the opposition would have won if they had presented a united front, but vanity and ambition got in the way.

Vanity and ambition also resurfaced shortly after the elections as several MPs, unable to stomach the prospect of life on the opposition benches, cynically defected to the KANU and were welcomed with glee. Loyalty to the voters who had elected them on an opposition ticket was apparently of no concern to these MPs. The press cried foul, accusing KANU of having bought them. They were probably right but the evidence was, naturally, scant.

In many ways, though, KANU needn't have bothered, as the opposition went on to make complete fools of themselves by literally coming to blows over which of the three leaders was to occupy the leader of the opposition's chair in the parliament. It was a pathetic display of childish fractiousness and it's still going on today. All of the opposition parties, but particularly FORD-Kenya and FORD-Asili, have frequently been shaken to their foundations by some very transparent blood-letting over leadership. In an early 1996 by-election, the voter turn-out was an incredible 4.5%! KANU 'won', of course, but what a hollow victory!

In 1995, a new party was launched to draw all the opposition under one umbrella and agree on a single presidential candidate to contest the next elections. The party was Safina, founded by Richard Leakey (whom Moi had sacked as director of the Kenya Wildlife Service), Raila Odinga (Oginga Odinga's son and the FORD-Asili MP for Langata constituency), Paul Muite (a prominent lawyer) and other vocal opposition MPs. Moi was well aware of Leakey's international reputation and his ability to raise election funding from overseas. The party was refused registration and Leakey was vilified almost daily for weeks. He was accused of being a white supremacist and neocolonialist, harassed wherever he went and, on one occasion, beaten up. Whites should stay out of Kenyan politics and concern themselves only with business, Moi thundered. Apparently, being a Kenyan-born citizen bestowed no political rights on anyone who happened to be white. It was racism at its best.

Despite all the invective, Safina has made some headway in bringing the opposition together – except for Mwai Kibaki (DP) – but, equally it may lead to nothing, given the personalities of the protagonists.

Meanwhile, KANU has been doing its best to silence any credible contenders for State House other than the present incumbent. In 1990 the erudite former minister for Foreign Affairs, Dr Robert Ouko, was murdered shortly after returning from the USA, and the inquiry into his death has dragged on inconclusively ever since. The same goes for Koigi Wamwere, who was held in remand in a Nakuru jail for years and was only acquitted in 1996 of a charge of attacking a police station with the intent of stealing weapons. Likewise, Professor George Saitoti, the Vice President, after an unwise slip of the tongue regarding his presidential aspirations, was forced to utterly debase himself in public and beg for forgiveness for even thinking about it. But the *pièce de résistance* was KANU's 1996 announcement that it was planning to change the constitution to allow Moi another term in office if he wins the next election (at present he is barred from a further term as president).

A great deal depends on the outcome of the next election (scheduled for December 1997) and, as far as the continuation of aid is concerned, something serious has to be done about clearing up the backlog of corruption and embezzlement cases involving billions of Kenyan shillings. Most of these cases have been going on for years with no resolution in sight. The Goldenberg, Trust Bank and Kamlesh Pattni scandals alone amount to close to KSh 20 billion.

And political survival is not the government's only concern. Kenya still has one of the highest population growth rates of any country in the world (around 3%). The strain on health and educational facilities is already showing, and the situation seems unlikely to improve. Add to this the hundreds of thousands of people of working age who are unable to find work, and you have a recipe for increased social turmoil and political instability.

GEOGRAPHY
Kenya straddles the equator and covers an area of some 583,000 sq km, which includes around 13,600 sq km of inland water in the form of part of Lake Victoria. It is bordered to the north by the arid bushlands and deserts of Ethiopia and Sudan, to the east by Somalia and the Indian Ocean, to the west by Uganda and Lake Victoria, and to the south by Tanzania. The main rivers in Kenya are the Athi/Galana and the Tana.

The country can be roughly divided into four main zones: the coastal belt, the Rift Valley and central highlands, western Kenya, and northern and eastern Kenya.

Coastal Belt
This area covers some 480 km of Indian Ocean littoral, including coral reefs and beaches, the Lamu archipelago, the Tana River estuary (Kenya's principal river) and a narrow, low-lying and relatively fertile strip of land suitable for agriculture. Beyond this, the terrain rises fairly steeply towards the central plateau and gives way to bushland and scrub desert.

Rift Valley & Central Highlands
These regions form the backbone of the country and it's here that Kenya's scenery is at its most spectacular. The lake-studded Rift Valley runs the whole length of the country from Lake Turkana to Lake Magadi and is peppered with the cones of extinct volcanoes. It's bounded on the eastern side by the thickly forested slopes of the Aberdare mountains and, further to the east, by the massif of Mt Kenya – Africa's second highest mountain at 5199m. This is the most fertile area of the country and the lower slopes of the mountains are intensively cultivated. Nairobi, the capital, sits at the southern end of the central highlands.

Western Kenya
The west of the country consists of an undulating plateau stretching from the Sudanese border to Tanzania in the south. The area around the shores of Lake Victoria is particularly fertile, well watered and intensively cultivated, and is also home to Mt Elgon (Kenya's second highest mountain at 4321m). Further south the land gradually merges into scrub and savannah, and is suitable only for cattle grazing; however, it's here that Kenya's largest and most popular wildlife sanctuaries are situated – Masai Mara, Amboseli and Tsavo. To the south of Amboseli rises the spectacular massif of Mt Kilimanjaro – Africa's highest mountain (5895m).

Northern & Eastern Kenya
These two regions cover a vast mountainous area of bushland, scrub and desert, where rainfall is sparse and the land is suitable only for cattle grazing. It's this area where Kenya is at its wildest and most untouched by the modern world.

GEOLOGY
The major geological feature in Kenya is the Great Rift Valley, a huge depression which extends for nearly 5000 km down to Mozambique in south-eastern Africa.

The valley system consists of a series of troughs and areas of uplift known as swells. The troughs, generally 40 to 55 km wide, are

Extensive volcanic activity (as shown above) resulted in East Africa's Rift Valley, one of the world's most extensive rifts. The volcanic activity produced Mt Kilimanjaro, Mt Kenya and Mt Elgon.

found along parallel fault lines, and make up most of the lakes and escarpments in East Africa. The swells form on either side of the troughs, and it's here that the mighty peaks of Kilimanjaro, Mt Kenya and Mt Elgon are found – all extinct volcanoes. The floor of the Rift Valley is still dropping, although at the rate of a few mm per year you are hardly likely to notice!

The Rift Valley is certainly not one long, well-formed valley with huge escarpments either side, although this classic geography does occur in places (the Rift Valley Province is one such location). Sometimes there are a series of small scarps, or even just a single scarp on one side (such as the Nkuruman Escarpment east of Masai Mara). In some cases uplift has occurred between parallel fault lines, leading to the formation of spectacular mountain ranges such as the Ruwenzoris on the Uganda-Zaïre border.

CLIMATE

Because of Kenya's diverse geography, temperature, rainfall and humidity vary widely, but there are effectively four zones about which generalisations can be made.

The undulating plateau of western Kenya is generally hot and fairly humid with rainfall spread throughout the year, falling mostly in the evenings. The greatest precipitation is usually during April when a maximum of 200 mm may be recorded, while the lowest falls are in January with an average of 40 mm. Temperatures range from a minimum of 14°C or 18°C to a maximum of 30°C to 34°C.

The central highlands and Rift Valley enjoy perhaps the most agreeable climate in the country, though there's quite a variation between the hot and relatively dry floor of the central Rift Valley and the snow-covered peaks of Mt Kenya. Rainfall varies from a minimum of 20 mm in July to 200 mm in April and falls essentially in two seasons – March to May (the 'long rains') and October to December (the 'short rains'). The Aberdare mountains and Mt Kenya are the country's main water catchment areas, and falls of up to 3000 mm per year are often recorded. Average temperatures vary from a minimum of 10°C or 14°C to a maximum of 22°C to 26°C.

The vast semi-arid bushlands, deserts and lava flows of northern and eastern Kenya are where the most extreme variations in temperature are to be found, ranging from highs of up to 40°C during the day in the deserts, dropping down to 20°C or less at night. Rainfall in this area is sparse and when it does fall it often comes in the form of violent storms. July is generally the driest month and November the wettest. The average annual rainfall varies between 250 and 500 mm.

The fourth climatic zone is the coastal belt, which is hot and humid all year round, though tempered by coastal sea breezes. Rainfall ranges from a minimum of 20 mm in February to a maximum of 300 mm in May. The annual average is between 1000 mm and 1250 mm. Average temperatures vary little throughout the year, ranging from a minimum of 22°C to a maximum of 30°C.

ECOLOGY & ENVIRONMENT
Pressure for Land

The pressure for land in Kenya is enormous due to the high population growth. This problem applies in particular to people who live in the immediate vicinity of national parks and reserves: not only is the land reserved for animals, but these same animals often wander outside the parks, causing tremendous amounts of damage in the process.

On Maasai land between the Amboseli and Tsavo national parks, the local people have tried a new approach and established their own wildlife sanctuary. This is one of the very few options left for people who have had much of their land gazetted as parks or reserves and placed off limits. Another option is to start another type of tourism project, such as a lodge, but as this requires investment capital it is only possible for the well-off few. Still another is to plough up the land and grow wheat, something the government is keen to encourage in its drive for self-sufficiency. Planting, however, creates more conflicts between the Maasai and the animals, as wildlife corridors disappear and animals have to cross previously unfenced land.

What can be done about the conflict between people and animals is anyone's guess, but the solution will not be easy. Compensating local people from the tourist revenue raised by national parks and reserves is one approach which has gained favour recently. But in practice, the amount of money which finds its way back to the

Wildlife Conservation

As Kenya relies so heavily on tourism for income, and because it's the animals which people have chiefly come to see, the government has placed a high priority on wildlife conservation and the eradication of poaching. To this end, in the late 1980s it appointed well-known palaeontologist Richard Leakey (son of Louis Leakey famed for discovering ancient human fossil remains in the Rift Valley in the 1950s) as head of the Kenya Wildlife Service.

Following Leakey's appointment, corrupt wildlife officials were sacked and the anti-poaching units beefed up, to the extent that 200 US-trained paramilitary personnel were deployed in 1990 on shoot-to-kill patrols. The measures have had a large degree of success, despite the fact that Richard Leakey was sacked in 1994 and replaced by an individual with a much lower profile. Extremely stiff penalties for poaching are now in effect.

Yet despite the risks, poaching still goes on, although on a much smaller scale than in previous years. It's easy to see the reasons for poaching. There is big money in ivory and rhino horn, and as long as the Taiwanese government and various Arab governments – notably the two Yemens, Oman and Kuwait – refuse to ban their importation, the slaughter of Kenya's wildlife is likely to continue. One kg of ivory is worth about US$300 wholesale and rhino horn is US$2000 a kg (or up to US$30,000 for a single horn). In the Middle East rhino horn is prized for dagger handles whilst in China and Korea, in powdered form, it's a supposed aphrodisiac.

Although poaching had been going on for many years, it took on a new dimension in 1972 as a result of the drought in north-eastern Africa which rendered some 250,000 Somali pastoralists destitute as their sheep, goats and camels died by the million. Many drifted south, armed with weapons ranging from bows and arrows to WWII guns, and found poaching to be a suitable antidote to poverty. Meanwhile, corruption in the Kenya Wildlife Service deepened, with officials taking bribes in return for turning a blind eye to the poachers' activities. By 1976, it was plain that the number of elephants being slaughtered by poachers far exceeded those dying as a result of drought and deforestation and it was estimated that there were over 1300 poachers operating within Tsavo National Park alone.

Worse was yet to come. In 1978, waves of Somalis hungry for ivory and rhino horn, and encouraged by official corruption, swept across the border and into the national parks, only this time they came with modern automatic weapons issued to them by the Somali government during the 1977 war with Ethiopia. They killed everything in their path including any Kenyan tribal poachers they came across. By the end of the decade, some 104,000 elephants (about 62% of the total) and virtually the entire rhino population had been slaughtered.

There was little improvement during the early 1980s despite the setting up of anti-poaching patrols armed with modern weapons, high-speed vehicles and orders to shoot on sight. Part of the reason was the patrols' reluctance to engage the Somalis, who have a reputation for toughness and uncompromising violence. By 1989, however, following the murder of George Adamson by poachers in the Kora National Reserve (as he was saving the lives of orphaned wildlife) as well as attacks on tourists in other national parks, the Kenyan government signalled its determination to seriously address the problem. ■

people is very small indeed. Currently, the Kenya Wildlife Service receives a paltry US$13 million a year, mostly from park entry fees. Given that something like 8% of the country is set aside for nature conservation, it is a very small sum. One answer could be to increase the entrance fees to the national parks, so that witnessing these superb wildlife spectacles is a privilege rather than the relatively cheap experience it is today. Of course this is hardly likely to encourage the tourist trade, but unless the local people are properly compensated for their land, it's not inconceivable that the great wildlife reserves of Kenya will become little more than large 'safari parks', reminiscent of those found in the West.

Environmental Problems

It is the tourist industry which is the cause of some of Kenya's major environmental problems, and once again, tough measures are called for. Parks such as Amboseli and Masai Mara are crisscrossed with tracks and crawling with tourist minibuses. The problem is particularly bad in the Mara, where minibuses seem to go pretty much where they please, as regulations are not policed by the local Narok council that administers the reserve.

The lodges within the parks themselves also create problems. Foremost among these is their use of firewood, a valuable and scarce resource – a recent survey found that each of the lodges and tented camps around Masai Mara used, on average, 100 tonnes of firewood in a year.

FLORA & FAUNA
Flora

Kenya's flora is notably diverse because of the country's range of physiographic regions. The vast plains of the south are characterised by distinctive flat-topped acacia trees, interspersed with the equally distinctive bottle-shaped baobab trees and thorn bushes.

On the slopes of Mt Elgon and Mt Kenya the flora changes with altitude. Thick evergreen temperate forest grows between 1000

and 2000m, giving way to a belt of bamboo forest up to about 3000m. Above this height is mountain moorland, characterised by the amazing groundsel tree *(Dendrosencio)*, with its huge cabbage-like flowers, and giant lobelias with long spikes. In the semidesert plains of the north and north-east, the vegetation cover is unremarkable yet very characteristic – thorn bushes seem to go on forever. In the northern coastal areas mangroves are prolific and the trees are cut for export, mainly to the Middle East for use as scaffolding; mangrove wood is termite resistant and is in high demand.

Fauna

Kenya has such a dazzling array of wildlife that game-viewing in the national parks is one of the main attractions of a visit to this country. All of the 'big five' (lion, buffalo, elephant, leopard and rhino) can be seen in at least two of the major parks, and there's a huge variety of other less famous but equally impressive animals.

To aid identification of animals while you're game-spotting on safari, refer to the Safari Guide on page 31. For a full treatment of Kenya's animals, Collins' *A Field Guide to the Mammals of Africa* has excellent colour plates to aid identification, as does the smaller *A Field Guide to the Larger Mammals of Africa*, also by Collins. The main trouble with both these books is the relatively poor index (which lists many animals only by their Latin names) and the frequent placement of colour plates far from the actual description of the animals in question. *Animals of East Africa* has good descriptive notes of the animals' habits and appearance, but the sketches are not the greatest and the notes on distribution are out of date.

The bird life is equally varied and includes ostriches, vultures and eagles, a wide variety of water birds such as flamingos, storks, pelicans, herons, ibis and cormorants, and others such as the yellow weaver birds which you'll see everywhere. The best reference guide for twitchers is *A Field Guide to the*

Minimising Your Impact

In their quest for the perfect photo opportunity, some drivers do crazy things. A healthy dose of common sense goes a long way, but too many drivers are under too much pressure to please their clients, with little regard for the effects on the wildlife. In the interests of the animals, please observe the following:

- Never get too close to the animals and back off if they are getting edgy or nervous. On a safari I once took, a female cheetah (with cub) became extremely agitated when she was totally surrounded and hemmed in by a dozen minibuses, all full of excited visitors trying to get their 'shot'. She reacted by dropping the cub and bolting.
- Never get out of your vehicle, except at designated points where this is permitted. The animals may look tame and harmless enough, but this is not a zoo – the animals are wild and you should treat them as such.
- Animals always have the right of way. Don't follow predators as they move off – you try stalking something when you've got half a dozen minibuses in tow.
- Keep to the tracks. One of the biggest dangers in the parks today is land degradation from too many vehicles crisscrossing the countryside. Amboseli's choking dust is largely a result of this. Likewise, Masai Mara in November 1992 looked, from the air, as though the East African Rally had been run entirely in the park. There were tyre tracks literally everywhere and they were clearly acting as drainage channels for the rain. If that continues, there won't be much grassland left.
- Don't light fires except at camp sites, and dispose of cigarettes with care.
- Don't litter the parks and camp sites. Unfortunately, the worst offenders are often the safari drivers and cooks who toss everything and anything out the window, and leave camp sites littered with all manner of crap. It won't do any harm to point out to them the consequences of what they're doing, or clean it up yourself.

Birds of East Africa by John G Williams. It is widely available in Kenya.

Endangered Species

Most of Kenya's major predators and herbivores have become endangered because of the continuous destruction of their natural habitat by people in search of agricultural and grazing land – particularly that adjacent to the national parks and game reserves.

The black rhino is probably Kenya's most endangered species, and its population has been ravaged by poachers over the years. Fortunately, it has been the subject of some major conservation efforts in recent years and its numbers are once again on the rise, although there are still very few in the wild. Rhino sanctuaries, complete with electric fencing, have been established in Tsavo and Lake Nakuru national parks, and the Aberdares is also due to be fenced in the future.

While the elephant is not technically endangered, it is still the target of poachers and large numbers are killed each year. Following the international ban on ivory, which was enforced by the UN Convention on International Trade in Endangered Species (CITES) in 1989, the number of elephants killed illegally in Kenya fell from over 2000 in 1988-89 to just over 200 in 1992-93.

GOVERNMENT & POLITICS

Kenya is a multiparty state, with the Kenya African National Union (KANU) being the ruling party. The major opposition parties (in order of numbers of seats held) are FORD-Asili, FORD-Kenya and the Democratic Party (DP). The government consists of the president, who holds executive power, and a single legislative assembly which consists of 188 members, the attorney general, the speaker, and 10 members who are nominated by the president. There's a high degree of political patronage.

The judiciary were, until 1987, independent of government pressure and free to interpret both the constitution and the laws passed by the legislative assembly. In that year, however, parliament rushed through a bill giving the president the right to dismiss judges without recourse to a tribunal, thus effectively silencing them as a source of opposition. The unpopular measure has yet to be repealed.

As far as the independence and freedom of action of government ministers is concerned, it would be fair to say that it's very limited. Indeed, it would not be inappropriate to slightly misquote Louis XIV's classic statement: *'L'état? C'est Moi!'*

ECONOMY

The cornerstone of Kenya's capitalist economy is agriculture, which employs around 80% of the population, contributes some 29% of the GDP and accounts for over 50% of the country's export earnings. The principal food crops are maize, sorghum, cassava, beans and fruit, while the main cash crops are coffee, tea, cotton, sisal, pyrethrum and tobacco. The bulk of the food crops are grown by subsistence farmers on small plots of land, whereas most of the cash crops originate from large, privately owned plantations employing contract labour (though there's a significant input from smaller growers). Coffee and tea are the largest of the agricultural export earners with annual production being around 120,000 tonnes and 160,000 tonnes respectively.

While such figures might be a healthy sign for the country's balance of payments, there's a great deal of discontent among the small farmers and labourers, who are paid a pittance for the tea and coffee they produce or pick. In 1989-90, the country witnessed riots over this paltry sum. The dispute was handled badly by the Kenya Tea Development Authority (KTDA), and although several heads rolled and price increases were promised, it was all too little too late. Small growers regularly have to wait up to a year or more to be paid. The situation is similar in the coffee sector and exacerbated by internationally imposed quotas which limit Kenya's ability to dispose of its stockpile.

On the other hand, tourism has replaced coffee as the country's largest export earner, although arrivals have dropped off since 1992 due to the tribal clashes in western Kenya, and the nation's perceived political instability and general lack of security. Each

year around 700,000 people visit Kenya, contributing more than US$200 million to the country's economy.

In addition to agriculture and tourism, Kenya has a relatively well developed industrial base which accounts for some 20% of GDP, though the bulk of this industry is concentrated around Nairobi and Mombasa. The principal products include processed food, beer, vehicles and accessories, construction materials, engineering, textiles, glass and chemicals. Initially, this sector of the economy was developed with import substitution in mind, but the bias has now changed in favour of joint-venture, export-oriented industries as a result of the increasing deficit in the balance of payments and IMF loan conditions. (The IMF have returned to Kenya after being thrown out in March 1993.) Kenya's external debt of around US$8 billion is still considered to be low, but the most worrying aspect is the high proportion of the country's foreign exchange earnings which go into servicing foreign debt – currently around 35%.

Mining is a relatively small contributor to GNP and is centred around the extraction of soda and fluorspar for export. There are other minerals, which include silver, gold, lead and limestone, but these have yet to be developed commercially.

Kenya's major export trading partners are the UK (17%), the EU (45%), the USA (about 5%) and Germany (12%).

Some 70% of domestic energy requirements are imported, but geothermal projects are being developed: there are four hydro-electric plants in operation along the Tana River and a hydroelectric plant was recently completed in the Turkwel Gorge. Kenya's major sources of imports are the EU (39%), the UK (about 18%), Japan (9%), Germany (8%) and the USA (5%).

Inflation is currently running at about 11%, and GDP per capita is US$320.

POPULATION & PEOPLE

Kenya's population stands at around 28 million and is made up almost entirely of Africans, with small (although influential) minorities of Asians (about 80,000), Arabs (about 40,000) and Europeans (about 40,000). The population growth rate of around 3% is one of the highest in the world and is putting great strain on the country's ability to expand economically and to provide reasonable educational facilities and other urban services. It has also resulted in tremendous pressure to increase the area of land under cultivation.

Africans

There are more than 70 tribal groups among the Africans, although the distinctions between many of them are already blurred and are becoming more so as Western cultural values become more ingrained. Traditional values are also disintegrating as more and more people move to the larger towns, family and tribal groups become scattered and the tribal elders gradually die off. See the Tribal Groups & Cultures section on p. 78 for more information.

Yet even though the average African may have outwardly drifted away from tribal traditions, the tribe is still the single most important part of a person's identity. When two Africans meet and introduce themselves they will almost always say right at the outset what tribe they are from. Although nominally Christian for the most part, a surprising number of people still practise traditional customs. Some of the more brutal customs, such as clitoridectomy (female circumcision), were outlawed by the British, usually with the aid of the local missionaries, but circumcision still remains the main rite to pass from childhood to adulthood for boys.

The most important distinguishing feature between the tribes is language. The majority of Kenya's Africans fall into one of two major language groups: the Bantu and the Nilotic. The Bantu people arrived in East Africa in waves from West Africa over a period of time from around 500 BC. Among the Bantu the largest tribal groups are the Kikuyu, Meru, Gusii, Embu, Akamba, Luyha and Mijikenda.

The Nilotic speakers migrated to the area from the Nile Valley some time earlier but then had to make room for the migrations of Bantu-speaking people. Nilotic speaking groups include the Maasai, Turkana, Samburu, Pokot, Luo and Kalenjin. Together, these tribal groups account for more than 90% of the total African population in Kenya. The Kikuyu and the Luo are by far the most numerous groups, and between them hold practically all the positions of power and influence in the country.

A third language grouping, and in fact the first migrants into the country, are the Cushitic speakers, who occupy the north-east of the country and include such tribes as the El-Molo, Somali, Rendille and the Galla.

On the coast, Swahili is the name given to the local people who, while having various tribal ancestries, have in common the fact that they have been mixing, trading and intermarrying both among themselves and with overseas immigrants for hundreds of years.

Kenya has one of the world's highest population growths, so you'll encounter plenty of children.

Asians

The economically important Asian minority is made up largely of people of Indian descent whose ancestors originated from the western state of Gujarat and from the Punjab. Unlike the situation in Uganda, sense prevailed and the Asians here were not thrown into exile, largely because their influence was too great. (Uganda is still trying to get its economy back on track.)

India's connections with East Africa go back centuries to the days when hundreds of dhows used to make the trip between the west coast of India or the Persian Gulf and the coastal towns of East Africa every year. In those days, however, the Indians came as traders and only a very few stayed to settle. This all changed with the building of the Mombasa-Uganda railway at the turn of the century. In order to construct it, the British colonial authorities brought in some 32,000 indentured labourers from Gujarat and Punjab. When their contracts expired many of them decided to stay and set up businesses. Their numbers were augmented after WWII with the encouragement of the British.

Since they were an industrious and economically aggressive community, the Indians soon controlled large sectors of the economies of Kenya, Tanzania and Uganda as merchants, artisans and financiers. Not only that, but they kept very much to themselves, regarding the Africans as culturally inferior and lazy. Few gave their active support to the black nationalist movements in the run-up to independence, despite being urged to do so by Nehru, India's prime minister. And when independence came, like many of the white settlers, they were very hesitant to accept local citizenship, preferring to wait and see what would happen. To the Africans, therefore, it seemed they were not willing to throw in their lot with the newly independent nations and were there simply as exploiters.

As is well known, Uganda's Idi Amin used this suspicion and resentment as a convenient ruse to enrich himself and his cronies. Uganda's economy collapsed shortly after the expulsion of the Asian community, since Amin's henchmen were incapable of running the industries and businesses which the Asians had been forced to leave.

For a time in the 1970s it seemed that there was little future for Asians in Africa. Governments were under heavy pressure to 'Africanise' their economies and job markets. Even in Kenya thousands of shops owned by Asians who had not taken out Kenyan nationality were confiscated in the early 1970s and Asians were forbidden to trade in the rural areas. Those days appear to have passed and African attitudes towards Asians have mellowed. What seemed like a widespread demand that they should go 'home' has been quietly dropped; the lesson of what happened to the economy of Uganda when the Asians were thrown out is one reason for this.

EDUCATION

Primary school education is provided free by the government, but is not compulsory. Over 5½ million children attend around 15,000 primary schools, while the country's 2500 or so secondary schools cater to around 600,000 students.

There are four universities, with a total enrolment of around 35,000 students: the University of Nairobi (established in 1956) and Kenyatta University (1972), both in Nairobi; Egerton University (1939) in Nakuru; and Moi University (1984) in Eldoret.

Illiteracy runs at the alarmingly high rate of around 30%.

ARTS

Music

Indigenous Kenyan pop music does exist, but it is nowhere near as well known as styles such as *soukous* from Zaïre, which dominate the local scene.

The style known as *benga* is the contemporary dance music of Kenya today. It originated among the Luo people of western Kenya, and became popular in the area in the 1950s. It has since spread throughout the country.

The music is characterised by clear electric

guitar licks and a bass rhythm. The guitar in the modern bands takes the place of the traditional *nyatiti* (folk lyre), while the bass guitar replaces the drum, which originally was played by the nyatiti player with a toe ring. Some well-known exponents of benga include Shirati Jazz, Victoria Jazz and Ambira Boys.

Popular bands today play a mix of music, heavily influenced by benga, soukous and Western music, with lyrics generally in Swahili. These include bands such as Them Mushrooms and Safari Sound.

The live-music scene in Nairobi is quite fluid, but good places to try include the International Casino at Museum Hill, the Sirona Hotel in Parklands and the Landmark Hotel in Westlands. There are a number of places in the suburbs, but you'll need a taxi or your own transport. Try the Bombax Club at Dagoretti Corner on the Langata Road, the Cantina Club at the entrance to Wilson Airport and the Simba Saloon at the Carnivore Restaurant just past Wilson Airport. The *Daily Nation* has good listings on weekends, but doesn't usually give the addresses of the advertised places.

Literature

Heinemann's African Writers Series has arguably the best range of contemporary African authors (see the list of writers included in the series inside each book). Two of Kenya's best authors are Ngugi wa Thiong'o and Meja Mwangi, whose books are a good introduction to what's happening in East African literature at present. Ngugi is uncompromisingly (but somewhat dogmatically) radical, and his harrowing criticism of the neocolonialist politics of the Kenyan establishment landed him in jail for a year, lost him his job at Nairobi University and forced him into exile. His books, surprisingly, are not banned in Kenya even though he was considered a dangerously subversive thorn in the side of the government. Meja Mwangi sticks more to social issues and urban dislocation but has a brilliant sense of humour which threads its way right through his books. All the titles below are published by Heinemann.

Titles worth reading by Ngugi wa Thiong'o include *Petals of Blood*, *A Grain of Wheat*, *Devil on the Cross* and *Weep Not Child*. Titles by Meja Mwangi include *Going Down River Road, Kill me Quick* and *Carcass for Hounds*. All these titles are published by Heinemann.

Another author whose books are well known even outside Africa is Chinua Achebe. Although Achebe is a Nigerian and his material is drawn from his experiences in that country, many of the themes and issues are relevant to contemporary East Africa. His most famous title is *Things Fall Apart* (Heinemann, 1958). *Ant Hills of the Savannah*, a much more recent publication, is also well worth reading.

Another Nigerian author who writes about similar themes is Elechi Amadi. Try his *The Concubine*.

For writing by women in Africa try *Unwinding Threads*, a collection of short stories by many different authors from all over the continent.

SOCIETY & CONDUCT
Refugees & the Dispossessed

As Kenya is a relatively stable country, with opportunities to make a living or at least receive hand-outs from tourists, it is a natural magnet for refugees from strife-torn neighbouring countries. Nairobi, Mombasa and, to a lesser degree, the coastal resort towns are the favoured destinations. You'll come across plenty of refugees on your travels, although it's relatively easy for these people to remain anonymous if they can make enough money to stay off the streets.

There's nothing remarkable about this – it happens all over the world. What is remarkable in Kenya is the number of single young mothers – many of them are Kenyan but there are also those from Uganda, Sudan, Ethiopia and Rwanda. The break up of many traditional communities as a result of colonial policies that were designed to bring people into the money economy, and the continuation of this system under postcolonial regimes, has led to the large-scale movement of people to urban areas. Most arrive with nothing and are forced to live in overcrowded shantytowns (some 60% of Nairobi's population lives in these places) with little hope of anything resembling a steady job with reasonable pay. As a result, all the symptoms of urban alienation can be found in these places, and drunkenness, theft and rape (particularly of schoolgirls) are fairly commonplace. But such problems aren't confined to the major urban areas: they appear to be fairly widespread everywhere outside of traditional tribal areas.

As far as the girls are concerned, once they become pregnant they're expelled from school (in other words, it's the end of their educational prospects) and, as likely as not, rejected by their families too. In 1986, the number of young girls who found themselves in this position was 11,000 (according to official figures) and the number has been rising steadily ever since. The options for such girls are extremely limited. A few shelters do exist (usually run by Christian organisations), but it's only the lucky few who get in; for the rest, it's very poorly paid domestic work or the flesh market.

Laws regarding the responsibilities of paternity in Kenya either don't exist or are hardly ever enforced – it's definitely a man's world – and establishment Kenyan society remains tight-lipped about the problem. What society remains even more tight-lipped about is the practice of well-to-do Kenyan families recruiting little girls from the bush as domestic servants. Those recruited are even more circumspect.

Though clothed and fed and, if lucky, paid a pittance which varies between US$1 and US$16 a month, these children work on average 15 to 17 hours a day with no days off. Some get no pay at all, with just food and clothing provided in lieu of salary. The reason their parents push them into this hellish existence, apart from the wages which they expect to recoup, is the hope that their children will acquire a training and education of sorts. The reality is often quite different. These girls are often raped by either the man of the house or his sons and thrown out when they become pregnant; as

likely as not, those girls also join the flesh market.

Whatever you may think of prostitution, life without a good income is hard in Kenya. Minimal accommodation rentals, even in rough areas of Nairobi, are around US$50 a month; in better areas it's much more. Add decent clothes and footwear and medical attention when necessary, and that's a lot of money to be made, even to make ends meet – let alone save anything. It's not surprising, therefore, that those who do manage to get their heads above water head for the bars and discos frequented by expatriate workers and tourists, since it's more lucrative and there is the vague possibility of marriage or, at least, a long-term friendship.

Of course, it isn't just pregnant young girls who find themselves dispossessed. The conditions under which young boys have to work in the coffee, sisal and rice plantations are equally onerous and many find their way onto the streets of Nairobi (so-called 'parking boys'), Mombasa and the coast ('beach boys'), along with other jobless adult males.

Blaming the government for this state of affairs is all too easy for those from rich Western countries but is, to a large degree, unfair. Because of Kenya's high birth rate and the limited funds available, the government is already flat out keeping pace with the demand for schools and hospitals, developing the transport infrastructure and paying interest on its foreign loans. Given this, it's unlikely that much can be done in the foreseeable future for those who fall under the category of Kenya's dispossessed.

Cultural Considerations

Dress Despite their often exuberant and casual approach, Kenyans are generally quite conservative, and are particularly concerned with modesty in dress. Many travellers seem to get around in T-shirts and shorts, which is acceptable (just) in most areas, but you should be more circumspect on the Muslim-dominated coast, particularly in Lamu. Here women should wear tops that keep the shoulders covered and skirts or pants which reach at least to the knees. Shorts on men are likewise not particularly appreciated.

When doing official business with people such as civil servants and embassy staff, your position will be much enhanced if you're smartly dressed and don't look like you've just spent five weeks in the back of a truck (even if you have!).

Child Prostitution Child prostitution is prevalent in Kenya, particularly in Nairobi and the tourist areas of the coast where so-called 'sex tourism' is big business. Although the government is signatory to at least one UN convention aimed at protecting children, it has been less than vigorous in tackling the problem.

It is illegal to engage in sexual activity with children under the age of 14 (!), and even though people caught doing so may be dealt with leniently in Kenya, they may also be liable to legal action in their own country.

Photographing People Kenya's wildly photogenic tribal people are generally less than wildly enthusiastic about being photographed, and with good reason. See the section under Photography in the Facts for the Visitor chapter for more information.

RELIGION

It's probably true to say that most Kenyans outside the coastal and eastern provinces are Christians of one sort or another, while most of those on the coast and in the eastern part of the country are Muslim. Muslims make up some 30% of the population. In the more remote tribal areas you'll find a mixture of Muslims, Christians and those who follow their ancestral tribal beliefs.

Christianity

As a result of intense missionary activity from colonial times to the present, just about every Christian sect is represented in Kenya, from Lutherans and Catholics to Seventh Day Adventists and Wesleyans. The success which all these sects have enjoyed would be quite mind-boggling if it were not for the fact that they have always judiciously combined Jesus with education and medicine – two commodities in short supply until recently in Kenya. Indeed, there are still many remote areas of Kenya where the only place you can get an education or medical help is at a mission station, and there's no doubt that those who volunteer to staff them are dedicated people.

On the other hand, the situation is often not as simple as it might at first appear. As with Catholicism in Central and South America, which found it necessary to incorporate native deities and saints into the Roman Catholic pantheon in order to placate local sensibilities, African Christianity is frequently a combination of traditional and Christian beliefs. This is especially so where a tribe has strong ancestral beliefs. There are also many pure, home grown African Christian sects which owe no allegiance to any of the major Western cults. The only thing they have in common is the Bible, though their interpretation of it is often radically different. It's worth checking out a few churches while you're in Kenya, and even if you can't understand the words, you'll certainly be captivated by what only Africans can do with such beauty and precision – unaccompanied choral singing.

The upsurge of home grown Christian sects has much to do with cultural resurgence, the continuing struggle against neocolonialism, and the alienation brought about by migration to urban centres far from tribal homelands. Some of these sects are distinctly radical and viewed with alarm by the government. The Tent of the Living God, for instance, was denounced by the president as being anti-Christ and three of its leaders were arrested at a gathering in Eastleigh, Nairobi, in late January 1990. The charges against them were thrown out of court the following week and the men released, but the government's action was perhaps an indication of how it intends to deal with such perceived threats to the status quo in the future.

It isn't just the radical sects which worry the government, however. During the agitation for the introduction of a multiparty political system, even mainstream church leaders took to criticising the government from the relative safety of their pulpits. Many were denounced and some came so close to the bone that they were accused of treason and there were calls for their arrest, although none were actually arrested.

Islam

Most Muslims belong to the Sunni branch of the faith and, as a result, the Sunni communities have been able to attract substantial Saudi Arabian funding for schools and hospitals along the coast and elsewhere.

Only a small minority belong to the Shia branch of Islam and most are to be found among the Asian community. On the other hand, Shiites have been coming to East Africa from all over the eastern Islamic world for centuries, partially to escape persecution but mainly for trading purposes. They didn't come here to convert souls, and there was a high degree of cooperation between the schismatic sects and the Sunnis, which is why there's a total absence of Shiite customs in Swahili culture today.

Among the Asian community there are representatives of virtually all Shiite sects, but the most influential are the Ismailis – followers of the Aga Khan. As with all Ismailis, they represent a very liberal version of Islam and are perhaps the only branch of the faith which is strongly committed to the education of women at all levels and their participation in commerce and business. It's obvious that the sect has prospered well in Kenya, judging by all the schools and hospitals dedicated to the Aga Khan which you will come across in most urban centres.

Hinduism

Hinduism is a self-contained religion which concerns only those born into it. You'll come across a considerable number of temples in the larger urban areas where most people of Indian origin live. There are literally scores of different sects of Hinduism to be found in Kenya – too numerous to mention here – and many are economically quite influential.

For a superb and very detailed account of each and every Asian-derived sect of both Islam and Hinduism see *Through Open Doors – A View of Asian Cultures in Kenya*, by Cynthia Salvadori. This is a large-format, hardback book with many illustrations, and is on sale in most of Nairobi's bookshops.

LANGUAGE

English and Swahili (correctly known as Kiswahili) are the official languages and are taught in schools throughout Kenya, but there are many other major tribal languages, including Kikuyu, Luo, Kikamba, Maasai and Samburu as well as a plethora of minor tribal languages. Most urban Kenyans and even tribal people involved in the tourist industry speak English so you shouldn't experience too many problems making yourself understood. Italian and German are also spoken by many Kenyans but usually only among those associated with the tourist trade on the coast.

It's extremely useful, however, to have a working knowledge of Swahili, especially outside urban areas and in remote parts of the country, since this will open doors and enable you to communicate with people who don't speak English. It's also the most common language which speakers of different tribal languages use to communicate with each other. Even tribespeople who haven't been to school will usually be able to speak *some* Swahili. If you're planning on visiting Tanzania you'll find it extremely useful, as it's now the official language there (though English is still used extensively).

Another language you'll come across in Kenya, one which is spoken almost exclusively by the younger members of society, is Sheng. Essentially a patois, it's a fairly recent development and, like Swahili, is still evolving. It's composed of a mixture of Swahili and English along with a fair sprinkling of Hindi, Gujarati, Kikuyu and several other Kenyan tribal languages. It originated in the colonial days as a result of the employment of African nannies by whites to look after their children.

Unless you can speak reasonable Swahili,

you probably won't realise Sheng is being spoken since it does sound quite similar to Swahili. One of the indications that it's being spoken is the initial greeting between friends. The greeting will be *'Sassa!'*. The response to this can be, *'Besht'*, *'Mambo'* or *'Fit'* (pronounced almost like 'feet'). There is then an option to continue in Sheng or any other mutually intelligible language. For more Swahili terms see the Food section in Facts for the Visitor.

Lonely Planet's *Swahili phrasebook* by Robert Leonard gives you a more complete overview.

Pronunciation

Vowels Swahili vowels are pronounced as follows:

a	as the 'a' in 'father'
e	between the 'e' in 'better' and the 'a' in 'may'
i	as the 'ee' sound in 'bee'
o	as the 'o' in 'old'
u	as the 'oo' in 'too'

Double vowels, or any two vowels together, are pronounced as two separate syllables. There are no diphthongs as in English. Thus *saa* (time/hour) is pronounced 'sa-a', and *yai* (egg) is pronounced 'ya-i'.

Consonants Some consonants require a bit of explanation:

dh	as the 'th' in 'this'
ky	as the 'ch' in 'chat'
th	as the 'th' in 'thing'
ny	as the 'ñ' in Spanish *señora*
ng'	as the 'ng' in 'sing'
gh	like a 'g', but more of a gargle
r	in English closer to a 'd', but 'r' will also be understood

Word Stress

In words with more than two syllables, the stress generally falls on the second last syllable.

Greetings & Civilities

It is considered rude to speak to someone without first greeting them, so even if you only want directions, greet the person first. It's the English equivalent of 'excuse me'.

Hello.	*Jambo* or *Salama*

(There is also a respectful greeting used for elders: *shikamoo*. The reply is *marahaba*.)

Welcome.	*Karibu*
Goodbye.	*Kwaheri*
Thank you.	*Asante*
Thanks very much.	*Asante sana*
You're welcome.	*Karibu*
Yes.	*Ndiyo*
No.	*Hapana*

Small Talk

How are you?	*Habari?*
I'm fine, thanks.	*Nzuri.*
What's your name?	*Unaitwa nani?*
My name is ...	*Jina langu ni*
Where are you from?	*Unatoka wapi?*
I come from ...	*Mimi ninatoka*
Where do you live?	*Unakaa wapi?*
I live in ...	*Ninakaa*
How are things in ...?	*Habari ya ... ?*
Fine.	*Nzuri*
No problem.	*Hakuna matata*
It is ...	*Ninaitwa ...*
How was the journey?	*Habari ya safari?*
I don't understand.	*Nisamehe sifahamu.*
white people	*Wazungu*
white person	*Mzungu*

Getting Around

I want to go to ...	
	Mimi nataka kwenda ...
Is this the way to ... ?	
	Hii njia ya ... ?
How much to go to ... ?	
	Shillingi ngapi kwenda ... ?

When does the ... leave?	*... inakwenda saa ngapi?*
bus	*basi*
train	*treni*
truck/car	*gari*

boat	*boti*	restaurant	*hoteli ya chakula*
share taxi	*gari ndogo*	toilet	*choo*

Drive slowly.	*Endesha pole pole.*
Wait a minute.	*Ngoja kidogo.*
Stop here.	*Simama hapa.*

On Safari

Look there.	*tazama pale*
What is there?	*iko nini pale?*
What animal is that?	*huyo mnyama gani?*

ticket	*tikiti*
airport	*kiwanja cha ndege*
bus station	*stesheni ya basi*
railway station	*stesheni ya treni*
taxi	*teksi*
right	*kwa kulia*
left	*kwa kushoto*

antelope	*pofu/kulungu*
bird	*ndege*
crocodile	*mamba*
elephant	*ndovu/tembo*
gazelle	*swulu/swara/paa*
giraffe	*twiga*
hippopotamus	*kiboko*
hyena	*fisi*
lion	*simba*
monkey	*tumbili*
rhinoceros	*kifaru*
snake	*nyoka*
water buffalo	*nyati*
zebra	*punda milia*

Accommodation

Where is a ... ?	*Wapi ... ?*
hotel	*hoteli ya kulalia*
very good hotel	*hoteli mzuri sana*
guesthouse	*nyumba ya wageni*

Do you have a room for ... ?	*Kuna rumu ya ... ?*
one person	*mtu moja*
two people	*watu wahili*

Shopping

Where is a/the ... ?	*Wapi ... ?*
chemist/pharmacy	*duka la dawa*
bookshop	*duka la vitabu*
grocery	*duka*
market	*sokoni*

How much is the room?	*Rumu ni shillingi ngapi?*
I'd like to see the room.	*Nataka kuona rumu tafadhali.*
Is there hot water?	*Kuna maji ya moto?*

I want to buy ...	*Mimi nataka kununua ...*
Do you have ... ?	*Kuna ... ?*
There is.	*Kuna*
There isn't.	*Hakuna*
How much?	*Ngapi?*
This is very expensive.	*Hii ni bei ghali sana.*

for one day	*kwa siku moja*
for a week	*kwa wiki mzima*
shower	*shawa*
bath	*bafu*
fan	*feni*
sheet	*shiti*
towel	*tauli*
key	*ufunguo*
noisy	*kelele*

too big	*kubwa*
too small	*kidogo*
more	*zaidi*

Around Town

Where is a/the ...?	*Wapi ... ?*
bank	*benki*
hotel	*hoteli ya kulalia*
hospital	*hospitali*
police station	*stesheni ya polisi*
post office	*posta*

clothing	*nguo*
insect repellent	*dawa ya mdudu*
laundry detergent	*omo*
mosquito coil	*dawa ya mbu ya kuwashia*
soap	*sabuni*
toilet paper	*karatasi ya choo*

toothpaste   *dawa ya meno*

Time

Bear in mind that Swahili time and Western time differ by six hours, although unless you get right out into the small towns this should be no cause for confusion.

What is the time?	*Saa ngapi?*
It's 8 o'clock.	*Saa nane.*
When?	*Saa ngapi?*
today	*leo*
tomorrow	*kesho*
yesterday	*jana*
hour	*saa*
week	*wiki*
month	*mwezi*
year	*mwaka*

Days of the Week

Monday	*Jumatatu*
Tuesday	*Jumanne*
Wednesday	*Jumatano*
Thursday	*Alhamisi*
Friday	*Ijumaa*
Saturday	*Jumamosi*
Sunday	*Jumapili*

Numbers

1	*moja*
2	*mbili*
3	*tatu*
4	*nne*
5	*tano*
6	*sita*
7	*saba*
8	*nane*
9	*tisa*
10	*kumi*

The 'teens' are *kumi na* ... (10 plus ...), the 20s *ishrini na* ... (20 plus ...) and so on. The hundreds are *mia*, and the thousands *elfu*.

11	*kumi na moja*
12	*kumi na mbili*
20	*ishrini*
30	*thelathini*
40	*arobaini*
50	*hamsini*
60	*sitini*
70	*sabini*
80	*themanini*
90	*tisini*
100	*mia*
200	*mia mbili*
1000	*elfu*
2126	*elfu mbili mia moja ishrini na sita*

Health & Emergencies

I am ill.	*Mimi mgonjwa.*
Please call a doctor.	*Tafadhali wewe umwite daktari.*
I hurt here.	*Ninaumwa hapa.*
I'm pregnant.	*Nina mimba.*

pharmacy	*duka la dawa*
dentist	*daktari la meno*
doctor	*daktari*
hospital	*hospitali*
medicine	*dawa*

Watch out!	*angalia*
Leave me alone!	*niache*
I'm lost.	*nimepotea*
I've been robbed.	*nimeibiwa*

Facts for the Visitor

PLANNING
When to Go
There are a number of factors to take into account when considering what time of year to visit Kenya. The main tourist season is January and February, as the weather at this time of year is generally considered to be the best – hot and dry. It's also when you'll find the largest concentrations of bird life on the Rift Valley lakes, and the animals in the game parks tend to congregate more around the watercourses as other sources dry up, making them easier to spot.

From June to September could be called the 'shoulder season' as the weather is still dry. This is also the time of that visual extravaganza – the annual wildebeest migration into the Masai Mara Game Reserve from the Serengeti.

During the long rains (from March to May) and the short rains (from October to December) things are much quieter – places tend to have rooms available and accommodation prices come down. The rains generally don't affect your ability to get around and see things (although Amboseli National Park can be flooded out), it's just that you may get rained on, especially in the late afternoon. This is especially so in the highlands and the west of the country.

Maps
Lonely Planet's *Kenya travel atlas* provides the handiest, most accurate maps available and is a great companion to this guidebook. The *Tourist Map of Kenya*, printed and published in Kenya, gives good detail as does the *Kenya Route Map*.

Macmillan publishes a series of maps to the game parks and these are not bad value at KSh 250 each.

The Public Map Office next to the Kenyatta Conference Centre in Nairobi has a stock of government survey maps covering the whole country. The most popular ones (Mt Kenya, Mt Elgon and those covering the game parks) are often out of stock but it's worth getting hold of these maps if possible.

Many of their other Survey of Kenya maps, other than those available in the bookshops, are not available to the general public without official authorisation. This is hard to get and takes time so if you're a tourist with limited time you can forget it. Even people with credentials, such as Kenyan residents and members of the Mountain Club of Kenya (MCK), have great difficulty or find it impossible to get hold of detailed maps of the country.

What to Bring
Bring the minimum. One thing that many travellers in Kenya find once they actually get there is that they have far too much gear. This is not only an uncomfortable inconvenience, it also means that instead of taking back some special reminders of Kenya you'll be taking back the same extra pullover and jeans that you set off with. Unless it's absolutely essential, *leave it at home!*

A rucksack (backpack) is far more practical than an overnight bag, and is essential if you plan to climb Mt Kenya or do any amount of walking. It is worth buying a good-quality bag right at the start – African travel soon sorts out the good stuff from the junk, and if it's the latter you've opted for you'll be cursing it the whole way.

What type of pack you buy is largely a matter of personal preference. We find that the travel packs with the straps which zip into a compartment in the back are excellent. Although expensive, they are a compromise solution to a number of different problems; however, they are not really suited for specialised activities such as climbing or serious walking.

A day pack is a worthwhile item, if only for keeping your camera dry and out of the incredible dust which seems to permeate every crack and crevice when you're on safari. For those reasons and for security, it needs to be one which zips shut. Quite a few travellers use the local *kiondos* (woven baskets) which are fine if they suit your purpose.

A sleeping bag is more or less essential if you are travelling overland beyond Kenya or planning to climb mountains, but within the country itself there are enough hotels for you not to need one. On the other hand, carrying a sleeping bag and closed-cell foam mat does give you a greater degree of flexibility and means that if you take a safari you know you'll have adequate gear. Sleeping bags are the one thing which all camping safari companies require you to provide.

There's always much discussion about the pros and cons of carrying a tent, and basically it boils down to what sort of travelling you want to do, and how much weight you're prepared to carry. As with a sleeping bag, a tent is not necessary if you're just travelling from town to town, but carrying your own portable shelter opens up a whole stack of exciting possibilities. The same applies to carrying a stove and cooking gear, so give some careful thought as to what you want to do, and how. On the other hand, the full range of camping equipment can be hired from various places in Nairobi (principally Atul's on Biashara St) and from certain hotels elsewhere in the country (principally the Naro Moru River Lodge on the western side of Mt Kenya).

Clothes need to be both practical and take into account local sensibilities. Although Kenya straddles the equator, the large variations in altitude lead to equally large variations in climate. The coast is hot and steamy year-round, while Nairobi and the western highlands get decidedly cool in the evenings in July and August, so you need to carry one decent warm pullover as well as warm-weather gear. A windproof and waterproof jacket also comes in handy, particularly during the rainy seasons.

Overlooked by many people but absolutely indispensable is a good pair of sunglasses. The amount of glare you experience in the bright tropical light is not only uncomfortable but can damage your eyes. A

hat which shades your face and neck is also well worth considering. A water bottle is well worth any slight inconvenience it may cause. It needs to be unbreakable, have a good seal, and hold at least one litre.

Other useful items are a Swiss Army knife, a small sewing kit (including a few metres of fishing line and a large needle for emergency rucksack surgery), a 10m length of light nylon cord for a washing line along with a handful of clothes pegs, and half a tennis ball makes a good fits-all washbasin plug.

Most toiletries – soap, shaving cream, shampoo, toothpaste, toilet paper, tampons – are available throughout the country.

The one thing that you're really going to appreciate in Kenya is a pair of binoculars. When out in the game parks you can put them to constant use and they are essential for identifying the dozens of species of mammals and birds that you'll come across. If you don't plan on going to the game parks they are still handy just for the scenery, or perhaps for trying to spot that potential lift coming over the horizon when you're stuck out in the north somewhere...

HIGHLIGHTS

Without doubt it is the game parks which attract people to Kenya – the wildlife viewing here is still probably the best and most easily accessible in Africa. The Masai Mara Game Reserve is the number one attraction, but other parks such as Amboseli, Tsavo and Samburu also provide great viewing. Bird-watchers will also be well satisfied with a visit to Kenya. The Rift Valley lakes of Baringo, Bogoria, Naivasha and Nakuru are all excellent for bird-watching.

For the really adventurous, Kenya offers some exciting prospects. Climbing the snowy heights of Mt Kenya, the second highest peak in Africa, is a superb experience and one which doesn't require specialised equipment. Other options include camel (or even donkey) safaris with Samburu tribespeople in the semidesert regions of the north; white-water canoeing; hiking safaris; fishing and ballooning.

People looking for activities requiring

slightly less energy will find the beaches of the coast the perfect place to chill out for a while. And it doesn't have to be purely hedonistic either, as there is a rich history and also the strong Swahili coastal culture to delve into. Also see the table on pages 40-41.

TOURIST OFFICES
Local Tourist Offices
Considering the extent to which the country relies on toursim, it's incredible to think that there's not even a tourist office in Nairobi.

There's not much available in the way of printed information either. There are a couple of free pamphlets which go some way towards filling the gap. They are the monthly *Tourist's Kenya*, and the quarterly *What's On*, which also covers Uganda and Tanzania. Both contain articles on subjects of tourist interest plus selective listings of hotels, restaurants, airlines, embassies, banks, safari and car-hire companies, train and boat schedules, and a considerable amount of advertising (which is why they're free). You can pick them up at the larger hotels and at travel agencies.

The only other tourist offices in the country are the ones in Mombasa on Moi Ave (☎ (011) 311231) and in Malindi on Lamu Rd.

Tourist Offices Abroad
The Ministry of Tourism maintains a number of overseas offices including:

France
    5 Rue Volney, Paris 75002 (☎ (01) 42 60 66 88; fax 42 61 18 84)
Germany
    Hochstrasse 53, 6 Frankfurt A M (☎ (069) 282552; fax 239239)
Hong Kong
    1309 Liu Chong Hing Bank Building, 24 Des Voeux Rd, Central (☎ 2523-6053)
Japan
    Yurakucho Building, 1-10 Yurakucho, 1 Chome, Chiyoda-ku, Tokyo (☎ (03) 214-4595)
Sweden
    Birger Jarlsgatan 37, 11145 Stockholm (☎ (08) 218300; fax 200030)

Switzerland
    Bleicherweg 30, CH8039 Zurich (☎ (01) 202-2244; fax 202-2256)
UK
    25 Brook's Mews (off Davies St) Mayfair, London (☎ (0171) 355-3144; fax 495-8656)
USA
    9100 Wilshire Blvd, Los Angeles, CA 90212 (☎ (213) 274-6634; fax 859-7010)
    424 Madison Ave, New York, NY 10017 (☎ (212) 486-1300; fax 688-0911)

VISAS & DOCUMENTS
Visas
Visas are required by all except nationals of some Commonwealth countries (nationals of Australia, New Zealand and Sri Lanka and British passport holders of Indian, Pakistani and Bangladeshi origin require visas), Denmark, Ethiopia, Germany, the Republic of Ireland, Italy, Norway, Spain, Sweden, Turkey and Uruguay. Those who don't need visas are issued a Visitor's Pass on entry which is valid for a stay of up to six months. Three months is the average, but it depends what you ask for.

The cost of a three-month, single-entry visa is roughly the local equivalent of US$30, though this does vary. Two photos (sometimes three) are required but you normally do not have to show an onward ticket or a letter from a travel agent confirming that you have booked one. Visas remain valid for a period of three months from the date of issue. Apply well in advance for your visa especially if doing it by mail – they can take up to two weeks in some countries (eg Australia). Kenyan visa applications are simple and straightforward in Tanzania and Uganda, and payment is accepted in local currency.

Visas are also available on arrival at Jomo Kenyatta International airport in Nairobi for US$20. Transit visas issued at the airport are valid for three days only and are definitely not extendable.

If you enter Kenya through a land border no-one will ever ask you for an onward ticket or 'sufficient funds'. This isn't always the case if you enter by air. A lot depends on what you look like, whether you're male or female, what you write on your immigration

HIGHLIGHTS

	REGION	COMMENTS

Historical

Fort Jesus
Mombasa's Portuguese fort, built in 1593 changed hands nine times between 1631 and 1875; it's now a museum.

The Coast — The Old Town's biggest attraction is well worth a visit, especially Omani house in the fort's north-western corner.

Gedi
The mysterious and extensive ruins of this Arab-Swahili town are among the principal historical monuments on the coast.

The Coast — Excavations indicate that the town was founded in the 13th century and was inexplicably abandoned in the 17th or 18th century.

Lamu
The island is home to Kenya's oldest town which has changed little over the centuries.

The Coast — Access is by diesel-powered launch from the mainland. Shela beach is one of the most relaxing places you'll ever visit.

Activities

Diving/Snorkelling
Diving is excellent at the marine national parks of Malindi and Watamu. It's even better at the Shimoni and Wasini islands, although they are less accessible and developed.

The Coast — You can rent a glass-bottom boat at Malindi to see the amazing variety of coral and fish.

White-Water Rafting
A day trip from Nairobi starts above the Sagana on the Athi River, finishing above the Masinga Dam. An exciting three-day trip takes you from Yatta Gap to Tsavo Safari Camp.

Around Nairobi — Of the two major rivers in Kenya, the Athi/Galana and Tana, only the former has substantial rapids, chutes and waterfalls.

Beaches
The beach at Diani is one of the best; Tiwi Beach is more low-key and camping on the beach is available. Lamu boasts some of the finest beaches on the coast.

The Coast — Beaches south of Mombasa are white coral sand and are protected by a coral reef that excludes sharks.

Trekking
Mt Kenya (5199m) is Africa's second highest mountain and its gleaming and eroded snow-covered peaks act as a magnet for trekkers, particularly from mid-January to late February and late August to September.

The Central Highlands — Mt Kenya's highest peaks, Batian and Nelion, can only be reached by mountaineers, but trekkers can reach the third highest, Point Lenana (4985m). The views are simply stunning.

Dhow Trips
The main form of travel around the Lamu archipelago, which boasts more dhows than anywhere else off the East African coast. Dhows began to be used as a form of transport from the 8th century onwards.

The Coast — One of Kenya's most worthwhile and memorable experiences; make sure you take a hat and sunblock as there is rarely any shade on board.

	REGION	COMMENTS
Safaris		
Wildlife Safaris They typically start and end in either Nairobi or Mombasa and are conducted through Kenya's world-renowned national parks; there are usually two, sometimes three, game drives per day.	National Parks & Reserves	All budgets are catered for: camping safaris for the budget-conscious to lodge and tented camp sites for those who want luxury.
Balloon Safaris Hot-air balloon flights depart daily from both Keekorok Lodge and Fig Tree Lodge in Masai Mara National Reserve and include a champagne breakfast on the plains.	Western Kenya	Not to be missed, a silent dawn glide is an absolutely superb way of viewing the savannah plains and the animals, without the intrusion of vehicles and dozens of other tourists.
Cycling Safaris The best options are a three-day Masai Mara combined trip (walking/cycling) or a six-day trip, again through the heart of Maasai land.	Various	Doing your own thing entails confronting the dangers of cycling along main roads in Kenya and the major off-road problems of punctures from thorn trees.
Camel Safaris Most of them take place in the Samburu and Turkana tribal areas between Isiolo and Lake Turkana.	Northern Kenya	A superb way of getting off the beaten track and into areas where vehicle safari's don't go. An unrivalled desert experience among the nomads of Kenya's north.
National Parks & Reserves		
Masai Mara National Reserve The highlight is no doubt the annual wildebeest migration when literally millions of these ungainly beasts move north from the Serengeti in July and August in search of lush grass, before turning south again around October.	Western Kenya	Virtually everyone who visits Kenya goes to this 320 sq km of open grassland dotted with flat-topped Acacia trees. This is the Kenyan section of the Serengeti Plains and wildlife abounds.
Amboseli National Park The best reasons for visiting this park are its dramatic setting against the backdrop of Mt Kilimanjaro, and the chance of spotting a black rhino.	Southern Kenya	Although there's not the huge profusion of game found in the Masai Mara, the game here is easy to spot. There are also huge herds of elephants.
Kakamega Forest Reserve A superb slab of virgin tropical rainforest in the heart of an intensively cultivated agricultural area. Home of a number of primates and over 330 species of birds.	Western Kenya	The forest itself comprises a number of habitats but is generally very dense. This reserve is well worth the minimal effort required to get to it.
Lake Baringo Of Kenya's 1200 different species of birds, more than 450 species have been sighted at this freshwater lake. The lake has many islands (two of them inhabited).	The Rift Valley	A spectacular sight and a very mellow place to visit. One of the islands is called 'Devil's Island' and locals claim it is haunted.

card and which immigration officer you deal with. If it's fairly obvious that you aren't intending to stay and work then you'll generally be given the benefit of the doubt. Put yourself in a strong position before you arrive: look smart, and write the name of an expensive hotel on your immigration card in the appropriate section.

So long as your visa remains valid you can visit either Tanzania or Uganda and return without having to apply for another visa. This does not apply to visiting any other countries.

Visa Extensions Visas can be renewed in Nairobi at the immigration office (☎ (02) 332110), Nyayo House (ground floor), on the corner of Kenyatta Ave and Uhuru Highway; at the office in Mombasa (☎ (011) 311745), or at immigration on the 1st floor of Reinsurance Plaza, corner of Jomo Kenyatta Highway and Oginga Odinga Rd in Kisumu during normal office hours.

Remember that you don't need a re-entry visa if you're only going to visit Tanzania or Uganda *as long as your visa remains valid.* Staff at the immigration offices are generally friendly and helpful.

Other Visas Since Nairobi is a common gateway city to East Africa and the city centre is easy to get around, many travellers spend some time here picking up visas for other countries which they intend to visit. If you are going to do this you need to plan ahead because some embassies only accept visa applications in the mornings, others only on certain days of the week. Some take 24 hours to issue, others 48 hours. Some visas (Sudan, for instance) may have to be referred to the country's capital city, but this is rare. See the Embassies list later in this chapter for details of addresses and office hours.

Burundi
    The embassy is currently not issuing visas and will tell you to get one on arrival at the border.

Ethiopia
    In theory, the embassy here only issues visas to people who have no Ethiopian Embassy in their own country. In practice, anyone can get one, although you may have to come up with a reason why you didn't get one before leaving home. One-month visas cost US$63, require one photo and take 48 hours to issue. Applications must be submitted before noon.

Rwanda
    Double-entry, seven-day transit visas cost KSh 1500; one-month visas cost KSh 2000, require two photos and are delivered the same day if you apply before noon. If you are travelling overland, it's much cheaper (US$20) to get a visa on arrival at the border.

Somalia
    The embassy does not presently function and, in fact, anyone can get into Somalia at present without a visa.

Sudan
    Visas are difficult to get because of the civil war and all applications have to be referred to Khartoum. An onward ticket is necessary, so get one of these before you apply.

Tanzania
    The cost of a visa depends on your nationality and ranges from US$55 for British nationals, US$45 for Americans, US$26 for Japanese, US$16 for Germans, to US$10 for others. One photo is required and visas take half an hour to issue. Visas are also available on arrival at Namanga, Kilimanjaro airport (Arusha), Dar es Salaam airport and at Zanzibar.

Uganda
    Most nationalities don't require visas. For those that do they cost up to US$25, require two photos and are delivered the same day if you apply before noon.

Zaïre
    Visa fees are the same for all nationalities. Single-entry/multiple-entry visas cost KSh 2500/4000 for a month; KSh 4500/6000 for two months, and KSh 6500/7500 for three months. Two photos are required and visas are delivered the same day if you apply before 11 am.

Travel Insurance

Get some! A travel insurance policy to cover theft, loss and medical problems is a wise idea. There are a wide variety of policies and your travel agent will have recommendations (though not necessarily informed recommendations or personal experience). See the Health Insurance section under Health later in this chapter.

Driving Licence & Permits

If you plan on doing any driving, your licence from home is sufficient.

Carnets When bringing a foreign-registered vehicle into Kenya, it must be covered by a *carnet de passage*. The purpose of a carnet is to allow an individual to take a vehicle into a country where duties would normally be payable, without the necessity of having to pay those duties. It's a document which guarantees that if a vehicle is taken into a country but not exported, then the organisation which issued it will accept responsibility for payment of import duties. Carnets can only be issued by national motoring organisations and before they will issue such a document they have to be absolutely sure that if the need to pay duties ever arises they would be reimbursed by the individual to whom the document is issued. The amount of import duty can vary considerably but generally speaking, it's between one and 1½ times the new value of the vehicle.

To get a carnet you need to make an application to a national motoring organisation in the country where your vehicle is registered. They will issue you with an indemnity form for completion either by a bank or an insurance company. Once this is completed and a bond deposited with a bank or a premium paid to an insurance company, the motoring organisation issues a carnet. The cost of the carnet itself is minimal. The whole process generally takes about a week to complete.

EMBASSIES

Kenya has diplomatic representation in many countries. Where there is no Kenyan embassy or high commission, visas can be obtained from the British Embassy or high commission.

Kenyan Embassies Abroad

Kenya maintains the following embassies and consulates abroad:

Australia
    QBE Building, 33 Ainslie Ave, Canberra, ACT 2601 (☎ (06) 247-4788; fax 257-6613)

Belgium
    1-5 Avenue de la Joyeuse, 1040 Brussels (☎ (02) 230-3065; fax 230-8462)
Canada
    415 Laurier Ave, Ottawa, Ontario, KIN 6R4 (☎ (613) 563-1773; fax 233-6599)
Egypt
    7 El Mohandes Golal St, Mohandessen, Giza, Cairo (☎ (091) 345-3628; fax 344-3400)
Ethiopia
    Fikre Miriam Rd, PO Box 3301, Addis Ababa (☎ (01) 610303; fax 611433)
France
    3 Rue Cimarosa, 75116 Paris (☎ (01) 45 53 35 00; fax 45 53 95 32)
Germany
    Villichgasse 17, 5300 Bonn-Bad Godesburg 2, Micael Plaza, (☎ (0228) 356042; fax 358428)
India
    E-66 Vasant Marg, Vasant Vihar, 110057 New Delhi (☎ (011) 687-6538; fax 687-6550)
Italy
    Via Icilio No 14, 00153 Rome (☎ (06) 578-1192; fax 5742-2788)
Japan
    24-3 Yakumo, 3 Chome, Meguru-ku, Tokyo 152 (☎ (03) 723-4006; fax 723-4488)
Netherlands
    Niewe Parklaan 21, 2597 The Hague (☎ (070) 350-4215; 355-3594)
Nigeria
    52 Oyinkan Abayomi Drive, Ikoyi, PO Box 6464, Lagos (☎ (01) 682768; fax 685532)
Pakistan
    Sector G-613, House 8, St 88, PO Box 2097, Islamabad (☎ (051) 211243; fax 212542)
Rwanda
    PO Box 1215, Kigali (☎ 82774; fax 86234)
South Africa
    302 Brooke St, Menlo Park, Pretoria (☎ (012) 342-5066)
Sudan
    Street 3 Amarat, PO Box 8242, Khartoum (☎ 43758; fax 452264)
Sweden
    Birger Jarlsgatan 37, 2tr, 10395 Stockholm (☎ (08) 218300; fax 209261)
Tanzania
    NIC Investment House, Samora Ave, PO Box 5231, Dar es Salaam (☎ (051) 46362; fax 46519)
Uganda
    Plot No 2030, Muyenga Kansanga Rd, PO Box 5220, Kampala (☎ (041) 267386; fax 267369)
UK
    45 Portland Place, London W1N 4AS (☎ (0171) 636-2371; fax 323-6717)
USA
    2249 R St NW, Washington DC 20008 (☎ (202) 387-6101; fax 462-3829)

Zaïre
> 4002 Ave de l'Ouganda, BP 9667, Zone Degombe, Kinshasa (☎ (012) 33205)

Zambia
> Harambee House, 5207 United Nations Ave, PO Box 50298, Lusaka (☎ (01) 227938; fax 263150)

Zimbabwe
> 95 Park Lane, PO Box 4069, Harare (☎ (04) 792901; fax 723042)

Foreign Embassies in Kenya

Countries which maintain diplomatic missions in Kenya include:

Australia
> Riverside Drive, Nairobi (PO Box 39341); open Monday to Thursday 7.45 am to 4.30 pm and Friday 7.45 am to 12.30 pm (☎ 445034; fax 444617)

Belgium
> Limuru Rd, Muthaiga, Nairobi (PO Box 30461); open Monday to Friday 8.30 am to 12.30 pm (☎ 741564; fax 741568)
> Mitchell Cotts Building, Mombasa (☎ 220231; fax 312617)

Burundi
> Development House, Moi Ave, Nairobi (PO Box 44439); open Monday to Friday 8.30 am to 12.30 pm and 2 to 5 pm (☎ 218458; fax 219005)

Canada
> Comcraft House, Haile Selassie Ave, Nairobi (PO Box 30481); open 7.30 am to 4 pm (☎ 214804; fax 226987)

Denmark
> HFCK Building, Koinange St, Nairobi (PO Box 40412); open Monday to Friday 7.45 am to 3 pm (☎ 331088; fax 331492)

Djibouti
> Comcraft House, Haile Selassie Ave, Nairobi (PO Box 59528); open weekdays 8.30 am to 3 pm (☎ 339633; fax 339168)

Egypt
> Harambee Plaza, Haile Selassie Ave, Nairobi (PO Box 30285); open 9 am to 3.30 pm (☎ 225991; fax 21560)

Eritrea
> Rehema House, Westlands, Nairobi (PO Box 38651), open weekdays 8.30 am to 12.30 pm and 2 to 5.30 pm (☎ 443163; fax 443165)

Ethiopia
> State House Ave, Nairobi (PO Box 45198); open 8.30 am to 12.30 pm and 2 to 5 pm (☎ 723027; fax 723401)

France
> Barclays Plaza, Loita St, Nairobi (PO Box 41784); open 8.30 am to noon (☎ 339783; fax 220435)

Germany
> Williamson House, 4th Ngong Ave, Nairobi (PO Box 30180); open 8.30 am to 12.30 pm (☎ 712527; fax 714886)
> Palli House, Nyerere Ave, Mombasa (☎ 314732; fax 314504)

Greece
> IPS Building, Kimathi St, Nairobi (PO Box 30543); open 9 am to 2 pm (☎ 340722; fax 216044)

India
> Jeevan Bharati Building, Harambee Ave, Nairobi (PO Box 30074); open 8.30 am to 1 pm and 1.30 to 4.30 pm (☎ 222566; fax 334167)

Israel
> Bishops Rd, Nairobi (PO Box 30107); open 8 am to 1 pm and 2 to 5 pm (☎ 722182; fax 715966)

Italy
> Jubilee Building, Moi Ave, Mombasa (☎ 314705; fax 316654)

Japan
> ICEA Building, Kenyatta Ave, Nairobi (PO Box 60202); open 8.30 am to 12.30 pm and 2 to 4.30 pm (☎ 332955; fax 216530)

Malawi
> Waiyaki Way, Westlands, Nairobi (PO Box 30453); open 9 am to 12.30 pm and 2 to 4.30 pm (☎ 440569; fax 440568)

Mauritius
> Union Towers, Moi Ave, Nairobi (PO Box 49326); open 8.30 am to 12.30 pm and 2 to 5 pm; this is also the Air Mauritius office (☎ 330215)

Mozambique
> 159 Kyuna Road, Kyuna, Nairobi (PO Box 66923); open weekdays 9 am to noon (☎ 581857; fax 582478)

Netherlands
> Uchumi House, Nkrumah Ave, Nairobi (PO Box 41537); open 9 am to 12.30 pm (☎ 227111; fax 339155)
> ABN Bank Building, Nkrumah Rd, Mombasa (☎ 311043)

New Zealand
> Minet-ICDC House, Mamlaka Rd, Nairobi (PO Box 47383); (☎ 722467; fax 722549)

Pakistan
> St Michael's Rd, Westlands, Nairobi (PO Box 30045); open 8.30 am to 1 pm and 1.30 to 3.30 pm (☎ 443911; fax 443803)

Rwanda
> International House, Mama Ngina St, Nairobi (PO Box 48579); open 8.30 am to 12.30 pm and 2 to 5 pm (☎ 334341; fax 336365)

Seychelles
> Agip House, Waiyaki Way, Westlands, Nairobi (PO Box 20400); open 9 am to noon and 2.30 to 4 pm (☎ 445599; fax 441150)

Somalia
There is currently no functioning Somali embassy.

South Africa
Lonrho House, Standard St, Nairobi (PO Box 42441); open weekdays 8.30 am to 12.30 pm and 1.30 to 4.30 pm (☎ 228469; fax 223687)

Spain
Bruce House, Standard St, Nairobi (PO Box 45503) (☎ 335711; fax 332858)

Sudan
Minet-ICDC House, Mamlaka Rd, Nairobi (PO Box 74059); open 8.30 am to 3.30 pm (☎ 720853)

Sweden
International House, Mama Ngina St, Nairobi (PO Box 30600); open 8.30 am to 5 pm (☎ 229042; fax 218908)
Alba Petroleum, Miji Kenda Rd, Mombasa (☎ 314065; fax 492804)

Tanzania
Continental House, corner of Uhuru Highway and Harambee Ave, Nairobi; PO Box 47790; open 8.30 am to noon (☎ 331056; fax 218269)
Palli House, Nyerere Ave, Mombasa; open weekdays from 8.30 am to 12.30 pm and 2.30 to 5 pm. (☎ 229595; fax 227077).

Uganda
Uganda House, Baring Arcade, Kenyatta Ave, Nairobi (PO Box 60853); open 8.30 am to 12.30 pm and 1.30 to 5 pm (☎ 330801; fax 330970)

UK
Visa & Immigration Section, Bruce House, Standard St, Nairobi (PO Box 30465); open 8.30 to 11.30 am and 1.30 to 3.30 pm (☎ 335944; fax 333196)
Note: From January 1997 the embassy is on Upper Hill Rd, west of the city centre.

USA
Moi Ave, Nairobi (PO Box 30137); open 7.30 am to 12.30 pm and 1.15 to 4.15 pm (☎ 334141; fax 340838)

Zaïre
Electricity House, Harambee Ave, Nairobi (PO Box 48106); open 8.30 am to 12.30 pm and 2 to 5 pm (☎ 229771)

Zambia
Nyerere Rd, Nairobi (PO Box 48741); (☎ 724796; fax 718494)

Zimbabwe
Minet-ICDC House, Mamlaka Rd, Nairobi (PO Box 30806); open 8.30 am to 12.30 pm and 2 to 4.30 pm (☎ 721045; fax 726503)

CUSTOMS

There are strict laws about wildlife products; the export of products made from elephant, rhino and sea turtle are prohibited. The collection of coral is also not allowed.

Always check to see what permits are required, especially for the export of any plants, insects and shells.

The other usual regulations apply – 250g of cigarettes, one litre of alcohol, and other personal items such as cameras, laptop computers and binoculars can all be brought in.

MONEY
Costs

The cost of budget accommodation in Kenya is very reasonable so long as you're happy with communal showers and toilets. Clean sheets are invariably provided and sometimes you'll also get soap and a towel. For this you're looking at KSh 200 a single and KSh 300 a double and up. If you want your own bathroom, costs rise to around KSh 300 a single and KSh 450 a double. It can be slightly cheaper on the coast but more expensive in Nairobi.

There are plenty of small cafes in every town, usually concentrated in a certain area. They cater to local people and you can get a traditional meal for around KSh 100 or KSh 200. Often the food isn't up to much but sometimes it can be excellent. For just a little bit more, the Indian restaurants are great value. Some offer all-you-can-eat lunches for around KSh 250. The food is not only tasty but you won't need to eat for the rest of the day either. A splurge at a better class restaurant is going to set you back between KSh 500 and KSh 1000.

The price of beer and soft drinks depends entirely on where you buy them. They're obviously cheapest bought from a supermarket (around KSh 35 for a beer). Using this as a benchmark figure, you would be paying around 30% more for them in a basic bar, slightly more than double in a better class bar or restaurant, and up to eight times as much in a five-star hotel!

Public transport is very reasonable and the trains are excellent value. To travel from one end of Kenya to the other (Mombasa to Malaba) on the train in 2nd class is going to cost you KSh 3750. In 3rd class it's less than half that. Buses are priced about halfway between the 3rd and 2nd-class train fares.

The thing that is going to cost you most in Kenya is safaris. A three-day safari, for instance, with companies which cater for budget travellers is priced from around US$180; seven days costs from US$400. This includes transport, food, hire of tents, national park entry fees, camping fees and the wages of the guides and cooks. In other words, more or less everything except a few drinks and tips.

Car hire is even more expensive and is probably out of reach of most budget travellers. A 4WD Suzuki costs from KSh 4600 per day with unlimited mileage; petrol is extra. If you don't want 4WD then a small car, such as a Nissan Sunny, costs around KSh 3200 per day.

Note: The prices used in this book are as quoted by the organisation concerned, and may sometimes be in dollars and sometimes in Kenyan shillings. Whether costs are quoted in US$ or KSh makes no difference as payment is always in local currency.

Carrying Money

Never carry large amounts of cash around, especially if you have a preference for money belts which are worn outside your clothes. Those worn under your clothes are much less enticing to would-be thieves, of which there are no shortage. See the Dangers and Annoyances section later in this chapter for a complete rundown on personal security.

Currency

The unit of currency is the Kenyan shilling (KSh), which is made up of 100 cents. Notes in circulation are KSh 1000, 500, 200, 100, 50, 20 and 10; there are new ('copper') coins of KSh 1, 5 and 10. These are quite small and as yet not in wide circulation. Old ('silver') coins are much bigger and heavier, and come in the denominations of KSh 5 (seven-sided) and KSh 1, and 50, 10 and 5 cents. Note that most public telephones in Nairobi and other major towns have been modified to only accept 'copper' coins; a major pain as they are not that easy to find.

Currency Exchange

After a period of instability in the early 1990s, the Kenyan shilling has stabilised, and now hovers around the US$1 = KSh 55 to KSh 60 mark.

Australia	A$1	=	KSh 45
France	1FFr	=	KSh 11
Germany	DM1	=	KSh 37
United Kingdom	UK£1	=	KSh 93
USA	US$1	=	KSh 55

While most major currencies are accepted in Nairobi and Mombasa, once away from these two centres you'll run into problems with currencies other than US dollars, pounds sterling, French francs and German marks.

If you are going to be travelling elsewhere in East Africa, play it safe and carry dollars – it makes life much simpler.

Changing Money

With the deregulation of the money supply, foreign exchange bureaus (forex) have popped up all over the place, and these are the preferred places to change money these days. Their rates are competitive, and they don't charge commission. The rates for the main bureaus in Nairobi are published in the *Daily Nation* newspaper.

Banks will change money, but they charge commission, in some cases pretty steep ones. They also take a lot longer than the forex bureaus, are open shorter hours and are generally less convenient.

Black Market

Once again, the deregulation of the money supply has knocked the black market on the head. Despite this, you still get characters sidling up beside you in Nairobi or Mombasa to whisper the magic words: 'Change Money?'. While they might promise enticing rates, in reality they can't offer any more than the banks or forex, and are just trying to lure you into a situation where they can relieve you of some of your cash. Give them a big miss.

Tipping

With such an active tourist industry, Kenya is a country where tipping is expected. Obviously there's no need to tip in the very basic African eateries or hotels, on *matatus* (local minibuses) or when using other public transport. In better restaurants 5 to 10% of the bill is the usual amount, although in these a service charge of 10% will often have been included on the bill (though it's debatable whether the employees ever get it).

If you take a safari then it's also expected that you tip your driver, guide and cook. The majority of employees in this industry earn low wages so it's suggested you be as generous as you feel able to. Around KSh 150 per day per employee is about the right amount. This is the cost per person, and how much you give obviously depends on whether they have worked well to make your safari enjoyable. ■

POST & COMMUNICATIONS

The Kenyan postal system is run by the government Kenya Posts & Telecommunications Corporation (KPTC; known disparagingly as 'kaput'). Despite this, the postal system is very reliable. Letters sent from Kenya rarely go astray but do take up to two weeks to reach Australia or the USA. Incoming letters to Kenya take around a week to reach Nairobi.

Parcels or books sent by surface mail take up to 4½ months to arrive – but they do get there.

Postal Rates

The airmail rates (in KSh) for items posted from Kenya are:

Item	Africa	Europe	USA & Australia
letter	17.50	20.00	25.00
postcard	9.50	13.00	17.50
aerogram	14.50	14.50	14.50

Sending Mail

Kenya is a good place from which to send home parcels of goodies, or excess gear. In the main post office in Nairobi you'll often see at least a couple of people busily taping and wrapping boxes to send home. You have to take the parcel *unwrapped* to be inspected by customs at the post office not later than 3.30 pm. You then wrap and send it. The whole process is very simple and, apart from wrapping the parcel, takes only a few minutes.

There's usually no-one selling wrapping material outside the post office in Nairobi so you need to bring along your own cardboard, paper, tape and string. The cheapest place to get this stuff is the supermarket on Koinange St between Kenyatta Ave and Standard St. Otherwise go to Biba on Kenyatta Ave at the junction with Muindu Mbingu St. Cardboard boxes are usually available free of charge or for a few shillings at supermarkets.

Receiving Mail

Letters can be sent care of poste restante in any town. Virtually every Africa overland traveller uses Nairobi as a mail drop and so the amount of mail in poste restante here is amazing. The vast majority of it finds its way into the correct pigeonholes though there's naturally the occasional mistake. Most of the mistakes are entirely the fault of the letter writer. Make sure your correspondents write your name in block capitals and underline the surname.

Some travellers use the American Express Clients Mail Service and this can be a useful alternative to poste restante. Officially you are supposed to have an Amex card or be using their travellers' cheques to avail yourself of this service but no check of this is made at the office in Nairobi. The postal addresses in Nairobi and Mombasa are:

American Express Clients Mail Service
    Express Kenya Ltd, PO Box 40433, Nairobi
    Express Kenya Ltd, PO Box 90631, Mombasa

The Nairobi office is in Bruce House on Standard St (☎ (02) 334722), while the Mombasa office is on Nkrumah Rd (☎ (011) 312461).

Telephone

The phone system works reasonably well, although it can take a number of attempts to get an international connection depending on the time of day.

International Calls International calls from Kenya are expensive. To Europe or the USA the rate is US$3 per minute, to Australia and New Zealand it's US$4 per minute. From a private phone it's marginally cheaper.

International calls are easy to make from major towns where you can either go through the operator or dial yourself on a private line.

Phone cards are available at the Nairobi Extelcoms office and at the Kenyatta Conference Centre in denominations of KSh 200, KSh 400 and KSh 1000 but the supply of them is erratic. If phone cards are available, there are card phones in Posta Rd near the main post office in Nairobi, and another two in the Extelcoms office on Haile Selassie Ave. There are also two in the lobby of the Kenyatta Conference Centre and these are by far the best to use as there's little background noise there. Mombasa, Malindi, Lamu, Nakuru and Kisumu each have at least one card phone at their main post office.

Operator-connected calls are also easy to make. The Extelcoms office in Nairobi is open from 8 am to midnight. Again, the Kenyatta Conference Centre is the best place to ring from as there's an international call office in the lobby and this is much quieter and less frantic than the Extelcoms office. It is only open until 6 pm, however.

In other towns, calls can be made from the post office, although there may be some delay in getting through to the international operator in Nairobi.

It's possible to make reverse-charge (collect) calls, but only to the UK, Europe and the USA.

Calls put through a hotel operator from your room will be loaded at between 25 and 50% so check what they're going to charge you before making a call.

Local Calls Local and long-distance calls are also quite straightforward. There are public phone boxes in every town and these all seem to work. The only problem is that there aren't enough of them, especially in Nairobi where you'll often find a queue of four or five people at each box. Local calls cost KSh 3, while long-distance call rates vary depending on the distance. Call boxes in Nairobi accept only new ('copper') KSh 1 or KSh 5 coins. Elsewhere the boxes are slowly being converted, and will usually have 'copper coins only' scribbled on them in black marker pen if they are ones that have been converted.

When making a local call, make sure you put a coin into the slot first (regardless of what you insert after that). If you don't, you may have problems making your call.

Calls to Tanzania and Uganda are only long-distance calls, not international. The telephone codes for the main towns and cities in Kenya are as follows:

Diani Beach	0127
Eldoret	0321
Isiolo	0165
Kakamega	0331
Kericho	0361
Kilifi	0125
Kisii	0381
Kisumu	035
Kitale	0325
Lamu	0121
Malindi	0123
Maralal	0368
Mombasa	011
Nairobi	02
Naivasha	0311
Nakuru	037
Nanyuki	0176
Nyahururu	0365
Nyeri	0171
Thika	0151
Voi	0147
Watamu	0122

E-mail
E-mail is still in its early stages, and thus far there are two providers in Nairobi, one of which is set up for taking casual e-mail. See the Internet & E-mail section in the Nairobi chapter for details.

BOOKS

Large-format, hardback, photo-essay books on Africa are becoming easier to find in western bookshops. However, you will be hard-pressed to find a good selection of novels, plays and biographies by contemporary African authors, even though many of them are published by the African branches of major western publishing companies. Heinemann's African Writers Series offers a major collection of such works but they're generally only available in Nairobi and Mombasa. In Western countries, they're to be found only in specialist bookshops.

Most books are published in different editions by different publishers in different countries. So, a book might be a hardcover rarity in one country while it's readily available in paperback in another. Fortunately, bookshops and libraries search by title or author, so your local bookshop or library is well placed to advise you on the availability of the recommendations that follow.

Lonely Planet

Africa on a shoestring covers more than 50 African countries, concentrating on practical information for budget travellers. *East Africa* covers the region in considerably more detail, with information on Tanzania, Uganda, Rwanda, Burundi and eastern Zaïre.

Trekking in East Africa by David Else covers a selection of treks and expeditions in the mountains and wilderness areas of Kenya, Tanzania, Uganda and Malawi, and has plenty of advice and general information about trekking in this part of the world.

Lonely Planet's *Swahili phrasebook* will help you solve most of your basic language problems in Kenya. And the *Kenya travel atlas* is also a great companion to this guide.

Guidebooks

Insight Kenya, edited by Mohammed Amin & John Eames, is another of the popular APA guidebook series with many excellent photographs and a lively text. It concentrates more on the country's history, its peoples, cultures, sights and wildlife rather than on practical information and is a good book to read either before you go or while you're there.

Guide to Mt Kenya & Kilimanjaro, edited by Iain Allan, has been written and added to over the years by dedicated enthusiasts, but is mainly directed at skilled climbers and mountaineers. It contains information on the rock and ice routes, but also has some (very dated) trail descriptions, maps, photographs, descriptions of fauna, flora, climate and geology, even mountain medicine.

More recent practical guides to East Africa which would be excellent companions to the one you are reading are those by David Else. The *Camping Guide to Kenya* covers every camp site in Kenya – the cities, national parks and mountain areas – and contains information and advice for campers and backpackers venturing off the main routes into the more remote areas. *Mountain Walking in Kenya* covers a selection of walking routes through the mountain and highland regions of Kenya including everything from easy strolls around Lake Naivasha to longer hikes on Mt Kenya. There's an equipment guide as well as accurate maps and colour photographs.

Travel

Journey to the Jade Sea by John Hillaby, recounts this prolific travel writer's epic trek to Lake Turkana in northern Kenya in the days before the safari trucks began pounding up the dirt. Other books to look for include *Initiation* by JS Fontaine, *A Bend in the River* by VS Naipaul and *Travels in the Congo* by André Gide.

Two women's accounts of life in East Africa earlier this century have been recent best sellers. *Out of Africa* by Karen Blixen (Isak Dinesen) has also been made into a hugely popular movie. *West with the Night* by Beryl Markham has also been a major best seller.

History, Politics & Economics

There are numerous books on the history of Africa which include *The Penguin Atlas of African History* by Colin McEvedy, *A Short History of Africa* by Roland Oliver & JD

Fage, and *The Story of Africa* by Basil Davidson. Also excellent reading is *The Africans – A Triple Heritage* by Ali A Mazrui, which was published in conjunction with a BBC TV series of the same name.

For the origins and development of the coastal Swahili culture and how it has been affected by the arrival of the Portuguese in the Indian Ocean, the standard work is *The Portuguese Period in East Africa* by Justus Strandes. For a radical African viewpoint of the effects of colonialism in general, Walter Rodney's *How Europe Underdeveloped Africa* is well worth a read.

Worthwhile contemporary accounts include the extremely readable but rather discouraging *The Africans* by David Lamb. Or there's *The Making of Contemporary Africa* by Bill Freund, and *A Year in the Death of Africa* by Peter Gill. On contemporary Kenyan politics, it's well worth reading Oginga Odinga's *Not Yet Uhuru* and *Detained – A Prison Writer's Diary* by Ngugi wa Thiong'o, for a radically different view from that put out by the Kenyatta and Moi regimes.

Not exclusively about Africa but very relevant to bilateral and multilateral aid issues, is the *Lords of Poverty* by Graham Hancock, an exposé of the bungling and waste perpetrated by the UN, IMF, World Bank and others.

The *Africa Review* an annual production by World of Information, offers an overview of the politics and economics of every African country as well as detailed facts and figures. It's well balanced and researched and makes no attempt to curry favours with any particular regime.

General

There are some excellent, but quite expensive, photo-essay hardbacks which you may prefer to look for in a library. They include *Journey though Kenya*, by Mohammed Amin, Duncan Willets & Brian Tetley. There is a companion volume entitled *Journey through Tanzania* by the same authors.

Other colourful books on the region include *Africa Adorned* by Angela Fisher;

Ivory Crisis by Ian Parker & Mohammed Amin; *Isak Dinesen's Africa* by various authors; *Africa: A History of a Continent* by Basil Davidson; and *Through Open Doors: A View of Asian Cultures in Kenya* which is by Cynthia Salvadori. She also co-authored with Andrew Fedders *Peoples & Cultures of Kenya*.

In addition to the above, there's also a surfeit of large-format, hardback books on the various tribal societies of Kenya, especially the Maasai and Samburu, which you'll see in the bookshops of Nairobi and Mombasa.

Flora & Fauna Guides

A Field Guide to the Larger Mammals of Africa by Jean Dorst & Pierre Dandelot, together with *A Field Guide to the Birds of East Africa* by JG Williams & N Arlott, should suffice for most people's interest in the national parks and wildlife reserves.

ONLINE SERVICES

As with everything, the World Wide Web has a wealth of information – and a lot of dross – on Africa and Kenya. The following places have some interesting information and are good links to related sites:

Africa Online
   www.africaonline.com
   www.africaonline.com/AfricaOnline/newsstand.
   html
Kenya Human Rights Initiative
   www.spidergraphics.com/khr/khrdef.html
University of Pennsylvania African Studies Dept
   www.sas.upenn.edu

NEWSPAPERS & MAGAZINES

Tabloid newspapers are printed in both English and Swahili. Of the three English-language papers, the best is the *Daily Nation*, which has both local and overseas coverage, and is well worth reading on a daily basis if you want to get a feel for what's happening in the country. It has the best cartoons, doesn't shirk from criticising the government and exposing corruption, but balances this with a similar attitude towards the opposition parties. The others are the *Kenya Times* (the KANU party rag) and the *Standard*.

There is also a good range of locally produced magazines in both English and Swahili. Principal among these is the *Weekly Review* which is the Kenyan equivalent of Time/Newsweek. Radicals berate this magazine as being a tool of government propaganda but it does, nevertheless, discuss issues in much greater detail than any of the daily newspapers and it's well worth a read.

The *East African* is a decent weekly paper published by the Nation group, which is also available in Uganda.

The *East African Chronicle* is an interesting business weekly. Probably the best for in-depth articles which pull no punches is the *Economic Review*, which is also a weekly paper.

Foreign newspapers (up to a week old) in English, French, Italian and German are readily available in Nairobi and Mombasa but vary greatly in price depending on where you buy them.

Current affairs magazines such as *Time, Newsweek, New African* and *South* are also widely available at a controlled price which is printed on the front cover. *New African* is the best of the bunch if you're looking for detailed coverage of African affairs and events. It's published monthly.

RADIO & TV

The Kenyan Broadcasting Corporation (KBC) has radio transmissions in English, Swahili and more specialised languages such as Hindi and African languages.

The BBC World Service and Voice of America transmit to East Africa on short wave around 12 hours a day and have programmes in English and Swahili. The *Daily Nation* prints the programmes each day. Although BBC frequencies change from time to time, the main ones to try if you have a short-wave radio include: 17885, 15420 and 9630 kHz.

There are two TV channels – KBC and KTN. The latter is better except that it no longer produces its own independent news programmes but takes them from KBC.

Films

With its wide, sweeping landscapes and superb scenery, Kenya has been the location for many feature films. Unfortunately the quality of the films does not always match the quality of the backdrop!

Films shot in Kenya include the 1950s Tarzan movies, *King Solomon's Mines* in 1950, the pretty awful *White Mischief*, featuring Sarah Miles and John Hurt, and the 1985 film depiction of the life of Karen Blixen, *Out of Africa*, which starred Robert Redford and Meryl Streep.

A more recent offering is the 1990 *Mountains of the Moon*, which dramatised the historic journey of Burton and Speke in their search for the source of the Nile. ■

Many programmes are imported from Europe, the USA and Australia.

M-Net cable TV from South Africa is the most recent addition to the scene in Kenya. Most mid-range and better hotels subscribe to the service, so you can watch CNN, BBC and a host of movie and sports channels.

PHOTOGRAPHY
Film

You'll find Kodak and Fuji 64, 100, 200 and 400 ASA slide film readily available in Nairobi and Mombasa, but 800 ASA is harder to find. The same is true for colour-negative film.

As an indication of price, 36-exposure slide film in Nairobi costs KSh 400, 36-exposure colour print film is KSh 200.

Wildlife Photography

For serious wildlife photography a SLR (single lens reflex) camera which can take long focal length lenses is necessary. If all you have is a little generic 'snapomatic' you may as well leave it behind. Although they are becoming more sophisticated these days, the maximum focal length is around 110 mm – still too small for getting decent shots.

Zoom lenses are best for wildlife photography as you can frame your shot easily to get the best composition. This is important as the animals are constantly on the move.

The 70 to 210 mm zoom lenses are popular and the 200 mm is really the minimum you need to get good close-up shots. The only problem with zoom lenses is that with all the glass (lenses) inside them they absorb about 1½ 'f' stops of light, which is where the 200 and 400 ASA film starts to become useful.

Telephoto (fixed focal length) lenses give better results than zoom lenses but you're limited by having to carry a separate lens for every focal length. A 400 or 500 mm lens brings the action right up close, but again you need the 200 or 400 ASA film to make the most of them. You certainly need a 400 or 500 mm lens if you're keen on photographing bird life.

Another option is to carry a 2x teleconverter, which is a small adaptor which fits between the lens and the camera body, and doubles the focal length of your lens, so a 200 mm lens becomes 400 mm. These are a good cheap way of getting the long focal length without having to buy expensive lenses. They do, however, have a couple of disadvantages. The first is that, like the larger lenses themselves, a teleconverter uses about 1½ 'f' stops of light. Another disadvantage is that, depending on the camera and lens, teleconverters can make it extremely difficult to focus quickly and precisely, which is an important consideration when both you and the animals are on the move.

When using long lenses a tripod can be extremely useful, and with anything greater than about 300 mm it's a necessity. The problem here is that in the confined space of the hatch of a minibus (assuming you'll be taking an organised safari) it is impossible to set up the tripod, especially when you are sharing the confined space with at least three or four other people. Miniature tripods are available and these are useful for setting up on the roof of the van, although you can also rest the lens itself on the roof, provided that the van engine is switched off to stop any vibration.

Whatever combination of camera, lenses and accessories you decide to carry, make sure they are kept in a decent bag which will protect them from the elements, the dust, and the knocks they are bound to receive. It's also vital to make sure that your travel insurance policy includes your camera gear if it gets stolen.

Camera Hire & Repair

If you don't have the inclination or the resources to buy expensive equipment but you know a bit about photography, it is possible to hire SLR cameras and lenses in Nairobi. The best place to do this is Expo Camera Centre (☎ (02) 221797), Jubilee Exchange, Mama Ngina St. It's busy here every day of the working week both with local businesses and tourists so you know it must be reliable and that the prices will be competitive.

Expo also has a well-equipped repair shop where you can leave an ailing camera to be repaired with confidence. They do an excellent job but they're not cheap (neither is anyone else).

Film Processing

There are plenty of one-hour film-processing labs in Nairobi, and at least one in all other major towns. They can handle any film speeds. The cost is reasonable and the results just as good as what you'd get back home. Three good places are Expo Camera Centre, Camera Experts and the lab next to the Coffee House, all on Mama Ngina St. The lab also has a wide variety of film for sale.

Developing of print films is not cheap at around US$15 for 36 exposures. Developing and mounting of slide film is cheap, however, and it saves you the worry of taking exposed film through dodgy airport X-ray machines. It costs KSh 285 for a roll of 36 and takes four hours, but can only be done in Nairobi.

Photographing People

As is the case in any country where you are a tourist, this is a subject which has to be approached with some sensitivity. People such as the Maasai and the Samburu have had so many rubbernecks pointing cameras at them for so many years that they are utterly sick to death of it – with good reason. There are even signs up in Namanga and Amboseli saying that it is prohibited to take photos of the Maasai. This doesn't mean that you can't, but just that you'll have to pay for it. Much as you may find this abhorrent, it is nevertheless an aspect of the tourism industry you'll just have to accept – put yourself in their position and try to think what you'd do.

It is of course possible to take pictures of people with zoom lenses but, most of the time, what's the point? By paying or giving some sort of gift, you'll not only get a better picture by using a smaller lens but you'll have some interaction with your subject. You might even get an invitation to see the family (and possibly photograph them).

TIME
Time in Kenya is GMT/UTC plus three hours all year round.

One thing that must be borne in mind is that Swahili time is six hours out of kilter with the way we tell the time, so that noon and midnight are 6 o'clock (*saa sitta*) Swahili time, and 7 am and 7 pm are 1 o'clock (*saa moja*). Just add or subtract six hours from the time you are told and hopefully from the context you'll be able to work out whether the person is talking about am or pm! You don't come across this all that often unless you speak Swahili but you still need to be prepared for it.

ELECTRICITY
Kenya uses the 240-volt system. The power supply is usually reliable and uninterrupted in most places though there are occasional failures. Power sockets are of the three-square-pin variety as used in the UK, although some older buildings have round-pin sockets. Bring a universal adaptor if a power supply is important to you.

HEALTH
Travel health depends on your predeparture preparations, your day-to-day health care while travelling and how you handle any medical problem or emergency that does develop. While the list of potential dangers

can seem quite frightening, with a little luck, some basic precautions and adequate information few travellers experience more than upset stomachs.

Travel Health Guides
There are a number of books on travel health:

Staying Healthy in Asia, Africa & Latin America, Dirk Schroeder, Moon Publications, 1994. Probably the best all-round guide to carry, as it's compact but very detailed and well organised.
Travellers' Health, Dr Richard Dawood, Oxford University Press, 1995. Comprehensive, easy to read, authoritative and also highly recommended, although it's rather large to lug around.
Where There is No Doctor, David Werner, Macmillan, 1994. A very detailed guide intended for someone, like a Peace Corps worker, going to work in an underdeveloped country, rather than for the average traveller.
Travel with Children, Maureen Wheeler, Lonely Planet Publications, 1995. Includes basic advice on travel health for younger children.

Predeparture Planning
Health Insurance A travel insurance policy to cover theft, loss and medical problems is a good idea. The policies handled by STA Travel and other student travel organisations are usually good value. Some policies offer lower and higher medical-expense options but the higher ones are chiefly for countries such as the USA which have extremely high medical costs. Make sure you check the small print:

- Some policies specifically exclude 'dangerous activities' which can include scuba diving, motorcycling, even trekking. If such activities are on your agenda you don't want that sort of policy. A locally acquired motor-cycle licence may not be valid under your policy.
- You may prefer a policy which pays doctors or hospitals direct rather than you having to pay on the spot and claim later. If you have to claim later make sure you keep all documentation. Some policies ask you to call back (reverse charges) to a centre in your home country where an immediate assessment of your problem is made.
- Check that the policy covers ambulances or an emergency flight home. If you have to stretch out you will need two seats and somebody has to pay for them!

Medical Kit It's wise to carry a small, straightforward medical kit. The kit should include:

- Aspirin or paracetamol (acetaminophen in the US) – for pain or fever.
- Antihistamine (such as Benadryl) – useful as a decongestant for colds and allergies, to ease the itch from insect bites or stings, and to help prevent motion sickness. There are several antihistamines on the market, all with different pros and cons (eg a tendency to cause drowsiness), so it's worth discussing your requirements with a pharmacist or doctor. Antihistamines may cause sedation and interact with alcohol so care should be taken when using them.
- Antibiotics – useful if you're travelling well off the beaten track, but they must be prescribed and you should carry the prescription with you. Some individuals are allergic to commonly prescribed antibiotics such as penicillin or sulpha drugs. It would be sensible to always carry this information when travelling.
- Loperamide (eg Imodium) or Lomotil for diarrhoea; prochlorperazine (eg Stemetil) or metaclopramide (eg Maxalon) for nausea and vomiting. Antidiarrhoea medication should not be given to children under the age of 12.
- Rehydration mixture – for treatment of severe diarrhoea. This is particularly important if travelling with children, but is recommended for everyone.
- Antiseptic such as povidone-iodine (eg Betadine), which comes as a solution, ointment, powder and impregnated swabs – for cuts and grazes.
- Calamine lotion or Stingose spray – to ease irritation from bites or stings.
- Bandages and Band-aids – for minor injuries.
- Scissors, tweezers and a thermometer (note that mercury thermometers are prohibited by airlines).
- Cold and flu tablets and throat lozenges.
- Insect repellent, sunblock, chapstick and water purification tablets.
- A couple of syringes, in case you need injections away from Nairobi or Mombasa. (Ask your doctor for a note explaining why they have been prescribed.)

Ideally antibiotics should be administered only under medical supervision and should never be taken indiscriminately. Take only the recommended dose at the prescribed intervals and continue using the antibiotic for the prescribed period, even if the illness seems to be cured earlier. Antibiotics are quite specific to the infections they can treat. Stop immediately if there are any serious reactions and don't use the antibiotic at all if you are unsure that you have the correct one.

In Kenya, if a medicine is available at all it will generally be available over the counter and the price will be much cheaper than in the west. However, be careful if buying drugs, particularly where the expiry date may have passed or correct storage conditions may not have been followed. Bogus drugs are not uncommon and it's possible that drugs which are no longer recommended, or have even been banned in the west, are still being dispensed.

Health Preparations Make sure you're healthy before you start travelling. If you are embarking on a long trip make sure your teeth are OK; there are lots of places where a visit to the dentist would be the last thing you'd want.

If you wear glasses take a spare pair and your prescription.

If you require a particular medication take an adequate supply, as it may not be available locally. Take the prescription or, better still, part of the packaging showing the generic rather than the brand name (which may not be locally available), as it will make getting replacements easier. It's wise to have a legible prescription or a letter from your doctor with you to show that you legally use the medication.

Immunisations Vaccinations provide protection against diseases you might meet along the way. For visitors to Kenya no immunisations are required by law, but it is a good idea to take precautions, especially if you will be travelling off the beaten track.

It is important to understand the distinction between vaccines recommended for travel in certain areas and those required by law. Essentially the number of vaccines subject to international health regulations has been dramatically reduced over the last 10 years. Currently yellow fever is the only vaccine subject to international health regulations – vaccination as an entry requirement is a requirement when re-entering the USA,

Australia and European countries after visiting Kenya.

Occasionally travellers face bureaucratic problems regarding cholera vaccine even though all countries have dropped it as a health requirement for travel. Under some situations it may be wise to have the vaccine despite its poor protection, eg for the trans-Africa traveller. This is not necessary if you are only visiting Kenya.

On the other hand a number of vaccines are recommended for travel in certain areas. These may not be required by law but are recommended for your own personal protection.

Most travellers from western countries will have been immunised against various diseases during childhood but your doctor may still recommend booster shots against measles or polio, diseases still prevalent in many developing countries. The period of protection offered by vaccinations differs widely and some are contraindicated if you are pregnant.

All vaccinations should be recorded on an International Health Certificate, which is available from your physician or government health department.

Plan ahead for getting your vaccinations: some of them require an initial shot followed by a booster, while some vaccinations should not be given together. It is recommended you seek medical advice at least six weeks prior to travel.

In Kenya, immunisations are available from the government health centre at City Hall in Nairobi. Vaccinations which travellers to Kenya should consider include:

Tetanus & Diphtheria Boosters are necessary every 10 years and protection is highly recommended.

Polio A booster of either the oral or injected vaccine is required every 10 years to maintain our immunity from childhood vaccination. Polio is a very serious, easily transmitted disease which is still prevalent in Kenya.

Typhoid Available either as an injection or oral capsules. Protection lasts from one to five years depending on the vaccine and is useful if you are travelling for long in rural, tropical areas. You may get some side effects such as pain at the injection site, fever, headache and a general unwell feeling. A single-dose injectable vaccine, which appears to have few side effects, is now available but is more expensive. Side effects are unusual with the oral form but occasionally an individual will have stomach cramps.

Hepatitis A The most common travel-acquired illness which can be prevented by vaccination. Protection can be provided in two ways – either with the antibody gamma globulin or with a vaccine called Havrix 1440. Havrix 1440 provides long-term immunity (possibly more than 10 years) after an initial course of two injections and a booster one year later. It may be more expensive than gamma globulin but certainly has many advantages, including length of protection and ease of administration. Since it is a vaccine it will take about three weeks to provide satisfactory protection – hence the need for careful planning prior to travel. Gamma globulin is not a vaccination but a ready-made antibody which has proven very successful in reducing the chances of hepatitis infection. It should be given as close as possible to departure because it is at its most effective in the first few weeks after administration and the effectiveness tapers off gradually between three and six months.

Hepatitis B Persons who should receive a hepatitis B vaccination include anyone who anticipates contact with blood or other bodily secretions, particularly those who intend to stay in the country for a long period of time and children. The vaccination course comprises three injections given over a six-month period then boosters every three to five years. The initial course of injections can be given over as short a period as 28 days then boosted after 12 months if more rapid protection is required.

Yellow Fever Protection lasts 10 years and is recommended. You usually have to go to a special yellow-fever vaccination centre. Kenya is considered by the WHO to be a yellow fever area, so vaccinations are required for re-entry to Europe, Asia or Australia. Note that vaccination is contraindicated during pregnancy but if you must travel to a high-risk area it is probably advisable.

Meningococcal Meningitis Vaccination is recommended for travellers to Kenya and East Africa. A single injection will give good protection against the A, C, W and Y groups of the bacteria for at least a year. The vaccine is not, however, recommended for children under two years because they do not develop satisfactory immunity from it.

Rabies A rabies vaccination involves having three injections over 21 to 28 days and should be considered by those who will spend a month or longer in Kenya, especially if they are cycling, handling animals, caving, travelling to remote areas, or children (who may not report a bite). If someone who has been vaccinated is bitten or scratched by an animal they will require two booster injections of vaccine.

Cholera Not required by law but occasionally travellers face bureaucratic problems on some border crossings. Protection is poor and it lasts only six months. It is contraindicated in pregnancy.

Basic Rules

Care in what you eat and drink is the most important health rule; stomach upsets are the most likely travel health problem (between 30 and 50% of travellers in a two-week stay experience this) but the majority of these upsets will be relatively minor. Don't become paranoid; trying the local food is part of the experience of travel, after all.

Water The number-one rule is *don't drink the water* and that includes ice. If you don't know for certain that the water is safe always assume the worst. Reputable brands of bottled water or soft drinks are generally fine. Take care with fruit juice, particularly if water may have been added. Milk should be treated with suspicion, as it is often unpasteurised. Boiled milk is fine if it is kept hygienically. Tea or coffee should also be OK, since the water should have been boiled.

The simplest way of purifying water is to boil it thoroughly. Vigorously boiling for five minutes should be satisfactory; however, at high altitude water boils at a lower temperature, so germs are less likely to be killed.

Simple filtering will not remove all dangerous organisms, so if you cannot boil water it should be treated chemically. Chlorine tablets (Puritabs, Steritabs or other brand names) will kill many but not all pathogens, including giardia and amoebic cysts. Iodine is very effective in purifying water and is available in tablet form (such as Potable Aqua), but follow the directions carefully and remember that too much iodine can be harmful.

Tincture of iodine (2%) can also be used. Four drops of tincture of iodine per litre or quart of clear water is the recommended dosage; the treated water should be left to stand for 20 to 30 minutes before drinking. Flavoured powder will disguise the taste of treated water and is a good idea if you are travelling with children.

Micropur water filters are useful for long trips. They filter out parasites, bacteria and viruses, and although expensive they are more cost-effective than buying water.

Food Salads and fruit should be washed with purified water or peeled where possible. Ice cream is usually OK if it is a reputable brand name, but beware of street vendors' icecream and of ice cream that has melted and been refrozen. Shellfish such as mussels, oysters and clams should be avoided as well as undercooked meat, particularly in the form of mince. Steaming does not make shellfish safe for eating.

If a place looks clean and well run and if the vendor also looks clean and healthy, then the food is probably safe. In general, places that are packed with travellers or locals will be fine, while empty restaurants are questionable. The food in busy restaurants is cooked and eaten quite quickly with little standing around and is probably not reheated.

Nutrition If your food is poor or limited in availability, if you're travelling hard and fast and therefore missing meals, or if you simply lose your appetite, you can soon start to lose weight and place your health at risk.

Make sure your diet is well balanced. Eggs, tofu, beans, lentils and nuts are all safe ways to get protein. Fruit you can peel (bananas, oranges or mandarins for example) is usually safe (melons can harbour bacteria in their flesh and are best avoided) and a good source of vitamins. Try to eat plenty of grains (including rice) and bread. Remember that although food is generally safer if it is cooked well, overcooked food loses much of its nutritional value. If your diet isn't well balanced or if your food intake is insufficient, it's a good idea to take vitamin and iron pills.

In hot weather make sure you drink enough – don't rely on feeling thirsty to indicate when you should drink. Not needing to urinate or very dark yellow urine is a danger sign. Always carry a water bottle with you on long trips. Excessive sweating can lead to loss of salt and therefore muscle cramping. Salt tablets are not a good idea as a preventative, but in places where salt is not used much adding salt to food can help.

Medical Problems & Treatment

Self-diagnosis and treatment can be risky, so wherever possible seek qualified help. Although we do give drug dosages in this section, they are for emergency use only. Medical advice should be sought where possible before administering any drugs.

In Nairobi an embassy or consulate can usually recommend a good place to go for such advice. So can five-star hotels, although they often recommend doctors with five-star prices. (This is when that medical insurance really comes in useful!) In some places standards of medical attention are so low that for some ailments the best advice is to get on a plane and go somewhere else.

Sunburn In the tropics, the desert or at high altitude you can get sunburnt surprisingly quickly, even through cloud. Use a sunscreen and take extra care to cover areas which don't normally see sun – eg your feet. A hat provides added protection, and you should also use zinc cream or some other barrier cream for your nose and lips. Calamine lotion is good for mild sunburn.

Prickly Heat Prickly heat is an itchy rash caused by excessive perspiration trapped under the skin. It usually strikes people who have just arrived in a hot climate and whose pores have not yet opened sufficiently to cope with greater sweating. Keeping cool but bathing often, using a mild talcum powder or even resorting to air-conditioning may help until you acclimatise.

Heat Exhaustion Dehydration or salt deficiency can cause heat exhaustion. Take time to acclimatise to high temperatures and make sure you get sufficient liquids. Wear loose

---

Vital Signs

A normal body temperature is 98.6°F or 37°C; more than 2°C (4°F) higher is a 'high' fever. A normal adult pulse rate is 60 to 80 beats per minute (children 80 to 100, babies 100 to 140). You should know how to take a temperature and a pulse rate. As a general rule the pulse increases about 20 beats per minute for each 1°C rise in fever.

Respiration (breathing) rate is also an indicator of illness. Count the number of breaths per minute: between 12 and 20 is normal for adults and older children (up to 30 for younger children, 40 for babies). People with a high fever or serious respiratory illness (like pneumonia) breathe more quickly than normal. More than 40 shallow breaths a minute usually means pneumonia. ■

---

clothing and a broad-brimmed hat. Do not do anything too physically demanding.

Salt deficiency is characterised by fatigue, lethargy, headaches, giddiness and muscle cramps and in this case salt tablets may help. Vomiting or diarrhoea can deplete your liquid and salt levels. Anhydrotic heat exhaustion, caused by an inability to sweat, is quite rare. Unlike the other forms of heat exhaustion it is likely to strike people who have been in a hot climate for some time, rather than newcomers.

Heat Stroke This serious condition, which can also be fatal, can occur if the body's heat-regulating mechanism breaks down and the body temperature rises to dangerous levels. Long, continuous periods of exposure to high temperatures can leave you vulnerable to heat stroke. You should avoid excessive alcohol or strenuous activity when you first arrive in a hot climate.

The symptoms are feeling unwell, not sweating very much or at all and a high body temperature (39°C to 41°C). Where sweating has ceased the skin becomes flushed and red. Severe, throbbing headaches and lack of coordination will also occur, and the sufferer may be confused or aggressive. Eventually the victim will become delirious or convulse. Hospitalisation is essential, but meanwhile get victims out of the sun, remove their clothing, cover them with a wet sheet or towel and then fan continually.

Fungal Infections Fungal infections, which occur with greater frequency in hot weather, are most likely to occur on the scalp, between the toes or fingers (athlete's foot), in the groin (jock itch or crotch rot) and on the body (ringworm). You get ringworm (which is a fungal infection, not a worm) from infected animals or by walking on damp areas, like shower floors.

To prevent fungal infections wear loose, comfortable clothes, avoid artificial fibres, wash frequently and dry carefully. If you do get an infection, wash the infected area daily with a disinfectant or medicated soap and water, and rinse and dry well. Apply an antifungal cream or powder like the widely available Tinaderm. Try to expose the infected area to air or sunlight as much as possible and wash all towels and underwear in hot water as well as changing them often.

Hypothermia Too much cold is just as dangerous as too much heat, particularly if it leads to hypothermia. If you are trekking on Mt Kenya be prepared.

Hypothermia occurs when the body loses heat faster than it can produce it and the core temperature of the body falls. It is surprisingly easy to progress from very cold to dangerously cold due to a combination of wind, wet clothing, fatigue and hunger, even if the air temperature is above freezing. It is best to dress in layers; silk, wool and some of the new artificial fibres are all good insulating materials. A hat is important, as a lot of heat is lost through the head. A strong, waterproof outer layer is essential, as keeping dry is vital. Carry basic supplies, including food containing simple sugars to generate heat quickly and lots of fluid to drink. A space blanket is something all travellers in cold environments should carry.

Symptoms of hypothermia are exhaustion, numb skin (particularly toes and fingers), shivering, slurred speech, irrational or violent behaviour, lethargy, stumbling, dizzy spells, muscle cramps and violent bursts of energy. Irrationality may take the form of sufferers claiming they are warm and trying to take off their clothes.

To treat mild hypothermia, first get the person out of the wind and/or rain, remove their clothing if it's wet and replace it with dry, warm clothing. Give them hot liquids – not alcohol – and some high-kilojoule, easily digestible food. Do not rub victims, instead allow them to slowly warm themselves. This should be enough to treat the early stages of hypothermia. The early recognition and treatment of mild hypothermia is the only way to prevent severe hypothermia, which is a critical condition.

Altitude Sickness Acute Mountain Sickness or AMS occurs at high altitude and can be fatal. The lack of oxygen at high altitudes (over 2500m) affects most people to some extent. It may be mild (benign AMS) or severe (malignant AMS) and occurs because less oxygen reaches the muscles and the brain at high altitude, requiring the heart and lungs to compensate by working harder. Symptoms usually develop during the first 24 hours at altitude but may be delayed up to three weeks. Symptoms of benign AMS include headache, lethargy, dizziness, difficulty sleeping and loss of appetite. Malignant AMS may develop from benign AMS or without warning and can be fatal. These symptoms include breathlessness, dry cough (which may progress to the production of pink, frothy sputum), severe headache, lack of coordination and balance, confusion, irrational behaviour, vomiting, drowsiness and unconsciousness.

In benign AMS the treatment is to remain resting at the same altitude until recovery, usually a day or two. Paracetamol or aspirin can be taken for headaches. If symptoms persist or become worse, however, descent is necessary; even 500m can help. The treatment of malignant AMS is immediate descent to a lower altitude. There are various drug treatments available but they should never be used to avoid descent or enable further ascent by a person with AMS.

A number of measures can be adopted to prevent acute mountain sickness:

- Ascend slowly – have frequent rest days, spending two to three nights at each rise of 1000m. If you reach a high altitude by trekking, acclimatisation takes place gradually and you are less likely to be affected than if you fly direct.
- The altitude at which a person sleeps is an important factor. It is always wise to sleep at a lower altitude than the greatest height reached during the day. Also, once above 3000m, care should be taken not to increase the sleeping altitude by more than 300m per day.
- Drink extra fluids. The mountain air is dry and cold and moisture is lost as you breathe.
- Eat light, high-carbohydrate meals for more energy.
- Avoid alcohol, it may increase the risk of dehydration occuring.
- Avoid sedatives.
- Avoid the drugs acetazolamide (Diamox) and dexamethasone even though they have been recommended for prevention of AMS. They can reduce the symptoms, but they also mask warning signs; severe and fatal AMS has occurred in people taking these drugs. In general they are not recommended for travellers.

Motion Sickness Eating lightly before and during a trip will reduce the chances of motion sickness. If you are prone to motion sickness try to find a place that minimises disturbance – near the wing on aircraft, close to midships on boats, near the centre on buses. Fresh air usually helps; reading and cigarette smoke don't. Commercial motion-sickness preparations, which can cause drowsiness, have to be taken before the trip commences; when you're feeling sick it's too late. Ginger (available in capsule form) and peppermint (including mint-flavoured sweets) are natural preventatives.

Diarrhoea Despite all your precautions you may still get a mild bout of travellers' diarrhoea but a few rushed toilet trips with no other symptoms is not indicative of a serious problem. Moderate diarrhoea, involving half-a-dozen loose movements in a day becomes more of a nuisance.

Dehydration is the main danger with any diarrhoea, particularly for children where dehydration can occur quite quickly. Fluid replacement remains the mainstay of management. Weak black tea with a little sugar, soda water, or soft drinks allowed to go flat and diluted 50% with water are all good. With severe diarrhoea a rehydrating solution is necessary to replace minerals and salts. Commercially available ORS (oral rehydration salts) are very useful; add the contents of one sachet to a litre of boiled or bottled water. In an emergency you can make up a solution of eight teaspoons of sugar to a litre of boiled water and provide salted cracker biscuits at the same time. You should stick to a bland diet as you recover.

Lomotil or Imodium can be used to bring relief from the symptoms, although they do not actually cure the problem. Only use these drugs if absolutely necessary – eg if you *must* travel. For children under 12 years Lomotil and Imodium are not recommended. Under all circumstances fluid replacement is the most important thing to remember. Do not use these drugs if the person has a high fever or is severely dehydrated.

In certain situations antibiotics may be indicated:

- watery diarrhoea with blood and mucus (in this situation gut-paralysing drugs like Imodium or Lomotil should be avoided)
- watery diarrhoea with fever and lethargy
- persistent diarrhoea not improving after 48 hours
- severe diarrhoea, if it is logistically difficult to stay in one place

The recommended drugs (adults only) would be either norfloxacin (400 mg) twice daily for three days or ciprofloxacin (500 mg) twice daily for three days.

The drug bismuth subsalicylate has also been used successfully. It is not available in some countries. The dosage for adults is two tablets or 30 ml and for children it is one tablet or 10 ml. This dose can be repeated every 30 minutes to one hour, with no more than eight doses in a 24-hour period.

The drug of choice in children would be co-trimoxazole (Bactrim, Septrin, Resprim) with dosage dependent on weight. A five-day course is given.

Ampicillin has been recommended in the past and may still be an alternative.

Giardiasis The parasite causing this intestinal disorder is present in contaminated water. The symptoms are stomach cramps, nausea, a bloated stomach, watery, foul-smelling diarrhoea and frequent gas. Giardiasis can appear several weeks after you have been exposed to the parasite. The symptoms may disappear for a few days and then return; this can go on for several weeks. Tinidazole, known as Fasigyn, or metronidazole (Flagyl) are the recommended drugs for treatment. Either can be used in a single treatment dose.

Dysentery This serious illness is caused by contaminated food or water and it is characterised by severe diarrhoea, often with blood or mucus in the stool. There are two kinds of dysentery. Bacillary dysentery is characterised by a high fever and rapid onset; headache, vomiting and stomach pains are also symptoms. It generally does not last longer than a week, however it is highly contagious.

Amoebic dysentery is often more gradual in the onset of symptoms, with cramping abdominal pain and vomiting less likely; fever may not be present. It is not a self-limiting disease: it will persist until treated and can recur and cause long-term health problems.

A stool test is necessary to diagnose which kind of dysentery you have, so you should seek medical help urgently. In case of an emergency the drugs norfloxacin or ciprofloxacin can be used as presumptive treatment for bacillary dysentery, and metronidazole (Flagyl) for amoebic dysentery.

For bacillary dysentery, norfloxacin (400 mg) twice daily for seven days or ciprofloxacin (500 mg) twice daily for seven days are the recommended dosages.

If you're unable to find either of these drugs then a useful alternative is co-trimoxazole 160/800 mg (Bactrim, Septrin, Resprim) twice daily for seven days. This is a sulpha drug and must not be used by people with a known sulpha allergy.

In the case of children the drug co-trimoxazole is a reasonable first-line treatment. For amoebic dysentery, the recommended adult dosage of metronidazole (Flagyl) is one 750 to 800-mg capsule three times daily for five days. Children aged between eight and 12 years should have half the adult dose; the dosage for younger children is one-third the adult dose.

An alternative to Flagyl is Fasigyn, taken as a two-gram daily dose for three days. Alcohol must be avoided during treatment and for 48 hours afterwards.

Cholera Cholera vaccination is not very effective. The bacteria responsible for this disease are waterborne, so attention to the rules of eating and drinking should protect the traveller.

Outbreaks of cholera are generally widely reported, so you can avoid such problem areas. The disease is characterised by a sudden onset of acute diarrhoea with 'rice water' stools, vomiting, muscular cramps, and extreme weakness. You need medical help – but treat for dehydration, which can be extreme, and if there is an appreciable delay in getting to hospital then begin taking tetracycline. The adult dose is 250 mg four times daily. It is not recommended for children aged eight years or under nor for pregnant women. An alternative drug is Ampicillin. Remember that while antibiotics might kill the bacteria, it is a toxin produced by the bacteria which causes the massive fluid loss. Fluid replacement is by far the most important aspect of treatment.

Viral Gastroenteritis This is caused not by bacteria but, as the name suggests, by a virus. It is characterised by stomach cramps, diarrhoea, and sometimes by vomiting and/or a slight fever. All you can do is rest and drink lots of fluids.

Hepatitis Hepatitis is a general term for inflammation of the liver. There are many causes of this condition: drugs, alcohol and infections are but a few.

Hepatitis A This is quite a common disease in Kenya.

The symptoms are fever, chills, headache, fatigue, feelings of weakness and aches and pains, followed by loss of appetite, nausea, vomiting, abdominal pain, dark urine, light-coloured faeces, jaundiced skin and the whites of the eyes may turn yellow. In some cases you may feel unwell, tired, have no appetite, experience aches and pains and be jaundiced. You should seek medical advice, but in general there is not much you can do apart from resting, drinking lots of fluids, eating lightly and avoiding fatty foods. People who have had hepatitis must forego alcohol for six months after the illness, as hepatitis attacks the liver and it needs that amount of time to recover.

The routes of transmission are via contaminated water, shellfish contaminated by sewerage, or foodstuffs sold by food handlers with poor standards of hygiene.

Hepatitis E This is a very recently discovered virus, of which little is yet known. It appears to be rather common in developing countries, generally causing mild hepatitis, although it can be very serious in pregnant women.

Care with water supplies is the only current prevention, as there are no specific vaccines for this type of hepatitis. At present it doesn't appear to be too great a risk for travellers.

Hepatitis B This is also a very common disease, with almost 300 million chronic carriers in the world. Hepatitis B, which used to be called serum hepatitis, is spread through contact with infected blood, blood products or bodily fluids, for example through sexual contact, unsterilised needles and blood transfusions, or via small breaks in the skin. Other risk situations include having a shave or tattoo in a local shop, or having your body pierced. The symptoms of type B are much the same as type A except that they are more severe and may lead to irreparable liver damage or even liver cancer. There is no treatment for hepatitis B.

Hepatitis C This is another recently defined virus. It is a concern because it seems to lead to liver disease more rapidly than hepatitis B.

The virus is spread by contact with blood – usually via contaminated transfusions or shared needles. Avoiding these is the only means of prevention, as there is no available vaccine.

Hepatitis D Often referred to as the 'Delta' virus, this infection only occurs in chronic carriers of hepatitis B. It is transmitted by blood and bodily fluids. Again there is no vaccine for this virus, so avoidance is the best prevention. The risk to travellers is certainly limited.

Typhoid Typhoid fever is yet another gut infection that travels the faecal-oral route – ie it is contaminated water and food that are responsible. Vaccination against typhoid is not totally effective and it is a dangerous infection; medical help must be sought.

In its early stages typhoid resembles many other illnesses: sufferers may feel like they have a bad cold or flu on the way, as early symptoms are a headache, a sore throat, and a fever which rises a little each day until it is around 40°C or more. The victim's pulse is often slow relative to the degree of fever present and gets slower as the fever rises – unlike a normal fever where the pulse increases. There may also be vomiting, diarrhoea or constipation.

In the second week the high fever and slow pulse continue and a few pink spots may appear on the body; trembling, delirium, weakness, weight loss and dehydration are other symptoms. If there are no further complications, the fever and other symptoms will slowly diminish during the third week. However you must get medical help before this because typhoid is very infectious and because pneumonia (acute infection of the lungs) or peritonitis (perforated bowel) are common complications.

The fever should be treated by keeping the victim cool and dehydration should also be watched for.

The drug of choice is ciprofloxacin at a dose of one gram daily for 14 days. It is quite expensive and may not be available. The alternative, chloramphenicol, has been the mainstay of treatment for many years. In many countries it is still the recommended antibiotic but there are fewer side affects with Ampicillin. The adult dosage of chloramphenicol is two 250-mg capsules, four times a day. Children aged between eight and 12 years should have half the adult dose; younger children should have one-third the adult dose.

People who are allergic to penicillin should not be given Ampicillin.

Worms These parasites are most common in rural, tropical areas and a stool test when you return home is not a bad idea. They can be present on unwashed vegetables or in undercooked meat and you can pick them up through your skin by walking in bare feet. Infestations may not show up for some time, and although they are generally not serious, if left untreated they can cause severe health problems. A stool test is necessary to pinpoint the problem and medication is often available over the counter.

Tetanus This potentially fatal disease is found worldwide, occurring more commonly in undeveloped tropical areas. It is difficult to treat but is preventable with immunisation. Tetanus occurs when a wound becomes infected by a germ which lives in soil and in the faeces of horses and other animals, so clean all cuts, punctures or animal bites. Tetanus is also known as lockjaw, and the first symptom may be discomfort in swallowing, or stiffening of the jaw and neck; this is followed by painful convulsions of the jaw and whole body.

Rabies Rabies is a fatal viral infection found in many countries, including Kenya, and is caused by a bite or scratch from an infected animal. Dogs are noted carriers as are monkeys and cats. Any bite, scratch or even lick from a warm-blooded, furry animal should be cleaned immediately and thoroughly. Scrub with soap and running water, and then clean with an alcohol or iodine solution. If there is any possibility that the animal is infected medical help should be sought immediately to prevent the onset of symptoms and death. In a person not immunised against rabies this involves having five injections of vaccine and one of immunoglobulin over 28 days starting as soon as possible after the exposure. Even if the animal is not rabid, all bites should be treated seriously as they can become infected or can result in tetanus.

Meningococcal Meningitis This is a bacterial infection of the lining of the brain. Sub-Saharan Africa is considered the 'meningitis belt' and the meningitis season falls at the time most people would be attempting the overland trip across the Sahara – the northern winter before the rains come.

This very serious disease attacks the brain and can be fatal. A scattered, blotchy rash, fever, severe headache, sensitivity to light and neck stiffness which prevents forward bending of the head are the first symptoms. Death can occur within a few hours, so immediate treatment is important.

Treatment is large doses of penicillin given intravenously, or, if that is not possible, intramuscularly (ie in the buttocks).

Tuberculosis (TB) Tuberculosis is a bacterial infection which is widespread in many developing countries. It is usually transmitted from person to person by coughing but may be transmitted through consumption of unpasteurised milk. Milk that has been boiled is safe to drink, and the souring of milk to make yoghurt or cheese also kills the bacilli. Typically many months of contact with the infected person are required before the disease is passed on so it is not considered a serious risk to travellers.

The usual site of the disease is the lungs, although other organs may be involved. Most infected people never develop symptoms. In those who do, especially infants, symptoms may arise within weeks of the infection occurring and may be severe. In most, however, the disease lies dormant for many years until, for some reason, the infected person becomes physically run down. Symptoms include fever, weight loss, night sweats and coughing. Vaccination against tuberculosis may prevent serious disease so is recommended especially for young children who are likely to be heavily exposed to infected people.

Bilharzia Bilharzia is carried in water by minute worms. The larvae infect certain varieties of freshwater snails found in rivers, streams, lakes and particularly behind dams. The worms multiply and are eventually discharged into the water surrounding the snails.

The worm enters through the skin, and the first symptom may be a tingling and sometimes a light rash around the area where it entered. They attach themselves to your intestines or bladder, where they produce large numbers of eggs. Weeks later, when the worm is busy producing eggs, a high fever may develop. A general feeling of being unwell may be the first symptom; once the disease is established abdominal pain and blood in the urine are other signs. The infection often causes no symptoms until the disease is well established (several months to years after exposure) and damage to internal organs irreversible.

Avoiding swimming or bathing in fresh water where bilharzia is present is the main method of preventing the disease. In Kenya, unless you know definitely that water is bilharzia free, assume the worst and be aware that even deep water can be infected. Bilharzia is present in Lake Victoria. If you do get wet, dry off quickly and dry your clothes as well. Seek medical attention if you have been exposed to the disease, even if you don't have any symptoms, and tell the doctor your suspicions, as bilharzia in the early stages can be confused with malaria or typhoid. If you cannot get medical help immediately, praziquantel (Biltricide) is the recommended treatment. The recommended dosage is 40 mg/kg in divided doses over one day. Niridazole is an alternative drug.

Diphtheria Diphtheria can be a skin infection or a more dangerous throat infection. It is spread by contaminated dust contacting the skin or by the inhalation of infected cough or sneeze droplets. Frequent washing and keeping the skin dry will help prevent skin infection. The mainstay of treatment of the diphtheria throat infection is an intravenous infusion of diphtheria antitoxin. The antitoxin is produced in horses so may be associated with allergic reactions in some people. Because of this it must be administered under close medical supervision.

Sexually Transmitted Diseases Sexual contact with an infected sexual partner spreads these diseases. While abstinence is the only 100% preventative, using condoms is also effective. Gonorrhoea, herpes and syphilis are the most common of these diseases; sores, blisters or rashes around the genitals, discharges or pain when urinating are common symptoms. Symptoms may be less marked or not observed at all in women. Syphilis symptoms eventually disappear completely but the disease continues and can cause severe problems in later years. The treatment of gonorrhoea and syphilis is with antibiotics.

There are numerous other sexually transmitted diseases, for most of which effective treatment is available. However, there is no cure for herpes and there is also currently no cure for AIDS.

HIV/AIDS HIV, the Human Immunodeficiency Virus, may develop into AIDS, Acquired Immune Deficiency Syndrome. HIV is a huge problem in Kenya, and the statistics are frightening. Not only are the health services being stretched way beyond limits – it's estimated that 50% of Kenyan hospital cases are HIV related – but life expectancy is dropping rapidly, and it has been estimated that by the turn of the century Kenya will have one million AIDS orphans.

Any exposure to blood, blood products or bodily fluids may put the individual at risk. In many developing countries transmission is predominantly through heterosexual

sexual activity. This is quite different from industrialised countries where transmission is mostly through contact between homosexual or bisexual males, or via contaminated needles shared by IV drug users. Apart from abstinence, the most effective preventative is always to practise safe sex using condoms. It is impossible to detect the HIV-positive status of an otherwise healthy-looking person without a blood test.

HIV/AIDS can also be spread through infected blood transfusions; donors in Kenya are rarely screened for HIV/AIDS. It can also be spread by dirty needles – vaccinations, acupuncture, tattooing and ear or nose piercing can be potentially as dangerous as intravenous drug use if the equipment is not clean. If you do need an injection, ask to see the syringe unwrapped in front of you, or better still, take a needle and syringe pack with you overseas – it is a cheap insurance package against infection with HIV.

Fear of HIV infection should never preclude treatment for serious medical conditions. Although there may be a risk of infection, it is very small indeed.

Malaria This serious disease is spread by mosquito bites. Symptoms include headaches, fever, chills and sweating which may subside and recur. Without treatment malaria can develop more serious, potentially fatal effects.

It is extremely important to take malarial prophylactics. Antimalarial drugs do not prevent you from being infected but kill the parasites during a stage in their development.

There are a number of different types of malaria. The one of most concern is falciparum malaria. This is responsible for the very serious cerebral malaria. Falciparum is the predominant form in many malaria-prone areas of the world. Contrary to popular belief cerebral malaria is not a new strain.

The problem in recent years has been the emergence of increasing resistance to commonly used antimalarials like chloroquine, maloprim and proguanil. Newer drugs such as mefloquine (Lariam) and doxycycline (Vibramycin, Doryx) are often recommended for chloroquine and multi-drug-resistant areas. Expert advice should be sought, as there are many factors to consider when deciding on the type of antimalarial medication, including the area to be visited, the risk of exposure to malaria-carrying mosquitoes, your medical history, and your age and pregnancy status. It is also important to discuss the side-effect profile of the medication, so you can work out some level of risk versus benefit ratio. It is also very important to be sure of the correct dosage of the medication prescribed to you. Some people have inadvertently taken weekly medication (chloroquine) on a daily basis, with disastrous effects. While discussing dosages for prevention of malaria, it is often advisable to include the dosages required for treatment, especially if your trip is through a high-risk area that would isolate you from medical care. The main messages are:

1. Primary prevention must always be in the form of mosquito-avoidance measures. The mosquitoes that transmit malaria bite from dusk to dawn and during this period travellers are advised to:
   - wear light coloured clothing
   - wear long pants and long sleeved shirts
   - avoid highly scented perfumes or aftershave
   - use a mosquito net – it may be worth taking your own
   - use mosquito repellents containing the compound DEET on exposed areas (overuse of DEET may be harmful, especially to children, but its use is considered preferable to being bitten by disease-transmitting mosquitoes)
2. While no antimalarial is 100% effective, taking the most appropriate drug significantly reduces the risk of contracting the disease.
3. No-one should ever die from malaria. It can be diagnosed by a simple blood test. Symptoms range from fever, chills and sweating, headache and abdominal pains to a vague feeling of ill-health, so seek examination immediately if there is any suggestion of malaria.

Contrary to popular belief, once a person contracts malaria he/she does not have it for life. Two species of the parasite may lie dormant in the liver but they can also be eradicated using a specific medication. Malaria is curable, as long as the person seeks medical help when symptoms occur.

Anti-malarial drugs are available in pharmacies in Nairobi. Lariam (mefloquine) costs KSh 1200 for four tablets; Paludrine tablets are KSh 15 each.

Dengue Fever There is no prophylactic available for this mosquito-spread disease; the main preventative measure is to avoid mosquito bites. A sudden onset of fever, headaches and severe joint and muscle pains are the first signs before a rash starts on the trunk of the body and spreads to the limbs and face. After a further few days, the fever will subside and recovery will begin. Serious complications are not common but full recovery can take up to a month or more.

Yellow Fever This disease is endemic in many African countries between 15° north and 15° south of the equator, but not including Kenya. This viral disease is transmitted to humans by mosquitoes; the initial symptoms are fever, headache, abdominal pain and vomiting. There may appear to be a brief recovery before the disease progresses to more severe complications, including liver failure. There is no medical treatment apart from keeping the fever down and avoiding dehydration, but yellow fever vaccination gives good protection for 10 years. Vaccination is an entry requirement for some countries, predominantly for those travellers coming from an infected area.

Filariasis This is a mosquito-transmitted parasitic infection which is found in many parts of Africa, including Kenya. There is a range of possible manifestations of the infection, depending on which filarial parasite species has caused the infection. These include fever, pain and swelling of the lymph glands; inflammation of lymph drainage areas; swelling of a limb or the scrotum; skin rashes and blindness. Treatment is available to eliminate the parasites from the body, but some of the damage they cause may not be reversible. Medical advice should be obtained promptly if the filariasis infection is suspected.

Typhus Typhus is spread by ticks, mites or lice. It begins with fever, chills, headache and muscle pains followed a few days later by a body rash. There is often a large painful sore at the site of the bite and nearby lymph nodes are swollen and painful. Treatment is with tetracycline, or chloramphenicol under medical supervision.

Tick typhus is spread by ticks. Trekkers in southern Africa may be at risk from cattle or wild-animal ticks. Seek local advice on areas where ticks pose a danger and always check your skin carefully for ticks after walking in a danger area such as a tropical forest. A strong insect repellent can help, and serious walkers in tick areas should consider having their boots and trousers impregnated with benzyl benzoate and dibutylphthalate.

Sleeping Sickness In parts of tropical Africa, including Kenya, tsetse flies can carry trypanosomiasis or sleeping sickness. They pass it on by biting large, warm-blooded animals and are responsible for the lack of horses and cows in some areas. The tsetse fly is about twice the size of a housefly and recognisable by the scissorlike way it folds its wings when at rest.

Only a small proportion of tsetse flies carry the disease but it is best to try to avoid being bitten; there is no immunisation. The flies are attracted to large moving objects such as safari buses, to perfume and aftershave, and to colours like dark blue. Swelling at the site of the bite, five or more days later, is the first sign of infection; this is followed within two to three weeks by fever. The illness is serious but responds well to medical attention.

Cuts & Scratches Skin punctures can easily become infected in hot climates and may be difficult to heal. Treat any cut with an antiseptic such as povidone-iodine. Where possible avoid bandages and Band-aids, which can keep wounds wet.

Coral cuts are notoriously slow to heal and if they are not adequately cleaned small pieces of coral can become embedded in the wound. Avoid coral cuts by wearing shoes when walking on reefs, and clean any cut thoroughly with sodium peroxide if available.

Bees, Spiders & Scorpions Bee and wasp stings are usually painful rather than dangerous. Calamine lotion or Stingose spray will give relief and ice packs will reduce the pain and swelling. There are some spiders with dangerous bites but antivenenes are usually available. Scorpion stings are notoriously painful although not fatal in this part of the world. Scorpions often shelter in shoes or clothing.

Snakes To minimise your chances of being bitten always wear boots, socks and long trousers when walking through undergrowth where snakes may be present. Don't put your hands into holes and crevices, and be careful when collecting firewood.

Snake bites do not cause instantaneous death and antivenenes are usually available. Keep the victim calm and still, wrap the bitten limb tightly, as you would for a sprained ankle, and then attach a splint to immobilise it. Then seek medical help, if possible with the dead snake for identification. Don't attempt to catch the snake if there is even a remote possibility of being bitten again. Tourniquets and sucking out the poison are now comprehensively discredited.

Bedbugs & Lice Bedbugs live in various places, but particularly in dirty mattresses and bedding. Spots of blood on bedclothes or on the wall around the bed can be read as a suggestion to find another hotel. Bedbugs leave itchy bites in neat rows. Calamine lotion or Stingose spray may help.

All lice cause itching and discomfort. They make themselves at home in your hair (head lice), your clothing (body lice) or in your pubic hair (crabs). You catch lice through direct contact with infected people or by sharing combs, clothing and the like. Powder or shampoo treatment will kill the lice and infected clothing should then be washed in very hot water.

Leeches & Ticks Leeches may be present in damp rainforest conditions; they attach themselves to your skin to suck your blood. Trekkers often get them on their legs or in their boots. Salt or a lighted cigarette end will make them fall off. Do not pull them off, as the bite is then more likely to become infected. An insect repellent may keep them away. You should always check your body if you have been walking through a potentially tick-infested area as ticks can cause skin infections and other more serious diseases (see Typhus earlier).

If a tick is found attached, press down around the tick's head with tweezers, grab the head and gently pull upwards. Avoid pulling the rear of the body as this may squeeze the tick's gut contents through the attached mouth parts into the skin, increasing the risk of infection and disease. Smearing chemicals on the tick will not make it let go and is not recommended.

Women's Health
Gynaecological Problems Poor diet, lowered resistance due to the use of antibiotics for stomach upsets and even contraceptive pills can lead to vaginal infections when travelling in hot climates. Maintaining good personal hygiene, and wearing skirts or loose-fitting trousers and cotton underwear will help to prevent infections.

Yeast infections, characterised by a rash, itch and discharge, can be treated with a vinegar or lemon-juice douche, or with yoghurt. Nystatin, miconazole or clotrimazole suppositories are the usual medical prescription. Trichomoniasis and gardnerella are more serious infections; symptoms are a smelly discharge and sometimes a burning sensation when urinating. Male sexual partners must also be treated, and if a vinegar-water douche is not effective medical attention should be sought. Metronidazole (Flagyl) is the prescribed drug.

Pregnancy Most miscarriages occur during the first three months of pregnancy, so this is the most risky time to travel as far as your own health is concerned. Miscarriage is not uncommon, and can occasionally lead to severe bleeding. The last three months should also be spent within reasonable distance of good medical care. A baby born as early as 24 weeks stands a chance of survival, but only in a good modern hospital. Pregnant women should avoid all unnecessary medication, but vaccinations and malarial prophylactics should still be taken where possible. Additional care should be taken to prevent illness and particular attention should be paid to diet and nutrition. Alcohol and nicotine, for example, should be avoided.

WOMEN TRAVELLERS

Sexual harassment of women is far less prevalent in Kenya than in many countries for white women. If you're black and walking the streets alone after 7 pm, there's a very good chance you'll be arrested, accused of being a whore and pressured into bribing your way out. Refuse to pay and you could well spend the night in a cell at the central police station, be taken to court the following morning and fined KSh 1000. According to some people to whom this has happened, you break no ice protesting your innocence even if you're married and your husband happens to be back at a hotel room or elsewhere. It can even happen if you're a black woman in the company of a white man. The obvious way around this is to take taxis at night if you're going anywhere.

White women come under the category of 'tourists' and enjoy a somewhat dubious though privileged status. If you're a white woman, you may get the occasional hassle but it's rarely persistent if treated with the cold shoulder. There are certain areas in Nairobi where you wouldn't want to walk alone at night, but that applies equally to men, though usually for different reasons.

In country areas women need to exercise caution not to place themselves in situations where if a problem arose they would not be able to alert someone. Attacks on foreign women (and indeed, men) are on the increase, and the attacks often happen in isolated places.

GAY & LESBIAN TRAVELLERS

In this part of the world the official attitude towards homosexual activities is one of disdain if not outright hostility. There is no public discussion of homosexuality. In practice, it's a different matter but discretion is the better part of valour, as homosexual acts are illegal and penalties are harsh. People will approach you on occasion and, in some places, it's pretty obvious what's going down.

DISABLED TRAVELLERS

Think seriously before coming to Kenya if you fit into this category. Only top-end hotels have elevators and you'd find it particularly difficult to use public transport – only the London taxi cabs are spacious enough to accommodate a wheelchair. Likewise, there are no toilet facilities for disabled people.

TRAVEL WITH CHILDREN

This presents few problems other than those you would encounter anywhere else in the world. Africans in general are very friendly, helpful and protective towards children (and their mothers). On the other hand, if you want reasonable toilet and bathroom facilities, you'd be advised to stay in a mid-range hotel. You'd also be well advised to avoid feeding your children street food. Canned baby foods, powdered milk, disposable nappies and the like are available in most large supermarkets in the major towns and cities but not elsewhere. Your major concern if they get sick is good medical facilities. These are few and far between. Your fallback here is a pharmacy. Most of these stock the usual range of medicines and you will not need a doctor's prescription to buy them.

Most hotels will not charge you for a child under two years of age. For those between two and 12 years old sharing the same room as their parents it's usually 50% of the adult rate. You'll also get a cot thrown in for this price. Likewise, most reasonable restaurants will cater for children – smaller portions at a comparable price.

For further invaluable advice see Lonely Planet's *Travel with Children* by Maureen Wheeler.

DANGERS & ANNOYANCES
Crime
It is a sad fact that crime is rife in Kenya, and it ranges from petty snatch theft and mugging right on up through violent armed robbery and car-jacking and even goes into the white-collar ranks and above. Rarely does one come across a country where such lawlessness is so ingrained that it's basically accepted as part of life. It certainly doesn't help that the authorities are not only unable but also seem unwilling to do anything to clean the place up. Indeed it could be argued that the authorities are among the worst offenders.

As a visitor to Kenya this means that, while there is no need to be paranoid that every person you see or meet is a potential crook, you definitely do need to keep your wits about you at all times. From a visitor's point of view, the situation is worst in the areas with the highest concentration of tourists, namely, Nairobi, Mombasa and the coast. Simple snatch thefts and robbery with minimal force are the most common problems, and many, many people are relieved of their valuables on a daily basis. The worst instances involve armed robbery or other violence which has ended in the death of some tourists. The problem is certainly not limited to attacks on tourists, but obviously they make pretty juicy targets.

This is a great shame and certainly mars many peoples' visit to Kenya. There are some wonderful people in Kenya, but unfortunately many visitors are forced onto the defensive for so much of the time they simply never get to meet them. Instead they come away with a very negative view of the country. This is hugely damaging to Kenya's tourism industry (its number one foreign exchange earner) and is to a large extent responsible for the dramatic slump in tourism numbers the country now finds itself going through. As long as the authorities are prepared to sit back and continue to cream off as much as they can while doing nothing to ensure the safety of visitors to their country (let alone local Kenyans) they are running the risk of killing the golden goose.

Not only that but they also run the risk of the entire country ultimately sliding into the sort of chaotic mire which characterises many African countries but which, up until now, Kenya has managed to avoid.

Theft
The time when you face the biggest risk is within the first couple of days of arriving in the country. The people who make a living by relieving people of their possessions can often spot new arrivals by their uncertain movements and general unfamiliarity with the place. This is particularly true in Nairobi, and in fact the number of people who get their passports and money knocked off on the No 34 public bus in from the airport is amazing. The thieves use the 'instant crowd' technique, you'll find yourself jostled and before you know it your bag or money-belt strap has been slashed. Unless you are familiar with the place, it's probably better to pay out the KSh 900 for a taxi.

Never leave your gear unattended anywhere as chances are it won't be there when you get back, no matter how short a time you are away. In hotel rooms your gear is generally safe but use your common sense – in some places (particularly the real cheapies/brothels) the door locks are purely cosmetic. In Nairobi the danger of theft of your possessions from your hotel room has to be weighed against the real risk of having them ripped off on the street. If your hotel and room is secure, it's probably safer to leave valuables there. If you are going out raging at night, only carry as much money as you're likely to need, and leave everything else in your hotel. If your hotel has safety deposit boxes, leave your valuables there.

The place to carry your passport, money and other precious documents is in a pouch against your skin, either around your waist or your neck. Neither method is foolproof but both give a measure of security and make it much harder to lose things. Leather pouches are far more comfortable to have against your skin than synthetic ones, and the moisture from perspiration is far less likely to turn your precious documents into a soggy pulp.

Small pouches and other wallets worn on the outside of your clothes are like flashing beacons to a thief as are the ubiquitous money belts ('bum bags'), yet they continue to be immensely popular. Advertise your valuables, and someone will be watching you. Day packs, especially in Nairobi, instantly classify you as a tourist (and probably one who hasn't been around too long). Elsewhere, they're not quite such a beacon. Minimise the risk by wearing them on your front rather than your back.

Never walk the streets of Nairobi or Mombasa wearing jewellery or a watch which is clearly visible – unfortunately snatch thefts are very commonplace at any hour of the day, even in seemingly safe places.

If you are the victim of a snatch theft, think twice before yelling 'Thief!' Nairobi people hate thieves, pursue them with a vengeance and, if they can catch them, mete out instant, brutal and often lethal punishment on the spot. One or more thieves lose their lives every day in Nairobi for this. The police may intervene, but not always.

Confidence Tricks In Nairobi the chances are you'll come across people who play on the emotions and gullibility of foreigners. People with tales about being 'refugees' can sound very convincing as they draw you into their net but they all end up asking for money. If you do give any, expect to be 'arrested' by 'plain-clothes police', complete with fake ID cards, who then extract a 'fine' from you on the basis that 'it's illegal to give money to foreigners'. Stories such as this abound and the number of travellers who get taken in – sometimes to the tune of hundreds of dollars – is legend. The best policy is to ignore all such requests for money even though by doing this you'll occasionally be turning down what is a genuine request for help.

Another trick in Nairobi is the envelope full of money which gets dropped on the footpath in front of you. The idea is that, as you are reaching to pick it up, someone else (the accomplice of the person who dropped it) grabs it and then suggests to you that, as you both found it, you should go somewhere and share your 'good luck'. If you go along the only thing that will be shared is your money in a side alley somewhere.

Another tried and tested con trick starts out with a 'student' approaching you with a photocopied sponsorship form headed by the name of a school. They tell you their school needs funds to buy equipment and ask you to give a donation. Look at the form and you'll find the names of two or three wonderfully philanthropic foreigners who have apparently donated vast amounts of Kenyan shillings to this worthy cause. If you fall for this then you need your head examined. If the person proves persistent, just ask them to go along with you to a telephone so you can confirm that the request is genuine and that the person is a registered student at the school in question.

The story changes each week. Whatever works gets pumped for all it's worth.

In Nakuru they don't lack ingenuity either. A trick that has been popular for years involves tourists with cars. Locals splash oil on your wheels, then tell you that your wheel bearings, differential or something else has failed, and then direct you to a nearby garage where their friends will 'fix' the problem – for a substantial fee. We've even had reports of oil being splashed on the back wheels and then the driver being told that the rear differential had failed even though the car was front wheel drive! Another vehicle trick is that people on the side of the road will gesticulate wildly to you as you are driving along, indicating that your front wheels are wobbling. Chances are that if you stop you'll be relieved of your valuables.

Mugging
Foreigners (and even experienced expatriates) do occasionally get mugged, but if you're sensible the chances of it happening to you are small. There are certain places in Nairobi and on the coast where it's not recommended to walk at night (see those chapters for details), but other than that it's just a matter of common sense: don't go out

drinking in the nightclubs or bars carrying your valuables and then go rolling home down the street; don't wear your wealth, or you become a very tempting target. Leave valuable jewellery at home, keep cameras out of sight and don't pull out wads of money to pay for something. Always have enough small change for everyday transactions handy and keep the rest concealed. Take a cue from the taxi drivers of Nairobi who stash their money in at least half a dozen places on their body and in various articles of clothing.

Lastly, be wary on crowded matatus. It's not the ragamuffins you should watch but those who appear to be well dressed and on their way home from work. Plenty of these people work the matatus and you, as a tourist, are just one of their targets. Kenyans get hit, too.

And, if you do get mugged, don't listen to anyone who swears blind that he/she can get back what you've lost because they know 'the scene'. You'll end up several hours later being told a sob story or simply never see the person again.

BUSINESS HOURS
Government offices are open Monday to Friday from 8 or 8.30 am to 1 pm, and 2 to 5 pm. Some private businesses are also open on Saturday mornings from around 8.30 am to 12.30 pm.

Banking hours are Monday to Friday from 9 am to 2 pm. Banks are also open on the first and last Saturday of the month from 9 to 11 am.

Public Holidays
January	New Year's Day
March-April	Good Friday
	Easter Monday
1 May	Labour Day
1 June	Madaraka Day
10 October	Moi Day
20 October	Kenyatta Day
12 December	Independence Day
25 December	Christmas Day
26 December	Boxing Day

Nairobi and Mombasa both have branches of Barclays Bank which stay open until 4.30 or 5 pm Monday to Saturday. The branch at Nairobi airport is open 24 hours. Foreign exchange bureaus are open much longer hours, but still only on weekdays.

ACTIVITIES
Diving & Snorkelling
Malindi, Watamu, Shimoni and Wasini Island are the spots for scuba diving, the latter two being preferred. At Watamu, diving is from a boat not far offshore. A typical anchor dive is made at 12 to 15m depth. Visibility is often only fair and in fact Kenyan diving visibility has a poor reputation due to the plankton in the water. There are, however, usually plenty of fish in the water even if the coral is not that spectacular. For more information contact the Dive Shop at the Driftwood Club in Malindi, or the Ocean Sports Hotel at Watamu. Possibilities at Shimoni and Wasini Island, in the extreme south, are covered in The Coast chapter.

Windsurfing
Most of the resort hotels south and north of Mombasa have sailboards for hire, and the conditions are ideal – the waters are protected by the offshore reefs and the winds are usually reasonably strong and constant. The going rate at most places seems to be about KSh 250 per hour, plus more if you need instruction.

Beaches
One of the great attractions of Kenya is the superb beaches which line the coast. Many travellers find themselves staying much longer than they anticipated. This is real picture postcard stuff – coconut palms, dazzling white sand and clear blue water. The only problem is that for the most part the resort hotels have a virtual monopoly on accommodation, although there are a couple of budget options both south and north of Mombasa.

The beach at Diani is one of the best although it's lined solidly with resort hotels. Tiwi Beach, between Diani and Mombasa, is much more low-key and you can camp right on the beach at the Twiga Lodge. There are similar possibilities north of Mombasa, although at certain times of year seaweed accumulates on the beach in huge quantities. Lamu doesn't suffer this problem and has some of the best beaches on the coast.

Desert Exploring

There's the opportunity to experience this on either side of Lake Turkana and for a considerable distance south of there on the eastern side of the lake. For most travellers, this is one of the highlights of their trip to Kenya.

On the western side, access to the lake is easy with a bitumen road all the way from Kitale, and there's at least one bus and often a matatu or two every day in each direction. If you're heading up this way then don't miss the opportunity of exploring the Cherangani Hills east of the Kitale–Lodwar road using the Marich Pass Field Studies Centre as your base. Either side offers many challenging possibilities. It's also home to the Turkana, Samburu and Rendille tribespeople who, like the Maasai, have hung on to their traditional ways. It's certainly an area which you shouldn't miss at any cost.

Trekking & Walking

Mt Kenya is the obvious one, but other promising and relatively unexplored territory includes Mt Elgon on the Uganda border, the Cherangani Hills north of Kitale, the Matthews Range and Ndoto Mountains north of Isiolo, and even the Ngong Hills close to Nairobi. For more information refer to the relevant chapters in this book or contact the Mountaineering Club of Kenya (MCK) at its clubhouse at Wilson airport (meetings every Tuesday at 8.30 pm – visitors welcome), or in Nairobi (☎ (02) 501747), PO Box 45741, Nairobi.

Gliding

The Gliding Club of Kenya has its headquarters in Mweiga near Nyeri in the Aberdares, and there are flights every day except Monday. For more information contact the Gliding Club of Kenya (☎ (0156) 22467), PO Box 926, Nyeri.

Ballooning

Balloon safaris in the game parks are an absolutely superb way of seeing the savannah plains and of course the animals, but without the intrusion of vehicles and dozens of other tourists doing the same thing. The most popular of these trips is that in the Masai Mara Game Reserve.

The hot-air balloons depart daily from both Keekorok Lodge and the Fig Tree Lodge just after dawn and return around mid-morning. The flight includes a champagne breakfast on the plains. The cost is US\$360. Bookings can be made through Adventures Aloft (☎ (02) 220592), Eagle House, Kimathi St, PO Box 40683, Nairobi; the Fig Tree Lodge; Block Hotels (☎ (02) 540780), PO Box 47557, Nairobi; or directly at Keekorok Lodge.

There's another outfit which offers balloon trips in Taita Hills Game Reserve. Bookings for this can be made through the Hilton International (☎ (02) 334000), PO Box 30624, Nairobi.

Fishing

The Kenya Fisheries Department operates a number of fishing camps in various parts of the country. They are really only an option if you have your own transport as the sites are off the main roads. Before you head off you need to get a fishing licence from the Fisheries Department. Advance bookings are not taken so it's just a matter of turning up at the site. For full details of the exact locations of the camps, see the Fisheries Department in Nairobi; the office is near the Nairobi National Museum.

White-Water Rafting

Rafting is still in its infancy in Kenya, perhaps because of the limited possibilities – there are only two major rivers in Kenya, the Athi/Galana and Tana. The Tana flows through relatively flat country so it's sluggish and unsuitable for rafting. The Athi/Galana, on the other hand, has substantial rapids, chutes and waterfalls. The only outfit which can fix you up with a trip down this river is operated by Mark Savage (☎ (02) 521590), PO Box 44827, Nairobi.

A day trip from Nairobi consists of putting in just above Sagana on the Athi River and finishing about four km above the Masinga Dam. The trip starts with about two km of mild rapids followed by six km of smooth water and then two km of Grade 4-plus rapids without a breather and another two km of the same grade but with a few calm stretches for bailing out. This is followed by portage around a waterfall and a further 13 km of smooth water to the take-out point.

There's also an exciting three-day trip available from Yatta Gap on the Athi down to Tsavo Safari Camp (74 km).

WORK

It's difficult, though by no means impossible, for foreigners to find jobs. The most likely areas in which employment might be found are in the safari business, teaching, advertising and journalism but, except for teaching, it's unlikely you'll see them advertised and the only way you'll find out about them is to spend a lot of time getting to know resident expatriates. You will also need to be able to prove that you have the relevant qualifications and/or experience in the field. Basically the rule of thumb is that if an African can do the job there's no need to hire a *mzungu* (white person).

The most fruitful area in which to look for work, assuming that you've had some experience and have the relevant skills, is the 'disaster industry'. Nairobi is awash with UN and other aid agencies servicing the famines in Somalia and southern Sudan, and the refugee camps along the Kenyan border with those countries, and the relief efforts in Rwanda. But remember that the work is tough, often dangerous and the pay low. To find such work you would, again, have to spend a lot of time getting to know the expatriates involved in this.

Freelance work in the fields of journalism, literature and the film industry is also possible but, if you get involved in this, make sure you have a cast-iron contract for the work which you do. Too many people neglect to

do this, go ahead on a kiss and a promise, don't get paid and/or see their work ripped-off or shelved and end up tearing their hair out.

Work permits and resident visas are not the easiest of things to arrange either. A prospective employer may be able to arrange them relatively painlessly but, usually, you would find yourself spending a lot of money and time at Nyayo House (immigration).

For those interested in volunteer work, Voluntary Service Overseas (317 Putney Bridge Rd, London SW15 2PN, (0181) 780 2266; fax 780-1326) can provide placements for professionals.

ACCOMMODATION

Kenya has a good range of accommodation from the very basic KSh 150 a night budget hotels to luxury tented camps in the national parks for up to US$500 a night!

Kenyan residents should bear in mind that most places have separate rates for residents, and these are often considerably less than the non-resident rates. Rates quoted throughout this book are non-resident rates unless otherwise stated.

Camping

There are enough opportunities for camping that it is worth considering bringing a tent. It is also possible to hire camping equipment in Nairobi and elsewhere but it's not the sort of lightweight gear you could carry without a vehicle.

There are camp sites in just about every national park and game reserve and these are usually very basic. There'll be a toilet block with a couple of pit toilets, and usually a water tap, but very little else. Private sites are few and far between but where they do exist they offer more in the way of facilities. Often it's possible to camp in the grounds of a hotel but this is obviously not an option in the bigger towns where space is limited.

Camping out in the bush is also possible though you would be advised to ask permission first. On the coast this is not advisable and sleeping on the beaches would be just asking for trouble.

Just in case you thought that the tented camps in the game parks might be a cheap option – forget it. They are luxury camps with all the facilities laid on, and high prices. The 'tents' barely justify the name – they usually just have canvas or mosquito netting for walls, but otherwise have a roof and bathroom. High, shoulder and low-season pricing policies apply equally to these places as they do to the top-end hotels.

Hostels

The only youth hostels affiliated with Hostelling International (HI) are in Nairobi and Malindi. They are fine, but not so cheap and there's better options available.

There are other places which call themselves 'youth hostels' but are not members of HI. Some are good, others less so.

Hotels

Real bottom-end hotels (known everywhere as boardings & lodgings – 'hotels' are often only restaurants and hotels second. This in itself is not a problem as long as you don't mind the noise, disruption and general atmosphere. Most places don't mind renting out rooms all night, although in some you get distinctly strange looks when they discover that not only do you want the room for the whole night, but that you want to spend it alone! These places are also not all that clean – you'll have to ask for clean sheets and the shared bathrooms smell – and the rooms are often claustrophobic cells. On the other hand, you do occasionally come across cheap places which are clean and pleasant places to stay, so don't dismiss them totally; there's usually at least one cheap boarding & lodging in each town. On the plus side, they are cheap; expect a single/double room to cost around KSh 150/250.

Things improve dramatically if you have a dollar or two more to spend, though there are always exceptions. For KSh 300/500 a single/double, you will usually get a clean room with private bath (soap and towel supplied). These places often have a restaurant and bar (usually noisy). The only real advantages you get over the cheap places are your own bathroom and toilet and a degree of security.

Those who prefer a mid-range hotel are well catered for. If you're willing to spend KSh 600 to KSh 1000 a night then you can expect all the basic comforts and sometimes even touches of luxury such as towels, soap and toilet paper, clean sheets and beds, a table and chair; and often a telephone and room service.

At the top end of the market, accommodation ranges from better than the average mid-range to the five-star international chain hotels which provide the lot with prices to match. These start at around KSh 1200/1500 for a single/double and head up from there. Some of these places are old colonial buildings with bags of atmosphere, but most are modern and vary from characterless to the luxurious. The resort hotels on the coast and the lodges in the game parks also fall into this category, although some of the latter are superb places to stay if you can afford it – having animals come to drink at the salt lick in front of your lodge as you sit on the verandah sipping a cool drink is just great, but pleasures such as this can set you back up to US$300 per person for full board, depending on the season that you are visiting in.

If you intend to stay in any of the top-range hotels, it's important to know that the price depends on the season. The high season generally runs from 16 December to 31 March and from 1 July to 31 August. The shoulder season is from 1 September to 15 December and the low season from 1 April to 30 June. There's generally also an additional supplement over the Christmas and New Year periods.

Although most middle-range and top-end places quote prices in US dollars, payment in local currency is the accepted thing.

FOOD
Local Food

For the main part, Kenyan cuisine consists largely of stodge filler with beans or a (tough) meat sauce and is really just survival food for the locals – maximum filling-up potential at minimum cost. It is still possible to eat cheaply and well although the lack of variety becomes tedious after a while. People with carnivorous habits are far better served by the local food than vegetarians.

The most basic local eateries (usually known as *hotels* or *hotelis)* hardly warrant being called restaurants. These places usually have a limited menu and are open only for lunch – the main meal of the day. If you're on a tight budget you'll find yourself eating in these places most of the time. However, if you have the resources, even in the smaller towns it's usually possible to find a restaurant that offers more variety and better food at a higher price. Often these places are connected with the mid-range and top-end hotels.

The only place where any sort of distinctive African cuisine (other than *nyama choma*, or barbecued goat's meat) has developed is on the coast where the Swahili dishes reflect the history of contact with the Arabs and other Indian Ocean traders – coconut and spices are used heavily and the results are generally excellent.

As might be expected with the large number of Asians in Kenya, there are also large numbers of Indian restaurants. In addition, many hotels are owned by Indians and the choice of food available on their menus reflects this. If you like this cuisine, you'll have no problems even in the smaller towns though most of these restaurants are confined to Nairobi and Mombasa. Indian food also offers the best choice for vegetarians.

Sambusas are probably the most common snack and are obvious descendants of the Indian samosa. They are deep-fried pastry triangles stuffed with spiced mince meat. Occasionally you come across sambusas with vegetable fillings, but this is usually only in the Indian restaurants. If you can find them freshly made and still warm, sambusas can be excellent. However, more often by the time you get them they are at least several hours old, are cold and have gone limp and greasy from the oil saturation.

Another item that fits into the pure starch category is that curious beast known as the *mandazi*. It's a semisweet, flat doughnut and, once again, when they're fresh they can be very good. They are usually cooked and eaten at breakfast time – often dunked in tea. Should you decide to eat one later in the day, chances are it will be stale and hard.

Something that you don't come across very often but which makes an excellent snack meal is *mkate mayai* (literally 'bread eggs'). This was originally an Arab dish and is now found in countries as far ranging as Kenya and Singapore. Basically it's a wheat dough

Nyama Choma

If you had to name a national dish in Kenya, *nyama choma* (barbecued goat's meat) would probably be it. In recent years it has become almost a fetish amongst Africans and expatriates alike and, to cater for the demand, dozens of places have opened up offering just that. Sometimes it's good; sometimes it's as tough as old leather. What you get is what you choose from a refrigerated selection of various cuts which you buy by the kg. Once it's barbecued, it's brought to your table by a waiter and sliced into bite-sized pieces along with a vegetable mash (often *matoke* which are plantains). It's not a cheap option but not that expensive either.

The trouble with nyama choma, if you've ever had any culinary experience, is that in no way does it resemble (except in the most expensive establishments) anything similar to marinated and seasoned barbecued meat. Most of the time, you'll take years off the life of your teeth chewing it and end up spending more time with a tooth pick than you spend eating. Marinating and the use of herbs, let alone basting, have yet to reach Kenya.

Nevertheless, the Kenyan middle class regard an invitation to nyama choma (and copious quantities of Tusker lager) as a special night out. So don't let us put you off – try it! Maybe this is how Africans keep their beautiful, healthy teeth. ■

which is spread into a thin pancake, filled with minced meat and raw egg and then folded into a neat parcel and fried on a hotplate.

Seemingly on every second street corner someone is trying to make a few shillingi selling corn cobs roasted on a wire grille over a bed of hot coals. You pay only KSh 5 for these. Another street-corner snack is deep-fried yams, eaten hot with a squeeze of lemon juice and a sprinkling of chilli powder.

Main Dishes Basically it's meat, meat and more meat, accompanied by starch of some sort. The meat is usually in a stew with perhaps some potato or other vegetables thrown in, and is often as tough as an old boot. Beef, goat and mutton are the most commonly eaten meats.

The starch comes in four major forms: potatoes, rice, *matoke* and *ugali*. Matoke is mashed plantains (green bananas), while ugali is maize meal which is cooked up into a thick porridge until it sets hard. It's then served up in flat bricks. It's incredibly stodgy, almost totally devoid of any flavour and tends to sit on the stomach like a royal corgi, but most Kenyans swear by it. It's certainly the equivalent of mashed potato for the Poms or sticky rice for the Chinese and Koreans but it certainly isn't a culinary orgasm. Freshly cooked it's palatable; when stale, just about inedible. Naturally, you must try it at least once and some travellers actually get to like it, but don't hold your breath! The main thing it has going for it is that it's cheap.

Roast chicken and steak are popular dishes in the more up-market restaurants of the bigger towns. Food in these places differs little from what you might get at home. Cooked red kidney beans are always an alternative to meat and are widely available in local eateries.

Menus, where they exist in the cheaper places, are usually just a chalked list on a board on the wall. In better restaurants they are usually just in English.

The following food list gives some of the main words you are likely to come across when trying to decipher Swahili menus or buy food in the market.

Useful Words

boiled	*chemka*
bread	*mkate*
butter	*siagi*
cup	*kikombe*
curry	*mchuzi*
egg(s)	*yai (mayai)*
food	*chakula*
fork	*uma*
fried	*kaanga*
glass	*glasi*
hot/cold	*moto/baridi*
hot (spicy)	*hoho*
Indian bread	*chapati*
knife	*kisu*
napkin	*kitambaa*
pepper	*pilipili*
plate	*sahani*
raw	*mbichi*
ripe	*mbivu*
roast	*choma*
table	*mesa*
teaspoon	*kijiko*
salt	*chumvi*
sauce	*mchuzi*
soup	*supu*
sugar	*sukari*
sweet	*tamu*
yoghurt	*maziwalala*

Vegetables & Grains

aubergine	*biringani*
cabbage	*kabichi*
capsicum	*pilipili baridi*
carrots	*karoti*
cassava	*muhogo*
garlic	*vitunguu saumu*
kidney beans	*maharagwe*
lettuce	*salad*
maize-meal porridge	*ugali*
mashed plantains	*matoke*
onions	*vitunguu*
plantains	*ndzi*
potatoes	*viazi*
rice	*wali*
spinach	*sukuma wiki*
boiled spinach	*sukuma wiki*

tomatoes	*nyana*
vegetables	*mboga*
vegetable stew	*mboga*

Meat & Fish

beef	*nyama ya ngombe*
kebabs	*mushkaki*
meat	*nyama*
meat stew	*karanga*
mutton, goat	*nyama ya mbuzi*
pork	*nyama ya nguruwe*
steak	*steki*
crab	*kaa*
fish	*samaki*
lobster	*kamba*
squid	*ngisi*

Fruit

This is where Kenya excels. Because of the country's varied climate, there's an excellent array of fruits. The tropical ones are especially good. Depending on the place and the season you can buy mangoes, papaya, pineapple, watermelon, oranges, guavas, custard apples, bananas (many varieties) and coconuts. Prices are cheap and the quality very high.

bananas	*ndizi*
coconut (green)	*dafu*
coconut (ripe)	*nazi*
custard apples	*stafeli*
dates	*tende*
fruit	*matunda*
grapefruits	*madanzi*
guava	*pera*
limes	*ndimu*
mangoes	*maembe*
oranges	*machungwa*
papayas	*paipai*
passionfruit	*pasheni*
pineapples	*mananasi*
sugar cane	*miwa*
watermelon	*tikiti*

Fast Food

Fast food has taken off in a big way and virtually every town has a place which serves food that rates high in grease and low in price. Fried chips with lashings of lurid tomato sauce are a basic filler, but sausages, eggs, fish and chicken are also popular. In Nairobi there are literally dozens of these places, and they can be handy places to pick up a snack.

Vegetarian

Vegetarians are not well catered for. Away from the two main cities there are virtually no vegetarian dishes to accompany the starch. Beans are going to figure prominently in any vegetarian's culinary encounters in Kenya! Buying fresh fruit and vegetables in the market can help relieve the tedium.

Self-Catering

Preparing your own food is a viable option if you are camping and carrying cooking gear. Every town has a market and there's usually an excellent range of fresh produce available.

DRINKS

Nonalcoholic Drinks

Tea & Coffee Despite the fact that Kenya grows some of the finest tea and coffee in the world, getting a decent cup of either can be difficult.

Tea *(chai)* is the national obsession and is drunk in large quantities. It bears little resemblance to what you might be used to but as long as you look on it as just a different hot drink and not actually tea it can be quite good. Be warned that it is generally very milky and horrendously sweet. Chai is made the same way in Kenya as it is in India: all the ingredients (tea, milk and masses of sugar) are put into cold water and the whole lot is brought to the boil and stewed. Finding a good honest cup of tea is virtually impossible outside the fancy restaurants. For tea without milk ask for *chai kavu*.

Coffee is similarly disappointing. Instant coffee is generally used, and in small quantities, so, once again, you're looking at a sweet milky concoction. However, as each cup is individually made it's somewhat easier to order one tailored to your own liking.

Soft Drinks All the old favourites are here, including Coke, Pepsi and Fanta, and they go under the generic term of soda. As with beer, prices vary depending on where you buy. In most places you pay around KSh 15 per bottle but in the more exclusive places you can pay up to KSh 70.

Juice There are no such predictable prices for freshly squeezed fruit juices which range from KSh 30 to KSh 150 per glass.

The main juice you'll find available everywhere is passionfruit juice. It is always fresh and very good. It is known locally simply as passion, although it seems a little odd asking a waitress whether she has passion and how much it costs!

Alcohol

Beer Kenya has a thriving local brewing industry and formidable quantities of beer are consumed. Go to just a tiny group of *dukas* (local stores) by the side of the road somewhere and chances are one of them will either be a bar, or it will stock beer. Sure, it won't be cold, but then even in the most up-market places beer is available both chilled and warm. 'Why warm?' you might ask as your face wrinkles in horror! Most Kenyans appear to prefer it that way.

The beer names are White Cap, Tusker and Pilsner (all manufactured by Kenya Breweries Ltd) and they're sold in 500 ml bottles. They are basically the same product with different labels (though there is a discernible difference in taste). The same company manufactures export-quality 300 ml beers – Export and Premium – and these are slightly stronger and more expensive. Guinness is also available but tastes and looks nothing like the genuine Irish article.

Kenya Breweries also has a draught version of Tusker which is very good but only available in a few places. Check the price before ordering – in some places it's cheaper than the bottled variety; in others it costs more.

Beers are cheapest bought from a supermarket where a 500 ml bottle will cost you around KSh 35. Bought from a normal bar, you are looking at KSh 70. Bought at a bar in a five-star hotel it can cost up to KSh 200.

Wine Kenya has a fledgling wine industry and the Lake Naivasha colombard wines are said to be quite good. This is something that cannot be said about the most commonly encountered Kenyan wine – papaya wine. It tastes foul and even the smell is unbearable.

On the other hand, you can get cheap imported European and even Australian wine by the glass for around KSh 150 in Nairobi restaurants. This is expensive when compared to the price of beer but is actually not too bad given that it is imported.

Local Brews Although it is strictly illegal to brew or distil liquor it still goes on. *Pombe* is the local beer, is usually a fermented brew made with bananas or millet and sugar and shouldn't do you any harm. The same cannot be said for the distilled drinks, known locally as *chang'a*, often effective poisons. Various percentages of methyl alcohol creep into the brew. They'll blind you if you're lucky; kill you if you're not. Leave it alone!

ENTERTAINMENT
Cinemas

There are cinemas in Nairobi, Mombasa and other major towns. The fare varies from Indian masala to trashy Hollywood ultra-violence. The Nairobi cinemas usually have fairly recent Hollywood releases. The price is a bargain, usually around KSh 100 or less.

Discos

Africans love to party and you'll always find a disco in the main towns. Nairobi has half a dozen, and they are great places to spend an evening. Single men may find that in some places they are outnumbered by unattached African women. Once again, entry is cheap.

Bars

Almost equal to the African love of dancing is the African love of beer – they consume massive amounts of the stuff, and there are bars everywhere. These range from flash five-star places where waiters wear bow-ties, to local dukas where the beer is warm, the floor earthen and the noise level high.

TRIBAL GROUPS & CULTURES

Kenya is home to more than 70 tribal groups; this section provides an introduction to some of these people and their diverse cultures.

Akamba

The region east of Nairobi towards Tsavo National Park is the traditional homeland of the Akamba people *(Ukambani)*. They migrated here from the south several centuries ago in search of food, mainly the fruit of the baobab tree which was accorded great nutritional value.

The Akamba were great traders and ranged all the way from the coast to Lake Victoria and up to Lake Turkana. Ivory was one of the main barter items but locally made products such as beer, honey, iron weapons and ornaments were also traded. They used to obtain food stocks from the neighbouring Maasai and Kikuyu, as their own low-altitude land was relatively poor and couldn't sustain the increasing population which followed their arrival in the area.

In colonial times the Akamba were highly regarded by the British for their intelligence and fighting ability and were drafted in large numbers into the British army. Thousands lost their lives in WWI. When it came to land, however, the British were not quite so respectful and tried to limit the number of cattle the Akamba could own (by confiscating them) and also settled more Europeans in Ukambani. The Akamba response was the formation of the Ukamba Members Association, which marched en masse to Nairobi and squatted peacefully at Kariokor Market in protest. After three weeks the administration gave way and the cattle were eventually returned to the people.

All adolescents go through initiation rites to adulthood at around the age of 12, and have the same age-set groups common to many of Kenya's peoples. The various age-set rituals involve the men, and the women to a lesser extent, gaining seniority as they get older.

Young parents are known as 'junior elders' *(mwanake* for men, *mwiitu* for women) and are responsible for the maintenance and upkeep of the village. Once his children are old enough to become junior elders themselves, the mwanake goes through a ceremony to become a 'medium elder' *(nthele)*, and later in life a 'full elder' *(atumia ma kivalo)* with the responsibility for death ceremonies and administering the law. The last stage of a person's life is that of 'senior elder' *(atumia ma kisuka)* with responsibility for the holy places.

Akamba subgroups include Kitui, Masaku and Mumoni.

Gusii

The Gusii inhabit an area in the western highlands east of Lake Victoria. The area is dominated by Nilotic-speaking groups with just this pocket of the Bantu-speaking Gusii.

Being a relatively small group, the Gusii were always on the move following influxes of other groups into their existing lands. After migrating to the Mt Elgon area sometime before the 15th century, the Gusii were gradually pushed south by the advancing Luo, and over the next couple of centuries came into conflict with the Maasai and the Kipsigis. They finally settled in the hills here as the high ridges were easier to defend. Having fought hard for their autonomy, the Gusii were unwilling to give it up to the British and suffered heavy losses in conflicts early this century. Following these defeats, the men were conscripted in large numbers into the British army.

The Gusii family typically consists of a man, his wives and their married sons, all living together in a single compound. Large families serve two purposes: with high infant mortality rates the survival of the family is assured, and the large numbers facilitate defence of the family enclosure. Initiation ceremonies are performed for both boys and girls, and rituals accompany all important events. Death is considered not to be natural but the work of 'witchcraft'. The Gusii were primarily cattle keepers but also practised some crop cultivation, and millet beer was often important at big occasions.

As is the case with many of Kenya's ethnic groups, medicine men *(abanyamorigo)* had a highly privileged and respected position. Their duty was to maintain the physical and mental wellbeing of the group – doctor and social worker combined. One of the more bizarre practices was (and still is) the removal of sections of the skull or spine to aid maladies such as backache or concussion.

Kalenjin

'Kalenjin' is a name formulated in the 1950s to describe the group of peoples previously called the Nandi by the British. The Nandi tag was erroneous as the people were all Nandi-speakers (one of many dialects) but were not all Nandis; the other groups included Kipsigis, Marakwet, Pokot and Tugen (arap Moi's people). The word *kalenjin* means 'I say to you' in Nandi.

The Kalenjin people occupy the western edge of the central rift valley area which includes Kericho, Eldoret, Kitale, Baringo and the Mt Elgon area. They first migrated to the area west of Lake Turkana from southern Sudan around 2000 years ago and gradually filtered south as the climate changed and the forests dwindled.

Although originally pastoralists, most Kalenjin groups took up agriculture. Some, however, such as the Okiek, stuck to the forests and to a hunter-gatherer existence. Beekeeping was a common activity and the honey was used not only in trade but also for brewing beer.

As with most tribes, Kalenjin have age-sets into which a man is initiated after circumcision and remains for the rest of his life. Polygamy was widely practised. Administration of the law is carried out at the *kok* – an informal gathering of the clan's elders and other interested parties in the dispute. Unusually, the doctors were usually women and they used herbal remedies in their work. Other specialist doctors practised trepanning – taking out pieces of the skull to cure certain ailments – which is also practised by the Bantu-speaking Gusii of the Kisii district.

Kikuyu

The Kikuyu number more than three million and their heartland is the area around Mt Kenya. The original Kikuyu are thought to have migrated to the area from the east and north-east over a period of a couple of hundred years from the 16th century, and were actually part of the group known as Meru. Basically they overran the original occupants of the area such as the Athi and the Gumba, although intermarriage and trading did take place.

The Kikuyu's new land was bordered by the Maasai and although there were periods of calm between the two groups, there were also times when raids were carried out against each other's property and cattle. Both groups placed a high value on cattle. Intermarriage was not uncommon between them and they share a number of similarities – particularly in dress, weaponry, and dancing – as a result of their intermingling.

The administration of the clans *(mwaki)*, made up of many family groups *(nyumba)*, was originally taken care of by a council of elders with a good deal of importance being placed on the role of the witch doctor, medicine man and the blacksmith. Traditionally the Kikuyu god (Ngai) is believed to reside on Mt Kenya *(Kirinyaga* – the 'mountain of brightness', 'mountain of whiteness' or 'black and white peak spotted like ostrich feathers') which accounts for the practice of orientating Kikuyu homes with the door facing Mt Kenya.

Initiation rites for both boys and girls are important ceremonies and consist of circumcision in boys and cliterodectomy in girls (the latter now rarely practised), accompanied by elaborate preparations and rituals. Each group of youths of the same age belong to an 'age-set' *(riika)* and pass through the various stages of life (with associated rituals) together.

Subgroups of the Kikuyu include Embu, Ndia and Mbeere.

Luo

The Luo people live in the west of the country on the shores of Lake Victoria. Along with the Maasai, they migrated south from the Nile region of Sudan around the 15th century. Although they clashed heavily with the existing Bantu-speaking people of the area, intermarriage and cultural mixing occurred.

The Luo are unusual amongst Kenya's ethnic groups in that circumcision is not practised in either sex. The tradition was replaced by something that one can imagine being almost as painful – the extraction of four or six teeth from the bottom jaw. Although it is not a common practice these days, you still see many middle-aged and older people of the region who are minus a few bottom pegs.

Although originally cattle herders, the Luo have adopted fishing and subsistence agriculture. The family group consists of the man, his wife (or wives) and their sons and daughters-in-law. The house compound is enclosed by a fence, and includes separate huts for the man and for each wife and son. (There is a good reconstruction of a Luo homestead in the grounds of the Kisumu Museum.)

The family group is a member of a larger grouping of families *(dhoot)*, several of which in turn make up a group of geographically related people *(ogandi)* each led by a chief *(ruoth)*. Collectively the ogandi constitute the Luo tribe. As is the case with many tribes, great importance is placed on the role of the medicine man and the spirits.

DAVID WALL

Witch doctors are an important component of Kikuyu traditional beliefs and the doctors are held in high regard.

DAVID ELSE

DAVID ELSE

DAVID ELSE

DEBRA TAN

Most Samburu tribespeople lead a traditional lifestyle. Their culture is very similar to the Maasai with whom they share the same language.

HUGH FINLAY

DEBRA TAN

DEBRA TAN

Turkana women's beads are not just colourful decorations, they also tell a story of the events in their lives (top left & right). The El Molo people rely partly on tourism for their income, selling crafts at places such as Lake Turkana (bottom).

DAWN DELANEY

GREG ELMS

TONY WHEELER

The Maasai are the most well known of Kenya's tribal people, and their name is synonomous with their striking red dress and beaded jewellery. They also have a reputation as fierce warriors; young male warriors can look startling with ochre covered faces.

Maasai

It is the Maasai more than anyone who have become a symbol of 'tribal' Kenya. With a reputation (often exaggerated) as fierce warriors and a supercillious demeanour, the Maasai have largely managed to stay outside the mainstream of development in Kenya and still maintain their cattle herds in the area south of Nairobi straddling the Tanzanian border.

They first came to the region from the Sudan and eventually came to dominate a large area of central Kenya until, in the late 19th century, they were decimated by famine and disease, and their cattle herds routed by rindepest. Up until the Masai Mara National Reserve was created in the early 1960s, the Maasai had plenty of space for their cattle grazing, but at a stroke much of this land was put off limits. As their population increased (both the cattle and the Maasai) pressure for land became intense and conflict with the authorities constant. Settlement program-mes have only been reluctantly accepted as Maasai traditions scorn agriculture and land ownership is a foreign concept.

Another consequence of the competition for land is that many of the ceremonial traditions can longer be fulfilled. Part of the ceremony where a man becomes a warrior *moran* involves a group of young men around the age of 14 going out and building a village *manyatta* after their circumcision ceremony. Here they spend as long as eight years alone, and while the tradition and will survives, the land is just not available.

Tourism provides an income to some, either through selling everyday items (gourds, necklaces, clubs and spears), dancing or simply posing for photographs. However, while a few can make a lot of money from tourism the benefits are not widespread.

The colourful Maasai live a nomadic lifestyle, wandering throughout the year, with their main source of food being their cattle.

DAVID ELSE

Meru

The Meru arrived in the area north-east of Mt Kenya from the coast sometime around the 14th century following invasions of that area by Somalis from the north. The group was led by a chief known as the *mogwe* up until 1974 when the incumbent converted to Christianity and denied his son from inheriting the role. A group of tribal elders *(njuuri)* were all-powerful and along with the mogwe and witch doctor would administer justice as they saw fit – which often consisted of giving poison-laced beer to an accused person. Other curious practices included holding a newly born child to face Mt Kenya and then blessing it by spitting on it, and witch doctors might eliminate one of their rival's sons by putting poison on the circumcision blade.

Subgroups of the Meru include the Chuka, Igembe, Igoji, Tharaka, Muthambi, Tigania and Imenti.

Samburu

Closely related to the Maasai, and in fact speaking the same language, the Samburu occupy an arid area directly north of Mt Kenya. It seems that when the Maasai migrated to the area from Sudan, some headed east (and became the Samburu) while the bulk of them continued south to the area they occupy today.

As is often the case, age-sets are an integral part of the society and the men pass through various stages before becoming a powerful elder at the top of the ladder. Circumcision is practised in both sexes; with the girls it is only done on the day of marriage, which is usually when she is around 16 years old. Men are often in their thirties by the time they pass out of warriorhood and become elders qualified to marry.

Samburu males go through the stages of being junior and then senior warriors, followed by junior and finally senior elders.

DAVID ELSE

Swahili

Although the people of the coast do not have a common heritage, they do have a linguistic link – Kiswahili (commonly referred to as Swahili), a Bantu-based language which evolved as a means of communication between Africans and foreign traders such as Arabs, Persians and the Portuguese. As might be expected with such diverse input, the Swahili language borrows words from Arabic, Hindi, Portuguese and even English. The word *swahili* is a derivative of the Arabic word for coast – *sahel*.

Arab traders first started plying the coast in their sailing dhows sometime before the 7th century, arriving with the north-east monsoon and sailing home on the south-west monsoon. The main exports were ivory, tortoiseshell and leopard skins, while items such as glass beads from India and porcelain from as far afield as China found their way here.

After the 7th century Islam booame a strong influence as traders began settling along the coast. Today the majority of the coastal people are Muslims, although it's a world away from the puritanical forms of Islam which prevail in some places in the Middle East.

Swahili subgroups include Bajun, Siyu, Pate, Mvita, Fundi, Shela, Ozi, Vumba and Amu (residents of Lamu).

Turkana

The Turkana are another of Kenya's more colourful (and warlike people). Originally from the Karamajong district of north-eastern Uganda, the Turkana number around 250,000 and live in the virtual desert country of Kenya's north-west. Due to their isolation, the Turkana are probably the least affected by the 20th century of all Kenya's people.

Like the Samburu and the Maasai (with whom they are linguistically linked), the Turkana are cattle herders first, although more recently they have taken up fishing the waters of Lake Turkana and even growing the occasional crops, weather permitting. But unlike the other two tribes, the Turkana have discontinued the practice of circumcision.

The traditional dress of the Turkana people is amazing, as is the number of people who still wear it – catching a bus up in the north-west is a real eye-opener for a first-time visitor. The men cover part of their hair with mud which is then painted blue and decorated with ostrich and other feathers. The main garment they wear, despite the blast-furnace heat of the region is a woollen blanket (usually a garish modern checked one) which is worn around the shoulder.

Traditional accessories include a small wooden stool carved out of a single piece of wood (used either as a pillow or a stool), a wooden stick with a distinctive shape, and a wrist knife. Both the men and the women wear with great flourish the lip plug through the lower lip. The women wear a variety of beaded and metal adornments, much of it indicating to the trained eye events in the woman's life. A half skirt of animal skins and a piece of block cloth are the only garments worn, although those days pieces of colourful cloth are not uncommon for use as baby slings.

Tattooing is also common and usually has special meaning. Men are tattooed on the shoulders and upper arm each time they kill an enemy – the right shoulder for killing a man, the left for a women; it's surprising the number of men you still see with these markings. Witch doctors and prophets are held in high regard and tattooing on someone's lower stomach is usually a sign of witch doctors' attempts to cast out an undesirable spirit rather than any sort of decoration.

CRAFT OF KENYA

You'll find some beautiful local craft work in Kenya, including:

Fabrics & Batik

Kangas and *kikois* are the local sarongs and serve many purposes. Kangas are colourful prints on thin cotton. Each bears a Swahili proverb and they are sold in pairs, one to wrap around your waist and one to carry a baby on your back, though you can buy one if you prefer. Biashara St in Mombasa is the kanga centre in Kenya, and you'll pay upwards of KSh 200 for a pair, depending on quality.

Kikois are made of a thicker cotton and just have stripes. They are originally from Lamu and this is still the best place to buy them, although the kanga shops in Mombasa also stock them. They are also made into travellers' clothes in Lamu.

Batik cloth is another good buy and there's a tremendous range, but the better prints are not cheap. The cheapest are printed on cotton and you can expect to pay around KSh 400 for one measuring about one metre square, but the price also varies depending on the artist. Batiks printed on silk are of superior quality and the prices are usually in the thousands rather than hundreds of shillings.

Makonde

Makonde carvings, which are made from ebony, a very black and very heavy wood, are the best pieces of woodcarving to buy and also the most expensive. This genre of carving had its origins in the highlands on either side of the Ruvuma River in southern Tanzania, but, because of its popularity, has been copied by other carvers all over East Africa. Created with inspiration, attention to detail and an appreciation of the life force which motivates its imagery, makonde is a superbly unique art form. Unfortunately, too many imitators create inferior products. Much of what is passed off as ebony is actually lighter (and cheaper) wood blackened with Kiwi boot polish; it's further degraded by the often slapdash quality of the carving. A quality piece of makonde carving is always superbly finished.

Before you buy any of this type of carving, do the rounds of the expensive craft shops in Nairobi and see what it ought to look like. Better still, buy it in Tanzania where it's much cheaper anyway. And, when you've seen the real thing, don't become too obsessed with ebony: there are some excellent Kenyan carvers who use local hardwoods and employ Kiwi boot polish as the finish.

Basically, there are two forms of this art – the traditional and the modern – and they're instantly distinguishable. The modern stuff is pure Modigliani, though the carvers have doubtless never heard of the man or seen any of his works.

The best pieces are to be found in the expensive craft shops and were probably made in Tanzania, but you shouldn't pass up the opportunity of having a good look at what is hawked around the bars of Nairobi. Some of it is good; most of it is rubbish. If you're interested, heavy bargaining is necessary.

Sisal Baskets

Sisal baskets, or *kiondos*, are probably the most distinctive Kenyan souvenir and are now popular and widely available in the West. They are still an excellent buy and the range is staggering – take a look in the market in Nairobi (although prices there are expensive). They come in a variety of sizes, colours and configurations with many different straps and clasps. Expect to pay around KSh 100 for a basic basket, and up to around KSh 300 for a large one with a leather 'neck'. Some of the finer baskets have the bark of the baobab tree woven into them and this bumps up the price considerably.

Soapstone

Soapstone carvings from Kisii in the west of Kenya are the main sculptural offering on sale. The soft, lightly coloured soapstone is carved into dozens of different shapes, from ashtrays to elephants. The best place for buying Kisii soapstone carvings is not in Kisii, as you might expect, but in Kisumu on Lake Victoria. The only problem is that it's extremely heavy and a kg or two of dead weight in your rucksack is not something to be taken lightly.

Elephant Hair Bracelets

On the streets of Nairobi you'll undoubtedly be approached by hawkers trying to sell you 'elephant hair' bracelets. Despite all the protestations to the contrary, these bracelets are made from reed grass (which is then covered in boot polish), from slivers of cow horn, or simply from plastic. You can safely assume that none of them are the real McCoy. ∎

THINGS TO BUY

Kenya is an excellent place for souvenirs, although much of the cheap stuff available is just pure junk mass-produced by hand for the tourist trade. Look carefully at what's available before parting with your money. It is illegal to export some wildlife products; see the Customs section in this chapter.

Nairobi and Mombasa are the main centres but many of the items come from the various regions, so it's often possible to pick up the same at source, although you then have the problem of transporting it.

The best buys include *makonde* carvings, sometimes made from ebony (but often softer woods stained with boot polish), *kiondos* (woven sisal baskets), jewellery and tribal souvenirs, including colourful Maasai beaded jewellery, the decorated *calabash* (dried gourds) and spears and shields. There are also batiks, local sarongs *(kangas* and *kikois)*, soapstone carvings from Kisii in the west of Kenya, and paintings.

It's possible to pick up something which will look good in your living room back home without spending a fortune but, these days, something of genuine quality and artistry is going to cost real money because there are many skilful artists around who produce works of genuine art (as opposed to tourist tat) and know that there are quite a few tourists around who are very discerning and will pay big bucks for quality. This particularly applies to makonde carvings, jewellery and paintings. In some cases, you can be talking about thousands of US dollars.

If you're interested in quality artwork, spend time doing the rounds of the shops and galleries which deal in it.

Getting There & Away

Unless you are travelling overland, flying is the most convenient – and just about the only – way of getting to Kenya. Nairobi is the main hub for flights and the route on which you are most likely to get a relatively cheap ticket, but it's worth checking out cheap charter flights to Mombasa from Europe too.

Buying an ordinary economy-class ticket is not the most economical way to go, but it does give you maximum flexibility and the ticket is valid for 12 months.

Students and those under 26 (under 29 in the USA) can often get discounted tickets so it's worth checking first with a student travel bureau (such as STA Travel) to see if there is anything on offer. Another option is an advance-purchase ticket which is usually between 30% and 40% cheaper than the full economy fare, but has restrictions. You must purchase your ticket at least 21 days in advance (sometimes more) and you must stay away for a minimum period (usually 14 days) and return within 180 days (sometimes less). The main disadvantage is that stopovers are not allowed and if you have to change your dates of travel or destination then there will be extra charges to pay. Stand-by fares are another possibility. Some airlines will let you travel at the last minute if there are seats available just before departure. These tickets cost less than the economy fare but are usually not as cheap as the advance-purchase fares.

Of all the options, however, the cheapest way to go is via the so-called 'bucket shops'. These are travel agencies which sell discounted tickets. Airlines only sell a certain percentage of their tickets through bucket shops so the availability of seats can vary widely, particularly in the high season. You have to be flexible with these tickets, although if the agents are sold out for one flight they can generally offer you something similar in the near future.

Most of the bucket shops are reputable organisations, but be careful as there is always the occasional fly-by-night operator who sets up shop, takes your money for a bargain-basement ticket and then either disappears or issues you with an invalid or unusable ticket. Check carefully what you are buying before you hand over money.

Bucket shops generally advertise in newspapers and magazines and there's a lot of competition and different routes available so it's best to telephone first and then rush round if they have what you want.

AIR
North America

In the USA, the best way to find cheap flights is by checking the Sunday travel sections in the major newspapers such as the *Los Angeles Times* or *San Francisco Examiner-Chronicle* on the west coast, and the *New York Times* on the east coast. The student travel bureaus are also worth trying – STA Travel or Council Travel.

North America is a relative newcomer to the bucket-shop traditions of Europe and Asia so ticket availability and the restrictions attached to them need to be weighed against what is on offer with the more traditional advance-purchase or full economy fares.

Return tickets to Nairobi from New York cost about US$2600 in the low season (1 November to 14 December, 16 January to 24 March and 11-14 April), and US$3000 in the high season (15 December to 15 January, 25 March to 10 April, 15 June to 30 September). From Los Angeles a return ticket costs about US$3000 in the low season and US$3400 in the high season.

If you shop around, it's possible to get cheaper tickets.

From Canada, Air France offers flights from Toronto to Nairobi for US$2580 in the low season and US$2953 in the high season.

It may well be cheaper in the long run to fly first to London from the east coast of the USA using Virgin Atlantic (from around US$251 one way or US$439 return in the low season, and $329 one way and $573 return in the high season), or stand-by on the other airlines for a little more, and then buy a bucket-shop ticket from there to Kenya with or without stopovers. But you must do your homework to be sure of this. All the main magazines which specialise in bucket-shop advertisements in London will mail you copies so you can study current prices before you decide on a course of action.

Europe

You can find bucket shops by the dozen in London, Paris, Amsterdam, Brussels, Frankfurt and a few other places too. In London, there are several newspapers with lots of bucket-shop ads which will give you a good idea of current fares, as well as specialist magazines catering entirely to the travel industry.

Trailfinder is a magazine put out three times a year by Trailfinders and is available free at all their branches. Their branches dealing with long-haul travel (including Africa) are at 42-50 Earls Court Rd, London W8 6FT (☎ (0171) 938-3366), and 194 Kensington High St, London W8 7RG (☎ (0171) 938-3939). Trailfinders can fix you up with all your ticketing requirements for anywhere in the world as well as providing information on insurance, immunisation and books. Trailfinders has been in business for years and can be highly recommended. All the staff are experienced travellers so they speak your language. It's open Monday to Saturday from 9 am to 6 pm (7 pm on Thursdays). There are branch offices at 58 Deansgate, Manchester M3 2FF (☎ (0161) 839-6969), 2 McLellan Galleries, 254-284 Sauchiehall St, Glasgow G2 3EH (☎ (0141) 353-2224), 48 Corn St, Bristol BS1 1HQ (☎ (0117) 929 9000) and 22-24 The Priory, Queensway, Birmingham, B4 6BS (☎ (0121) 236-1234).

The Africa Travel Centre (☎ (0171) 387-1211), 4 Medway Court, 21 Leigh St, London WC1H 9QX, specialises in travel to and around Africa and has discount flights to most major cities in Africa as well as details on safaris which you can book in advance if you care to. Office hours are Monday to Friday from 9.30 am to 5.30 pm and on Saturdays from 10 am to 2 pm. As with Trailfinders, the Africa Travel Centre is highly recommended.

The price of airline tickets from London to Nairobi is around UK£220 one way and UK£350 return. The airlines used are generally Aeroflot and Eastern European and Middle Eastern airlines but this isn't always the case. Also check out Africa Travel System (☎ (0171) 630-5434) at Glen House, Stag Place, Victoria, London SW1E 5AG, which specialises in airline tickets to Africa.

There is no advantage in buying a one-way ticket to Nairobi and then another one-way ticket back to Europe from there. You'll end up paying more than if you bought a return ticket in the first place. You may also run foul of immigration on arrival in Kenya without an onward ticket and be forced to buy one on the spot – an expensive exercise.

A round-the-world (RTW) ticket is another option if you have the time, but very few of these tickets include Nairobi. Johannesburg is the most common African stopover. For example, a London, Johannesburg, Perth, Sydney, San Francisco, Orlando, Washington, London ticket costs around UK£800.

Remember that discounted tickets cannot generally be paid for with a credit card. You must pay with cash or with a bank cheque.

Asia

You may safely assume that flying is the only feasible way of getting between the Indian subcontinent and Kenya. There are plenty of flights between East Africa and Bombay due to the large Indian population in East Africa. There are bucket shops of a sort in New Delhi, Bombay and Calcutta.

Typical fares from Bombay to Nairobi are around US$580 return with a three month ticket, US$750 return with a one year ticket. One-way fares cost US$415. Ethiopian Airlines and Kenya Airways offer flights, as do Pakistan International Airlines (PIA), via Karachi.

In Nairobi there are a travel agents offering tickets to Karachi, Islamabad, New Delhi,

Bombay and Calcutta. Most of these will be with Air India or PIA.

Australasia

For Australians and New Zealanders there are a number of route options to Africa. There are direct connections with Qantas from Perth to Harare and Johannesburg twice a week, and with South African Airways direct to Johannesburg, also twice a week. A return ticket from Sydney or Melbourne to Harare costs around A$1700 to A$2000, depending on the season. From there to Nairobi it's going to cost an additional A$800 or so for a return ticket.

Another option between Australia and Africa is the weekly Air Mauritius flight from Perth to Mauritius, from where there are twice-weekly flights to Nairobi. The fare is A$2000 from Sydney or Melbourne, and you can have a stopover in Mauritius if you wish.

The most recent routing from the east coast of Australia is with EgyptAir, which flies to Cairo from Sydney, twice a week, with twice-weekly connections on to Nairobi. Return fares from Sydney or Melbourne range from A$1866 to A$2144 depending on the season.

It obviously makes sense for Australasians to think in terms of a RTW ticket or an Australia/New Zealand to Europe round-trip ticket with stopovers in Asia and Africa. It shouldn't be too much trouble for a travel agency to put together a ticket which includes various Asian stopovers plus a Nairobi stopover. Having Nairobi added to such a ticket bumps up the price a little and you may have to go through several travel agencies before you get satisfaction as many of them know very little about deals via Africa.

It's probably best to start your search for a ticket by looking in the travel section of the Saturday issue of either the *Sydney Morning Herald* or the *Age* and by visiting a student travel bureau.

Ethiopia

Both Ethiopian Airlines and Kenya Airways operate regular direct flights between Nairobi and Addis Ababa.

Sudan

Kenya Airways and Sudan Airways operate direct flights between Khartoum and Nairobi.

Tanzania

The cheapest regular flights from Tanzania to Kenya are between Dar es Salaam and Nairobi on Kenya Airways. A one-way full economy fare is US$136 plus US$20 departure tax. There are also flights between Zanzibar and Mombasa (US$55). However, as these are very popular, you'll need to book ahead if you want to be sure of getting a seat.

Two other international flights you may be interested in are those operated by Eagle Aviation (☎ (011) 434480 Mombasa, and c/o Skyland Safaris in Zanzibar ☎ (054) 31744). It flies on Monday, Wednesday and Sunday in either direction between Mombasa and Kilimanjaro (for Arusha and Moshi), departing Mombasa at 8.30 am and Kilimanjaro at 10.30 am. The flight takes one hour and 10 minutes. It also flies every Thursday and Friday in either direction between Mombasa and Zanzibar, departing Mombasa at 7 am and Zanzibar at 9 am on Thursday, and Mombasa at 7 am and Zanzibar at 5 pm on Friday. The flight takes one hour and costs US$55.

Air Victoria flies Mwanza-Nairobi (Wilson airport) on Wednesday, Friday and Sunday, and Western Airways flies Mwanza-Nairobi on Monday and Friday. The flights from Mwanza to Nairobi cost US$160 with Air Victoria and US$150 with Western Airways and take about 1¾ hours. In Mwanza bookings should be made through Fourways Travel Service (☎ (068) 40653, PO Box 990, Pamba, Mwanza. Credit cards are not accepted despite the stickers on the door.

LAND
Ethiopia

The border crossing at Moyale is frequently used by travellers and overland trucks and presents few problems. Beware that when crossing into Kenya you will be asked for your vaccination card here which must have valid cholera and yellow fever stamps. Those without cards are refused entry into Kenya.

The only transport between Moyale and Marsabit are trucks. These take two to four days and cost KSh 500 to Marsabit and KSh 600 to KSh 1000 to Isiolo.

All vehicles, including buses travelling between Marsabit and Isiolo or Marsabit and Moyale, must travel in convoy. The reason for this is to minimise the danger of attack from *shiftas* (bandits).

There are buses going north from the Ethiopian side of Moyale but they start early at around the break of dawn. A few km out of town, you'll encounter the first of many police check points. At the border, ensure your passport is stamped both by immigration (at the checkpost) and customs (100m further on), otherwise you will be sent back to the border from here. If there are any Tupperware smugglers on board (seriously!), then expect a long delay. Customs rules allow passengers to bring in only one item of any particular sort per person so don't be too surprised if you're asked to wear a sweater or carry an umbrella. It's a bizarre sight seeing up to 60 people turfed off the bus by the police, all of them with the same umbrella design! – but perfectly legal.

Somalia

There's no way you can get overland from Kenya to Somalia at present (unless you're part of a refugee aid convoy). Even if you attempted it, the Kenyan police or the army would turn you back. Moreover, the entire border area is infested with well-armed Somali shifta making any attempt to cross it a dangerous and foolhardy venture.

Sudan

As with Somalia, there's no way you can get overland between Kenya and Sudan at present. The furthest north you're going to get is Lokichokio, and you'll be lucky to get that far unless you're with a refugee aid convoy.

Tanzania

Bus There are several land connections by bus between Kenya and Tanzania.

Mombasa to Dar es Salaam Hood Bus/Cat Bus has departures from Mombasa to Dar es Salaam via Tanga on Monday, Tuesday and Friday at 9 am. In the opposite direction, it departs Dar es Salaam for Mombasa via Tanga on Tuesday, Wednesday and Friday at 9 am. Officially, the journey from Mombasa to Tanga takes about eight hours and to Dar es Salaam about 12½ hours but, in practice, it can take as long as four hours to clear all 50 or so passengers through both border posts at Horohoro/Lunga Lunga so the journey time may be that much longer. The fare between Mombasa and Dar es Salaam is KSh 400 (TSh 4000 in the opposite direction). The bus office in Dar es Salaam is on Msimbazi St, close to the Kariakoo Market and the Caltex station. In Mombasa, it's on Kenyatta Ave.

The road between Dar es Salaam and Tanga is surfaced and in good condition but from there to the border it's diabolical. From the border to Mombasa you're back on a good tarmac road.

No-one but a masochist would do this journey the hard way by taking a bus first to Tanga followed by another one from there to the border and yet another from there to Mombasa. For a start, there's a six km walk between the two border posts and hitching is well-nigh impossible. Once on the Kenyan side, however, there are frequent matatus for the one hour journey to Mombasa. Doing it this way could take you the best part of two days.

Nairobi to Arusha & Moshi Between Nairobi and Arusha there's a choice of normal buses and minibus shuttles. All of them go through the border posts without a change.

The minibus shuttles vary slightly in price but all take the same amount of time (four hours). One of the cheapest is Riverside Shuttle (☎ (057) 8323 Arusha) which has its office next to the Chinese restaurant on Sokoine Rd in Arusha. It departs Nairobi to Arusha daily at 8.30 am from opposite the Norfolk Hotel on Harry Thuku Rd. In the opposite direction, from Arusha to Nairobi, it departs daily at 2 pm. The fare is TSh 7000 or KSh 1000 and the shuttle will drop you at any downtown hotel at either end on request. Simply tell the driver where you want to get off. At the Nairobi end, you can be dropped off at Jomo Kenyatta international airport on request.

Slightly more expensive is the Davanu Shuttle (☎ (057) 4311 Arusha and (02) 222002 Nairobi) which has its office at Windsor House, 4th Floor, University Way, Nairobi, and at the Adventure Centre, Goliondoi Rd, Arusha. It departs Nairobi for Arusha daily at 8.30 am and 2 pm, and Arusha for Nairobi daily at 8 am and 2 pm. The fare is TSh 8000 or KSh 1000. As with Riverside, Davanu will drop you at any downtown hotel at either end on request. Be careful with both companies regarding fares as they will initially attempt to charge you the equivalent of US$25 (Riverside) and US$30 (Davanu) if you're a nonresident. Simply telling them you're going to check out prices with their rivals usually does the trick.

Much cheaper is Arusha Express, which operates full-sized buses and has its office in among the cluster of bus companies down Accra Rd in Nairobi. In Arusha, the office is at the bus station. It operates a daily service leaving Nairobi at 8.30 am and costs KSh 400 or TSh 3000 and takes about four hours. It returns to Nairobi the same day around 2 pm.

Getting through customs and immigration on all the above buses is straightforward. The only snag you might encounter is being approached by touts who claim to work for the bus company and are employed to get you through the border crossing. This they will do (unnecessary) and in the process claim that officially you have to change US$50 to enter Tanzania, and will offer a ridiculous exchange rate. Don't fall for it.

It's also easy, but less convenient, to do this journey in stages, and since the Kenyan and Tanzanian border posts are next to each other at Namanga, there's no long walk involved. There are frequent matatus (TSh 700) and share-taxis (TSh 1300) from Arusha to Namanga every day. The taxis normally take about 1½ hours, though there are a number of kamikaze drivers who are totally crazy and will get you there in just one hour. From the Kenyan side of the border, there are frequent matatus (three hours, KSh 200) and share-taxis (two hours, KSh 300) to Nairobi, which go when full. Both have their depot outside the petrol station on Ronald Ngala St, close to the junction with River Rd in Nairobi.

Nairobi to Dar es Salaam Direct buses between Nairobi and Dar operate roughly every second day from each city. In Nairobi the buses park outside the Arusha Express office in Accra Rd, and will have a sign on the bus door giving departure time (some travel by day, others at night); tickets can be booked with the bus crew who hang out on the bus.

The journey takes 10 to 12 hours and costs KSh 1000.

Voi to Moshi The crossing between Voi and Moshi via Taveta is also reliable as far as transport goes (buses, matatus and share-taxis), as long as you go on a Wednesday or Saturday, which are the market days in Taveta. A matatu between Voi and Taveta (along a bumpy road) takes 2½ hours and costs KSh 200. From Taveta to Holili (the Tanzanian border), however, it's a three km walk, but there are also *boda-boda* (bicycle taxis) for TSh 300. From Holili there are plenty of matatus and share-taxis to Moshi. A matatu from Holili to Moshi will cost you TSh 400 and take about 45 minutes.

Kisii to Musoma/Mwanza There are no direct buses between Kenya and Tanzania through the Isebania border, and doing it in stages is a pain in the arse. The road between Mwanza and Musoma is terrible and between there and the border it's diabolical. Once over the border, it's plain sailing on tarmac roads but you'll need a night's sleep at Kisii before continuing. There's very little traffic on the road between the Isebania border and Musoma so give yourself plenty of time and don't count on lifts with overland companies, the UN or other NGOs. Ideally, you need your own vehicle.

Serengeti to Masai Mara If you look at any detailed map of the Serengeti National Park and Masai Mara Game Reserve, you'll see that there's a border crossing between Bologonja and Sand River, and so you would assume it's possible to cross here. It is if you're crossing *from* Kenya *to* Tanzania, assuming you have the appropriate vehicle documentation (insurance and temporary entry permit). But officially, it isn't possible to cross in the opposite direction because you must pay the park entry fee to Masai Mara and you must pay it in Kenyan shillings, which you ought not to have since, under Kenyan currency regulations, you're not allowed to export them. And the nearest place where you *might* be able to change money is at Keekorok Lodge, 10 km away. Just imagine! In practice, the border guards/park officials are very helpful, so if you just happen to have a sufficient stash of Kenyan shillings to pay the park entry fees, then like Nelson with his blind eye at Trafalgar, it's a question of 'I see no ships'. There is, of course, no public transport along this route.

Train Through service to Tanzania has recently recommenced, with a once-weekly connection between Voi and Moshi. From Voi the departure is on Saturday at 5 am, arriving at Moshi at 11.30 am. The return trip leaves Moshi at 2 pm, arriving in Voi at 7.10 pm. The fare from Voi to Taveta is KSh 330/175 in 1st/2nd class; Voi to Moshi is KSh 475/255.

Uganda

The main border post for overland travellers is Malaba, with Busia being an alternative if you are coming from Kisumu.

Bus Akamba operates two direct buses between Kampala and Nairobi daily which cost KSh 900 (USh 18,000), depart at 7 am and 7 pm, and the journey takes around 12 to 14 hours. Its office in Kampala is on

Dewinton St; in Nairobi it's on Lagos Rd. Akamba also has its daily Royal service, which is real luxury with large seats similar to 1st-class in an aircraft. There are only three in each row! Tickets cost KSh 2100 (USh 42,000), and the price includes a meal at the halfway point (Eldoret).

Mawingo also operates daily buses at 3 pm. These are marginally cheaper than Akamba (USh 16,000 from Kampala), but are more crowded and take up to 15 hours.

You can do the journey in stages: there are frequent matatus until the late afternoon between Kampala (three hours, USh 5000) or Jinja (two hours, USh 5000) and Malaba (Uganda), and in either direction between Tororo and Malaba (less than one hour, USh 250). The road is in excellent condition, although it does mean that the drivers can get up to terrifying speeds. Luckily, there's not much traffic on this road except close to Kampala.

The Ugandan and Kenyan border posts are about one km from each other at Malaba and you can walk or take a boda-boda.

On the Kenyan side several companies run daily buses between Malaba and Nairobi which depart at around 7.30 pm to arrive at about 5.30 am the next day. The fare is KSh 450 with Akamba. If you prefer to travel by day there are plenty of matatus between Malaba and Bungoma which take about 45 minutes. If you stay in Bungoma overnight there are plenty of cheap hotels to choose from. From Bungoma there are several daily buses to Nairobi which leave at about 8 am and arrive about 5 pm the same day.

The other entry point into Kenya from Uganda is via Busia further south. There are frequent matatus between Jinja and Busia and between Busia and Kisumu. Akamba has direct buses on this route which connect Kisumu and Kampala. The buses leave Kisumu daily at noon, and cost KSh 600.

Train The recent increase in East African cooperation has led to the reintroduction of a classic rail journey, between Nairobi and Kampala. This is an excellent way to travel between the two capitals, and the border crossing is a breeze as the immigration officials come through the train and you don't even have to leave your compartment. The Kenya Railways train is hauled by Kenyan locomotives and staffed by Kenyan crew on the Kenyan side; Ugandan locos and crew take over on the Ugandan side. The spirit of cooperation is not total however – the picture of Moi in the buffet car remains up the whole way and Museveni doesn't get a look in!

Departure from Nairobi is at noon on Tuesday, arriving in Kampala on Wednesday at 9.30 am. The fare is KSh 4400/3520 in 1st/2nd class, which includes bedding and meals. From Kampala the departure is 4 pm on Wednesday, arriving in Nairobi at 2.40 pm on Thursday, and the fares are USh 57,850/35,300 in 1st/2nd class. The train is often subject to delays of anything up to six hours.

There are also trains from Nairobi to the border at Malaba via Nakuru and Eldoret on Friday and Saturday at 3 pm, arriving at Malaba the next day at 8 am. The fares are KSh 2630/1820 in 1st/2nd class including meals and bedding. In the opposite direction they leave Malaba on Saturday and Sunday at 4 pm, arriving in Nairobi the following morning.

BOAT
Tanzania
Sea It's possible to go by dhow between Mombasa, Pemba and Zanzibar but sailings are very infrequent these days. What is much more reliable is the ferry, MS *Sepideh*, operated by Zanzibar Sea Ferries Ltd (☎ 33725 Zanzibar, ☎ 38025 Dar es Salaam, ☎ 56210 Pemba, ☎ 311486 Mombasa), which connects Mombasa with Tanga, Pemba, Zanzibar and Dar es Salaam. The schedule varies according to the season, but it's usually twice a week in either direction. The fares are US$65 Mombasa-Dar es Salaam, US$50 Mombasa-Zanzibar, US$45 Tanga-Zanzibar, US$40 Mombasa-Tanga or Mombasa-Pemba, US$30 Tanga-Pemba or Pemba-Zanzibar and US$25 Zanzibar-Dar es Salaam.

Lake Victoria Until early 1996 there was a ferry service which connected Kisumu (Kenya) with Mwanza (Tanzania) on Lake Victoria once a week, but the ship which serviced this route, the MV *Bukoba*, sank in May 1996. It's likely that the schedules of the other two boats – the MV *Victoria* and the MV *Serengeti* – will have been altered so that the two ports are connected again but you'll have to make enquiries. Even when the two ports were connected, cancellations were frequent.

Originally the boat left Mwanza at 6 pm on Thursday, arriving in Kisumu at 10 am the following day, then departed at 6 pm on Friday arriving back in Mwanza at 10 am on Saturday. The fare from Kisumu is KSh 1200/950/600 in 1st/2nd/3rd class, and bookings can be made at the port office from 8 am to noon and 2 to 4 pm weekdays.

LEAVING KENYA
The airport departure tax for international flights is US$20. This is payable in either US dollars cash, the equivalent in other major foreign currencies or Kenyan shillings.

Warning
The information in this chapter is particularly vulnerable to change: prices for international travel are volatile, routes are introduced and cancelled, schedules change, special deals come and go, and rules and visa requirements are amended. Airlines and governments seem to take a perverse pleasure in making price structures and regulations as complicated as possible. You should check directly with the airline or a travel agent to make sure you understand how a fare (and ticket you may buy) works. In addition, the travel industry is highly competitive and there are many lurks and perks.

The upshot of this is that you should get opinions, quotes and advice from as many airlines and travel agents as possible before you part with your hard-earned cash. The details given in this chapter should be regarded as pointers and are not a substitute for your own careful, up-to-date research. ■

Getting Around

AIR
Kenya Airways

Kenya Airways, the national carrier, connects the main cities of Nairobi, Mombasa, Kisumu and Malindi. It's advisable to book in advance and essential to reconfirm 48 hours before departure if you're coming from either Malindi or Kisumu and have to connect with an international flight from either Nairobi or Mombasa airports. Otherwise you may well find that your seat has been reallocated. The flight schedules and fares can be found in the respective city chapters.

The main Kenya Airways booking office in Nairobi is in the Barclays Plaza building on Loita St (☎ (02) 823456).

Private Airlines

There are also a number of private airlines operating light aircraft which connect the main cities with smaller towns and certain national parks. The airlines are Air Kenya Aviation (☎ (02) 501421), Prestige Air Services (☎ (02) 501211), and Eagle Aviation (☎ (02) 603593, and they all operate out of Nairobi's Wilson Airport and/or Mombasa's Moi Airport.

These airlines connect Nairobi with Mombasa, Kisumu, Nanyuki, Malindi, Lamu and the national parks/reserves of Amboseli, Masai Mara and Samburu. Flight schedules can be found under the relevant sections.

BUS

Kenya has a network of regular buses, matatus (normally minibuses), share-taxis and normal private taxis. The cheapest form of transport is by bus, followed by matatu, share-taxi (Peugeot services) and lastly private taxi (expensive). There's not a great deal of difference in journey times between normal buses and matatus, but there's a huge difference in safety.

Bus fares are generally about halfway between what you would pay on the railways

in 2nd class but journey times are quicker. Unlike the trains, which usually travel at night, many buses travel during the day so you may prefer to take a bus if you want to see the countryside. All but one of the bus companies are privately owned but some of them run better buses than others. Akamba Bus Service has the most comprehensive network, and has a pretty good safety record. The government bus line, KBS Stagecoach, runs modern buses, including some double-deckers, to the main towns and is also reliable and safe. Of the other private companies, Coastline, Goldline and Malindi Bus are also OK.

Some Kenyan towns have what you might call a 'bus station', although this is often nothing more than a dirt patch. In others each bus company will have its own terminus though these are often close to each other. There are exceptions and these are indicated on the street maps. Matatu and share-taxi ranks sometimes use the same stations as buses but this isn't always the case, especially in Nairobi.

There are also a number of private 'shuttle buses' which connect Nairobi with Mombasa and with Arusha and Moshi in Tanzania. They're more comfortable than ordinary buses since they only take around 18 passengers but they are at least two to three times more expensive than ordinary buses. Their schedules can be found in the Nairobi and Mombasa sections.

MATATU

The way that most local people travel is by vehicles known as matatus. (The name comes from 'three', because when matatus first started running it cost three coins to travel.) These can be anything from small, dilapidated Peugeot 504 pick-ups with a cab on the back, to shiny, brightly painted 20-seat minibuses complete with mega-decibel stereos, as found in Nairobi. The majority of those which do the long-distance runs, however, are white Nissan minibuses. Most matatu drivers are under a lot of pressure from their owners to maximise profits so they tend to drive recklessly and overload their vehicles. They also put in long working days. Stories about matatu smashes and overturnings in which many people are killed or injured can be found daily in the newspapers. Of course, many travellers use them and, in some cases, there is no alternative, but if there is (such as a bus or train) then take that in preference. The Mombasa to Nairobi road is notorious for smashes.

As in most East African countries, you can always find a matatu which is going to the next town or further afield so long as it's not too late in the day. Simply ask around among the drivers at the park. Matatus leave when full and the fares are fixed. It's unlikely you will be asked for more money than the other passengers.

TRAIN

Kenyan trains are a very popular form of travel, despite the fact that the rolling stock, tracks and other essential works have been allowed to deteriorate. The trains generally run on time and are considerably safer than travelling by bus or matatu. Passenger lines run from Mombasa on the coast to Malaba on the Kenya-Uganda border via Voi, Nairobi, Nakuru and Eldoret with branch lines from Nakuru to Kisumu and Voi to Taveta. The other branch lines, which do not operate passenger services are the Nairobi to Nanyuki, Gilgil to Nyahururu, or Eldoret to Kitale branches.

Classes

First class consists of two-berth compartments with a washbasin, drinking water, a wardrobe and a drinks service. There's a lockable door between one compartment and the adjacent one so, if there are four of you travelling together, you can make one compartment out of two, if you wish. They're usually very clean. What you cannot do is lock the door of your compartment from the outside when you go for meals.

Second class consists of four-berth compartments with a washbasin and drinking water supply. Third class is seats only. All the compartments have fans. Sexes are separated in 1st and 2nd class unless you book the whole compartment. Again, compartments aren't lockable from the outside, so don't leave any valuables lying around and maybe padlock your rucksack to something.

Third class can get a little wearing on the nerves on long journeys especially if they are overnight (which most are). Second class is more than adequate in this respect and 1st class is definitely a touch of luxury as far as budget travel goes.

Reservations

You must book in advance for both 1st and 2nd class – two to three days is usually sufficient – otherwise you'll probably find that there are no berths available and you will

---

Matatus

Matatus are not just transport. They are Kenya's contribution to world culture. These gaudily painted minibuses, featuring 200-decibel stereo systems pumping out disco beats at bone-conduction level have a crew of three: the driver, who normally hasn't slept for three days, keeping himself going by chewing *miraa* shoots (from a bush which contains a natural amphetamine); the conductor, who extracts fares from reluctant passengers; and the tout, a veritable Daddy Cool whose aerial gymnastics on the outside of the minibus ought to be an Olympic event. The tout performs these antics to attract customers.

All Nairobi matatus are individually named and some of the popular ones on the Eastleigh run include 'Public Enemy', 'Undertaker', 'Get in & Die', 'Florida 2000', 'You Move with the Best', and 'You Die Like the Rest'. Driving standards and the frequency of fatal accidents justify these names, yet despite this, matatus are still the preferred mode of local transport. ■

have to go 3rd class. Visa credit cards are accepted for railway bookings. If you're in Malindi and planning on taking the train from Mombasa to Nairobi, bookings can be made with travel agencies and major hotels in Malindi, or by calling the station yourself. Compartment and berth numbers are posted up about 30 minutes prior to departure.

Meals & Bedding

Most trains have a dining car which provide dinner and breakfast. Meals on the trains used to be quite an experience with plentiful and cheap four-course meals served on starched white linen by smartly dressed waiters. Sadly, these days the meals are nothing special, and the level of service is generally mediocre but that's of little consequence since you pay for them anyway in the price of the ticket whether you want them or not. Cold beer is available at all times either in the dining car or you can have it delivered to your compartment.

Bedding is provided in 1st and 2nd class and is also included in the price of your ticket.

CAR & 4WD

If you are bringing your own vehicle to Kenya you should get a free three-month permit at the border on entry, so long as you have a valid *carnet de passage* for it. If you don't have a carnet you should be able to get a free one-week permit at the border on entry after which you must get an 'authorisation permit for a foreign private vehicle' at Nyayo House, Kenyatta Ave, Nairobi, which costs a few dollars but a lot of time queuing. Before you do this, however, get in touch with the Automobile Association of Kenya which is in the Hurlingham shopping centre (signposted) in Nairobi.

When you are driving your own vehicle there are certain routes in north-east Kenya where you must obtain police permission before setting out. This is just a formality but there will be a roadblock to enforce this. The main stretch where this applies is between Isiolo and Marsabit where all transport must travel in convoy at a particular time of day

unless you're turning off to go somewhere else (such as Samburu National Park, Wamba or Maralal).

Foreign registered vehicles with a seating capacity of more than six people are not allowed into Kenyan game parks and reserves. The regulation is in force mainly to keep out the overland trucks.

Road Conditions

Kenyan roads are generally in good condition and many are excellent but, to a degree, it depends on which party the local member of parliament belongs to. If it's KANU (the ruling party) they'll be good, elsewhere watch out for potholes. The main exception to this is the Mombasa to Malaba road via Nairobi (the A104). This is the main road through the country and it not only takes Kenyan traffic but all of the heavy trucks bound for Uganda, Rwanda, Burundi and eastern Zaïre so it takes a constant battering. There are many long excellent sections but, equally, there are others in need of repair – especially between Nairobi and Mombasa. If a truck forces you off the road along one of the narrow sections on this road you can virtually say goodbye to your entire suspension and, possibly, your life. Drive very carefully along this road and at all costs avoid driving at night.

The roads in the north and north-east and in the national parks are all gravel, usually in a reasonable state of repair though there are long sections of corrugated gravel in some parts. Driving on these, at the necessary speed to avoid wrecking a vehicle, can be agony on your kidneys after several hours, especially if you're on a bus which has had a double set of unyielding springs fitted to it. Naturally, there are washouts on some of these gravel roads during the rainy seasons and, under these circumstances, journey times can be considerably longer. If a bridge gets washed out, you'll either have to turn back or wait.

Right up in the north on the eastern side of Lake Turkana, especially in the Kaisut and Chalbi deserts, you can make good headway in the dry season, and the roads (which would be better described as tracks) are often surprisingly smooth and in good condition. This is certainly true of the road from Wamba to North Horr via Parsaloi, Baragoi, South Horr and Loyangalani, except for the *luggas* (dry riverbeds) between Wamba and Parsaloi for which you'll need 4WD.

After rain, however, it's another story, particularly on the flat parts of the deserts. They turn into treacherous seas of mud, often as much as a metre deep in places. Only a complete fool would attempt to drive in these circumstances without 4WD, sand ladders, adequate jacking equipment, shovels, a tow rope or wire, drinking water and spare metal jerry cans of fuel. This is particularly true of the stretches of track between North Horr and Maikona and on any of the tracks leading off the Marsabit to Isiolo road through the Losai National Reserve.

To get out of the mud, if you're really stuck, you're going to be entirely dependent on the small number of vehicles which *may* pass by and *may* stop and help (they won't want to get stuck either), or on a passing herd of camels. It's going to cost you money either way. Not only that, but you can sometimes drive for hours only to find that it's impossible to cross a river, which may not even exist in the dry season, and have to drive all the way back again. Fuel is very difficult to find in this region and is usually only available at mission stations for up to three times what you would pay for it in Nairobi – and they'll only sell you a limited amount. Make adequate preparations if you are driving your own vehicle.

Fuel Costs

In Nairobi, petrol costs KSh 35 per litre; diesel is somewhat cheaper at KSh 27.

Car & 4WD Rental

Hiring a vehicle to tour Kenya (or at least the national parks) is a relatively expensive way of seeing the country but it does give you freedom of movement and is sometimes the only way of getting to the more remote parts of the country. On the other hand, if you're sharing costs, it's quite a feasible option.

There are a number of factors to take into consideration before deciding what type of vehicle to take and which company to go through, and there's no real substitute for sitting down with pen and paper and working out as near as possible what the total cost will be. To do this you'll need as many hire-charge leaflets as you can get hold of and a distances table.

The other major consideration is what type of vehicle is going to be suitable to enable you to get where you want to go. At times other than the rainy season, a 2WD vehicle may be perfectly adequate in some parts of the country including Masai Mara Game Reserve, Amboseli and Tsavo national parks (at least on the main access routes of the latter), but it won't get you to the east side of Lake Turkana and would restrict your movements in the Aberdare and Meru national parks and the Buffalo Springs and Samburu game reserves. Most companies also have a policy of insisting that you take a 4WD vehicle if you're going upcountry and off the beaten track.

Rental Costs This is something of a minefield since the daily/weekly base rates vary quite a lot as do the km (mileage) charges. What initially looks cheap often works out just as expensive as anything else. To give you some idea of average costs, the base rates for a 2WD saloon car are between KSh 950 to KSh 1500 per day plus KSh 8.50 to KSh 15 per km (usually with a daily minimum of either 50 or 100 km) plus collision damage waiver insurance (CDW) of between KSh 600 and KSh 900 per day and theft protection insurance waiver (TPW) of around KSh 600 per day (see Insurance later). Daily unlimited km rates vary between KSh 3900 (one day) and KSh 3200 (eight to 30 days) plus the two insurance rates quoted above.

In the next category, an average small 4WD vehicle such as a Suzuki Sierra costs between KSh 1200 and KSh 1500 per day plus KSh 12 to KSh 15 per km (usually with a daily minimum of either 50 or 100 km) plus CDW of between KSh 600 and KSh 900 per day and TPW of around KSh 600 per day. Daily unlimited km rates vary between KSh 4600 (two to seven days) and KSh 3200 (eight to 30 days) but conditions may apply here depending on how many km you want (see Minimum Mileage Conditions later). The lower price includes, say, 500 km and the higher price, say, 1200 km. To these daily rates you must add KSh 600 to KSh 800 CDW per day plus around KSh 600 TPW per day but, again, some companies include the insurance costs in these rates; others do not.

In the highest category – a 4WD Isuzu Trooper or Mitsubishi Pajero, for example – daily rates vary between KSh 2000 and KSh 2500 plus KSh 25 and KSh 30 per km (usually with a daily minimum of 50 or 100 km) plus CDW of between KSh 900 and KSh 1100 per day and TPW of around KSh 750. Daily unlimited km rates vary between KSh 5100 (two to seven days) and KSh 7400 (eight to 30 days) but conditions may apply depending on how many km you want. To these rates you must add KSh 900 to KSh 1100 CDW per day plus around KSh 750 to KSh 900 per day TPW per day but, again, some companies include the insurance costs in these rates.

Value Added Tax Whatever the total charges come to on your hire – hire rate, insurance, fuel top-up, km charges, etc – you will be charged 15% value added tax (VAT) on top of the lot. You can argue the hind leg off a donkey about the patently obvious fact that VAT has already been previously added to some of the costs but you'll be wasting your breath. The Kenyan tax man doesn't understand such logic and anyone who runs a company in Kenya knows this too so they're not going to leave themselves short. End of story. This is Kenya.

Minimum Mileage Conditions Some of the so-called 'unlimited' km rates are not quite that. Some have a ceiling of 500 to 1200 km per week free after which you pay the excess at the normal km rate. Some companies also offer the option of 500 km or 1200 km per week free of charge with corresponding lower or higher base rates. If you are renting on a daily basis, some companies have a 50 km or 100-km minimum charge, regardless of whether you travel this far or not. If you're not planning on going too far then it may be more economical to opt for the lower free km rate.

Insurance The only way to cover yourself against damage to the hire vehicle and other property is to take out Collision Damage Waiver (CDW) insurance. The thing to really look out for here is the excess payable by you in the event of a collision. With the larger and generally more reputable companies (Avis, Hertz, Europcar, Central, among others) it's generally around KSh 2500 and a very generous KSh 2000 with Central. With others (Glory, Market, Payless, Habib's, et al.), however, it's as high as KSh 40,000, and this is over and above the KSh 600 to KSh 1100 or so you pay per day for insurance in the first place! What sort of CDW insurance leaves you liable for KSh 40,000 excess? Insurance? What insurance!? You *must* establish what the excess is before renting a vehicle or you could be in for a nasty shock if someone stoves into you and writes the car off. Even if the excess is high, however, it's essential to be insured and remember that tyres, tools and windscreens are always excluded from CDW insurance.

The other insurance you must have is Theft Protection Waiver (TPW). Some companies include this in the CDW insurance; many do not. As with CDW, you must know whether you are insured for this as car theft is becoming increasingly common in Kenya, and if your vehicle is ripped-off and you're not insured, you'll be up for the full value of the vehicle. Do you know how much vehicle is worth in Kenya? Don't even think about it. Not only that, but without such insurance, some companies stipulate that you will be liable, 'up to the value stated by the company'. In other words, think of a number and double it. That leaves you with no legal rights except to pay what they demand. Even if you have TPW, some of the cheaper car hire companies have an excess of KSh 40,000 which you are liable for. The more expensive companies do not and, yet again, Central comes out on top with a liability of just KSh 2000.

Deposits There's a wide variation in the deposits charged on hired vehicles. It's usually the estimated total hire charges (base rate and km) plus whatever the excess is on the CDW. You can cover this with either cash or signed travellers' cheques (returnable). The most convenient way to do it is by using a credit card.

Drivers' Licences & Minimum Age An international driver's licence or your own national driving licence is standard. Some companies stipulate a minimum age of 23 years but with others it is 25. There are occasionally stipulations about endorsements on licences (clean licences preferred) and that you must have been driving for at least two years. You will also need acceptable ID such as a passport.

Maintenance Although it's not always the case, it's probably true to say that the more you pay for a vehicle, the better condition it will be in. It's worth paying attention to this, especially if you're planning on going a long way. It doesn't necessarily mean that all the cheaper companies neglect maintenance but, as our feedback mail indicates, some certainly do.

The other factor related to maintenance is what the company will do for you (if anything) in the event of a major breakdown. The major companies *may* deliver you a replacement vehicle and make arrangements for recovery of the other vehicle at their expense, but with most companies you'll be entirely responsible for getting the vehicle fixed and back on the road. Only when you return it will you be refunded and you'll need receipts to prove what you spent.

Seasonal Discounts It's a good idea to do some footwork during the low season as some of the more expensive companies offer

substantial discounts of up to 40% on their normal rates during this period.

One-Way Rates If you want to hire a vehicle in one place and drop it off in another there will be additional charges to pay. These vary depending on the vehicle, the company and the pick-up and drop-off locations. With some companies it's free but in most cases it would be wise to count on KSh 7500 between Nairobi and Mombasa and KSh 1500 between Mombasa and Malindi.

Driving to Tanzania Only the larger (and more expensive) companies cater for this and there are additional charges. Briefly, these are about KSh 12,000 for documentation, insurance, permits etc.

Rental Agencies At the top end of the market are two companies:

Avis
    Koinange St, Nairobi (☎ (02) 336794)
    Moi Ave, Mombasa (☎ (011) 223048)
    Sitawi House, Malindi (☎ (0123) 20513)
    Two Fishes Hotel, Diani Beach (☎ (0127) 2101)
    Jomo Kenyatta International Airport, Nairobi (☎ (02) 822186)
Hertz
    Muindi Mbingu St, Nairobi (☎ (02) 331960)
    Jomo Kenyatta International Airport, Nairobi (☎ (02) 822339)
    Moi Ave, Mombasa (☎ (011) 316333)
    Moi International Airport, Mombasa (☎ (011) 433211)
    Moi Ave, Malindi (☎ (0123) 20040).

In much the same league but somewhat less expensive on weekly rates is Europcar at Bruce House, Standard St, Nairobi (☎ (02) 334722), and also in the Times building, Nkrumah Rd, Mombasa (☎ (011) 215917), and in Malindi (☎ (0123) 30556). It also has branch offices at Jomo Kenyatta International Airport in Nairobi (☎ (02) 822348), Moi International Airport in Mombasa (☎ (011) 433780), and at Diani Sea Lodge at Diani Beach (☎ (0127 2114).

Somewhat cheaper but very reliable companies with well-maintained vehicles include:

Central Rent-a-Car
   Fedha Towers, Standard St, Nairobi (☎ (02) 222888; fax 339666)
Glory Car Hire
   Diamond building, Tubman Rd, Nairobi (☎ (02) 2250224; fax 331533)
   Moi Ave, Mombasa (☎ (011) 313561/221159)
   Ngala building, Lamu Rd, Malindi (☎ /fax (0123) 20065)
Habib's
   Agip House, Haile Selassie Ave, Nairobi (☎ (02) 220463)
Market Car Hire
   Market Service Station, on the corner of Koinange & Banda Sts, Nairobi (☎ (02) 225797)
Payless Car Hire
   Hilton Hotel, Nairobi (☎ (02) 223581; fax 223384)
   Mombasa (☎ (011) 222629; fax 221282)
   Malindi (☎ (0123) 31643; fax 31645)
   Diani (☎ (0127) 2276)

Central Rent-a-Car is certainly the best in this category with a well-maintained fleet of fairly new vehicles and a good back-up service. Its excess liability on CDW is also the lowest (KSh 2000), and its insurance rates include *both* TPW and CDW insurance.

Glory has some decent cars but also has some real bombs. Market and Payless are owned by the same people and their excess liability on CDW would leave you penniless if you did have an accident (KSh 40,000), but then so would Glory which has the same excess.

BICYCLE

Bicycles are basically only in use in cities and there's not many of them. Virtually everybody travels by matatu. Anyone foolish enough to risk cycling along main roads in Kenya must be considered suicidal. The exception would be in the countryside and off the main roads. Always assume that the vehicle approaching you from behind is going to knock you off the road so get off it before it reaches you. This obviously makes cycling tedious but it's better than ending up on a mortuary slab.

The hills of Kenya are not particularly steep but can be long and hard. You can expect cover around 80 km per day in the hills of the western highlands, somewhat more where the country is flatter. Be wary of cycling off road as punctures from thorn trees are a major problem.

HITCHING

Hitching is usually good on the main roads and may well be preferable to travelling by matatu, but if you are picked up by an African driver and are expecting a free lift then make this clear from the outset. Most will expect a contribution at least. Hitching to the national parks, on the other hand, can be very difficult since most people either go on a tour or hire their own vehicle. Apart from that, once you get to the park lodges or camping areas, you will be entirely dependent on persuading other tourists with their own vehicles to take you out with them to view game since walking in the parks is generally forbidden. Although many travellers hitchhike, it is not a totally safe way of getting around. Just because we explain how hitching works does not mean we recommend it.

BOAT
Lake Victoria Ferry

Ferries connect Kisumu with Kendu Bay and Homa Bay, and Homa Bay with Mfangano Island, but the service is very limited. The schedule for the lake ferries can be found in the Kisumu section.

Dhow

Sailing on a dhow along the East African coast is one of Kenya's most worthwhile and memorable experiences. There's nothing quite like drifting along the ocean in the middle of the night with the moon up high, the only sounds the lapping of the waves against the side of the boat and subdued conversation. It's enjoyable at any time of day, even when the breeze drops and the boat virtually comes to a standstill.

There are no creature comforts aboard these dhows so when night comes you simply bed down wherever there is space. You'll probably get off these boats smelling of fish since fish oil is used to condition the timbers of the boat – nothing that a shower won't remove! Take drinking water and food with you although fish is often caught on the way and cooked up on deck over charcoal. Just imagine yourself on Magellan's or Francis Drake's circumnavigation of the world and you'll have it about right except it will only take a few days instead of three years and you won't have to do any pillaging! Dhows can be picked up in Lamu but there are also possibilities in Mombasa.

Many of the smaller dhows these days have been fitted with outboard motors so that progress can be made when there's no wind. The larger dhows are all motorised and some of them don't even have sails.

If you have the money (US$60), check out the Tamarind Dhow cruises which leave from the Tamarind Restaurant in Nyali on the mainland opposite Mombasa island – see the Mombasa section for details.

Safaris

ORGANISED VEHICLE SAFARIS

There are essentially two types of organised safaris – those where you camp and those where you stay in game lodges or luxury tented camps at night. Whichever you choose, safaris typically start and end in either Nairobi or Mombasa, though there are a number of exceptions to this. Apart from transfer to and from Nairobi or Mombasa and driving from one park to another, once you're in a park you'll be taken on a number of game drives – usually two and sometimes three per day. Each drive typically lasts two to 2½ hours and the best (in terms of sighting animals) are those in the early morning and late afternoon when the animals are at their most active. The vehicles used for these drives are six to eight-seater minibuses with roof hatches, Land Rovers, or open-sided trucks.

As a general rule, you'll be left to your own devices between late morning and around 3 pm (except for lunch) though, if you're on a camping safari, you may well be taken to a lodge in the early afternoon to

relax over a cold beer or have a swim in the pool. You may also be taken to a lodge after the late-afternoon game drive for the same thing before returning to camp for dinner.

Camping Safaris

Camping safaris cater for budget travellers, for the young (or young at heart) and for those who are prepared to put up with discomfort. They are no-frills safaris, with none of life's little luxuries such as flush toilets, running water or iced drinks. Such safaris can be quite demanding depending on where you go, and you'll be expected to lend a hand. You'll end up sweaty and dusty and there may well be no showers available – even cold ones. On the other hand, you're in for an authentic adventure in the African bush with nothing between you and the animals at night except a sheet of canvas and the embers of a dying fire. It's not at all unusual for elephants or hippos to trundle through the camp at night, or even the occasional lion, and, so far, no-one has been eaten or trampled on.

Another plus for these safaris is that you'll probably find yourself with travellers from the four corners of the earth. Truck safaris may have as many as half a dozen different nationalities on board.

The price of your safari will include three meals a day cooked by the camp cook(s), though on some safaris you'll be expected to lend a hand in the preparation and clean up. Food is of the 'plain but plenty' variety.

The price will also include all the necessary camping gear except a sleeping bag which you must provide or hire locally. The tents provided sleep two people as a rule and you'll be expected to erect and dismantle it yourself, though there are some safaris where the camp is taken on ahead of you and the tents erected by the staff, or where companies have permanent tented camps sites. If you're a single traveller, you'll be expected to share a tent with someone else. If you don't want to do that then you'll be up for a 'single supplement' of between 20% to 25% on the price of the safari which will secure you a tent of your own. Mosquito nets are generally not provided so you'll have to hire one yourself or bring along insect repellent either in the form of coils or a skin cream.

You'll need to bring clothing and footwear sufficient to cover you for hot days and cold nights but the amount of baggage which you'll be allowed to bring is limited. Excess gear can usually be stored at the safari company's offices. Don't forget to bring along a torch (flashlight) and pocket-knife – the company will provide kerosene lanterns for the camp but it's unlikely they'll be left on all night.

There are also a number of somewhat more expensive camping safaris available which utilise permanent camp sites with pre-erected tents fitted with mosquito nets, beds and sheets and which have showers.

Remember that at the end of one of these safaris your driver/guide and the cook(s) will expect a reasonable tip. This is only fair since wages are low and these people will have made a lot of effort to make your trip a memorable one. Be generous here. Other travellers are going to follow you and the last thing anyone wants to find themselves closeted with is a disgruntled driver/guide who couldn't care less whether you see game or not. A good tipping guide is around KSh 150 per guide/cook per person per day – in other words, what you would spend on a round of drinks between just two people.

Lodge & Tented Camp Safaris

The other type of safari is for those who want luxury at night and in between game drives. The accommodation is in game lodges or luxury tented camps. There are plenty of beautifully conceived and superbly located lodges in the main national parks where you can expect a fully self-contained room, cottage or tent, cuisine of an international standard, a terrace bar with ice-cold drinks, a swimming pool and videos and plenty of staff to cater for all your requirements. Many of these lodges overlook a watering hole or salt lick so you can sit on the viewing terrace and watch the animals from there. The watering hole or salt lick will usually be floodlit at night. Some of the lodges put out bait or salt

to encourage certain animals to visit the spot and while this is often very contrived, it usually guarantees you a sighting of animals which you'd be very lucky to see otherwise, leopards in particular.

There's obviously a considerable difference in price for these safaris as opposed to camping, and most of the people who go on them are package tourists with expectations and attitudes of mind quite dissimilar to those who opt for a camping safari. For them it's essentially a holiday rather than in-depth involvement in Africa, its people and wildlife. It's the African bush at arm's length. On the other hand, if you have the money, it's worth staying at the occasional lodge just for the contrast and many lodges do go to great lengths to bring Africa as close as possible to you in terms of design, location and decor.

Lodge safaris will cost you up to four times what a camping safari costs, sometimes considerably more. Luxury tented camps are no less expensive than lodges and the more exclusive ones cost up to twice as much as a lodge. They are for people to whom money is no object and who want to experience what it must have been like in the days of the big-game hunters, except that they'll be stalking game with cameras rather than guns.

Routes

Whether you take a camping safari or a lodge safari, there's a whole plethora of options available ranging from two days to 15 days and, in some cases, up to six weeks, though the longer trips would take you to neighbouring countries as well. If possible, it's best to go on a safari which lasts at least five days and preferably longer since otherwise a good deal of your time will be taken up driving to and from the national parks and Nairobi. You'll also see a great deal more on a longer safari and have a much better chance of catching sight of all the major animals. Remember that sightings of any particular animal cannot be guaranteed but the longer you spend looking, the better your chances are. A longer safari will also give you the opportunity of having some involvement with the local tribespeople.

A three-day safari typically takes you either to Amboseli or Masai Mara. A four-day safari would take you to Amboseli and Tsavo, to Amboseli and Masai Mara or to Samburu and Buffalo Springs but you'd be pushing it to get three parks in four days. A five-day safari would take you to Amboseli and Tsavo, or to Masai Mara and Lake Nakuru; whereas a six-day safari would take you to lakes Nakuru, Bogoria and Baringo plus Masai Mara, or to Lake Nakuru, Masai Mara and Amboseli. On a seven-day safari, you could expect to visit at least two of the Rift Valley lakes plus Masai Mara and Amboseli, whereas on an 11-day safari you would take in two or more of the Rift Valley lakes plus Masai Mara, Amboseli and Tsavo; or Samburu and Buffalo Springs, Meru, Lake Nakuru and Masai Mara.

Most of the safari companies cover the above standard routes but some also specialise in different routes designed to take you off the beaten track. There are, for instance, safaris which take in Masai Mara, Lake Victoria, Mt Elgon, Saiwa Swamp and Nakuru, and others which take in Mt Kenya, Samburu and Buffalo Springs, Nyahururu, Lake Nakuru and Masai Mara. Other safaris visit Shaba, rather than Samburu and Buffalo Springs, where you'll hardly see another vehicle. There are also others which will take you to Marsabit National Park in the far north, but they're very few and are generally part of a safari to Lake Turkana.

Some companies also offer safaris to Lake Turkana which range from six to 10 days. The shorter trips take one or other of the standard routes – Nairobi, Nakuru, Nyahururu, Maralal, Baragoi, South Horr and Loyangalani or Nairobi, Isiolo, Maralal, Baragoi, South Horr and Loyangalani. The longer trips detour from this route and take you to either or both of Samburu and Buffalo Springs National Reserves and either Meru National Park or Shaba National Reserve. There are also combination safaris which include a vehicle safari to Lake Turkana and a camel safari in the Matthews Range or the Ndoto Mountains. A full description of the options available can be found in the Lake Turkana Safaris section later on.

Costs

There's a lot of competition for the tourist dollar among the safari companies, and prices for the same tour are very similar. The trouble is, there are now so many safaris to choose from which offer similar itineraries and options that it's not that easy to compare prices. It depends what you want, though it's still generally true that the longer you go for, the less it costs per day.

For camping safaris with no frills you are looking at an all-inclusive price of around US$70 to US$80 per day on a reducing scale the longer you are out. The price includes transport, food (three meals per day), park entry and camping fees, tents and cooking equipment. The price per day for safaris over 11 days tends to rise somewhat since there's a lot more organisation involved and you'll be going to remote areas where there are no services available so everything has to be trucked in.

Unfortunately, the situation is not as simple as the above suggests. While it may be OK to use the above figure as a benchmark, prices vary widely. A three-day safari to Amboseli and Masai Mara or Amboseli and Tsavo varies from US$180 to US$570. A five-day safari to Amboseli and Masai Mara or to the Rift Valley and Amboseli varies from US$300 to US$800; and a seven-day safari to Amboseli, Masai Mara and the Rift Valley or to Amboseli, Masai Mara and Samburu varies from US$400 to US$1000 or more. In other words, you must do some legwork. Collect as many company leaflets as you can (about a morning's work), decide where you want to go, compare prices, work out what's included and what isn't, and then make your choice. Remember that, generally, you get what you pay for. A high degree of personal involvement in camp chores and a willingness to eschew creature comforts usually guarantees a low price. If you want the opposite, it will cost you more. No-one works for nothing.

The prices for safaris which involve staying in lodges or tented camps are considerably higher. Here you're looking at a minimum of US$180 per person per night in the lodges and up to US$350 in the luxury tented camps.

The above prices are based on the assumption that you will share accommodation (a tent or room) with one other person. If you don't want to do this then you'll have to pay what's called a 'single room supplement'. This is generally around 20% to 25% extra and sometimes up to 50%.

Departure Frequency

This varies a lot from company to company and depends on the season. In the high season, many companies have daily or every second day departures to the most popular game parks – Amboseli, Masai Mara and Tsavo – since there's high demand. To the less frequented parks such as Samburu and Buffalo Springs, Shaba and Meru, they generally leave only once or twice per week. Safaris to Lake Turkana are usually only once weekly. In addition, most companies will leave for any of the most popular game parks at any time so long as you have a minimum number of people wanting to go – usually four. In the low season, there are fewer departures.

It obviously makes a lot of sense to either book ahead or to get a group together rather than just turn up and expect to leave the very next morning. Advance booking is essential for the Lake Turkana safaris since they're heavily subscribed. It's also essential for any of the more exotic options described in the Other Safaris section.

Choosing a Company

There is no doubt that some safari companies are better than others. The main factors which make for the difference are the quality and type of vehicles used, the standard of the food, and the skills and knowledge of the drivers/guides. It's equally true that any company can take a bunch of people on safari one week and bring them back fully satisfied,

and yet the following week take a different set of people on the same safari and end up with a virtual mutiny. That's an extreme example, but whether a company gets praised or condemned can hinge on something as simple as a broken spring which involves having to wait around for most of the day whilst a replacement vehicle is sent out from Nairobi.

The other major factor to take into consideration before you decide to go with any particular company is whether they actually operate their own safaris with their own vehicles or whether they are just agents for other safari companies. If they're just agents then obviously part of what you pay is their commission but the most important thing here is, if anything goes wrong or the itinerary is changed without your agreement, you have very little comeback and you'll be pushing shit uphill to get a refund. We get letters about this all the time from travellers to whom this all has happened.

Unfortunately, the situation isn't that easy to avoid. It's a minefield working out which are genuine safari companies and which are just agencies. Go into any office in Nairobi and, naturally, they all have their own vehicles and, of course, they'll compensate you at the end of the safari if anything goes seriously wrong. Not so if they're just agents. They will already have paid the lion's share of what you gave them to the company which actually provided the vehicles and staff so that gives them very little room to manoeuvre. Likewise, there's no way that the actual safari company is going to provide the agency with a refund.

It's perfectly obvious that quite a few so-called safari companies are merely agencies. Simply pick up half a dozen leaflets from various companies and compare the wording – you'll find that quite a few are identical!

On the other hand, quite a lot of genuine safari companies put out leaflets giving the impression that they do every conceivable safari under the sun. They don't. They may well do quite a lot of them with their own vehicles and staff and take personal responsibility for them but, in many cases, especially as regards Mt Kenya treks, gorilla safaris to Uganda/Zaïre and the national parks of Tanzania (Serengeti, Ngorongoro, Lake Manyara, Mt Kilimanjaro etc), they will be on-selling to another company or a Tanzanian company which specialises in these. This doesn't mean they're out to rip you off. If a company operates its own safaris, it has a reputation to look after and it will only be on-selling to companies that it trusts and which have a record at least the equal of its own.

If you find shopping around too daunting you might consider going to a travel agent (see the Travel Agents section in the Nairobi chapter). However, if you are looking for a real bottom-end safari, you are likely to get a better price by shopping around as negotiation is then possible.

Another aspect of Kenya's safari business is that there's a good deal of client swapping between companies whose vehicles are full and those which aren't. You may find yourself on a certain company's safari which is not the one you booked through. The reputable companies won't do this without informing you but the agents certainly will. Getting swapped onto another company's safari isn't necessarily a bad thing but make sure that the safari you booked and paid for is what you get. There is an organisation called the Kenyan Association of Tour Operators (KATO) to which most reputable safari companies belong so you have *some* recourse to appeal in case of conflict but it's essentially a paper tiger.

Despite the pitfalls mentioned here, there are many reliable companies offering camping safaris which have their own vehicles and an excellent track record. The following companies have been listed alphabetically, and are not in any order of preference, reliability or cost.

This is by no means an exhaustive list of companies which offer camping safaris nor is there necessarily any implication that others are unreliable – though some are. On the other hand, we do get hundreds of letters from travellers every year describing their experiences with various safari companies. Some get consistently good reports and others get variable reports, but there are some which get consistently bad reports. If you do choose a company not listed here don't blame us if you get into strife but do tell us what the problem was and what was done about it (if anything).

Best Camping Tours

2nd floor, Nanak House, corner of Kimathi and Banda Sts, PO Box 40223, Nairobi (☎ 229667; fax 217923)

This is a popular and reliable company which offers budget camping safaris on all the main routes including Amboseli or Masai Mara (three to four days); Amboseli and Tsavo (four days); Amboseli, Tsavo, the Rift Valley lakes and Masai Mara (eight days); Mt Kenya, Samburu, Nakuru and Masai Mara (eight days); Amboseli, Mt Kenya, Samburu, Nakuru and Masai Mara (eight days); and many other options. Average cost is around U\$80 per day.

Blackwing Safaris

PO Box 42532, Nairobi (☎/fax 891241)

This small company caters for discerning clients who want flexibility and quality and who don't want to be crammed into the usual safari minibus. Safaris are only three clients or less at a time and can be arranged for any duration within Kenya or Tanzania. Safaris cost a standard US\$360 a day per person assuming a minimum of five days but this includes the lot – all transport, transfer to and from Nairobi airport, first and last nights at the Boulevard Hotel in Nairobi, all food and drink (including beer, wine and spirits), all park entry and camping fees, and the full range of camping and safari equipment.

Bushbuck Adventures

Barclays Bank building, Kenyatta Ave, PO Box 67449, Nairobi (☎ 212975; fax 218735)

Bushbuck is a small company and its emphasis is on passenger comfort and conservation. As a result, it's relatively expensive but part of the profits go back into conservation projects. Its main emphasis is on customised safaris for individuals and groups. The price of these safaris ranges from US\$360 per person per day for one person to US\$88 per person for 18 people.

Come to Africa Safaris Ltd

3rd floor, Rehema House, between Kaunda and Standard Sts, PO Box 69513, Nairobi (☎ 213186; fax 213254)

This company covers most of the national parks in Kenya (as well as Tanzania) and also has its own permanent tented camp – the Mara Hippo Camp – in Masai Mara. All its safaris cost a standard US\$70 per person per day, and are popular among budget travellers.

Exotic Safaris

1st floor, South Wing, Uniafric House, Koinange St, PO Box 54483, Nairobi (☎ 338811; fax 245767)

We receive consistently good reports of this company, which offers a full range of safaris along the standard routes. It also offers an eight-day Turkana safari – see later.

Gametrackers Camping Safaris

1st floor, Kenya Cinema Plaza, Moi Ave, PO Box 62042, Nairobi (☎ 338927, 222703; fax 330903)

Also long-established and reliable, this company offers a whole range of both camping and lodge safaris. It also offers a number of much longer safaris such as a four-week Mountain Gorilla Safari (US$890), a five-week Southern Africa Safari (US$855), and a nine-week Africa in Depth Safari (US$1425). It also covers the national parks of Tanzania, Mt Kenya treks, Lake Turkana and a camel safari (details of the last three below).

Departures for the shorter trips vary between once a week and 10 times a month. For the longer trips it's usually once a week and for the four and five-week safaris it's once a month.

Ketty Tours

Moi Ave (PO Box 82391), Mombasa (☎ 315178; fax 311355)

This company specialises partly in short tours of the coastal region (Wasini, Shimba Hills, Gedi etc) but it also offers camping safaris to all the usual parks ranging from two to 10 days. The average cost per person per day is US$80.

Safari-Camp Services

Barclays Plaza, PO Box 44801, Nairobi (☎ 330130; fax 212160)

This company was one of the first in Kenya and has been operating successfully for two decades. You'll hear nothing but praise about them. It was also the originator of the legendary 'Turkana Bus'. Safari Camp Services is very much concerned with authenticity, good organisation and value for money.

Its Turkana Bus is one of the best (see below) and its Wildlife Bus, which visits Samburu, Lake Nakuru and Masai Mara is just as good (seven days, US$505, departures once a fortnight on Saturday). There are also 'lodge-equivalent' camping safaris for those who prefer somewhat better facilities.

Safari Camp Services also takes in camel safaris (see below), the coast, and Lake Nakuru and Masai Mara (five days, US$360, departs once a fortnight).

Safari Seekers

5th floor, Jubilee Insurance Exchange building, Kaunda St, PO Box 9165, Nairobi (☎ 226206; fax 334585)

Ground floor, Diamond Trust Arcade, Moi Ave, PO Box 88275, Mombasa (☎ 220122; fax 228277).

This company has been operating for some years and gets consistently good reports. It also has its own permanent camp sites in Amboseli, Samburu and Masai Mara. Safari Seekers offers both camping and lodge safaris in Kenya (ex-Nairobi and Mombasa) and Tanzania (ex-Arusha) as well as mountain climbing in Kenya. All of these it operates itself. Camping safaris cost US$80 to US$85 per person per day all inclusive except for sleeping bags (US$10 per person per trip). Departures are at least once a week or anytime assuming a minimum of four people. Safari Seekers also offer a choice of 10 lodge/ luxury tented camp safaris which will depart any day assuming a minimum of two people and average US$230 per person per day all inclusive.

Special Camping Safaris Ltd

Karen Shopping Centre, PO Box 51512, Nairobi (☎ /fax 882541)

This small company offers Amboseli and Tsavo (four days, US$350), Masai Mara (four days, US$350), Masai Mara and the Rift Valley lakes (six days, US$510), and a Game Safari 'special' which takes in Masai Mara, Lakes Naivasha, Nakuru, Bogoria and Baringo, Maralal, Samburu and Mt Kenya (10 days, US$800). It also has a 10-day Turkana expedition (details below). Departures are once a week for the shorter trips and once a fortnight for the longer ones.

Savuka Tours & Safaris

3rd floor, Pan Africa House, Kenyatta Ave, PO Box 20433, Nairobi (☎ 725907, 725108)

This outfit is not a member of KATO but we've had good reports of it from its customers. It has a permanent camp site in Masai Mara.

Tour Africa Safaris Ltd

3rd Mezzanine floor, Corner House, cnr Mama Ngina and Kimathi Sts, PO Box 34187, Nairobi (☎ 336767; fax 338271)

Ground floor, NSSF House, Nkrumah Rd, Mombasa (☎ 316172; fax 316197)

TAS specialises in longer distance safaris such as to the gorillas in Zaïre, Tanzanian national parks and southern African countries, but it does have two safaris exclusively in Kenya. The first is the 'Big Simba Expedition' which takes in Lake Nakuru and Masai Mara and involves staying at TAS' exclusive luxury tented camp in the Mara (five days, US$395, departures once a week). The other is a seven-day 'Wildlife Safari' which takes in Samburu, Lake Nakuru and Masai Mara.

Up-Market Companies If you don't want to camp but prefer to stay in a lodge each night then check out:

Abercrombie & Kent Ltd

6th & 7th floor, Bruce House, Standard St, PO Box 59749, Nairobi (☎ 228700; fax 215752)

African Tours & Hotels
Utalii House, Uhuru Highway, PO Box 30471, Nairobi (☎ 336858; fax 218109)
Nkrumah Rd, PO Box 90604, Mombasa (☎ 223509; fax 311022)

Inside Africa Safaris
Wabera St between Mama Ngina and Kaunda Sts, PO Box 59767, Nairobi (☎ 223304; fax 215448)

Pollman's Tours & Safaris
Koinange St, PO Box 45895, Nairobi (☎ 544373; fax 544639)
Taveta Rd, PO Box 84198, Mombasa (☎ 312565; fax 314502)

United Touring Company
Fedha Towers, cnr Muindi Mbingu and Kaunda Sts, PO Box 42196, Nairobi (☎ 331960; fax 331422)
Moi Ave, PO Box 84782, Mombasa (☎ 316333; fax 314549).

Vacational Tours & Travel Ltd
Nairobi Hilton, PO Box 44401, Nairobi (☎ 337392; fax 210530)

In this category Inside Africa Safaris come up consistently cheaper, assuming a minimum of eight people, than the others but its safari options are limited to the Aberdares, Amboseli, Masai Mara, Lake Nakuru and Samburu plus a number of coastal trips (eg Shimba Hills and Taita Hills), and none of its safaris is longer than six days. Also, its prices rise dramatically if there are less than eight in the group. As an example, its price for a four-day Masai Mara and Lake Nakuru safari is US$495 per person assuming eight people but US$690 if you're a group of only three people and US$580 if you're a group of five people. By contrast, UTC's price for the same thing is a standard US$815 (high season) and US$635 (low season) and Abercrombie & Kent's price for the same thing is US$574 (high season) and US$518 (low season). Pollman's prices are about intermediate between Inside Africa and UTC/Abercrombie & Kent.

As with camping safaris, however, things are not quite as simple as the above might indicate. UTC's and Abercrombie & Kent's prices assume double occupancy of a room or tent. If you're a single traveller and don't want to share then you'll be up for 'single room supplement' which is typically 10% extra on top of the above rates.

Departure frequency is another factor to take into consideration. UTC and Abercrombie & Kent have daily departures on their shorter safaris and guaranteed weekly departures on their longer trips whereas Inside Africa, which is a much smaller company, will not guarantee regular departures unless your group is large enough (or willing to pay the higher prices for a smaller group).

OTHER SAFARIS
Lake Turkana Safaris

There can be few travellers who come to Kenya who do not relish the idea of what amounts to a pilgrimage through the semi-arid wilds of Samburu and up to the legendary Lake Turkana (The Jade Sea). To get an idea of the sort of country you will pass through on this journey, refer to the East of Turkana section in the Northern Kenya chapter.

These safaris all use open-sided 4WD trucks which take up to 18 people along with two to three staff (cook, driver and courier) and you will need to set aside a minimum of seven days to complete the journey. There are others which take longer (10 days) and give you a better appreciation of this part of Kenya and its peoples, and there are even longer ones which incorporate a camel safari. All of them terminate at Loyangalani on the shores of Lake Turkana before returning south. The routes taken are fairly standard but what you see en route depends on how long the safari lasts. Some take in Lake Bogoria and Lake Baringo and others take in Samburu and Buffalo Springs national reserves: others take in both of these. Virtually all of them pass through Maralal where you spend the night.

The following list of recommended safari companies which offer trips to Lake Turkana is listed alphabetically and not in any order of preference or price.

Bushbuck Adventures
Barclays Bank building, Kenyatta Ave, PO Box 67449, Nairobi (☎ 212975; fax 218735)
Bushbuck offers Lake Turkana safaris but it keeps well away from the usual route, instead taking in the Matthew's Range, the Ndoto Mountains and Shaba National Game Reserve. It also offers a

longer 'Northern Frontier Expedition' which takes in Samburu, the Ndoto Mountains, Lake Turkana and North Horr and, like the previous tour, keeps well away from the usual route.

Exotic Safaris & Travel

1st floor, Uniafric House, Koinange St, PO Box 54483, Nairobi (☎ 338811; fax 245767)

Exotic offers an eight-day Turkana safari which goes via Lake Baringo and South Horr on the way north, and Maralal and Samburu National Reserve on the way back. The price is US$455 all inclusive except for sleeping bags, and departures are any day assuming a group of four people or more.

Gametrackers

1st floor, Kenya Cinema Plaza, Moi Ave, PO Box 62042, Nairobi (☎ 338927; fax 330903)

This company offers two eight-day options to Lake Turkana and one of the options takes in Marsabit National Park – the only company to do this. The first option takes in Lake Baringo, South Horr, Lake Turkana, the Nabuyotom volcano on the southern shore of the lake (by power boat), Maralal and the Samburu National Reserve. It costs US$415 and there are two departures per month. The other option goes first to Samburu National Reserve (two days) and then heads for Marsabit after which it crosses the Chalbi Desert and over to Lake Turkana. From Lake Turkana it returns to Nairobi via Maralal. This safari costs US$415 and departs twice a month.

Gametrackers also offers a combined Lake Turkana and camel safari that lasts 10 days – see below under 'Camel Safaris'.

Safari Camp Services

PO Box 44801, Barclays Plaza, Nairobi (☎ 28936, 330130; fax 212160)

This is the group that blazed the trail 20 years ago and recently celebrated its 1000th departure. There are two options: the Turkana Bus and the Vanishing Africa safari. The Turkana Bus is the economy option and takes in Maralal, Lake Turkana, Wamba and Samburu National Reserve. It takes seven days, costs around US$400, and departures are two to five times a month, depending on the season. Vanishing Africa is somewhat more up-market and uses Land Cruisers for transport. This 14-day safari takes in Masai Mara, lakes Naivasha, Nakuru and Baringo, Maralal, South Horr, Lake Turkana, and Samburu National Reserve and utilises lodge accommodation wherever possible – private camp sites elsewhere. As a result, it's considerably more expensive at US$2870 and only departs once a month. The prices are all inclusive except for a sleeping bag and alcoholic drinks.

Safari Camp Services also offers a combined Turkana Bus safari with a camel safari in the Matthews Range/Ndoto Mountains which lasts 14 days in total and costs US$799 all inclusive.

Special Camping Safaris

Gilfillan House, Kenyatta Ave, PO Box 51512, Nairobi (☎ 338325; fax 211828)

This company takes the usual route but its safari lasts 10 days and takes in a night on the slopes of Mt Kenya. The cost is US$600 and there are two departures each month except during April, May and November when there are no departures.

Yare Safaris

1st floor, Union Towers, Mama Ngina St, PO Box 63006, Nairobi (☎ /fax 214099)

Yare offers three Turkana options: the Turkana Charge (for those in a big hurry – six days, US$390), the Turkana Run (for those in slightly less of a hurry – seven days, US$370) and the Turkana Trail (for those with more time at their disposal – 10 days, US$530). Departures are fortnightly throughout the year. Yare has a good reputation and is a popular choice.

Camel Safaris

This is a superb way of getting right off the beaten track and into areas where vehicle safaris don't or cannot go. Camel safaris offer maximum involvement in areas of Kenya which the 20th century has hardly touched, if at all. Most of them take place in the Samburu and Turkana tribal areas between Isiolo and Lake Turkana and you'll have plenty of opportunity to become accustomed to the pace of nomadic life and to mingle with the indigenous people. You'll also encounter wildlife though, naturally, sightings of any particular animal and in what numbers cannot be guaranteed.

You have the choice of riding the camels or walking alongside them (except in a few spots where you will be forced to dismount). The camels are led by experienced Samburu *morani* (warriors) and accompanied by English-speaking guides of the same tribe who are well-versed in bush lore, botany, ornithology and local customs. Most travelling is done as early as possible in the cool of the day and a camp site established around noon. Following lunch, you are free to relax during the heat of the day and, in the evening, while the sleeping arrangements and dinner are being organised by the staff, take a walk (along with a guide if you choose). Hot showers are normally available before drinks and dinner are served around a camp fire.

All the companies provide a full range of camping equipment (two-person tents, as a rule) and ablution facilities, but they vary in what they require you to bring along. Some even provide alcoholic drinks, though normally you pay extra for this. The typical distance covered each day is between 15 and 18 km so you don't have to be super fit. Far more important is flexibility and a good positive attitude, since no two safaris are exactly alike.

Yare Safaris also host the annual Maralal International Camel Derby from its lodge and camp site at Maralal. The derby includes a full day of races in Maralal on the Saturday of the last week of October, plus a longer 18-day endurance race. For full details see the Maralal section in the Northern Kenya chapter.

The following list of recommended companies which offer camel safaris has been listed alphabetically, and not in any order of preference or price.

Camel Trek Ltd
PO Box 15076, Nairobi (☎ 891079; 891716)
Camel Trek is a small, reliable company which has treks starting from Isiolo. Departures are weekly from mid-December through March, and from July to mid-October, and the cost is US$644 for a five-day safari and US$517 for three-nights. Return transport from Nairobi is available for US$55.

Desert Rose Camels
PO Box 44801, Nairobi (☎ 228936; fax 212160)
Safaris cover the Matthews Range, Ndoto Mountains and Ol Doinyo Nyiru between Wamba and South Horr. The exact route depends on the season, the number of days you have available and personal interests. You will be accompanied by experienced Samburu camel handlers and guides. All baggage, camping equipment and food and drink are transported by camels. There are, of course, camels for riding, too.
Desert Rose prefer a minimum of six days for a safari and for this the rates are US$160 per person per day (10 people) going gradually up to US$226 per person per day (five people) and US$424 (two people) and US$752 (one person). These rates include all food and drink (including wine and beer), camping equipment, and a medical kit.

Gametrackers
1st floor, Kenya Cinema Plaza, Moi Ave (PO Box 62042), Nairobi (☎ 338927; fax 330903)
This company offers a 10-day combined camel safari and vehicle safari, which starts and finishes in Nairobi, but the camels are used exclusively for transporting baggage: you have to walk alongside them. The trip takes in the Ndoto Mountains and Lake Turkana (reached by vehicle). There are departures twice a month (on a Monday) except during April, May and November and the cost is US$550 per person which includes all transport, food and camping equipment (except sleeping bags).

Yare Safaris Ltd
1st floor, Union Towers, Mama Ngina St, PO Box 63006, Nairobi (☎/fax 214099)
Yare offers a seven-day safari although only five days are actually spent on safari since the first and last days involve transfer from and to Nairobi. Overnight accommodation the night before and after the trek is in double self-contained *bandas* (thatched huts) at Yare's Maralal club and camp site. The actual trek starts at Barsalinga on the Ewaso Nyiro River (which flows through Samburu and Buffalo Springs game reserves) and it leaves every Saturday. You may walk or ride as you wish but a support vehicle carrying the bulk of your luggage, the tents and supplies plus any personal needs such as beer, spirits and soft drinks will go ahead of the camels to the next camp site. This is not an arduous safari but neither is it luxury. A flexible and positive attitude of mind is the most important thing to have. The cost is US$450 per person which includes everything except a sleeping bag, items of a personal nature and alcoholic drinks (which you can purchase at the club before departure).

Walking & Cycling Safaris

For the keen walker and those who don't want to spend all their time in a safari minibus, there are a number of options.

Bike Treks
PO Box 14237, Nairobi (☎ 446371; fax 442439)
This company offers both walking and cycling as well as combined walking/cycling safaris. Its shortest safari is a three-day Masai Mara combined trip which costs US$285 and includes transport to and from Nairobi, all camping equipment, food and bicycles but excludes park fees and tips. A more substantial safari is the six-day walking trip (US$720) in the Loita plains and hills of Maasailand west and south of Narok which includes a full day game viewing drive in the Masai Mara Game Reserve.
For cyclists, there's a six-day safari, again through

the heart of Maasailand including a full day's game drive in Masai Mara National Reserve which costs US$720 including everything except park entry and public camp-site fees and tips. A minimum of three people guarantees departure on any of these safaris.

Bushbuck Adventures

Gilfillan House, Kenyatta Ave, PO Box 67449, Nairobi (☎ 212975; fax 218735)

Bushbuck is a small company and its emphasis is on passenger comfort and conservation. It's relatively expensive but part of the profits go back into conservation projects. Its main emphasis is on customised safaris for individuals and groups. The price ranges from US$390 per day for a one person safari to US$160 per person for 12 people (in two vehicles).

Gametrackers

1st floor, Kenya Cinema Plaza, Moi Ave, PO Box 62042, Nairobi (☎ 338927; fax 330903)

This company offers a four-day walking safari into the Aberdare National Park. There are up to five departures each month except during May and November when there are none and the cost is US$315 per person (minimum five people).

Hiking & Cycling Kenya

4th floor, Arrow House, Koinange St, PO Box 39439, Nairobi (☎ 218336; fax 228107)

This company specialises in hiking safaris although they all involve some transport by road and/or boat. All are camping safaris. Its 10-day safari takes you to Lake Turkana in the footsteps of Count Teleki. On the way back to Nairobi, by vehicle, you visit Maralal and Samburu National Reserve.

There's also a 14-day walking and boating safari which takes in the Mara River, Lake Nakuru, Mt Elgon, the Cherangani Hills and Lake Turkana. It includes game drives through Masai Mara and a visit to the remote Sibiloi National Park (by boat) at the north-eastern end of Lake Turkana. It's one of the few opportunities you will have to visit Sibiloi (hardly any other safari company includes this park on their itineraries).

Samburu Trails Trekking Safaris

PO Box 56923, Nairobi (☎ 505139; fax 502739)

This company offers walking safaris in Samburuland. There are two options, both starting from Isiolo. These are comfortable safaris with everything provided including tents, camp beds and bedding, safari showers, tables and chairs. All the equipment is transported by donkeys so it's a good idea to keep your personal baggage down to a minimum. The cost is US$125 per person per day (or US$60 per person for larger groups). Set aside a minimum of five days for either trek.

Sirikwa Safaris

PO Box 332, Kitale

This outfit is run by Jane & Julia Barnley from

their farmhouse/guesthouse and camping site about 20 km outside Kitale on the Lodwar road. They can arrange bird-watching trips to the Cherangani Hills along with a guide (KSh 600 per day for a guide) as well as trips to Saiwa Swamp National Park, Marich Pass, Mt Elgon and the Kongelai Escarpment.

White-Water Rafting

For a totally different safari experience, there's white water rafting.

Savage Wilderness Safaris Ltd

PO Box 44827, Nairobi (☎ 521590; fax 501754)

This outfit is the only one of its kind in Kenya. Depending on water levels, rafting trips of up to 450 km and of three weeks duration can be arranged, though most trips last between one and four days during which you cover up to 80 km.

One of the most popular short trips (one day's duration) is on the Tana River, north-east of Nairobi. The first of the rapids is only class (or grade) 3 followed by three km of class 2 and 3 (ideal for learning some of the basic skills needed to tackle the larger rapids further on). That's followed by six km of calm scenic water where birdlife abounds. The last six km are the most exciting, consisting of class 3, 4 and, at certain water levels, class 5 rapids interspersed with short sections of calmer water. This trip departs anytime there are two or more customers and costs US$95 per person.

Another of the popular short trips is the three-day adventure on the Athi River, south-east of Nairobi between Tsavo East and West national parks. These trips leave any day of the week subject to a minimum of four passengers and cost US$320 per person with additional days at US$45.

The last rafting possibility is along the Ewaso Nyiro River, north-west of Isiolo. This trip takes a minimum of three days. It's a scenic river all the way and there's plenty of wild game to be seen. This trip costs US$380 per person with additional days at US$105.

The above prices are inclusive of transport, high quality food, soft drinks, beer, and, where applicable, tents, airbeds and sleeping bags. You are also provided with all necessary equipment – life jackets, helmets etc. National park entry and camping fees are not included but the usual itineraries do not enter parks.

The most exciting times to go on these white-water rafts are from late October to mid-January and from early April to late July when water levels are at their highest. The Tana River generally maintains a higher water level longer than the Athi.

Balloon Safaris

Viewing a game park from the vantage point of a hot-air balloon is a magnificent experience which you won't ever forget – but it is expensive! The experience of floating silently above the plains with a 360° view of everything beneath you, without safari buses competing for the best photo opportunity, is incomparable. It's definitely worth saving for.

The flights typically set off at dawn and go for about 1½ hours after which they put down and you tuck into a champagne breakfast. After that, you'll be taken on a game drive in a support vehicle and returned to your lodge. At present, these flights are only available in the Masai Mara and they cost around US$360.

Adventures Aloft
  Eagle House, Kimathi St, PO Box 40683, Nairobi (☎ 221439)
  This company operates out of Mara Fig Tree Lodge and you can either book in Nairobi, at the Fig Tree Lodge, or any other lodge in Masai Mara.
Balloon Safaris Ltd
  Wilson Airport, PO Box 43747, Nairobi (☎ 502850)
  This company operates out of Keekorok Lodge so you can either book through Block Hotels in Nairobi (☎ 540780; fax 540821) or at Keekorok Lodge or any other lodge in Masai Mara. The flights depart from Keekorok Lodge.

Flying Safaris

These safaris essentially cater only for the rich and those interested in sport fishing. They centre around Rusinga Island in Lake Victoria. A light aircraft collects you from your nearest Masai Mara airstrip in the early morning and returns you in time for lunch or an afternoon game drive. In the meantime a motorboat takes you out on Lake Victoria where you can feed and photograph African Fish-Eagles and go fishing for Nile perch – the largest freshwater fish in Africa. Angling gear is provided. Bookings can be made through Lonrho Hotels Kenya (☎ 216940; fax 216796), PO Box 58581, Nairobi.

Mt Kenya Climbs

All the details of organised climbs up this mountain are to be found in the Mt Kenya section in the National Parks chapter.

SAFARIS FURTHER AFIELD

Quite a few companies in Nairobi offer safaris to the Tanzanian game parks of Lake Manyara, Ngorongoro Crater, Serengeti and Tarangire but most of them are just agencies for Tanzanian safari companies based in Arusha so you might as well go there and organise things yourself. It would certainly cost less than doing it in Kenya since you won't be paying the agency's commission. On the other hand, there are a few companies in Nairobi which specialise in long distance safaris to the north, west and south of Kenya. While most of these take in up to three of the Kenyan national parks, the main focus is elsewhere. The options here range from two to eight weeks, the longer ones taking you to Zimbabwe, Botswana or South Africa.

One of the most popular of these long-range safaris is to the mountain gorillas of Zaïre/Uganda. A two-week trip there would typically go through Kenya and Uganda and return the same way, taking in several of the Kenyan and Ugandan national parks along the way. A three-week trip would take you first to the gorillas via Uganda (including several national parks along the way) and return to Kenya by looping through Tanzania along the southern shore of Lake Victoria taking in the Serengeti and Ngorongoro.

Another possibility is a safari to Ethiopia taking in all the major sights (Addis Ababa, Lalibela, Gondar, Axum etc). This is possible in four weeks but is something of a rush. Better are the five and six-week safaris taking in Lake Turkana and Marsabit National Park on the way up to the Ethiopian border at Moyale. These trips start and finish in Nairobi.

The trips going south are usually one way and generally terminate in either Harare (Zimbabwe) or Cape Town (South Africa). Depending on the amount of time you wanted to spend, they would take you through Tanzania, Malawi, Zimbabwe, Botswana, Namibia and South Africa. Some of the longer trips might include a visit to the gorillas before heading south.

Recommended companies offering extended safaris include the following.

Gametrackers

1st floor, Kenya Cinema Plaza, Moi Ave, PO Box 62042, Nairobi (☎ 338927; fax 330903)

This company offers a four-week Gorilla Safari to Zaïre via Uganda on the outward journey and returning via Tanzania, taking in several national parks. The cost is US$890 plus a group kitty of US$250 plus the cost of visas and national park fees (US$325), a total of US$1465. Departures are monthly except in August and November.

Its five-week Southern Africa Safari takes in Tanzania, Zanzibar, Malawi, Zimbabwe and Botswana including several national parks. The tour terminates in Harare. This costs US$855 plus a group kitty of US$165 plus the cost of visas and optional side trips/activities (US$380 if you take them all). Departures are approximately monthly except in April, August and December.

Flight Centres

This company is the main Nairobi-based company offering long-distance safaris. Flight Centres offer a choice of 14 long-distance safaris and they're all consistently cheaper than what anyone else has on offer.

Flight Centres offer two gorilla safaris. The shorter two-week trip starts and ends in Nairobi and goes via Uganda taking in three national parks en route in addition to the gorillas. It costs US$400 plus US$330 food kitty. The longer three week safari does a loop through Tanzania on the return leg and takes in five national parks in addition to the gorillas before terminating in Mombasa. It costs US$650 plus US$475 food kitty. Both of these prices include everything except visa costs and a sleeping bag.

For Ethiopia, there's a choice of safaris with the longer ones incorporating Lake Turkana and Marsabit National Park. The four-week trip costs US$650 plus US$150 food kitty; the five-week trip costs US$700 plus US$175 food kitty, and the six-week trip costs US$750 plus US$200 food kitty. All of these prices include the lot except for visa costs and a sleeping bag.

It also offers a 14-day and a 20-day safari of the game parks of Kenya and Tanzania which take in Masai Mara, lakes Naivasha and Nakuru, Thomson's Falls, Serengeti and Ngorongoro and cost US$790 (plus US$150 food kitty) and US$950 (plus US$195 food kitty), respectively, including everything except visa costs and a sleeping bag.

Its safaris to southern Africa are all one-way only and vary from 18 days to 57 days depending on how many countries you want to visit and where you want to end up – Harare, Victoria Falls or Cape Town. The costs range from US$600 plus US$10 food kitty for a three-week trip to US$1250 plus US$500 food kitty for the 57-dayer.

DO-IT-YOURSELF SAFARIS

This is a viable proposition in Kenya if you can get a group together to share the costs of renting a vehicle and camping equipment. The details of renting a suitable vehicle can be found in the Car & 4WD Rental section earlier in this chapter.

Doing it yourself has several advantages over organised safaris. The main one is flexibility – you can go where you want, stop whenever you like and stay as long as you like. You don't have to follow the standard tourist routes. Another is that you can choose your travelling companions. The main disadvantage is the extra effort you have to put in to organise the safari – hiring equipment, buying food and drink, cooking and agreeing among yourselves where you want to go and which route to take. It can also be a worry if none of you have mechanical skills or the necessary tools and the vehicle breaks down. There's also the security of the vehicle and contents to think about if you want to leave it somewhere and go off walking. If you do this then you'll have to pay someone to guard it. Lastly, there's the question of maps, especially if you intend to get right off the beaten track. Reasonably good large-scale maps are available in Kenya but the detailed ones are unavailable without going through a great deal of red tape. This means you could find yourself out in the middle of nowhere with not a clue where you're going and have to backtrack.

If you want to hire camping equipment (anything from a sleeping bag to a folding toilet seat, tent or mosquito net) the best place to go to is Atul's (☎ (02) 225935), Biashara St, Nairobi. Hire charges have to be paid in full before commencement of hire as well as a deposit for each item. The deposits are refunded when hired items are returned in good condition. Identification, such as a passport, is required.

The items for hire are far too numerous to mention here, but there is a list which you can pick up for KSh 30. Advance booking is highly recommended and saves a lot of time. If you'd like a list before going to Kenya, write to PO Box 43202, Nairobi.

As far as costs go, it's probably true to say that organising your own safari is going to cost at least as much and usually more than going on a cheap organised safari, but how much more depends on a lot of factors – mainly the cost of hiring a vehicle, fuel and what sort of food you want to eat along the way. You'll have to work this out yourself.

Safari Guide

ANTELOPES

Bongo
(Tragelaphus eurycerus)
Swahili: *bongo*

The large, striped bongo antelope is rarely seen. About your only chance of sighting one is in Aberdare National Park. They live close to water in dense forest, only leaving the forest cover to graze at night in open clearings.

The bongo stands around 120 cm high at the shoulder and measures around 250 cm from head to tail. Mature males are a beautiful dark mahogany-brown colour, while the females are a much lighter reddish-brown. Both sexes have distinctive vertical white stripes on the body, never less than nine, never more than 14. Horns are sported by both males and females, and these are slightly spiralling (lyre shaped) with yellow tips, with those on the male being slightly shorter and sturdier than on the female.

The bongo grazes mainly on leaves and will often stand on its hind legs to increase its reach. It also digs for roots with its horns. Bongo are usually found in small family herds although bulls often lead a solitary existence, meeting up with other animals only to mate.

Bushbuck
(Tragelaphus scriptus)
Swahili: *pongo*

Although the small bushbuck antelope exists in fairly large numbers in most of Kenya's game parks, it is a shy, solitary animal and is rarely sighted.

Standing at about 80 cm at the shoulder, the bushbuck is chestnut to dark brown in colour with a variable number of white vertical stripes on the body between the neck and rump, as well as (usually) two horizontal white stripes lower down which give the animal a 'harnessed' appearance. There are also a number of white spots on the upper thigh and a white splash on the neck. Females are reddish brown. Horns are usually only grown by males but females have been known to grow them on rare occasions. They are lyre shaped with gentle spirals and average about 30 cm in length.

Bushbuck are rarely found in groups of more than two and prefer to stick to areas with heavy brush cover. When startled they take off and crash loudly through the undergrowth. They are nocturnal animals and browsers yet rarely move far from their chosen spot. Though shy and elusive they can be aggressive and dangerous when cornered. Their main predators are leopard and python.

Kirk's Dik Dik
(Madoqua kirki)
Swahili: *dik dik*

Kirk's dik-dik is the more common of the two dik-diks found in Kenya (the other is Gunther's dik-dik, found only in Marsabit National Park & Reserve) and is commonly seen in Nairobi, Tsavo, Amboseli and Masai Mara reserves. Its name comes from the 'zic-zic' call it makes when alarmed.

The dik-dik is a tiny antelope, standing only around 35 cm at the shoulder. It is a reddish-brown colour on the back, with lighter flanks and white belly. Size is usually the easiest way to identify a dik-dik, but other telltale marks are the almost total lack of a tail and the tuft of dark hair on the forehead. Horns (found on the males only) are so short (around six cm) that they are often lost in the hair tuft.

Dik-dik are usually seen singly or in pairs and are often found in exceedingly dry places – it seems they don't have a great dependence on water. They are territorial creatures, each pair occupying an area of around five hectares. They are mainly nocturnal but can be seen grazing in acacia scrub in the early morning and late afternoon; like so many animals they rest in the heat of the day.

The females bear a single offspring twice a year. After six months the young dik-dik reaches sexual maturity and is then driven out of the home territory.

Common or Bush Duiker
(Sylvicapra grimmia)
Swahili: *nsya*

This is the most common of the duikers, of which there are at least 10 species. Even so, they are not often sighted as they are largely nocturnal, usually only live in pairs and prefer areas with good scrub cover. They are known to exist in Marsabit, Tsavo, Nairobi, Amboseli, Meru and Masai Mara reserves.

The duiker stands only 60 cm at the shoulder, is a greyish light-brown colour with white belly and a dark brown vertical stripe on the face. The horns (males only) are short (around 20 cm), pointed, and grow straight.

Duikers are widely distributed and can be found in a variety of habitats ranging from open bush to semi-desert and up to the snow line of the highest mountains except for bamboo forest and rainforest. This ability to survive in many different habitats explains their survival in cultivated areas where other herbivorous species have been exterminated.

They are almost exclusively browsers and only rarely eat grasses though they appear to supplement their diet with insects and guinea fowl chicks. They are capable of doing without water for long periods but will drink it when available.

Eland
(Tragelaphus oryx)
Swahili: *pofu*

The eland looks similar to some varieties of cattle seen on the Indian subcontinent, and is found in Nairobi, Marsabit, Tsavo and Masai Mara parks/reserves.

The biggest of the antelopes, the eland stands about 170 cm at the shoulder and a mature bull can weigh up to 1000 kg. Horns are found on both sexes and these are spiralled at the base, swept straight back and grow to about 65 cm. Males have a much hairier head than the females, and their horns are stouter and slightly shorter. They are a light greyish-brown in colour, and bear as many as 15 vertical white stripes on the body, although these are often almost indistinguishable on some animals.

The eland prefers savannah scrub to wide open spaces, but also a·oids thick forest. It grazes on grass and tree foliage in the early morning and late afternoon, and is also active on moonlit nights. It needs to drink once a day, but can go for a month or more without water if its diet includes fodder with high water content.

Eland are usually found in groups of around six to 12, but there may be as many as 50 in a herd. A small herd normally consists of several females and one male, but in larger herds there may be several males, and there is a strict hierarchy. Females reach sexual maturity at around two years and can bear up to 12 calves in a lifetime. The young are born in October-November.

Gerenuk
(Litocranius walleri)
Swahili: *swala tiga*

The gerenuk is probably the easiest of all antelopes to identify because of its inordinately long neck, which accounts for its Swahili name, *swala tiga*, meaning giraffe-gazelle. Its distribution is limited to Meru, Samburu, Tsavo and Amboseli national parks.

Growing to around 100 cm at the shoulder, the gerenuk is a dark fawn colour on the back which becomes much lighter on the sides and belly. The horns (found on the male only) curve gently backward and grow up to 40 cm long.

The gerenuk's habitat ranges from dry thorn bush country to semidesert and its food consists mainly of the tender leaves and shoots of acacia bushes. It is quite capable – in the same way as a goat – of standing on its hind legs and using one of its forelegs to pull down the higher branches of bushes to get at the leaves and shoots. Also like goats, they are quite capable of doing without water.

Grant's Gazelle
(Gazella granti)
Swahili: *swala granti*

This is one of the most common antelopes and exists in large numbers in Nairobi, Amboseli, Masai Mara, Tsavo and Marsabit reserves.

Grant's gazelle are most easily identified by their colouring and long horns: sandy brown on the back, clearly demarcated from a lighter colour on the flanks and white belly, and white around the tail and hind legs. They are not a large gazelle, standing around 90 cm at the shoulder. Horns are found on both sexes and are heavily ridged with around 25 rings; in the male they grow to around 60 cm (although they often appear longer because of the relatively small body) and curve gracefully and evenly up and back, usually with some outward curving as well; in the female the horns are much shorter but follow the same pattern.

You usually come across herds of Grant's gazelle in open grassy country where there is some forest cover, although they are also occasionally found in heavily wooded savannah country. Herd size is usually between 20 and 30, with one dominant male, does and young. Food consists mainly of leaves and grass. As water is obtained through dietary intake these gazelles do not need to drink.

Greater Kudu
(Tragelaphus strepsiceros)
Swahili: *tandala mkubwa*

The greater kudu is one of the largest of the antelopes but it's a rare sight and only found in any numbers in Marsabit National Park & Reserve. Elsewhere, kudu prefer hilly country with fairly dense bush cover. The kudu stands around 1.5 metres at the shoulder and weighs up to 250 kg, yet it's a very elegant creature, light grey in colour, with broad ears and a long neck. The sides of the body are marked by six to 10 vertical white stripes and there is a white chevron between the eyes. Horns are carried only by the males and are both divergent and spiralling.

Kudu live in small herds of up to four or five females with their young but these often split up during the rainy season. The males are usually solitary though occasionally they band together into small herds.

They are mainly browsers and only seldom eat grasses but are capable of eating many types of leaves which would be poisonous to other animals.

Although somewhat clumsy animals when on the move, they are capable of clearing well over two metres when jumping.

Hartebeest
(Alcelaphus buselaphus)
Swahili: *kongoni*

The hartebeest is a medium-sized antelope and is found in Nairobi, Tsavo, Amboseli and Masai Mara parks. It is easy to recognise as it has a long, narrow face and distinctively angular short horns (on both sexes) which are heavily ridged. Colouring is generally light brown on the back, becoming paler towards the rear and under the belly. The back slopes away from the humped shoulders. They prefer grassy plains for grazing but are also found in lightly treed savannah or hills.

The hartebeest feeds exclusively on grass, and usually drinks twice daily, although it can go for months without water if necessary.

They are social beasts and often intermingle with animals such as zebras and wildebeest. Their behaviour is not unlike the wildebeest's, particularly the head tossing and shaking.

Sexual maturity is reached at around 2½ years and calving goes on throughout the year, although there are peak periods in February and August. Predators are mainly the large cats, hyena and hunting dogs.

Impala
(Aepyceros melampus)
Swahili: *swala pala*

The graceful impala is one of the most common antelopes and is found in virtually all national parks and reserves in large numbers.

A medium-sized antelope, it stands about 80 cm at the shoulder. The coat is a glossy rufous colour though paler on the flanks with the underparts, rump, throat and chin being white. A narrow black line runs along the middle of the rump to about halfway down the tail and there's also a vertical black stripe on the back of the thighs but, unlike in Grant's gazelle, this does not border the white buttocks. It's also distinguishable from Grant's gazelle by having a tuft of long black hair above the heels of the hind legs. Only the males have horns which are long (averaging 75 cm), lyre-shaped and curve upwards as they spread.

Impala are gregarious animals; each male has a 'harem' of up to 100 females, though more usually around 15 to 20. Males without a 'harem' form bachelor groups. Fierce fighting occurs between males in rutting season, otherwise they're quite placid animals.

One of the most noticeable characteristics of impala is their speed and prodigious ability at jumping. They are quite capable of clearing 10m in a single jump lengthwise or three metres in height and this they frequently do even when there are no obstacles in their path.

Impala are both browsers and grazers and are active during the day and by night. They are quite highly dependent on water but are capable of existing on just dew for fairly long periods. Their main predators are leopard, cheetah and hunting dogs.

HUGH FINLAY

Klipspringer
(Oreotragus oreotragus)
Swahili: *mbuzi mawe*

The distinctive klipspringer inhabit rocky outcrops in Tsavo, Amboseli, Masai Mara, Marsabit and Meru reserves.

Standing about 50 cm at the shoulder, they are easily recognised by their curious 'tip-toe' stance (the hooves are designed for balance and grip on rocky surfaces) and the greenish tinge of their speckled coarse hair. Horns (found on the male only) are short (10 cm) and widely spaced.

Klipspringer are most often seen on rocky outcrops, or in the grassland in the immediate vicinity, and when alarmed they retreat into the rocks for safety. They are amazingly agile and sure-footed creatures and can often be observed bounding up impossibly rough rock faces. These antelope can also go entirely without water if there is none around, getting all they need from the greenery they eat. They are most active just before and after midday, and single males often keep watch from a good vantage point. The klipspringer is usually found in pairs, or a male with two females, and inhabits a clearly defined territory.

Klipspringer reach sexual maturity at around one year, and females bear one calf twice a year. Calves may stay with the adult couple for up to a year, although young males usually seek their own territory earlier than that.

Predators are mainly the leopard and the crowned eagle, but also include jackal and baboon.

Lesser Kudu
(Tragelaphus imberbis)
Swahili: *tandala ndogo*

The lesser kudu is a smaller model of the greater kudu, the major differences being the lack of a beard, more numerous and more pronounced vertical white stripes on the body, and two white patches on the underside of the neck. As with the greater kudu, only the males have horns. The coat colour varies from brownish grey to blue-grey. It stands around a metre high at the shoulder.

Kudu usually live in pairs accompanied by their fawns though females occasionally form small herds. They are very shy animals and spend much of the day hiding in dense bush, only moving out of cover to feed in the early morning and at dusk. This makes them difficult to spot.

Kudu are browsers and feed on a mixture of leaves, young shoots and twigs and, though they drink regularly if water is available, they are capable of doing without it for relatively long periods – more so than the greater kudu.

The most likely places you will find them are Tsavo and Marsabit national parks where they prefer the drier, more bushy areas.

Oribi
(Ourebia ourebi)
Swahili: *taya*

Not unlike a duiker in appearance, the small oribi is relatively uncommon, and your best chance of spotting one is in the Masai Mara reserve.

The oribi's most distinguishing mark, although you'll need binoculars to spot it, is a circular batch of naked black skin below the ear – it is actually a scent gland. Another useful indicator is the tuft of black hair on the tip of the short tail. Otherwise the oribi is a uniform golden brown with white on the belly and insides of the legs. Short straight horns about 10 cm in length are found on the males only.

Oribi usually graze in grassy plains with good shelter. If water is available they will drink willingly but can also go without it entirely. When alarmed they bolt and then make bouncing jumps with a curious action – all four legs are kept completely stiff. It is thought this helps them to orient themselves in places with poor visibility. After 100m or so they stop and assess the danger.

Oribi are usually found in pairs and are territorial. Sexual maturity is reached at around one year, and the females bear one calf twice a year.

Being quite small, the oribi have many predators, including the larger cats.

Oryx
(Oryx gazella callotis)
Swahili: *choroa*

The fringe-eared or Kilimanjaro oryx *(Oryx gazella callotis)* is found in Kenya's Amboseli and Tsavo national parks and is a large antelope standing around 120 cm at the shoulder. The coat is a sandy fawn with a black spinal stripe which extends to the tip of the tail. The underparts are white and separated from the lower flanks by another black stripe. There are also two black rings just above the knee of the forelegs.

The related galla oryx *(Oryx gazella gallarum)* is reddish-grey and is most commonly seen in the Marsabit reserve and along the Tana River. (Note that the oryx species name may also be referred to as *beisa*.)

Both types of oryx have ovate, pointed ears with the main distinguishing feature being, as the name suggests, a tuft of black hair on the ears of the fringe-eared one. Oryx are easy to distinguish from other antelopes due to their straight, very long and heavily ridged horns which are carried almost parallel. Both the males and females have horns. These horns come into their own when the animal is forced to defend itself. Held down between the forelegs, they are formidable weapons and used to impale an enemy.

Oryx are principally grazers but will also browse on thorny shrubs. They are capable of doing without water for long periods but will drink daily if it is available.

Herds vary from five to 40 individuals and sometimes more though the bulls are usually solitary. Oryx are often found in association with zebra and Grant's gazelle.

Reedbuck
(Redunca redunca)
Swahili: *tohe*

The best places to spot the dusty brown reedbuck is in Nairobi and Amboseli national parks, and they are occasionally seen in Tsavo National Park.

The reedbuck is a medium-sized antelope, standing around 80 cm high at the shoulder. The most distinctive features are the forward curving horns (found on the males only) and the bushy tail. The underbelly, inside of the thighs, throat and underside of the tail are white.

The reedbuck frequents open grassy plains or hills and is never found more than around eight km from a water supply. It is very territorial and is found in small groups of up to 10 animals. The groups usually consist of an older male and accompanying females and young. Its diet consists almost exclusively of grass but does include some foliage.

At mating time males fight spiritedly. After reaching sexual maturity at around 1½ years, females bear one calf at a time.

The bohor reedbuck's main predators include the big cats, hyena and hunting dogs.

Roan Antelope
(Hippotragus equinus)
Swahili: *korongo*

The roan antelope is one of Kenya's less common antelope species. The best place to see one is in the Shimba Hills National Reserve, where they have been translocated from other parts of the country, although there are still a few small herds in Masai Mara.

The roan is the third largest of the antelopes after eland and kudu. It measures up to 150 cm at the shoulder and bears a striking resemblance to a horse. The coat varies from reddish fawn to dark rufous with white underparts and there's a conspicuous mane of stiff, black-tipped hairs which stretches from the nape to the shoulders. Under the neck, there's another mane of sorts consisting of long dark hairs. The ears are long, narrow and pointed with a brown tassel at the tip. The face is a very distinctive black and white pattern. Both sexes have curving backswept horns which can measure up to 70 cm.

Roan are aggressive by nature and fight from a very early age – a characteristic which frequently deters predators. For most of the year they live in small herds of up to 20 and sometimes more, led by a master bull, but in the mating season, the bulls become solitary and take a female out of the herd. The pair stay together until the calf is born after which the females form a herd by themselves. They eventually return to their former herd. Herds congregate during the dry season.

Being principally grazers, roan rarely move far when food is plentiful but they are susceptible to drought and during such periods they may be constantly on the move.

Sable Antelope
(Hippotragus niger)
Swahili: *pala hala*

Also found only in the Shimba Hills National Reserve, the sable antelope is slightly smaller than its cousin the roan, but is more solidly built. The colouring is dark brown to black, with white face markings and belly. Both sexes carry long backswept horns which average around 80 cm, those of the male being longer and more curved.

The sable antelope is active mainly in the early morning and late afternoon, and is found in herds of up to 25 and sometimes more in the dry season. They are territorial and each group occupies a large area, although within this area individual males have demarcated territories of up to 30 hectares. Sable feed mainly off grass but leaves and foliage from trees account for around 10% of their diet.

Females start bearing calves at around three years of age, and the main calving times are January and September.

Like the roan, the sable is a fierce fighter and has been known to kill lions when attacked. Other predators include the leopard, hyena and hunting dog.

Sitatunga
(Tragelaphus spekei)
Swahili: *nzohe*

The sitatunga is a swamp antelope with unusual elongated hooves which give it the ability to walk on marshy ground without sinking. It is restricted solely to the Saiwa Swamp National Park near Kitale, and it's well worth a visit to this small, walkers-only park.

Very similar to the bushbuck in appearance, except that the coat of the male is much darker and the hair of both sexes much longer and shaggier, the sitatunga stands something over one metre at the shoulder. The females have a lighter, reddish coat and the males have twisted horns up to 90 cm long. It is a fairly shy antelope and sightings are not all that common. A good swimmer, the sitatunga will often submerge itself almost completely when alarmed.

It feeds largely on papyrus and other reeds and is usually nocturnal though in places where it remains undisturbed it can be diurnal. Animals normally live singly or in pairs but sometimes come together in small herds numbering up to 15.

Thomson's Gazelle
(Gazella thomsonii)
Swahili: *swala tomi*

The small and frisky Thomson's gazelle is instantly recognisable by the black slash across the side which separates the brown back from the white underbelly. They are very common in the plains country, such as in Amboseli, Masai Mara and Nairobi reserves, but rare in different habitats such as Tsavo National Park.

Standing around 60 cm at the shoulders, the 'Tommy' is one of the smaller antelopes. Horns on the male grow to about 30 cm and almost straight with just a gentle curve towards the tips; in the female the horns are straighter and much shorter. Another easy to identify characteristic is the short black tail which seems to be constantly twitching. Along with the oribi, Tommys also do the stiff-legged bouncing jump when alarmed.

Group size varies: one old (largely territorial) male may be accompanied by anything from five to 50 females, or there may be herds of up to 500 young males without territory. When food is plentiful the herds tend to be smaller and more territorial. In times of drought herds of several thousand may gather and roam for food. They are often found in close proximity to other animals, including wildebeest and Grant's gazelles.

Sexual maturity is reached at around one year but males only mate after establishing their own territory, which occurs sometime after two years of age. Calving occurs throughout the year though tends to peak at the end of the rainy season.

Being a small animal, Tommys have many predators, including the big cats, hunting dogs, hyena and serval.

HUGH FINLAY

HUGH FINLAY

Topi
(Damaliscus lunatus)
Swahili: *nyamera*

The topi is not unlike the hartebeest in appearance, but is a dark almost purplish colour and has black patches on the rear thighs, front legs and face. Its horns, which are found on both sexes, also differ in shape from the hartebeest in curving gently up, out and back. Although fairly widely distributed in East Africa, in Kenya it is only found in Masai Mara where it exists in large numbers.

A highly gregarious antelope which lives in herds numbering from 15 up to several hundred individuals, topi congregate at certain times of year in gatherings of up to 10,000 in preparation for a migration to fresh pastures. They are often found mingling with wildebeest, hartebeest and zebra.

In the mating season, bulls select a well-defined patch of ground which is defended against rivals and this is where mating takes place. At this time females are free to wander from one patch to another. After mating, the herds split into single-sex parties.

Topi are exclusively grazers and prefer flood plains which support lush pasture though they are capable of thriving on dry grasses which other antelopes will not eat. When water is available they drink frequently but they are also capable of surviving long periods without water so long as there is sufficient grass available.

Their main predator is the lion.

TONY WHEELER

HUGH FINLAY

Waterbuck

Defassa or common waterbuck
(Kobus ellipsiprymnus)
Swahili: *kuru*

The defassa waterbuck is a fairly solid animal and is easily recognisable by its thick, shaggy, dark brown coat, and white inner thighs. It is fairly common and easily seen in Nairobi and Nakuru national parks, and in Masai Mara. A second variety, the ringed waterbuck (also *Kobus ellipsiprymnus*), so-called because of the white ring around its rump, is also seen in Marsabit, Tsavo and Amboseli parks. Both varieties have white facial and throat markings.

Only the males have horns, and these curve gradually outwards then grow straight up to a length of about 75 cm. As you might expect from the name, waterbuck are good swimmers and readily enter the water to escape from predators. Their habitat is always close to water, and males have marked territories by the water's edge. Females and younger males tend to wander at random through male territories. Herds are small and usually consist of cows, calves and one mature bull – the other bulls live in small groups apart from the herd.

The bulk of the waterbuck's diet is grass but it does eat some of the foliage of trees and bushes.

Sexual maturity is reached at just over one year, although a male will not become the dominant bull in the herd until around five years of age.

Waterbuck are usually only preyed on when other food is scarce. The reason being that when mature the flesh is tough and has a distinct odour. Predators such as lion, leopard and hunting dogs go for the young calves and females.

HUGH FINLAY

TONY WHEELER

Wildebeest (Gnu)
Blue wildebeest or brindled gnu
(Connochaetes taurinus)
Swahili: *nyumbu*

Wildebeest are to the African savannah what the bison once were to the North American prairies. Numbering in their millions in certain areas, particularly Masai Mara and over the border in Serengeti, they are unmistakable for their prehistoric appearance. Wildebeest (also known as blue wildebeest or brindled gnu) are well known for their eccentric behaviour which includes loud snorting, tossing and shaking of the head, bucking, running around in circles and rolling in the dust (thought to be a reaction to the activity of the botfly larva which manage to find their way right up into their nostrils). They are heavily built with a massive head and wild mane, are somewhat clumsy, and have been described as having the forequarters of an ox, the hind parts of an antelope and the tail of a horse.

TONY WHEELER

Their sheer numbers, nevertheless, are testimony to their superb adaptation to the environment.

Almost entirely grazers, they are constantly on the move in search of good pasture and water, and their annual migration between the Serengeti and Masai Mara (and vice versa) has to be one of the world's most spectacular sights. Thousands lose their lives in this annual event – drowning in rivers, being taken by crocodiles and other predators or just through sheer exhaustion. The migration north from Serengeti takes place in July and the return trip from Masai Mara in October.

They're very gregarious animals and are usually seen in large herds numbering up to tens of thousands in association with zebra, Thomson's gazelle and other herbivores.

During the mating season, groups of up to 150 females and their young are gathered together by one to three bulls which defend a defined territory against rivals even when on the move. There's apparently no hierarchy among the bulls and, at the end of the mating season, the breeding herds are reabsorbed into the main herds.

Although they graze in a scattered fashion without any apparent social organisation during the rainy season, they coalesce around water holes and remaining pasture in the dry season. Wildebeest prefer to drink daily and will walk up to 50 km to secure water but are capable of surviving for up to five days without it. They're also a noisy animal when grazing, constantly producing a series of snorts and low-pitched grunts.

Their main predators are lions, cheetahs and hunting dogs though hyena are also very partial to young calves.

BIRDS

Flamingo
(Phoenicopterus minor, Phoenicopterus ruber)
Swahili: *heroe*

Flamingo are found by the million in Kenya. They are attracted by the proliferation of algae and crustaceans which thrive in the soda lakes of Baringo, Bogoria, Nakuru and Magadi in the Rift Valley, and Lake Natron across the border in Tanzania.

There are always some birds at each lake but large concentrations seem to move capriciously from one to another over a period of years. Lake Nakuru is the current hot spot but this may well change. It is thought that the changing water levels may be one reason why they change locations. Whatever lake they are presently at, the best time of the year for flamingo viewing is in January-February when they form huge pink masses around the shores of the lakes.

Flamingo have a complicated and sophisticated system for filtering the foodstuffs out of the water. This is because the highly alkane water would be toxic if consumed in large quantities. The deep-pink lesser flamingo, *Phoenicopterus minor*, filters algae and diatoms out of the water by vigorous suction and expulsion of the water in and out of its beak several times per second. The minute particles are caught on fine hairlike protrusions which line the inside of the mandibles. This is all done with the bill upside down in the water. The suction is created by the movement of the thick and fleshy tongue which lies in a groove in the lower mandible and works to and fro like a piston. Where the *Phoenicopterus minor* obtains its food largely by sweeping its head to and fro and filtering the water, the greater flamingo, or *Phoenicopterus ruber*, is more a bottom feeder and supplements its algae diet with small molluscs, crustaceans and other organic particles from the mud. It has been estimated that one million lesser flamingo consume over 180 tons of algae and diatoms daily!

GREG HERRIMAN

TONY WHEELER

Ostrich
(Struthio camelus)
Swahili: *mbuni*

The very distinct and instantly identifiable ostrich is the largest living bird. It is widely distributed throughout the savannah plains of Kenya, and so is most widely seen in the southern parks and reserves – Masai Mara, Amboseli and Tsavo.

The adult ostrich stands around 2.5m high and weighs as much as 150 kg. The neck and the legs are bare, and all these areas of bare skin turn bright red in breeding males. The bushy plumage on the males is black, with white feathers in the redundant wings and the tail. The females are a uniform greyish brown and are slightly smaller and lighter than the males. The ostrich's long and strong legs can push it along at up to 50 km/h.

The Ostrich tends to be territorial and is rarely seen in groups of more than six individuals. It feeds on leaves, flowers and seeds of a variety of plants. When feeding, the food is gradually accumulated in the top of the neck and then passes down to the stomach in small boluses, and it's possible to see these masses of food actually moving down the neck.

The ostrich breeds in the dry season, and the males put on quite an impressive courtship display. Having driven off any possible rival males, the male trots up to the female with tail erect, then squats down and rocks from side to side, simultaneously waving each wing in the air alternately. Just for good measure the neck also waves from side to side. The males may couple with more than one female, in which case the eggs of all the females (up to five) are laid on the same nest, and so it may contain as many as 30 eggs. The eggs are incubated by the major female (the one first mated with) by day, and by the male at night. The other female birds have nothing further to do with the eggs or offspring.

TONY WHEELER

Vulture
Nubian vulture
(Torgos tracheliotus)
Swahili: *gushu*

Vultures are a large, eagle-like bird belonging to the Accipitridae family, of which hawks and eagles are also members. There are a whole range of different species, the most common ones in Kenya being the Egyptian *(Neophron percnopterus)*, hooded *(Necrosyrtes monachus)* and white-headed vulture *(Trigonoceps occipitalis)*. Others include Ruppell's vulture *(Gyps ruppellii)*, a common nester in Kenya's Hell's Gate National Park, and also the white-backed vulture *(Gyps bengalensis)*, found in all East African national parks. Vultures prefer savannah country with high concentrations of game.

These large birds, with a wing span of up to three metres and weighing up to five kg, feed almost exclusively by scavenging. They are fairly inefficient fliers and so rely to a large degree on finding rising hot-air thermals on which to glide and ascend. For this reason you won't see them in the air until well into the morning when the upcurrents have started.

African vultures have no sense of smell and so depend totally on their excellent eyesight, and that of their colleagues, for locating food. Once a kill or a fallen animal has been sighted a vulture will descend rapidly and await its turn at the carcass. Of course other vultures will follow the first downwards and in this chain reaction they may come from as far afield as 50 km. They are very efficient feeders and can rapidly strip flesh from bone, although they are not good at getting a start on a completely intact carcass. A large group of vultures (and they congregate in groups, often of up to 100) can strip an antelope to the bone in half an hour. Because they are poor fliers, however, vultures often cannot fly with a belly full of food and so after gorging will retreat a short distance and digest their meal.

HUGH FINLAY

TONY WHEELER

BUFFALO

(Syncerus caffer)
Swahili: *mbogo*

The buffalo is another animal which appears in great numbers in all the major parks, with the exception of Nairobi National Park.

The massive animal is said to be the most dangerous (to humans) of all African animals and should be treated with caution, although for the most part they will stay out of your way. Females protecting young calves, and solitary rogue bulls, are the most aggressive, and having 800 kg of angry animal thundering towards you is no joke.

Both sexes have the distinctive curving horns which broaden and almost meet over the forehead, although those in the female are usually smaller. The buffalo's colour varies from dark reddish brown to black.

Buffalo are often found in herds of 100 or more and never stray too far from water, especially in the dry season. When food and water are plentiful the herds often disperse. They are territorial in that they have a home range of about 50 km outside of which they don't stray.

CARNIVORES

Cheetah
(Acinonyx jubatus)
Swahili: *duma*

The cheetah is one of the most impressive animals you can hope to see – sleek, streamlined and menacing. It's found in small numbers in all of Kenya's major game reserves – Nairobi, Amboseli, Masai Mara, Tsavo, Samburu, Buffalo Springs, Marsabit and Meru.

Similar in appearance to the leopard, the cheetah is longer and lighter in the body, has a slightly bowed back and a much smaller and rounder face. It stands around 80 cm at the shoulder, measures around 210 cm in length (including the tail) and weighs anything from 40 to 60 kg.

When undisturbed, the cheetah hunts in early morning or late evening, although these days with the number of tourist vehicles around, it is often found hunting at midday when the rubbernecks are back in the lodges stuffing their faces and the poor animal has a chance to stalk some dinner undisturbed. This forced change in habit is particularly stressful for the cheetah as it relies on bursts of tremendous speed for catching its prey, and this speed (up to 110 km/h) is only sustainable for a very short time. Obviously, as the midday heat is much greater than morning or afternoon, hunting for the cheetah becomes much more difficult. During a hunt the cheetah stalks its prey

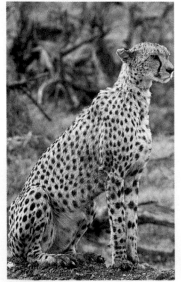

HUGH FINLAY

as close as possible and then sprints for 100 metres or so; if by that time it hasn't caught its victim, it will give up and try elsewhere. The prey (usually small antelope) is brought to the ground often with a flick of the paw to trip it up. Other food includes hare, jackal and young wart hog.

Cheetah cubs reach maturity at around one year but stay with the mother much longer than that as they have to learn hunting and survival skills. Cubs are usually born in litters numbering from two to four, and the main breeding period is from March to December.

The cheetah rarely fights but predators (mainly of cubs) include lion, leopard and hyenas.

Civet

(Viverra civetta or Civetticus civetta)
Swahili: *fungo*

The civet is a medium sized omnivore around 40 cm high at the shoulder and 90 cm long (excluding the tail), with some canine features and short, partially retractile claws. Its coat of long coarse hair is basically grey but with a definite and variable pattern of black spots over most of the body, along with two black bands stretching from the ears to the lower neck and two black bands around the upper part of the hind legs. The tail is bushy at the base becoming thinner towards the tip, held out straight when the animal is on the move, and black except for three to four greyish bands near the base. The head is mostly greyish white and the ears are quite small, rounded and tipped with white hairs.

Civet are solitary, nocturnal animals which hide in thickets, tall grass or abandoned burrows during the day and so are rarely sighted. The most likely places to spot one are in Marsabit or Tsavo West reserves, although they are also known to inhabit Nairobi, Amboseli and Masai Mara.

It has a very varied diet consisting of rodents, birds and their eggs, reptiles, amphibians, snails, insects (especially ants and termites) as well as berries, the young shoots of bushes and fruits.

Litters consist of up to four cubs and these have a similar, though slightly darker colouring.

The other conspicuous feature of the civet is the presence of musk glands in the anal region which produce a foul-smelling oily substance used to mark territory. This musk is used in the manufacture of perfumes; in Western countries it is collected from animals held in captivity.

Genet
Small spotted or common genet
(Genetta genetta)
Swahili: *kanu*

Unlike the civet, the genet distinctly resembles the domestic cat though the body is more elongated and the tail longer and bushier. The coat is long and coarse with a prominent crest along the spine. The basic colour varies from grey to fawn and is patterned from the neck to the tail with roundish dark brown to blackish spots. The tail is banded with nine to 10 similarly coloured rings and has a whitish tip. The large-spotted or rusty-spotted genet *(Genetta tigrina)*, is similar in appearance to the common genet, but has a brownish-black spinal stripe and larger spots.

The genet lives in savannah and open country and is a very agile tree climber but not frequently sighted since it is entirely nocturnal. During the day it sleeps in abandoned burrows, rock crevices, hollow trees or up on high branches and seems to return to the same spot each day. The animals live singly or in pairs.

Its prey is generally hunted on the ground though it will climb trees to seek out nesting birds and their eggs. Like the domestic cat, it stalks prey by crouching flat on the ground. Its diet consists of a variety of small animals (mostly rodents), birds, reptiles, insects and fruits. It is well known for being a wasteful killer, often eating only a small part of the animals it catches.

Litters typically consist of two to three kittens. Like the domestic cat, the genet spits and growls when angered or in danger.

Hunting Dog
(Lycaon pictus)
Swahili: *mbwa mwitu*

The hunting dog is the size of a large domestic dog and is found in all the reserves, or where there is a high concentration of game animals.

The dog's unusual coloration makes it quite an ugly creature – the black and yellowish splotches are different in each animal, ranging from almost all black to almost all yellow. The only constant is the white tail tip. Prominent physical features are the large rounded ears.

Hunting dogs tend to move in packs ranging from four or five up to as many as 40. They are efficient hunters and work well together. Once the prey has been singled out and the chase is on, a couple of dogs will chase hard while the rest pace themselves; once the first two tire another two step in and so on until the quarry is exhausted. Favoured animals for lunch include gazelle, impala and other similar sized antelope. They rarely scavenge, preferring to kill their own.

Hunting dog cubs are usually born in grass-lined burrows in litters averaging seven, although litters of up to 15 are not unheard of. By six months they are competent hunters and have abandoned the burrow. The hunting dog has no predators, although unguarded cubs sometimes fall prey to hyena and eagle.

Hyena
(Crocuta crocuta)
Swahili: *fisi*

The spotted hyena is a fairly common animal throughout most of Kenya and especially where game is plentiful. Bearing a distinct resemblance to dogs, it is a large, powerfully built animal with a very sloping back, broad head and large eyes but with rather weak hindquarters. The sloping back is what gives the animal its characteristic loping gait when running. Its coat is short, dull grey to buff and entirely patterned with rounded blackish spots except on the throat. Its powerful jaws and teeth enable it to crush and swallow the bones of most animals except the elephant.

Hyena are mainly nocturnal animals but are frequently seen during the day, especially in the vicinity of lion or cheetah kills impatiently waiting for their turn at the carcass along with vultures. Otherwise, the days are spent in long grass, abandoned aardvark holes or in large burrows which they dig out up to a metre below the surface of the soil. It's a very noisy animal and when camping out in the bush at night you'll frequently hear its characteristic and spine-chilling howl which rises quickly to a high-pitched scream. This is only one of the sounds which the spotted hyena emits. Another is the well known 'laugh', though this is generally only produced when the animal finds food or is mating.

The hyena has highly developed senses of smell, sight and sound, all important in locating food (carrion or prey) and for mutual recognition among pack members and mating pairs.

TONY WHEELER

Hyena are well known as scavengers and can often be seen following hunting lions and hunting dogs, usually at a respectable distance, though they will occasionally force these animals to abandon their kill. On the other hand, although carrion does form an important part of their diet, hyenas are also true predators and are more than capable of bringing down many of the larger herbivores. To do this they often form packs to run down wildebeest, zebra and gazelle, and are able to reach speeds of up to 60 km/h. They also stalk pregnant antelope and, when the female gives birth, snatch and kill the newly born foal and occasionally the mother too. Domestic stock are also preyed on.

In the mating season, hyena assemble in large numbers especially on moonlit nights. All hell breaks loose on these occasions and the noise is incredible. The gestation period is about 110 days and litters number up to four though usually less. The young are born in the mother's burrow. The pups are weaned at around six weeks old and become independent shortly afterwards.

Humans are the hyena's main enemy, though lions and hunting dogs will occasionally kill or mutilate hyenas if they get too close to a kill. Although they are reputed to be cowardly, you're advised to keep your distance from them as they do occasionally attack humans sleeping in the open.

TONY WHEELER

GEOFF CROWTHER

HUGH FINLAY

Jackal

Common or golden jackal
(Canis aureus)
Swahili: *bweha*

There are two species of jackal found in Kenya: the common or golden jackal, and the black-backed jackal *(Canis mesomelas)*, which is a common sight in the major reserves. The black back which gives it its name is usually more silvery than black, is wide at the neck and tapers to the tail. The golden jackal is similar, though without the back markings. Although the jackal is in fact a dog, its bushy tail and long ears are more like a fox.

The jackal is mostly a scavenger and so is commonly seen in the vicinity of a kill. The jackal will hunt for itself – insects, small mammals, birds, and the occasional small antelope. They are also found around human settlements and will attack sheep, poultry and calves.

Jackal are territorial and a pair will guard an area of around 250 hectares. Cubs are born in litters of five to seven and, although they don't reach maturity until almost a year old, they usually leave the parents when just two months old.

Enemies of the black-backed jackal include the leopard, cheetah and eagle.

Leopard

(Panthera pardus)
Swahili: *chui*

The leopard is perhaps the most graceful and agile of the large cats. A powerfully built animal which uses cunning to catch its prey, it is present in all the major game reserves but is difficult to find as it is nocturnal and spends the day resting on branches of trees, often up to five metres above the ground. It is as agile as a domestic cat in climbing such trees and this is also where it carries its prey so that it's out of the way of other scavengers which might contest the kill.

The leopard's coat is usually short and dense with numerous black spots on a yellowish background. The underparts are white and less densely spotted. In addition, the coats of leopards found in open country are generally lighter than those in wooded country.

Leopard are solitary animals except during the mating season when the male and female live together. The gestation period is three months and a litter usually consists of up to three cubs. They prey on a variety of birds, reptiles and mammals including large rodents, rock hyrax, wart hog, smaller antelopes and monkeys (especially baboon), and occasionally take domestic animals such as goat, sheep, poultry and dogs. This wide range of prey explains why they are still able to survive even in areas of dense human settlement long after other large predators have disappeared. But their presence is generally unwelcome since they occasionally turn human-eater. It also explains why they are found in very varied habitats ranging from semidesert to dense forest and as high as the snow line on Mt Kenya and Kilimanjaro.

Lion

(Panthera leo)
Swahili: *simba*

Lion are one of the main attractions of the game reserves and are found in all the main ones. They spend most of the day lying under bushes or in other attractive places and when you see a pride stretched out in the sun like this, they seem incredibly docile. It is possible to drive up very close to them in a vehicle – they either don't sense humans or realise that humans in vehicles are not a threat. Whatever the case, don't be tempted to get out of a vehicle at any time in the vicinity of a lion. Loud noises and sudden movement also disturb them. They're at their most active for around four hours in the late afternoon, then spend the rest of the time laying around.

GREG HERRIMAN

Lion generally hunt in groups, with the males driving the prey towards the concealed females who do most of the actual killing. Although they cooperate well together, lions are not the most efficient hunters – as many as four out of five attacks will be unsuccessful. Their reputation as human-eaters is largely undeserved as in most circumstances they will flee on seeing a human. However, once they have the taste for human flesh, and realise how easy it is to make a meal of one, lions can become habitual killers of people. This mostly occurs among the old lions which no longer have the agility to bring down more fleet-footed animals.

Lion are territorial beasts and a pride of one to three males and accompanying females (up to 15) and young will defend an area of anything from 20 to 400 sq km, depending on the type of country and the amount of game food available.

TONY WHEELER

Lion cubs are born in litters averaging two or three. They become sexually mature by 1 ½ years and males are driven from the family group shortly after this. Lions reach full maturity at around six years of age. Unguarded cubs are preyed on by hyena, leopard, python and hunting dogs.

GREG HERRIMAN

Mongoose
Banded mongoose
(Mungos mungo)
Swahili: *kicheche*

The banded mongoose (the one most commonly found in Kenya) is usually seen in groups in Tsavo, Amboseli and Masai Mara reserves. It is brown or grey in colour and is easily identifiable by the dark bands across the back which stretch from the shoulder to the tail. The animal is about 40 cm in length and weighs between 1.3 and 2.3 kg.

Mongoose are very sociable animals and live in packs of between 30 and 50 individuals which stay close to one another when foraging for prey. They are often very noisy, having a wide variety of sounds which they use to communicate with each other. When threatened they growl and spit in much the same manner as a domestic cat. Being diurnal animals, they prefer sunny spots during the day but retire to warrens – rock crevices, hollow trees and abandoned anthills – at night. A pack frequently has several warrens within its territory.

The mongoose's most important source of food are insects, grubs and larvae but they also eat small amphibians, reptiles, birds' eggs, fruits, berries and birds. Their main predators are birds of prey though they are also taken by lion, leopard and hunting dogs. Snakes rarely pose a danger since these would-be predators are attacked by the entire pack and the snake is frequently killed.

Mongoose are one of the creatures which have become very habituated to humans in some places and come right up to the game lodges scavenging for scraps.

Serval
(Felis serval)
Swahili: *mondo*

The serval is a wild cat, about the size of a domestic cat but with much longer legs. It is found in all the major game reserves in Kenya.

The serval's colouring is a dirty yellow with large black spots which follow lines along the length of the body. Other prominent features are the large upright ears, the long neck and the relatively short tail. It stands about 50 cm high and measures 130 cm including the tail. Being a largely nocturnal animal, the serval is usually only seen in the early morning or late evening. It lives on birds, hares and rodents and is an adept hunter – it catches birds in mid-flight by leaping into the air.

Serval cat young are born in litters of up to four and although independent at one year, don't reach sexual maturity until two years of age.

ELEPHANT

(Loxodonta africana)
Swahili: *ndovu* or *tembo*

Everyone knows what an elephant looks like so a description of them is unnecessary except perhaps to mention that African elephants are much larger than their Asian counterparts and that their ears are wider and flatter. A fully grown bull can weigh up to 6½ tonnes and sometimes more. In Kenya they are found in all the major game parks with the exception of Nairobi National Park where they would be too destructive to the environment to make their long term presence viable. They have been encountered as high as 3600m on the slopes of Mt Kenya.

GEOFF CROWTHER

The tusks on an old bull can weigh as much as 50 kg each, although 15 kg to 25 kg is more usual. The longest tusks ever found on an elephant in Kenya measured 3.5m! Both the males and females grow tusks, although in the female they are usually smaller. An elephant's sight is poorly developed but its senses of smell and hearing are excellent.

Elephant are gregarious animals and are usually found in herds of between 10 and 20 individuals consisting of one mature bull, a couple of younger bulls, cows and calves, though herds of up to 50 individuals are sometimes encountered. Old bulls appear to lose the herding instinct and often lead a solitary existence, only rejoining the herd for mating. Herds are often very noisy since elephant communicate with each other by a variety of sounds, the most usual ones being various rumbles produced through the trunk or mouth. The most well known elephant sound, however, is the high-pitched trumpeting which they produce when frightened or in despair and when charging.

HUGH FINLAY

Herds are on the move night and day in order to secure sufficient water and fodder, both of which they consume in vast quantities – the average daily food intake of an adult is in the region of 250 kg. They are both grazers and browsers and feed on a wide variety of vegetable matter including grasses, leaves, twigs, bark, roots and fruits and they frequently break quite large trees in order to get at the leaves. Because of this destructive capacity, they can be a serious threat to a fragile environment especially in drought years and are quite capable of turning dense woodland into open grassland over a relatively short period of time. Because of Africa's rapidly increasing human population and the expansion of cultivated land, they also come into conflict with farmers when they destroy crops such as bananas, maize and sugar cane.

The other essential part of an elephant's diet are various mineral salts which they obtain from 'salt licks'. These are dug out of the earth with the aid of their tusks and swallowed in considerable quantities.

Elephant breed year-round and the period of gestation is 22 to 24 months. Expectant mothers leave the

HUGH FINLAY

GREG HERRIMAN

herd along with one or two other females and select a secluded spot where birth occurs. They rejoin the herd a few days later. Calves weigh around 130 kg at birth and stand just under a metre high. They're very playful and guarded carefully and fondly by their mothers until weaned at two years old. After that, they continue to grow for a further 23 years or so, reaching puberty at around 10 to 12 years. An elephant's life span is normally 60 to 70 years though some individuals reach the ripe old age of 100 and even longer.

GIRAFFE

Rothschild's Giraffe
(Giraffa camelopardalis rothschild)
Swahili: *twiga*

Rothschild's giraffe, one of three types of giraffe common to East Africa, is found in western Kenya around Lake Baringo, and Uganda. The Masai giraffe *(Giraffa camelopardalis tippelskirchi)* is more widespread in Kenya and is found in all the parks south and west of Nairobi. Rothschild's is paler and more thickset than the Masai, with less-jagged patches, and is usually unmarked below the knee. The Masai giraffe has irregular, star-shaped patches and is usually buff-coloured below the knee. However, it is often difficult to identify a particular giraffe type because individual and regional variations in colour and pattern are wide.

TONY WHEELER

The average male stands around 5.5m; females are mere midgets at 4.5m. Horns are found on both sexes, but are merely short projections of bone covered by skin and hair. These are all that's left of what would once have been antlers. Despite the fact that the giraffe has such a huge neck, it still has only seven vertebrae – the same number as humans.

Reticulated Giraffe
(Giraffe camelopardalis reticulata)
Swahili: *twiga*

The reticulated giraffe differs from the Masai and Rothschild's giraffes in both colouring and pattern. It is a deeper brown and its body has a much more regular 'tortoiseshell' pattern, with white rather than buff-coloured outlines. It is found in the north and north-east of the country – Meru, Marsabit and Samburu reserves. You can easily come across them at the side of the road between Isiolo and Marsabit but probably the biggest herds are to be seen in Samburu and Buffalo Springs reserves.

Giraffe graze mainly on acacia tree foliage in the early morning and afternoon; the rest of the time they rest in the shade. At night they also rest for a couple of hours, either standing or lying down.

GEOFF CROWTHER

HIPPOPOTAMUS

(Hippopotamus amphibius)
Swahili: *kiboko*

In Kenya the hippo is found in greatest numbers in Masai Mara but can also be observed at Amboseli, Nairobi and Tsavo national parks and at Lake Baringo. At Tsavo there is a submarine viewing tank but the hippo are not very cooperative and seem to have deserted the immediate area.

Hippo are too well known to need description except to note that these huge, fat animals with enormous heads and short legs vary between 1350 kg and 2600 kg when fully grown. Their ears, eyes and nostrils are so placed that they remain above water when the animal is submerged.

Hippo generally spend most of the day wallowing in shallow water, coming out to graze only at night. They are entirely herbivorous and feed on a variety of grasses in pastures up to several km away from their aquatic haunts. They are voracious feeders and can consume up to 60 kg of vegetable matter each night. They urinate and defecate in well-defined areas – often in the water in which case they disperse the excreta with their tails.

Hippo are very gregarious animals and live in schools of 15 to 30 individuals though, in certain places, the schools can be much larger. Each school consists about equally of bulls and cows (with their calves) and, like other herd animals, there's an established hierarchy. Hippos may appear to be placid but they fight frequently among themselves for dominance and this is especially so among the males. The wounds inflicted in such fights are often quite horrific and virtually every hippo you see will bear the scars of such conflicts. They're not normally dangerous to humans unless cornered or frightened but you should definitely keep your distance. They may look sluggish but they are capable of running at considerable speed.

Hippo breed all year and the period of gestation is around 230 days. The cows give birth to a single calf either in the water or on land and suckle it for a period of four to six months after which it begins to graze on a regular basis. Sexual maturity is reached at about four years old and the life span is about 30 years (longer in captivity).

The only natural predators of hippo are lion and crocodile which prey on the young. Though hippo occasionally foul up fishing nets, they're considered to be beneficial since their wallowing stirs up the bottom mud and their excreta is a valuable fertiliser which encourages the growth of aquatic organisms.

GEOFF CROWTHER

GEOFF CROWTHER

GEOFF CROWTHER

GEOFF CROWTHER

HYRAX or DASSIE

(Procavia capensis)
Swahili: *pimbi*

The species of hyrax you're most likely to encounter (especially on Baboon Cliffs in Nakuru National Park but also in Nairobi, Tsavo, Masai Mara and Marsabit reserves) is the cape rock hyrax *(Procavia capensis)* or cape dassie. It's a small but robust animal about the size of a large rabbit with a short and pointed snout, large ears and thick fur. The tail is either absent or reduced to a stump.

Hyrax are extremely sociable animals and live in colonies of up to 60 individuals, usually in rocky, scrub-covered locations. They're diurnal, feeding mostly in the morning and evening on grass, bulbs and roots, and on insects such as grasshoppers and locusts. During the rest of the day they can be seen sunning themselves on rocks and chasing each other in play. Where habituated to humans, they are often quite tame but in other places, when alarmed, they dash into rock crevices uttering shrill screams. Their senses of hearing and sight are excellent.

Hyrax breed all year and the period of gestation is about seven months – a remarkably long period for an animal of this size. Up to six young are born at a time and the young are cared for by the whole colony. Predators include leopard, hunting dogs, eagle, mongoose and python.

Despite being such a small creature, hyrax are more closely related to the elephant than any other living creature by virtue of certain common physical traits.

PRIMATES

Baboon
(Papio cynocephalus)
Swahili: *nyani*

The yellow baboon is just one of at least seven sub-species of baboon and is the one most commonly sighted in Kenya. The other relatively common one is the olive baboon *(Papio anubis),* most often seen in Nairobi National Park. The main difference between the two is that the olive baboon has long facial hair and a mane on the shoulders, especially the males.

Baboon have a dog-like snout which gives them a much more aggressive and less human-like facial appearance than most other primates. They are usually found in large troops (of up to 150 animals, with a dominant male) which will have a territorial area ranging from two to 30 sq km. They spend most of the time on the ground searching for insects, spiders and birds' eggs. The baboon have also found that the lodges in the game parks are easy pickings, especially when

GEOFF CROWTHER

idiotic tourists throw food to them so they can get a good snap with the Instamatic.

Eastern Black & White Colobus
(Colobus guereza caudatus)
Swahili: *mbega*

This forest-dwelling colobus monkey is a handsome creature found only in the forest parks – Mt Kenya, Mt Elgon, Aberdare and Saiwa Swamp.

The monkey is basically black but has a white face, bushy white tail and a white 'cape' around the back which flows out behind when the monkey moves through the trees – an impressive sight. An average colobus measures about 140 cm, of which about 80 cm is tail, and weighs from 10 kg to 23 kg.

The black and white colobus spends most of its time in the forest canopy and is easily missed unless you keep a sharp eye out. It is unusual for them to leave the trees; they get most of their water from small puddles formed in the hollows of branches and trunks. Colobus monkey are usually found in troops of up to 12 animals, consisting of a dominant male, females and young. Newborn monkeys are initially white, gaining their adult coat at around six months.

Greater Bushbaby
(Galago crassicaudatus)
Swahili: *komba*

Looking more like an Australian possum, the bushbaby is in fact a small monkey and is about the size of a rabbit. It is found in all major reserves, although being a nocturnal creature it is rarely sighted by day. The head is small with large rounded ears and, as might be expected on a nocturnal animal, relatively large eyes. The thick fur is dark brown and the bushbaby sports a thick bushy tail. Your average bushbaby measures around 80 cm in length, of which the tail is around 45 cm, and weighs less than two kg.

The lesser bushbaby *(Galago senegalensis)* is about half the size of the greater bushbaby. It is a very light grey in colour and has yellowish colouring on the legs.

Vervet
Green monkey or grivet
(Cercopithecus aethiops)
Swahili: *tumbili*

The playful vervet is the most common monkey in Kenya and is seen in parks and reserves throughout the country. It is easily recognisable with its black face fringed by white hair, and yellowish-grey hair elsewhere except for the underparts which are whitish. The males have an extraordinary bright blue scrotum.

Vervets are usually found in groups of up to 30 and are extremely cheeky and inquisitive – they are often very habituated to humans. Normally they live in woodland and savannah but never in rainforest or semidesert areas.

TONY WHEELER

RHINOCEROS

(Diceros bicornis)
Swahili: *kifaru*

GREG HERRIMAN

One of Africa's most sought-after species by poachers, the numbers of black rhino in Kenya have fallen dramatically in the past, though they are now once again on the increase, thanks to some determined conservation efforts. They are now thought to number around 500, compared with around 20,000 in 1970!

Rhino are one of the more difficult animals to sight, simply because they're so few in numbers compared to other wildlife. They are seen in Amboseli quite often, and also in Masai Mara, Tsavo East (rarely), Nairobi National Park and Nakuru. Rhino usually feed in the very early morning or late afternoon; at other times they tend to keep out of sight.

The eyesight of the rhino is extremely poor and it relies more on its keen senses of smell and hearing. Usually when alarmed it will flee from perceived danger, but if it decides to charge it needs to be given a wide berth, though with its poor eyesight chances are it'll miss its target anyway. Rhinos have been known to charge trains and even the carcasses of dead elephants!

A rhino's territory depends on the type of country and the availability of food, and so can be as little as a couple of hectares or as much as 50 sq km. The diet consists mainly of leaves, shoots and buds of a large variety of bushes and trees.

Rhino reach sexual maturity by five years but females do not usually become pregnant for the first time until around seven years of age. Calves weigh around 40 kg at birth and by three months of age weigh around 140 kg. Adult animals weigh in at anything from 1000 kg to 1600 kg! They are solitary animals, only coming together for some days during mating. Calves stay with the mother for anything up to three years, although suckling generally stops after the first year.

GREG HERRIMAN

WART HOG

(Phacochoerus aethiopicus)
Swahili: *ngiri*

Although there are a number of wild-pig species in Kenya, the one you're most likely to see is the wart hog. It is found in all the major parks – Amboseli, Masai Mara, Nairobi, Tsavo, Meru, Marsabit and Samburu.

The wart hog gets its name from the somewhat grotesque wart-like growths which grow on its face. They are usually found in family groups of a boar, a sow and three or four young. Their most (or perhaps only) endearing habit is the way they turn tail and trot away with their thin tufted tails stuck straight up in the air like some antenna.

The males are usually bigger than the females, measuring up to one metre and weighing as much as 100 kg. They grow upper and lower tusks; the upper ones curve outwards and upwards and grow as long as 60 cm; the lower ones are usually less than 15 cm.

Wart hog live mainly on grass, but also eat fruit and bark, and, in hard times, will burrow with the snout for roots and bulbs. They rest and give birth in abandoned burrows or sometimes excavate a cavity in abandoned termite mounds. The young are born in litters of up to eight, although two to four is far more usual.

TONY WHEELER

TONY WHEELER

ZEBRA

(Equus burchelli, Equus grevyi)
Swahili: *punda milia*

TONY WHEELER

Zebra are one of the most common animals in the Kenyan parks and are widely distributed. You'll find them in great numbers in Nairobi, Tsavo, Amboseli, Samburu, Buffalo Springs, Maralal and Marsabit reserves as well as Masai Mara where they are present in the thousands.

Zebra often intermingle with other animals, most commonly the wildebeest but also topi and hartebeest.

There are two species to be seen in Kenya, the most common being Burchell's zebra which is found in all the western and southern parks all the way up to Samburu and Maralal. In the more arid north-west and north-east, however, the most common species is the Grevy's zebra which differs from Burchell's in having much narrower and more numerous stripes, prominent, broad, rounded ears, and a pure white underbelly.

Some taxonomists classify Burchell's zebra into various 'races' or subspecies but this is a contentious issue since it is impossible to find two zebras exactly alike even in the same herd. What is more certain is that although Burchell's and Grevy's zebra often form mixed herds over much of their range, they do not interbreed in the wild.

GEOFF CROWTHER

Zebra are grazers but will occasionally browse on leaves and scrub. They need water daily and rarely wander far from a water hole, though they appear to have considerably more resistance to drought than antelope.

Reproductive rituals take the form of fierce fights between rival stallions for control of a group of mares. The gestation period is about 12 months and one foal is born at a time.

The most usual predator is the lion, though hyena and hunting dogs will occasionally take zebra too.

GEOFF CROWTHER

Nairobi

Mark Knopfler could almost have been singing about Nairobi when he wrote *Telegraph Road*. Until the late 19th century there was nothing there. It was just a watering hole for the Maasai. Then came the Mombasa to Uganda railway, with its 32,000 indentured Indian labourers from Gujarat and the Punjab, along with their British colonial overlords intent on beating the German colonial push for the Ugandan heartland. Being approximately halfway between Mombasa and Uganda and a convenient place to pause before the arduous climb into the highlands, it quickly became tent city.

Much of the area was still a foul-smelling swamp at this time and game roamed freely over the surrounding plains, yet by 1900 it had become a town of substantial buildings and five years later succeeded Mombasa as the capital of the British East Africa protectorate. Since then it has gone from strength to strength and is now the largest city between Cairo and Johannesburg. Yet, in terms of the world's largest cities, Nairobi is still small with a population of about 1.5 million. You can walk from one end of the central business district to the other in 20 minutes. And where else in the world would you be able to see lions, cheetahs, rhinos and giraffes roaming free with the tower blocks of a city as a backdrop?

It's a very cosmopolitan place – lively, interesting, pleasantly landscaped and a good place to get essential business and bureaucratic matters sewn up. This is no Third World capital city though there are some very overcrowded slums on the outskirts and across the Nairobi River from Kirinyaga Rd. The latter are periodically bulldozed away and burnt down by the city council in the interests of hygiene but it takes only days for them to regenerate!

Like most cities, Nairobi has its crowded market and trading areas, its middle class/office workers' suburbs and its spacious mansions and flower-decked gardens for the rich

and powerful. The first is an area full of energy, aspiration and opportunism where manual workers, exhausted matatu drivers, the unemployed, the devious, the down-and-out and the disoriented mingle with budget travellers, whores, shopkeepers, high-school students, food-stall vendors, drowsy security guards and those with life's little illicit goodies for sale. It's called River Rd – though, of course, it spans more than just this road itself. One of the funniest yet most poignant yarns about an area such as this is to be found in a novel by Kenyan author Meja Mwangi called *Going Down River Road* (Heinemann, African Writers Series). I'd recommend this book to anyone and especially travellers passing through Nairobi. Even if you are not staying in this area you should make a point of getting down there one day just to see how the other half lives on the wrong side of Tom Mboya St.

Elsewhere in Nairobi are all the things you won't have seen for months if you've been hacking your way across the Central African Republic and Zaïre from West Africa or making do with the shortages in Zambia and Tanzania. Things like the latest films on big screens, bookshops, restaurants, cafes and bars full of travellers from all over the world, offices where you can get things done with the minimum of fuss, foreign exchange bureaus where you can change travellers' cheques in a matter of minutes and a poste restante where you can sort out your own letters from the pile. There's also excellent photographic shops, express mail and fax services and even e-mail service providers. It's a great place to stay for a week or so but if you stay too long it can get expensive because almost everyone you meet wants to do the same as you did when you first arrived – splurge at the restaurants, drink their fill in the bars and rage until dawn in the discos.

Unfortunately these days Nairobi is also getting a reputation as one of Africa's most lawless cities, and the city authorities seem unable, or unwilling, to tackle the problem. Petty crime is rife, and other more serious crimes are not infrequent.

Orientation

The compact city centre is in the area bounded by Uhuru Highway, Haile Selassie Ave, Tom Mboya St and University Way. The main bus and railway stations are within a few minutes walk of this area, while the main budget travellers' accommodation area is centred around Latema Rd, just east of Tom Mboya St on the fringe of the bustling and somewhat sleazy River Rd area.

To the west of the centre is one of the more enlightened bits of Nairobi town planning – Uhuru Park. It's a much needed lung for this increasingly crowded city and is a pleasant place in the daytime. At night it becomes a mugger's paradise and should be avoided.

Directly west of Uhuru Park, and still within walking distance of the centre (but *don't* walk at night!), are some of the city's better middle and top-range hotels, the youth hostel, a number of government ministries and the hospitals. Beyond here are the sprawling upper-middle class suburbs of Kilimani, Upper Hill and Hurlingham with their large detached houses and carefully tended gardens surrounded by high fences, and guarded by *askaris* (private security guards) along with prominent signs warning that the premises are patrolled by 'Ultimate Security', 'Total Security', 'Securicor' and the like. These signs are surely one of the most enduring impressions of suburban Nairobi.

North of the centre is the university, the national museum, the International Casino and one of Nairobi's original colonial hotels, the Norfolk. Beyond here is Westlands, almost a self-contained satellite city of Nairobi proper and another of the city's upper-middle class suburbs. North-east of the centre is Parklands, which is home to many of Nairobi's Asian minority and where the Aga Khan Hospital is to be found.

Going east, there are the bustling and predominantly African suburbs of Eastleigh and Pangani along with the country bus station.

Eastleigh, these days, is so full of Somali refugees that it's dubbed 'Little Mogadishu' by the locals. All manner of illicit and nefarious activities go on here though you'll remain blissfully unaware of this unless you actually live there for some time.

South of the city is the industrial area, the sprawling modern suburbs of Embakasi, Nairobi 'B' and 'C' and Nairobi West, Nairobi National Park, Wilson Airport and, even further south and off to the east, Jomo Kenyatta International Airport which is connected to the city by an excellent dual carriageway.

Maps There are many maps of Nairobi available in the bookshops but probably the best is the *City of Nairobi: Map & Guide* (Survey of Kenya) in English, French and German which has a red front cover with partially coloured photographs on the back cover. It covers the suburbs as well as having a detailed map of the central area. If you're going to be staying for a long time, however, the *Nairobi A to Z* (Kenway Publications, KSh 230), by RW Moss, is worth buying.

Information

Tourist Office In a city the size of Nairobi, and in a country which relies so heavily on tourism, it seems inconceivable that there is no tourist office, but there isn't.

What there is are two free booklets which you can pick up at the better class hotels, the Thorn Tree Cafe, car hire companies and the like. Both booklets have a substantial amount of advertising – no surprise in that, but it would help considerably if they made a little more effort to get their facts right and their maps accurate.

The better of these two publications is *Tourist's Kenya* which comes out usually about once a month and attempts to cover everything of interest in 95 fold-out pages. They don't do a bad job and it's well worth getting hold of a copy.

The other freebie is *What's On* which is published monthly and covers not just Kenya but also Tanzania and Uganda. It's glossier but much less informative and is almost bereft of prices. It also contains some terribly written articles which Tourist's Kenya doesn't even attempt. Still, it's better than nothing.

Foreign Consulates See the Facts for the Visitor chapter for a full list of diplomatic missions in Nairobi.

Money At Jomo Kenyatta International Airport the branch of Barclays Bank is open 24 hours a day, seven days a week. In Nairobi, the bank's branch on the corner of Kenyatta Ave and Wabera St is open Monday to Saturday from 9 am to 4.30 pm.

Changing money at a bank in Nairobi these days, however, is time-consuming and you're liable to be charged commission on travellers' cheques. It's much quicker and more convenient to change at a forex bureau and most of these charge no commission on cheques. They're found on virtually every street in the city centre including Mama Ngina St (Crown), Standard St (Finerate), Kenyatta Ave (Taipan and Chase), Muindi Mbingu St (Nairobi) and Utalii St. Up in Westlands there's only one choice – the Travellers Forex Bureau in the basement of The Mall shopping centre. All of them display the day's rates for European and North American currencies and some will also take Australian and New Zealand currencies. Exchange rates are pretty standard, and are published daily in the business pages of the *Daily Nation*.

American Express (☎ 334722) at Express Travel Kenya, Bruce House, Standard St, is open Monday to Friday from 10 am to 4 pm. It can issue travellers' cheques in the normal manner but cannot cash them.

Post & Communications The GPO is on Haile Selassie Ave. A new post office on Kenyatta Ave has been under construction for several years now and will probably remain in that condition for some time to come. The office on Haile Selassie is open Monday to Friday from 8 am to 5 pm and Saturday from 9 am to noon. The poste restante is well organised and you are allowed to look through as many piles as you

like, plus there's no charge for letters collected. The only trouble is that the counter which deals with it is also one of the few which sells stamps, so the queues are often long.

With the huge volume of poste restante mail here it's not surprising that some letters get misfiled but it doesn't happen too often. As a favour to other travellers you should pull out any letters you come across which are misfiled so the clerk can get them into the right pile.

This post office is also the best one from which to post parcels. The contents of all parcels sent overseas have to be inspected by the post office staff before being sealed so don't arrive with a sealed parcel or you'll have to pull it apart again. Bring all packing materials with you as there are none for sale at the post office. One of the cheapest places to buy good packing materials is at the supermarket on Koinange St opposite the new post office. Otherwise, try Biba on Kenyatta Ave at the Muindi Mbingu St intersection.

If you just want stamps, the small post office on Moi Ave just north of Kenyatta Ave is much more central. There's also a post office on the ground floor of the Kenyatta Conference Centre.

American Express (☎ 334722) in Bruce House, on Standard St (PO Box 40433) also has its client mail service.

Private couriers, DHL, can be found on the ground floor of International House, Mama Ngina St, and also on Mpaka Rd in Westlands.

Telephone The Extelcoms office is on Haile Selassie Ave, almost opposite the post office. It is open from 8 am to midnight and you can make direct dial calls yourself from here with a phone card or go through the operator. You can also do this at the post office on the ground floor of the Kenyatta Conference Centre and, if there's no conference in progress, it's much quieter here than in the Extelcoms office. There are more card phones on Posta Rd, opposite Nyayo House.

There's also a number of private agencies in the centre of town which offer international telephone services but their charges are higher than at the Extelcoms office. Count on about KSh 290 per minute to anywhere in Europe, North America and Africa and KSh 390 per minute to anywhere in South America, Asia, and Australasia.

In Westlands, the best place to make an international call is at Finance & General in the basement of The Mall shopping centre. There's never a queue here and it's comfortable. Credit cards are accepted.

The telephone code for calls to Nairobi from anywhere in Kenya, Uganda and Tanzania is 02.

Fax The Extelcoms office also offers telex and fax services which are much cheaper than any of the private agencies which offer these services, though you must be prepared to wait in a queue for a short while.

As with telephone calls, there are numerous private agencies offering fax services in the city centre but you need to shop around before sending one as the price of sending a one-page fax can vary from KSh 600 to KSh 1000.

In Westlands you can do it either with Finance & General (cheaper) in the basement of The Mall shopping centre or at CopyCat (more expensive) in the Sarit Centre.

Internet & E-Mail There are at least two service providers in Nairobi. They are Thorn-Tree E-Mail (☎ 229650), Embassy House, on the corner of Harambee Ave and Parliament Rd, and Form-Net Africa (☎ 245630), Finance House, Loita St.

Of these two, only Thorn-Tree, which is run by a company called Omega Microsystems, caters to casual e-mail users. The charges are very reasonable (around KSh 20 per page) and the service excellent.

Travel Agencies To get the best possible deal on an international airline ticket, first make the rounds of the airline offices to ascertain the standard price and then make the rounds of the travel agencies. Always get several quotes as things change constantly.

NAIROBI

PLACES TO STAY
2 Mrs Roche's
3 Sirona Hotel
6 Boulevard Hotel
9 YMCA
10 Norfolk Hotel
11 West End Lodgings
17 YWCA
19 Serena Hotel
21 Fairview Hotel
22 Panafric Hotel

24 Heron Court Hotel
25 Milimani Hotel
26 Sagret Hotel
27 Lenana Mount Hotel
29 Hurlingham Hotel
31 Youth Hostel
34 Upper Hill Campsite

PLACES TO EAT
28 China Town
Restaurant & Fredz

OTHER
1 Aga Khan Hospital
4 Nairobi National Museum
5 Snake Park
7 International Casino
8 Australian High Commission
12 Text Book Centre
13 Kariokor Market
14 Country Bus Station
15 Peugeot Taxis to Namanga (Tanzania)
16 Zambian High Commission
18 Sudan & Zimbabwe Embassies
20 All Saints' Cathedral
23 Ethiopian Embassy
30 Hurlingham Shopping Centre
32 Nairobi Hospital
33 Kenyatta Hospital
35 National Library
36 Railway Museum

See Central Nairobi Map (pages 156-7)

One of the best agencies to go to (if not the best) is Flight Centres (☎ 210024; fax 334207; e-mail fcswwat@arcc.or.ke), 2nd floor, Lakhamshi House, Biashara St. This company has been doing discounted airline tickets for years and what they don't know probably isn't worth knowing. They also offer a visa service and can advise about safari companies and they also run many of their own.

Also recommended is Let's Go Travel (☎ 340331; fax 336890) which is on Standard St, opposite Bruce House and close to the intersection with Koinange St. This long-established company not only handles all travel requirements, but also puts out a number of very useful lists, including one detailing current accommodation prices around the country.

Bookshops There is a good selection of bookshops in the city centre. The Nation Bookshop is on the corner of Kimathi St and Kenyatta Ave, next door to the New Stanley Hotel, and around the corner on Kenyatta Ave is the Westland Sundries Bookshop – both are excellent.

On Mama Ngina St there's Prestige Books, next to the 20th Century Cinema. There are others in the city centre but they don't carry the same range.

Outside of the immediate city centre there is the Text Book Centre on Kijabe St at the back of the Norfolk Hotel which carries a vast range of books and stationery including everything relevant to Africa. It also has a branch on the ground floor of the Sarit Centre, Westlands.

Libraries The main public library in Nairobi is the Kenya National Library (☎ 227871), Ngong Rd. It's open Monday to Friday from 9.30 am to 6 pm. The other library is the McMillan Memorial Library (☎ 221844), Banda St. It's open Monday to Friday from 9 am to 5 pm and Saturday from 9.30 am to 1 pm.

Cultural Centres All the foreign cultural organisations have libraries which are open to the public and are free of charge except for the American Cultural Center and British Council which are for members only. The French, Japanese and German cultural centres all welcome travellers. The addresses are:

Alliance Française
ICEA building, Ground floor, Kenyatta Ave (☎ 340054); open Monday to Friday from 8.30 am to 5.30 pm and on Saturday from 8.30 am to 1 pm

American Cultural Center
National Bank building, Harambee Ave (☎ 334141 ext 343); open Monday, Tuesday and Thursday from 9 am to 5 pm, Wednesday from 9 am to noon and Friday from 9 am to 4 pm

British Council
ICEA building, Mezzanine floor, Kenyatta Ave (☎ 334855); open Tuesday to Friday from 10 am to 6 pm and Saturday from 10 am to 1 pm

Goethe Institute
Maendeleo House, on the corner Monrovia and Loita Sts (☎ 224640); open Monday to Friday from 10 am to 5 pm

Italian Cultural Institute
Corner House, 15th Floor, Mama Ngina St (☎ 337356 ext 45); open Monday and Tuesday from 8 am to 1 pm and 2 to 6 pm and Wednesday to Friday from 8 am to 2 pm

Japan Information Centre
Postbank House, on the corner of Market and Banda Sts (☎ 340520); open Monday to Friday from 8.30 am to 12.30 pm and 2 to 4 pm

Nairobi Cultural Institute
This centre in Ngong Rd (☎ 569205) has various lectures as well as other functions of local cultural interest.

Camping Equipment If you want to hire camping equipment (anything from a sleeping bag to a folding toilet seat, tent or mosquito net) the best place to go to is Atul's (☎ 225935), Biashara St. It has the lot and is open Monday to Friday from 8.30 am to noon and 2 to 5 pm and on Saturday from 8.30 am to noon and 2.30 to 4 pm. Hire charges have to be paid in full before commencement of hire as well as a deposit for each item. The deposits are refunded when hired items are returned in good condition. The best way to leave a deposit is in the form of countersigned travellers' cheques. Identification, such as a passport, is required.

Photography For passport-size photographs, the cheapest place to go is the machine under the yellow and black sign 'Photo Me', a few doors up Kenyatta Ave from the Nation Bookshop on the corner of Kimathi St. It costs KSh 100 for four prints and takes about three minutes. There's another machine on the corner of Tom Mboya St and Accra Rd. You can also get passport photos from the photography shop in Kimathi House opposite the New Stanley Hotel; they are marginally more expensive.

For camera repairs or equipment rental the best place is Expo Camera Centre (☎ 221797), Jubilee Exchange, Mama Ngina St. They're also very reliable for developing and printing/mounting of both colour print and slide film. Alternatively, try Camera Experts, also on Mama Ngina St, or the Camera Maintenance Centre in the Hilton Arcade.

Laundry There are no launderettes in Nairobi so you either do your own washing or have it done through your hotel. Virtually all hotels offer a laundry service but, if you're on a budget, check prices first – it can turn out surprisingly expensive.

Dry cleaning can be done at one of several places in Nairobi but is not particularly cheap. The most convenient are Diplomat on Kenyatta Ave between Loita and Koinange Sts, and White Rose on Kaunda St between Koinange and Muindi Mbingu Sts.

Medical Services If you need medical treatment try Dr Sheth on the 3rd floor of Bruce House on Standard St. This doctor has his own pathology laboratory if you need blood or stool tests. He charges KSh 800 per consultation plus laboratory fees. There is also a dentist on the same floor.

Otherwise go to outpatients at either Nairobi Hospital (☎ 722160), off Valley Rd, or the Aga Khan Hospital (☎ 740000), Third Parklands Ave, both of which have much the same scale of charges as Dr Sheth. At Nairobi Hospital a consultation costs KSh 660, the treatment is competent and major credit

The striking Jama Mosque is close to Muindi Mbingu Street. The stunning exterior is worth a look, however, entry is not always available to travellers.

cards are accepted. Avoid the Kenyatta National Hospital, because although it's free, treatment here is possibly worse than the ailment, according to local residents. The place is certainly bereft of any semblance of 'bedside manner'.

You can get vaccinations at City Hall Clinic, Mama Ngina St. It is open for jabs from 8.30 am to noon and 2.30 to 4 pm Monday to Friday. The vaccines vary in price with yellow fever and typhoid being the most expensive (KSh 400) and cholera and meningitis the cheapest (KSh 150). If you're concerned about clean needles being used – and you should be! – then bring your own.

If you want a gamma globulin shot (for hepatitis A) go to Dr Sheth (3rd floor, Bruce House, Standard St). The charge is KSh 800.

Emergency In case of emergency you could try the police on ☎ 717777, or simply dial ☎ 999. What response you would get I'm not sure.

For a medical emergency call the Aga Khan Hospital (☎ 740000), as it is reliable and has a 24-hour casualty section.

EARS Medivac (☎ 566683) is one of a number of private companies which provide ambulance service and emergency air evacuation.

Dangers & Annoyances You'll often hear Nairobi referred to as 'Nairobbery' by residents, both Kenyan and expatriate, and you'll certainly read about robberies and muggings, some of them violent, in the newspapers almost daily. This is something you should bear seriously in mind and act in a manner which will minimise your chances of becoming a victim. See the Dangers & Annoyances section in Facts for the Visitor for more information.

Other specific precautions you should take are:

Do not walk from the city centre to any of the hotels on Milimani Rd or to the youth hostel, YMCA or YWCA after dark. Uhuru Park is infamous for its muggers. Take a taxi. That KSh 200 fare could save you everything you've got.

Avoid walking alone at night carrying valuables in any of the streets between Tom Mboya and Kirinyaga (the River Rd area). If that's unavoidable, take with you only as much as you can afford to lose.

National Museum

The Kenya National Museum is on Museum Rd off Museum Hill which itself is off Uhuru Highway, and is well worth a couple of hours.

One of the museum's major exhibits is the Peoples of Kenya portraits display by Joy Adamson (of *Born Free* fame). In the late 1940s she was commissioned by the government to record the traditional cultures of the local people, and went on to paint over 600 images, some of which stand in the museum today. This Ethnography Gallery also houses exhibits on the material culture of the various Kenyan tribal groups.

With so many important fossil sites in Kenya, it's no surprise that the museum has some excellent fossil displays in its Prehistory Gallery, and a stunning re-creation of a prehistoric rock art site.

There's also an extraordinary cast on the floor which clearly records the footprints of three people (actually thought to be *Homo erectus*, probably our direct ancestors) which were laid down as they walked across a bed of volcanic ash nearly four million years ago!

Birders should be well satisfied with the Bird Gallery, as it houses more than 900 stuffed and mounted specimens, including all the ones you're likely to see on any trip to Kenya.

The museum also houses the recently refurbished Gallery of Contemporary East African Art, which provides a space for local artists to exhibit and sell their work.

Anyone heading for the coast should check out the Lamu Gallery, wehich has a fine display of the coastal Swahili culture, including the distinctive carved wooden doors which adorn traditional coastal houses.

Opening hours are from 9.30 am to 6 pm daily and admission is KSh 200 (KSh 100 for children).

Snake Park

The Snake Park, opposite the museum, has living examples of most of the snake species found in East Africa – some of them are in glass cages, others in open pits. There are also tortoises and crocodiles. Hours and entry charges are the same as for the museum.

National Archives

Right opposite the Hilton Hotel on Moi Ave is the National Archives. It is regarded by many as better than the National Museum and entry is free. It contains more than the usual documents you'd expect to find in such a building, including photographs of Mzee Kenyatta and Moi visiting different countries, and exhibitions of handicrafts and paintings.

Opening hours are from 8 am to 5 pm Monday to Friday.

Railway Museum

The Railway Museum is on Station Rd – follow the railway tracks until you are almost at the bridge under Uhuru Highway or walk across the small piece of vacant land next to the Haile Selassie Ave roundabout on Uhuru Highway.

In addition to the displays of old steam engines and rolling stock, the museum will give you a good idea of Kenya's history since the beginning of the colonial period. There's also a scale model of the venerable MV *Liemba* which plies the waters of Lake Tanganyika between Mpulungu (Zambia) and Bujumbura (Burundi).

Unfortunately this place looks a little sad

The Kima Killer

Early this century when the railway line was being pushed through from Mombasa to Kampala and beyond, a remarkable incident occurred at Kima, a small siding on the line, about 110 km along the track south-west of Nairobi.

A rogue lion had been terrorising the track gangs and had in fact claimed a few victims. In an attempt to eradicate this menace, a superintendent of Uganda Railways stationed in Mombasa, Charles Ryall, decided to mount a night vigil in a railway carriage specially positioned at the Kima siding. The station staff wanted nothing to do at all with the escapade and had locked themselves firmly in the station buildings.

Ryall left the carriage door open, in the hope that the lion would be lured in, and sat back with rifle at the ready and waited. Inevitably he fell asleep and just as inevitably the lion showed up. The struggle that ensued caused the sliding door on the compartment to shut and the lion was trapped inside with a firm grip on Ryall's neck. Accompanying Ryall in the carriage were two European merchants who were travelling to Nairobi and had hitched a ride with Ryall, agreeing to the overnight stop in Kima. So petrified were they that one of them ducked into the toilet and bolted the door, while the other watched transfixed as the lion wrested the body out of the train window!

A reward was offered by Ryall's mother for the capture of the offending lion but it was only after a trap, baited with a live calf, was devised that the human-eater was snared. It seems there was no reason for the lion to have turned human-eater as it was a healthy beast and there was an abundance of game animals in the vicinity – supposedly it just developed a liking for human flesh.

The railway carriage involved in this incident is today preserved in the Nairobi Railway Museum, while the tombstone of Ryall, which bears the inscription 'He was attacked whilst sleeping and killed by a man-eating lion at Kima', is in the Hill Cemetery, also in Nairobi. ■

these days. The outdoor displays are slowly but surely rotting away, while a number of the interior displays have simply gone. It's a great shame as there is no lack of volunteer groups (local and foreign) who are willing to come and restore the old rolling stock; it seems the Kenya Railways administration just couldn't care less.

The museum is open daily from 8 am to 4.45 pm; entry is KSh 50.

Parliament House

Like to take a look at how democracy works in Kenya? If so, you can get a permit for a seat in the public gallery at parliament house on Parliament Rd or, if parliament is out of session, you can tour the buildings by arrangement with the sergeant-at-arms.

Art Galleries

There's not much in Nairobi in the way of art galleries. At the museum there's the Gallery of Contemporary East African Art, which is worth a look. Of the private galleries, the Gallery Watatu in Lonrho House, Standard St, is the oldest established and has fairly regular exhibitions as well as a permanent display.

Kenyatta Conference Centre

There is a viewing level on the 28th floor of the centre but the revolving restaurant hasn't operated for years. If you'd like to go up there, it costs KSh 100. You're allowed to take photographs from the viewing level. Access is sometimes restricted when there's a conference in progress.

Activities

Clubs & Societies There are lots of specialist clubs and societies in Nairobi, many of which welcome visitors. Most of the foreign cultural organisations have film and lecture evenings (usually free of charge) at least once or twice a week. Give them a ring and see what they have organised or browse through the entertainment sections of the local daily newspapers. In addition to these, some local clubs you may be interested in contacting include:

East African Wildlife Society
   Nairobi Hilton, PO Box 20110, Nairobi (☎ 748170)
   This society is in the forefront of conservation efforts in East Africa and it publishes an interesting bimonthly magazine, *Swara*. Membership costs US$35 which includes subscription to *Swara* (US$70 if you want the magazine sent by airmail rather than surface mail).
Mountain Club of Kenya (MCK)
   PO Box 45741, Nairobi (☎ 501747)
   The club meets every Tuesday at 8 pm at the clubhouse at Wilson Airport. Members frequently organise climbing weekends at various sites around the country. Information on climbing Mt Kenya and Kilimanjaro is available on the same evening.

Sports The following clubs all offer facilities for tennis, squash and cricket, and some also cater for football and hockey. They are all private clubs and membership fees apply.

Impala Club
   Ngong Rd, Nairobi (☎ 568684)
Nairobi Club
   Ngong Rd (☎ 725726)
Nairobi Gymkhana
   Corner of Rwathia and Forest Rds (☎ 742804)
Parklands Sports Club
   Ojijo Rd (☎ 742938)

Swimming Pools Most of the international tourist hotels have swimming pools which can be used by non-guests for a daily fee of around KSh 200. The YMCA on State House Rd also has a large pool with springboard which you can use for KSh 80.

Organised Tours
There's not much in the way of organised tours of Nairobi, simply because there's not a great deal to see. If you are keen, contact Let's Go Travel (☎ 340331) who can organise a two-hour tour for around KSh 1800 per person.

Tours to the sights around Nairobi are easy to find, and take in places such as the Bomas of Kenya, the Karen Blixen Museum and the Nairobi National Park. Anything which includes the national park is going to be expensive as there is the US$20 park entry fee to pay.

Places to Stay – bottom end

Camping The best place to camp in Nairobi is *Upper Hill Campsite* (☎ 720290), Menengai Rd, off Hospital Rd, which is itself off Ngong Rd. It offers camping for KSh 150 per person in green, shady surroundings. If you don't have camping equipment there's dormitory accommodation available for KSh 250 as well as a few private double rooms. The site is enclosed by a high fence and guarded 24 hours a day and is favoured by overland truck companies as well as independent travellers. Facilities include hot showers, a mellow bar, restaurant (open for breakfast, lunch and dinner), fireplace with comfortable chairs, a library, collection of games and a covered workshop for vehicle maintenance. You can also store excess baggage here safely. It's a great place to stay, close to the city (15 minutes walk) and people are very friendly.

You could once say the same of *Mrs Roche's*, on Third Parklands Ave opposite the Aga Khan Hospital, a place which has been making travellers welcome for over 25 years. Unfortunately 'Ma', as she's affectionately known by long-time travellers, appears to have lost the plot these days and spends too much time drinking Tusker lager and not attending to security at the camp. Many travellers have had theft problems recently. It's suggested you be very security conscious if you choose to stay. All this is a great pity as Ma Roche's is situated in a pleasant residential area among trees and flowering shrubs and there are cheap places to eat, drink and shop in the immediate vicinity. Camping costs KSh 100 per night plus KSh 50 for a vehicle with dormitory beds at KSh 200 per person. To get to Mrs Roche's, take a matatu from the junction of Latema Rd and Tom Mboya St right outside the Odeon Cinema. There'll be a sign 'Aga Khan' in the front windscreen. Tell the driver you're heading for Mrs Roche's. It's well known.

Youth Hostel Also worth considering is the *Nairobi Youth Hostel* (☎ 721765), on Ralph Bunche Rd between Valley and Ngong Rds. It was completely refurbished and extended a few years ago and although it is still a good place to meet other travellers, the prices have risen dramatically and it's not the bargain it once was.

The hostel is very clean, well run, stays open all day and there's always hot showers. The wardens here are very friendly and will lock up gear safely for you for a small charge. On a day-to-day basis there are lockers to keep your gear in when you go out, but you must supply your own lock. The notice board here is also worth a look for travel partners, things to sell, etc. A bed in a 16-bed dorm is KSh 350, in a three or four-bed room it's also KSh 350 while in a twin room it's KSh 400.

Any matatu or bus which goes down either Valley or Ngong Rds will drop you at Ralph Bunche Rd. The No 8 matatu which goes down Ngong Rd is probably the most convenient. You can pick it up either outside the Hilton Hotel or on the corner of Kenyatta Ave and Uhuru Highway. If you're returning to the youth hostel after dark don't be tempted to walk back from the centre of the city. Many people have been robbed. Always take a matatu or taxi (KSh 200).

Hotels – City Centre There is a very good selection of budget hotels in Nairobi and the majority of them, except for two very popular places outside the city centre, are between Tom Mboya St and River Rd so if you find that one is full it's only a short walk to another. Virtually all the hotels in the city centre suffer from pretty chronic water shortages. Often there is only water for a couple of hours a day, so getting a shower at some of these places can be a bit of an ordeal. The area also has a bad reputation for theft and muggings, especially at night. Be careful around here.

Many of the cheaper hotels, such as the Iqbal and the New Kenya Lodge, will store baggage for you, usually for a small daily charge. However, you're advised not to leave anything valuable in your left luggage.

The *New Kenya Lodge* (☎ 222022), on River Rd at the Latema Rd intersection, is a bit of a legend among budget travellers and

Central Nairobi

0   125   250 m

NAIROBI

PLACES TO STAY
2	Nairobi Safari Club
3	Suncourt Hotel
4	Parkside Hotel
7	Meridien Court Hotel
11	Marble Arch Hotel
15	New Kenya Lodge
16	New Safe Life Lodging
18	Hotel Greton
19	Bujumbura Lodge
20	New Kenya Lodge Annex
23	Sirikwa Lodge
25	Oriental Palace Hotel
26	Iqbal Hotel
37	Terminal Hotel & Dove Cage Restaurant
38	Embassy Hotel
39	Grand Regency Hotel
47	Inter-Continental Hotel
55	Sixeighty Hotel
66	New Stanley Hotel, Nation Bookshop & Thorn Tree Cafe
68	Oakwood Hotel
72	Hilton Hotel
74	Ambassadeur Hotel
75	Solace Hotel
77	Dolat Hotel
78	Terrace Hotel
79	Hotel Gloria
81	Princess Hotel
99	Hotel Hermes

PLACES TO EAT
9	Dhaba Restaurant, Nyama Choma Terrace & Bar
10	Supreme, Mayur & Zam Zam Restaurants
14	Bull Cafe
24	Malindi Dishes
28	Nairobi Burgers
30	Minar Restaurant
33	Slush Happy Eater
36	Kenchic Inn, Hoggers Eating Place & Afro Unity Bar
40	Hard Rock Cafe & Kenya Airways (Barclays Plaza)
44	Harvest Cafe
45	Nyama Choma Stalls (NSSF Market)
51	Beneve Coffee House
54	Calypso & Dragon Pearl Restaurants (Bruce House)
56	Great Chung Wah Chinese Restaurant
58	La Scala
60	Cafe Helena & Coffee Bar
61	Trattoria Restaurant
62	Pasara Cafe & Rickshaw Chinese Restaurant
67	Supermac
69	Caprice
70	Jax Restaurant
71	l'ora blu
76	New Bedona Cafe
96	Tamarind Restaurant & American Cultural Center

continued next page

OTHER
1   Police
5   Bus Stop (for Westlands)
6   Maasai Market (Tuesday)
8   Moi Ave Post Office
12 Akamba Bus Office
13 Bancko Tours & Travel
17 DPS Peugeots (Share-taxis)
21 Coast Bus, Mawingo, Goldline,
    Arusha Express
22 Matatus for Embu, Isiolo & Nanyuki
27 Modern Green Day & Night Bar
29 Nakumatt Supermarket
31 McMillan Memorial Library
32 Jama Mosque
34 Flight Centres
35 Atul's (Camping Gear)
41 New Florida Nightclub
42 City Market
43 Air Zimbabwe & Air Tanzania (Chester
    House)
46 Immigration (Nyayo House)
48 Bus & Matatu Stop (for Hurlingham &
    Milimani)
49 New GPO (under construction)
50 Let's Go Travel
52 Holy Family Cathedral
53 City Hall
57 Ugandan High Commission
59 Central Rent-a-Car
63 Prestige Books, Dancing Spoons Cafe
    & Wine Bar/20th Century Cinema
64 Rwandan Embassy, DHL & British
    Airways
65 Expo Camera Centre
73 National Archives
80 KBS Stagecoach Bus Station
82 Florida 2000 Nightclub
83 Kenya Cinema Plaza & Zanze Bar
84 Zaïre Embassy (Electricity House)
85 Law Courts
86 Kenyatta Conference Centre
87 Public Map Office
88 Ministry of Foreign Affairs
89 Office of the President
90 Jomo Kenyatta's Mausoleum
91 Parliament House
92 Tanzanian High Commission
93 Thorn-Tree E-Mail (Embassy House)
94 Main Post Office (GPO)
95 Extelcoms
97 Air India & Indian High Commission
    (Jeevan Bharati Building)
98 US Embassy

still one of the cheapest places, though many people feel it's a bit past it these days. There's always an interesting bunch of people from all over the world staying there. Accommodation is basic but clean and there's

supposedly hot water in the evenings but you should not count on that. Singles/doubles, which have shared bathroom facilities, cost KSh 200/300.

The same people who own this also have the *New Kenya Lodge Annex* (☎ 338348) just around the corner on Duruma Rd. Prices here are the same as the old place but it lacks the atmosphere of the former. Some of the rooms don't even have windows and security is not what it could be. All the same, it's still quite popular, the staff are friendly and the notice board makes interesting reading.

The nearby *Iqbal Hotel* (☎ 220914), on Latema Rd, has been equally popular for years and is still a pretty good place. There's supposedly hot water available in the morning but you have to be up early to get it. Singles/doubles here cost KSh 200/400 with shared facilities. Baggage is safe and there's a storeroom where you can leave excess gear if you are going away for a while. The Iqbal's notice board is always a good place to look for just about anything.

Also on Latema Rd, the *Sunrise Lodge* is clean, secure and friendly and there's usually hot water in the mornings and evenings. It costs KSh 300/400 for singles/doubles with shared bathroom facilities including a simple breakfast or KSh 240/360 without breakfast. The front two rooms overlooking the street are the largest and have a balcony but they are right next door to the Modern Green Day & Night Bar which rages 24 hours a day, 365 days a year, so if you want a quiet room take one at the back. If you're looking for material for a novel, on the other hand, then take one of the two front rooms.

If the above three places are full there are three others on Dubois Rd, just off Latema Rd. The *Bujumbura Lodge* (☎ 228078) is very basic and a bit rough around the edges, but it's clean and quiet and very secure. The toilets and showers are clean and there is erratic hot water. It's good value at KSh 170/220 for singles/doubles with shared facilities. The *Nyandarua Lodging* and the *New Safe Life Lodging* (☎ 221578) are very similar and cost the same but the single rooms are just glorified closets. Make sure you ask what the check-out time is as it's often very early.

None of the other rock-bottom hotels in this area can seriously be recommended. They're just brothels or somewhere for drunks with a few *shilingi* left to sleep off their hangovers.

Moving up the scale, there are several hotels in the same area which are somewhat more salubrious. One of the cheapest is the *Hotel Gloria* (☎ 228916), on Ronald Ngala St almost at the Tom Mboya St intersection. Rooms here are reasonable value at KSh 600/800 for a single/double. All rooms have bath and hot water, and the price includes breakfast. The only problem here is that most of the rooms cop the noise and car exhaust fumes from the street below and it's quite horrendous.

A couple of doors along from the Gloria is the *Terrace Hotel* (☎ 221636) which has rooms with bath and hot water for KSh 350/450. It doesn't win any prizes for friendliness and some of the rooms are noisy, but overall it's not a bad place.

One of the best places in the budget category is the *Dolat Hotel* (☎ 222797), on Mfangano St, which is very quiet and costs KSh 480/600 for singles/doubles and KSh 960 a triple with own shower (no hot water). The sheets are changed daily, the rooms kept spotless and there's usually 24-hour water. It's a good, secure place with friendly management and quite a few travellers stay here.

Lastly, there's the very quiet and secure *West End Lodgings* (☎ 750524) on Kijabe St, north of the Norfolk Hotel, which is clean and has helpful staff. It's only a few cents more than the Iqbal for a double room, yet is far removed from the noise of Latema Rd.

The 'Y's There is both a *YMCA* (☎ 724066) and *YWCA* (☎ 724699) in Nairobi. The former is on State House Rd and the latter on Mamlaka Rd off Nyerere Rd and both of them are popular places to stay. The YMCA offers dorm beds for KSh 310 and mid-range singles/doubles with shared bathroom facilities for KSh 500/800. It also has singles/doubles with attached bathrooms for KSh

800/1200. All these prices include breakfast. Other meals are available for KSh 180 (lunch) and KSh 190 (dinner). Unless you're a member, you must buy temporary membership to stay here which costs KSh 50.

The YWCA offers much the same types of rooms and dorm beds as the YMCA but it's marginally cheaper and takes only couples and single women. It's also more difficult to get into because it's used by many students and young workers on a residential basis due to its even cheaper monthly rates. Like the YMCA, it has its own dining room with all meals available. You also have to pay a temporary membership fee of KSh 50 to stay here.

Places to Stay – middle
City Centre The *Solace Hotel* (☎ 331277) is on the horrendously noisy Tom Mboya St – the matatu drivers here honk and rev their engines to drum up business, and it goes on nonstop from early morning until late at night; it makes a mockery of the hotel's name. Rates are KSh 1320/1650 for small singles/doubles with attached bathrooms, and triples are KSh 1930, all including breakfast. It's somewhat overpriced and the extra money seems to be mainly for a carpet and phone in the room. If you do stay here make sure you get a room away from the street.

The *Sirikwa Lodge* (☎ 333838) on the corner of Munyu and Accra Rds is a good place in the middle bracket, although it's perhaps overpriced these days. For KSh 700/900 you get a clean room with bath, hot water, a phone and breakfast. Accra Rd is somewhat quieter than Tom Mboya St so this place is not a bad bet.

Two other quiet places, both of them on Tsavo Rd between Latema and Accra Rds, are the *Hotel Greton* (☎ 242891) which offers rooms with attached bathrooms, including hot showers, for KSh 800/950 a single/double and KSh 1300 for triples, including breakfast, and the *Grand Holiday Hotel* (☎ 214159) which has singles/doubles with attached bathrooms for KSh 950/1200 and triples for KSh 1800, including breakfast.

NAIROBI

Further away from this area, on Tom Mboya St down towards Haile Selassie Ave, is the *Princess Hotel* (☎ 214640). The rooms are somewhat shabby these days, but they have their own bathroom and cost KSh 450/580 including a good breakfast. Like all places on Tom Mboya St, the quietest rooms are at the back, though the street is nowhere near as noisy here as further up near Accra Rd. The hotel has its own bar and restaurant. The food is good and the staff friendly.

Right at the bottom of Moi Ave at the junction with Haile Selassie Ave is the *Hotel Hermes*. The staff here are friendly and pretty laid back and huge singles/doubles with attached bathrooms cost KSh 800/1000 including breakfast.

Across the other side of the city centre, west of Moi Avenue, there's a choice of three reasonably priced hotels which are very popular with travellers. Best value is the recently redecorated *Terminal Hotel* (☎ 228817; fax 220075) on Moktar Daddah St near the junction with Koinange St. It's spotlessly clean; soap, towels and toilet paper are provided and there's hot water around the clock. Security is excellent, the rooms are generally quiet and there's a notice board downstairs. Singles/doubles with attached bathrooms cost KSh 880/1100 and triples KSh 1300. Children sharing with their parents are charged KSh 50 per day. You can also store excess baggage here for KSh 30 per article per day.

Nearby, but a somewhat older place, is the *Embassy Hotel* (☎ 224087; fax 224534) on Biashara St between Koinange and Muindi Mbingu Sts. All the rooms have attached bathrooms, there's hot water and soap, towels and toilet paper are provided. Small singles here cost KSh 800. Normal singles/doubles are KSh 900/1000 with triples at KSh 1200. Breakfast is not included but is available for KSh 150. The hotel has its own bar and restaurant.

Also nearby is the *Parkside Hotel* (☎ 214154) on Monrovia St which runs alongside Jeevanjee Gardens. The staff here are very friendly and the hotel has its own restaurant. It's a little more expensive than

the previous two but still very good value at KSh 1380/1780 for singles/doubles and KSh 2600 for triples including breakfast. All the rooms have attached bathrooms with hot showers.

Round the block from the Parkside on University Way opposite the junction with Harry Thuku Rd is the *Suncourt Hotel* (☎ 221418; fax 217500). All the rooms here have attached bathrooms and cost KSh 1500/2550 for singles/doubles and KSh 3250 a triple. They also have 'executive' rooms at KSh 2350/3150 for singles/doubles and KSh 3600 for triples. Breakfast is not included but all meals are available in the hotel's restaurant.

Not too far from the Suncourt or the Parkside is the *Meridian Court Hotel* (☎ 333916; fax 333658), Muranga'a Rd off Moi Ave, which has rooms at much the same price. It's a modern building and singles/doubles are KSh 1950/2650 with triples at KSh 2950.

Back into the very heart of town, the *Oakwood Hotel* (☎ 220592; fax 332170), PO Box 40683, Kimathi St, right opposite the New Stanley Hotel, is a good choice. It's a very pleasant place to stay and the 23 rooms, all with attached bathrooms, are quite spacious and definitely comfortable plus they have a TV/video. The rates for residents are KSh 1700/2400 for singles/doubles and KSh 2850 for triples. Nonresident rates for the same thing are US$50/60 and US$75 but this is definitely negotiable and you can pay in Kenyan shillings in any case. Breakfast is included in the rates. The hotel has its own restaurant and a very cosy bar with a balcony overlooking the street below.

Re-entering the Latema Rd/River Rd area again, there are two up-market hotels in this down-market part of town. The cheapest is the relatively new *Oriental Palace Hotel* (☎ 217600; fax 212335) on Taveta Rd which is a huge, quite luxurious place used principally by businessmen. Standard singles/doubles for residents are KSh 2290/2790 or KSh 2790/3260 for deluxe rooms. For non-residents the rates are US$54/72 for standard singles/doubles and US$72/84 for deluxe rooms. Breakfast is not included. The hotel has a bar and a good Indian restaurant.

Even more expensive is the new *Marble Arch Hotel* (☎ 245720; fax 245724), Lagos Rd, which has 40 spacious rooms all with wall-to-wall carpeting, wood panelling, telephone, TV/video and a bathroom/toilet. It costs KSh 3100/4400 for singles/doubles and KSh 5600 a triple. There's also a suite for KSh 9750. Children between the ages of three and 12 years are charged 75% of the above rates. Breakfast is included in the price of a room. The hotel has its own coffee shop, restaurant, bar and business centre. On the basis of the facilities which this hotel provides it really belongs in the top-end category. The only problem with including it there is its location and that, for a top-end hotel, is a crucial factor. Basically, they got it wrong.

Milimani/Hurlingham Most of the other mid-range hotels are along Milimani, Ralph Bunche and Bishops Rds but there are others scattered around the fringes of the city centre and particularly in Westlands. Many of them are very popular with travellers as well as UN and NGO staffers.

Very popular indeed with travellers and expatriates on contract work is the *Heron Court Hotel* (☎ 720740; fax 721698), Milimani Rd, PO Box 41848. It's a large place, all the rooms have attached bathrooms with hot water, there's a swimming pool, sauna and massage parlour and guarded residents' car park. It's very good value at KSh 750/890 for singles/doubles with soap, towels and toilet paper provided. There are also apartments with a double bedroom, separate lounge with balcony, bathroom and fully equipped kitchen for KSh 900/1050. Breakfast is not included in the room rates. The staff here are friendly and helpful but you're advised not to leave valuables in your room – use the safe at reception. At the front of the hotel is one of Nairobi's most popular bar/restaurants, Buffalo Bill's, which is open daily from early morning until around 11 pm.

Right at the top of Milimani Rd at the Ralph Bunche Rd intersection is the *Sagret*

Hotel (☎ 720934), PO Box 18324, which is of a somewhat higher standard than the Heron Court and offers singles/doubles with attached bathrooms for KSh 1925/2950 and triples for KSh 3500 including breakfast. If you stay for a minimum of one week there's a 10% discount on these rates. The hotel has its own bar and restaurant (very popular for nyama choma) and accepts Visa and MasterCard. There's also plenty of parking space.

In between the Sagret and the Heron Court is the *Milimani Hotel* (☎ 720760; fax 722430), PO Box 30715. This is a huge, rambling place popular with expatriates on contract and charges KSh 2700/3780 for singles/doubles with attached bathrooms and KSh 5290 for triples including breakfast for residents. Children between the ages of two and 12 years are charged 50% of the adult rates. There are also more expensive apartments complete with fully equipped kitchens. Facilities at the hotel include a swimming pool, bar, beer garden, restaurant and guarded parking. Meal prices in the restaurant here are KSh 450 (buffet lunch) and KSh 500 (dinner).

Turning left at the Milimani/Ralph Bunche Rds junction and going about 50m, you come to the *Lenana Mount Hotel* (☎ 717044; fax 218809), Ralph Bunche Rd, PO Box 40943. This a fairly small but very pleasant hotel with facilities which include a swimming pool, restaurant and two bars as well as 24-hour room service. It's pretty good value at KSh 2800/4100 including breakfast. Casual meals here cost KSh 150 (breakfast), KSh 200 (lunch) and KSh 230 (dinner).

On Bishops Rd at the back of the Panafric Hotel is the *Fairview Hotel* (☎ 723211; fax 721320), PO Box 40842. Billed as 'the country hotel in the city' (with some justification due to its pleasant garden and quiet location), it offers singles/doubles with shared bath for KSh 2300/3700 or KSh 2800/4400 with private bath. There are also family units and balcony doubles for KSh 4800. All the rooms have a telephone, TV and video service, and prices include breakfast. Other meals average around KSh 400 (set menu) and there's an authentic African buffet every Tuesday and Friday for the same price. The bar has draught Tusker. Guests are entitled to use the swimming pool at the Panafric Hotel.

The long-established *Hurlingham Hotel* (☎ 721920), PO Box 43158, on Argwings Kodhek Rd, west of the Hurlingham shopping centre, is also a popular place to stay. Set in a large garden, it exudes a rustic charm but it's small and often full. Many of the people who stay here return time and time again, so it's best to ring in advance and make sure a room is available. There's a bar and restaurant and it costs KSh 1000/1600 with breakfast. All the rooms have shared facilities.

Parklands A popular place to stay here is the *Sirona Hotel* (☎ 742730), Kolobot Rd, off Forest Rd, on the fringes of Parklands. It's sometimes used by safari companies to accommodate their clients. It's a quiet place and costs KSh 1050/1500 for 'executive' singles/doubles and KSh 1400/1950 for 'VIP' singles/doubles including breakfast. There's a large restaurant and bar area (decorated with some excellent prints of Ernest Watson's paintings – check out 'Night Life at the Studio'), a beer garden, a pool table and ample safe parking. Most major credit cards are accepted.

Places to Stay – top end

In a city the size of Nairobi there are naturally many top-range hotels, some of them in the city centre and others outside this immediate area. If you are planning on staying in one it is worth booking through one of the travel agencies in town, instead of paying the so-called 'rack rates', as an agency can often get you a considerable discount. At the Serena, for example, it's possible to get a discount of nearly 40% by booking through United Touring Company.

City Centre On Muindi Mbingu St, between Standard St and Kenyatta Ave, is the *Six-eighty Hotel* (☎ 332680; fax 332908), PO Box 43436. This is a large hotel and good

value at KSh 3375/4230 for standard singles/ doubles and KSh 5085 for triples. Deluxe singles/doubles are KSh 4050/5075 with triples at KSh 6100. Breakfast is not included. The hotel has its own terrace bar and restaurant and, although the food in the restaurant is quite good, the terrace bar is nothing special – it's like a wind tunnel. They also put on live bands occasionally, usually at the weekends in the bar.

Better value and with considerably better facilities and a garden setting is the *Boulevard Hotel* (☎ 227567; fax 334071), Harry Thuku Rd, PO Box 42831. It offers rooms with bathroom, balcony, telephone and radio for KSh 3600/4300 for a single/double and KSh 4800 a triple including taxes but excluding breakfast. Facilities include a swimming pool, tennis court, restaurant, barbecue, bar, and beer garden. If you hear stories about the swimming pool being dangerous on account of out-of-control matatus plunging into it off adjacent Chiromo Rd, you can put your mind at rest. That did happen on two occasions in the past but now a fence has been erected which you'd need a tank to get through.

The *Ambassadeur Hotel* (☎ 336803; fax 211472), PO Box 30399, is right in the city centre on Moi Ave and is part of the Sarova Hotels chain. Unfortunately there is no escaping the fact that this place is terribly shabby and run-down, which is a great pity given the excellent location. It has singles/ doubles with attached bathrooms for US$40/ 50 excluding breakfast (US$7 extra). The hotel has a bar and, on the ground floor, a good restaurant with lunch/dinner for around KSh 500.

Also in the centre is the *New Stanley Hotel* (☎ 333233; fax 229388), PO Box 30680, on the corner of Kimathi St and Kenyatta Ave. It was built in 1907 and despite numerous subsequent renovations still has a touch of colonial charm. Singles/doubles (including breakfast and taxes) cost KSh 3850/4600 for residents or US$103/138 for nonresidents. There are also more expensive suites. All the rooms are air-conditioned with colour TV (including cable) and have direct-dial telephones. Facilities include a rooftop swimming pool, two restaurants, a ballroom, bar, health club and shops. At street level, there's the popular Thorn Tree Cafe, though the food here is mediocre and service can be agonisingly slow.

Nairobi's *Hilton Hotel* (☎ 334000; fax 339462), PO Box 30624, on Mama Ngina St near Moi Ave, has all the usual Hilton facilities including a rooftop swimming pool, and the rooms are very well appointed. Singles/doubles here go for US$128/166, while executive rooms with breakfast and complimentary bar are US$225/257, but to all these prices you must add a total of 33% in taxes!

The nearby *Inter-Continental Hotel* (☎ 335550; fax 210675), PO Box 30353, on City Hall Way, is an excellent place since its recent refurbishment. There is of course a swimming pool, as well as business centre, a couple of restaurants and bars, and an airport shuttle bus. Room rates are US$160/200, plus 27% taxes.

Close to the top of the line (though they bill themselves as the *creme de la creme*) you'll find the *Norfolk Hotel* (☎ 335422; fax 336742), PO Box 40064, on Harry Thuku Rd; the *Nairobi Serena Hotel* (☎ 725111; fax 725184), PO Box 46302, the edge of Central Park between Kenyatta Ave and Nyerere Rd, and the *Nairobi Safari Club* (☎ 330621; fax 331201; e-mail nsclub@arcc.or.ke), PO Box 43564, University Way.

The Norfolk is the oldest of Nairobi's hotels – it was built in 1904 – and was *the* place to stay in the old days. It's still extremely popular among those with a taste for nostalgia and the money to spend. All the old world charm has been retained despite facilities having been brought up to international standards. Singles/doubles in the main block cost US$210/220 plus there are suites for US$275 to US$410 and cottages for US$410 to US$570. Residents are charged KSh 6000 for singles or doubles. The prices do not include breakfast which is an extra KSh 350. Other meals are available for KSh 770 each. The Norfolk, which is owned by Lonrho Hotels, has a popular terrace bar (The Lord Delamere) and restaurant.

The Nairobi Serena is a much more recent hotel and imaginatively designed. It's owned by the Serena Lodges group and has singles/doubles for US$165/195 with suites for US$250 to US$430 plus a 10% service charge, 2% training levy and 15% VAT. It has all the facilities you'd expect from a five-star hotel. Even Jimmy Carter stays here. Meals cost US$12 (breakfast), US$18 (lunch) and US$20 (dinner) plus taxes.

The Nairobi Safari Club is a very modern building overlooking Nairobi University and has a very imposing entrance and lobby. All the rooms here are suites and the price includes temporary membership, although this doesn't entitle you to a jolly thing. The ordinary suites are priced at US$195/225 for singles/doubles plus there are presidential suites for US$485 a single or double. Note that these rates include taxes.

Top of the line is the *The Grand Regency Hotel* (☎ 211199; fax 217120), PO Box 57549, Loita St, which is at the centre of a long drawn-out legal battle between the owner, Kamlesh Pattni, and the Central Bank of Kenya. It's the ultimate in luxury (although it is done in dubious taste) and costs KSh 8000 to KSh 12,000 a single and KSh 11,000 to KSh 15,000 a double with suites ranging from KSh 24,500 to KSh 70,000. It's where the politicians bring people when they want to talk about megabuck loans and deals.

Up on the 'border' of Westlands and Parklands is the *Mayfair Court Hotel* (☎ 740920; fax 748823), PO Box 66807, Parklands Rd. This is a large, colonial-style hotel situated in its own beautifully maintained grounds and offers standard singles/doubles at US$110/145 and superior rooms at US$135/170 for singles/doubles including breakfast. Children aged between three and 12 years are charged 50% of the adult rates. There are two swimming pools, a health club, the popular Mischiefs Bar and a free shuttle bus service every hour to the city centre.

Milimani A little outside of the city centre where Kenyatta Ave turns into Valley Rd is the *Panafric Hotel* (☎ 720822; fax 726356), PO Box 30486. Part of the Sarova Hotels

NAIROBI

chain, it's a large, multistorey modern hotel with all the facilities you'd expect. Rooms here cost KSh 2950/4200 a single/double, plus there are more expensive suites. Prices include breakfast and all taxes.

Westlands Just beyond the main Westlands roundabout off Waiyaki Way is the *Landmark Hotel* (☎ 448713/7; fax 448977), PO Box 14287, which is part of the Block Hotels chain. It's a pleasant place to stay and was recently refurbished. Room rates are US$76/110 for singles/doubles including breakfast. There is also a free shuttle bus for guests between the hotel and the centre of town.

Thika Road A few km out of the centre on the Thika Rd is the swish *Safari Park Hotel* (☎ 802493; fax 802477), PO Box 45038. Set on a 25-hectare site, this hotel features soaring makuti roofs, lots of woodwork, a huge landscaped pool and lush gardens. It's certainly an escape from the city centre, and there's a separate casino complex on the site. Other facilities include a fitness centre, as well as tennis and squash courts. All the rooms have cable TV, mini-bar and four-poster beds, and the cost is US$155/180, or

PLACES TO STAY
2   Landmark Hotel
13 Mayfair Court Hotel & Mischiefs

PLACES TO EAT
1   Minar Restaurant (Sarit Centre Shopping Centre)
3   New Pizza Garden
9   Beijing Restaurant
10 Westlands Rendezvous
11 Stop Italia
12 Chinese Corner Restaurant
14 Nirula & Open House Restaurants
15 Mauriya Indian Restaurant
16 Manchurian Restaurant
17 Jiangsu Chinese Restaurant (Soin Shopping Arcade)
20 Zee Café & Haandi (The Mall Shopping Centre)

OTHER
4   Gypsie Bar
5   Meatmasters & Westland Sundries Bookshop
6   Service Stations
7   Market
8   Undugu Craft Shop
18 Post Office
19 Bus & Matatu Stands
21 Bus & Matatu Stands
22 Eritrean Embassy, Thai Cuisine Restaurant & Palakhi Indian Restaurant (New Rehema House)

there are double suites ranging from US$210 to US$700, all plus 27% taxes. Although it is quite a way from the city centre, there is a free shuttle bus into town every hour on the half hour from 8.30 am to 10.30 pm. The buses leave the city centre on the hour from 9 am to 11 pm from outside the Nakumatt supermarket on the corner of Kenyatta Ave and Kimathi St.

Places to Eat

For most people with limited means, lunch is the main meal of the day and this is what the cheaper restaurants cater for. That doesn't mean that they're all closed in the evening (though quite a few are). It does mean, however, that what is available in the early evening is often what is left over from lunch time and the choice is limited. If you want a full meal in the evening it generally involves eating from a mid-range (or better) restaurant, or from a barbecue attached to a bar.

Nairobi is replete with restaurants offering cuisines from all over the world – Italian, Spanish, Japanese, Chinese, Korean, Indian, Lebanese, and Thai. There are also steak houses, seafood specialists etc and at many places the prices are surprisingly reasonable. For around KSh 450 per person you can eat well at quite a few of them. For KSh 600 to KSh 750 per person you'd be looking at a banquet and if you spent that much at some of them you'd hardly need to eat anything the next day.

While there is a good selection of restaurants in the city centre, increasing numbers of restaurants are opening up in the suburbs, which makes it difficult if you don't have transport as taxis are expensive. The two main eating centres away from the downtown area are the Westlands shopping centre, about two km north of the centre along Uhuru Highway, and the Yaya Centre, about three km west of the centre on Argwings Kodhek Rd in Hurlingham.

Cheap Cafes & Restaurants There are a lot of very cheap cafes and restaurants in the Latema Rd/River Rd area and at the top end of Tom Mboya St where you can pick up a

very cheap, traditional African breakfast of mandazi (a semisweet doughnut) and tea or coffee. Most of these places would also be able to fix you up with eggs and the like. Since many of them are Indian-run, they also have traditional Indian breakfast foods like samosa and idli (rice dumplings) with a sauce.

The *Malindi Dishes* restaurant in Gaberone Rd is well worth trying at least once. As the name suggests, the food here has the Swahili influence of the coast, and so coconut and spices are used to rev up what is otherwise pretty ordinary cuisine. Main dishes are around KSh 100 to KSh 150 and the usual snacks and burgers are also available.

Also in this area is the *New Bedona Cafe* opposite the Dolat Hotel on Mfangano St. The food here is mostly fried, but it's cheap and the place is kept very clean. Another ultra-cheap cafe which is fairly popular is the *Bull Cafe* around the corner from the New Kenya Lodge on Ngariama Lane.

For a good solid meal (mixing western and local cuisine) such as steak and matoke (mashed plantains and maize) or maharagwe (kidney beans), try the *Cafe Helena* on Mama Ngina St opposite the City Hall. It's only open at lunch time and is popular with businesspeople. Meals are priced at around KSh 120 and are excellent value. The *Coffee Bar* next door is similar although more expensive. Another place at this end of town is the *Beneve Coffee House* on the corner of Standard and Koinange Sts. It has a tasty selection of self-service food ranging from stews to curries, fish and chips, sambusa, pasties and a host of other choices. It's good value.

Very popular with the lunch time business crowd is the *Jacaranda Cafe* in the Phoenix House Arcade between Kenyatta Ave and Standard St. A hamburger, chips and salad costs around KSh 150.

An excellent place for submarine sandwiches, cakes and decent coffee is the *Pasara* cafe on Standard St. This self-service place has an open-air patio and an indoor nonsmoking area, and newspapers and magazines are available for reading while you eat. They also do a good breakfast here for KSh 280.

If you're staying at Mrs Roche's up in Parklands, the *Stop 'n' Eat* tin shed just up the road offers ugali (maize meal) and ngombe (beef) at very modest prices.

Kenya is the home of all-you-can-eat lunches at a set price and Nairobi has a wide choice of them, most offering Indian food. One of the best is the *Supreme Restaurant* on River Rd at the roundabout, which offers an excellent Indian (Punjabi) vegetarian thali for KSh 220. It also has superb fruit juices.

Excellent value for breakfast and lunch in the city centre is the *Calypso* in the basement of Bruce House, Standard St. Here you can choose from a limited set menu (including meat and seafood) or the buffet lunch. Count on spending around KSh 250. It's a very popular place to eat at lunch times (despite the sloppy service) so get there early if you don't want to wait for a table. Try the fish pili pili – it's delicious.

Another good place to go for lunch and well-cooked, straightforward food is the *Harvest Cafe* on Kenyatta Ave between Koinange and Loita Sts. It's a very pleasant spot to eat and the service is brisk.

The *Jax Restaurant* on the 1st floor of the Old Mutual building, Kimathi St, is a very popular place for lunch. It offers a wide selection of beautifully prepared hot meals, and has an open-air section. The weekday lunch time buffet features Indian and continental dishes, and is good value at KSh 275. Also good value are the burgers, which come with the ubiquitous chips and salad, from KSh 130. It's open from 8 am to 5 pm Monday to Saturday.

Equally popular at lunch time is the *Dancing Spoons Wine Bar* on the 1st floor of the 20th Century Cinema on Mama Ngina St. It has an excellent range of western-style dishes at very reasonable prices (KSh 150 to KSh 250). Directly above (on the 2nd floor) is the wine bar – if you prefer to sit in here rather than the restaurant section, you can still order meals from downstairs. The entrance to this place is the same as for the cinema.

If you're up in Westlands at lunch time, there are several places where you can find a snack lunch cheaply. They include the *Zee Cafe*, in the basement of The Mall shopping centre; the *Open House Restaurant* on the ground floor under Nirula on Mpaka Rd which offers Indian mini-meals; and the *Westlands Rendezvous* on Woodvale Grove which offers African and European-style meals in its open-air cafe for KSh 120 to KSh 220. The manager of the Rendezvous is very friendly, the food is good and beer is available. It's open up until 8 pm. There's also a popular coffee shop with snacks on the ground floor of the Sarit Centre.

If you don't mind spending a little over the odds, the pizzas in the Landmark Hotel's *New Pizza Garden* are excellent and cost between KSh 175 and KSh 200. It also has a range of other dishes at about the same price, and there's live music on Sunday afternoon. The pizza garden is just over the road from the actual hotel and alongside Waiyaki Way.

Fast Food That well-known English staple, fish and chips, has caught on in a big way in Nairobi and there are scores of places offering it. They're all cheap but the quality varies from greasy and stale to excellent. The number of customers in the shop is one way to separate the good from the mediocre but the best way is to poke your nose inside and to take a look at the chips. If you smell anything stale or the chips are soggy, give the place a miss.

Very popular at lunch time for fish and chips is *Supermac* on Kimathi St (directly opposite the Thorn Tree Cafe) on the mezzanine floor of the shopping centre there. It not only offers some of the best fish and chips in Nairobi, but also serves sausages, salads and fruit juices.

Also recommended for this type of fast food is the *Prestige Restaurant*, in Tsavo Lane off Latema Rd, which offers large servings of sausage, chips and salad for KSh 100. It's popular with local people.

The hamburger is all-conquering in Nairobi too, though, surprisingly, none of the US chains have got a foothold in Kenya yet.

Too much competition from Indian entrepreneurs perhaps? Or perhaps they don't grow the right variety of potatoes in Limuru? What has got a solid foothold is the *Wimpy* chain which has branches on Kenyatta Ave, Tom Mboya St and Mondlane St. These places have the usual range of snacks and meals (burgers, sausages, eggs, fish, chicken, milk shakes etc) costing up to KSh 200. They are open from 7.30 am to 9.30 pm.

Another good cafe for a meal of burgers, fish or chicken with a mountain of chips and salad for around KSh 170 to KSh190 is *Nairobi Burgers* on Tom Mboya St right opposite the end of Latema Rd. Sweets, soups and ice cream are also served – it's a very popular place.

Also on Tom Mboya St, down near the Princess Hotel, is the *Pipes Restaurant*. This is a US-style, fast food place with all the usual junk-food snacks.

For take-away chicken & chips, you can't beat the amazingly popular *Kenchic Inn*, on the corner of Moktar Daddah and Muindi Mbingu Sts. It sells a phenomenal number of roast chickens every day.

Breakfast The *Growers Cafe* on Tom Mboya St is deservedly popular with both local people and travellers and the prices are reasonable. Food on offer includes eggs (boiled or fried), sausages and other hot foods, fruit salads (with or without yoghurt) and good coffee. Right upstairs is the *Swara Restaurant*, which also does a decent mandazi and tea breakfast, as well as good-value buffet lunches featuring Kenyan food.

If you're staying in the Koinange St area, the *Dove Cage Restaurant* on Moktar Daddah St next to the Terminal Hotel is an excellent little place. A full breakfast with juice and coffee sets you back around KSh 140, and the service is fast and friendly. Very similar is *Calypso* in the basement of Bruce House on Standard St where you can get an English-style breakfast for KSh 120.

For a breakfast splurge, try one of the buffets at a major hotel. The *Illiki Cafe* on the ground floor of the Ambassadeur Hotel on Moi Ave is excellent value. Here you can

tuck in for KSh 390. It offers the works – a variety of juices, milk, yoghurt, cereals, porridge, eggs, bacon, beans, sausages, toast, fruits, cakes – you name it.

Most of the other top-end hotels also do buffet breakfasts, although they are more expensive. The best value is offered by the *New Stanley Hotel* where a continental buffet breakfast costs KSh 450, or a full English breakfast is KSh 650. At the *Hilton* you're looking at about the same while the *Inter-Continental* charges KSh 550/750. If you'd like to breakfast in colonial nostalgia then the *Norfolk Hotel* would have to be the choice. A full continental/English breakfast here costs KSh 700/750.

More Expensive Restaurants The choice here is legion and spans many cuisines. Most of them are mentioned in the *Tourist's Kenya*, though there's no indication of prices.

Most of the more expensive restaurants are licensed and offer beer, wine and spirits but the major exceptions are the Indian vegetarian restaurants which usually offer only fruit juices and tea or coffee. Virtually all these restaurants accept credit cards.

Indian The *Mayur Restaurant* (☎ 331586), above the Supreme Restaurant (see Cheap Cafes & Restaurants) has been famous for superb Indian vegetarian food for years. It's not bad value at KSh 250/280 for a buffet lunch/dinner, but the hushed atmosphere can be a bit daunting.

Also excellent is the *Minar Restaurant* (☎ 229999) in Banda St, which specialises in Mughlai dishes and offers buffet lunches and à la carte dinners. Expect to pay around KSh 500 for a three-course dinner including coffee but excluding alcoholic drinks. The restaurant is licensed, the service friendly and the restaurant is open from noon to 2 pm and 7 to 10.30 pm daily. It also has branches at the Yaya Centre (☎ 561676), Argwings Kodhek Rd, Hurlingham; and at the Sarit Centre (☎ 748340), Westlands. All three of the Minar restaurants have a delicious all-you-can-eat buffet lunch on Sundays with a vast array of dishes (Indian and continental) and desserts all for KSh 425 including tax. These Sunday buffets are superb value so forget about breakfast on Sunday morning. Credit cards are accepted.

The *Zam Zam Restaurant* (☎ 212128), just off Kilome Rd near the top end of River Rd, is a modern place with pleasing decor and good service. The food is good, and remarkably cheap, yet this place remains relatively poorly patronised, perhaps because of its location close to River Rd. Main dishes are all under KSh 250 and the servings are generous.

Another good and relatively cheap place is the *Safeer Restaurant* (☎ 336803) in the Ambassadeur Hotel. Despite appearances, this place is not expensive and two people can eat well here for KSh 600 including a couple of beers. The food is mainly north Indian, and there are complimentary salads, chutney and pickle.

Out at Westlands there are three excellent Indian restaurants. The best of the lot, according to local residents, is the *Haandi* (☎ 448294/5) on the 1st floor of The Mall shopping centre. It's open every day including public holidays from 12.30 to 2.30 pm and 7.30 to 10.30 pm. Judge for yourself. Beautifully conceived and divided into three parts is the *Mauriya Indian Restaurant* on the corner of Mpaka and Muthithi Rds. It's a luxurious place and plainly has no interest in catering to the lunch time crowds as it's only open for dinner from 7.30 pm to 1.30 am daily. This is where you come for a long, languorous dinner with your lover. Credit cards? They'll do nicely, thankyou very much. Lastly, there's the newly opened *Palakhi Indian Restaurant* in New Rehema House at the junction of Rhapta Rd and Ring Road Westlands not far from the Westlands roundabout.

West African The *West African Paradise Restaurant* (☎ 741396) is in Rank Xerox House in Westlands. It offers a wide range of food from a number of West African countries and dishes include poulet yassa (chicken with onions and garlic sauce), jollof (rice with onions), and fufu (maize). It's

quite different food and is well worth a try if you haven't been to West Africa. The restaurant is open daily from 9.30 am to 9.30 pm.

Chinese Nairobi has a reasonable selection of Chinese restaurants although none of them are particularly cheap. Probably the cheapest is the *Great Chung Wah*, opposite the Sixeighty Hotel on Muindi Mbingu St. The KSh 250 lunch-time platter is good value and à la carte dishes cost from KSh 200 to KSh 300.

The *Hong Kong Restaurant* (☎ 228612) in College House on Koinange St is very popular at lunch time and the food is good but the decor and furnishings are a bit sparse. The soups here at KSh 150 to KSh 180 make a meal in themselves, but if you have room for more, main dishes cost around KSh 200 to KSh 300.

In Shankardas House, on Moi Ave near the Kenya Cinema complex, is the stylish *Pagoda Restaurant* (☎ 227036). Again, the food here is mainly Szechuan, and you can expect a complete meal to come to around KSh 600 with drinks.

The *Dragon Pearl* (☎ 340451), in Bruce House on Standard St, also has good Chinese food at prices comparable to the other more expensive restaurants. It's open daily for lunch and dinner.

Rated as the best Chinese restaurant in town by some residents is the *Rickshaw Chinese Restaurant* (☎ 223604), in Fedha Towers, Standard St. It has an extensive menu and the food is delicious. Again, you can expect to spend at least KSh 600 per person here.

Also very good if you're staying in the Milimani area is the *China Town Restaurant* on Ralph Bunche Rd adjacent to the Lenana Mount Hotel.

Up in Westlands are another four Chinese restaurants. They all compete with each other in terms of excellence of cuisine and mellow surroundings. Top of the line is probably the *Jiangsu Chinese Restaurant* on the 2nd floor of the Soin shopping arcade. This is a huge place but very classy – so classy, in fact, it's only open for dinner so adjust your wallet accordingly. Round the corner from here is *Nirula* on Mpaka Rd at the junction with Muthithi Rd. It has an open rooftop area as well as a closed section; credit cards are accepted. A stone's throw from here is the *Chinese Corner Restaurant* which is somewhat cheaper but just as good. The *Beijing Restaurant* (☎ 447494), Woodvale Grove, is also very good. It's open from 10.30 am to 2.30 pm and 6 to 10.30 pm and accepts credit cards.

Mongolian The only place you'll find this cuisine is at the *Manchurian Restaurant* (☎ 444263/4), Brick Court, on the corner of Mpaka Rd and Brookvale Grove in Westlands. Here you choose from a range of marinated meats, vegetables, condiments and spices and have your meal cooked in front of you on giant hot plates. A meal costs around KSh 400 (excluding drinks) and you can go back as many times as you like for more of the same or something else so don't pile everything onto the first plate! The secret of putting your own banquet together here is modesty over several dishes. It's open Monday to Saturday from 12.30 pm (lunch) and 7.30 pm (dinner). Credit cards are accepted.

Thai The *Bangkok Restaurant* (☎ 751311), Rank Xerox House, Parklands Rd, Westlands, has been in business now for a number of years and has a good reputation for authentic Thai food. It's open daily from 12.30 to 2.30 pm and 6 to 10.30 pm. Another Thai restaurant has recently opened on the top floor of New Rehema House at the junction of Rhapta Rd and Ring Road Westlands not far from the Westlands roundabout. This is the *Thai Cuisine Restaurant* which is open for lunch and dinner daily. At either place you can eat well for KSh 400 per person.

Italian For Italian food there is the long-running and very popular *Trattoria* (☎ 340855) on the corner of Wabera and Kaunda Sts. It is open daily from 8.30 am to 11.30 pm and

both the atmosphere and the food are excellent. There's a wide choice on the menu and à la carte is available at lunch time. In the evening it's all à la carte. A soup, main course, salad, dessert and a carafe or two of house chianti will relieve you of around KSh 600 to KSh 700 per person. As you might expect, the ice cream here is superb.

Probably just as good, but lacking the same reputation (and therefore, prices), is *La Scala*, on Standard St near Muindi Mbingu St. This place specialises in Italian food but also has western dishes such as steaks and burgers. Pizzas and pasta dishes cost KSh 150 to KSh 190, steaks are KSh 260. It's open daily from 7 am to midnight and is very popular with Kenyans looking for a modestly priced decent meal in pleasant surroundings.

Also worth a try is the *Marino Restaurant* (☎ 227150), 1st floor, National Housing Corporation building, Aga Khan Walk, just off Haile Selassie Ave. It has a spacious interior dining area as well as an open-air patio and is open from 9 am to 2 pm and 7 to 10 pm Monday to Saturday; closed on Sunday. There's a wide range of Italian and continental dishes available with main courses priced from KSh 190 to KSh 300.

Also good is the *Capolinea* in The Mall shopping centre at Westlands. This is more of a cafe-style place, and this is reflected in the prices – around KSh 90 to KSh 170 for snacks and sandwiches.

Another excellent place away from the centre is the *La Cucina* (☎ 562871) in the Yaya Centre in Hurlingham. It has everything from pasta to steak, home delivery is available, and there's an attached wine bar. Prices are a bit on the high side, but it's still popular.

The new *l'ora blu* should be open by now. It is a restaurant, wine bar, disco and live-music venue on the corner of Kimathi and Mama Ngina Sts. In its previous incarnation as the Foresta Magnetica it served excellent Italian food and had a fine atmosphere, although it wasn't all that cheap. As the management hasn't changed it should still be worth a look.

Greek & Middle Eastern At the Yaya Centre in Hurlingham there's the *Sugar & Spice (Zorba the Treat)* (☎ 562876) which is a modest place serving a wide variety of snacks. Also here is the *Patra Bakery*, an informal eatery serving Middle Eastern favourites such as felafel (KSh 150) and doner kebabs (KSh 180).

Japanese There's one Japanese restaurant in the city centre, the *Akasaka* (☎ 333948), which you'll find on Standard St opposite Bruce House between Koinange and Muindi Mbingu Sts. It's done out in traditional Japanese style and there's even a tatami room which you can reserve in advance though mostly it's table and chairs. It offers the full range of Japanese cuisine including tempura, teriyaki and sukiyaki as well as soups and appetisers. A full meal costs KSh 400 to KSh 800 per person. It's licensed and open daily from 12.30 to 2 pm for box lunches, and from 6 to 9 pm for dinner.

Korean The only Korean restaurant in Nairobi is the *Restaurant Koreana* in the Yaya Centre, Hurlingham. The food is excellent and authentic but it's expensive. A full meal costs around KSh 800 to KSh 1000 and the restaurant is licensed. It's open from noon to 2.30 pm and 6 to 10.30 pm Monday to Saturday and closed Sunday.

Ethiopian The *Daas* Ethiopian restaurant is in an old house, some distance from the centre off Ngong Rd (signposted) about halfway between Kenyatta Hospital roundabout and the Adams Arcade shopping centre. The décor includes many Ethiopian artefacts and there's often live music in the evenings. Meals are based around excellent unleavened bread and are eaten with the fingers. Expect to pay around KSh 400 to KSh 500 per person for a full meal including drinks.

Seafood The best seafood restaurant in Nairobi is the *Tamarind* (☎ 338959) in the National Bank building on Aga Khan Walk, between Harambee and Haile Selassie Aves.

It offers a wide selection of exotic seafood dishes, and culinary influences range from European to Asian to coastal Swahili. The cuisine is superb as are the surroundings which are decorated in a sumptuous Arabic-Moorish style. Eating here is definitely a major night out as most main courses are priced well over KSh 400 with crab and prawn dishes up to KSh 750. There's also a special vegetarian menu. It's open for lunch Monday to Saturday from 12.30 to 1.45 pm and daily for dinner from 6.30 to 9.45 pm.

Western A good restaurant for plain meat and vegie dishes (eg sausages and mashed potato) is the *Zanze Bar* (☎ 222532) on the top floor of the Kenya Cinema Plaza, Moi Ave, though a range of other dishes are also available. It's open for lunch and dinner daily but is not strictly a restaurant alone – more a combination of bar, wine bar, live music venue and restaurant. You can also play chess, darts and backgammon here. The food is good, reasonably priced (around KSh 250 per person), but you must pay an extra KSh 100 entry in the evenings (free during the day).

The *Hard Rock Cafe* (☎ 220802), on the mezzanine floor, Barclays Plaza, Loita/Market Sts, has become very popular since it opened up a few years ago. It's a much more spacious and interesting place than its sister establishment in Mombasa and the food is good though not particularly cheap at around KSh 250 to KSh 350 for a main course. It's open daily from 9 am to 2 am and there's secure parking available in the building.

Not strictly western (since it does pizzas and Indian dishes, too) but exclusively vegetarian is the *Slush Happy Eater* (☎ 220745), Tubman Rd off Kimathi St. In addition to grilled sandwiches and hot drinks it also offers fresh juices and dessert.

Nyama Choma For steak eaters who haven't seen a decent doorstep since they left Argentina, Australia, Uruguay or the USA and are looking for a gut-busting extravaganza then there's no better place than the *Carnivore* (☎ 501709), out at Langata just past Wilson airport. Whether it's lunch or dinner you take there's always beef, pork, lamb, ham, chicken, sausages and at least three game meats (such as ostrich, eland, hartebeest, crocodile, often wildebeest or zebra). The roasts are barbecued on Maasai spears and the waiters carve off hunks onto your plate until you tell them to stop. Prices include salads, bread, desserts and coffee. Meals here can be surprisingly cheap given the amount you receive and you're looking at KSh 885 for lunch from Monday to Saturday and KSh 985 on Sunday; dinner is priced at KSh 985 daily. This is a very popular tourist restaurant and the car park is usually overflowing with tourist buses. There's also a disco in the Simba Saloon on Wednesday and usually a live band on Saturday night. To get there take bus No 14, 24 or 124 and tell the conductor where you are going; the restaurant is a one-km signposted walk from where you are dropped off. It's easy to hitch back into the centre when you're ready to go. Otherwise, negotiate for a taxi.

For something a little less extravagant there's the *Nyama Choma Terrace & Bar*, above the Dhaba Restaurant at the top end of Tom Mboya St. This is a decent little place which on weekdays has nyama choma as well as a number of other Kenyan dishes, and it's very cheap. Quite a lot of the press corps come here though it's actually the bar they're most interested in.

Highly rated by residents, particularly Africans, is the nyama choma at the *Sagret Hotel*, Milimani Rd. Any day of the week you pass here, you'll see clouds of delicious-smelling smoke rising from the restaurant. The food is OK, relatively cheap and there's usually a good crowd though service can be slow. It's best to come here with a group of at least four people because you have to choose a hunk of meat from the refrigerated display and there'll be enough meat on each to feed at least four people. Chips or kenyege are available with the roast. Count on around KSh 200 to KSh 300 per person plus drinks. It's open for lunch and dinner everyday.

A definite step down the scale, but worth it for the atmosphere, are the 20 or more wooden shacks of the NSSF Market on the corner of Loita St and Kenyatta Ave. Here you can eat good choma for around KSh 80, and also sample many other Kenyan dishes such as matoke and kenyege. This is a very popular place among the city's office workers, and although foreigners are a rare sight here, you'll be warmly welcomed. Also good are the stalls at the Kariokor Market, across the river east of the city centre.

For authentic, no-frills Nairobi nyama choma the only place to go is the suburb of Kilmichael, some distance from the centre out past Pangani and Eastleigh. It's certainly not for the squeamish as the goats are slaughtered only a few metres away from where you eat and are then barbecued right in front of you, but there's no doubting the freshness of the meat! This is not a place to go to alone, however, as the people here are not used to seeing wazungu and while it's not threatening, it's best to be in the company of a reliable Kenyan. You probably wouldn't find it on your own anyway. African prices apply here so it's cheaper than anywhere else you'll find. Even Smith Hempstone, a former American ambassador to Kenya, once came here, much to the displeasure of the government – Kilmichael isn't exactly ambassadorial territory.

Entertainment

Cinema Nairobi is a good place to take in a few films and at a price substantially lower than what you'd pay back home, but if you don't want scratched films then go to one of the better cinemas such as *Kenya Plaza* on Moi Ave, or *20th Century* on Mama Ngina St. Expect to pay KSh 80 to KSh 100 to see a film. The cheaper ones are on Latema Rd and include the *Odeon* and *Embassy*. The *Cameo* on Kenyatta Ave is also relatively cheap. There are also two good drive-ins if you have the transport: both have snack bars and bars.

Discos There's a good selection of discos in the centre of Nairobi and there are no dress rules, though there's an unspoken assumption that you'll turn up looking half-decent.

Perhaps the most popular disco in the centre of town is the *Florida 2000* on Moi Ave near City Hall Way. The entry fee depends on the night but is between KSh 120 and KSh 180 for men and half that for women and it's open until 6 am. If you want a break from Maria Carey and Black Box, there's a bar and restaurant upstairs which is often just as lively as the mayhem below.

Also very popular is the *New Florida* (known locally as the 'Mad House'), near the corner of Koinange and Banda Sts, which is a mushroom-shaped building above a petrol station! This is a much smaller place than the 2000 though entry charges are the same. It stays open until 6 am and there's a downstairs bar/restaurant where you can find temporary respite from the madness. There are floor shows at about 1 am at both of the Floridas and the dancers are good but it's pretty kitsch.

Another popular disco in the centre is *Visions* on Kimathi St which is open daily except Monday from 9 pm. Less popular but more down-to-earth is the *Hollywood* on Moktar Daddah St between Koinange and Muindi Mbingu Sts where the entry charges are the same as the Floridas.

Further out of town is *Bubbles* at the International Casino, Westlands Rd/Museum Hill, just off Uhuru Highway. This disco is favoured by young people of Asian origin so it's not quite as gutsy as the Floridas.

If you're in the Milimani Rd area, check out *Fredz* next door to the China Town Restaurant on Ralph Bunche Rd. It's open in the evenings from around 6 pm but the disco doesn't fire up until later on. If you get there early there's no cover charge.

There's a live band/disco every Wednesday night at the *Simba Saloon* at the Carnivore in Langata but entry costs KSh 200 per person. There's usually a good crowd and it makes a refreshing change from the more enclosed and crowded space of the discos in town.

Beer in all these places is reasonably priced but other drinks, especially imported liquors, are more expensive. Snacks and meals are available at all of them.

Theatre The *Phoenix Theatre*, Parliament Rd, has a small auditorium which hosts professional productions by the local Nairobi Players drama group, but it's quite expensive. Check with local papers to see what's on.

Live Music In the next block to the Florida 2000 on Moi Ave and on the top floor of the Kenya Cinema Plaza, is the *Zanze Bar*, which has live music most nights. This bar offers a good alternative to the discos, and there's a small cover charge. Drinks are reasonably priced and the toilets have a blackboard on which you can scrawl jokes or obscenities.

Zingara Percussion is a local group which performs every Saturday afternoon at the *Hoggers Eating Place* on Muindi Mbingu St opposite Jeevanjee Gardens.

Much further out of town, right by the roundabout at Dagoretti Corner on Ngong Rd, is the *Bombax Club* which has live bands every Thursday, Friday, Saturday and Sunday night. Unlike many of the other discos and bars mentioned in this section, this one is frequented mainly by local Kenyans with only a sprinkling of wazungu, but the atmosphere is very friendly and convivial. Again, there's a small cover charge. To get there, take a minibus or matatu to Dagoretti Corner from Kenyatta Ave outside Nyayo House, or share a taxi (about KSh 300 to KSh 400).

Jazz For a classy night out try the *Jazz Cafe* at the Yaya Centre in Hurlingham. This is both a restaurant and live music venue, and is well worth a look.

Pubs/Bars The *Thorn Tree Cafe* in the New Stanley Hotel on the corner of Kimathi St and Kenyatta Ave is something of a meeting place for tourists, although the service is generally supercilious and snail-slow. Perhaps this is just a ploy by the management to discourage 'shabby' travellers who might lower the tone of the place. Whatever the case, if you sit down between 11 am and 2 pm and 5 and 7 pm for a drink you'll have to order something to eat as well. The best thing about the Thorn Tree is the notice board where you can leave personal messages (but not advertisements of any kind, such as things for sale, or a request for people to join a safari).

The trouble is, if you pass up the Thorn Tree Cafe, there's not a lot of choice left in terms of bars in the city centre except in the seedy Latema/River Rd area. The *Zanze Bar* is OK during the day but there's a cover charge after 6 pm (presumably to keep out the riffraff). You can forget about the bars at the Hotel Inter-Continental and the Hilton Hotel as they're too expensive (KSh 120 for a bottle of beer) and the *Porterhouse* on Mama Ngina St opposite International House is cosy but essentially the haunt of Asian businessmen. The bar at the *Cameo* cinema on Kenyatta Ave is a bit rough and ready and has a noisy jukebox and the *Afro Unity Bar* on the Muindi Mbingu St side of Jeevanjee Gardens is even more rough and ready, though it does attract students from the nearby Nairobi University and is never dull. One bar which is OK but very quiet is on the 1st floor of the Oakwood Hotel and has a balcony overlooking Kimathi St. It's far from lively but the beers are normal price and cold.

Another rough and ready Nairobi institution is the *Modern Green Day & Night Bar*, on Latema Rd next to the Sunrise Lodge. This place is open 24 hours a day, 365 days a year and the front door has never been closed since 1968. The authorities tried to close it for one day in 1989 during a national census but couldn't find the doors! It used to be a lively place for an educational evening out. These days it seems to have passed its use-by date; late at night, which used to be the liveliest time, it seems that half the patrons are comatose, the other half very nearly so, the juke box lies idle and the atmosphere is, well, downbeat.

Much livelier than the Modern Green is the *Friendship Corner* bar across the road. This tiny place is another 24-hour bar and really kicks on. You'll come across all manner of people here in various stages of inebriation.

Outside of the city centre, the most popular bar among foreigners and expats is *Buffalo Bill's* at the Heron Court Hotel, Milimani Rd. While it's open all day every day until around 11 pm, it only livens up from about 5.30 pm onwards. Meals and snacks are available throughout the day and night plus nyama choma from around 6.30 pm until closing. It's here that you'll meet all of Nairobi's eccentrics, adventurers, entrepreneurs, safari operators, NGO employees, disco queens, hookers and bullshit artistes. Beers cost KSh 70, warm or cold. There's disco music most nights of the week but nowhere to dance.

Further up Milimani Rd at the junction with Ralph Bunche Rd and at the back of the Eagle Star Apartments is the *Candle Bar* (otherwise known as the *Half London*). It's an earthy and quite popular little place illuminated by kerosene lanterns. Beers are cheap (KSh 40).

Even further up Milimani Rd on the right-hand side is the *Salama Hotel Annexe*. This bar and restaurant occupies an old colonial-style house. It's a friendly place and gets very lively most evenings. Beers are cheaper here than at Buffalo Bill's and the music is not as intrusive.

Those looking for more genteel surroundings in which to sip their beer could try the *Ngong Hills Hotel* on Ngong Rd, the beer gardens at the *Boulevard* or *Landmark* hotels, or the *Lord Delamere* bar at the *Norfolk Hotel*.

Up in Westlands there are three other bars which are well worth considering if you have your own wheels or don't mind the taxi fare. *Gypsies*, at the back of Ring Road Westlands opposite Barclays Bank and close to the Landmark Hotel, is a very popular bar, with decent food and good music. It's relatively quiet and there are no hassles and it basically stays open for as long as there are still sufficient people drinking. Friday night is the night to go along to *Mischiefs* at the Mayfair Court Hotel, Parklands Rd, on the 'border' between Westlands and Parklands. It's packed out on this night with a garrulous crowd of mainly wazungu. Mischiefs has an excellent sound system and good bar snacks.

Ngong Races

Every second Sunday for most of the year there's horse racing at the Ngong Racecourse. It's a very genteel day out, and with an entry fee of KSh 50 for the members' enclosure or just KSh 20 in the public enclosure, it's hardly going to break the bank. There's betting with the bookies or the tote, and while the odds you get are hardly going to set the world on fire, it's great fun to have a punt. You can bet as little as KSh 20 so even the most impecunious should be able to afford a flutter.

Local cynics will tell you that all the races, like everything else in the country, are rigged. It may well be true, but it hardly seems to matter. There's a good restaurant on the ground floor of the grandstand and two bars with beer at regular bar prices. If you don't have transport back to town it's easy enough to find a lift if you talk to people in the members' enclosure. Bus or matatu No 24 from the city centre goes right past the racecourse to the Karen shopping centre. ■

Things to Buy

Nairobi is a good place to pick up souvenirs although you do need to shop around. The City Market on Muindi Mbingu St has a good range of items, particularly kiondo baskets, and there's a whole gaggle of stalls in Kigali St behind the Jama Mosque. It's all a bit of a tourist trap and you need to bargain fiercely. There are also hundreds of stalls selling the same sorts of wares along just about every tiny alley which branches off from Biashara St between Muindi Mbingu and Tom Mboya Sts.

Even though they originated in Tanzania (and they're still much cheaper there), makonde woodcarvings are very popular in Nairobi and the shops are full of them. Most of the examples you will see are actually made in Ukambani (the land of the Kamba tribe).

At the cheaper end of the market, it's worth looking at the examples which hawkers bring around to the bars where tourists congregate. Buffalo Bill's at the Heron Court Hotel is one of the best places. The quality of the carving varies a lot, but if you're not in a hurry then you can find some

really fine examples at bargain-basement prices. Expect to pay around half to two-thirds of the price first asked.

Another craft item you can find in profusion both at stalls and inside shops are soapstone carvings including chess sets. These originate from the Kisii area of western Kenya but you'll be hard-pressed to find them there. Nakuru is where you'll find them at their cheapest however there's not a lot of price difference between there and Nairobi. The chess sets, of which there are many different designs, are an absolute bargain.

If you're not into bargaining, or want top-quality stuff, there are plenty of 'fixed-price' souvenir shops around although, even at these, they'll usually give you a 'special price' if you are obviously not a Hilton hopper. One of the better shops is on the corner of Kaunda and Wabera Sts, and another on Tubman Rd near the corner of Muindi Mbingu St.

Travellers with more cash at their disposal should think seriously about buying fine art, particularly paintings. There are some superb artists in Kenya and their work is only on the verge of being internationally recognised. It's possible that it will take off in the same way that Australian Aboriginal art did some years ago.

A good place to check out what's happening in this genre is the Gallery Watatu on the 1st floor of Lonhro House, Standard St. There's a permanent display here, much of which is for sale, plus they have regular auctions. Bring your cheque book with you or a credit card. Almost nothing goes for less than KSh 15,000 and for the crème de la crème, you're looking at about KSh 50,000 to KSh 100,000, however the champagne and the vol-au-vents are complimentary. It is also worth checking out the Gallery of East African Contemporary Art which is at the museum.

If you want to get kitted out in the latest designer 'white hunter' safari gear, there are literally dozens of shops selling all the requisite stuff at outrageous prices. But do you really want to look like an absolute nerd that's only ever seen the inside of a luxury tented camp?

The Spinners Web describes itself as a 'consignment handicraft shop' which sells goods made in workshops and by self-help groups around the country. It has some superb items, including hand-knitted jumpers, all sorts of fabrics and the huge Turkana baskets. The shop is on Waiyaki Way, Westlands, near Viking House.

The gift shop of the East African Wildlife Society in the arcade of the Hilton Hotel has a range of souvenirs and interesting knick-knacks, many of them with an animal theme. It's well worth shopping here as the proceeds go towards conserving Kenya's wildlife rather than to conserving the lifestyles of rich Kenyans.

If you're out in the Langata area, there's another couple of places worth investigating. The Ostrich Park has, apart from ostriches, a craft centre with an artisans' workshop, and you can see the items being made. See the Around Nairobi section for details. On Langata South Rd, between Langata Rd and Langata itself, is Utamaduni (☎ 891798). This consists of 18 separate shops which each have one room in a large house. The range of crafts is excellent, the quality good and the prices correspondingly high. On the plus side, an unspecified percentage of the profits goes to Kenya Wildlife Services. It's very much tourist orientated but if you're in the area is worth a look. There's also a good cafe here.

For a much less touristy atmosphere try the Kariokor Market east of the centre on Racecourse Rd in Eastleigh. It's a few minutes ride by bus or taxi. Another place out of the centre is the Undugu crafts shop in Woodvale Grove, Westlands, behind the market. This is a nonprofit organisation which supports community projects in Nairobi.

The Maasai Market is an informal market where Maasai women sell beaded jewellery, gourds, baskets and other Maasai crafts. It only takes place on Tuesdays from around 9 am to mid-afternoon, and has changed location a couple of times in recent years.

Currently it's held at the top end of Moi Ave, on the corner of Slip Rd.

Getting There & Away
Air Airlines with offices in Nairobi include:

Aeroflot
    Corner House, Mama Ngina St (☎ 220746)
Air France
    Fedha Towers, Muindi Mbingu (☎ 217512)
Air India
    Jeevan Bharati House, Harambee Ave (☎ 334788)
Air Madagascar
    Hilton Hotel (☎ 225286)
Air Malawi
    Sixeighty Hotel, Muindi Mbingu St (☎ 333683)
Air Mauritius
    Union Towers, Moi Ave (☎ 229166)
Air Rwanda
    Mama Ngina St (☎ 332225)
Air Tanzania
    Chester House, Koinange St (☎ 336224)
Air Zaïre
    Arrow House, Monrovia St (☎ 222271)
Air Zimbabwe
    Chester House, Koinange St (☎ 339522)
British Airways
    International House, 8th floor, Mama Ngina St (☎ 334362)
Cameroon Airlines
    Rehani House, 9th Floor, Koinange St (☎ 224743)
EgyptAir
    Hilton Arcade (☎ 226821)
El-Al Airlines
    KCS House, Mama Ngina St (☎ 228123)
Ethiopian Airlines
    Bruce House, Standard St (☎ 330837)
Gulf Air
    International House, Mama Ngina St (☎ 214444)
Japan Airlines (JAL)
    International House, Mama Ngina St (☎ 220591)
Kenya Airways
    Barclays Plaza, 5th Floor, Loita St (☎ 229291)
KLM
    Fedha Towers, Muindi Mbingu St (☎ 332673)
Lignes Aerienne (Seychelles)
    Rehema House (☎ 340481)
Lufthansa
    AM Bank House, University Way (☎ 335819)
Olympic Airways
    AM Bank House, University Way (☎ 219532)
Pakistan International Airlines (PIA)
    ICEA building, Kenyatta Ave (☎ 333900)
Royal Swazi
    Re-Insurance Plaza, Mezzanine Floor, Taifa Rd (☎ 339351)
South African Airways
    Lonrho House, Standard St (☎ 229663)

NAIROBI

Sudan Airlines
    UTC building, General Kago St (☎ 225129)
Virag
    Lonrho House, 6th Floor, Standard St (☎ 220961)
Uganda Airlines
    Uganda House, Kenyatta Ave (☎ 221354)

Kenya Airways is the main domestic carrier and operates from Nairobi's Jomo Kenyatta International airport. There are 12 flights weekly to Kisumu (USS$44 one way), five flights weekly to Malindi (US$83 one way) and 59 flights weekly to Mombasa (US$83 one way). Fares can be paid either in US dollars or in local currency.

Make sure you reconfirm flights 48 hours before departure.

In addition to Kenya Airways, the privately-owned Air Kenya Aviation (☎ 501601), Wilson airport, connects Nairobi with a number of centres:

destination	fare	frequency
Amboseli	US$70/125	daily
Lamu	US$118/236	daily
Malindi	KSh4680/9630	twice weekly
Masai Mara	US$87/150	twice daily
Mombasa	KSh 4680/9360	nine weekly
Nanyuki	US$105/180	daily
Samburu	US$70/115	daily

All fares are one way/return

The check-in times for all the above flights is half an hour before departure and the baggage allowance is 15 kg. All the flights are nonsmoking.

Bus In Nairobi most long-distance bus offices are along Accra Rd near the River Rd junction. For Mombasa there are numerous companies (such as Coast Bus, Crossline, Akamba, Mawingo, Malindi Bus, Takrim, and Tawfiq) doing the run, both by day and night. They all cost KSh 300 and the trip takes around seven to eight hours with a meal break on the way.

Akamba is the biggest private bus company in the country and has an extensive network. It's not the cheapest, but is probably the safest and most reliable company. The office is conveniently located on Lagos Rd, just off Latema Rd and very close to Tom Mboya St. Apart from the Mombasa service (KSh 420), it also has daily connections to Isiolo, Nyeri, Meru (KSh 200), Kakamega (KSh 420), Kitale (KSh 400), Chogoria, Embu and Kisumu. If you're heading for Uganda there are three daily Akamba buses direct to Kampala. See the Getting There & Away chapter for details.

The government KBS Stagecoach company is another large, reliable operator and runs coaches to the major cities and towns from its depot just off Ronald Ngala St not far from the country bus station. To the major destinations – Kisumu, Malaba, Eldoret, Kitale – it uses double-decker buses. The Stagecoach fares are on a par with Akamba's fares; the buses are well maintained and the drivers somewhere approaching sane.

For all other destinations, buses leave from the main country bus station just off Landies Rd, about 15 minutes walk southeast of the budget hotel area around Latema Rd. It's a huge but reasonably well-organised place, and all the buses have their destinations displayed in the window so it's just a matter of wandering around and finding the one you want. There is at least one daily departure and often more to virtually every main town in the country, and the buses leave when full. For more details see Getting There & Away for each place.

Shuttle Minibus A good option for travel to or from Mombasa, but also more expensive than the large buses, are the shuttle services run by two companies – Sav-Line and The Connection. They both offer air-con, 18-seater minibuses for KSh 900 per person one way which will drop you off anywhere in the two city centres. Bookings for Sav-Line should be made at Savage Camping Tours (☎ 228236), Diamond Trust House, Moi Ave, Nairobi. Bookings with The Connection can be made at Inside Africa Safaris (☎ 223304), Wabera St, Nairobi, and at Tamana Holidays (☎ 315208), Moi Ave, Mombasa.

HUGH FINLAY

TONY WHEELER

HUGH FINLAY

airobi is the youngest and most modern city in East Africa (top). Haggling is expected at
 many markets (middle). Enjoy the leisurely pace at the Ngong racecourse (bottom).

Jewellery & Tribal Souvenirs

Most of the jewellery on sale in Kenya is of tribal origin although very little of it is the genuine article. The colourful Maasai beaded jewellery is the most striking and the most popular, and items include earrings and the sets of three 'collars', all made with brightly coloured beads.

Other Maasai items include the decorated calabash – dried gourds used to store a mixture of blood and milk which is then left to ferment for a few days before it is drunk. Before the mixture is placed in the gourd specific grasses are burnt inside it, and the soot deposit imparts a certain flavour and aids in fermentation. As you might imagine, these gourds often smell a bit, but are quite strikingly decorated with Maasai beads. Spears and shields are also popular, although these days they are made specifically for the tourist trade.

One of the best places to pick up Maasai souvenirs is at Namanga on the Tanzanian border. This is where most minibuses headed for Amboseli National Park stop for a few minutes, so prices are outrageous. However, with some persistent bargaining you can reduce the prices to realistic levels. They know as well as you that the prices they ask are ridiculous, but there are plenty of well-heeled tourists passing through here who have more money than sense. For instance, the starting price for earrings is KSh 100 per pair, but they are quite happy to sell them for Ksh 10; similarly expressed an interest in a calabash and was quoted Ksh 500 – and eventually paid Ksh 35!

Tribal souvenirs are bought cheaper out in the bush away from the tourist circuits but buying still demands judicious haggling. ■

ROGER JONES

Above: Popular souvenirs are the bright and bold jewellery worn by Maasai women.

Below: Nairobi Market sells tribal souvenirs such as decorative dried gourds.

DAWN DELANEY

Share-Taxi The share-taxi is a good alternative to that dangerous and heart-stopping mode of transport – the matatu. Although you're still likely to be whisked along at breakneck speed, at least it will be in a vehicle that is not carrying twice its rated capacity and has at least a sporting chance of stopping in a hurry if the need arises. Share-taxis are usually Peugeot 505 station wagons which take seven passengers and leave when full. They are much quicker than the matatus as they go from point to point without stopping, and of course are more expensive. Like matatus, most of the share-taxi companies have their offices around the Accra and River Rds area.

DPS (☎ 210866) on Dubois Rd is typical of these companies and has daily Peugeots to Kisumu (KSh 500, four hours), Busia (KSh 700), Nakuru (KSh 200, two hours), Malaba on the Ugandan border (KSh 500), Kitale (KSh 500), and Kericho (KSh 350). On any of these services you can pay an extra KSh 20 for the front seat. These departures are only in the mornings so you need to be at the office by around 7 am, and it's a good idea to book one day in advance.

Tanzania Taxis for the Tanzanian border at Namanga leave from the top side of the service station on the corner of Ronald Ngala St and River Rd. Most people prefer to take either a bus direct from Nairobi to Arusha, or a shuttle minibus. See the Getting There & Away chapter for details.

Train The booking office at Nairobi railway station (☎ 335160) is open from 8 am to 7 pm daily.

Nairobi railway station also has a left-luggage office which is open daily from 8 am to noon and 1 to 6.30 pm. It costs KSh 50 per item per day.

Mombasa Trains run from Nairobi to Mombasa every day in both directions at 7 pm and the journey takes about 13 hours. The fares for nonresidents are KSh 2750 in 1st class and KSh 1930 in 2nd class. These prices include dinner, breakfast and bedding whether

you want them or not – there's no discount if you don't want them. This is a popular run so in the high season book your tickets as far in advance as possible, although you shouldn't have any trouble two or three days beforehand.

Kisumu The Nairobi to Kisumu trains depart daily at 6 pm arriving at Kisumu at 7.10 am the next day. In the opposite direction they depart daily at 6 pm arriving at Nairobi at 6.20 am the next day. The fares are KSh 1925 in 1st class and KSh 1320 in 2nd class. This is also a popular route and the train is often heavily booked. If that's the case you may have to rely on the extra coach which is added on the day of departure if demand warrants.

Uganda From Nairobi to the Ugandan border at Malaba there are trains on Friday and Saturday at 3 pm arriving at 8.45 am the next day. In the opposite direction they depart Malaba on Saturday and Sunday at 4 pm and arrive at 9 am the next day. The fares are KSh 2639 in 1st class and KSh 1820 in 2nd class, and again, the fares include meals and bedding. En route to Malaba these trains go through Naivasha, Nakuru (KSh 740/910), Eldoret (KSh 1930/1320) and Bungoma.

There's also a direct Nairobi to Kampala train once a week. See the Kenya Getting There & Away chapter for details.

Car & Motorcycle All the major companies, and many smaller ones, have offices in the city centre, and the bigger ones such as Avis and Hertz have desks at the airport. A comprehensive description of car hire, and a list of companies, can be found in the Getting Around chapter.

Hitching For Mombasa, take bus No 13, 34 or 109 as far as the airport turn-off and hitch from there. For Nakuru and Kisumu, take bus No 23 from the Hilton to the end of its route and hitch from there. Otherwise start from the junction of Chiromo Rd and Waiyaki Way (the extension of Uhuru Highway) in Westlands.

For Nanyuki and Nyeri take bus No 45 or 145 from the central bus station up Thika Rd to the entrance of Kenyatta National University and hitch from there. Make sure you get off the bus at the college entrance and not the exit. It's very difficult to hitch from the latter. Otherwise, start from the roundabout where Thika Rd meets Forest and Muranga'a Rds.

Getting Around

The Airport The Jomo Kenyatta International airport is 15 km out of town off the road to Mombasa. The cheapest way of getting into town is on the city bus No 34 *but* (and this is a big but) you must keep your wits about you! The number of people who have been ripped off on this bus doesn't bear thinking about. The usual story is that an 'instant crowd' forms, you are jostled and before you know it your bag or money pouch has been slashed or ripped off. It's not much of an introduction to Kenya, so take a taxi. There is generally no problem catching the No 34 city bus *to* the airport because, by then, you'll be familiar with Nairobi. The fare is KSh 20 and the trip takes about 45 minutes, more in peak periods.

The best way to or from the airport is by taxi, and this is really the only option if you have a dawn or late-night flight. The standard fare is KSh 900 from the airport to the city centre. To share a taxi to the airport, check out the notice boards at the Iqbal and the New Kenya Lodge or ask around fellow travellers. As your bargaining position is better in the city, taxis to the airport shouldn't cost more than KSh 750 during the day; late night or early morning you may pay more. Discount Travel Services (☎ 219156; fax 225299) offers an airport shuttle service for KSh 500 per person, with pick-up or drop-off anywhere in the city centre. Book in advance.

To Wilson airport (for light aircraft services to Malindi, Lamu etc) you can take bus or matatu Nos 15, 31, 34, 125 and 126 from Moi Ave opposite the US Embassy. The fare is KSh 15. A taxi from the centre of town will cost you KSh 300 to KSh 400 depending on

the driver. The entrance to the airport is easy to miss; get off at the BP station.

Bus Buses are the cheapest way of getting around Nairobi, but hopefully you won't need to use them much. Forget about them in rush hours if you have a backpack – you'll never get on and if by some Herculean feat you manage to do that, you'll never get off!

Useful buses include No 34 to the airport (catch it from the northern side of Kenyatta Ave, or Moi Ave opposite the US Embassy); No 46 from outside the new post office on Kenyatta Ave for the Yaya Centre in Hurlingham (KSh 9), or No 23 from Moi Ave at Jeevanjee Gardens for Westlands (KSh 8).

Matatu Matatus are also packed during peak hours, but are not bad at other times, the main disadvantage being that the drivers are crazy. Matatus are frequent and only slightly more expensive than the buses; you need to be super-vigilant though because they're a pickpocket's paradise. Never take your hand off your valuables and have small change handy for the fare. Matatus follow the same routes as buses, and can be caught in the same places.

Taxi Other than the fleet of London cabs (which belong to the son of the most prominent politician in the country), Nairobi taxis rate as some of the most dilapidated and generally unroadworthy buckets of bolts that ever graced a city street. Taxis cannot usually be hailed on the street (because they don't cruise for passengers) but you can find them parked on just about every second street corner in the city centre. They also hang out at the railway station and outside most of the main hotels. At night, you'll find them outside bars and the nightclubs.

The cabs are not metered but the fares charged are remarkably standard and few cabbies attempt to overcharge, though they're reluctant to give change if it's KSh 20 or less. KSh 200 gets you just about anywhere within the city centre. The same is true from Ralph Bunche Rd or Milimani Rd to the main post office though they some-

---

Creative Parking

Though the wildlife parks may be Kenya's premier tourist attraction, it's worth strolling around Kenya's other park – Nairobi's kerbsides – to observe the imaginative and often unbelievable way in which drivers utilise every inch of space to park their frequently scratched and battered vehicles. It's virtually impossible to find a spot to park in central Nairobi any day during business hours except Sunday so if there's the slightest possibility of parking another vehicle between two others in any way whatsoever then someone is going to do it! This is often at 90° to the adjoining cars with no thought about what happens to either the front or back ends. Neither pavements nor parking meters are any impediment to these people or the danger of having either end wiped out by either harassed pedestrians or kamikaze KBS bus drivers. If there's simply not an inch to spare that's just too bad and double parking becomes the order of the day. How you get a car out of this miasma is your problem – not that of the people who've boxed you in.

Parking wardens there certainly are, as well as fines for 'illegal' parking but the deterrent effect of them is minimal and, in any case, always negotiable to a degree.

The best areas to view this spectacle are between Kenyatta Ave and University Way and anywhere between Tom Mboya St and the Nairobi River. ■

---

times ask for a bit more as it involves backtracking down the other side of Haile Selassie Ave. From the city centre to anywhere in Westlands is around KSh 300 (for locals it's KSh 200). To the Carnivore restaurant from the city centre it is KSh 550.

Bicycle By all means ride a bicycle in Nairobi – if you have a suit of armour, a crash helmet and a constitution of iron. Personally, we wouldn't contemplate it. If you're not run over you'll certainly be run off the road on numerous occasions. No-one is going to give you any room or consideration at any time. Basically, it's dangerous.

Around Nairobi

In addition to the attractions listed below, there is also Nairobi National Park, easily the most accessible in the country. (See the National Parks & Reserves chapter.)

THE BOMAS OF KENYA

The Bomas of Kenya (☎ 891801) is a cultural centre at Langata – a short way past the entrance to the national park, on the right-hand side as you head out from Nairobi. Here you can see traditional dances and hear songs from the country's 16 ethnic groups amid authentically re-created sur-

roundings, though the dances are all done by one group of professionals rather than representatives of the tribes themselves. There is a daily performance at 2.30 pm (3.30 pm at weekends). Entry costs KSh 300 for adults and KSh 150 for children. There's the usual clutter of souvenir shops around the site.

If you are not on a tour, bus or matatu No 15, 125 or 126 from outside Development House, Moi Ave, will get you there in about half an hour. Get off at Magadi Rd, from where it's about a one-km walk (signposted).

OSTRICH PARK

The Ostrich Park (☎ 891051) is about one km further along Langata Rd, well signposted right opposite the turn-off for Langata itself. This makes a good family excursion, where you can feed ostriches, see artisans at work making handicrafts, and there's also a good kids' playground.

The park is open daily and entry is KSh 200 (KSh 100 for children).

LANGATA GIRAFFE CENTRE

The Langata Giraffe Centre is on Gogo Falls Rd about one km from the Hardy Estate shopping centre in Langata, about 18 km from central Nairobi. Here you can observe and hand-feed Rothschild giraffes from a raised circular wooden structure which also houses a display of information about giraffes. Although the centre is mainly aimed

Around Nairobi

1. Safari Park Hotel
2. Bombax Club
3. Ngong Racecourse
4. Karen Shopping Centre
5. Karen Blixen Museum
6. Langata Giraffe Centre
7. Ostrich Park
8. Bomas of Kenya
9. Nairobi National Park Main Gate & Animal Orphanage
10. Carnivore Restaurant
11. Wilson Airport
12. East Gate (Nairobi National Park)
13. Jomo Kenyatta International Airport

See Nairobi Map (pages 148-9)

See Nairobi National Park Map (page 3(6))

at local schoolchildren, it is also a popular tourist drawcard.

Across the road but still part of the centre is a small patch of forest through which you can make a one-km, self-guided forest walk. Booklets (KSh 20) are available from the ticket office.

The centre is open from 9 am to 5.30 pm daily. Admission costs KSh 250 (KSh 70 for children). To get there from the centre take matatu No 24 to the shopping centre in Langata and walk from there.

KAREN BLIXEN MUSEUM

This is the farmhouse which was formerly the residence of Karen Blixen, author of *Out of Africa*, and was presented to the Kenyan government at independence by the Danish government along with the adjacent agricultural college. As you're probably aware from the film of the same name starring Robert Redford and Meryl Streep, this is where Karen Blixen lived between 1914 and 1931. She arrived in Kenya at the age of 29 to marry her second cousin, the Swedish Baron von Blixen-Finecke, who had bought a farm in the area. The marriage failed and she became bankrupt forcing her to sell the farm amidst a series of personal tragedies which eventually left her life in shreds and forced her to leave Kenya. The house was bought by the Danish government in 1959.

The museum is open daily from 9.30 am to 6 pm and entry costs KSh 200. It's right next door to the Karen College on Karen Rd about two km from Langata Rd.

Getting There & Away

A No 111 bus or matatu from Moi Ave will get you there in about 40 minutes at a cost of KSh 30. Alternatively, take public bus No 27 from Kenyatta Ave or from the corner of Ralph Bunche and Ngong Rds to Karen village (the shopping centre) and change to a No 24 matatu there. A taxi will cost you about KSh 850 one way.

NGONG HILLS

Ngong and Karen, to the west of Nairobi, along with Limuru, to the north, were the

sites where many white settlers set up farms and built their houses in the early colonial days. The transformation they wrought was quite remarkable so that, even today, as you catch a glimpse of a half-timbered house through woodland or landscaped gardens full of flowering trees, you could imagine yourself to be in the Home Counties of England or some other European location. And, yes, the eucalypts which you see growing everywhere were an Australian import.

There are some excellent views over Nairobi and down into the Rift Valley from various points in the Ngong Hills, but it's unwise to go wandering around alone as people have been mugged here, especially at weekends. What you really need to get a feel for these areas is your own car or, alternatively, that of a resident who is willing to drive you around the place.

Places to Stay & Eat

There's nowhere to stay in this area of Nairobi but there is an excellent place to eat and drink. This is the *Horseman* (☎ 882033) at Karen shopping centre on Langata Rd. Here you have a choice of three restaurants (two open-air and one indoors) and a very popular bar (with draught beer) all set in a leafy compound complete with its own pond and croaking frogs. It's straight out of rural Surrey, England. The food in the restaurants (one of which offers barbecued game meats) is excellent though it is relatively expensive. The bar is often packed in the evenings and usually stays open late.

LIMURU

Limuru possibly has even more of a 'European' feel than the Ngong Hills, except that there are vast coffee and tea plantations blanketing the rolling hills cut by swathes of conifer and eucalypt forest. It's up here that you'll find the *Kentmere Club* (☎ (0154) 41053; fax 40692), Limuru Rd, Tigoni. This is the quintessential white settlers' club – even more so than the Norfolk Hotel in Nairobi.

The club consists of a series of low, intimate, wooden cottages with shingle roofs bathrooms and open fires connected to each other by quaint walkways and bridges. The main block is built in the same style and houses a restaurant and a superb re-creation of an English country pub with low ceilings, exposed beams and log-burning fireplaces. If you'd like to rent a cottage the cost is KSh 2050/3000 for singles/doubles with breakfast. Half-board rates are KSh 2700/4300. It's a very peaceful place, and the restaurant is excellent.

About 10 km beyond the Kentmere Club, and well signposted, is the *Waterfalls Inn* (☎ (0154) 40672) with its picnic site, waterfall, viewing point and restaurant. Admission costs KSh 300 per car (with up to five passengers) on weekends, KSh 150 on weekdays. Although mainly used by day-tripping picnickers, the extensive grounds can also be used for camping (KSh 250 per person). It's a very relaxing place during the week, although you really need your own transport as there are no public transport routes close by. Pony and horse riding is also available at KSh 60.

Another thing you can do in the area is to visit a tea farm. If you've never done this before then it's worth a day out. Visits are organised by Mitchell's *Kiambethu Tea Farm* (☎ (0154) 40756) at Tigoni, about 35 km north-east of Nairobi. Here you'll be shown the whole process of tea production as well as taken on an accompanied walk into the forest to see the colobus monkeys. Visits of the tea farm take place every day starting at 11 am and finish at 2.30 pm. The cost is KSh 1000 which includes tea and biscuits when you get there and lunch at the end of the tour which includes beer, wine, sherry and home-made ice cream. Groups are preferred and visits are by prior arrangement only. A tour from Nairobi costs US$55 per person, including transport and lunch. Contact Let's Go Travel (☎ 340331) in Nairobi.

Getting There & Away
KBS public bus No 116 will take you fairly close to the farm. If you have your own transport, take Limuru Rd (C62) past City Park and turn left at Muthaiga roundabout. Seven km further on you reach Ruaka village

where you turn right by the signpost for Nazareth Hospital and onto D407 Limuru Rd (otherwise known as Banana Rd). This takes you past the Kentmere Club, and the signposted turn-off to the Waterfall Inn.

THIKA
Despite its fame due to the popular *Flame Trees of Thika* novel, the town itself comes as something of a disappointment – there's not even many flame trees in evidence! It's appeal lies in the fact that it makes a great escape from the madness of urban Nairobi just 38 km down the road. If you want to get the feel for a small Kenyan agricultural service town, yet still be in commuting range of Nairobi, it could be just the place.

The town's only 'attraction' as such is **Chania Falls**, one km from the centre of town and on the edge of the busy Nairobi–Nyeri road (which thankfully bypasses Thika). The falls are quite small but there's a good view of them from the up-market Blue Post Hotel, which is a pleasant place to stop for a beer.

Places to Stay & Eat
If you decide to stay, there's a good choice of accommodation, particularly in the mid-range area as it seems Thika is also a popular weekend conference venue.

There's a number of similar boarding & lodgings. The *3 in 1* is typical, and costs KSh 150/250 for singles/doubles with shared facilities. It's passably clean and not too noisy. Another possibility is the *Sky Motel*.

Possibly the best value rooms in town are at the *12th December Hotel* (☎ (0151) 22140) near the post office. Large doubles cost KSh 500, and singles KSh 400, all including breakfast, though in a double room two people only get one breakfast!

Also worth a look is the *Sagret Hotel* (☎ (0151) 21786) where the rooms are a little smaller but all have private bath and balcony, and the price includes breakfast. Small vehicles can be parked securely in the hotel courtyard; larger vehicles remain on the street. The cost for rooms here is KSh 600/900.

PLACES TO STAY
5 Special Service Hotel
6 Sagret Hotel
8 3 in 1 Hotel
9 Kairo Mountain Hotel
11 Sky Motel
18 12th December Hotel
25 Chania Tourist Lodge

PLACES TO EAT
4 Twiga Bar
7 Rwambogo Bar & Restaurant
12 Ngaguro Café
14 Macvast Executive Restaurant Two

OTHER
1 Hindu Temple
2 Sikh Temple
3 Jain Temple
10 Local Matatus
13 Matatus to Nbi, Nyeri, Nakuru & Naivasha
15 Shell Petrol Station
16 Clock Tower
17 Standard Charter Bank
19 Post Office
20 Kenya Commercial Bank
21 Caltex Petrol Station
22 Barclays Bank
23 AGIP Petrol Station
24 Total Petrol Station
26 BP Petrol Station
27 Buses to Garissa

NAIROBI

Thika

Not to Scale

Further up the range is the *Chania Tourist Lodge* (☎ (0151) 22547), though it is poor value compared with the Sagret. Rooms here are somewhat overpriced at KSh 750/900.

The *Blue Post Hotel* (☎ (0151) 22241) is a reasonable up-market place set uncomfortably close to the very busy highway. Nevertheless, it's a pleasant place and probably worth the KSh 850/1200 charged for the rooms. The hotel has the best restaurant in Thika.

All the mid-range hotels have their own restaurants. For a good meal in a regular restaurant try the amazingly named *Macvast Executive Restaurant Two*! Here the waiters are all done up with pink pinstriped shirts and bow ties, but the prices are low and the menu extensive.

Getting There & Away

Matatus leave from a number of places around Thika. The main matatu stand, used mostly by local matatus, is near the Sagret Hotel. Most long-distance matatus – to Nairobi, Nakuru, Naivasha, Nyeri and Embu – leave from behind Barclays Bank. The trip to Nairobi only takes 45 minutes and costs KSh 30.

The Coast

> This cannot be less than natural beauty, the endless sand, the reefs, the lot, are completely unmatched in the world.
>
> **Ernest Hemingway**

The coast of Kenya is one of the country's main attractions. It offers a combination of historical sites, trading ports with a strong Arab-Muslim influence, superb beaches and diving opportunities – an area not to be missed.

Mombasa is the coast capital, if you like, and is the first port of call for most people after leaving Nairobi. It is an old trading port with a history going back at least to the 12th century, and the old city here shows heavy influence of the town's previous rulers – the mosques and the Portuguese fort in particular. It has a steamy humid climate but is a pleasant place nonetheless. Unfortunately, many people are in such a rush to get to the beach that they really only transit Mombasa, which is a pity as the city, particularly the old part, is well worth exploring.

To the north it's much the same story, with Malindi being the big coastal resort centre, but there's a couple of interesting attractions here as well – the historical site of Gedi just a short bus ride to the south, and the excellent diving on the coral reef in the offshore Malindi and Watamu marine national parks.

Head further north and you come to the island of Lamu – a beautiful Arab-influenced town which has been something of a travellers' mecca for years and still draws visitors by the thousands. Despite this it retains the very distinctive personality which attracted people to it in the first place – an easy-going unhurried pace, traditional architecture, and a unique culture which owes a great deal to its Muslim roots.

The people of the coast are the Swahili, and it's here that Kiswahili (Swahili) – the lingua franca of the modern nation – evolved as a means of communication between the local inhabitants and the Arab traders who first began plying their dhows up and down this coast sometime before the 7th century. Other influences also shaped the language and there is a smattering of not only Arabic but also Portuguese, Hindi and English words.

History

The first traders here appear to have been Arabs from the Persian Gulf who sailed south along the coast during the north-east monsoon, sailing home north with the south-west monsoon. By the 12th century some substantial settlements had developed, mainly on islands such as Lamu, Manda, Pemba and Zanzibar, as these provided greater security than the coast itself. The main export trade in this early part was in ivory, tortoiseshell and leopard skins, while items such as glass beads from India and porcelain from as far afield as China were finding their way here.

From the 12th to the 15th centuries settlements grew and a dynasty was established at Kilwa (in present-day Tanzania). By the end of this period Mombasa, Malindi and Paté (in the Lamu archipelago) were all substantial towns. The inhabitants were largely Arab but there were also significant numbers of African labourers. Intermarriage was common and, culturally, the settlements were more closely connected with the Islamic Persian Gulf than they were with inland Kenya. Although all these city-states had this common heritage and cultural link, they were all virtually independent and were often vying with one another for power.

So preoccupied were they with their own internal struggles that the coastal centres were quite unprepared for the arrival of the Portuguese in 1498. Before long they were paying tribute to the Portuguese and by 1506 the Portuguese had sacked and gained control of the entire coast. In the century which followed, the Portuguese had raided

Mombasa on two further occasions and built the beautiful defensive Fort Jesus in that city.

Trade was the main interest of the Portuguese and they concentrated their activities in that area. They did not exercise direct control over the administration of the coastal cities – just kept them in line and dependent.

Not all the locals were happy with this arrangement and trouble started for the Portuguese with local uprisings in the 17th century. They were mainly inspired by the disaffected Sheikh Yusuf of Mombasa, who spent most of his time in conflict with the Portuguese, and in fact occupied Fort Jesus in Mombasa after murdering the Portuguese commandant there in 1631. With the help of the sultans of Oman, the Portuguese were defeated and Fort Jesus occupied by 1698.

The Omani dynasties flourished and Mombasa and Paté became the pre-eminent spots on the coast, although both were defeated by Lamu in 1810. The internecine struggles of the various Omani factions led to Zanzibar coming into ascendancy, which in turn led the rulers of Mombasa to seek British assistance. The British, however, were reluctant to intervene and jeopardise their alliance with Seyyid Said, the Omani ruler, as their route to India passed close to Muscat. Before long the whole coast was under the control of the Omani ruler.

It was in this period of Omani rule that the slave trade flourished. Up until this time it had been carried out only on a small scale, but soon the newly established clove plantations on Zanzibar required labourers, and from there slaves were shipped to the Persian Gulf and beyond. It was also this increase in economic activity that brought the first Indian and European traders into the area. Trade agreements were made with the Americans (1833), the British (1839) and the French (1844), and exports to India also flourished – ivory, cloves, hides and coconut oil were all important. This increase in trade led Seyyid Said to transfer his capital from Muscat to Zanzibar in 1840, and decreased his reliance on the slave trade for revenue. He was thus able to sign a treaty banning the export of slaves to the Middle East.

THE COAST

Despite the fact that the British East Africa Company took over administration of the interior of the country, a 10-mile-wide (16-km-wide) coastal strip was recognised as the sultan's patch and it was leased from him in 1887, first for a 50-year period and then permanently. In 1920 the coastal strip became the British protectorate, the rest of the country having become a fully fledged British colony.

Mombasa

Mombasa is the largest port on the coast of East Africa. It has a population of nearly half a million of which about 70% are African, the rest being mainly Asian with a small minority of Europeans. Its docks not only serve Kenya, but also Uganda, Rwanda, Burundi and eastern Zaïre. The bulk of the town sprawls over Mombasa Island which is connected to the mainland by an artificial causeway which carries the rail and road links. In recent years Mombasa has spread onto the mainland both north and south of the island.

Large Mombasa may be but, like Dar es Salaam in Tanzania to the south, it has retained its low-level traditional character and there are few high-rise buildings except in the very centre of the city. The Old Town between the massive, Portuguese-built Fort Jesus and the old dhow careening dock remains much the same as it was in the mid-19th century, asphalt streets and craft shops apart. It's a hot and steamy town, as you might expect being so close to the equator, but an interesting place to visit.

History

Mombasa's history goes back to at least the 12th century when it was described by Arab chroniclers as being a small town and the residence of the King of the Zenj – Arabic for black Africans. It later became an important settlement for the Shirazis and remained so until the arrival of the Portuguese in the early 16th century. Determined to destroy the

Arab monopoly over maritime trade in the Indian Ocean, especially with regard to spices, the Portuguese, under Dom Francisco de Almeida, attacked Mombasa with a fleet of 23 ships in 1505. After 1½ days it was all over and the town was burnt to the ground. So great was the quantity of loot that much of it had to be left behind, for fear of overloading the ships, when the fleet sailed for India.

The town was quickly rebuilt and it wasn't long before it regained its commanding position over trade in the area, but peace didn't last long. In 1528, another Portuguese fleet under Nuña da Cunha arrived on the East African coast too late to catch the southwestern monsoon which would take them to India, so they were forced to look around for temporary quarters. Naturally, Mombasa was in no mood to welcome them but, unfortunately, Mombasa was at that time engaged in bitter disputes with the kings of Malindi, Pemba and Zanzibar. An alliance was patched together and the Portuguese were again able to take Mombasa, but sickness and constant skirmishing over many months eventually decided the outcome. The city was again burnt to the ground and the Portuguese sailed for India.

The Portuguese finally made a bid for permanency in 1593 with the construction of Fort Jesus, but in 1631 they were massacred to the last person in an uprising by the townspeople. The following year a Portuguese fleet was sent from Goa and Muscat to avenge the killings but was unable to retake the town. By this time, however, the Mombasan ruler had decided that further resistance was useless and, having reduced the town to rubble and cut down all the fruit trees and palms, he withdrew to the mainland. It was reoccupied without a fight by the Portuguese the following year. Portuguese hegemony in the Indian Ocean was on the wane by this time, not only because of corruption and nepotism within Portuguese ranks, but because of Dutch, French and English activity in India and South-East Asia.

The 17th century also saw the rise of

Oman as a naval power and it was the Omanis who, in 1698, were the next to drive the Portuguese from Mombasa after a 33-month siege in which all the defenders were slaughtered. Even this disaster wasn't enough to convince the Portuguese that their days were over and Mombasa was reoccupied. However, the end finally came in 1729 following an invasion by an Arab fleet, a general uprising of the population in which Portuguese settlers were slaughtered, and an abortive counteroffensive which involved the entire military resources of the viceroyalty of Goa.

In 1832 the Sultan of Oman moved his capital from Muscat to Zanzibar and from then until Kenya's independence in 1963 the red flag of Zanzibar fluttered over Fort Jesus. Meanwhile, the British became active along the East African coast. In their attempts to suppress the slave trade, they interfered increasingly in the affairs of Zanzibar until, in 1895, the British East Africa protectorate was set up with Mombasa as the capital (until it was moved to Nairobi) and the Sultan of Oman's possessions were administered as a part of it. When independence came, the Sultan's coastal possessions were attached to the new republic.

During the protectorate years the British confirmed Mombasa's status as East Africa's most important port by constructing a railway from Mombasa to Uganda. It was completed in 1901 using indentured labourers from Gujarat and Punjab in India – hence the origin of Kenya's (and Uganda's and Tanzania's) Asian population.

Orientation

The heart of Mombasa is Digo Rd/Nyerere Ave off which three main roads – Moi Ave, Haile Selassie Rd and Jomo Kenyatta Ave – branch north-west and a fourth – Nkrumah Rd – branches south-east towards the Old Town. The railway station is approximately in the centre of the island at the end of Haile Selassie Rd whereas most of the bus companies have their terminals along Kenyatta Ave.

Maps The best map you can buy of Mombasa is the Survey of Kenya's *Mombasa Island & Environs*, last published in 1977. Many of the street names have changed, but little else.

Information

Tourist Office The regional tourist office (☎ 311231) is just past the famous tusks on Moi Ave and is open Monday to Friday from 9 am to noon and 2 to 4.30 pm, and on Saturdays from 9 am to noon. It stocks very few leaflets but the staff are friendly and helpful and will ring up places free of charge to check on tariffs, visa requirements or whatever, but they do tend to be geared to big spenders – mainly those who want to stay at a beach resort hotel – as opposed to budget travellers.

It's worth picking up a copy of the free monthly *Kenya Coast Tourist Guide* which is available from major hotels, travel agencies and car hire companies. It contains listings of virtually all the hotels, restaurants, discos, water-sports outfits and bus companies in Mombasa and along the coast as well as feature articles about particular places. Beware of what is said about any place in these articles since the glowing praise is clearly focused on securing their continued advertising.

Embassies As Mombasa is an important port and tourism town, a number of countries maintain diplomatic offices here. See the Embassies section in the Facts for the Visitor chapter for details.

Money The branch of Barclays Bank on Moi Ave, 250m west of the Digo Rd/Moi Ave junction, is open Monday to Friday from 9 am to 3 pm (4.30 pm for forex transactions) and on the first and last Saturday of the month from 9 to 11 am. There are also a number of foreign exchange bureaus bureaus which include Pwani Forex Bureau on Digo Rd opposite the main market and the Fort Jesus Forex Bureau right in front of the entrance to the fort. They're both open Monday to Saturday from 8 am to 5 pm. The exchange rates are generally slightly lower

THE COAST

THE COAST

Mombasa

0   250   500 m

To Airport, Mapuka
Causeway & Nairobi

To Malindi, Lamu
& Northern Beaches

See Central Mombasa Map (page 193)

*Mombasa
Harbour*

Dhow
Dock

See Mombasa Old Town
Map (page 190)

Jumhuri
Park

Sports
Grounds

Fort
Jesus

*Kilindini
Harbour*

Cricket
Club

Golf
Course

To Tanga, Shelly,
Tiwi & Diani
Beaches

To Shelly Beach

1 Hospital	10 CPK Guest House
2 Hotel Sapphire	11 Local Bus &
3 Train Station	Matatu Stand
4 Swahili Curry Bowl	12 Oceanic Hotel
5 Chinese Overseas	13 Florida Nightclub
Restaurant	14 Portuguese Ruins
6 Tourist Office	('The Hermitage')
& 'The Tusks'	15 State House
7 Manson Hotel	16 Hospital
8 New Outrigger Hotel	17 Tamarind Restaurant
9 Yacht Club	

than in Nairobi, especially for travellers' cheques.

Outside of these hours it's possible to change money at one or other of the major hotels in Mombasa or at the beach resort hotels north and south of Mombasa, although their exchange rates are relatively poor.

American Express is represented by Express Kenya (☎ 312461), PO Box 90631, Nkrumah Rd.

Post & Communications The GPO is on Digo Rd and is open Monday to Friday from 8 am to 6 pm and on Saturday from 9 am to noon.

The telephone area code for Mombasa is 011.

Bookshops There are two main bookshops: Bahati Book Centre and Bahari Bookshop, both of them on Moi Ave. These are the two which carry the greatest selection of stock as well as stationery requisites. There are others on Nkrumah Rd but they sell mainly school textbooks and stationery.

Books If you'd like more details about Mombasa's stirring history, the best account is to be found in *The Portuguese Period in East Africa* (East African Literature Bureau, 1971), by Justus Strandes, which can be bought in most good bookshops in Nairobi and Mombasa.

Before you set off on a tour of the Old Town of Mombasa get a copy of the booklet *The Old Town Mombasa: A Historical Guide* (Friends of Fort Jesus), by Judy Aldrick & Rosemary Macdonald. It can be bought from the tourist office, Fort Jesus, or one of the bookshops on Moi Ave. This excellent guide is an essential companion for an exploration of this part of town and has photographs, drawings and a map.

Also well worth buying is *Fort Jesus* by James Kirkman, which gives a detailed account of the history of the Fort, as well as pointing out the salient features. It is available from the fort, the bookshops and sometimes the tourist office.

Medical Services The two best hospitals in Mombasa are the Aga Khan Hospital (☎ 226182), Vanga Rd, and the Mombasa Hospital (☎ 312099). At both of these you must pay for all services and medication so have that travel insurance handy.

Emergency Two numbers to call are the police hot line (☎ 222121) and Africa Air Rescue (☎ 312405, 24 hours).

Motoring Organisations The Automobile Association of Kenya or AAA (☎ 26778) has its office just north of the tourist office on the road which connects Aga Khan Rd with the railway station. It has a few road maps and may be of use if you have specific questions about road or traffic conditions.

Dangers & Annoyances A few years ago Mombasa acquired a bad reputation as a place for snatch-and-run thieves and muggers. That era now appears to have passed as far as the city itself is concerned but it is still the case on the beaches north and south of town. Do not, under any circumstances, walk along beaches carrying valuables at any time of day or night. Nine times out of 10 you'll be relieved of them. One other thieves' paradise is the Likoni ferry where a number of tourists have had their cameras snatched recently.

The Old Town

The Old Town isn't as immediately interesting as the fort, but it's still a fascinating area to wander around in. Early morning or late afternoon is the best time to walk around; there's more activity then, but it's very quiet in the middle of the day.

Though its history goes back centuries, most of the houses in the Old Town are no more than 100 years old but you'll come across the occasional one which dates back to the first half of the 19th century. They represent a combination of styles and traditions which include the long-established coastal Swahili architecture commonly found in Lamu, various late-19th century Indian styles and British colonial architecture with

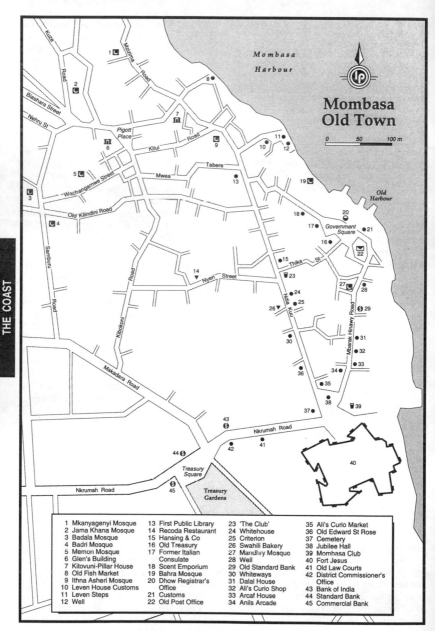

Mombasa Old Town

1	Mkanyagenyi Mosque	13	First Public Library	23	'The Club'	35	Ali's Curio Market
2	Jama Khana Mosque	14	Recoda Restaurant	24	Whitehouse	36	Old Edward St Rose
3	Badala Mosque	15	Hansing & Co	25	Criterion	37	Cemetery
4	Badri Mosque	16	Old Treasury	26	Swahili Bakery	38	Jubilee Hall
5	Memon Mosque	17	Former Italian	27	Mandhry Mosque	39	Mombasa Club
6	Glen's Building		Consulate	28	Well	40	Fort Jesus
7	Kitovuni-Pillar House	18	Scent Emporium	29	Old Standard Bank	41	Old Law Courts
8	Old Fish Market	19	Bahra Mosque	30	Whiteways	42	District Commissioner's
9	Ithna Asheri Mosque	20	Dhow Registrar's	31	Dalal House		Office
10	Leven House Customs		Office	32	Ali's Curio Shop	43	Bank of India
11	Leven Steps	21	Customs	33	Arcaf House	44	Standard Bank
12	Well	22	Old Post Office	34	Anils Arcade	45	Commercial Bank

its broad, shady verandahs and glazed and shuttered windows.

There are very few houses constructed entirely of coral rag, however. Most are of wattle and daub though they may include coral here and there. Most of the old palm thatch or tile roofing has been replaced with corrugated iron as well. What does remain are many examples of the massive, intricately carved doors and door frames characteristic of Swahili houses in Lamu and Zanzibar. It seems that when anyone of importance moved from these towns to Mombasa they brought their doors with them or had them newly made up to reflect their financial status. Of course, they're not as numerous as they used to be, either because of the ravages of time, or because they have been bought by collectors and shipped abroad. There is now a preservation order on those remaining so further losses should hopefully be prevented.

It's not just carved doors that you should look out for, though. Almost as much effort was put into the construction of balconies, their support brackets and enclosures. Fine fretwork and lattice work are a feature of the enclosures, reflecting the Muslim need for women's privacy. Sadly, quite a few of these were damaged or destroyed along Mbarak Hinawy Rd in the days when oversized trucks used the road for access to the old port.

By 1900, most of the houses in the main streets were owned by Indian businesspeople and traders whilst Mbarak Hinawy Rd (previously called Vasco da Gama St) and Government Square had become the centre for colonial government offices, banks, consulates and business or living quarters for colonial officials. Ndia Kuu housed immigrant entrepreneurs from India and Europe. The colonial headquarters at this time were situated in Leven House on the waterfront overlooking the old harbour, but shortly afterwards they were moved to Government Square and, in 1910, moved again up the hill to Treasury Square above Fort Jesus.

In later years, as Mombasa expanded along what are today the main roads, many of the businesses which had shops and offices in the Old Town gradually moved out, leaving behind ornate signs, etched glass windows and other relics of former times. Their exact location is described in *The Old Town Mombasa: A Historical Guide*.

You can start your exploration of the Old Town anywhere you like but the main points of interest are marked on the street map. There is a notice in Government Square saying that photography of the old harbour area (but not the buildings) is prohibited. It's doubtful how serious the authorities are about this since it's hard to see what is so sensitive about the place, but if you want pictures of it there are plenty of narrow streets leading off to the waterfront between the square and the Leven Steps where no-one will bother you.

Fort Jesus

The Old Town's biggest attraction dominates the harbour entrance. Begun in 1593 by the Portuguese, it changed hands nine times between 1631 and 1875. These days it's a museum and is open daily from 8.30 am to 6 pm. Entry costs KSh 200 for nonresidents and KSh 30 for residents (KSh 100 and KSh 10, respectively, for children under 12 years old). There are no student reductions.

It's well worth a visit and it's easy to pass a couple of hours here. Early morning is the best time as the air is still cool and the rest of the tourists are still in bed.

The fort was designed by an Italian architect, Joao Batista Cairato, who had done a lot of work for the Portuguese in Goa. He incorporated some ingenious elements into the design, such as the angular configuration of the walls, making it impossible for would-be invaders to lay siege to one wall without being sitting ducks for soldiers in one of the other walls.

The most interesting features today include the **Omani house** in the San Felipe bastion in the north-western corner of the fort. Built in the late 18th century it has served different functions as the purpose of the fort changed – it was the chief warder's house when the fort was a prison in the early

20th century. The view of the Old Town from the roof here is excellent.

The **museum** along the southern wall is built over what was the barracks rooms for the garrison. The exhibits are mostly ceramics but include other interesting odds and ends which have either been donated from private collections or dug up from various sites along the coast. The origins of many of the pieces are a reflection of the variety of cultures which has influenced the coastal culture – Chinese, Indian, Portuguese and Persian. Also displayed in the museum are finds from the Portuguese frigate *Santo António de Tanná* which sank off the fort during the siege in 1697.

The **western wall** of the fort is probably the most interesting and includes an Omani audience hall (now covered by a second storey but still complete with official inscriptions – and unofficial graffiti) and the Passage of the Arches – a passage cut through the coral giving access to the outer part of the fort, although it was later blocked off.

Harbour Cruises

Those looking for a luxury dhow cruise around the harbour should book a trip with Tamarind Dhow (☎ 229520) by calling direct or through Southern Cross Safaris, A La Carte Centre, Ratna Square (☎ 471948). This is a superb way of seeing the harbour, the Old Town and Fort Jesus from the water to the accompaniment of a gourmet meal, cocktails and a live band. You can even dance if you can still move after the meal! The food is excellent and prepared by chefs from the restaurant of the same name. The dhow itself is a motorised, ocean-going boat with an upper and main deck. The cruise, which starts from the jetty below the Tamarind Restaurant, takes you first down the harbour to Fort Jesus and then back up the harbour under Nyali Bridge, where it anchors for about an hour before returning to the jetty. There are two trips a day: the lunch-time cruise at 12.30 pm (two hours, cold seafood buffet, US$22) and the evening cruise at 6.30 pm (four hours, hot seafood or steak dinner, complimentary cocktail, US$65).

Prices include transport to and from your hotel.

A different type of dhow trip can be done with Kenya Marineland (☎ 485248) which is situated at Mtwapa Creek, some way up the coast going north. To join this trip you will be picked up from your hotel and taken to Kenya Marineland. After a tour of the Marineland you set sail for the open sea, weather permitting, and then return to Mtwapa Creek for lunch at the waterside restaurant. After lunch you set sail again up Mtwapa Creek finally returning to Kenya Marineland. On the return journey you will be entertained by acrobats, fire-eaters and limbo dancers. The trip lasts approximately four hours and costs KSh 1250 per person including transfer to and from your hotel, a barbecue lunch and entrance fees to the Marineland park, aquarium and snake farm.

There's also another outfit called Jahazi Marine Ltd (☎ 472213) which offers nighttime dhow cruises on Monday and Thursday for US$65. The price includes a sundowner cruise, with a cocktail, past Mombasa Old Town and the fort, a barbecue at Bamburi Nature Park, a torch-lit safari through the park, a visit to the casino and the Bora Bora Nightclub and transfers to and from your hotel.

Places to Stay

There's a lot of choice for budget travellers and for those who want something slightly better, both in the centre of the city and on the mainland to the north and south. Accommodation up and down the coast from Mombasa Island itself is dealt with later in this chapter.

Places to Stay – bottom end

One of the cheapest places to stay and just about habitable is the *Cozy Guest House* (☎ 313064), on Haile Selassie Rd, though we have had reports that women get hassled here. Singles/doubles cost KSh 260/400 with shared facilities. All the rooms have fans but due to chronic water problems the toilets can stink. The guesthouse will most likely be full if you get there late in the day.

THE COAST

PLACES TO STAY
1 New People's Lodge
6 Unity Guest House
12 Glory Bed & Breakfast
15 Excellent Guest House
16 New Al Jazira Hotel
   & Lucky Guest House
17 Cosy Hotel
18 Glory Guest House
19 Polana Hotel
20 Hotel Hermes
24 Hotel Splendid
26 Glory Guest House
30 Evening Guest House
33 Kilindini Guest House
42 New Palm Tree Hotel

PLACES TO EAT
13 Blue Room Restaurant
14 Indian Ocean Restaurant
23 Splendid View Restaurant
25 Pistachio Ice Cream
   & Coffee Bar
27 Le Bistro
29 Casablanca
   Restaurant & Bar
32 Mombasa Coffee House
35 Blue Fin Restaurant
36 Al Sultan Restaurant
38 Cafe Palacio
39 Hard Rock Cafe
44 Capri Restaurant,
   Air Kenya Aviation &
   Prestige Air Services
45 Fontanella Restaurant

OTHER
2 Buses & Matatus
  to Malindi & Lamu
3 Coast Bus
4 Bus Station
5 Cat Bus
7 Mawingo Buses
8 Akamba Bus
9 Malindi Taxi Bus
10 Pwani Forex Bureau
11 Market
21 Main Post Office (GPO)
22 Sheik Jundoni Mosque
28 Bahati Book Centre
31 Barclays Bank
34 Bahari Bookshop
37 Craft Stalls
40 Toyz Disco
41 Kenya Airways
43 Express Kenya (American
   Express) & Europcar
   Prestige Air Services
46 Fort Supermarket
47 Cathedral
48 US, Tanzanian &
   German Consulates

Central
Mombasa

0   100   200 m

Close by on Shibu Rd are the *New Al Jazira Hotel* and the *Lucky Guest House* (☎ 220895) which have singles/doubles with shared bath (no fans) for KSh 150/300. If you choose the Lucky then don't be too surprised if you have to wake up the staff on arrival. The entire lot of them were fast asleep when we arrived one day at 11 am.

Right in the centre of town on Digo Rd at the junction with Hospital Rd is the newly opened *Glory Bed & Breakfast* (☎ 314557) which has clean singles/doubles for KSh 400/500 with shared bathroom facilities. The price includes breakfast. Don't confuse this hotel with the two branches of the Glory Guest House, which are more expensive, or with the Glory Hotel Annexe at the back of the Casablanca, off Mnazi Moja Rd, which is basically a brothel. The name 'Glory' has proliferated around Mombasa in the last few years like mushrooms after rain.

Also good value in this range and convenient for the city centre is the *Evening Guest House* (☎ 221380), Mnazi Moja Rd, which has simple but very clean rooms at KSh 310 a single with shared bathroom facilities and KSh 410/500 for singles/doubles with attached bathroom. All the rooms have a fan and the hotel has its own restaurant. Reception is in the courtyard through the restaurant.

Around the corner from the Evening Guest House is the *Glory Hotel Annexe*. The rooms here are acceptable and include clean bedding, a fan and a washbasin, and the communal showers and toilets are scrubbed out regularly but it's basically a brothel. The price for a room varies but assume KSh 500 a double.

Another budget hotel at the northern end of the city centre, and one which has been popular for years, is the *New People's Lodge* (☎ 312831), on Abdel Nasser Rd right next to where the buses leave for Malindi and Lamu. Some travellers rate this place very highly and it certainly compares very well in price with the others but it is a little tatty and the rooms which face onto the main road are very noisy. The air also stinks of diesel fumes because bus drivers always rev their engines for up to an hour before they actually leave.

The management is friendly, and gear left in the rooms is safe. Rooms cost KSh 103/287 a single/double with shared showers and toilets, and KSh 235/414 a single/double with private facilities. There are also three, four and five-bed rooms with shared facilities. All the rooms have fans, the sheets are clean and the water in the showers is generally lukewarm. It's a large place and is rarely full. There's also a good, cheap restaurant downstairs.

Not far from the tourist office and similar in price to the other budget hotels is the quiet *Kilindini Guest House* off Shibu Rd.

Unless you just want a doss-house or are simply desperate then give the *Hydro Hotel*, Digo Rd at the Kenyatta Ave junction, the *Down Town Lodge*, Hospital Rd, the *Visitor's Inn*, corner of Haile Selassie and Shibu Rds, and the *Mvita Hotel*, corner of Hospital and Turkana Sts, a miss. The Mvita, in particular, has been allowed to decay into an appalling state of repair but, more importantly, it has become a hang-out for thieves who will not only break into your room but set you up for a mugging once you go outside. The management will not lift a finger to help you if this happens and the police are even less cooperative.

Places to Stay – middle

At the very bottom end of this category, but really good value and with a friendly manager, is the *Excellent Guest House* (☎ 311744) on Haile Selassie Rd. It offers bed and breakfast in rooms with bathrooms, mosquito nets, towel, soap, toilet paper and fans for KSh 700/900 for singles/doubles. All the rooms have a balcony and they're very well maintained.

Slightly more expensive is the *Hotel Splendid* (☎ 220967) on Msanifu Kombo St, a large place which is rarely full. It's a bit of a dive and far from splendid but it's relatively clean and has singles/doubles with attached bathrooms for KSh 800/950. The prices include breakfast. It's an old place and there's a popular rooftop restaurant which gets sea breezes in the evenings.

Better value and more modern but in a

somewhat less congenial part of town is the *Unity Guest House* (☎ 221298) just off Msanifu Kombo St. Singles with shared bathroom facilities cost KSh 400 and doubles/triples with own bathroom cost KSh 700/1125. There are also doubles with attached bathrooms, with air-con for KSh 1500. Prices include breakfast. It's a Muslim hotel so there's no bar and alcoholic drinks are prohibited.

Another well-maintained hotel in this category is the *Hotel Hermes* (☎ 313599) on Msanifu Kombo St near the Sheik Jundoni Mosque. The rooms are pleasant and most of them overlook the street but, because it's such good value for money, it's often full. Doubles (no singles) with attached bathrooms and air-con cost KSh 900 including breakfast.

Slightly further afield is the *Glory Guest House* (☎ 313204) on Shibu Rd. The rooms are a bit on the small side but are spotlessly clean and well maintained. Singles/doubles with attached bathrooms with fan cost KSh 600/800 plus there are singles/doubles with air-con for KSh800/1000. They also have a few singles/doubles with shared bathroom facilities for KSh 400/700. Breakfast is included in the price. There is a branch of this hotel on Haile Selassie Rd which offers bed and breakfast for KSh 400/700 with shared bathroom facilities and KSh 500/800 for singles/doubles with attached bathrooms. The standards at the two hotels are much the same.

Top value in this range is the *New Palm Tree Hotel* (☎ 312169), on Nkrumah Rd. All the rooms here are on the 1st and 2nd floor surrounding a spacious courtyard furnished with tables and chairs. A comfortable, spotlessly clean room with attached bathroom and fan costs KSh 897/1170 a single/double including breakfast. The staff are friendly and helpful, you can leave gear safely in the rooms and the hotel has its own bar (cheap, cold beers) and restaurant (tasty food at a reasonable price). It's popular with travellers.

Places to Stay – top end
One of the cheaper top-end hotels is the modern *Manson Hotel* (☎ 222356), on Kisumu Rd. It has 84 rooms with attached bathrooms which cost KSh 900/1200 a single/double without air-con and KSh 1300/1500 with air-con. Prices include breakfast. The hotel has a restaurant (exclusively vegetarian food) but no bar.

Similar in price and also some distance from the centre but close to the railway station, is the new *Hotel Sapphire* (☎ 491657) on Mwembe Tayari Rd. All the rooms have attached bathrooms with air-con and cost KSh 1800/2500 for singles/doubles, KSh 3300 for triples, all including breakfast. Facilities include the Mehfil Restaurant which serves Mughlai and continental dishes.

Much more centrally situated in the heart of the city is the brand new *Polana Hotel* (☎ 222168), Maungano Rd, close to the junction of Haile Selassie Rd and Msanifu Kombo St. It's a huge modern hotel with 140 rooms all of them fully air-con with bath, shower, mini-bar, TV (including CNN) and international direct-dial telephones. Singles/doubles including breakfast cost KSh 1930/2910. Facilities include a restaurant, bar, laundry service and in-house parking.

Superbly located overlooking the Indian Ocean and with a range of amenities which include Indian, Chinese and Italian restaurants, a swimming pool, casino and an open-air bar in a garden setting, is the relatively modern *Oceanic Hotel* (☎ 311191) off Oceanic Rd, not far from the Likoni ferry. Air-con rooms with attached bathrooms in this five-storey hotel cost KSh 1500/1800 a single/double and triples KSh 2100 including breakfast. All the rooms face the sea and most major credit cards are accepted. Considering the price, it's good value and the staff are friendly and helpful. Nonresidents can use the pool for KSh 100 per day.

Top of the range is the *New Outrigger Hotel* (☎ 220822), set in landscaped gardens leading down to Kilindini Harbour on the western side of Mombasa Island. All the rooms have attached bathrooms, with air-con and a balcony facing the harbour. Singles/doubles cost KSh 2300/3300 including breakfast. The hotel is under Belgian

THE COAST

management, the cuisine is French and there's a swimming pool.

Places to Eat

Mombasa has a good range of restaurants. If you are putting your own food together, or want to stock up with goodies to take down the coast, the Fort supermarket on Nyerere Ave is well stocked as is Nakumatt on Digo Rd. A wide variety of fruit and vegetables are available in the central market on Digo Rd next to the Hydro Hotel.

Places to Eat – cheap

If you are just looking for fish or chicken with chips try the *Blue Fin Restaurant*, on the corner of Meru Rd and Msanifu Kombo St. There's very little variety but it's not a bad place. There's a better choice at the *Blue Room Restaurant* on Haile Selassie Rd. which is a serve-yourself, fast-food joint offering a whole range of western and Indian staples such as sausages, samosas, pakoras, chips and the like at KSh 30 per piece, as well as burgers from around KSh 100, and pizzas from KSh 150 to KSh 250 depending on toppings. It's very clean, the food is fresh and there's no waiting. It's recommended for an inexpensive breakfast, lunch or late afternoon snack.

Slightly cheaper snacks of the same variety can be found at the *Indian Ocean Restaurant* on Msanifu Kombo St but it also offers lunch-time and evening specials of Swahili and Indian food for around KSh 150 (up to KSh 250 if you want prawns, for example). This restaurant is highly recommended and is open daily from 7 am until 8.30 pm. Specials are chalked up on a blackboard outside the restaurant.

If you're staying at either the Cosy Guest House or the New Al Jazira Hotel, the *Kencoast Cafe* opposite has delicious local dishes at really cheap prices. Service is very friendly.

Recommended for breakfast and snacks is the *Sky Bar & Restaurant* on Moi Ave not far from the tusks. You can eat a main meal here (chicken and chips, for instance) for around KSh 125. Similar is the *Franco Restaurant*

just beyond the tusks opposite the tourist office which is open seven days a week and offers buffet lunches and fruit juices at a very reasonable price.

The *Mombasa Coffee House* on Moi Ave is a good place for fresh coffee and snacks, and you can also buy coffee beans here.

Indian Food Since many of the restaurants in Mombasa are Indian-owned you can find excellent curries and thalis and at lunch time (from 12.30 to around 3 pm) there is often a cheap, substantial set meal available.

One such place is the popular *New Chetna Restaurant*, on Haile Selassie Rd directly under the Cozy Guest House. The food here is south Indian vegetarian (with dishes such as masala dosa and idli) and sweets. An all-you-can-eat set vegetarian lunch costs KSh 150.

Excellent tandoori specialities can be found at the very popular *Splendid View Restaurant*, Maungano Rd, which is opposite, but not part of, the Hotel Splendid. Food on offer includes chicken, lamb, fruit juices and lassis and you can eat well here for around KSh 150. There are tables outside and inside. The restaurant is open Monday to Saturday from 11.30 am to 2 pm and 4 to 11.30 pm, and on Sunday from 4.30 to 11.30 pm. It's very popular with local Asians so you know it must be good.

Swahili Food For coastal Swahili dishes made with coconut and coconut milk, the *Swahili Curry Bowl*, on Tangana Rd off Moi Ave, is recommended. Prices are reasonable. It's also one of *the* places for coffee and ice cream. Don't bother trekking out here on a Sunday as it's closed then.

Another excellent place, and one you should try at least once, is the *Recoda Restaurant* on Nyeri St in the Old Town. It's a hugely popular place among the locals and the tables are set up along the footpath. The atmosphere is great and the waiters are keen to explain what is available that day – usually dishes such as beans in coconut, grilled fish, meat, superb chapatis and salad. You may well find yourself coming back here each night. This is a Muslim restaurant so there are no alcoholic drinks and it's closed all day until after sunset during Ramadan.

Places to Eat – more expensive

Going up in price, the rooftop restaurant in the *Hotel Splendid* catches the breeze in the evenings and has surprisingly moderate prices (from KSh 100 for a main meal), though the food is only mediocre. Don't come here with any ideas of having a quick meal, as the service is far from lightning fast.

The new Hotel Sapphire also has the *Mehfil Restaurant* which serves Mughlai and continental dishes as does the *Al Sultan Restaurant* on Meru Rd close to the junction with Msanifu Kombo Rd but the latter is closed for the entire month of Ramadan.

The *Pistachio Ice Cream & Coffee Bar* is a small cafe near the Hotel Splendid. Not only does it have excellent ice cream, but the fruit shakes are great. The buffet lunch or dinner for KSh 150 is not bad value although the selection is limited. À la carte dishes such as spaghetti are also served. It's open daily from 9 am to 10 pm.

For Chinese food you could try the *Chinese Overseas Restaurant* (☎ 221585) on Moi Ave, just north of the tusks on the left-hand side. Main dishes are priced around KSh 250 to KSh 300.

The *Fontanella Restaurant* is in a shady courtyard on the corner of Digo Rd and Moi Ave. The extensive menu runs the whole gamut from fish and chips through steaks to lobster thermidor but it's quite expensive with main dishes ranging from KSh 250 to KSh 350. Consider it something of a splurge unless you're just here for a quiet beer or snack.

For a modest splurge, head for *Le Bistro* (☎ 229470), on Moi Avenue, close to the tusks. This restaurant and cocktail bar is owned and run by the same Swiss Germans who own the Pistacchio and it's open daily from breakfast to late at night. Both the atmosphere and the food, which includes pizza, pasta, steak and seafood, are excellent. Expect to pay around KSh 100 for a starter and from KSh 210 to KSh 300 for a main

dish though there are considerably cheaper snacks such as toasted sandwiches and hamburgers as well as lunch-time specials chalked up on the board outside. Beers are cold and reasonably priced plus there's a fairly extensive wine menu (a bottle of chianti, for instance, costs around KSh 800).

Tasty continental-style food as well as a number of tandoori specialities can be found at the new *Casablanca Restaurant & Bar*, Mnazi Moja Rd, for around KSh 250. It's very popular with westerners and Africans alike and consists of a double-storey, makuti-roofed, open-air bar/restaurant which is open all day until very late. It has an excellent music system, TVs and a disco each evening. It attracts much the same clientele as Buffalo Bill's in Nairobi but the food is streets ahead and there's no hassle plus the beers *are* cold – not lukewarm.

The *Cafe Palacio* (☎ 226149) at the junction of Moi Ave and Digo Rd attempts to be Mombasa's answer to McDonald's and Kentucky Fried Chicken but in this it fails miserably. The chicken is certainly very tender and well cooked but far from hot, the fish is tired and tasteless and the chips are cold and soggy. Worst of all are the so-called 'fruit juices' which are just watered-down synthetic cordial. We didn't try any of the seven varieties of pizza or the doner kebabs – maybe they're better – but you'll reel at the bill which will be around KSh 250 to KSh 300 for what is essentially a very mediocre meal.

Those keen to dine in an atmosphere as far removed from Kenya as anyone could imagine, and to choose from a range of dishes named after famous musicians, should try the *Hard Rock Cafe* (☎ 222221) Nkrumah Rd, next door to Kenya Airways. It's all somewhat contrived and it's nowhere near as well designed as the Nairobi Hard Rock but it's popular with package tourists and local yuppies. Before you go for a meal here you need to be absolutely certain that a constant bombardment of heavy rap music will be conducive to the digestive process. A main course plus a drink will set you back around KSh 400 to KSh 500.

Mombasa's best restaurant by far – at least as far as the island itself is concerned – is the *Capri Restaurant* (☎ 311156), in Ambalal House, Nkrumah Rd, opposite Kenya Airways. Originally set up by a Swiss man and still with a European head chef, the food is superb with a range of continental and seafood dishes as well as a well-stocked cellar of European wines. Nowhere in the island itself compares. It's open daily for lunch and dinner but closed on Sunday and public holidays. Expect to pay around KSh 500 to KSh 600 for a full meal without wine or beer. Attached to this restaurant is the *Hunters' Bar* which is a good place for an ice-cold beer in air-con surroundings as well as somewhat cheaper meals (around KSh 250 to KSh 300 for a main dish) encompassing a range of daily specials. The Hunters' is very popular at lunch times with local office workers. Wildlife conservationists should be aware that the walls of the bar are festooned with hunting trophies from a bygone era and the guy who shot them certainly wasn't a greenie. Even so, the atmosphere is very mellow and the staff are cheerful.

Down on the ground floor of the same building is a branch of the restaurant called the *Arcade Cafe* (open from 8.30 am to 5.30 pm) which serves coffee, fruit juices, milk shakes, pizza, hot dogs, meat pies, sandwiches and ice cream.

Head and shoulders above all the rest is the *Tamarind Restaurant* (☎ 471747) on the foreshore across from the Old Dhow Harbour in Nyali. This is a beautifully conceived, part open-air restaurant in Swahili style and festooned with bougainvillea. The food is superb, the service impeccable and the restaurant is open for lunch and dinner every day. Prices reflect the calibre of the place but it's well worth the splurge. You won't find better seafood anywhere in Kenya. Expect to pay at least KSh 1000 per head and considerably more if you take wine with your meal. Even a beer costs KSh 115 here. It's very popular in the evenings with discerning people who have money to spend.

Entertainment

The best nightclub/disco is the *New Florida Casino & Nightclub* on Mama Ngina Drive. Built right on the seashore and enclosing its own swimming pool, it's owned by the same people who run the Florida clubs in Nairobi. The atmosphere is much the same but here there are three open-air bars as well as an enclosed dancing area. Entry costs KSh 150 for men and KSh 70 for women (slightly more on Friday and Saturday nights) or KSh 50 per person on Sunday afternoon until 8 pm.

If you're looking for a slightly quieter night without the endless booming rap music of the Florida then give *Toyz*, on Baluchi St off Nkrumah Rd, a spin. Entry costs KSh 100 per person, the main part is air-con and there's an upstairs, open-air area where you can get away from the noise. Beers are advertised as costing KSh 60 but, as the night grinds on, they miraculously transform into KSh 70 so keep an eye on your bill.

Things to Buy

While Mombasa isn't the craft entrepôt you might expect it to be, it's still not too bad. The trouble is that there are a lot of tourists and sailors who pass through this port with lots of dollars to shed in a hurry. Bargains, therefore, can take a long time to negotiate. The main craft stall area is along Moi Ave from the roundabout with Nyerere Ave to Msanifu Kombo St. Many specialist craft shops have sprung up in recent years in the Old Town close to Fort Jesus, especially along Mbarak Hinawy Rd and Ndia Kuu.

Along Moi Ave it's mainly makonde woodcarvings, soapstone chess sets and animal or human figurines, basketwork, drums and other musical instruments, and paintings.

Biashara St, which runs west of the Digo Rd intersection, is the centre for fabrics and kangas or kikoi, those colourful, beautifully patterned, wraparound skirts complete with Swahili proverbs, which most East African women (who aren't Hindus) wear even if they wear it under a buibui (black wraparound skirt). You may need to bargain a little over the price (but not too much). What you get is generally what you pay for and, as a rule, they cost around KSh 300 a pair (they are not sold singly). Assuming you are willing to bargain, the price you pay for one will reflect the quality of the cloth. Buy them in Mombasa if possible. You can sometimes get them as cheaply in Nairobi but elsewhere prices escalate rapidly.

Getting There & Away
Air Kenya Airways flies between Nairobi and Mombasa in either direction at least five times daily. Most of these flights are nonstop but some go via Malindi. The fare from Nairobi to either Mombasa or Malindi is KSh 4680 one way. If you're relying on these flights to get back to Nairobi to connect with an international flight, then make absolutely sure you have a confirmed booking or, preferably, go back a day before.

International destinations served from Mombasa are Zanzibar and Kilimanjaro (for Arusha and Moshi). See the Kenya Getting There & Away chapter for details.

Three companies with lighter twin-prop planes operate flights from Mombasa to Malindi and Lamu. They are Air Kenya Aviation (☎ Mombasa 229777), Eagle Aviation Ltd (☎ Mombasa 316054) and Prestige Air Services Ltd (☎ Mombasa 21443). Both Air Kenya and Prestige Air Services have offices on the ground floor of Ambalal House, Nkrumah Rd. Each company has two flights per day in either direction between Mombasa and Lamu (US$85) via Malindi (US$28). The baggage allowance is 15 kg per person on Air Kenya and 10 kg on the other two companies' flights. Most of the time you won't be hassled if your baggage weighs over this amount but, even if you are, excess charges are minimal (KSh 35 per kg).

Air Kenya Aviation also flies south from Mombasa to Ukunda (for Diani Beach) twice a week (US$25).

Bus & Matatu In Mombasa bus offices are mainly along Jomo Kenyatta Ave except for Malindi Bus which is on Abdel Nasser Rd. For buses and matatus to the south of Mombasa you first need to get off the island via the Likoni ferry (see Boat in the later Getting Around section).

Nairobi For Nairobi, there are many departures daily in either direction (mostly in the early morning and late evening) by, among others, Coast, Crossline, Mawingo, Takrim, Tawfiq, Taita, Malindi and Akamba. The fare is KSh 300 and the trip takes from seven to eight hours including a meal break about halfway. Most of these companies have at least four departures daily, usually two in the early morning and two at night, while Malindi Bus has six departures daily at 8.30, 9 and 9.30 am, and 8, 9 and 10 pm.

Safer and more comfortable but more expensive are the shuttle services in either direction run by two companies. They are Sav-Line and The Connection. They both offer air-con, 18-seater minibuses for KSh 900 per person one way which will drop you off anywhere in the two city centres. Bookings for Sav-Line should be made at Savage Camping Tours (☎ 228236), Diamond Trust House, Moi Ave, Nairobi. Bookings with The Connection can be made at Inside Africa Safaris (☎ 223304), Wabera St, Nairobi, and at Tamana Holidays (☎ 315208), Moi Ave, Mombasa.

Malindi To Malindi there are also many departures daily in either direction from early morning until late afternoon by several bus companies and matatus. Buses take up to 2½ hours; matatus about two hours. In Mombasa they all depart from outside the New People's Hotel, Abdel Nasser Rd. See the Malindi section for more details.

It's possible to go straight through from Mombasa to Lamu but most travellers stop en route at Malindi.

Tanzania For Tanga, Dar es Salaam and Morogoro in Tanzania, Hood Bus/Cat Bus has departures three times a week. See the Kenya Getting There & Away chapter for details.

Share-Taxi Shared taxis from Mombasa to Malindi are expensive these days. Assume

KSh 4000 for the car shared between four people. You may occasionally get one for KSh 3500 if you speak Swahili. If you're alone, you can fly for the same amount.

Train Trains to or from Nairobi operate in either direction at 7 pm, arriving the next day at 8.30 am. The fares are KSh 2750 in 1st class and KSh 1930 in 2nd class. Fares include dinner, breakfast and bedding (whether you want them or not). You should make a reservation as far in advance as possible as demand sometimes exceeds supply. The booking office at the station in Mombasa is open daily from 8 am to noon, and 2 to 6.30 pm.

The left-luggage service at the railway station costs KSh 12 per item per day. It's open from 8 am to noon and 2 to 6.30 pm Monday to Saturday, and from 7.30 to 10 am and 2 to 6.30 pm on Sunday.

Boat Depending on the season, it's possible to get a ride on a dhow to Pemba, Zanzibar or Dar es Salaam in Tanzania, but departures are very infrequent; the ferry is much more reliable. See the Kenya Getting There & Away chapter for details.

Getting Around

The Airport Kenya Airways operates a shuttle bus from its Nkrumah Rd office at 10.20 am, and 2.20 and 5.40 pm. There's a regular public bus which goes to the airport and costs a few shillings. Any 'Port Reitz' matatu will take you past the airport turn-off (ask to be dropped off) from where it's about a 15-minute walk. The standard taxi fare is KSh 700 although the initial price starts at KSh 1000.

Taxi Even for short distances, taxi drivers will attempt to charge you whatever they think they can get out of you so you must bargain but, if you're going to spend a lot of time in Mombasa, get down to the New Florida Nightclub outside of which is a board detailing what you should be paying for specific journeys. Otherwise, assume KSh 200 from the railway station to the city centre and

KSh 700 between the city centre and the airport. A 'taxi' can be anything from a well-maintained London cab to a beaten-up old wreck you can't even open the door of and which the police will stop at every opportunity demanding *kitu kidogo* ('a little something').

Car & Motorcycle All the major hire companies and many of the smaller outfits have branch offices in Mombasa. Most of them (such as Avis, Payless and Glory) are on Moi Ave. Europcar is on Nkrumah Rd. Details of hire charges and conditions can be found under Rental Agencies in the Kenya Getting Around chapter.

Boat The Likoni ferry connects Mombasa Island with the southern mainland and runs at frequent intervals throughout the night and day. There's a crossing every 20 minutes on average between 5 am and 12.30 am; less frequently between 12.30 and 5 am. It's free to pedestrians; KSh 17 for a car. To get to the ferry from the centre of town take a Likoni matatu from outside the GPO on Digo Rd.

South of Mombasa

The real attractions of the coast south of Mombasa are the beaches, and although it is basically all resort hotels, there are a few options for the budget traveller – at Tiwi and Diani beaches.

All the beaches are white coral sand and are protected by a coral reef so there is no danger from sharks when you go swimming. Tiwi is probably the best beach since it's less developed though, like Shelly, it suffers from large amounts of floating seaweed, depending on the season. Diani doesn't have this to anywhere near the same extent but in some places much of the sand has been washed away leaving just a coral bed.

SHELLY BEACH
Shelly Beach is the closest beach to Mombasa and as such, is not a bad place to swim if you just want to day-trip from

Mombasa, though, at times, it's like pea soup because of the seaweed problem. There is no budget accommodation available here so forget it for a long stay unless you have plenty of money.

Places to Stay

The cheapest place to stay, but some distance from the beach, is the *CPK Guest House* (☎ (011) 451619) not far from the Likoni ferry. It's a pleasant place, and costs KSh 350 per person with breakfast.

One of the few places to stay on the beach itself (other than renting a holiday let) is the *Shelly Beach Hotel* (☎ (011) 451001), about three km from the Likoni ferry. As far as resort hotels go it's not a bad place, and seems to be popular with British tour groups. Most people seem to prefer swimming in the pool rather than in the sea just a few metres away. Half-board rates are KSh 1400/2000 for singles/doubles, more with air-con. In the off season it should be possible to get a reduction on these rates.

Further south are *Savannah Cottages* (☎ (011) 23456) which have air-con holiday lets with fully equipped kitchens, bathrooms, lounge and dining areas, and double bed-rooms with twin-bunk beds.

Getting There & Away

From the Likoni ferry, take the first turn to the left after the bus stand. From here it's a 30-minute walk and there are occasional matatus and enough traffic to make hitching possible. The Shelly Beach Hotel has its own transport into town, but you pay extra for this.

TIWI BEACH

Next along the coast is Tiwi Beach, also about two or three km off the main coast road, along either one of two gravel tracks (only one of which is signposted 'Tiwi') which wind their way through the coastal scrub. This is the best beach to head for if you're on a budget and/or have your own camping gear. It's also the least developed, though there's not much in the way of beachfront which isn't already spoken for.

Twiga Lodge, Coral Cove Cottages, Minilets, Tiwi Villas, Capricho Beach Cottages, Sand Island Beach Cottages

Southern Palms Beach Resort, Golden Beach Hotel, African Papaya Night Club & Restaurant, Diani Reef Grand Hotel, Diani Complex, Leisure Lodge & Casino, Leopard Beach Hotel, Coral Beach Cottages, Galaxy Chinese Restaurant

Kaskazi Beach Hotel, Diani Beach Shopping Centre, Trade Winds Hotel & Dan Trench's, Restaurant Maharani, Diani Sea Resort, Ali Barbour's Restaurant, Diani Sea Lodge, Hähnchen Grill & Nightclub

Two Fishes Hotel, Snake Park, Jadini Beach Hotel/Africana Sea Lodge, Nomad Beach Hotel, Paradise Ocean Village Club, Lagoon Reef Hotel, Robinson Baobab Club, White Rose Villas

Four Twenty South, Diani Beachalots, Vulcano Restaurant, Le Paradis Cottages, Diani Beach Cottages, Boko Coco le Mer Restaurant, Galu Supermarket, Galu Sea Lodge

Beaches South of Mombasa

0   5   10 km

The good thing here is that the hotels are low key, consisting mainly of individual cottages with a central bar and restaurant appealing to independent travellers. It's a totally different world from the package tourist ghetto of Diani Beach. You'll find the prices also reflect this difference.

The thing which you must do at this beach is book in advance if you intend to stay during the high season (January, April to early July, August to early September and Christmas/New Year), otherwise you may well find them full, although with the current downturn in tourism that is becoming less likely. Even so, it's wise to book ahead for the self-catering lodges at *any* time of year.

The last thing you need to know is that you'll have to bring all your own food and drink if you're staying at a self-catering lodge, though you could, of course, arrange to eat at a lodge which has a restaurant and bar.

From north to south, the hotels are: Sand Island Beach Cottages, Capricho Beach Cottages, Maweni Beach Cottages, Tiwi Villas, Coral Cove Cottages, Twiga Lodge, Minilets and Tiwi Beachalets. Most of these are signposted on the main road.

Activities

Next to the Twiga Lodge is a small outfit called Tiwi Divers, which offers good snorkelling and diving expeditions. Snorkelling is KSh 500 and lasts about two hours. If you just want to snorkel out from the beach, gear can be hired for around KSh 250 per day.

Places to Stay & Eat

Cheapest of the lot (but only by a small margin) is the very popular *Twiga Lodge* (☎ (0127) 51267). It is certainly *the* place to camp along the coast as you can pitch your tent just a few metres from the water plus there's plenty of shade. Camping costs KSh 120 per person, and includes access to good showers and toilets. Single/double rooms go for KSh 500/1000 with breakfast plus there are cottages accommodating four people for KSh 1000 (plus KSh 250 for each extra bed if there are more than four people). There's a restaurant, bar and shop. It's a good place

to stay as there's usually an interesting mix of people here.

Right next door to the Twiga Lodge are the *Coral Cove Cottages* (☎ (0127) 51062). The cottages here are similar in price to those at Twiga Lodge and range from having no facilities to being fully self-contained (complete with cooking equipment). It's a very pleasant place to stay and popular with young expatriate workers.

South of Twiga Lodge are the *Minilets* (☎ (0127) 51059), a collection of small, cottages with attached bathrooms, connected to the beach by a series of paved walkways. Singles/doubles are good value at KSh 600/800, and there's a bar and restaurant. This is a popular place among foreign workers living in Nairobi.

Going further north, *Tiwi Villas* (☎ (0127) 51265) is an attractive complex, on top of a small cliff, with a swimming pool, bar and restaurant. A double cottage here costs KSh 900, and one which sleeps four people KSh 1500.

Further up the coast, the *Capricho Beach Cottages* (☎ (0127) 51231) are a collection of one, two and three-bedroom cottages with lounge/dining room, bathroom, verandah and a full range of cooking equipment. You must provide your own bed linen and mosquito nets, though these can be hired with advance notice. A two-person cottage ranges from KSh 1345 in the off season to KSh 1450 in the high season. A cottage sleeping six people ranges from KSh 2460 to KSh 3000. The complex has its own swimming pool.

Beyond here, the *Sand Island Beach Cottages* (☎ (0127) 51233) is another group of self-catering cottages similar to those at Capricho which range in price between KSh 1345 and KSh 1440 for two people, up to KSh 2457 and KSh 3475 for six people, depending on the season. Bed linen and mosquito nets must be brought with you unless arranged in advance.

Getting There & Away

The buses and matatus drop you at the start of the gravel access road, from where it's a three-km (45-minute) walk. This road is notorious for muggings so, unless you're part of a group (in which case you can assume you're safe), wait for a lift. There are no buses or matatus but there are quite a few cars so you shouldn't have to wait too long. Taxis also run between the beach and highway.

DIANI BEACH

Diani is a package-tourist hotel/resort complex. If you're an independent traveller looking for a patch of authentic Kenyan coast and a mellow atmosphere, chances are you'll hate it here. The promotional literature looks very alluring and the architecture can be very imaginative but the clientele is dreadful.

At least, that's the story as far as the tarmac stretches at the back of this beachfront development. Further south, it does change and you get back into something resembling the Kenyan coast before the 'developers' got here. It's in this area that you'll find Dan Trench's, which is the only budget accommodation that you'll find on this part of the coast.

As at Tiwi beach, it's a good idea to make advance booking for any of the cheaper places at Diani during the high season otherwise you'll find them full, though some sort of accommodation can usually be found at any time at Dan Trench's.

Information

The village of Ukunda on the main Mombasa to Tanzania highway is the turn-off point for Diani Beach. It's here that you'll find the nearest post office plus a number of basic lodging houses. From here a tarmac road runs about two km down to a T-junction with the beach road which runs several km in either direction north and south. Along this beach road is everything which Diani has to offer.

Dangers & Annoyances

Do not walk along the road from Ukunda to the beach road. It's notorious for muggings. Avoiding walking is no problem as there are plenty of matatus (and KBS buses) running

backwards and forwards all day on their way to or from Likoni. Similarly, don't walk along the beach from Diani to Tiwi. The place where you cross the creek that divides the two is known locally as Machete Point, and many travellers have been done over here. If you do decide to walk, make sure it is at low tide, as the creek crossing is quite deep at high tide and you'll need to swim across.

Places to Stay – bottom end

The only cheap place is *Dan Trench's* (PO Box 8, Ukunda), behind the Trade Winds Hotel. It's not signposted, but if you turn off when you see the sign for the Trade Winds, it's on the right before you get to the Trade Winds entrance gate. This place is well set up for budget travellers and there's a range of accommodation options. Camping costs KSh 150 per person per night (no tents for hire), and there are single/double rooms at KSh 250 per person per night. There's also a few apartments with kitchen, bathroom, lounge and verandah at KSh 600 per day. It's a mellow place, and there are no security problems. If you're staying here you can use the beach and bar at the Trade Winds Hotel.

Places to Stay – middle

The only places in this category, and even these are not cheap, are the lodges and cottages south of the tarmac on the beach road.

At the southern end, after two km of potholed dirt road, is the *Galu Sea Lodge*, a pleasant two-storey building with a swimming pool. Next, heading north, you come to the Galu supermarket then the Boko Boko Coco le Mer Restaurant followed by the *Diani Beach Cottages* (☎ (0127) 3471) at US$55/75 for singles/doubles with half board. All major credit cards are accepted.

Next up are *Le Paradis Cottages*, the Vulcano Restaurant and *Diani Beachalets* (☎ (0127) 2180). At the latter, there's a range of rooms, with attached bathrooms, ranging from KSh 1050 in the high season (KSh 750 in the low season) for one bedroom, up to KSh 1600 in the high season (KSh 1250 in the low season) for four bedrooms, all plus 17% tax.

Further north still, at the beginning of the tarmac, is the popular *Four Twenty South* (☎ (0127) 2065). Here there are a number of different cottages which cost from KSh 1200 a double in the high season (KSh 850 in the low season) plus KSh 300 for each extra person. Bookings can be made through Let's Go Travel in Nairobi.

Unless indicated, all the above places to stay are self-catering and kitchen facilities are provided.

Beyond this point you're looking at major expense and the sort of ennui that only major resort complexes can offer.

Places to Stay – top end

The other hotels along this beach cost megabucks and are basically for those who have got money to burn. They range in price from US$40/50 a single/double to US$55/75 in the low season to *double* and *triple* that in the high season with full board.

With the downturn in tourism at the coast, those who are staying here have usually paid a fraction of these prices as part of an all-inclusive package from Europe. If you just want to stay for a night or two, ring around, as you should be able to get a significant discount.

All the resorts offer much the same – air-con rooms, swimming pool, bars, restaurant, usually a disco, and some have water sports equipment for hire. The better ones (and there are quite a few) have been designed with the environment and local architectural styles in mind; others are not so special.

From north to south along the strip the hotels are as follows (prices are for singles/doubles unless otherwise stated):

Southern Palms Beach Resort – KSh 2500/3500 with half board (low season); KSh 3500/5000 in the high season (☎ (0127) 3721)

Golden Beach Hotel – US$60/90 with half board (low season); US$120/160 in the high season (☎ (0127) 2625)

Indian Ocean Beach Club – US$74/148 with half board (low season); US$147/227 in the high season

Diani Reef Grand Hotel – US$103/144 with half board (low season); US$146/220 in the high season. There are also more expensive deluxe rooms (☎ (0127) 51215).

Leisure Lodge & Casino – US$100/130 with full board (low season); US$140/152 in the high season. There are also more expensive suites (☎ (0127) 2011).

Leopard Beach Hotel – US$60/90 with full board (low season); US$120/180 in the high season. There are also more expensive suites and cottages (☎ (0127) 2111).

Kaskazi Beach Hotel – US$100/140 for singles/doubles including breakfast (low season); US$120/150 in the high season (☎ (0127) 3725)

Trade Winds Hotel – US$50/100 with full board (low season); US$100/130 (high season)

Diani Sea Lodge – US$120/160 with full board in the high season (☎ (0127) 2115)

Two Fishes Hotel – US$57/98 with half board (low season); US$112/144 in the high season (☎ (0127) 2101)

Jadini Beach Hotel/Africana Sea Lodge – US$50/85 with half board (low season); US$87/120 in the high season (☎ (0127) 2269)

Nomad Beach Hotel – US$60/90 for a one-bedroom banda including breakfast; US$111/150 for a three-bed banda/cottage; US$130/170 for a four-bed banda/cottage (☎ (0127) 2155)

Safari Beach Hotel – US$57/95 with half board (low season); US$97/135 in the high season (☎ (0127) 2357)

Lagoon Reef Hotel – US$55/90 with half board (low season); US$124/170 in the high season (☎ (0127) 2627)

The Trade Winds Hotel and the Golden Beach Hotel are part of the African Tours & Hotels group. Bookings can be made through them at PO Box 30471, Nairobi (☎ (02) 336858).

The Lagoon Reef Hotel is part of the Reef Hotels group. Bookings can be made through Mombasa (☎ (011) 471771).

The Safari Beach Hotel, Jadini Beach Hotel and the Africana Sea Lodge are all part of the Alliance Hotels group (☎ (02) 332825).

The Indian Ocean Beach Club belongs to Block Hotels (☎ (02) 540780) in Nairobi.

Places to Eat

Diani beach is well supplied with shopping centres so you needn't bring everything with you from Ukunda village if you are self-catering, though the fruit and vegetables are naturally more expensive on the beach road than they are in Ukunda.

One of the largest complexes is the Diani Beach shopping centre, not far from the Trade Winds Hotel. It has a supermarket, bank, doctor's surgery, boutiques and a branch of Glory Car Hire. Further north there is Quinnsworth supermarket and, further north again, is the Diani Complex which has a supermarket, a branch of the Kenya Commercial Bank, a boutique and an Indian restaurant. Way down south beyond the tarmac and not far from the Galu Sea Lodge, is the Galu supermarket which is OK for basics but carries only a limited range of goods.

If you're staying at the southern end of the beach off the tarmac, there's the *Vulcano Restaurant da Lina* which is an excellent place to eat, though a bit of a splurge. It's open every night from 7 pm until late and offers a range of classic Italian dishes as well as seafood (lobster, prawns, crabs, calamari and fish).

Back on the tarmac about halfway towards the T-junction are a cluster of restaurants and nightclubs. Here you'll find the *Hähnchen Grill & Nightclub* (which, as the name suggests, is a German restaurant), *Temura's Restaurant* and the *Restaurant Maharani*. The latter is an Indian restaurant and is open daily from 7 to 11 pm as well as for lunch on Saturday and Sunday from 12.30 to 3 pm. In the same area but down a track on the opposite side of the road is *Ali Barbour's* which is an expensive seafood restaurant set in a coral cave between the Trade Winds Hotel and the Diani Sea Lodge.

North of the T-junction are the *Galaxy Chinese Restaurant* (which is next to the Quinnsworth supermarket) and the *Shan-e-Punjab* Indian restaurant in the Diani Complex. Beyond here, not far from the Diani Reef Grand Hotel, is the *African Papaya Nightclub & Restaurant*.

Apart from the above, many of the beach hotels offer buffet lunches and dinners at weekends which are open for non-guests. Make enquiries as to which currently offer the best deals and/or food. Most are priced in the KSh 500 to KSh 800 range.

Entertainment

Apart from the discos in the hotels (which you may have difficulty getting into if you're not a guest), there are at least four discos independent of the hotels. Because the clientele is more mixed in these discos they're more lively and worth checking out.

Opposite the Two Fishes Hotel is the *Bush Baby Nightclub*, an open-air restaurant and nightclub which is not a bad place for a bop. Not too far from here is the nightclub at the Hähnchen Grill (see Places to Eat). Almost next door to this is the *Shakatak Disco*. It's probably the best of the lot and entry is free although drinks are expensive.

Lastly, way up near the northern end of the tarmac, is the *African Papaya Nightclub & Restaurant* (see the earlier Places to Eat section).

Getting There & Away

Diani is the most accessible beach if you are dependent on public transport. From the Likoni ferry there are KBS buses (No 32) every 20 minutes or so from early morning until around 7 pm. The fare is minimal and the trip takes about 30 minutes.

Plenty of matatus make the trip from Likoni to Diani. They do the journey slightly faster and cost a little more.

When the buses and matatus get to Diani they first head north along the Diani beach road then turn around and go to the southern end of the bitumen where they turn again and head for Likoni. Just tell the driver where you want to get off.

SHIMONI & WASINI ISLAND

Shimoni is right out at the end of a small peninsula 76 km south of Likoni, and not far from the Tanzanian border. There's not a great deal here apart from the Shimoni Reef Lodge, but it's the headquarters of the Kisite Marine National Park.

Wasini Island itself is just off the coast of the Shimoni Peninsula. It's well wooded and unspoilt and is the perfect place to relax and experience a Swahili culture virtually un-touched by the 20th century and tourism. There are no cars, roads or running water and the only electricity comes from generators.

On a wander around you can come across Muslim ruins, local women weaving mats, men preparing for fishing by mending nets and making fish traps, huge old baobab trees and the extensive 'coral gardens' with its odd-shaped stands of old coral that you can walk through (except at certain times of year when the sea floods it).

Kisite Marine National Park
To visit this park, which is offshore to the south-east of Wasini Island, you'll need to go by boat. See the park headquarters in Shimoni to make arrangements. Entry to the park costs US$6 for nonresidents and KSh 100 for residents. Boats to take you there cost KSh 300 per person (less than 12 people) or KSh 150 per person (12 or more people). If the sea is rough, the boats don't sail so keep an eye on the weather and tides.

Snorkelling & Diving
In addition to the boats which can be hired from the Kisite park headquarters in Shimoni, Masood Abdullah (who runs the Mpunguti Restaurant on Wasini Island) can arrange trips to the marine park. He has his own dhow as well as masks and snorkels.

Kisite Dhow Tours in Diani, which oper-ates out of the Jadini Beach Hotel (☎ (0127) 2269) offers full-day tours from Shimoni jetty for US$65 from Diani. This includes transport, snorkelling in the marine park and a seafood lunch. You would be hard pressed to organise it for much less on your own.

Diving safaris off Pemba channel (spec-tacular!) and dhow trips to Kisite Marine National Park can also be arranged from the Shimoni Reef Hotel, but they are expensive.

Places to Stay & Eat
The only place to stay at Shimoni is the *Shimoni Reef Lodge* (☎ (011) 471771 in Mombasa; 9 in Shimoni), which is beauti-fully situated on a bluff overlooking the channel to Wasini Island. The facilities are excellent and it's a very mellow place to stay. The price for singles/doubles with half board is US$55/90 in the low season, US$124/166 in the high season.

Across the channel on Wasini Island, the only accommodation is at the *Mpunguti Res-taurant*, run by Mr Masood Adullah. You can camp here if you have your own gear for KSh 100 per person per night or rent a very clean and pleasant room for KSh 800/1200 (half board). Cooking facilities are available for those who prefer self-catering (fish, coconuts, maize flour and rice are for sale in Shimoni and on Wasini, but very little else).

Masood is a very affable character and well organised, and the traditional Swahili food he turns out is delicious. Alcoholic drinks must be brought with you from the mainland – there are none available on the island.

The only other accommodation in the area is the *Pemba Channel Fishing Club*, which charges US$110/180 for full board, however it does not take children under eight years old.

Getting There & Away
There are a couple of direct buses and matatus daily between Shimoni and Likoni. Hitching is also a possibility.

From Likoni there are taxis available to Shimoni, or you can take one of the few KBS buses which do the trip daily. You could also take a matatu towards Lunga Lunga and get off at the Shimoni turn-off, but you'd then have to hitch the 14 km from the main road to Shimoni. It's not that difficult – even the locals do it.

Once at Shimoni (unless you intend to stay at the Shimoni Reef Lodge) you'll have to negotiate a dhow ride across the channel. The price for this depends to a degree on who you meet on arrival, how many there are of you and how affluent you look. If you assume KSh 600 for the boat (round trip) you won't be too far wrong.

The same people who run the dhows will also take you to the reefs for snorkelling for much the same price but you'll have to negotiate a price for the hire of snorkelling gear.

North of Mombasa

MOMBASA TO KILIFI
Like the coast south of Mombasa, the north coast has been well developed almost two-thirds of the way up to Kilifi with resort complexes which take up much of the beach frontage. Most of them cater to package tourists on two to three-week holidays from Europe but there is scope for individual initiative here and there, though only the Jauss Farm at Vipingo and the 'youth hostel' at Kikambala genuinely fall into the budget accommodation bracket.

As with Shelly and much of Tiwi beaches south of Mombasa, the northern beaches are plagued with seaweed which clogs them and makes swimming an often unpleasant experience. Only at the expensive resort hotels are people employed to minimise this inconvenience by raking it into piles and either burning it or burying it. Elsewhere you literally have to jump into the soup.

Going north from Mombasa the names of the beaches are Nyali, Bamburi, Shanzu, Kikambala and Vipingo.

Mamba Crocodile Village
Mamba Village (☎ (011) 472709) is north of Mombasa on the mainland opposite Nyali Golf Club in the Nyali Estate. It's a crocodile farm set among streams, waterfalls and wooden bridges. If you've never seen a crocodile farm with reptiles ranging from the newly born to the full grown, here's your chance; if you have, give it a miss. This is a typical collection of concrete and wire-mesh cages with thousands of young crocodiles up to five years old, and a few token, fully grown adults to pull in the punters. You pay through the nose to see them, too, even though the owners of the farms are probably making megabucks selling skins to Gucci and the like. Entry costs KSh 400 for nonresidents and KSh 150 for residents

(for children its KSh 280 and KSh 60, respectively).

Bamburi Quarry Nature Trail
Further up the coast, this nature trail (☎ (011) 485729) has been created on reclaimed and reforested areas damaged by cement production activities which ceased in 1971. Once the forest was established, the area was restocked with plants and animals in an attempt to create a mini replica of the wildlife parks of Kenya. At present, animal species represented include eland, oryx, waterbuck, buffalo, wart hog, bush pig, various monkeys and many different varieties of birds. There's also what the owners claim to be an 'orphan' hippo which was introduced as a baby from Naivasha and which has remained bottle-fed ever since. A likely story!

The complex also includes a fish farm, crocodile farm, reptile pit and plant nursery. The centre is open daily from 2 to 5.30 pm. Feeding time is at 4 pm. To get there take a public bus to Bamburi Quarry Nature Trail stop (signposted) on the main Mombasa to Malindi road.

Places to Stay – bottom end
There are very few cheap places to stay on the beaches north of Mombasa. Even places way back from the beach with nothing special going for them can be remarkably expensive.

One of the few genuine cheapies is the *Kanamai Conference Centre* (☎ (0125) 32046) at Kikambala Beach which was previously a youth hostel but is no longer affiliated. Dormitory beds are KSh 200 in either two, six or 10-bed rooms, while one-bedroom cottages are KSh 880, two-bedroom KSh 1700, and three-bedroom KSh 2640. All the cottages have bathrooms. Meals are available for KSh 130 for breakfast, KSh 200 for lunch and KSh 250 for dinner – expensive for what is basically ugali and chicken stew. The trouble with this place is getting there. First you have to take a matatu to Majengo on the Mombasa to Kilifi road (from near the New People's Hotel in Mombasa). Get off when you see a yellow

THE COAST

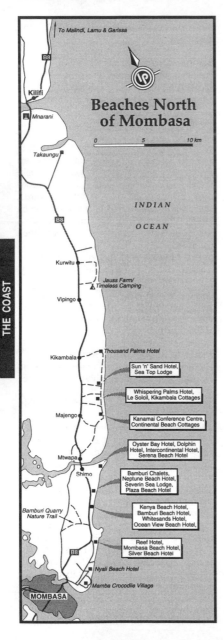

Beaches North of Mombasa

To Malindi, Lamu & Garissa

Kilifi

Mnarani

Takaungu

INDIAN

OCEAN

Kurwitu

Jauss Farm/
Timeless Camping

Vipingo

Thousand Palms Hotel

Kikambala

Sun 'n' Sand Hotel,
Sea Top Lodge

Whispering Palms Hotel,
Le Solcil, Kikambala Cottages

Majengo

Kanamai Conference Centre,
Continental Beach Cottages

Oyster Bay Hotel, Dolphin
Hotel, Intercontinental Hotel,
Serena Beach Hotel

Mtwapa

Shimo

Bamburi Chalets,
Neptune Beach Hotel,
Severin Sea Lodge,
Plaza Beach Hotel

Bamburi Quarry
Nature Trail

Kenya Beach Hotel,
Bamburi Beach Hotel,
Whitesands Hotel,
Ocean View Beach Hotel,

Reef Hotel,
Mombasa Beach Hotel,
Silver Beach Hotel

Nyali Beach Hotel

Mamba Crocodile Village

MOMBASA

0   5   10 km

THE COAST

sign saying 'Kanamai Conference Centre'. Go down the dirt track by this sign for about 300m and then turn left at the fork. Continue for about three km and you'll find it on the left-hand side by the beach. It's a long, hot walk and lifts are few and far between. With a backpack it's a major effort.

Close by, a little further to the north along the track which runs parallel to the beach, are the *Continental Beach Cottages* (☎ (0125) 32077) which are good value at KSh 1070 per person in the high season (KSh 1200 with breakfast), dropping to KSh 770 in the low season. Accommodation is in one and two-bedroom cottages each with lounge, kitchen, bathroom and air-con. It's rarely full and there's a good swimming pool, bar and restaurant and a pleasant beach. Cheap meals (omelette and chips and curries) are available for around KSh 170. As with the Conference Centre, the only problem about this place is getting there; taxis are expensive.

Right next door to the Continental is *Kikambala Cottages* (☎ (0125) 32032), a very basic place with no pool or restaurant. However, the cottages are comfortable enough, and cheap at KSh 1950 with two bedrooms, bathroom, lounge, and kitchen with fridge. As there are no shops or cheap restaurants nearby you need to be fairly self-sufficient here .

If you're staying at either of the above places and want a change of scene or a cold beer, the Whispering Palms Hotel is about 15 minutes walk north along the beach. Breakfasts here cost KSh 330 and you can use the swimming pool for KSh 200 per day.

A little further north, just behind the Sun 'n' Sand Hotel and about three km off the main coast road, is the *Sea Top Lodge* (☎ (0125) 32184), a small hotel which seems to be a bar first and a hotel second. The cost is KSh 550 for a small but clean double room. There are a few small dukas nearby and the beach is a short walk away. With a little discretion you could probably use the facilities at the Sun 'n' Sand.

Further up the coast at Vipingo, about 40 km north of Mombasa, there is *Timeless Camping* (☎ (0125) 32218) on the Jauss

TONY WHEELER

HUGH FINLAY

HUGH FINLAY

TONY WHEELER

Mombasa's Old Town exudes historic charm with the 16th century Fort Jesus at its entrance, traditional houses lining the streets and swaying dhows in the old harbour. Further along the coast at Gedi are the extensive ruins of an Arab-Swahili town, including remains of a palace (bottom right).

DAVID ELSE

TONY WHEELER

TONY WHEELER

Dhows

Dhows have been sailing along the coast of East Africa for centuries and, until fairly recently, were the principal trading vessels used between the eastern coast of the continent and the Persian Gulf and India. They once numbered in the thousands but, since the turn of the century, they have declined rapidly in the face of competition from steamships. These days only a few make the journey to the Gulf. Those that remain confine themselves to sailing between the mainland and the offshore islands and between the islands themselves, and even then only in certain areas. Their romantic appeal, nevertheless, remains and a dhow trip around the Lamu archipelago is an extremely popular activity among travellers.

Essentially, all dhows are wooden vessels, either planked or dug out, along with a rudder, mast and lateen (triangular) sail. Like all sail boats, unless motorised they're completely dependent on the wind. Unlike boats with only square sails, they're capable of tacking into the wind.

Dhows are differentiated by size and shape. The largest are known as *jahazi*, which are planked, ocean going vessels with broad hulls and ruggedly designed to be capable of withstanding constant bumping along rocky shores and submerged coral reefs. They can have either one or two lateen sails. Most have woven coconut fibre matting fixed to their sides to reduce splash and a wooden 'eye' attached to each side of the bow below a decorated or carved tailboard. Dhows of this type built in the Lamu archipelago often have a perpendicular bow whereas those from Zanzibar have sloping bows. A jahazi often has a toilet hanging off the stern of the boat.

Motorised versions of the jahazi are known as *mtaboti* or *mchaboti*. The only difference is that these have an inboard motor instead of a sail.

Smaller craft go under a generic name of *mashua* and there are many different types. Around Lamu they're usually known as *kijahazi*. These dhows differ from the jahazi in being smaller, much narrower in the hull and having only one sail. They can be remarkably fast given a favourable wind and are the ones you're most likely to use for trips around Lamu.

Another common type of dhow, smaller still, is the *dau la mwao* – a sort of dugout canoe with a narrow hull, small mast and no keel which sits low in the water and is frequently used for transporting soil, sand and coral rag building blocks. Most do not have a square stern. A variation of this type from the Kizingitini area is the *mtori* which is somewhat smaller and faster and fitted with a keel. Decoration on the mwao and the mtori is restrained. It's interesting to note that the mwao is the nearest surviving relative to the *dau la utango* which was the most common type of dhow found along the coast during the 19th century.

There are excellent models of the various types of the dhow in the Lamu museum. ∎

family farm. It consists of a camp site, budget chalets, and two bungalows. The camp site is equipped with showers and toilets and costs KSh 100 per person per night. The budget chalets are fairly basic twin rooms with clean beds and mattresses, and toilets and showers have to be shared with those occupying the camp site. The cost for these is KSh 330 per person. The bungalows are fully equipped and cost KSh 3200 for the four-bed one, and KSh 4300 for the large bungalow which sleeps 10 people. Unfortunately, this place is pretty run-down these days. If arriving by public transport, get off at Vipingo village and ring from there; someone will come and collect you. If you have your own transport, you'll have to ask the way because there's no signpost. Don't walk in the area unaccompanied as there have been mugging incidents in the past.

Places to Stay – top end

Virtually all the other hotels along this stretch of the East African coast before you arrive at Kilifi are resort complexes and cater largely for package tourists from Europe. Most of them are so self-contained that many of those staying there hardly ever see anything of Africa other than Mombasa airport, the inside of minibuses, the hotel itself and black Kenyan waiters. As at the hotels south of Mombasa and at Malindi, many cater almost exclusively for one specific European nationality whether they be British, German or Italian (French people don't feature prominently in East African tourism). There's precious little intermingling.

All the hotels compete furiously with each other to provide the utmost in creature comforts, mellow surroundings, day trips and sports facilities and there's little to choose between them though it's generally true to say that the further you get from Mombasa, the cheaper and less ritzy they become.

Down at Nyali Beach – the closest to Mombasa – even places which don't face the sea and are in no way hotel resorts, and which you might imagine should be fairly cheap given the facilities they offer, can be surprisingly expensive. *Bamburi Chalets*

(☎ (011) 485706), for example, which offers cottages with two bunk beds, two normal beds, shower, cooking facilities, gas stove, refrigerator, and use of a swimming pool cost US$78 per night or US$117 with sea views. The *Cowrie Shell Apartments* (☎ (011) 485971) all have two bedrooms and face the sea, and cost US$58 to US$117 depending on the season. The *Baharini Chalets* (☎ (011) 486302) have only one bedroom and are much cheaper at US$23, but are not great value as there are no cooking facilities.

It's unlikely that if you intend to stay at any of the resort complexes that you'll be reading this book since you'd have reserved your hotel via an agent and your air fares would be included in a package deal. Should you wish to make your own arrangements for staying at any of the resort complexes, however, here's a selection of the hotels. Be warned, however, that walk-in rates are generally considerably higher than what you would pay as part of a package deal. You should also be warned that if you're an independent traveller, you'll feel distinctly out of place in many of these hotels. They definitely do not attract the most interesting element of humanity.

Nyali Beach The following resorts are at Nyali Beach:

Mombasa Beach Hotel – US$120/160 (half board) in the high season down to US$60/90 in the low season (☎ (011) 471861)

Nyali Beach Hotel – from US$136/209 (half board) in the high season down to US$62/124 in the low season (☎ (011) 471551)

Reef Hotel – US$88/132 (half board); add US$10 per person per day for full board (☎ (011) 471771)

Bamburi Beach Further north are the following hotels:

Bamburi Beach Hotel – US$55/70 in the high season and US$35/55 in the low season, all with half board (☎ (011) 485611)

Neptune Beach Hotel – singles/doubles with half board cost US$50/64 (☎ (011) 485701)

Ocean View Beach Hotel – US$70/109 with half board (☎ (011) 485601)

Plaza Beach Hotel – US$44/60 with half board
(☎ (011) 485321)

Severin Sea Lodge – singles/doubles with half board
from US$97/140 and twin suites for US$338
(☎ (011) 4855001)

Travellers' Beach Hotel – US$66/90 with half board
(☎ (011) 485121)

Whitesands Hotel – US$70/105 (half board); suites
US$215 to US$480 (☎ (011) 485926)

Shanzu Beach At Shanzu Beach are the
following resorts:

Dolphin Hotel – US$58/104 with full board (☎ (011)
485801)

Mombasa Intercontinental Resort US$70/140 with
breakfast; double suites US$270 to US$445
(☎ (011) 485811)

Oyster Bay Hotel – from US$42/57 with half board
(☎ (011) 485061)

Serena Beach Hotel – in the high season singles/
doubles with breakfast US$150/200; suites
US$250 and US$400. In the low season,
singles/doubles are US$65/130 with suites at
US$150 and US$300. Shoulder season prices are
in-between the two. All prices are subject to a
service charge (10%), training levy (2%) and
VAT (15%) (☎ (011) 485721).

Kikambala Beach Finally, Kikambala
Beach offers the following:

Whispering Palms Hotel – singles/doubles with full
board cost US$94/122 (low season), and US$120/
165 in the high season (☎ (0125) 32004)

Sun 'n' Sand Beach Hotel – US$52/104 in the low
season (half board); US$110/130 in the high
season; children are charged 50% of the adult rate
(☎ (0125) 32133)

Takaungu Right up at the top end of this
long line of beaches close to Kilifi is the
village of Takaungu. It's supposedly the
oldest slave port on the Kenyan coast to
Zanzibar is the oldest. It's worth a visit if you
have the time. The local people are very
superstitious and no-one goes down to the
beach at night except the fishers. If you can
speak Swahili you'll hear many weird stories
going around which date back to the time of
slavery. It's an interesting place right off the
beaten track where you won't meet many
other travellers.

Rooms can be rented in private houses in

Takaungu for around KSh 200 per night. Ask
at the teashops.

For those with slightly less limited
resources there's *Takaungu House* (☎ (02)
502491), a luxury house which is privately
owned and run. There are just three bedrooms, but other features include a
swimming pool, beach frontage, snorkelling,
water-skiing and deep-sea fishing on
request. The charge for full board is KSh
6400 per person.

KILIFI

Other than Mtwapa Creek, just north of
Mombasa, Kilifi is the first major break in
the coastline between Mombasa and Malindi.
It has been a backwater for many years,
ignored by developers yet coveted by discerning white Kenyans, artists, writers and
adventurers from various parts of the world
who have gradually bought up most of the land
overlooking the wide creek and the ocean and
built, in many cases, some quite stunning and
imaginative houses. They form a sort of
society within a society and keep largely to
themselves. Without an introduction, it's
unlikely you'll meet them though sailing a
yacht into the creek would probably secure
you an invitation! Kilifi Creek is a popular
anchorage spot for yachties in this part of the
world and you can meet them in the evening
at the Seahorse Inn off to the left of the main
road on the northern side of the creek.

So why stop off in Kilifi? The answer to
this is mainly for the contrast it offers to
Mombasa and Malindi, and for the Mnarani
ruins on a bluff overlooking the creek on the
Mombasa side. Very few travellers ever see
these ruins yet they're well preserved and
just as interesting as those at Gedi though not
as extensive. The beach, too, on either side
of the creek is very pleasant and doesn't
suffer from the seaweed problem which
plagues the beaches further south. The only
problem is access, which is mostly through
private property, though you can walk along
it from the old ferry landing at low tide.

The present district centre of Kilifi is on
the northern bank of the creek.

1 Mkwajuni Motel
2 Barclays Bank
3 Kilifi Cafeteria
4 Kenya Commercial Bank
5 Post Office
6 Covered Market
7 Kilifi Members Club
8 Bus Station
9 Tushauriane New Lodging
10 Sahani Tamu Restaurant
11 Mnarani Club
12 Dhows Inn
13 Mnarani Ruins

To Seahorse Inn (1 km)
To Malindi

Old Ferry Landing Stages

Kilifi Creek

Kilifi

Bars
Bars
Mnarani Village
To Mombasa

0   100   200 m

Note: Map to scale except Kilifi Creek, which is considerably wider than indicated

Information

Kilifi consists of the small village of Mnarani (or Manarani) on the southern bank of the creek and Kilifi itself on the northern bank. It's a small town which you can walk around within minutes.

There's a good variety of shops (including a small bookshop), a lively open-air market and an enclosed fruit and vegetable market, a post office, a number of basic hotels and two banks. Barclays Bank is open Monday to Friday from 9 am to 3 pm and on Saturday from 9 to 11 am. The Kenya Commercial Bank keeps the same hours.

Mnarani

Mnarani, on the southern bank of Kilifi Creek overlooking the ferry landing, was once one of the string of Swahili city-states which dotted the East African coast. Excavations carried out in 1954 showed that the site was occupied from the end of the 14th century to around the first half of the 17th

century after which it was destroyed by marauding Galla tribespeople.

The principal ruins here include the Great Mosque with its finely carved inscription around the mihrab (the niche in a mosque showing the direction of Mecca), a group of tombs to the north (including one pillar tomb), a small mosque dating from the 16th century, and also parts of the town wall and a gate. There's also a large and quite forbiddingly deep well whose shaft must go down at least as far as the low-tide level of the creek.

Mnarani was associated with **Kioni**, at the mouth of Kilifi Creek on the same side, and with **Kitoka**, about 3.5 km south of here on the northern bank of Takaungu Creek. A carved stone with an interlaced ornament, probably from a mihrab, was found at Kioni on the cliff above the creek and is presently in the Fort Jesus museum at Mombasa. The ruins at Kitoka include a mosque similar to the small mosque at Mnarani along with a few houses. All these settlements were subject to Mombasa.

The Mnarani ruins are just above the old southern ferry landing stage and the path to them (about 300m long) is prominently signposted on the main road. Entry costs KSh 200 for nonresidents and KSh 30 for residents (KSh 100 and KSh 10 for children) but there's often no-one there to collect the fee.

Places to Stay – bottom end
There are a number of cheap hardboard-cubicle doss-houses scattered around town but you'd have to be desperate to stay there as they're basically bars which make provision for 'short-time' customers.

About the only place where you'll find a half-decent bed is the *Tushauriane New Lodging* (☎ (0125) 22486) near the bus station. This is a recently constructed hotel, several storeys high, which offers good, clean, simple rooms with mosquito nets and shared bathroom facilities for KSh 150/300 a single/double.

The *Kingenda Guest House* close to the central market and the Kenya Commercial Bank, which you'll see advertised in several places around town, has no rooms despite claims to the contrary. It's just a bar and restaurant.

Places to Stay – middle
The best place in this range is the *Dhows Inn* (☎ (0125) 22028) on the main road south of Kilifi Creek opposite the entrance to the Mnarani Club. It's a fairly small place with a number of double rooms surrounding a well-kept garden. There's a lively and quite popular bar and restaurant. A room here with mosquito nets and bath costs KSh 550 per person including breakfast. If arriving by bus or matatu, get the driver to drop you right outside, rather than in Kilifi itself in which case you'll have the long walk across the bridge.

On the northern side of the bridge, just off the main road, is the *Mkwajuni Motel* (☎ (0125) 22472). Set in a spacious garden, the rooms are small but very clean and neat, each with a small patio and table and chairs.

The motel is only about 10 minutes walk into town. Single/double rooms cost KSh 600/850 including breakfast.

Places to Stay – top end
The large resort complex at Kilifi is the somewhat exclusive *Mnarani Club* on the southern side of Kilifi Creek and quite close to the Dhows Inn. It's one of the African Safari Club hotels and they do not encourage casual bookings so these must be made through Mombasa (☎ (011) 485520). The hotel caters largely to package tourists from Germany and Switzerland and it's these people who keep the craft-shop owners of Mnarani village smiling.

Despite its size, the Mnarani Club is hardly visible from the main road or even from a boat on the creek since it's constructed of local materials (including some enormous makuti roofs) and surrounded by beautifully landscaped gardens full of flowering trees and bougainvillea.

The other top-range hotel is the *Seahorse Inn* (☎ (0125) 22813), about 1.5 km off to the left of the main Mombasa–Malindi road on the northern side of the creek. It's a very pleasant place with individual bandas set in a coconut grove right on the banks of Kilifi Creek which, at this point, is a couple of km wide. To stay here will set you back KSh 2600/4300 for full board. Like the Mnarani Club, the Seahorse Inn is run by the African Safari Club, so the same applies with bookings.

If you're thinking of visiting either of these two hotels for the day it will cost you KSh 1500 (KSh 750 for children) including lunch, afternoon tea, all non-alcoholic drinks and use of the pool and all other sports facilities. African Safari Club members who are not guests pay a reduced fee of KSh 750 (KSh 375 for children).

Places to Eat
A cheap and very popular place to eat both for lunch and dinner is the *Tana Hotel* at the bus station. Standard Indo-African fare is on offer, and you can eat well here for around KSh 130 to KSh 180. It's closed all day until after sunset during Ramadan. Another popular

place, especially at lunch time, is the *Kilifi Cafeteria* though prices here are somewhat higher.

Across on the southern side of the creek, you can eat at the *Dhows Inn* which has a limited menu of meat and seafood dishes. The only trouble with eating here is that food takes forever to arrive and the quality is variable: sometimes it's good, sometimes it's almost inedible. The average price of a main course is around KSh 200.

For a splurge, go for lunch at the *Mnarani Club* or the *Seahorse Inn* but note the entry fee for non-guests (see previous section). Normally, casual visitors are not allowed in during the evening but this is probably negotiable – for a fee – with the manager.

Even more up-market is the very agreeable *Sahani Tamu Restaurant* on the northern side of the creek, opposite the Mnarani Club. The food here is mainly Italian and seafood and is very well prepared and presented. Main dishes such as spaghetti are in the KSh 200 to KSh 250 range, steaks are around KSh 350, and seafood dishes from KSh 500 to KSh 750. It's well worth the expense and makes a very pleasant evening out. The restaurant is open daily, except Tuesday, from 11 am to 2 pm and 6 to 10 pm.

Entertainment

For a spit-and-sawdust evening on Tusker or White Cap you can't beat the bars in Mnarani village of which there are several, but the amount of action depends largely on how many tourists brave the 200m or so of dirt road between the Mnarani Club and the village. Don't expect cold beers at any of these bars.

The bar at the *Dhows Inn* on the other hand is usually pretty lively and you can be assured of cold beer.

The *Mnarani Club* has a nightly floor show – usually of tribal dancing – followed by a live African band which plays until late. This is, however, a club hotel and it's unlikely they will let you in during the evening, although this is negotiable, for a fee. Look smart if you want to avoid a hassle or even a rejection.

For a far more informal evening pay a visit to the *Kilifi Members Club* on the northern side of the creek.

Getting There & Away

All the buses and matatus which ply between Mombasa and Malindi stop at Kilifi but getting on a bus at Kilifi to go to either Mombasa or Malindi can be problematical since they're often full. Matatus are a much better bet but, like the buses, can be very crowded.

WATAMU

About 24 km south of Malindi, Watamu is a smaller beach resort development with its own marine national park – part of the Marine National Reserve which stretches south from Malindi. The coral reef here is even more spectacular than at Malindi since it has been much less exploited and poached by shell hunters. In addition, underwater visibility is not affected by silt brought down into the sea by the Galana River.

The coast at Watamu is broken up into three separate coves divided by craggy and eroded headlands and there are a number of similarly eroded islands just offshore. The coral sand is a dazzling white and although there is some shade from coconut palms, you'll probably have to retreat to the cooler confines of a hotel bar or restaurant in the middle of the day. The most southerly cove is fronted entirely by beach resorts and exclusive private houses. The central cove also has a number of resorts, though they are not as extensive. The northern cove and part of the headland is covered by the rambling Watamu Beach Hotel at the back of which is the actual village of Watamu.

Before tourist development got underway here, Watamu was a mellow little fishing village of makuti-roofed cottages nestled beneath coconut palms and it still retains much of that atmosphere despite the intrusion of souvenir shops, bars and restaurants catering for the tourist hordes. In fact the contrasts are quite bizarre – it's one of the few places where you'll see package tourists in designer beach attire wandering down the dusty streets of an African village. A lot of development has taken place on the outskirts of the village and is clearly destined to continue. For independent travellers a visit to Watamu is probably not worth it, not only because of the very limited amount of reasonably priced accommodation, but also because most of the beach frontage is taken up by the resort hotels which makes access problematical. That's a pity, because it is a beautiful spot.

Information

There are branches of both Barclays Bank and the Kenya Commercial Bank in the village of Watamu. Barclays is open Monday to Friday from 9 am to 4.30 pm, and KCB is open Monday to Friday from 9 am to 1 pm and 3 to 5 pm, and on Saturday from 9 to 11 am.

Post & Communications There is a post office close to the junction of the coast road and the road to Gedi.

There's also a branch of Phone Home (☎ 32302) at the junction of the coast road and the road leading into Watamu village. This is a private company offering phone and fax services at fixed rates (more expensive than going through the post office in Malindi but less expensive than going through a hotel switchboard).

Watamu's telephone code is 0122.

Watamu Marine National Park

The actual coral reef lies between one and two km offshore and to get to it you'll have to hire a glass-bottomed boat. These can be arranged directly with the owners at the park entrance for KSh 2500 for two people including park fees or for KSh 3000 for a party of up to eight people excluding park fees. You can also arrange these boats through any of the large hotels though they will, of course, charge a commission for their services.

Entry to the park itself costs US$5 for nonresidents and KSh 100 for residents.

There are also boat trips to a group of **caves** at the entrance to **Mida Creek** which are home to a school of giant rock cod many of which are up to two metres long. Diving

equipment is usually necessary to get down to their level since, most of the time, they remain stationary on the bottom.

Places to Stay – bottom end

Budget accommodation has always been something of a problem in Watamu. There are a couple of cheap lodges in the village but they can't seriously be recommended. The *Blue Lodge* charges KSh 350 for a scruffy, stuffy and gloomy double room illuminated by the feeblest of globes – only for the desperate. The other alternative, *Sam's Lodge,* is no better, though it is marginally cheaper at KSh 300 for a double. Neither place has fans or mosquito nets – which are absolutely essential on the coast.

Another possibility in the village is a private house known as the *Maasai House*. It has only one double room with shared facilities and another room with an attached bathroom, both of which cost more than the above two lodges. There's a kitchen, big verandah, a garden with a well, and a housekeeper who will cook meals at a reasonable charge. It's a good place to meet the Samburu performers from the Watamu Beach Hotel.

Of the regular lodges, the best value is the family-run *Villa Veronica/Mwikali Lodge* (☎ 32083), opposite the Hotel Dante Bar & Restaurant. This is a very friendly and secure place which offers clean rooms with double bed, fan, mosquito nets, shower and toilet for KSh 600 and KSh 800 for a room with two double beds including breakfast. The only drawback to this place is that it's tucked into a hollow so you miss out on sea breezes.

The *Hotel Dante* itself is about the cheapest habitable place, and doubles with attached bathrooms (no singles) go for KSh 500 including breakfast. The rooms have fans and mosquito nets and there's a bar and restaurant but the swimming pool is empty.

The only other place that fits this price bracket is *Watamu Cottages* (☎ 32211), on the main access road to the village and about 15 minutes hot walk. These are a good deal at KSh 750 for a double, with bathroom, and including breakfast but are often full. The rooms are set in a pleasant garden which also has a swimming pool.

It may occasionally be possible to get a cheap room at the *Seventh Day Adventist Youth Camp* if there's no group there but don't count on it. You can also camp here if you have your own tent. The facilities are minimal though there is a gas cooker which you can use.

Places to Stay – middle

The best deal in this range is *Peponi Cottages* (☎ 32434). It consists of a small complex of two-storey, makuti-roofed units which are quite pleasant, if a little small. Each has mosquito netting on the windows, and a balcony runs the length of the buildings. There's also a small pool. The Italian owner is very pleasant and *sympatico* but, because it's small, it's often full. A double, with bathroom, costs KSh 1000 excluding breakfast.

On the main road leaving the village is the *Watamu Paradise Restaurant & Cottages* (☎ 32062) which has a number of cottages, mostly doubles though there are some triples. Depending on the standard, a double, with attached bathroom, without breakfast costs from KSh 1000 or KSh 1400 including breakfast. Doubles with shared facilities cost KSh 800 excluding breakfast and KSh 1200 including breakfast. All the rooms have a fan and mosquito nets. It's a very pleasant place to stay and there's a small swimming pool, bar, restaurant and a disco.

Down in the centre of Watamu village is the *Ascot Residence Hotel* (the telephone is out of order), PO Box 14, which is a sprawling walled complex containing numerous makuti-roofed cottages, a bar and restaurant and a huge swimming pool. It gives the appearance of being a top-end hotel but the prices don't reflect this. All the rooms have a fan, mosquito net, private verandah and have attached bathrooms. Doubles without breakfast cost from KSh 1000 or from KSh 1200 with breakfast. It's good value and the surroundings are very pleasant.

Also highly recommended is *Mrs Simpson's Guest House* (☎ 32023), PO Box 33, Watamu. Barbara Simpson has lived in Kenya

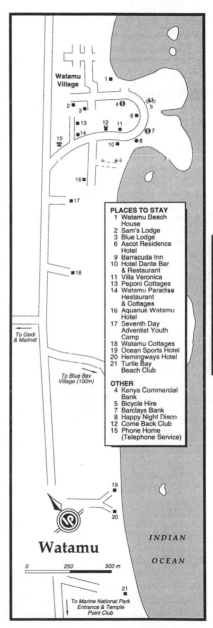

PLACES TO STAY
1 Watamu Beach House
2 Sam's Lodge
3 Blue Lodge
6 Ascot Residence Hotel
9 Barracuda Inn
10 Hotel Dante Bar & Restaurant
11 Villa Veronica
13 Peponi Cottages
14 Watamu Paradise Restaurant & Cottages
16 Aquarius Watamu Hotel
17 Seventh Day Adventist Youth Camp
18 Watamu Cottages
19 Ocean Sports Hotel
20 Hemingways Hotel
21 Turtle Bay Beach Club

OTHER
4 Kenya Commercial Bank
5 Bicycle Hire
7 Barclays Bank
8 Happy Night Disco
12 Come Back Club
15 Phone Home (Telephone Service)

Watamu Village

To Gedi & Malindi

To Blue Bay Village (100m)

Watamu

0   250   500 m

INDIAN OCEAN

To Marine National Park Entrance & Temple Point Club

THE COAST

for more than 70 years and has plenty of fascinating and amusing tales to entertain her guests with. The atmosphere is very homely and meals, cooked by Samson, are excellent. She has three double rooms with attached bathrooms for KSh 1600 per person for full board and including any laundry that you want doing. She can also organise snorkelling trips much cheaper than any of the resort hotels and she has a car available. The guesthouse is some 30 minutes walk from Turtle Bay towards Temple Point. Otherwise, ask the matatu driver to drop you at Plot 28.

Places to Stay – top end

Top-end hotels take up much of the beach frontage along each of the three coves. As at Malindi, they're mostly resort-type hotels which cater to package tourists' every need and are quite specific as to the European nationality which they appeal to – German, British or Italian – although that doesn't exclude others.

At the northern end and next to Watamu village is the rambling *Watamu Beach Hotel* (☎ 32001), where most of the German tourists stay. It's one of the many hotels operated by the African Safari Club, a German-based organisation, and casual bookings are not encouraged – they don't even know at the reception desk what the tariff is! If you want to stay, bookings can be made at the African Safari Club office in Mombasa (☎ (011) 485520). It's unlikely you'll stay here unless you've booked. African Safari Club members can use the facilities here for KSh 750 per day (KSh 375 for children). Nonmembers' rates for the same are KSh 1500 (KSh 750 for children) which includes lunch, afternoon tea and all nonalcoholic drinks.

At the northern end of the central cove is the *Barracuda Inn* (☎ 617074). This is an Italian-owned place which also discourages casual bookings. They will, however, let you stay if there's a vacancy. It's a huge place with numerous, double-storeyed cottages, all of them have attached bathrooms with air-con. Non-resident rates for singles/doubles are the equivalent of US$70/100 with half board and US$80/120 with full board. Resident rates are KSh 2600/4500 with half board and KSh 2800/5000 with full board. Non-guests can use the hotel facilities (pool, tennis courts and billiard table) for a negotiable fee (KSh 100 to KSh 200). There's an enormous bar and restaurant area under a soaring makuti roof.

Just beyond the Barracuda on the same entrance road is the *Aquarius Watamu Hotel* (☎ 32069), PO Box 96, Watamu. This is a new Italian-owned hotel with all the amenities of a resort complex. Prices depend on the season and range from KSh 1300 to KSh 3300 per person for bed and breakfast.

The southern cove sports four hotels, all of them of the resort variety. Closest to Watamu village is the *Blue Bay Village* (☎ 32626), which caters mostly to Italians. Full-board doubles vary from the equivalent of US$68 to US$115 including all taxes and service charges, depending on the type of room you take (standard, deluxe or superior). Single-room supplements vary between the equivalent of US$26 and US$30. Children aged between three and 12 years are charged at the equivalent of US$25 less. Half board rates are the equivalent of US$10 less than full-board rates.

Next along is *Ocean Sports* (☎ 32008), where the clientele is mainly British. It's much smaller than the other places and the facilities are fairly modest. It does, however, have excellent diving equipment and will take experienced divers out for a dive on the reef. Singles/doubles for nonresidents cost the equivalent of UK£46/60 and for residents KSh 3100/3900 with half board. Children between the ages of six and 12 years cost US$11 and KSh 1000, respectively. Most of the clientele are middle-aged and have children with them.

Hemingways (☎ 32256), which is next to Ocean Sports, is a much larger place and, again, caters largely to a British clientele. The rates here for nonresidents start at the equivalent of UK£86/115 a single/double including breakfast in the high season down to UK£45/60 in the low season but it depends what type of room you take. Suites go as high as UK£175 in the high season down to

UK£100 in the low season. Rack rates for residents start at KSh 6210/8280 up to KSh 8100/10,800 for singles/doubles including breakfast in the high season. Children up to the age of five years are free but from five to 12 years are entitled to a 10% discount. The prices include free transport to and from Malindi airport (by prior arrangement) and free snorkelling trips in the marine national park, excluding national park fees.

At the far end of the cove is the *Turtle Bay Beach Club* (☎ 32622) which caters to a mixture of nationalities – mainly British, Italian and German. Like the Watamu Beach Hotel, it's a huge, rambling place with all the usual facilities and water-sports equipment but it's definitely a club and you won't even get past the front gate unless you're a member so, if you're a casual visitor, forget it.

Right at the entrance to the marine park is the lavish *Temple Point Club* (☎ 32057) which caters to young Italians. This is a relatively new place complete with soaring makuti roofs but you can forget about it unless you're a member. They definitely do not encourage casual bookings.

Places to Eat

Budget eating facilities are at a premium in Watamu though it is possible to get simple meals at one or other of the local bars in the village – the *Ujamaa Restaurant*, attached to the bar of the same name, is one possibility. *Friend's Corner* is a small duka on the road between the Come Back Club and Villa Veronica. It has about the best cheap food in town, although the variety is limited.

The *Hotel Dante* is probably the best of the non-resort restaurants. The service is slow but there's warm beer and a juke box to distract you while you're waiting. Almost opposite is the *Come Back Club Restaurant*, but the food is not up to much and it's hard to think of a good reason to come back, except perhaps to dance in the disco which operates some nights.

For better meals at a reasonable price (for Watamu) head for the *Watamu Paradise Restaurant & Cottages* where you can get seafood and European-style meals for

between KSh 250 and KSh 400 (more for crab or lobster). There's also a bar with cold beers, and a disco most nights.

That's about the limit if you're an independent traveller but, if you have money to throw away, you could always take one of the buffet lunches at the resort hotels (where available). The price of these for non-guests, including use of facilities, falls into a very similar bracket to those charged at the Watamu Beach Hotel (see earlier) except on Sunday at either Ocean Sports or Hemingways where you can get an excellent buffet lunch for KSh 900 (KSh 450 for children). In the low season they're cheaper though the buffets are somewhat more modest.

Entertainment

For a disco not attached to a hotel there is the makuti-roofed *Happy Night Disco* next to the Hotel Dante. It operates nightly and entry costs KSh 50.

Getting There & Away

Matatus leave from the bus station in Malindi throughout the day. They cost KSh 25 to Watamu and take about 30 minutes. Most of these first go down to the Turtle Bay Beach Club after which they turn around and go to Watamu village. On the return journey they generally go direct from Watamu village to Malindi without first going down to the Turtle Bay Beach Club.

Getting Around

Bicycles can be hired for KSh 250 per day from Subira Bicycle Hire opposite the Ascot Residence Hotel.

Taxis can be found outside the Watamu Beach Hotel.

GEDI

Some four km from Watamu, just off the main Malindi–Mombasa road, are the famous Gedi ruins, one of the principal historical monuments on the coast. Though the ruins are extensive, this Arab-Swahili town is something of a mystery since it's not mentioned in any of the Portuguese or Arab chronicles of the time.

Excavations, which have uncovered such things as Ming Chinese porcelain and glass and glazed earthenware from Persia, have indicated the 13th century as the time of its foundation, however it was inexplicably abandoned in the 17th or 18th century, possibly because the sea receded and left the town high and dry, or because of marauding Galla tribespeople from the north. The forest took over and the site was not rediscovered until the 1920s. Even if you have only a passing interest in archaeology it's worth a visit.

Entry costs KSh 200 for nonresidents and KSh 30 for residents (less for students and children) and the site is open daily from 7 am to 6 pm. A good guidebook with map is for sale at the entrance for KSh 30.

The site is quite large and surrounded by two walls, the inner one of which was possibly built to enclose a smaller area after the city was temporarily abandoned in the 15th to 16th centuries.

In places it actually incorporates earlier houses into its structure. The site is lush and green with numerous baobab trees. Monkeys chatter in the tree tops, lizards rustle in the undergrowth and large, colourful butterflies flutter among the ruins.

The buildings were constructed of coral rag, coral lime and earth and some have pictures incised into the plaster finish of their walls, though many of these have deteriorated in recent years. The toilet facilities in the houses are particularly impressive, generally in a double-cubicle style with a squat toilet in one and a wash stand in the other where a bowl would have been used. Fancier versions even have double washbasins with a bidet between them.

The other notable feature of the site is the great number of wells, many of them remarkably deep.

Most of the interesting excavated buildings are concentrated in a dense cluster near the entrance gate. There are several others scattered around the site within the inner wall and even between the inner and outer walls. Outside the site, by the car park, there's a small museum with some items found on the site. Other items are exhibited in Fort Jesus in Mombasa.

The Tombs

On your right as you enter the site is the Dated Tomb, so-called because the Muslim date corresponding to 1399 has been deciphered. This tomb has provided a reference point for dating other buildings within the complex. Next to it is the Tomb of the Fluted Pillar which is characteristic of such pillar designs found up and down the East African coast. There's another good example of this kind of pillar in Lamu.

The Great Mosque

The Great Mosque originally dates from the mid-15th century but was rebuilt a century later, possibly as a result of damage sustained at the time of Gedi's first abandonment. The mosque is of typical East African design with a mihrab facing towards Mecca. You can see where porcelain bowls were once mounted in the walls flanking the mihrab.

The Palace

Behind the mosque are the ruins of the extensive palace which is entered through an arched door. Once through the doorway, you enter a reception court and then a large audience hall while to the left of this are numerous smaller rooms. Look for the many 'bathrooms' and the room flanking the audience hall with its square niches in the walls intended for lamps. Behind that room is another one with no doorway at all which would probably have been used to store valuables. Entry was by ladder through a small hatch high up in the wall. Beyond this is a kitchen area with a small but very deep well.

The Palace also has a particularly fine pillar tomb, while to the right is the Annexe with four individual apartments, each with its own courtyard.

The Houses

In all, 14 houses have been excavated at Gedi, 10 of which are in a compact group beside the Great Mosque and the Palace. They're named after particular features of

1	Museum
2	Office
3	Dated Tomb
4	Tomb of the Fluted Pillar
5	House of the Cistern
6	House of the Panelled Walls
7	Mosque of the Long Conduit
8	House of the Scissors
9	House of the Iron Lamp
10	House of the Ivory Box
11	House of the Sunken Court
12	House of the Venetian Bead
13	House of the Chinese Cash
14	Pillar Tomb
15	House on the West Wall
16	The Palace
17	The Great Mosque
18	House of the Long Court
19	Pillar Tomb
20	House of the Dhow
21	House of the Double Court
22	Mosque between the Walls
23	Mosque of the Three Aisles
24	Large House
25	Small Mosque
26	Mosque of the Sarcophagi
27	Mosque on the Wall

their design or after objects found in them by archaeologists. They include the House of the Cowries, House of the Cistern and House of the Porcelain Bowl.

Other Buildings
Follow the signposted path from the Tomb of the Fluted Pillar to the House of the Dhow and House of the Double Court with a nearby tomb. There are pictures in the wall plaster in these houses.

A path follows close to the inner city wall from the houses to the Mosque of the Three Aisles where you will also find the largest well in Gedi. Beside it is the inner wall of the East Gate from where a path leads to the Mosque Between the Walls; a path cuts back to the car park from here.

Alternatively, from the East Gate you can follow another path right around the inner circuit of the inner wall or divert to the Mosque on the Wall at the southern extremity of the outer wall. The House on the West Wall actually comprises several adjoining houses of typical design while at the northern end of the town there is the more complex North Gate.

Just outside the North Gate is a 'traditional' **Giriama tribal village**, and here the package tourists are entertained with 'traditional' Giriama dances. Unfortunately it's *very* contrived and the dancing girls' costumes look something like a cross between a Hawaiian skirt and a tennis outfit.

Butterfly Farm
This is situated just before the entrance to the Gedi ruins and is well worth a visit. Entry costs KSh 50.

Getting There & Away
Take the same matatu as you would to go to Watamu but get off at Gedi village where the matatu turns off from the main Malindi–Mombasa road. From there it's about a one-km signposted walk to the ruins along a *murram* road.

It's also possible to get a taxi to take you on a round trip from Malindi for about KSh 1000 with an hour or more to look around the site. This could be worth it if your time is limited and there's a small group to share costs.

MALINDI
Malindi was an important Swahili settlement as far back as the 14th century and often

rivalled Mombasa and Paté for control of this part of the East African coast. It was also one of the very few places where the early Portuguese mariners found a sympathetic welcome, and today you can still see the cross which Vasco da Gama erected as a navigational aid.

These days, on account of its beaches, it has experienced a tourist boom similar to that north and south of Mombasa, and resort hotels are strung out all the way along the coast. It still retains a recognisable African centre where commerce, business and everyday activities, which aren't necessarily connected with the tourist trade, continue. Outside this relatively small centre, Italian and, to a lesser extent, German entrepreneurs have transformed Malindi into tinsel and glitter suitable only for high rollers and those with money to burn.

There are now air-con piano bars, karaoke bars, a casino, glitzy shopping centres, discos and all the associated infrastructure necessary to keep package tourists fully distracted 24 hours a day and as distanced from the real Africa as their budgets will possibly allow. It's the perfect example of overkill. However, with the downturn in Kenya's tourist intake, the developers have taken a severe hiding.

Quite a lot of businesses have folded recently: even the Italian consulate has closed. Nevertheless, a meal, other than spaghetti or pizza, will still cost you two to three times as much as you would pay for the same thing in Mombasa or Lamu. Seafood, in particular, is outrageously priced. Still, if you want to pretend you're on the Italian riviera, here it is.

The beach is still there though it isn't anything special and it does have the drawback of suffering from the brown silt which flows out of the Galana River at the northern end of the bay during the rainy seasons. This can make the sea very muddy all the way down to the Vasco da Gama cross however generally not below that, so if you want to avoid this go to Silversands Bay or even further south closer to the marine national park.

Information
Tourist Office There is a tourist office next door to Kenya Airways on the Lamu road. The staff are helpful but have little useful information and very few leaflets.

Money Barclays Bank is open Monday to Friday from 9 am to 4.30 pm, and on Saturday from 9 to 11 am. The Standard Chartered Bank and the Trust Bank have much the same hours except that the Trust Bank is open half an hour later on Saturday morning.

Immigration There is an office next to the Juma Mosque and pillar tombs on the waterfront (see street map for location).

Post & Communications The post office is open for international telephone calls from 7 am to 7 pm Monday to Friday and 8 am to 2.30 pm on Saturday. There is also a card phone here but, as usual, the supply of cards is erratic. There's also a branch of Phone Home (☎ 31589) in the Malindi Complex on Lamu Rd which caters for international telephone and fax services.

Malindi's telephone code is 0123.

Warning Don't walk back to your hotel along the beach at night. In past years many people have been mugged at knife-point, although these days the beach appears to be safer. Go back along the main road (which has street lighting) or take a taxi. You also need to exercise caution if returning to Silversands camp site late at night.

Town Buildings
Malindi has a pedigree going back to the 12th century and was one of the ports visited by the Chinese junks of Cheng Ho between 1417 and 1419, before the Chinese emperor prohibited further overseas voyages. It was one of the few places on the coast to offer a friendly welcome to the early Portuguese mariners and to this day the pillar erected by Vasco da Gama as a navigational aid still stands on the promontory at the southern end of the bay. The cross which surmounts this pillar is of Lisbon stone (and it is therefore

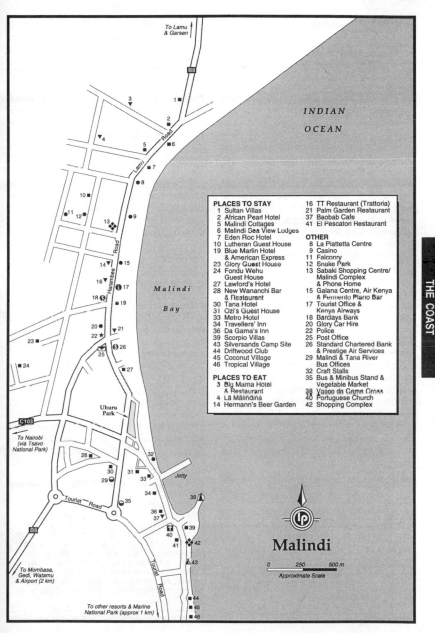

PLACES TO STAY
1 Sultan Villas
2 African Pearl Hotel
5 Malindi Cottages
6 Malindi Sea View Lodges
7 Eden Roc Hotel
10 Lutheran Guest House
19 Blue Marlin Hotel
& American Express
23 Glory Guest House
24 Fondu Wehu
Guest House
27 Lawford's Hotel
28 New Wananchi Bar
& Restaurant
30 Tana Hotel
31 Ozi's Guest House
33 Metro Hotel
34 Travellers' Inn
36 Da Gama's Inn
39 Scorpio Villas
43 Silversands Camp Site
44 Driftwood Club
45 Coconut Village
46 Tropical Village

PLACES TO EAT
3 Big Mama Hotel
& Restaurant
4 La Malindina
14 Hermann's Beer Garden

16 TT Restaurant (Trattoria)
21 Palm Garden Restaurant
37 Baobab Cafe
41 El Pescatori Restaurant

OTHER
8 La Piatteta Centre
9 Casino
11 Falconry
12 Snake Park
13 Sabaki Shopping Centre/
Malindi Complex
& Phone Home
15 Galana Centre, Air Kenya
& Fermento Piano Bar
17 Tourist Office &
Kenya Airways
18 Barclays Bank
20 Glory Car Hire
22 Police
25 Post Office
26 Standard Chartered Bank
& Prestige Air Services
29 Malindi & Tana River
Bus Offices
32 Craft Stalls
35 Bus & Minibus Stand &
Vegetable Market
38 Vasco da Gama Cross
40 Portuguese Church
42 Shopping Complex

INDIAN OCEAN

Malindi Bay

To Lamu
& Garsen

To Nairobi
(via Tsavo
National Park)

Uhuru Park

To Mombasa,
Gedi, Watamu
& Airport (2 km)

To other resorts & Marine
National Park (approx 1 km)

Jetty

Malindi

0   250   500 m
Approximate Scale

original) but the supporting pillar is of local coral.

There's also the so-called Portuguese church which Vasco da Gama is reputed to have erected and where two of his crew were buried – at least, that is what the curator will tell you. Maybe he's right but the graves of the sailors are certainly not the originals. Vasco da Gama was not carrying cement on his voyage around Africa! What is more plausible is that this church is the one which St Francis Xavier visited on his way to India. The rest of the compound is taken up by the graves of Catholic missionaries from the late 19th and 20th centuries. The site is run by the Kenya Museums authority so you're supposed to pay an entry fee but the curator is happy with KSh 50 as a contribution towards upkeep.

Not far to the north are a number of pillar tombs and the remains of a mosque and a palace. Other than this, however, little remains of the old town. The nearest substantial ruins from pre-Portuguese days are at Gedi, south of Malindi.

Malindi Marine National Park
The most popular excursion from Malindi is to the Malindi Marine national Park several km south of town past Silversands. Here you can rent a glass-bottomed boat to take you out to the coral reef. Masks and snorkels are provided though they're usually pretty well used and the quality is not what it might be. Fins can be rented for around KSh 100 from the kiosk on the beach inside the marine park gate.

The variety and colours of the coral and the fish are simply amazing and you'll be surprised how close you can get to the fish without alarming them. On the other hand, the area is getting a little overused and there's been a lot of damage to the coral – the boat people actually anchor on the coral itself. Shell collectors have also degraded the area. During the rainy season visibility is severely reduced by the silt in the water which gets washed in from the Galana River.

You can arrange these trips in Malindi – people come around the hotels to ask if you

are interested in going. The usual price is around KSh 600 per person which includes a taxi to take you to and from your hotel, hire of the boat and the park entry fee (US$5 for nonresidents and KSh 100 for residents). You may be able to get it for less if you bargain hard but you won't be able to knock too much off this price. The marine park is open daily from 7 am to 7 pm, but the boats only go out at low tide.

Snake Park
Yes, Malindi has the inevitable snake park. It's behind the Sabaki shopping centre/ Malindi Complex on the Lamu road and is open from 9 am to 6 pm daily. Entry is KSh 200 for nonresidents and KSh 100 for residents. Children are half price.

Falconry
The falconry has a number of caged birds of prey, as well as a huge tortoise which roams the grounds, and a chimp on a rope – fine if you like that sort of thing. The opening hours are 9 am to 5.30 pm and the entry fees are the same as for the snake park.

Scuba Diving
If you'd like to go scuba diving you can do this from the Driftwood Club at Silversands Bay. A dive costs the equivalent of US$40 plus the marine park entry fee of US$5 for nonresidents and KSh 100 for residents. There is also a diving school here for those who wish to learn, but it's not cheap at around the equivalent of US$450 for a course.

Deep Sea Fishing
Kenya is famous for the game-fishing opportunities off the coast. The Malindi Sea Fishing Club can organise trips at a cost of around the equivalent of US$470 per boat for four people including all equipment. Most of the resort hotels can also arrange these trips. It's not a good idea to arrange these trips from street touts, as some boats have no safety equipment, navigational aids or radios on board. ■

Places to Stay – bottom end

There are a number of cheap, basic lodges in the centre of town, but they're usually fairly noisy at night and you don't get the benefit of sea breezes or instant access to the beach. Best of the bunch is the *Tana Hotel* (☎ 20657) which has rooms with attached bathrooms, fan and mosquito nets for KSh 400/500 a single/double. There's no bar or restaurant here.

Also reasonable is the *Tana Ocean View Annexe* which has doubles with attached bathrooms for KSh 600 and singles with shared facilities for KSh 300. Much more basic is the *New Wananchi Bar & Restaurant* which costs KSh 150/180 for singles/doubles with shared facilities.

Most travellers prefer to stay in one of the hotels closer to the beach. The best in this area is probably *Ozi's Guest House* (☎ 20218) which is on the foreshore road. It's kept spotlessly clean, and safe lockers are available. The rooms, which all have fans and mosquito nets, cost KSh 350/600 for singles/doubles and KSh 850 for triples with breakfast. Bathrooms and toilets are shared between four rooms. The only problem here is that rooms on one side face the mosque, while those on the other side overlook the Malindi Bus depot – either way you'll be woken early.

Another popular place is the *Silversands Camp Site* (☎ 20412) two km south of town along the coast road. It costs KSh 90 per person to camp here (KSh 50 for children) and there are good toilets, saltwater showers, and freshwater taps but very little shade. Mattresses can be hired for KSh 20 per day. There's also a laundry service. There are also three types of tented banda for rent, the price for which depends on whether you stay two nights or less or three nights or more. The *Mzuri Huts* have attached bathrooms and cost KSh 450 for one night or KSh 1290 for three nights for a double.

The *White Huts* have two single beds, mosquito nets, screened windows, electric lights and lockable doors but shared showers and toilets for KSh 330 for one night or KSh 930 for three nights a double. The *Green Huts*, of which there are three, are actually tents under a makuti roof and cost KSh 270 for one night or KSh 780 for three nights a double. They have mosquito nets, private bathroom facilities and electric lights. There is no single-occupancy tariff, and prices are negotiable if you plan to stay for a while. Bicycles can be rented for KSh 160 per day or KSh 30 by the hour. There's a cafe on the site which does simple meals at a reasonable price but if you want to do your own cooking then you'll have to buy fruit and vegetables from the main market in town and anything else from the Oasis Complex a little further down the road to the south where there's a supermarket.

Also popular in the past has been the *Travellers' Inn*, on the beachfront road just south of the main part of town. It's hard to see the attraction of this place as the rooms are basic and somewhat gloomy, but it is kept clean and the owner is very friendly. Rooms with a fan and shared bathroom facilities cost KSh 350 for a double including breakfast (no singles) but there are no mosquito nets.

Da Gama's Inn (☎ 30295) is a relatively new place just south of the Travellers' Inn, though you wouldn't know this judging from the state of the place. Quite a few travellers stay here and the owner, James, is friendly and helpful and the restaurant is good. The cost of rooms is entirely negotiable but is on a par with the Travellers' Inn and includes breakfast. The rooms have fans but not necessarily mosquito nets.

Forget about the once-popular *Metro Hotel*, also on the sea-front, unless you're desperate and want to be bitten alive by mosquitoes. It has very basic singles/doubles for KSh 150/250 and triples for KSh 300.

Back up in town away from the beachfront, by far the best place is the *Fondo Wehu Guest House* (☎ 30017) in the western part of town. It's about 15 minutes walk from the bus station and well signposted both from Kenyatta and Lamu Rds. The place is run by an English woman and her Kenyan husband and is a very popular place to stay. Dorm beds in the airy upstairs dorm cost KSh 200, and comfortable singles/doubles will cost

KSh 350/500. The price includes an excellent breakfast and free laundry service. Tasty snacks are also available. Fondo will probably greet you on arrival.

Close by is the *Miami Guest House* (☎ 31029) which is a larger place with a rooftop restaurant which offers singles/doubles with attached bathrooms for KSh 450/750 and doubles with shared bathroom facilities for KSh 650. This is a Muslim hotel so alcoholic drinks are prohibited. Like Fondo Wehu, it's well signposted.

Excellent value is the *Lutheran Guest House* (☎ 21098) off the Lamu road at the back of the Malindi Complex and next to the Snake Park. It's a popular place to stay and deservedly so. The rooms are set around a quiet garden courtyard – very reminiscent of an Indonesian *losmen* – and are clean and well maintained as well as having a fan and mosquito nets. Rooms with shared bathroom facilities cost KSh 350/600 for singles/doubles and KSh 430/750 for singles/doubles with attached bathrooms, including breakfast. There are also two fully furnished cottages each having two bedrooms, a bathroom and a living room for KSh 900 per night or KSh 3500 per week but breakfast is not included. Alcoholic drinks are not permitted on the premises.

Places to Stay – middle

There are few places to stay in this price range and tariffs vary according to the season. *Malindi Cottages* (☎ 20304), out on the Lamu road, close to the Eden Roc Hotel, is one of the best. It consists of several fully furnished cottages surrounding a swimming pool. Each cottage has two bedrooms, a sitting room, kitchen, bathroom and verandah. Facilities include a refrigerator, gas cooker, cooking utensils, mosquito nets and fans. Each cottage sleeps up to five adults and costs KSh 1500 per night. There are also so-called single cottages with a double bed for KSh 600 per night.

Just beyond the Eden Roc Hotel on the Lamu road are *Malindi Sea View Cottages* (☎ 20439) which consists of a number of makuti-roofed cottages, some of them

divided in half to form two double rooms each with its own shower and toilet. The beds are enormous and have a full mosquito net plus there's a fan in each room but the water pressure in the showers is often very low. The prices here are KSh 1400 per person per night including breakfast negotiable down to KSh 1200 per night. The hotel has it's own swimming pool and there's a bar of sorts but the waiter can be hard to find.

Beyond the Sea View Cottages are two more hotels, both of a similar standard. The first is the *African Pearl Hotel* (☎ 20449) which is good value at KSh 1300/1600 for singles/doubles including breakfast. Kenyan residents pay KSh 1100/1400, respectively. The hotel has its own (dirty) pool, bar and restaurant. Next is *Sultan Villas* which is very similar in standard to African Pearl and offers singles/doubles at KSh 1200/1800 including breakfast. The hotel has its own (clean) pool.

Places to Stay – top end

Malindi's top-range hotels are strung out along the beachfront both north and south of the town centre. Some of them are very imaginatively designed and consist of clusters of makuti-roofed cottages in beautifully landscaped gardens full of flowering trees. Others are fairly standard beach hotels. All of them have swimming pools and other sporting facilities and many have a disco. They cater mostly, but not exclusively, to package tourists from Europe on two to three-week holidays and they all seem to pitch their business at a specific nationality – British, German or Italian. Very little intermingling seems to take place and you can definitely feel you've come to the wrong spot in some hotels if you don't belong to the dominant nationality. It's a common trait with package tourism anywhere in the world.

Most of the hotels impose a supplement over the Christmas and New Year periods which can be quite considerable (KSh 1000 and more is fairly typical), so bear this in mind if you intend to stay at this time of the year.

If being by the beach is important, it's also

worth bearing in mind that the hotels north of town do not have a beach frontage as there is a wide swathe of sand dunes here; those to the south of town are right on the beachfront.

Right in the town itself are *Lawford's Hotel* and the *Blue Marlin Hotel*, which are owned by a German company, Kenya-Hotels GmbH, though bookings can be made by ringing the hotels direct on ☎ 20440. Half board at either is KSh 3150/4200 for singles/doubles for nonresidents and KSh 2700/3600, respectively, for residents. Higher prices prevail in the high season.

North of town on the Lamu road is the *Eden Roc Hotel* (☎ 20480, fax 21225), one of the few hotels which seems to have a mixed clientele. It's also one of the few places with tennis courts, though these are not open to non-guests. The hotel is one of the older resorts in Malindi, and certainly not much imagination has gone into its design. The rates for nonresidents including breakfast are KSh 1804/2406 for singles/doubles in the bungalows, KSh 2060/2740 in the deluxe rooms and KSh 2943/3924 in the private suites. Resident rates for the same thing are KSh 1465/1954, KSh 1650/2200 and KSh 1854/2472, respectively.

South of town, the top-range hotels stretch all the way from the path leading to the Vasco da Gama monument down to Casuarina Beach and the Malindi Marine national Park.

First is *Scorpio Villas* (☎ 20194) which has 40 rooms in 17 cottages spread over some 1.5 hectares of beautiful tropical gardens, with three swimming pools and just 50m from Silversands Beach. All the cottages are fully furnished in Lamu style and come complete with your own house steward. There's an excellent restaurant and bar within the complex. It's Italian-owned and Italians form the bulk of the clientele. Bed and breakfast rates per person per night sharing a double room are from KSh 1700 and full-board rates from KSh 2300.

Further down the beach beyond the Silversands Camp Site is the *Driftwood Club* (☎ 20155, fax 30712). This was one of the first beach resorts to be built at Malindi and it's different from the other hotels as it's used

more by individual travellers rather than package groups. Although it gets more of a mixture of nationalities, the clientele is mainly British and white Kenyan. The club offers a variety of rooms from KSh 800/1300 for singles/doubles with fan and shared bathrooms to KSh 2900/3700 with air-con and private bathroom. There are also two luxury cottages each consisting of two air-con bedrooms, two bathrooms, living room and verandah which will sleep up to four people for KSh 10,800. Children between the ages of three and 11 years sharing with parents are charged KSh 500. All prices include breakfast. Full-board rates are also available. The bar, restaurant and other facilities are open to non-guests on payment of a temporary membership fee of KSh 100 per day or KSh 350 per week, so there's often an interesting mix of budget travellers hanging out by the pool.

Next down the beach is *Coconut Village* (☎ 20928, fax 30103), where the clientele is mainly Italian. Double rooms with full board cost KSh 2500 per person per night for non-residents and KSh 2100 for residents, depending on the time of year (and there are no less than six 'seasons'!). Half-board rates are KSh 2250 and KSh 1900 per person per night for nonresidents and residents, respectively. Children under two years old are free of charge and those under 12 pay 50% of the above rates. All prices include taxes and service charges. The hotel has a popular open-air, makuti-roofed discotheque which overlooks the beach. It operates once weekly on Wednesday night and entry for non-guests costs KSh 300.

Ignoring the *Malindi Beach Club*, which is a private club, next up is the *Tropical Village* and the *African Dream Village* (☎ 20442, fax 20119), both of which are owned by the same people. The clientele is mainly Italian. High-season rates including breakfast are KSh 2000/3500 for singles/doubles and low-season rates are KSh 900/1800. Shoulder-season rates fall between these two sets of prices. Full and half-board rates are also available. These two resort complexes are among the most imaginatively conceived of all the hotels in Malindi with huge soaring makuti-roofed areas for their bars and restaurants.

Further down the coast road is the *White Elephant Sea Lodge* (☎ 20223), which caters mainly to British tourists, but is presently undergoing renovations.

Turning left off the coast road towards the marine national park entrance are the *Dorado Cottages* (☎ 30104, fax 21459). Non-resident rates here in the low season for bed and breakfast are KSh 1800 per person per night. In the high season they are KSh 2450. Resident rates for the same thing are KSh 1550 and KSh 2100 per person per night, respectively. Full and half-board rates are also available. The clientele is mainly Italian.

Next along this road is *Jambo Village* (☎/fax 21245) which caters to a young crowd of various nationalities. Non-resident rates for bed and breakfast are KSh 2000/3800 for singles/doubles and for residents KSh 1800/3400.

Last up is the new *Stephanie Sea House* (☎ 20720, fax 20613) overlooking the marine national park, which is Italian-owned and caters mainly to Italians though not exclusively. This is probably one of the best places to stay and has an excellent beach completely free of seaweed as well as a crystal-clear sea uncontaminated with silt. There are five different 'seasons' and rates vary between the equivalent of US$25 per person per night through to US$35 to US$50 in the low, shoulder and high seasons for bed and breakfast. Transfers can be arranged to and from both Mombasa and Malindi airports for a fairly modest fee.

Places to Eat – cheap

There's not a lot of choice in this range unless you're keen on pizza or spaghetti. Cheap African-style meals can be found in the restaurants at the hotels in the centre of town. The *New Safari Hotel*, for instance, is a very popular place with the locals at lunch time but it's closed all day during the month of Ramadan.

Slightly more expensive but excellent value is the *Palm Garden* on Lamu road

opposite the petrol station. Food here is very tasty, and the place is usually packed with escapees from the resorts. The menu is mainly seafoods and curries. The front part of the restaurant serves snacks and light meals, while the makuti-roofed back section (entered from the side street) does full meals. Meals in the snack area include burgers and chips for around KSh 180, wiener schnitzel (KSh 250), steaks (KSh 220) and curries (KSh 200 to KSh 250).

Similar, and also good value, is the *TT Restaurant* (otherwise known as *Trattoria)* a little further up the Lamu road on the opposite side. It offers much the same meals as the Palm Garden and also has relatively cheap, cold beers.

Continuing up the Lamu road and in the centre of the Malindi Complex (signposted) is the *Golden Shell Restaurant* which offers a range of seafood and curry dishes at very reasonable prices varying between KSh 200 and KSh 300.

At the opposite end of town, it's possible to get fish and chips for around KSh 200 at the *Baobab Restaurant* on Vasco da Gama Rd but not all items on the menu are so reasonably priced. Some items go up as high as KSh 800 and I've seen so-called 'lunch-time specials' priced as high as KSh 750. What they do have here, however, are the cheapest, cold beers in town at KSh 45.

Not far from the Baobab is *El Pescatori Pizzeria & Grill Bar* which is worth checking out for lunch and dinner if you like pizza (from KSh 180) or spaghetti (from KSh 150). The rest of the menu, especially seafood, is just as highly priced as anywhere else in town.

Ozi's Guest House is also worth considering for reasonably priced curries (around KSh 150 to KSh 200) though they do have more expensive seafood dishes such as prawns, crab and lobster.

Places to Eat – more expensive

For a splurge, it's worth trying the *Driftwood Club* where you have to pay KSh 100 for temporary membership. This entitles you to the use of their swimming pool, hot showers, bar and restaurant. The prices are quite reasonable – lunch for KSh 450, dinner for KSh 550, good snacks (such as smoked sailfish and prawn sandwiches) from KSh 100, and à la carte seafood main dishes for KSh 200 to KSh 450. The Sunday curry lunch buffet is a bargain at KSh 250. It's very convenient if you are staying at the Silversands Camp Site.

I Love Pizza in front of the fishing jetty and close to the Metro Hotel is a popular place for a splurge. As you might expect, it serves Italian food (pizza and pasta for around KSh 250) and also more expensive meals such as chicken casserole and seafood dishes from KSh 450. It's open from noon to midnight daily.

In the northern part of town, near the disco and casino, are a couple of places which also cater primarily to the resort crowds. At *Hermann's Beer Garden* you are able to eat German and other continental dishes for KSh 300 and more. It's hardly the place you want for a quiet meal as the music is generally quite loud.

Right next door at the Stardust Club is the open-air *Putipu Restaurant*, where the emphasis is very much on Italian food. Main dishes are in the KSh 400 to KSh 750 range, while pizzas cost between KSh 220 and KSh 280.

Further north, off the Lamu road, you can also splurge at one of three places, all of them very close to each other. They are *Big Mama Hotel & Restaurant* (ex-*Eddie's* for which there's still a sign), *Ul-Nil's Poolside Bar & Restaurant* and *La Malindina*. They're all similarly priced so plan on spending at least KSh 600 to KSh 800 per person without drinks.

For superb gelati ice cream, the *Gelateria Bar* in the Sabaki shopping centre has a range of flavours, but it's not cheap. There's a similar place on the opposite side of the road next to the Italian restaurant which offers barbecued game meats.

Good coffee and cakes can be found at the *Karen Blixen Cafe* in the Galana Centre, Lamu Rd, which has tables and chairs in the courtyard.

Entertainment

Discos Because Malindi is a holiday resort there are a number of bars and discos to visit in the evening, some of which rock away until dawn. The most famous of them is the *Stardust Club* which generally doesn't get started until 11 pm and costs KSh 200 for women and KSh 300 for men (more on Saturday nights). Similar is *Club 28* next door to the Eden Roc Hotel.

There's also a disco at least once a week – usually on Wednesday – at *Coconut Village* past the Driftwood Club and, if you get there early enough, you won't have to pay the entry charge. It's a pleasant place to dance away the evening and you won't drown in perspiration as it's open-air under makuti roofs right on the beach. The bar is incredible and is worth a visit just to see it. It's built around a living tree with one of the branches as the bar top!

Bars The liveliest tourist bar is the makuti-roofed *Hermann's Beer Garden*, where the music is loud, the lighting subdued and the girls ever present.

Also fairly popular is the *Fermento Piano Bar* on the top floor of the shopping centre diagonally opposite the Sabaki Centre. This is a ritzy, air-con bar specialising in cocktails, though they also sell beers. Up until around 10 pm they show music videos; after that it's either live music or dreadful Italian karaoke. If it's the latter, you may decide that it's time to drift across the road to the Stardust Club.

The *Malindi Fishing Club*, right next to the Metro Hotel, may also be worth checking out if you're staying in the area. It's a very attractive, traditionally constructed building with a makuti roof. There's a bar and snacks are available. The clientele, mainly British, are friendly, beers are some of the cheapest in town, the only snag being the daily membership charge of KSh 50.

The *Malindi Golf & Country Club*, a couple of km north of town, is open to all comers on payment of a temporary membership fee. Apart from golf, there is tennis, a bar/restaurant, and a library.

If you want to do some serious gambling or simply have a flutter on the one-arm bandits (pokies, to the Aussies) along with the hordes of like-minded addicts then there's the *Casino* on the Lamu road. It has all the usual international games and you can bet as little as KSh 50 on most games. Entry is free and drinks are reasonably priced. It's open daily from noon until 5 am.

Things to Buy

There's a collection of at least 30 craft shops (tin shacks) on the beachfront near the mosque. Prices are reasonable, though you must, of course, bargain, and the quality is also reasonable. Crafts on offer include makonde carvings, wooden animal carvings, soapstone and wooden chess sets, basketware and the like. If you have unwanted or excess gear (T-shirts, jeans, cameras) you can often do a part-exchange deal with these people.

Getting There & Away

Air Three companies each operate two flights a day between Malindi and Mombasa (US$28) and between Malindi and Lamu (US$65). They are Air Kenya Aviation (☎ 30808), Galana Centre; Eagle Aviation Ltd (☎ 21258), next door to Express Kenya/ American Express; and Prestige Air Services Ltd (☎ 20861), next door to the Standard Chartered Bank. All these offices are on Lamu Rd.

Kenya Airways (☎ 20237) also flies from Malindi to Nairobi and Mombasa twice daily. If you're relying on these flights to get back to Mombasa or Nairobi to connect with an international flight then make absolutely sure you have a confirmed booking or, preferably, go back a day before.

Bus & Matatu Three bus companies operate between Mombasa and Malindi on a daily basis. They are Malindi Bus, Tana Express and the Faza Express. The first two have offices in Mombasa and Malindi but Faza Express only has offices in Mombasa and Lamu. There are several departures daily in

either direction which take about 2½ hours and cost KSh 60.

There are also matatus which do this run taking about two hours and cost a little more. There's no need to book in advance from Mombasa if you turn up early enough in the morning. In Mombasa the buses leave from outside the New People's Hotel from early morning until mid-afternoon. Matatus leave from the same place all day until late afternoon and go when full.

Both the buses and matatus *fly* up and down this coast road as though they were being pursued by a marauding army of shifta (bandits) in high-speed Land Cruisers, and they pack in as many punters as they possibly can. I counted 138 people on one such bus and that didn't include the driver and his mate!
Geoff Crowther

Between Malindi and Lamu there's only one bus line these days and that is the Faza Express. The reason for this is that the other lines have withdrawn their services because of the appalling state of the road and the danger of being held up by armed shifta – this despite the fact that the buses travel with an armed soldier on board. If you do decide to go by bus, you should be aware of the fact that there is a possibility that your bus may be held up by shifta toting AK47s in which case you'll be robbed or, at worst, robbed and shot. Make enquiries locally as to the current situation before setting off on this route.

There are two Faza Express buses to Lamu daily from Malindi which cost KSh 300 and leave from outside the New Safari Hotel in the centre of town at 8.30 am. There's no booking office so just turn up. These buses originate in Mombasa so they're usually pretty full on arrival and a writhing mass of flesh and bones on departure. It's a lousy eight-hour journey, if you're lucky; 11 hours if you're unlucky. Think seriously about flying if you can afford it.

Share-Taxi It's possible to find Peugeot 504 station wagons which do the journey between Malindi and Mombasa, but difficult in the opposite direction. They leave when full (seven passengers) and cost around KSh

400 per person (negotiable). You'll find them at the bus station in Malindi but only in the mornings. Commissioning a normal taxi to take you between Mombasa and Malindi or vice versa will cost you about KSh 4000.

Train You can make advance reservations for Kenyan Railways at most of the large hotels in Malindi and at travel agencies, but you'll be charged KSh 200 for the service. All they do for this is make a telephone call to Mombasa railway station. You can do it yourself (☎ (011) 312220) for a fraction of the cost. See the Mombasa Getting There & Away section for information on train fares and timetables.

Getting Around

You can rent bicycles from the Silversands Camp Site, from Ozi's Guest House and from some of the mid-range and lower top-end hotels. Charges are KSh 30 per hour or KSh 160 per day. This is probably the best way to get around town unless you prefer to walk.

Taxis are mainly concentrated along the Lamu Rd between the post office and the Sabaki Centre. Fares are basically the first figure which comes into the taxi driver's head so you need to negotiate but even a very short journey won't cost you much less than KSh 100. The fare to the airport is KSh 300 from anywhere along Lamu Rd and around KSh 200 from the town centre.

On the main street near the Blue Marlin Hotel, Glory Car Hire (☎ 20065), Hertz (☎ 20069), Avis, and Europcar all have offices. Payless Car Hire (☎ 311643) is up the gravel lane beside the Palm Garden Restaurant. It's advisable to book a car in advance if you want to be sure of getting the class and type of vehicle you want as the choice is limited and demand is high.

GARSEN

This is another nondescript town between Garissa and Lamu, on the one hand, and Malindi and Lamu on the other. There's absolutely no reason to stay here if you're on the only remaining bus line between Malindi and Lamu (the Faza Express) but, if you're hitching between Garissa and Lamu (there are no longer any buses between the two), it may be necessary. There are several basic hotels to choose from. The best is the *3-in-1 Lodging & Restaurant* which is fairly clean and has its own restaurant.

Lamu

In the early 1970s Lamu acquired a reputation as the Kathmandu of Africa – a place of fantasy and other-worldliness wrapped in a cloak of medieval romance. It drew all self-respecting seekers of the miraculous, the globetrotters, and that much maligned bunch of people called hippies. The attraction was obvious. Both Kathmandu and Lamu were remote, unique and fascinating self-contained societies which had somehow escaped the depredation of the 20th century with their culture, their centuries-old way of life and their architecture intact.

Though Kathmandu is now overrun with well-heeled tourists and the hippies have retired to their rural communes or into business as purveyors of the world's handicrafts, Lamu remains much the same as it has always been – to a degree.

With an almost exclusively Muslim population, it is Kenya's oldest living town and has changed little in appearance or character over the centuries. Access is still by diesel-powered launch from the mainland (though there's an airstrip on Manda Island) and the only motor-powered vehicle on the island, other than the occasional tractor, is that owned by the district commissioner. The streets are far too narrow and winding to accommodate anything other than pedestrians or donkeys. Men still wear the full length white robes known as *khanzus* and the *kofia* caps, and women cover themselves with the black wraparound buibui as they do in other Islamic cultures, although here it's a liberalised version which often hugs their bodies, falls short of the ankles and dispenses completely with the veil worn in front of the face.

There are probably more dhows to be seen here than anywhere else along the East African coast and local festivals still take place with complete disregard for camera-toting tourists. The beach at Shela is still magnificent and uncluttered and nothing happens in a hurry. It's one of the most relaxing places you'll ever have the pleasure to visit.

At least, that was the story until the mid-1980s. Since then a number of pressures have been threatening to undermine the fabric of this unique Swahili settlement. The most important of these during the late 1980s and early 1990s was tourism. In those days, during the high season, several hundred tourists would visit Lamu every day, either by air or overland by bus and launch. In the low season, the influx was considerably less but the perceived degradation of Lamu's social fabric attributed to tourism at the time prompted local newspapers to run scare stories under headlines such as, 'Lamu Under Siege'. They did have a point but the days of shock-horror seem to have passed and, with the downturn in Kenya's tourist industry over the last few years, the inflow of tourists, particularly budget travellers, has decreased to such a degree that many of the cheaper hotels have permanently closed their doors.

The other major pressure is population increase. It's expected that the town's current population of around 15,000 will increase to 30,000 by the end of the century. To accommodate and provide services for all those extra people is going to take some very sensitive planning. Even today, it's a well-known fact that Lamu schoolchildren fare worst in the national secondary school certificate examinations compared with the rest of the country. Redressing that deficiency is not going to be an easy task. While it may be true that tourism distorts economic patterns and centuries-old cultural values and can even destroy them, Lamu urgently needs an injection of cash for preservation, restora-

tion, creation of employment, schools and for a cleanup – particularly of the open drainage system. Tourism could be the source of that cash but the boom days are over – at least until the tourist industry picks up again.

What can be done about stabilising the population is another story entirely and a sensitive issue in a traditional Muslim culture. Yet, as the population expands and the demand for water and electricity increases, it's clear that Lamu faces a crisis at some point in the future. Water supplies on the island are very limited and the electricity generating station is running at well below 50% capacity with the bulk of the plant lying idle awaiting repair. When it will be repaired is anyone's guess.

History

The 20th century may have brought Lamu a measure of peace and tranquillity but it has not always been that way. The town was only of minor importance in the string of Swahili settlements which stretched from Somalia to Mozambique. Although it was a thriving port by the early 1500s, it surrendered without a fight to the early Portuguese mariners and was generally politically dependent on the more important sultanate of Paté which, at the time, was the most important island port in the archipelago. Until the late 1700s it did manage to avoid the frequent wars between the sultanates of Paté, Mombasa and Malindi following the decline of Portuguese influence in the area.

After that there followed many years of internecine strife between the various island city-states of Lamu, Paté, Faza and Siyu, which only ended in 1813 when Lamu defeated the forces of Paté in a battle at Shela. Shortly afterwards, Lamu became subject to the sultanate of Zanzibar which nominally controlled the whole of the coastal strip from Kilwa to the Somali border (under a British protectorate from 1890) until Kenya became independent in 1963.

Lamu had a slave-based economy (in common with the other Swahili coastal city-states) until the turn of the 20th century when the British forced the Sultan of Zanzibar to

THE COAST

Lamu

0   50   100 m

PLACES TO STAY
4   Buhari Hotel
5   Pole Pole Guest House
6   Peace Guest House
7   Kishuna Guest House
8   Pool Guest House
9   Yumbe House
11 Haludy Guest House
12 Stone House Hotel
15 New Kenya Lodge
16 Casuarina Rest House
18 Lamu Guest House
19 Petley's Inn
22 Amu House Annexe
24 Full Moon Guest House
26 Amu House
27 New Maharus Guest House
29 Lulu House
30 New Castle Lodge
40 Lamu Palace Hotel

PLACES TO EAT
3   Serena Vegetarian
    Restaurant
23 Bush Gardens Restaurant
25 Hapa Hapa Restaurant
28 Mid-Town Nyama Choma
36 New Star Restaurant
37 Rumours Gypsies Gallery
    & Air Kenya Aviation
38 Swahili Dishis
39 Labanda Restaurant
45 Coconut Juice Garden

OTHER
1   Door Carving Workshops
2   Jamaa Mosque
10 Swahili House Museum
13 Donkey Sanctuary
14 Craft Shop
17 Lamu Museum
20 Prestige Air Services
21 Standard Chartered Bank
31 Fort
32 Customs
33 Post Office
34 Market
35 Hospital
41 Lamu Book Centre
42 Riyadha Mosque
43 Police Club
44 Faza Express Bus Office

To Matondoni

To Mokowe (mainland)

INDIAN OCEAN

Main Jetty

Dhow Moorings

To Shela Beach, Civil Servants Club
& District Commissioner's Office

sign an anti-slavery agreement and subsequently intercepted dhows carrying slaves north from that island. All that cheap labour fuelled a period of economic growth for Lamu and traders grew rich by exporting ivory, cowries, tortoiseshell, mangrove poles, oil seeds and grains, and importing oriental linen, silks, spices and porcelain.

With the abolition of slavery in 1907, the economy of the island rapidly went into decline and stayed that way until very recently when increased receipts from tourism gave it a new lease of life. That decline, and its strong sense of tradition, is what has preserved the Lamu you see today. No other Swahili town, other than Zanzibar, can offer you such a cultural feast and an uncorrupted traditional style of architecture – if you can ignore the TV aerials.

Information
Tourist Office There's a seasonal tourist information counter on the waterfront near the jetty, but it's of limited use.

Money The Standard Chartered Bank and the Kenya Commercial Bank, both on the harbour front, are the only banks in Lamu. They're both open Monday to Friday from 9 am to 3 pm, and Saturday from 9 to 11 am. It's possible that the Standard Chartered Bank may have closed by now.

Post & Communications Lamu's telephone code is 01221.

Books There are some excellent books about Lamu and the Swahili civilisation. The best general account is *The Portuguese Period in East Africa* by Justus Strandes. This is a translation of a book originally published in German in 1899 with up-to-date notes and appendices detailing recent archaeological findings, some of which contradict Strandes' opinions. It's very readable.

Lamu: A Study of the Swahili Town, by Usam Ghaidan, is a very detailed study of Lamu by an Iraqi who was formerly a lecturer in architecture at the University of Nairobi and has since devoted his time to

research into the Swahili architecture of the north Kenyan coast. You can find both of the above books in most good bookshops in Nairobi or Mombasa and the latter at the museum in Lamu.

If you're going to stay long in Lamu the leaflet-map *Lamu: Map & Guide to the Archipelago, the Island & the Town* is worth buying at the museum bookshop.

Bookshops Apart from the museum, the Lamu Book Centre, close to Rumours Coffee Shop, has a small but reasonable selection of English-language novels and other books. It's also the only place where you can buy local newspapers, and international news magazines such as *Time* and *Newsweek*. It's open from 6.30 am to 12.30 pm and 2.30 to 9 pm.

Town Buildings
Lamu town dates back to at least the late 14th century when the Pwani Mosque was built. Most buildings date from the 18th century, but the lower parts and basements are often considerably older. The streets are narrow, cool and quiet and there are many small courtyards and intimate spaces enclosed by high walls. Traditionally, buildings were constructed entirely out of local materials – faced coral-rag blocks for the walls, wooden floors supported by mangrove poles, makuti roofs and intricately carved shutters for windows. This is changing gradually with the increasing use of imported materials and is one of the factors of great concern to conservationists.

One of the most outstanding features of the houses here, as in old Zanzibar, is the intricately carved doors and lintels which have kept generations of carpenters busy. Sadly, many of them have disappeared in recent years but the skill has not been lost. Walk down to the far end of the harbour front in the opposite direction to Shela and you'll see them being made.

Only a few of the mosques have minarets and even these are small affairs. This, combined with the fact that there's little outward decoration and few doors and windows cialising in books on Lamu and the Swahili culture.

Swahili House Museum

If the museum stokes your interest in Swahili culture then you should also visit this museum tucked away off to the side of Yumbe House (a hotel). It's a beautifully restored traditional house with furniture and other house wares as well as a pleasant courtyard. Entry charges and opening hours are the same as the main museum.

Lamu Fort

The building of this massive structure was begun by the Sultan of Paté in 1810 and completed in 1823. From 1910 right up to 1984 it was used as a prison. It has recently undergone complete restoration and now houses an impressive walk-through aquarium and natural history museum, as well as the island's library. Entry fees and opening times are the same as for the museum.

Donkey Sanctuary

One of the most unexpected sights on Lamu is the Donkey Sanctuary which is run by the International Donkey Protection Trust of Sidmouth, Devon, UK. Injured, sick or worn-out donkeys are brought here to find rest and protection. As in most societies where they're used as beasts of burden, donkeys are regularly abused or get injured so it's good to see something positive being done for their welfare. The sanctuary is right on the waterfront. Although the free clinic has been going since 1985, land for the sanctuary wasn't purchased until 4 July 1987, a day that is celebrated by the sanctuary's manager as Donkey Independence Day (it also just happens to coincide with America's Independence Day!).

The Beach

There's no beach on the Lamu town waterfront itself. What there is here is a muddy, garbage-strewn mess in urgent need of a major cleanup. For a white-sand beach and crystal-clear water you need to go to Shela, a 40-minute walk or 10-minute trip by dhow

---

Touts

Lamu used to be notorious for its touts and 'beach boys' who would meet you off the ferries from the mainland or from Manda Island airstrip and fill your head full of rubbish about the availability of accommodation and facilities at the various hotels on the island. That's all finished. Only licensed 'guides' are now allowed to do this sort of thing and their charges, though negotiable, are nominal. For whatever 'fee' you agree to, they'll take you to the hotel of your choice or to one which they recommend in your price range, and carry your bags, so there's no need to brush them off on arrival as just a nuisance. If you want them to, they'll even turn up at your hotel on a specified day and time to carry your bags down to the ferry (again, for an agreed 'fee'). ■

---

opening onto the street, makes them hard to distinguish from domestic buildings.

Both in Lamu and in Shela, private developers have recently been allowed to build ugly, modern hotels despite local pressure, but fortunately there is only one in each place. There has been quite an increase in the number of hotels and guesthouses, but as most of them have used existing buildings the fabric and atmosphere of the old town has, by and large, been retained.

Lamu Museum

A couple of hours spent in the Lamu Museum, on the waterfront next to Petley's Inn, is an excellent introduction to the culture and history of Lamu. It's one of the most interesting small museums in Kenya. There's a reconstruction of a traditional Swahili house, charts, maps, ethnological displays, models of the various types of dhow and two examples of the remarkable and ornately carved ivory *siwa* – a wind instrument peculiar to the coastal region which is often used as a fanfare at weddings. There's a good slide show available at the museum – ask to see it. Entry costs KSh 200 (KSh 100 for children) for nonresidents and KSh 30 (KSh 10 for children) for residents and the museum is open daily from 8 am to 6 pm.

The museum has a good bookshop spefrom Lamu. The beach starts at Peponi Hotel, circles around the headland and continues all the way along the Indian Ocean side of the island. The best part of the beach if you want waves is well past Peponi Hotel – there's no surf at Peponi because you're still in the channel between Lamu and Manda islands. It's possible to hire windsurfing equipment at Peponi for use in the channel.

Matondoni Village
You'll see many dhows anchored along the waterfront at Lamu and at Shela in the harbour at the southern end of town but if you want to see them being built or repaired the best place to do this is at the village of Matondoni.

To get there you have a choice of walking (about two hours), hiring a donkey, or hiring a dhow. If you choose the dhow it will cost KSh 500 per person (minimum five passengers) but it usually includes a barbecue fish lunch.

Walking there is a little more problematical until you find the track at the back of town and that is easier said than done as there are tracks leading every which way. Head first for the football pitch and then follow the telephone wires which go to Matondoni. Sounds easy doesn't it? It isn't, so you'll have to stop and ask directions from local people until you're sure you're on the right track.

Set off early if you are walking. It gets very hot later in the day. There's a small cafe in Matondoni village where you can get fish and rice for around KSh 80 as well as fruit juice. There are no guesthouses in the village but a bed or floor space can usually be arranged in a private house if you ask around. An impromptu group of travellers generally collects later in the afternoon so you can all share a dhow ride back to Lamu.

Kipongani Village
This is also worth a visit. Here local people make straw mats, baskets and hats. It's a friendly place, and tea and snacks can be arranged plus there's a beautiful empty beach nearby with waves.

Shela Village
Shela village, a 40-minute walk from Lamu, is a pleasant little village well worth a wander around. The ancestors of the people here came from Takwa when that settlement was abandoned in the late 17th century and they still speak a dialect of Swahili which is distinct from that of Lamu. Many have migrated to Malindi in recent years. Don't miss the famous mosque with its characteristic minaret at the back of Peponi Hotel. Many of the houses in this village have been bought up and restored by foreigners in the last few years, but while it has a surprising air of affluence, the languorous atmosphere remains unspoiled. Quite a few travellers prefer to stay in Shela rather than in Lamu town itself. It's certainly more convenient for the beach if that's your main interest.

To get to Shela, follow the harbour-front road till it ends and then follow the shore line. You will pass the new hospital built by the Saudi Arabian government and a ginning factory before you have to follow the shore line. If the tide is out, you can walk along the beach most of the way. When it's in, you may well have to do a considerable amount of wading up to your thighs and deeper. If that doesn't appeal, there is a track all the way from Lamu to Shela but there are many turn-offs so stay with the ones which run closest to the shore (you may find yourself in a few cul-de-sacs doing this as a number of turn-offs to the left run to private houses and end there). A popular alternative to walking there is to take one of the frequent motorised dhows which shuttle back and forth between Lamu and Shela. This costs KSh 50 per person assuming there are a minimum of two people.

Dhow Trips
Taking a dhow trip is almost obligatory, and it is a very relaxing way to pass a day. You'll constantly be approached while walking along the waterfront by people wanting to take you out for a trip. The cost is around KSh 300 per person for four or more people, KSh 400 for less than four people. Five is a comfortable number as the boats are not that

big. The price includes fishing and snorkelling, although both are largely fruitless exercises as it's virtually impossible to catch fish during the day, and the best snorkelling is a couple of hours away. A barbecue fish lunch on the beach at Manda is provided, supposedly with the fish you have caught but usually with fish provided by the captain. Make sure you take a hat and some sunblock as there is rarely any shade on the dhows, despite assurances to the contrary.

See the Islands Around Lamu section later in this chapter for details about longer dhow trips.

Places to Stay – bottom end

Lamu has been catering for budget travellers for some two decades and, up to two years ago, there were more budget hotels than you could point a stick at. That situation has now radically changed with the downturn in the tourist industry and many have put up the shutters so there's now only a limited choice. All the same, don't believe a word anyone tells you about there being running water 24 hours a day at any of these places. There often isn't. Water is not an abundant commodity on Lamu and restrictions are in force most of the year. It's usually only available early in the morning and early in the evening which, in most cases, means bucket showers only and somewhat smelly toilets.

Prices are remarkably consistent because of the competition for clientele though you obviously get what you pay for both in terms of facilities and position. A dormitory bed or space on the floor of a rooftop costs around KSh 100, a single room between KSh 150 and 250, and a double room KSh 300 to KSh 500. Almost all of these would involve sharing bathroom facilities but some of the higher priced doubles would have their own bathroom. Prices rise in the high season (August to September and around Christmas/New Year) by a factor of up to 50%; at other times there's plenty of scope for negotiation, particularly if you plan to stay for more than just a day or two. Instant discounts are offered to anyone who plans to stay three or more days. If a lodge is full when you

arrive but you like it a lot and want to be first in line for a room, they'll usually let you sleep on the roof or elsewhere until the following morning.

Where you stay initially will probably depend largely on what sort of room you are offered, what's available and who meets you getting off the ferry from the mainland.

If you plan on staying in Lamu for a while it's worth making enquiries about renting a house, so long as there's a group of you to share the cost. On a daily basis it won't be much cheaper (if at all) than staying at a lodge but on a monthly basis you're looking at a considerable saving. You can share them with as many people as you feel comfortable with or have space for and prices usually include a house steward. Some of the simpler houses can be very cheap indeed and include a refrigerator and cooking facilities. They're available in Lamu town itself but also at Shela and between Lamu and Shela. Some of them can be excellent value and very spacious. You need to ask around and see what is available. It's possible to find some remarkably luxurious places, especially around Shela.

Lamu Town Right on the waterfront is the *Full Moon Guest House* which is a friendly place with an excellent 1st-floor balcony overlooking the water. It costs KSh 250 per room (single or double) in the low season and KSh 500 in the high season, all with shared facilities.

In a similar category is the *New Kenya Lodge*, behind the Kenya Commercial Bank. It's fairly clean and has mosquito nets and cold bucket showers. The rooms cost KSh 250 to KSh 350.

Very good value, clean and simple, is the *Lamu Guest House* at the back of the Lamu Museum. There's a choice of different rooms here but the best are probably those on the top floor. Doubles with attached bathrooms with fan cost KSh 550 and KSh 650 and triples with the same facilities are KSh 750. There are also some doubles with attached bathrooms, but no fan for KSh 400.

Next to the fort is the *New Castle Lodge* which overlooks the main square and picks up sea breezes since it's fairly high up. It used to be very popular with backpackers but these days it's only just habitable. Singles/doubles with shared bathroom facilities cost KSh 150/300. The rooms have mosquito nets and fans. Give the nearby *Bahati Lodging* a wide berth. It's the pits and you wouldn't even stable pigs in there.

Way out the back of town through a maze of sandy alleyways about 15 minutes walk from the waterfront (assuming you don't get lost) is the *Peace Guest House* (☎ 3020) which is very clean, provides mosquito nets and charges KSh 170 (KSh 200) for a bed in a four-bed dormitory including breakfast, and KSh 500 (KSh 600 in the high season) for spacious, doubles with attached bathrooms, with fan. If you're staying more than three nights they'll offer you a discount of approximately 20%. You can also camp here for KSh 80 per tent including the use of kitchen facilities and a fridge. This is a very spacious place surrounded by gardens and flowering trees and has been popular for years though it is quite a way from the centre of town. It's signposted most of the way from the waterfront but you can still get lost in the last 300m.

Closer to the centre of town and back from the waterfront but one of the tallest buildings in Lamu is the *Pole Pole Guest House* which has 15 doubles with attached bathrooms, with fan, some of them with mosquito nets, for KSh 300 excluding breakfast. There's a spacious, makuti-roofed area on top of the hotel from which there are great views over the town and the waterfront.

At the top end of this range is the *Kishuna Guest House* at the back side of town. It's just a modern concrete block devoid of character but it's very clean and offers singles/doubles with attached bathroom for KSh 400/700 including breakfast. All the rooms have a fan and mosquito nets and you have a choice in the double rooms of twin beds or a double bed.

Shela Quite a few travellers, especially beach lovers, prefer to stay at Shela village rather than in Lamu itself. There is no real budget accommodation here unless you can negotiate a room with a local family or rent a whole house and share the cost with a bunch of other people.

If you're going to stay here for a while – and it seems most of the people who stay here do – then it's best to ask around for a house to rent and have a group together to share the cost. Many of the houses here are owned by expatriate foreigners (especially Italians) who have poured vast amounts of money into them but only live here for part of the year. Most of them have been very sensitively upgraded and some are stunning. Quite a lot of them can be rented out so ask around in the restaurants.

Places to Stay – middle
Lamu Town Good value in this range is the *Casuarina Rest House* (☎ 3123) which was formerly the police headquarters. It offers large, airy rooms with good views and is clean and well maintained but often full. It costs KSh 1000 to KSh 1500 a double depending on how long you intend to stay, but like all places it's negotiable to an extent, and prices are much lower in the off season. There's access to a large, flat, roof area.

More expensive but excellent value is the new *Stone House Hotel* (☎ 33544/33149) which has beautiful sea-facing doubles with attached bathrooms for KSh 1850 and others which don't face the sea for KSh 1700. Singles with attached bathrooms are KSh 1450 and singles with shared bathroom facilities are KSh 1300. All prices include breakfast. The hotel has its own superb rooftop restaurant (no alcoholic drinks) with excellent views over the town and waterfront.

Very similar in style and quality is *Lulu House* (☎ 33539) in the maze of streets behind the fort which is relatively new and costs KSh 750/1500 for singles/doubles with attached bathroom, including breakfast. The rooms are very pleasant, the staff friendly and there's a roof area, a table-tennis room and a safe to leave valuables.

Close to the main square is the *New Maharus Guest House* (☎ 33001). There's nothing 'new' about the place and some of the rooms are positively antediluvian plus it totally lacks character but it's relatively cheap at KSh 700/1000 for singles/doubles and KSh 1300 for triples in '1st Class' rooms, KSh 500/700 for singles/doubles and KSh 900 for triples in '2nd class' rooms and KSh 300/400 in '3rd class' rooms in the high season. In the low season you can take KSh 100 to KSh300 off these prices depending on the class of room. Prices include breakfast and the rooms in 1st and 2nd class have attached bathrooms. Third class rooms come with shared bathroom facilities. It's not great value.

One of the most beautiful places in this range is *Yumbe House* (☎ 33101; fax 33300), close to the Swahili House Museum. It's a four-storey traditional house surrounding a central courtyard which has been superbly and sensitively converted into a hotel with airy terraces and makuti roofs. All rooms have attached bathrooms (towels, soap and toilet paper are provided), spotlessly clean, and there are mosquito nets and fan. It's excellent value at KSh 960/1830 for singles/doubles and KSh 2560 a triple including breakfast in the low season and KSh 1020/2130 for singles/doubles and KSh 3050 for triples including breakfast in the high season.

Right on the waterfront is *Amu House* (☎/fax 33420). This hotel is a beautifully restored 16th-century house decorated with plaster carvings and furnished with local antiques. All the bedrooms have attached bathrooms and equipped with fans and some have private verandahs but they all have antique beds with mosquito nets. The hotel also has its own restaurant offering breakfast and dinner specialising in Swahili-style seafood. It's a great place to stay and costs KSh 1500/2000 for singles/doubles including breakfast. If you make a reservation in advance and arrive by air, they'll meet you at Manda airport.

Another good place in this range is the *Pool Guest House*, so-called because it has a small swimming pool, though this is invariably empty. It's a mellow maze of a place surrounding a shady courtyard and the rooms

vary quite a bit, some having waterfront views and sea breezes. All have attached bathrooms with two beds, mosquito nets, a fan and are excellent value at KSh 700 without breakfast in the low season (more in the high season). There's also a rooftop area with good views over town. The staff are friendly and helpful.

The *Buhari Hotel* (☎ 33172) is a fairly new place with a very pleasant rooftop area, but variable rooms. The downstairs rooms are small and gloomy, but the upstairs rooms, particularly those at the front, are very good and cost KSh 800 for a room with a double bed and KSh 1500 for a room with two double beds including breakfast. All rooms have attached bathrooms and have mosquito nets.

Also worth considering is the *Haludy Guest House*. Rooms with attached bathrooms in this spacious and airy place cost KSh 1200 to KSh 1700 in the high season, dropping to KSh 650 to KSh 900 in the low season. There's a fridge and cooking facilities for those who want to put their own meals together. The only problem with this place is finding someone to rent you a room.

Shela The only mid-range places in Shela are whole villas which, as previously described, are available for longer term rental (a couple of weeks or more). Typical is the *White Rock Pool House*, right on the foreshore close to Peponi Hotel, which sleeps up to 10 people and costs the equivalent of US$100 a day in the low season and US$120 in the high season. It comes complete with a house steward, cook and cleaners.

Places to Stay – top end
Lamu Town The best top-range hotel in Lamu itself is the historic *Petley's Inn* (☎ 33107; fax 33378) right on the harbour front next to the Lamu Museum. It was originally set up in the late 19th century by Percy Petley – a somewhat eccentric English colonist who ran plantations on the mainland at Witu until he retired to Lamu – thus making it one of the oldest hotels in Kenya. Unfortunately, it was gutted by fire in August 1993 during which many irreplaceable mementos

were lost forever. Instead of crying into his rum and coke, however, the manager saw this as an opportunity to completely revamp the hotel's layout, facilities and services. This has been done with an admirable sense of good taste – all the traditional features have been restored, including makuti roofs and woven blinds. It's a great place to stay. The bed and breakfast rates for sea-facing rooms with a balcony are KSh 2400/3000 for singles/doubles and KSh 3750 for triples. Standard rooms including breakfast cost KSh 2000/2750 for singles/doubles and KSh 3300 for triples. Facilities include a swimming pool, a bar on the ground floor and an excellent rooftop bar/restaurant (open to non-guests) which catches the sea breezes. There's a sensible seafood and meat menu which changes every day depending on what's fresh, the food is excellently cooked and prices are reasonable.

Also on the waterfront is what some people consider to be Lamu's latest blot on the landscape. Intrusive and large by Lamu standards it certainly is but *some* effort has been put into creating a recognisably Lamu façade. This is the Swiss-managed *Lamu Palace Hotel* (☎ 33272; fax 33104). All the rooms have attached bathrooms and have air-con and cost the equivalent of US$50/80 for singles/doubles and US$100 for triples including breakfast in the high season and the equivalent of US$35/55 for singles/ doubles and US$70 for triples including breakfast in the low season. These rates include boat transfer to and from Manda island airstrip. There's also a bar (the Chege Bar) which, like the restaurant, is open to non-guests.

Shela At the far end of Shela village and right on the beach is *Peponi Hotel* (☎ 33421/3; fax 33029) which is *the* place to stay if you want a top-range hotel at Shela. It consists of whitewashed cottages with their own verandahs facing the channel between Lamu and Manda islands and is reckoned to be one of the best hotels in the country, both in terms of its position, its facilities and the quality of the cuisine. The rates for bed and breakfast

in the standard rooms are the equivalent of US$130/170 for singles/doubles and in the superior rooms they are US$150/200. Full-board rates are US$150/220 in the standard rooms and US$180/270 in the superior rooms. Advance booking is essential. Motorised dhow transport between Manda airstrip and Peponi Hotel costs KSh 100 one way or KSh 500 by speedboat.

Peponi Hotel is a waters-ports centre and there are number of activities and equipment available both to guests and non-guests which include water-skiing (KSh 4000 per hour), windsurfing (KSh 500 to KSh 700 depending on the level of your skill), snorkelling (KSh 100 per day for the equipment alone), and scuba diving for certified divers between November and March (KSh 2350 for a single dive or KSh 4700 for two dives at two sites including lunch). It also offers full-moon dhow cruises for KSh 3500 (minimum eight people) including drinks, wine and a lobster dinner. Other facilities open to non-guests are the bar and the lunchtime barbecue area which serves very tasty fish and meat dishes at a reasonable price. The hotel is closed during May and June.

Also on the channel is *Kijani House* (☎ 33235; fax 33237), which has beautifully furnished rooms each with their own verandah arranged around a lush and colourful garden. Facilities include two swimming pools, and like Peponis, it is also closed in May and June. The cost here is the equivalent of US$70/90 for singles/doubles including breakfast in the standard rooms and US$85/ 120 in the superior rooms. Full-board rates are US$90/160 and US$105/190, respectively. Children between the ages of three and 12 are approximately half price. Boat transfers to and from Manda airstrip are free.

Immediately at the back of Peponi Hotel is the *Pwani Guest House* (☎ 33540), a small place with only three double rooms but very pleasant indeed. The spacious rooms all have two double beds as well as a child's cot and cost KSh 2000 a double including breakfast in the low season and KSh 2500 in the high season. All the rooms have attached bathrooms, hot water and mosquito nets plus there's a beautiful rooftop lounge area overlooking the channel.

In the centre of Shela village is the *Island Hotel* (☎ 33290; fax 245458; (02) 229880 in Nairobi), a superb traditional Lamu-style house with the romantic rooftop Barracuda Restaurant and only five minutes walk from the waterfront. The hotel has 14 rooms, including three family rooms, all of which have attached bathrooms. The rates are the same year-round and singles/doubles with bed and breakfast cost the equivalent of US$47/66 with triples at US$89. Full-board rates are US$65, US$103 and US$145, respectively. Children between the ages of three and 12 sharing their parents' room are charged US$11 for bed and breakfast and US$24 with full board. The room rates are inclusive of boat transfers to and from Manda island airstrip. The very good restaurant here is open to non-guests and prices are very reasonable. Swahili cuisine is the speciality. Starters are priced at KSh 100 to KSh 160 with main dishes at between KSh 240 (fish) and KSh 460 (crab) but it's not licensed to sell alcoholic drinks.

A good deal cheaper, and the place to stay if you want to do your own catering, is the *Shela Rest House* (☎ 33091) not far from the Island Hotel. It too has open makuti-roofed areas and sea views. Two-bedroom apartments with kitchen and fridge cost the equivalent of US$39 for three people and US$52 for four. It's a friendly place and the management can arrange for a cook to prepare your meals if you want a rest from doing it yourself.

Also reasonably priced is the *Shella Beach House* (☎ /fax 33420) which is owned by the same people who run Amu House in Lamu town. There are two rooftop bedrooms here and another one on the ground floor as well as a makuti-roofed sitting area and another one for dining. It costs KSh 1100/1500 for singles/doubles including breakfast.

Lastly there's the ugly three-storey blot on the foreshore that should never have got past the planning stage – the *Shela Beach Hotel*. This place sticks out like the proverbial dogs' balls but, fortunately – or unfortunately, seeing as it's still standing – construction has ceased and it's anyone's guess when it will be completed. It would be far better if it were demolished.

At the opposite (south-west) end of Lamu island is **Kipungani** where there's another top-end hotel called *Sea Breezes*. It's owned by Prestige Hotels and charges much the same as Petley's Inn.

Places to Eat – cheap
It's important to know that *all* of the cheap places to eat and many of the more expensive restaurants are closed all day until after sunset during the month of Ramadan. This leaves you with only three choices for breakfast (if your hotel doesn't provide this) and lunch. They are Petley's Inn, the Lamu Palace Hotel and Peponi Hotel.

One of the cheapest places to eat in Lamu is the *New Star Restaurant*. You certainly won't beat the prices and some people recommend it highly, but service can be slow (depending on what you order and the time of day). Fish and chips or rice costs KSh 150 to KSh 180.

Cheaper still is the very basic *Swahili Dishis* (sic) just off the waterfront. This tiny place caters purely for the locals and serves no-frills African food at rock-bottom prices. Another local eatery is the *Mid-Town Nyama Choma* cafe on the main square by the fort. There are no prizes here for culinary excellence, but for a cheap meat meal it's the place to go.

For consistently good food at a reasonable price there are a handful of very popular restaurants. The menus at all are pretty standard, with fish, seafood, steaks and curries. All do excellent juices and shakes. Despite the excellent seafood available, the seafood meals in Lamu are really quite basic.

Close by the dhow moorings is the *Labanda Restaurant* which, apart from the standard dishes, also does poulet yassa, a delicious Senegalese chicken dish for KSh 280. It also serves some vegetarian dishes, which are hard to find on Lamu.

For exclusively vegetarian fare head for the *Serena Vegetarian Restaurant*. This restaurant has been popular for years though under various names such as Coral Rock and Yoghurt Inn – there's still a sign at the front saying Yoghurt Inn. It has a good range of vegetarian dishes as well as banana pancakes, lassi and fruit juices. Expect to pay around KSh 150 to KSh 200 for main dishes. It's open daily but often closed on Tuesday during the low season.

Somewhat more expensive but extremely popular is the *Bush Gardens* on the waterfront, next door to the Hapa Hapa Restaurant. It's run by the very personable and energetic 'Bush Baby' who personally supervises the cooking which sometimes makes for slow service but guarantees you an excellent meal. Fish dishes (barracuda, tuna, snapper or shark) cost KSh 200, crab KSh 450, prawns KSh 350 and lobster KSh 750, all served with chips or coconut rice and salad. Fruit juices are also available. It's arguably the best seafood restaurant in Lamu.

Next door is the *Hapa Hapa Restaurant* which is also very good, and offers a similar range of dishes, including seafood and possibly the best fruit juices and milk shakes in town. Prices are similar to those at Bush Gardens, and it's also a very popular place, especially at breakfast time.

Juice lovers should pay at least one visit to the *Coconut Juice Garden* on the waterfront beyond the Lamu Palace Hotel heading for Shela. It serves excellent, cheap fruit juices and coconut milk.

Many travellers come across a man popularly called Ali Hippy who, for several years, has been offering travellers meals at his house. The meal usually includes lobster, crab, fish, coconut rice and vegetable stew and the whole family entertains you while you eat. Some people come away quite satisfied (it's definitely an unusual evening out) but the majority these days feel it's somewhat contrived, and indeed it's not unusual for the whole evening to be cancelled with no explanations – or refunds – given. Expect to pay around KSh 200. A number of other local families have begun to imitate Ali so don't be surprised if you're approached on the street with a similar proposal.

At Shela, the *Stop Over Restaurant* right on the beach is a popular place to eat or drink and prices are very reasonable though they only offer simple meals. Similar, and offering a slightly wider range, is the *Bahari Restaurant* on the foreshore between Kijani House and Peponi Hotel.

Places to Eat – more expensive

For an up-market snack or coffee, *Rumours* in the same building as Gypsies Gallery, on the street parallel to the waterfront, is worth a try. It's open from 8.45 am to 8.45 pm and is European-owned. It doesn't close during Ramadan.

The rooftop restaurant at *Petley's Inn* is a great place to eat and is surprisingly inexpensive considering the quality of the food. It's also open to non-guests. The menu is changed daily depending on what is fresh. The cheapest dishes are spaghetti, seafood curry and burgers (KSh 250). More expensive dishes include fish and steaks (KSh 300), prawns (KSh 350) and lobster (KSh 550). This is also one of the very few places where you can have a beer (KSh 60) or other alcoholic drink with your meal. It's open year-round for breakfast, lunch and dinner including during Ramadan.

For a splurge meal the range is strictly limited. The restaurant at the *Lamu Palace Hotel* is far from cheap and the food is quite patchy – some nights it's excellent, other times it's mediocre which is surprising seeing as the Swiss owner/manager used to run the Castle Hotel in Mombasa. There's also a bar here. The restaurant is open during Ramadan.

The rooftop restaurant at the *New Mahrus Hotel* touts itself as a classy restaurant but the food is only average and the hygiene suspect. Basically, you can forget about it.

For a modest splurge at Shela the *Barbecue Grill* at Peponi Hotel offers delicious food and is open to non-guests. There's a choice of both barbecued fish and meat and a superb range of salads and sauces.

For a romantic night out with excellent food go for dinner at the rooftop *Barracuda Restaurant* at the Island Hotel in Shela. It's

GEOFF CROWTHER

DAWN DELANEY

HUGH FINLAY

Lamu's architecture has a distinct Arab influence (top). Donkeys and pedestrians are the main traffic in the town's narrow, winding streets (middle). The waters off this unique Swahili settlement are dotted with wooden dhows, and they're totally at the mercy of the wind (bottom).

TONY WHEELER

HUGH FINLAY

GEOFF CROWTHER

The beautiful contrasts of Kenya's Rift Valley: stark cliffs around Lake Baringo; Lake Nakuru
sometimes home to pelicans and flamingos; the boiling hot springs around Lake Bogoria

open to non-guests and prices are reasonable. Starters go for KSh 100 to KSh 160 and main dishes range from KSh 240 (fish) to KSh 460 (crab). Lobster is more expensive.

Entertainment

Bars There are a number of places where you can get a beer in Lamu itself but only three of them have cold beers. One of them is the makuti-roofed terrace bar at *Petley's Inn* which is a very pleasant place to relax and catch the sea breeze. It's the most popular watering hole on the island and is open to non-guests. On the ground floor of the hotel there's an 'African' bar which serves warm beer at cheap prices.

The other place with cold beer is the bar at the *Lamu Palace Hotel* on the waterfront. It's also a good place to catch the breezes, and as you're on ground level it's interesting to watch the passing parade of pedestrians.

The *Police Club* by the police station serves warm beer. It's open in the evenings until fairly late and you don't have to be in the police force to get in.

There's another bar at the *Civil Servants' Club* which has a disco on some Friday and Saturday nights. Keep an eye out for advertising posters around the town. Entry costs KSh 100 and it's a good night out.

Out at Shela, *Peponi Hotel* is a mandatory watering hole and the beer here is always ice-cold. The bar is on the verandah overlooking the channel and beach. It's open all day until late at night and there's always a lively and friendly bunch of characters swapping stories, jokes and anecdotes.

Getting There & Away

Air Three companies each operate twice-daily flights from Lamu to Mombasa (US$85) and Malindi (US$65). They are Air Kenya Aviation (☎ 33445), Baraka House, next door to Rumours Cafe, Eagle Aviation (☎ 33313) and Prestige Air Services Ltd (☎ 33055). The last two have their booking offices on the waterfront in Lamu close to Petley's Inn.

The airport at Lamu is on Manda Island and the ferry across the channel to Lamu

costs KSh 50. You will probably be met by registered guides at the airport who will offer to carry your bags to the hotel of your choice for a small consideration (say, KSh 100).

Air Kenya Aviation (☎ 33445; (02) 501421 in Nairobi) operates daily flights in either direction between Lamu and Nairobi's Wilson airport (US$112).

Bus There's only one bus company which operates between Malindi and Lamu and vice versa and that is Faza Express. It has offices in Mombasa and Lamu but not in Malindi. The pick-up point in Malindi is at the New Safari Hotel in the centre of town. The fare between Malindi and Lamu is KSh 300 and between Mombasa and Lamu it's KSh 350. The journey between Malindi and Lamu takes about eight hours if you're lucky; 11 hours if you're unlucky. Two buses leave in either direction daily at 8.30 am from Malindi and 7 am from Lamu. The buses to and from Lamu arrive and depart from the ferry jetty on the mainland not far from Mokowe. Between here and Lamu you take a motorised ferry which costs KSh 50 per person and takes about 20 minutes (this means you have to get up early if travelling from Lamu to Malindi/Mombasa). The Faza Express office in Lamu is open daily from 8.30 am to 12.30 pm, 2.30 to 4.30 pm and 7 to 8.30 pm. Early booking is advisable as demand is heavy.

Refer to the Malindi section for details of the possible dangers of travelling by bus between Malindi and Lamu. Better still, think seriously about flying if you can afford it.

Dhow Other than trips around the Lamu archipelago, you *may* be able to find a dhow sailing to Mombasa but it's unlikely and you'll need to get permission first from the district commissioner. The journey takes two days on average and prices are negotiable.

Getting Around

Boat There are frequent ferries between Lamu and the bus terminal on the mainland (near Mokowe). The fare is KSh 50. Ferries between the airstrip on Manda Island and

THE COAST

Lamu also cost KSh 50. Between Lamu village and Shela there are plenty of motorised dhows in either direction throughout the day until around sunset which cost KSh 50 per person or KSh 200 for the boat. They'll take up to 10 people at a time. Expect to have to wade back to shore at the Lamu end but not at the Shela end.

There are also regular ferries between Lamu and Paté Island – see the following section for details.

Islands Around Lamu

A popular activity while you're in Lamu is to take a dhow trip to one of the neighbouring islands. You need a small group (six to eight people) to share costs if you're going to do this but it's very easy to put a group like that together in Lamu. Just ask around in the restaurants or the budget hotels.

Since taking tourists around the archipelago is one of the easiest ways of making money for dhow owners in Lamu, there's a lot of competition and you'll be asked constantly by different people if you want to go on a trip. Negotiation over the price and what is included is essential both to avoid misunderstandings and being overcharged. The price of day trips is usually settled quickly because a lot of travellers will have been on them and the cost will be well known.

Dhow trips are usually superb whoever you go with so it's unfair to recommend any particular dhow or captain but, if you're going on a long trip – say, three days – then it's a very good idea to check out both the dhow and the crew before committing yourself. Don't hand over any money until the day of departure except, perhaps, a small advance (say KSh 500 per person) for food. Also, on long trips, it's probably best to organise your own beer, soft drinks and bottled water supplies. Beer, incidentally, isn't easy to organise as there's no longer a Kenya Breweries depot in Lamu. Enquire at Petley's Inn or the police canteen. Lastly, remember that the person who touts for your business is often not the captain of the boat but an intermediary who takes a commission for finding you.

Dhows without an outboard motor are naturally entirely dependent on wind to get them anywhere, though poling – or even pushing – the boat is fairly common along narrow creeks and channels. If you have to pole the boat or you get becalmed out in the channels between the islands, there's no point in remonstrating with the captain. He's not God and there's nothing he can do about it, yet it's surprising how many people imagine otherwise. With that in mind, never go on a long trip if you have a deadline to meet. A three-day trip can occasionally turn into a five-day one, although this is unusual.

Likewise, dhows are dependent on the tides. You can't sail up creeks if the tide is out and there's not enough depth of water to float the boat. This will be the main factor determining departure and return times.

To give you some idea of what a longer dhow trip involves, see the boxed story on pp. 244-5 which gives a description of a dhow trip Geoff Crowther took with five others. It was written a few years ago but it's still current.

MANDA ISLAND
This is the easiest of the islands to get to since it's just across the channel from Lamu and almost everyone takes a half-day trip to the Takwa ruins at the head of the creek which almost bisects the island. The average cost of a dhow to this place is around KSh 1000 shared by however many people you can put together. Sometimes (but not always) this includes a barbecued fresh-fish lunch so settle this issue before you leave.

The extensive Takwa ruins are what remains of an old Swahili city which flourished between the 15th and 17th centuries and which attained a peak population of some 2500. It was abandoned for reasons unknown when the townspeople moved to Shela. The ruins consist of the remains of about 100 limestone and coral houses, all aligned towards Mecca as well as a mosque and tomb dating from 1683 (1094 by the

Islamic calendar). The settlement is surrounded by the remains of a wall and huge baobab trees dot the site. It's maintained by the National Museums of Kenya and entry costs KSh 200 (KSh 30 for residents).

Just off the north-east coast of Manda is **Manda Toto Island** which offers some of the best snorkelling possibilities in the archipelago. The reefs here are excellent and there are also good beaches. The only way to get here is by dhow and you need a full day to get there and back. There's no accommodation on Manda Toto itself.

Places to Stay
The only place to stay here is the *camp site* adjacent to the ruins but very few people stay here because the facilities are minimal.

Getting There & Away
The trip across to Manda takes about 1½ hours and can only be done at high tide as it's reached by a long mangrove-fringed inlet

which is too shallow at low tide. You may well have to wade up the final stretch, so wear shorts. Since you have to catch the outgoing tide, your time at the site will probably not be more than an hour.

It's possible to walk to the Takwa ruins from either the airstrip or the village of Ras Kitau but it's quite a long way and the paths are not too clear.

PATÉ ISLAND
There are a number of historical sites on Paté Island including Paté the town, Siyu, Mtangawanda and Faza. All are still inhabited – mainly by fishers and mangrove-pole cutters – but very little effort has been put into preserving or clearing the remains of the once powerful Swahili city-states and that's not likely to happen until tourist receipts warrant the expense. Indeed, the only foreigners who come to this island are those on dhow trips and the occasional archaeologist so you can expect to be a novelty and treated

Lamu Archipelago

A Dhow Trip to Kiwayu

After discussions with three different intermediaries in Lamu about trips to Kiwayu we made our choice and arranged to meet outside the Kisiwani Lodge at 6 am the next day. The price was fixed at US$120 for a three-day trip, or around US$6 per person per day including food. Meanwhile we purchased beers and soft drinks from the Kenya Breweries depot and dropped them off at the Kisiwani (the crews will generally do this for you but it will cost more).

Next morning the dhow finally turned up at 7.30 along with a crew of four and we set off in the direction of the channel between Manda Island and the mainland. Since the wind wasn't in the right direction, the dhow had to tack all the way to the channel by which time it was low tide. There was sufficient water in the channel to just keep the boat afloat – but the wind had dropped completely. There was no alternative but to pole and push the dhow all the way to the end of the channel and naturally we all lent a hand. It took hours.

Once out in the open sea again, the wind picked up and we were able to get close to Paté Island but again the wind dropped and the clouds burst. It looked very much like we and all our gear were about to get a soaking so it was with considerable relief that we discovered the crew had brought along an enormous sheet of plastic.

After the storm, the wind picked up again and we reached Mtangawanda by about 3.30 pm where we got off the boat and had a late lunch cooked by the crew. Despite only having one charcoal burner, they did an excellent job of this and the food was delicious.

We set off again about 4.30 pm and headed for Faza with a stiff side wind which enabled us to make good progress for the next two hours. After that it died completely and darkness fell. By 10 pm, it was obvious we were going nowhere that night so the anchor was dropped and a meal prepared (by torchlight!). By now we were all getting to know each other very well and there was a good rapport between crew and passengers. The tranquillity and beauty of a becalmed night at sea added immensely to this. After the meal, we all bedded down as best we could for a night of 14th-century discomfort.

By first light we discovered that seepage through the hull of the boat had brought the water level to well above the toe-boards so it was all hands on deck and bail out with anything to hand. Shortly after this, the wind picked up and we sped our way across the channel between Paté Island and Kiwayu, arriving at about 11 am off the tip of the island. At this point, all the passengers and one of the crew got off the dhow and went snorkelling among the reefs on the eastern side. The dhow, meanwhile, sailed on to Kiwayu village.

We caught up with the dhow again around 3 pm after walking along the beach and climbing over the ridge. Lunch was prepared by the crew (again delicious) and we settled down to an afternoon and evening of relaxation – sunbathing, fishing and exploring the village. Those with tents camped on the beach and the others took a banda at the camp site.

---

with friendly curiosity especially by the local children.

Accommodation and food on the island is easy to arrange with local families. The cost is negotiable but very reasonable. There are no guesthouses as such except at Faza but there are generally one or two simple restaurants which offer basic meals like bean or meat stews and tea.

Mosquitoes are a real pest and you're going to need insect repellent. Mosquito coils are for sale in the island's shops.

History

The origins of Paté are disputed. There are claims that it was founded in the 8th century by immigrants from Arabia, but recent exca-vations have produced nothing earlier than the 13th century when another group of Arabs, the Nabahani, arrived and gradually came to exert considerable influence over the other semiautonomous settlements along the coast.

By the time the Portuguese arrived in the early 16th century, Paté's fortunes were on the decline but were given a shot in the arm by the European mariners' interest in the silk cloth for which the town was famous and the introduction by the Portuguese of gunpowder. A number of Portuguese merchants reputedly settled here but their welcome was relatively short-lived, and by the mid-17th century their descendants had withdrawn to Mombasa following a series of uprisings by

Next morning brought heavy rain but by 11 am we were on our way back to Lamu with a strong tailwind and making excellent progress. Just off Faza, however, the wind died again and the captain (rightly) predicted there'd be no more that day so it was Faza for the night at his family's house. But it wasn't that simple getting off the boat! The tide was out and we couldn't sail up the creek to the town. It didn't look like a particularly feasible idea from the relative 'comfort' of the boat but, after some persuasion, we all jumped overboard with our packs on our heads and headed for the shore in thigh-deep water. There were no mishaps but a lot of jokes and laughter. Half an hour later we reached Faza.

The dhow was brought up at high tide and we were given three bedrooms to share at the family house. That evening a superb meal was prepared for us by the captain's family which we ate in the company of what must have been a good proportion of the town's younger children, all fascinated by this strange collection of wazungu that had turned up in town. Though we did offer, the family refused to take any money for the meal and the accommodation.

After the meal, the captain gave us his prediction about the winds next day – pretty pessimistic – and advised us to take the motor launch back to Lamu. The food was at an end, the last beers had been consumed with the meal that night and so, in the end, we all opted for the motor launch rather than another possible two days and a night back to Lamu. He did, on the other hand, firmly offer to take any or all of us back to Lamu on the dhow at no further cost if that's what we preferred.

All things considered, an excellent trip, superb value, great company, quite an adventure and I'd do it again.

Geoff Crowther

THE COAST

the Patéans against taxes imposed by the Portuguese authorities.

For the next half century or so, Paté regained some of its former importance and successfully fought off attempts by the Omani Arabs to take it over. Paté's harbour, however, had long been silting up and the city-state was eventually forced into using that of Lamu. The dependency created frequent tensions, particularly as Paté claimed sovereignty over Lamu, and the two were frequently at war. The final crunch came in 1812 when a Patéan army was soundly defeated at Shela. Thereafter, Paté faded into insignificance and lost all importance after the ruling family was driven out by Seyyid Majid in 1865 and was forced to set up the short-lived sultanate of Witu on the mainland.

Today, Paté resembles a down-at-heel Lamu. The narrow, winding streets and the high-walled houses are there but the streets are earthen and the coral-rag walls are unplastered. Its one redeeming feature is the Nabahani ruins which are just outside of town. These are quite extensive and include walls, tombs, mosques and houses. They're worth exploring but they've never been seriously excavated or cleared so it can be difficult to get around because of the tangle of vegetation. In addition to that, local farmers plant their tobacco crops among the ruins and have demolished substantial sections of the walls.

Getting There & Away

There is a motor launch which usually leaves Lamu for Mtangawanda (about two hours) and Faza (about four hours) three times a week on Monday, Wednesday and Friday (Tuesday, Thursday and Saturday in the opposite direction). The fare is KSh 150.

From Mtangawanda it's about an hour's walk to Paté town along a narrow footpath through thick bush and across tidal flats but you're unlikely to get lost as the path is easy to follow and you'll probably be walking it with local people who get off the launch.

The launch doesn't always call at Mtangawanda on the return trip from Faza to Lamu, so it's best to walk across to Faza and take it from there, paying a visit to Siyu on the way.

SIYU
History

Founded in the 15th century, Siyu was famous not for commerce or military opportunism but as a centre of Islamic scholarship and crafts. In its heyday (between the 17th and 19th centuries) it boasted some 30,000 inhabitants and was the largest settlement on the island though, today, less than 4000 people live here and there are few signs of its former cultural and religious influence.

Though one of the last upholders of coastal independence, Siyu's demise came in 1847 when it was occupied by the Sultan of Zanzibar's troops. The huge fort outside town dates from this period and is one of the largest buildings on the island. It's well worth a visit, as unlike many other Swahili relics, it has undergone considerable renovation.

The modern village displays little of Siyu's former glory and consists essentially of a sprawl of simple mud-walled and makuti-roofed houses.

Getting There & Away

The mangrove-lined channel leading up to Siyu is too shallow and silted up to allow the passage of anything but the smallest boats and so can't be reached directly from the sea by dhow or motor launch. The only feasible access is on foot either from Paté or Faza.

From Paté it's about eight km to Siyu along an earth track through the bush. The first part is tricky since there are turn-offs which are easy to miss so it's a good idea to take a guide with you as far as the tidal inlet. From here on it's easy as the path bears left and then continues straight through to Siyu. This last leg should take you about one hour.

FAZA
History

Faza has had a chequered history. It was destroyed by Paté in the 13th century and rebuilt in the 16th century only to be destroyed again by the Portuguese in 1586 as a result of its collaboration with the Turkish fleet of Amir Ali Bey. It was subsequently re-established and switched its allegiances to the Portuguese during their attempts to subdue Paté in the 17th century but declined into insignificance during the 18th and 19th centuries. These days it has regained some of its former importance after being chosen as the district headquarters for Paté Island which includes part of the Kenya mainland to the north.

Orientation

The modern town is quite extensive and includes a post office, telephone exchange, the district headquarters, a simple restaurant, two general stores and two guesthouses.

Things to See & Do

Faza has very little to offer in the way of interesting ruins. About the only thing there is in the town itself are the remains of the **Kunjanja Mosque** right on the creek front next to the district headquarters where the ferries anchor. Even so, most of it is just a roofless pile of rubble though there's a beautifully carved mihrab and some fine Arabic inscriptions above the doorway. Outside town is the tomb of Amir Hamad, commander of the Sultan of Zanzibar's forces, who was killed here in 1844 whilst campaigning against Siyu and Paté.

It's an interesting place to wander around and easy to strike up conversations with just about anyone – men, women or children. Most of the houses here are mud walled or coral-rag with makuti roofs though concrete and corrugated iron make an occasional appearance.

Places to Stay & Eat

The two guesthouses – *Lamu House* and *Shela House* – are essentially family residences but they're more than willing to turn over one or more bedrooms for your use and cook you a delicious evening meal if you need somewhere to stay. The price is negotiable and the families are very friendly.

The simple restaurant mentioned earlier offers bean stews, tea and mandazi for just a few cents and is a popular meeting place for the men of the town.

Getting There & Away

The inlet leading up to Faza from the main channel is deep enough at high tide to allow the passage of dhows and motor launches (though at low tide you'll have to walk in over the mud and sandbanks from the main channel).

There's a regular motor launch which connects Lamu with Faza via Mtangawanda three times a week on Monday, Wednesday and Friday (Tuesday, Thursday and Saturday in the opposite direction). The fare is KSh 150 and the journey takes four hours. From Faza to Lamu, the launch leaves at about 6 am but you need to be down by the district headquarters about half an hour before that as you have to be ferried out to the launch in small boats.

Getting to Siyu from Faza involves a two-hour walk through shambas and thick bush along an earth track. The first hour's walk as far as the disused airstrip is no problem, and there are generally people you can ask for directions if you're unsure. The second half is more confusing and you may need a guide so it might be best in the long run to take a guide with you all the way from Faza.

KIWAYU ISLAND

Kiwayu Island is at the far north-east of the Lamu archipelago and is included in the Kiunga Marine National Reserve. It acquired a reputation some years ago as an exclusive hideaway for rock stars and various other members of the glitterati, both local and foreign. It's unlikely you'll be rubbing shoulders with these people.

The main reason for coming here is to explore the coral reefs off the eastern side of the island which the tourist literature rates as some of the best along the Kenyan coast. That may be true but it's somewhat overrated (Watamu and Manda Toto island are better) yet the dhow trip there is definitely a highlight of a trip to Lamu and comes highly recommended.

The village on the western side of the island where the dhows drop anchor is quite small but it does have a general store with a few basics.

Places to Stay & Eat

Virtually the only place to stay here at a reasonable price is the *Kiwayu Camping Site* run by a man named Kasim. There used to be several very pleasant bandas to stay in here but, although they still exist, they've been allowed to fall into decay so don't expect anything special. The cost varies depending on which one you take but the 'tree house' is KSh 600 per night (sleeps three). Clean sheets, pillows and mattresses are provided as well as a kerosene lantern and mosquito coil. There are basic toilet and salt-water shower facilities. Campers can erect their tents here for KSh 150 including use of showers and toilets. You'll pay the same charge even if you camp on the beach below the site since this is also apparently owned by Kasim. There's a covered dining and cooking area for the use of both campers and banda dwellers.

Further up the coast across from Kiwayu on the mainland is the luxury lodge, *Munira*

Safari Camp, which costs the equivalent of US$80 per person per night with full board or US$50 per person per night for Kenyan residents. There's a speed launch from Lamu which takes less than an hour, or flights by Air Kenya Aviation from Lamu which take 10 to 15 minutes.

Getting There & Away
The only ways of getting to Kiwayu is by dhow, speedboat or air and, for most people, this would be part of a longer trip from Lamu by dhow with stopovers elsewhere. If there's sufficient wind, the return trip to Kiwayu from Lamu takes three days and two nights.

The Rift Valley

In Kenya the Rift Valley comes down through Lake Turkana, the Cherangani Hills, lakes Baringo, Bogoria, Nakuru and Naivasha, and then exits south through the plains to Tanzania. Together these areas make up some of Kenya's most interesting places to visit. Lake Turkana (see the Northern Kenya chapter) is a huge lake in the semidesert north, home to nomadic pastoralists and a world away from the tourist minibuses and fancy hotels of the south. The Cherangani Hills (see the Western Kenya chapter) provide some excellent walking opportunities and brilliant scenery – and hair-raising roads. More accessible are the central lakes which attract literally hundreds of bird and mammal species – they're a naturalist's dream and a visit to at least one of them is a must.

Volcanic activity is usually an accompaniment to rift valleys, and Kenya has several extinct volcanoes, the most prominent of which are Mts Longonot, Kenya and Kulal. Longonot is the most accessible, easiest to climb and certainly the most dominant feature of the landscape as you enter the Rift Valley from Nairobi. Mt Kenya, at 5200m, is a challenging climb, although Point Lenana, at 4985m, can be reached without specialist equipment. Kulal is more forbidding, unpredictable and harder to get to, being in the vicinity of Lake Turkana. Further south are the vast plains which are the home of the Maasai – and also home to a profusion of wildlife that you're not likely to come across anywhere else in the world. This is an area not to be missed.

What is known as the Rift Valley in Kenya is in fact part of the Afro-Arabian rift system which stretches some 6000 km from the Dead Sea in the Middle East, south through the Red Sea, Ethiopia, Kenya, Tanzania and Malawi to Mozambique. There's a western branch of the system which forms the string of lakes in the centre of the African continent: Albert and Edward, which make up part of the Uganda-Zaïre border; Kivu on the Zaïre-Rwanda border; and Tanganyika on the Tanzania-Zaïre border. This western arm joins up with the main system at the northern tip of Lake Malawi.

Soda Lakes

Because the shoulders of the rift (see the Rift Valley diagram on page 22) slope directly away from the valley, the drainage system in the valley is generally poor. This has resulted in the shallow lakes found along the valley floor in Kenya, some of which have no outlet. Due to high evaporation, the waters have become extremely concentrated and the high alkalinity from the area's volcanic deposits makes the perfect environment for microscopic blue-green algae and diatoms, which in turn provide food for tiny crustaceans and insect larvae. These in turn are eaten by certain species of soda-resistant fish.

The water of these soda lakes (Bogoria, Nakuru and Magadi in Kenya, and Lake Natron in Tanzania) may feel a little strange to the touch (it's soapy) and often doesn't smell too pleasant (though this is mostly due to bird droppings). However, the abundant algae, insect larvae, crustaceans and fish make these lakes a paradise to many species of water bird and they flock here in their millions.

Foremost among the birds is the deep-pink lesser flamingo *(Phoenicopterus minor)*, which feeds on the blue-green algae, and the pale-pink greater flamingo *(Phoenicopterus ruber)*, which feeds on the tiny crustaceans and insect larvae. Also numerous are various species of duck, pelican, cormorant and stork. The highest concentrations of these birds are found where food is most abundant and this varies from year to year and lake to lake. Lake Nakuru, for instance, sometimes almost dries up, forcing the birds to migrate to other soda lakes.

Another curious feature of the uplifting of the valley shoulders is the effect this has had on existing drainage patterns, although this of course happened in the last couple of million years. In Uganda, the uplifting caused the White Nile to form a pond (Lake Nyoga) after it left Lake Victoria, and to flow up what was previously a tributary and into the northern end of Lake Albert via a circuitous route. Prior to the uplift, the river had flowed direct from Lake Victoria into the southern end of Lake Albert.

Viewpoints
The best places to view the escarpments of the Rift Valley are from the viewpoints which are signposted along the Nairobi to Naivasha road, just past Limuru. Here the road descends into the valley and the views are stunning. Mt Longonot is directly in front while the plains of the Maasai sweep away to the south. Predictably, there are souvenir stalls at the viewpoints, but there are few bargains to be found because of the number of tourists who stop here.

The old road to Naivasha also descends into the rift in this area, and it's the route to take if you are heading for Mt Longonot or Masai Mara, as the new road runs direct to Naivasha. It's also the road used by heavy vehicles and is often in a diabolical state of disrepair. This road was originally built by Italian POWs in WWII, and there is a chapel at the bottom of the scarp.

Getting There & Around
Lakes Naivasha, Nakuru, Elmenteita and, to a lesser extent, Baringo are readily accessible to independent travellers without their own vehicle. There are plenty of buses and matatus and a rail link between Nairobi, Naivasha and Nakuru, and less frequent buses and matatus between Nakuru and Marigat/Kampi ya Samaki (for Lake Baringo). The other lakes, however, are more remote and there's no public transport. Hitching is very difficult and can be impossible. There's also the problem that lakes Nakuru and Bogoria are both in national parks/reserves, which you are not allowed to walk in – you must tour them in a vehicle. For details about these parks, and also the Rift Valley's Mt Longonot and Hell's Gate National Parks, see the National Parks & Reserves chapter.

Renting a vehicle may be expensive for budget travellers, but it would certainly work out cheaper for four people to hire a vehicle to visit Naivasha, Nakuru, Bogoria and Baringo than for them all to pay individually for safari-company tours. A one day tour of Lake Nakuru starting from Nairobi goes for around US$60 per person. A two day tour of lakes Nakuru, Bogoria and Baringo costs about US$180 per person. A car hired for several days and shared between four people would cost less than the total cost of a two day tour for four people.

NAIVASHA

There's very little of interest in the town of Naivasha itself. It's just a small service centre for the surrounding agricultural district. Most travellers just pass through here on the way to or from Mt Longonot, Lake Naivasha, Hell's Gate National Park and Nakuru. The main road skirts the town so if you're going directly from Nairobi to Nakuru you don't actually pass through Naivasha. It's a good place to stock up with supplies if you're planning a sojourn by the lake as there are very limited stocks in the dukas dotted along the lakeshore road.

The area around Naivasha was one of the first settled by wazungu, and the Delamere Estates, originally owned by Lord Delamere, surround the town and stretch away to the west towards Nakuru. Many of the plots around Naivasha are still European-owned, which is hardly surprising given that this was one of the stamping grounds of the Happy Valley set of the 1930s.

The town basically consists of two main roads and a handful of other streets, and everything is within walking distance.

Information

There are branches of Barclays Bank and the Kenya Commercial Bank on Moi Ave which are open during normal banking hours.

Places to Stay – bottom end

If you need to stay overnight in Naivasha there's a good range of budget hotels. The *Naivasha Super Lodge* has no doubles but the single beds are large enough for a couple; at KSh 150 these are not bad value.

For something a little less cosy try the *Olenkipai Boarding & Lodging* or the *Heshima Bar Boarding & Lodging*, both of which are adequate. The Heshima charges KSh 150/300 for a twin room with common bath.

Good value if you're alone is the *Othaya Annexe Hotel*, in Station Lane, which is clean and has singles (no doubles) for KSh 200 with common bath. The hotel has its own bar and restaurant.

Naivasha

0   100   200 m

1 Bus & Matatu Stand
2 Wambuku Hotel
3 Post Office
4 Ken-Vaoh Hotel
5 Barclays Bank
6 Heshima Bar Boarding
   & Lodging
7 Othaya Annexe Hotel &
   Naivasha Super Lodge
8 La Belle Inn
9 Sun Set Restaurant
10 Olenkipai Boarding
   & Lodging
11 Matatus to Kongoni
   (South Lake Rd)
12 Taxis
13 Naivasha Silver Hotel
   & Jolly Café
14 Matatus to Nairobi

There are plenty of other cheap places along Kariuki Chotara Rd.

Places to Stay – middle

For more salubrious lodgings the *Naivasha Silver Hotel* (☎ (0311) 20640) on Kenyatta Ave has rooms with hot water for KSh 300/400 a single/double. There's an upstairs bar and restaurant.

Places to Stay – top end

The best accommodation in town is the rustic *La Belle Inn* (☎ (0311) 20116) on Moi Ave, which is a popular rendezvous for local residents and a watering hole and meal stop for safari companies. The staff are friendly and rates are good value at KSh 1100/1500 for singles/doubles with shared bathroom facilities, or KSh 1500/1900 with private bath. Prices include breakfast. There's a guarded car park, and all credit cards are accepted.

The huge new *Ken-Vash Hotel* (☎ (0311) 30049), behind the post office, seems a little out of place in small-town Naivasha. The rooms are small, definitely nothing special, and for KSh 800/1200 including breakfast it's hard to see who they are going to get to fill this place.

Places to Eat

If you appreciate good food, there's essentially only one place to eat in Naivasha, *La Belle Inn*. The food is very reasonably priced and the outdoor terrace is a great place to have a beer or a meal despite the occasional clouds of dust raised by trucks on their way further west. It's open daily (all day) except Tuesday.

The *Jolly Cafe* next to the Silver Hotel on Kenyatta Ave is slightly less extravagant and has passable food. For good old no-frills African stodge try the Sun Set Restaurant on the corner of Kenyatta Ave and Kariuki Chotara Rd.

Getting There & Away

Bus & Matatu The main bus and matatu station is on Kariuki Chotara Rd. There are frequent buses and matatus to Nairobi (KSh 90), Nakuru (KSh 90), Nyahururu (KSh 120) and all points further west. Note that matatus to Nairobi leave from the matatu stand on Kenyatta Ave.

Train Travel from Naivasha to Nairobi by train is inconvenient as most of the trains pass through in the early hours of the morning. The trains to Kisumu and Malaba pass through in the late afternoon or evening. Unless you are prepared to travel 3rd class, make a booking in Nairobi before catching the train in Naivasha.

Hitching It's useless trying to hitch out of Naivasha town to Nairobi without first getting onto the main road. The accepted point for hitching, and where the main road passes closest to the town, is about 500m east of the bus station. It's about one km to the main road in either the Nakuru or Nairobi direction.

LAKE NAIVASHA

Naivasha is one of the Rift Valley's freshwater lakes and its ecology is quite different from that of the soda lakes. It's home to an incredible variety of bird species and a focus of conservation efforts in Kenya. Not everyone supports these efforts, however, and the ecology of the lake has been interfered with on a number of occasions, the most notable introductions being sport fish, commercial fish (such as Nile perch), the North American red swamp crayfish, the South American coypu (an aquatic rodent, also called a nutria, which escaped from a fur farm) and various aquatic plants including salvinia, which is a menace on Lake Kariba in southern Africa.

The lake has ebbed and flowed over the years, as half-submerged fencing posts indicate. Early in the 1890s it dried up almost completely but then it rose a phenomenal 15m and inundated a far larger area than it presently occupies. It currently covers about 170 sq km.

Since it's a freshwater lake which can be used for irrigation purposes, the surrounding countryside is a major production area of flowers, fresh fruit and vegetables as well as beef cattle for domestic consumption and export. There's even a vineyard on the eastern shore. The flower market has become a major industry in the Naivasha area, as all the shade houses indicate. It's incredible, but flowers picked here in the very early morning can be at the daily flower auctions in Holland the same day, and sell for little more than half the price of those produced in Europe!

Between 1937 and 1950 Lake Naivasha was Nairobi's airport! Imperial Airways and then BOAC flew Empire and Solent flying boats here on the four day journey from

Southampton. Passengers came ashore at the Lake Naivasha Hotel (now the Lake Naivasha Country Club), where buses would be waiting to shuttle them to Nairobi. The lake also featured strongly with the decadent Happy Valley settler crowd in the 30s.

For a full account of the history of European activity in the area, get hold of a copy of *Naivasha & the Lake Hotel* by Jan Hemsing, available from the Lake Naivasha Country Club.

Things to See & Do
On the western side of Lake Naivasha, past the village of Kongoni, there is a **crater lake** with lush vegetation at the bottom of a beautiful but small volcanic crater. If you have transport it's worth visiting. The crater is part of the Crater Lake Game Sanctuary, and entry costs KSh 100.

South of the lake is the Hell's Gate National Park which is well worth exploring and one of the few national parks in which you're allowed to walk (see the National Parks & Reserves chapter). On the eastern side of the lake is **Crescent Island**, a bird sanctuary which you can visit by boat (see Getting Around later in this section).

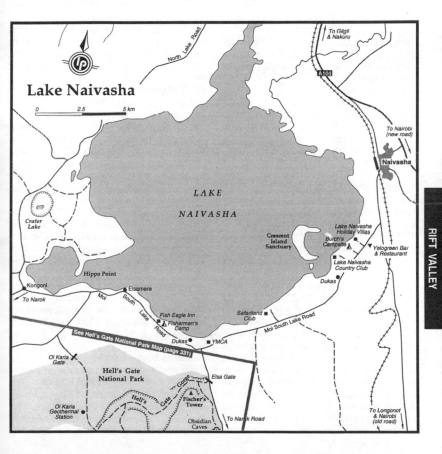

RIFT VALLEY

The mansion known as Oserian (or the Djinn Palace) which features in the book (and the dreadful movie) *White Mischief* is on the southern shore of the lake. It's privately owned and is not open to the public.

Elsamere

Almost opposite Hippo Point, a couple of km past Fisherman's Camp, is Elsamere, the former home of the late Joy Adamson of *Born Free* fame. She bought the house in 1967 with the view that she and her husband, George, might retire there. She did much of her writing from Elsamere right up until her murder in 1980. It seems George never spent much time there. It is now a conservation centre and open to the public daily from 3 to 6 pm. The entrance fee of KSh 250 includes afternoon tea on the lawn, a visit to the memorial room and a film-viewing of *The Joy Adamson Story*.

The only other way to visit is to stay here (see Places to Stay) or book in for a meal – lunch costs KSh 500, dinner KSh 600. Bookings can be made through the Elsamere Conservation Centre (☎ (0311) 21055; fax 21074), Moi South Lake Rd, PO Box 1497, Naivasha.

Places to Stay – bottom end

There are several budget accommodation possibilities on the lakeshore. The most popular is *Fisherman's Camp* (☎ (0311) 30088) on the southern shore. You can camp here for KSh 150 per person with your own tent, or there are tents for hire at KSh 200 per night. There are also fully self-contained *bandas* (round, concrete or mud-brick huts with makuti roofs) with four beds in each for KSh 500 per person, or a dorm at KSh 350 with bedding. They also have what is known as the *Top Camp* (up the hill across the other side of the road). Here they have a range of bandas, or you can camp. Firewood is for sale at both camps plus, at the main camp, there's a basic bar and restaurant. You can also rent boats between 8 am and 5 pm (see Getting Around). It's a very pleasant site with grass and shady acacia trees. Make sure you camp well away from overland trucks

unless you want to party all night, though finding a quiet spot isn't a problem as it's a huge site.

Another choice is the *YMCA* (☎ (0311) 30396), three km back towards Naivasha town close to the turn-off for Hell's Gate National Park. Although it's difficult to get down to the lakeshore from the YMCA, it's still a good camp site, especially if you intend to walk into Hell's Gate. Camping costs KSh 150 per person per night plus there are a number of somewhat spartan and run-down bandas for KSh 200 per person (children half-price). Firewood and bedding can be provided for a small charge. It gets busy here with school groups during school holidays. Bring all your own food and drink with you (the nearest dukas are about one km down the road towards Naivasha).

A third possibility is *Burch's Campsite* (☎ (0311) 21010) about one km beyond the Yelogreen Bar & Restaurant towards Fisherman's Camp. There's a range of accommodation options here, as well as a store selling basic provisions, including home-grown apples. Pitching your tent in the shady camp site costs KSh 150 per person, or there are basic but adequate twin-bed rondavels (bed and mattress only, no other bedding supplied) for KSh 450, or bigger, four-bed rondavels with attached bath for KSh 900 for a double, plus KSh 300 for each extra person. This includes bedding, cooking equipment and use of a gas stove. Campers and those in the basic rondavels have access to hot showers and a communal cooking area.

Lastly, you can also camp at the Safariland Club (see Places to Stay – top end), which is not a bad option as you have access to the hotel's other amenities. The cost is KSh 200 per person.

Places to Stay – middle

Right next door to the Fisherman's Camp is the *Fish Eagle Inn* (☎ (0311) 30306). This new place has a number of very cramped rooms around a spacious lawn. Quite how they justify the outrageous price of KSh 850 *per person* I'm not quite sure. Even the dormitory costs KSh 520! You can also camp here (KSh 200), but you can't get your vehicle down to the camp site, and there's little shade.

Places to Stay – top end
The *Safariland Club* (☎ (0311) 21013; fax 21216), is a top-end hotel with all the facilities you might expect. A single/double room with half board in the high season (December to March and July to August) costs US$83/121 (US$52/72 low season). There are also one-bedroom cottages for US$161 (US$112) and two-bedroom cottages for US$322 (US$224). The club accepts all the usual credit cards, and facilities include boat hire (US$27 per hour for four people, or US$9 per person to Crescent Island), horse riding, lawn tennis and table tennis. Nonresidents can use the swimming pool for KSh 250 per day.

Very similar is the *Lake Naivasha Country Club* (☎ (0311) 21004; fax 21161) and since it's part of the Block Hotels chain, bookings should be made through Nairobi (☎ (02) 540780; fax 543810). This hotel has a beautiful, expansive garden with access to the lake, a good kids' playground and a pool. They also have some interconnecting rooms, making it a good option for families. Singles/doubles with half board in the high season cost US$118/181 (US$51/102 low season) plus there are two-bedroom cottages for US$451 (US$254). Boat trips cost KSh 1000 per hour; to Crescent Island, which is just a short hop from here, the trip is KSh 800 return, and they will leave you on the island and pick you up later in the day – with a picnic lunch it's an excellent day excursion.

Virtually next door to the Country Club is the very pleasant *Lake Naivasha Holiday Villas* (☎ (02) 224998; fax 230962 in Nairobi). This smaller place consists of a number of very nice, spacious rooms at KSh 1400/2800 in the low season, KSh 4000/5000 in the high season for half board. The only drawback here is that there is no lake frontage.

Lastly there's the *Elsamere Conservation Centre* (☎ (0311) 21055; fax 21074), beyond

Fisherman's Camp. Here you can get a room in the grounds of Joy Adamson's former house with full board (the only choice) for KSh 3200 per person per night. Children under seven years of age are not allowed to stay since it's basically a research centre. It's a very pleasant place to stay and the staff are very friendly.

Places to Eat
If you're not eating at any of the above hotels or camp sites, there's the *Yelogreen Bar & Restaurant* near the eastern end of Moi South Lake Rd. It's a pleasant place for a cold beer, and the food is good and reasonably priced. However, you'll probably want your own transport to get here as it's more than one km from the nearest lake accommodation.

Getting There & Away
The usual access to Lake Naivasha is along Moi South Lake Rd. This also goes past the turn-off to Hell's Gate National Park (both the Elsa and Ol Karia gate entrances). There are fairly frequent matatus between Naivasha town and Kongoni on the western side of the lake. It's 17 km from the turn-off on the old Naivasha to Nairobi road to Fisherman's Camp and costs KSh 30.

Getting Around
Motorboats for game-viewing on Crescent Island can be hired from the Safariland Club and the Lake Naivasha Country Club.

Much cheaper rowing and motorised boats can be hired from Fisherman's Camp, but it's a long way from there to Crescent Island. Rowing boats (four people maximum) cost KSh 200 per hour, and small motorboats KSh 1000 per hour.

For land exploration, bicycles can be hired from Fisherman's Camp for KSh 250 per day.

LAKE ELMENTEITA
Like Lake Nakuru, Elmenteita is a shallow, soda lake with a similar ecology. Flamingos live here too, but in nowhere near the same numbers as at Nakuru. Elmenteita is not a national park, so you can walk around it and

there are no entry fees. However, there are few tracks and, as most of the shoreline is privately owned, there's a lot of fencing.

The easiest way to get there is to take a matatu along the Naivasha to Nakuru road and get off at one of the signposted viewpoints on the escarpment above the lake. You can either walk down from there or hitch a ride.

Places to Stay

The beautiful *Lake Elmenteita Lodge* (☎ (0367) 5040) has excellent views over the lake, and costs US$40/80 in the low season, or US$110/140 in the high season. Game drives can be arranged, and horse riding is offered at the trifling charge of US$18 per person per hour.

KARIANDUSI PREHISTORIC SITE

The Kariandusi site is signposted off to the right of the main road on the way from Naivasha to Nakuru. There's not much to see as the only excavation was carried out by Louis Leakey in the 1920s, although the small museum is worth a look.

NAKURU

Kenya's fourth largest town is the centre of a rich farming area about halfway between Nairobi and Kisumu on the main road and railway line to Uganda. It's here that the railway forks, one branch going to Kisumu on Lake Victoria and the other to Malaba on the Ugandan border and on to Kampala.

It's a pleasant town with a population of around 80,000 but is of interest mainly to those who work and farm in the area. The big draw for travellers is the nearby Lake Nakuru National Park with its usually prolific bird life; information about the park is detailed in the National Parks & Reserves chapter. The Menengai Crater and Hyrax Hill Prehistoric Site in the immediate area are both worth a visit (see later in this chapter).

Information

Nakuru has one foreign exchange bureau – it's on George Morara Rd (the highway) next to Marshalls (Peugeot dealers), a short walk west of the town centre.

Places to Stay – bottom end

The *Amigos Guest House* on Gusil Rd is a very friendly place to stay and the best value in this range. The rooms and bathroom facilities are passably clean, towels are provided and there's hot water. Singles/doubles with shared facilities cost KSh 250/300. Don't confuse this place with the other Amigos at the junction of Kenyatta Ave and Bondoni Rd. The other one isn't anywhere near as good and can be very noisy because of the upstairs bar.

Right in the centre of town is the *Shik Parkview Hotel* (☎ (037) 212345), on the corner of Kenyatta Ave and Bondoni Rd. It's a large place, but whoever designed it surely made a basic mistake since, although the single rooms have a private bathroom, the doubles do not! The beds are comfortable but what other furniture you get varies. Singles/doubles cost KSh 230/400 with common bath and breakfast; singles with private bathroom cost KSh 300. The rooms overlooking Kenyatta Ave are noisy. The best thing about this place is its proximity to the bus and railway stations.

You could also check out the *Shiriksho High Life Hotel* on Mosque Rd, which is conveniently close to the bus and matatu station but is not a great bargain. It's similar in price to the Shik Parkview, but none of the rooms have private bathroom.

Places to Stay – middle

Going up in price, an excellent choice is the *Mukoh Hotel* (☎ (037) 213516), on the corner of Mosque and Gusil Rds, which is clean and comfortable and has good views of the lake from the rooftop. Singles/doubles cost KSh 300/450 with private bath. Soap and towels are provided and there is erratic hot water. The hotel has its own bar and restaurant, and the management is very friendly.

Not far from the Mukoh and similar in quality is the *Carnation Hotel* (☎ (037) 43522) which has singles/doubles priced at

PLACES TO STAY
2 Waterbuck Hotel
8 Midland Hotel
16 Mukoh Hotel
17 Carnation Hotel
18 Amigos Guest House
20 Shik Parkview Hotel

PLACES TO EAT
7 Nakuru Coffee House
10 Oyster Shell Restaurant
19 Tipsy Restaurant

OTHER
1 Barclays Bank
3 Esso Petrol Station
4 Bethany Bookshop
5 Standard Chartered Bank
6 Pavement Craft Stalls
9 Barclays Bank
11 Gillani's Supermarket
12 Post Office
13 Town Hall
14 Police
15 Cathedral
21 Kenya Finance Bank
22 Market
23 Bus & Matatu Station

Nakuru

0   300   600 m

KSh 360/700 including breakfast. There's hot water in the bathrooms and the hotel has its own restaurant.

Places to Stay – top end

There's a choice of two top-end places in Nakuru. The *Midland Hotel* (☎ (037) 212155; fax 44517) on Geoffrey Kamati Rd is a rambling old place with rooms and attached bathroom with hot water for KSh 2000/2500 including breakfast. It has three bars (including the Long Bar) and two restaurants (one outdoor and one indoor).

Somewhat cheaper, and very pleasant, is the *Waterbuck Hotel* (☎ (037) 215672) on the corner of Government Ave and West Rd, which offers rooms with attached bathroom and balcony for KSh 1200/1300. The price includes a good breakfast. This is the low season price; expect to pay more at other times. The hotel has its own bar, restaurant and barbecue bar, and the staff are very friendly. Vehicles can be parked safely in the hotel compound, which is guarded 24 hours a day.

Further away from the centre of town on the road to Nairobi, and close to the turn-off for Hyrax Hill, is the modern *Hotel Kunste*

(☎ (037) 212140) which is a conference centre/hotel. Rates for its rooms with an attached bathroom are KSh 600/900 for a single/double including breakfast. Lunch or dinner costs KSh 250.

Further out, several km down the road towards Nairobi, is the *Stem Hotel* (☎ (037) 85432) which has rooms for KSh 1200 a double with half board. It's really only of interest to those with their own transport.

Places to Eat

For price and quality, the best place to eat is the *Tipsy Restaurant* on Gusil Rd. It's very popular with local people, especially at lunch time. Dishes include Indian curries, western food and lake fish. The food is very tasty and very reasonably priced – around KSh 90 to KSh 130 for main dishes.

The restaurant on the ground floor of the *Mukoh Hotel* is a good place for breakfast and also serves good meals and snacks. For just a coffee and a snack try the *Nakuru Coffee House* on the corner of Moi Rd and Kenyatta Ave. You can also buy roasted coffee beans there.

The open-air bar at the *Midland Hotel*, which offers barbecued chicken and a Sunday curry buffet (chicken or beef), is a popular place to eat, especially at lunch time. It's very reasonably priced at around KSh 170 to KSh 250 for main courses. The outside bar of the *Waterbuck Hotel* is also very similar.

Going up somewhat in price, one of the town's best restaurants is the *Oyster Shell Restaurant* (☎ (037) 40946), upstairs on Kenyatta Ave near the Club Rd corner. The menu is extensive and includes western, Indian, Mughlai and Indonesian dishes. It's open daily for lunch and dinner and is very reasonably priced; main dishes range between KSh 150 and KSh 250.

Entertainment

Apart from the bars mentioned earlier, there is one disco in Nakuru – the *XTC* above the Oyster Shell Restaurant. It's quieter than the discos in Nairobi, but it has excellent equipment and a good mixture of music. There is

no cover charge. Beers sell for normal bar prices.

Getting There & Away

Bus & Matatu The bus and matatu station is right in the thick of things at the eastern edge of town, near the railway station. It's a pretty chaotic place though generally it doesn't take too long to locate the bus, matatu or Peugeot you want. There are regular matatu/Peugeot departures for Naivasha (KSh 90), Nairobi (KSh 150/200), Nyahururu (KSh 80/100), Nyeri (KSh 150/180), Eldoret (KSh 150/200), Kericho (KSh 120/150), Kisii (KSh 220/250) and Kisumu (KSh 200/250).

Akamba buses also service Nairobi and points west. The only problem is that the Akamba depot is about one km west of town, at the Agip station on the main road out.

Other buses go to Eldoret (KSh 130), Nairobi (KSh 130) and Baringo (KSh 80), among other places.

Train As is the case with Naivasha, trains often come through in the middle of the night so you're better off going by road, as the buses and matatus arrive in the daytime only. The daily Kisumu and Nairobi trains come through at 11.30 pm and 1 am respectively, while the Malaba trains are on Friday and Saturday at 8 pm.

For Kampala, the weekly train from Nairobi comes through at 3 pm on Tuesday. The fare is KSh 3240/2590 in 1st/2nd class.

As for travel to Naivasha, you need to make an advance reservation in Nairobi if you're heading west and want 1st or 2nd class.

MENENGAI CRATER

Rising up on the northern side of Nakuru is the Menengai Crater, an extinct 2490m-high volcano. The crater itself descends to a maximum depth of 483m below the rim. You can drive right up to the edge, where there's one of those totally trivial signs telling you that you're five million km from some city halfway across the world.

To walk up to the crater takes a solid couple of hours, and it really is *up*, but still a very pleasant walk. The views back over Lake Nakuru are excellent, as are the views north to Lake Bogoria once you reach the top. About three-quarters of the way along there is a small group of dukas where you can get basic meals, soft drinks and, of course, the amber fluid. There's a map showing the crater's location on page 337.

LAKE BOGORIA

The two completely dissimilar lakes of Bogoria and Baringo are north of Nakuru off the B4 highway to Marigat and Lodwar. Lake Bogoria is a shallow soda lake and Lake Baringo a deeper freshwater lake. The B4 road is a superb, sealed highway the whole way to Kampi ya Samaki on the western shore of Lake Baringo.

Lake Bogoria covers an area of 30 sq km and has a maximum depth of nine metres. As with the other soda lakes in Kenya, Bogoria has no outlet and so the intense evaporation has led to high levels of salts and minerals. The result is that the lake supports no fish at all, but is ideal for blue-green algae, which is the staple food of the flamingos. For more information about Lake Bogoria see the National Parks & Reserves chapter.

LAKE BARINGO

Some 15 km north of the town of Marigat you come to the village of **Kampi ya Samaki** which is the centre for exploring Lake Baringo. This lake, like Naivasha, is fresh-water and, until fairly recently, used to cover around 170 sq km with a maximum depth of just 12m. Over the last few years, however, with the damming of the rivers which feed it for irrigation purposes, coupled with a drought, the level of the lake has shrunk so

---

Hyrax Hill Prehistoric Site

Just outside Nakuru on the Nairobi road, this prehistoric site is open daily from 9 am to 6 pm and admission is KSh 200. The small booklet, *Visitor's Guide to the Hyrax Hill Site*, is available from the museum there. For its location see the Lake Nakuru National Park map on page 337.

Archaeological excavations were first conducted here in 1937 although the significance of the site had been suspected by Louis Leakey since 1926. Further excavations have been conducted periodically, right up into the 1980s.

The finds at the site indicate three settlements were made here, the earliest possibly 3000 years ago, the most recent only 200 to 300 years ago. From the museum at the northern end you can take a short stroll around the site, starting with the North-East Village where 13 enclosures, or pits, were excavated. Only Pit D, investigated in 1965, is still open; the others have grown over. The North-East Village is believed to be about 400 years old, dated by comparison with the nearby Lanet site. A great number of pottery fragments were found at the site, some of which have been pieced together into complete jars and are displayed in the museum.

From the village the trail climbs to the scant remains of the stone-walled hill fort near the top of Hyrax Hill, which gave the site its name. You can continue up to the peak, from which there is a fine view of the flamingo-lined Lake Nakuru.

Descending from the hill on the other side you come to the Iron Age settlement where the position of Hut B and Hut C is clearly visible. Just north of these huts, a series of burial pits containing 19 skeletons was found. Since they were mostly male, and a number of them had been decapitated, it's possible they were killed in some sort of fighting. Unfortunately, souvenir seekers have stolen the bones that were displayed.

Virtually underneath the Iron Age site, a Neolithic site was discovered. The Iron Age burial pits actually topped a Neolithic burial mound, and a second Neolithic burial mound was found nearby. This mound is fenced off as a display. Between the burial mound and the Nairobi road are more Iron Age pits, excavated in 1974. The large collection of items found in these pits included a real puzzle – six Indian coins, one of them 500 years old, two of them dating from 1918 and 1919!

Finally, following the path back to the museum, there's a *bau* board in a large rock. This popular game is played throughout East Africa.

You are free to walk around the site yourself but a guide is useful. He'll expect a small tip at the end. ■

Lakes Baringo & Bogoria

Despite all this, Lake Baringo, with its islands (two of them inhabited) and encircling mountains, is still a spectacular sight and a very mellow place to visit. Boating trips are a popular activity and there's even a so-called 'Devil's Island' which local people will tell you is haunted. They don't mind taking you there during the day but at night they won't go near the place and say you can see flames and hear people screaming even though no-one lives on the island.

Activities

Other than bird walks, the most popular activity is boat rides on the lake and visits to the islands. Although these can be arranged at either Lake Baringo Club (expensive) or Robert's Camp (considerably cheaper), you can also make your own arrangements at the Fish Factory, a five minute walk from Robert's Camp – follow the path heading north along the fence line of Robert's. Here you will find what are basically out-of-work fishers many of whom still have their own fibreglass boats, powered by outboard motors. The prices for boat rides are pretty similar to those at Robert's Camp but it depends who you meet. Ask around for Joshua Lechiwgei, a friendly young Maasai, who has trained two fish eagles on the island of Ol Kokwe to come out to his boat and take out of the water the fish Joshua brings with him from the lake shore.

One-hour boat trips from Lake Baringo Club (see Places to Stay) cost KSh 800 per person (minimum two people), bird walks KSh 500 per person including transport, horse rides KSh 800 per hour and camel rides KSh 350 per half hour. The club also offers trips to Lake Bogoria for KSh 3000 per person (minimum two people), including park fees and transport, and to a nearby Njemps village for KSh 400 per person (minimum two people). The Njemps are a local tribe who live in villages around the lake shore and practice a mixture of pastoralism and fishing. The club has an arrangement with the headman of the village you visit so you're allowed to walk around freely and

alarmingly that the shoreline is now several hundred metres from where it used to be. And that isn't all. Soil erosion is so bad on the western perimeter of the lake that the seasonal *luggas* (creeks) which flow into the lake whenever there's a downpour bring down massive amounts of mud and silt so that the lake water is almost always muddy. It's also been over-fished to such an extent that the tilapia which are caught these days are rarely more than 15 cm long. This has virtually put the fishers out of business and brought to a halt the construction of a new fish-processing factory.

Baringo Wildlife

The lake supports many different species of aquatic animal and bird life as well as crocodile and herds of hippo which invade the grassy shore every evening to browse on the vegetation. You'll probably hear their characteristic grunt as you walk back to your tent or banda after dark or settle down for the night. They might even decide to crop the grass right next to your tent. If they do, stay where you are. They're not aggressive animals (they don't need to be with their bulk and jaws!) but if you frighten or annoy them they might go for you. And, despite all appearances, they can *move*! The crocodile is relatively small and, so far, there have been no recorded incidents of them attacking humans. They prefer goats, of which there are vast flocks around this area contributing seriously to deforestation and soil erosion.

Crocodile and hippo apart, Lake Baringo's main attraction is the bird life and the lake is the bird-watching centre of Kenya. People come here to engage in this activity from all over the world. Kenya has over 1200 different species of bird and more than 450 of them have been sighted at Lake Baringo. Some bird-watchers are so keen they're known as 'twitchers' since their primary concern seems to be to rack up sightings of as many different bird species as possible. It's a serious business and Lake Baringo Club even has a 'resident ornithologist' who leads bird-watching walks and gives advice to guests. A few years ago she set a world record for the number of species seen in one 24 hour period – over 300!

There's a constant twittering, chirping and cooing of birds in the trees around the lake, in the rushes on the lake and even on the steep face of the nearby escarpment. Even if you've had no previous interest in bird-watching, it's hard to resist setting off on a dawn bird walk and the highlight of the morning is likely to be a sighting of hornbills or the magnificent eagles which live almost exclusively on rock hyrax. ■

take photographs; you'll probably be hassled to buy some of the villagers handicrafts.

The facilities at the club are open to non-residents on payment of KSh 100 per person per day temporary membership on weekdays and KSh 150 on weekends, although this fee is waived if you're eating either lunch or dinner (KSh 850) there. Use of the swimming pool costs KSh 150 per person per day on top of the daily membership fee. If you arrive at the club by vehicle you probably won't be asked for the fee. At 7 pm each evening there's a slide show and commentary featuring some of the more common birds sighted in the area.

Places to Stay – bottom end

There's a great place to stay just before the village called *Robert's Camp* (☎ Kampi ya Samaki 3 through the operator) where you can camp for KSh 200 per person per night (KSh 100 for children under 12 years old). Bundles of firewood cost KSh 50. Facilities include clean showers and toilets. There are also three double bandas available for KSh 600 per person plus 15% tax. The bandas are

the best if there is one available, but demand is heavy at times and it would be wise to book one in advance through Mrs E Roberts, PO Box 1051, Nakuru. The bandas are beautiful, circular, grass-thatched, traditional-style houses which are as clean as a new pin and furnished with comfortable beds, a table and chairs and mosquito netting at the windows. Shower and toilet are separate and private cooking facilities are available for KSh 400. The people here are very friendly and there's a huge land tortoise which ambles around the grounds and appears to be used to the attention it receives. Other facilities include a store with an excellent selection of groceries, meat (fresh and processed) and dairy products, and a bar which is open daily from 8 am to noon and 1 to 8 pm. The bar will stay open later than 8 pm at a cost of KSh 20 per extra hour. You can also organise boat trips from here for KSh 1100 per hour for the boat (up to seven people).

If you're camping here then you need to exercise some common sense regarding the hippos. Although hippos may graze within just a metre of your tent at night, you should

RIFT VALLEY

stay at least 20m away from them when you can, especially if they have young ones. Don't frighten them in any way with headlights, torches (flashlights) or loud noises and don't use flash photography. No-one's ever been hurt by a hippo in over 10 years but they are wild animals and should be treated with respect.

If Robert's Camp bandas are full or you have no camping equipment then there's a choice of several basic lodges in Kampi ya Samaki. The best of these is the *Bahari Lodge* where all the drivers of safari vehicles stay. It's very clean and each room has two single beds with clean sheets and a blanket and (usually) a mosquito net. The cost is just KSh 100 per bed. Shower and toilet are shared. There's a bar/restaurant offering cheap, tasty meals and *cold* beers (KSh 40) – yes, they have a fridge. The *Hippo Lodge* at the entrance to the village is similarly priced but somewhat grubby.

Places to Stay – top end
Right next door to Robert's Camp is the *Lake Baringo Club*, one of the Block Hotels chain (☎ (02) 540780; fax 543810 in Nairobi). Singles/doubles with full board are US$39/78 in the low season and US$83/128 in the high season (July and August). Children under 12 years sharing a room with adults stay for free, and pay only for meals (50% of adult meal prices). The rooms here are very pleasant, the cuisine excellent and the staff very friendly. Facilities at the club include a swimming pool, dart boards, table-tennis table, badminton court, a library and a whole range of local excursions including boat trips and bird-watching trips accompanied by an expert.

While the Lake Baringo Club is an excellent place to stay, so too is the *Island Camp Baringo*, which is a luxury tented lodge sited on the extreme southern tip of Ol Kokwa Island in the lake. It's a beautifully conceived place, with a labyrinth of stone walls and steps set among flowering trees, and is the perfect hideaway. There are 25 double tents each with their own shower and toilet, and all of them have superb views over the lake.

Facilities at Island Camp include two bars, a swimming pool and watersports equipment. Full board costs US$141/187 for singles/doubles in the high season and US$69/138 in the low season inclusive of return boat transfer. Children between the ages of two and 12 years pay US$44 and KSh 985, respectively. For guests with their own vehicles, guarded parking is available in the village between the main street and the lakeshore. The locals can all point you in the right direction. The boats leave from a jetty at the far northern end of Kampi ya Samaki village. Bookings can be made either direct through Island Camp (☎ (071) 374069) or through Let's Go Travel (☎ (02) 340331; fax 336890) in Nairobi.

Places to Eat
If you're camping at Robert's Camp and doing your own cooking you need not bring your own food or equipment with you as all this is available at the camp itself. The shop at the site has an excellent range of fresh and packaged foods (see Places to Stay). The only things that are in short supply are fresh vegetables and fruit though there's a very limited supply available in Kampi ya Samaki. Marigat has a much better choice of these things.

Those who want to splurge can eat at the *Lake Baringo Club*. As you might expect, the meals here are excellent but it will cost you KSh 850 for either lunch or dinner. Beers at the club are very expensive at KSh 120 for a large Tusker. The club is also the only place where you can buy petrol and diesel between Marigat and Maralal.

Getting There & Away
There are three buses (KSh 80) per day in either direction between Kampi ya Samaki and Nakuru as well as a number of matatus (KSh 100) and Nissan minibuses (KSh 120). The journey takes between 1½ and two hours. From Kampi ya Samaki, two of the buses leave around 7 am. There's no regular schedule for the matatus and Nissans. If you have difficulty finding direct transport from Kampi ya Samaki to Nakuru at any time of

day, first take something to Marigat (KSh 20) and then arrange transport from there. From Marigat there are more frequent connections to Nakuru.

It's an interesting journey between Nakuru and Baringo since the country remains relatively lush and green until you pass the equator, where it almost immediately becomes drier and dustier and continues to get more barren and forbidding the further north you go. As you get near Marigat there are spectacular mountains, ridges and escarpments.

A gravel track connects Loruk at the top end of the lake with the Nyahururu to Maralal road. It's in good shape if you have your own transport. There's no public transport along this road and hitching is extremely difficult.

LAKE MAGADI

Lake Magadi is the most southerly of the Rift Valley lakes in Kenya and is very rarely visited by tourists because of its remoteness. Like most of the Rift Valley lakes, it is a soda lake and supports many flamingos and other water birds. It also has a soda extraction factory, hence the railway line there. Some years ago it was the site of a major rescue operation of young flamingos when drought threatened hundreds of thousands of them because of soda encrustation on their feathers – this doesn't affect the adults.

Magadi is quite different from the lakes to the north as it is in a semidesert area. Temperatures hover around the 38°C mark during the day and much of the lake is a semisolid sludge of water and soda salts. There is a series of hot springs around the periphery of the lake.

The town of Magadi is purely a company town, owned and built by the multinational, ICI.

Olorgasailie Prehistoric Site

Important archaeological finds were made at this site by Louis and Mary Leakey in the 1940s. Hand axes and stone tools thought to have been made by *Homo erectus* around half a million years ago were unearthed. While casts of some are on display in the Nairobi museum, most have been left in place, protected from the elements by shade roofs.

Places to Stay

At Olorgasailie there are three twin-bed bandas for rent at KSh 500. You need to bring all your own food, but water is available.

Getting There & Away

There is a rail link to the lakeshore which branches off from the main Nairobi to Mombasa line but there are no passenger services along it. There's also a minor road from Nairobi (the C58), along which two buses run daily. The first leaves Nairobi country bus station around 10 am, the other around 5 pm; return trips are at 6 am and 3 pm. Both buses pass the junction which leads to the archaeological site, about two km from the main road.

The Central Highlands

The Kenyan central highlands comprise the Aberdares, which begin around Limuru just north-west of Nairobi and continue on up to Maralal, plus the massif of Mt Kenya itself. They form the eastern wall of the Rift Valley and are the heartland of the Kikuyu people (see the Tribal Groups & Cultures section, starting on page 78). Within the main area are two national parks, Aberdare and Mt Kenya.

It's a very fertile region, well watered,

intensively cultivated and thickly forested. The climate, likewise, is excellent. Given these qualities, it's not surprising that the land was coveted by the white settlers who began arriving in ever increasing numbers once the Mombasa-Uganda railway was completed. Here they could grow anything year-round, particularly cash crops which were in demand in Europe. It's also not surprising that the Kikuyu eventually became so disenchanted with the alienation of their best land that war erupted between the two groups in the form of the Mau Mau Rebellion. It is probable that this event, more than any other, forced the British colonial authorities to reassess their position and ultimately to grant independence to the country.

While white Kenyan farmers still exist in considerable numbers in the area, their holdings have been reduced and much of the land parcelled out among the Kikuyu. Given the current level of population growth, it's anyone's guess how much longer this subdivision and further encroachment on the forest can continue before the environment is seriously threatened. Soil erosion is a major problem and many plots are too small to support a family. It's true there's still a great deal of forest remaining but with pressure on it for use as construction material and firewood (the most common form of fuel for cooking and heating) there are limits to the expansion of agricultural land. It's important to remember that much of Kenya is scrub and desert.

The Aberdares

Known to the Kikuyu as *Nyandarua*, 'drying hide', the Aberdares were named after the president of the Royal Geographical Society by the explorer Joseph Thomson in 1884. The lower eastern slopes were long cultivated by the Kikuyu while the higher regions, with peaks of up to 4000m and covered in dense forests and bamboo thickets, were left to the leopard, buffalo, lion and elephant. The arrival of the Europeans saw the establishment of coffee and tea plantations on the eastern side and wheat and pyrethrum farms on the western slopes. Most of this land has now been returned to the Kikuyu. Not all of the higher reaches of the Aberdares, however, are dense forest. There are also extensive areas of mist-covered moors along the ridges, and a good swathe of forest out of which the Aberdare National Park was created in 1950; for details see the National Parks & Reserves chapter.

NYERI

Nyeri is one of the largest towns in the central highlands, the administrative headquarters of Central province, and the usual gateway to Aberdare National Park. It's a lively place with an extensive market, several banks, hardware stores, vehicle-repair shops, bookshops and a plethora of other stores selling everything under the sun. It also has a good choice of hotels and restaurants.

It started life as a garrison town back in the early days of colonialism but was quickly transformed into a trading and social centre for white cattle ranchers, coffee growers and wheat farmers. Their watering holes, in the form of the White Rhino Hotel in town and the Aberdare Country Club at Mweiga are nostalgic reminders of their proclivities, though the White Rhino appears to have accepted inevitable decline. The Country Club, on the other hand, is magnificent and superbly maintained.

It's a very green area and is intensively cultivated for all manner of vegetables, sugar cane, citrus fruits, bananas, tea, coffee and even that Australian import, macadamia nuts. On a clear day, too (usually early morning), you can see Mt Kenya in all its snowcapped glory in the distance. Apart from these virtues, however, it's hardly the most magnetic town in Kenya and few travellers stay more than a couple of nights.

The Gliding Club of Kenya has its headquarters at Mweiga, just a short distance north of Nyeri. If you are into soaring, or would like to take a glide over the Aberdares, it's worth getting in touch with the managers Peter & Petra Allmendinger (☎ (0171) 2748), PO Box 926, Nyeri.

Places to Stay – bottom end

If you're down and out, there are some real dives here such as the *Bahati Boarding & Lodging* and the *New 7 Star Boarding & Lodging*. They're very primitive and can't seriously be recommended. Apart from that, the Bahati is usually full of semi-permanent residents. If you can get in, you're looking at KSh 100 to KSh 150 per person for a bed with shared bathroom facilities.

PLACES TO STAY
1 Outspan Hotel
2 Green Hills Hotel
3 White Rhino Hotel
6 Central Hotel
14 Bahati Boarding
& Lodging
15 New 7 Star
Boarding & Lodging
20 New Thingira
Guest House
29 Nyeri Star Hotel
31 Cedar Tree
Boarding & Lodging
32 Batian Grand Hotel

PLACES TO EAT
8 Uptown Cafe
9 People's Cafe
10 Cousin Cafe Bar
& Restaurant
23 Kenchic Inn
25 Batian Beer Garden/
Restaurant & Cinema

OTHER
4 Standard Chartered
Bank
5 Main Post Office
7 Automobile Association
of Kenya
11 Clock Tower
12 Kenya Commercial
Bank
13 Upper Bus &
Matatu Stand
16 Wamugi Bookshop
17 Nyeri Supermarket
18 City Hall
19 Mosque
21 Library
22 Barclays Bank
24 Clock Tower
26 Municipal Market
27 Lower Bus &
Matatu Stand
28 Vegetable Market
30 Post Office

Nyeri

0   75   150 m

On the other hand, there are two excellent budget hotels to choose from. The first one is the *Nyeri Star Hotel* (☎ (0171) 4213), close to the lower bus and matatu stand. This offers singles/doubles with attached bathroom for KSh 250/400 with towel and soap provided and there's hot showers. It's a friendly place, secure and has a popular bar and restaurant. Despite it's proximity to the bus station you can't hear the noise and it's rarely full as it's a large place.

The second place is the *New Thingira Guest House* (☎ (0171) 4769), just down the hill off the main road from Karatina. This is

also very good value at KSh 300/450 for singles/doubles with attached bathrooms. Breakfast is available for KSh 70. There's also a ground floor bar and restaurant.

Another one you could try if the above are full (unlikely) is the *Josmica Boarding & Lodging* on the top side of the lower bus station. Some of the rooms here have attached bathrooms.

Places to Stay – middle
One of the best in this range is the modern *Central Hotel* (☎ (0171) 4233) at the top end of town. Singles/doubles with their own

bathrooms with hot water cost KSh 450/550. They also have suites for KSh 650 but you're advised not to take one as they are directly above the bar area which can get very noisy. Other than that, the hotel is fine and the food which the restaurant serves is good and reasonably priced. There's also a guarded parking lot for residents.

For a touch of olde-worlde charm at about double the price, there's the old white settlers' watering hole, the *White Rhino Hotel* (☎ (0171) 30934). It's a popular place to stay, has several bars, a lounge, beer garden and a relatively cheap restaurant and offers rooms with attached bathroom at KSh 650/1000 for singles/doubles and triples for KSh 1300 including breakfast. There's also a guarded car park for residents.

More expensive but with modern facilities is the *Green Hills Hotel* (☎ (0171) 30604), across the valley from the White Rhino. This is a large place with 98 double rooms and seven cottages, a swimming pool, bar and restaurant. Singles/doubles with attached bathroom and including breakfast cost KSh 900/1500. Lunch and dinner are available for KSh 300. There's also a large guarded parking lot.

Top of the range is the modern *Batian Grand Hotel* (☎ (0171) 4451) which has singles/doubles with attached bathrooms including breakfast for KSh 1200/2200

(nonresidents) or KSh 800/1400 (residents). It's a very well appointed hotel and all the rooms have a radio and telephone. All the front rooms face Mt Kenya. There's also a good bar and restaurant and the food is excellent. There's a guarded parking lot and most credit cards are accepted.

Places to Stay – top end

About one km out of town is the *Outspan Hotel* (☎ (0171) 2424), one of the Block Hotels chain (☎ (02) 540780; fax 543810 in Nairobi). This is the check-in place for guests of the Treetops Lodge in the Aberdare National Park. It's sited in beautifully landscaped gardens opposite the golf course and has all the facilities you would expect from a top-end country hotel except that the Mt Kenya Bar has, in fact, no view of Mt Kenya at all – surely a major planning balls-up. Prices depend on the season and the type of accommodation you take. In the high season (16 December to 3 January and 1 April to 8 April) it costs US$66/101 for singles/doubles with half board, and single/twin cottages cost US$74/113. In the low season (9 April to 30 June) it's US$29/58 for singles/doubles, with single/twin cottages at US$33/66. Children between the ages of two and 12 sharing a room with their parents are charged at 50% of the adult rate.

The only other place in this price range

Baden Powell Museum

Nyeri is famous as the former home of Lord Baden Powell, the founder of the worldwide Scouts Movement. It was here in the cottage called Paxto, in the grounds of the Outspan Hotel, that he lived until his death and it's here that he was buried. The cottage was later occupied by Jim Corbett – 'destroyer of man-eating tigers in central India during the 1920s and 1930s', according to the plaque in front of the cottage. These days it's a museum packed with scouting memorabilia which bus loads of boy scouts and girl guides from all over the world tramp through every day. Just about everyone who visits leaves a memento so the place is awash with troop colours. Baden Powell's gravestone is in the garden at the front. Entry is free to members of the movement and KSh 50 to anyone else (how the curator tells the difference is anyone's guess).

It's ironic that a white colonist should be honoured in this manner in Nyeri yet one of Kenya's foremost independence fighters, General Dedan Kimathi, lies in an unmarked grave at the other end of town. Kimathi was captured by the British colonial authorities towards the end of the Mau Mau Rebellion and hanged in Kamiti prison – or so the western history books say. That, however, is not what is taught in Kenyan schools. They are taught that he was buried alive. That's hard to believe but who knows the truth? All the same, where's the headstone? ■

is the *Aberdare Country Club*, at Mweiga about 12 km north of Nyeri, which is part of the Lonrho Hotels Kenya group (☎ (02) 216940; fax 216796 in Nairobi). Like the Kentmere Club at Limuru and the Norfolk Hotel in Nairobi, this was once one of the quintessential white planters' watering holes and social foci except that these days it caters for the international leisure set and those with the money to burn on a night or two at The Ark. Full board (including temporary membership) costs US$120/156 for singles/doubles in the high season and US$74/123 in the low season. Children aged from two to 12 years sharing a room with their parents are charged US$44 at any time of year. All the rooms and cottages have excellent views of the plains below and across to Mt Kenya and the club is surrounded by its own, private 500 hectare wildlife sanctuary. Facilities at the club include a swimming pool, tennis courts, golf course, horse riding, game rides, walking safaris and trout fishing.

Places to Eat
The most reliable places for a meal are the *White Rhino Hotel* and the *Central Hotel* where you can eat well and relatively cheaply. Expect to pay around KSh 150 to KSh 200 for a main meal.

The very popular *Uptown Cafe* is worth a visit if you want cheap, tasty no-frills food. It offers a good range of food such as burgers, various curries and steaks. Two other cheap places for meals, snacks and coffee are the *People's Cafe* near the main post office and the *Cousin Cafe Bar & Restaurant*.

For fast food of the McDonald's-clone variety, try the *Kenchic Inn*, one of the many branches of this chain in Kenya. A quarter fried chicken with chips here costs KSh 120.

Getting There & Away
From the upper bus stand there are regular buses to Nyahururu, Nakuru, Thika, Nairobi (KSh 100) and Nanyuki, and less frequently to places further afield such as Meru and Eldoret. The buses to Nairobi may involve a change at Karatina so check before buying a ticket.

Nissan minibuses are more comfortable and faster between Nyeri and Nairobi and normally cost KSh 120 but can be up to KSh 160 if demand is high. A Peugeot share-taxi to Nairobi costs KSh 180. A Nissan minibus to Nanyuki costs KSh 80. To Nakuru, a Nissan minibus costs KSh 150 and a Peugeot taxi KSh 170.

NYAHURURU (THOMSON'S FALLS)
Nyahururu, or 'T Falls' as virtually everyone calls it, was one of the last white settler towns to be established in the colonial era and didn't really take off until the arrival of the railway spur from Gilgil (on the main Nairobi to Kisumu line) in 1929. The railway still operates but these days carries only freight. Nyahururu is one of the highest towns in Kenya (at 2360m) and the climate is cool and invigorating. The surrounding undulating plateau is intensively cultivated with maize, beans and sweet potatoes, and is well forested, mainly with conifers. The most interesting approach to the town is probably along the excellent road from Nakuru which snakes up and down through farmlands and forests and offers some spectacular views over the Aberdares.

The falls, on the outskirts of town, are named after Joseph Thomson who was the first European to walk from Mombasa to Lake Victoria in the early 1880s. They're a popular stopover for safari companies en route to Maralal and points further north and are well worth a visit. Formed by the waters of the Ewaso Narok River, the falls plummet over 72m into a ravine and the resulting spray bathes the dense forest below in a perpetual mist. A series of stone steps leads down to the bottom of the ravine and is the only safe access. Don't attempt to go down any other way as the rocks on the side of the ravine are often very loose. Up above the falls and partially overlooking them (though the view is obscured by a row of ugly souvenir shacks) is the old colonial watering hole, Thomson's Falls Lodge, which has retained much of its quaint atmosphere and is still the most interesting place to stay. The hotel grounds are a popular place for a Sunday picnic with local families.

Nyahururu has an inexplicably large population of street kids who hang around the bus station and will hassle you for small change. Have some handy if you don't want to be followed all the way up the street; they're very persistent.

Places to Stay – bottom end

The best place to stay if you have camping gear is the camp site at *Thomson's Falls Lodge*. It's very pleasant and costs KSh 300 per person per night with as much firewood as you need and hot showers included.

For those without camping equipment, there are several budget hotels in town. Good value is the *Good Shepherd's Lodge*, which offers rooms with attached bathrooms with towel and soap provided for KSh 140 a single (no doubles). It's very clean and there's a restaurant next door.

For solo male travellers the best bet is probably the quiet *Nyandarua County Council Guest House*, behind the post office and provincial headquarters. It only has single rooms (sharing not permitted), but they all have attached bathrooms with soap, towel and toilet paper provided. The cost is KSh 150 and there is a restaurant and TV room. The staff are very friendly.

Going up in price, the *Stadium Lodging* (☎ (0365) 22002) is quite good value at KSh 200/300 for singles/doubles with attached bathrooms with hot water. It's clean, there's a table and chair in each room and security is excellent.

Right opposite the bus stand is the *Cyrus Lodge* which has singles/doubles with attached bathrooms for KSh 120/170. The hotel has its own bar and restaurant.

The modern, five storey *Nyaki Hotel* (☎ (0365) 22313) is set back from the main road in the centre of town. It's very clean and quiet and costs KSh 200/750 for singles/doubles with attached bathrooms with

PLACES TO STAY
1 Thomson's Falls Lodge
3 Good Shepherd's Lodge
4 Nyaki Hotel & Restaurant
8 Karyandua County Council
   Guest House
17 Stadium Lodging
19 Baron Hotel
23 Cyrus Lodge

PLACES TO EAT
20 Tropical Bar & Restaurant

OTHER
2 Catholic Church
5 Hospital
6 Esso Petrol Station
7 Co-Op Bank of Kenya
9 Kenya Commercial Bank
10 Post Office
11 Barclays Bank
12 Town Hall
13 Police
14 Covered Market
15 BP Petrol Station
16 Open-Air Market
18 Clock Tower
21 Mosque
22 Bus & Matatu Station

To Rumuruti & Maralal

Thomson's Falls

To Nyeri & Nanyuki

Ewaso Narok River

To Nakuru

To Gilgil

Train Station (goods only)

Stadium

Nyahururu

0   125   250 m

CENTRAL HIGHLANDS

towels and soap provided, but the price does not include breakfast. The hotel has its own bar and restaurant.

There's also the *New Nyahururu Guest House* which offers rooms with attached bathrooms for KSh 150 per person.

Places to Stay – middle

The place to stay in this category if you have the money is *Thomson's Falls Lodge* (☎ (0365) 22006; fax 32170), overlooking the falls. Though it's no longer frequented by white planters, it exudes nostalgia and olde-worlde charm with its polished wooden floorboards and log fires. Accommodation is available either in the main building with its bar, lounge and dining room, or in separate cottages scattered over the well-maintained lawns. Rooms here have attached bathrooms with hot water and your own log fire, and cost KSh 1600/2000 for singles/ doubles, with triples at KSh 2800 including breakfast.

If you prefer modernity and a place in the centre then the *Baron Hotel* (☎ (0365) 32751) is the choice. It's clean and well organised and rooms with attached bathrooms with hot water go for KSh 350/600 a single/double, with suites at KSh 900, all including breakfast. The hotel has its own bar and restaurant and the food is good with a choice of three dishes each day – fish, meat or chicken. Prices are very reasonable.

Also in this category is the new *Kawa Falls Hotel* (☎ (0365) 32295), on the way out of town towards Gilgil. There are 83 rooms, all of them with attached bathrooms, but the hotel likes to think it's something special so it has both resident and nonresident rates which is ridiculous in a place like Nyahururu. Rates are KSh 550/900 for singles/doubles and KSh 1200/1500 for suites, all including breakfast. Clearly, there's room for negotiation here. You can't fill an 83 room hotel in Nyahururu at that price in a big hurry.

Places to Eat

Most of the budget hotels and many of the bars have a restaurant where you can get standard African food. Meals at the *Baron Hotel* are also excellent value.

For local colour and a barbecued meal, try the *Tropical Bar & Restaurant* around the corner from the Baron Hotel.

For a minor splurge – or if you're staying there – eat at *Thomson's Falls Lodge*. Breakfast, lunch and dinner are available, but you need to give advance warning if you intend to take your meal in the main dining room. A full English-style breakfast costs KSh 200. Three-course lunches or dinners with dessert and tea or coffee cost KSh 500. There's also an open-air grill which operates at lunch time and offers a variety of dishes, including soups and various types of nyama choma (barbecued meat). A meat dish will cost you about KSh 250. The lodge has the most interesting and one of the liveliest bars in town with deep, comfortable armchairs and blazing log fires. All facilities are open to nonresidents, including campers.

For those who want to prepare their own meals, there's an excellent choice of fruit, vegetables and meat in the covered market.

Entertainment

The *Baron Hotel* has a discotheque every Friday and Saturday night.

Getting There & Away

There are plenty of buses and matatus throughout the day until late afternoon in either direction between Nyahururu and Nakuru (KSh 100) and Nyeri (1½ hours, KSh 150). Other destinations served by regular matatus and buses include Nairobi (about two hours, KSh 200), Nanyuki (KSh 150) and Naivasha (1½ hours, KSh 150).

There's also at least one minibus per day in either direction between Maralal and Nyahururu which leaves early in the morning and costs KSh 200 to KSh 250 depending on the bus. Get there early if you want a seat. For the rest of the day, hitching is feasible but not easy. The road is surfaced as far as Rumuruti after which it's gravel or *murram* (dirt). Parts of this gravel road are in bad shape but it improves considerably the nearer you get to Maralal.

Around Mt Kenya

Mt Kenya is circled by an excellent tarmac road along which are the area's main towns – Naro Moru, Nanyuki, Meru and Embu, and Isiolo at the extreme north-eastern end. For details on climbing the mountain, see the National Parks & Reserves chapter.

NARO MORU

The village of Naro Moru, on the western side of the mountain, consists of little more than a string of small shops and houses, a couple of very basic hotels, a market, agricultural warehouses and the famous Naro Moru River Lodge, but it's the most popular starting point for climbing Mt Kenya. There's a post office here but no banks (the nearest are at Nanyuki and Nyeri).

The other important thing to bear in mind is that the Naro Moru River Lodge has an exclusive franchise on the mountain huts along the Naro Moru route, including those at the meteorological (Met) station, so you have to go to this lodge to make bookings. It's all been carefully calculated to sew up the market on this route but that doesn't prevent you from climbing independently as long as you're willing to camp and carry the appropriate equipment.

Places to Stay

There are a number of basic hotels in Naro Moru village but very few travellers who are intent on climbing the mountain stay here. Most stay at the Naro Moru River Lodge (just outside the village), at the Mt Kenya Hostel or the Mountain Stop Motel (both about halfway between Naro Moru and the Met Station) or at the Mountain Rock Hotel (halfway between Naro Moru and Nanyuki). Still, if you want to stay in the village, you can do that. There are four hotels: the *Naro Moru 82 Lodge; Naro Moru Hotel 86; Wananchi Tours Lodge* and the *Mountain View Hotel*. They're all much the same and you can get a bed for KSh 150 to KSh 200 but the best of the lot is the Mountain View Hotel.

The village apart, and if you're an independent traveller and intent on scaling the summit, think seriously about walking 12 km and staying at the *Mt Kenya Hostel & Campsite* on the way to the start of the Naro Moru trail. The original hostel burnt down several years ago but Joseph and James have since done a prodigious amount of work and rebuilt it so that it now has several well-appointed bedrooms, a kitchen, lounge and bathrooms. It's a great place to stay and very friendly, plus you can pick up information about the mountain since there are always people staying here who have either just come down or are about to go up. You can camp here for KSh 150 per person or take a bed for KSh 200 (there are 30 in total). They also have a fully equipped store of mountain gear for hire as well as a 4WD vehicle to take you to the park entrance/Met Station for KSh 2500 shared between up to nine people. You can hire guides, porters and cooks here, too (KSh 290 per day for guides and cooks and KSh 270 per day for porters). All meals are available here with advance notice.

Just outside the entrance to the hostel is the *Mountain Stop Motel* which has camping

for KSh 150 per person and 10 bandas (doubles) for KSh 250 per banda. Toilets and showers (hot water) are shared. There's a large bar/lounge area with a fireplace under a makuti roof, a barbecue and a separate small bar which is popular with local people. Meals are available on request. The owner, Solomon Wanjohi, is enthusiastic and helpful.

In the village itself, is the *Naro Moru River Lodge* (☎ (0176) 62622; fax 62212), which is about 1.5 km off to the left down a gravel track from the main Nairobi to Nanyuki road. It's essentially a top-range hotel set in landscaped gardens alongside the Naro Moru River, but it does have a well-equipped camp site with hot showers and toilets for US$4 per person per night and firewood at US$2 per load. Also at the camp site are dormitory bunkhouses where a bed costs US$6. Campers are entitled to use all the hotel facilities.

Those seeking a degree of luxury either before or after climbing the mountain have the option of 'standard' or 'superior' rooms with attached rooms or self-service cottages. In the low season (11 April to 30 June and 16 September to 15 December) the rooms cost US$30/55 a single/double in standard and US$40/65 in superior with half board. In the high season (16 December to 10 April and 1 July to 15 September), the rooms cost US$72/94 a single/double in standard and US$82/114 in superior. The self-service cottages vary in price depending on which one you take, and range between US$45 and US$105 per night. Between 22 December and 5 January there's a surcharge of US$20 per person per day.

Facilities at the hotel include a swimming pool, two bars, restaurant, secure parking and fishing opportunities.

The main reason for coming to this lodge if you're an independent traveller is that it's here you must book and pay for any of the mountain huts which you want to stay at along the Naro Moru route. Those at the Met Station cost US$8 and the ones at Mackinder's Camp US$11. Members of the Mountain Club of Kenya are entitled to a

DAVID ELSE

HUGH FINLAY

DAVID ELSE

enya's diverse natural attractions: Fischer's Tower, the 25m-high column of volcanic rock
Hell's Gate National Park; Thomson's Falls near Nyahururu; elephant herds constantly
n the move for water and fodder.

Mt Kenya's Unusual Alpine Flora

As in other alpine areas of the tropics such as the Andes, the Himalayas, Borneo and on neighbouring Mt Kilimanjaro, there are a number of unusual plant species on the upper slopes of Mt Kenya. Some of these are so distinct they are major features of the area. The most prominent are the giant lobelia and the giant groundsel.

The giant lobelia are unmistakable with their un-branched tree-like stems topped by a wild looking mop of thick, hairy leaves which, depending on the species, grow to a height of between two and nine metres. The hairs are an adaptation to the severe climate. The stems, nevertheless, remain largely non-woody. Like other lobelia species, the giants have blue to purple flowers borne in clusters on long, terminal spikes which project above the foliage. However, unlike the smaller annual species, giant lobelias flower only once in their lifetime.

There are three giant species found in Kenya. In the wetter forests between 1200m and 2700m high, the most usual is *Lobelia gibberoa* which grows to a height of up to nine metres. The other two, *Lobelia aberdairca* and *Lobelia telekii*, which grow to a height of two metres, are found between 2100m and 3400m, though some hardy individuals grow even as high up as 4600m. ∎

DAVID ELSE

Left: The giant lobelia flowers only once in its lifetime.

Below: Giant groundsels grow very slowly, live for about 120 years and flower every decade or so.

DAVID ELSE

25% discount on these prices and the accommodation charges at the lodge.

The other reason for coming to this lodge if you don't have a tent, cooking equipment or appropriate clothing is that it runs a comprehensive hire service which is open daily from 7 am to 1 pm and 2 to 8 pm. The charges are similar to those at Atul's in Nairobi and are detailed in the National Parks & Reserves chapter. The River Lodge can arrange transport to the park entry gates on either the Naro Moru or Sirimon trails. The charge is US$60 one way to the Naro Moru gate and US$90 one way to the Sirimon gate shared between up to six people.

There's also an excess baggage store which costs KSh 20 per piece per day. You can use this service whether you are a guest or not.

Seven km north of Naro Moru on the Nanyuki road is the *Mountain Rock Hotel* (☎ (02) 210051; fax 210051 in Nairobi), tucked away in wooded surroundings less than one km from the main road. This is the place to head for if you're intent on taking either the Sirimon or Burguret routes up Mt Kenya. It offers pleasant cottages each with hot showers and fireplaces for US$26/29 a single/double. 'Superior' rooms are also available and these cost US$32/39. There's also a well-equipped camp site with hot and cold water, toilets, cooking facilities, electricity and ample firewood for US$5 per person per night. All prices include taxes and service charges. Facilities at the hotel include a spacious dining room, two bars (one open-air), lounge, nyama choma barbecue and a beer garden. Patrick, who runs this hotel, is a very friendly and reliable person.

Horse riding (US$13 per hour), trout fishing (US$6.50 per hour including fishing rod and licence) and bird-watching are some of the activities which the lodge caters for, plus there are traditional dances performed when demand warrants it (US$5 per person with a minimum of six people).

The main reason for coming here, however, is to take one of the hotel's guided treks to the summit of Mt Kenya via the Naro Moru, Burguret or Sirimon routes. There is a whole range of these to choose from depending on where you want to go and how long you wish to take. The full range of possibilities is outlined in the section on climbing Mt Kenya in the National Parks & Reserves chapter.

Places to Eat

There are no restaurants worth a mention at Naro Moru so you'll either have to cook your own food or eat at the *Naro Moru River Lodge*. There's very little choice of food available at the shops in Naro Moru so bring your own or, if you have transport, go to Nanyuki to buy it.

Getting There & Away

There are plenty of buses, Nissan minibuses and Peugeot share-taxis from Nairobi and Nyeri to Nanyuki and Isiolo which will drop you off in Naro Moru. The fare from Nairobi to Naro Moru is around KSh 200 (more for a Peugeot) and the journey takes about 2½ hours. From Nyeri to Naro Moru the fare is KSh 50 and the journey takes a little over half an hour.

The Naro Moru River Lodge also operates a shuttle bus between the lodge and Nairobi assuming there's sufficient demand – minimum two people – and you must book 24 hours in advance. The fares are KSh 3000 per person one way and KSh 4000 return. In Nairobi you have to book the bus on the 1st floor of College House (☎ (02) 337501), University Way. In Naro Moru, book at the lodge itself.

The lodge also does transfers to Nanyuki airstrip for KSh 600 per person one way and KSh 900 return, and to the meteorological station for US$78, the park gate for US$39 or the trailhead on the Sirimon route for US$137.

NANYUKI

Nanyuki is a typical small country town about halfway along the northern section of the Mt Kenya ring road and a popular base from which to trek up the mountain via either the Burguret or Sirimon routes. It was founded by white settlers in 1907 in the days when game roamed freely and in large numbers over the surrounding grassy plains. The game has almost disappeared – shot by the settlers for meat and to protect their crops from damage by foragers – but the descendants of the settlers remain and the town has also become a Kenyan airforce base as well as a British army base for the joint manoeuvres conducted by the two armies each year. It's a fairly pleasant town and still has a faint ring of the colonial era to it. All the usual facilities are here, including banks, a post office and a good range of well-stocked stores.

Places to Stay – bottom end

The cheapest place is the *Nanyuki Youth Hostel* (☎ (0176) 2112) at the Emmanuel Parish Centre, Market Rd, but it's pretty basic, even dismal. The showers have only cold water. There are also some simple lodges, including the *Silent Guest House* and the *Juba Boarding & Lodging*.

More expensive but a popular place to stay is the *Josaki Hotel* (☎ (0176) 2181) which

has large, clean, singles/doubles with attached bathrooms with hot water for KSh 400/600 including breakfast. There's a bar and restaurant on the 1st floor which has cold beer for KSh 45. Secure parking is available.

Also popular, but not as good, is the *Sirimon Guest House* (☎ (0176) 32344) fronting the central park. It has singles/ doubles with attached bathrooms in the main hotel for KSh 170/320 or KSh 200/400 in the annexe.

Similar in price to the Sirimon is the *Jambo House Hotel* (☎ (0176) 22751), which is opposite the Josaki, and offers singles/doubles with attached bathrooms without breakfast for KSh 140/250 and triples for KSh 380. The hotel has its own bar and restaurant.

Also in this range is the *Nyako Boarding & Lodging*, but it's very difficult to find anyone to show you a room and, in any case, it's right next door to the matatu stand which makes it very noisy.

PLACES TO STAY
1 Simba Lodge
4 Sportsman's Arms Hotel
5 Nanyuki River Lodge
7 Nyakio Boarding & Lodging
9 Landview Boarding & Lodging
11 Juba Boarding & Lodging & Jambo House Hotel
12 Josaki Hotel
13 Sirimon Guest House
21 Silent Guest House
22 Youth Hostel

PLACES TO EAT
19 Marina Bar & Restaurant & Muneera's Restaurant

OTHER
2 Catholic Church
3 Nanyuki Sports Club
6 Bus & Matatu Stand
8 Market
10 Hindu Temple
14 Kenya Commercial Bank
15 Standard Chartered Bank
16 Cotton Cultures Souvenirs
17 Clock Tower
18 Barclays Bank
20 Post Office
23 Prison

Nanyuki

To Sweetwaters Rhino Reserve (28 km), Ol Pejeta Ranch (33 km) & Nyahururu

To Isiolo & Meru

To Naro Moru, Nairobi & Airport

Places to Stay – middle

A short distance from the centre of town off the Isiolo road is the *Simba Lodge*, not far from the Catholic church. Rooms with attached bathrooms in this comfortable and quiet hotel cost KSh 500/900 including breakfast. Soap and towel are provided and the hotel has its own cosy restaurant and bar. Vehicles can be parked in the hotel compound and are guarded by an askari. Credit cards are not accepted.

More convenient for the centre of town and tucked in alongside the Nanyuki River is the *Nanyuki River Lodge* (☎ (0176) 32523). This is quite a large place and offers singles/doubles with attached bathrooms including breakfast at KSh 550/850. There's a bar and restaurant where you can also eat lunch and dinner for KSh 200 (four courses). There's adequate guarded parking and a disco on Saturday nights (KSh 100 for men and KSh 50 for women).

Top of the line and a very pleasant place to stay is the newly refurbished *Sportsman's Arms Hotel* (☎ (0176) 22598; fax 22895), south-east of the town centre and across the river. This was once the white settlers' watering hole as the style of the building and the 10-acre landscaped gardens indicate. Some of the makuti-roofed cottages have been preserved for their nostalgia value but brand new ones have also been put up, complete with all modern facilities, so that there are now a total of 85 beds. B&B in the ordinary rooms here is KSh 1035/1495 for singles/doubles. There are also cottages at KSh 1811/2760 for singles/doubles including breakfast. Lastly, there are also self-catering cottages for KSh 2500/4500 for singles/doubles. Facilities at the hotel include an Olympic-sized heated swimming pool, a business centre, restaurant, three bars, a fitness club and a nightly disco in the Buccaneer Club.

Places to Eat

There are very few restaurants in Nanyuki which are not attached to hotels, so take your pick. The *Marina Bar & Restaurant* and *Muneera's Restaurant*, which are next to each other on the main road, are reasonable places to eat and the Marina is an expats' watering hole. For something more sophisticated, go for a meal at the *Sportsman's Arms*. It serves the best food in town.

Things to Buy

There are a number of souvenir stalls and shops set up around town, catering mostly to the British army. The Cotton Culture store on the main street has some interesting items, including beautiful woollen jumpers hand-knitted by a local women's cooperative.

Getting There & Away

Air Air Kenya Aviation (☎ (02) 501421; Wilson airport, Nairobi), flies daily from Nairobi to Nanyuki and Samburu and then back again to Nairobi via Nanyuki. It departs Nairobi at 9.15 am, Nanyuki at 10.10 am, Samburu at 10.50 am, Nanyuki at 11.30 am and arrives back in Nairobi at 12.15 pm. The fares are US$70 (Nairobi-Nanyuki), US$105 (Nairobi-Samburu) and US$40 (Nanyuki-Samburu) one way.

Bus There are daily buses, Nissan minibuses and Peugeot share-taxis from Nairobi (KSh 200 to KSh 250) and Isiolo (KSh 120) to Nanyuki as well as minibuses and matatus from Nyeri (KSh 60) and Nyahururu which run throughout the day.

For those with stamina, there's also an Arusha Express bus direct from Nanyuki to Mombasa and Malindi via Nairobi daily at 5 pm. The fare to Mombasa is KSh 500, or KSh 600 to Malindi. The booking office is directly opposite the clock tower on the main road through town.

AROUND NANYUKI

There are a number of accommodation possibilities in the vicinity of Nanyuki, although only one of them could be called cheap.

Closest to town is the *Mt Kenya Safari Club*, one of the Lonrho group (☎ (02) 216940; fax 216796 in Nairobi). This hotel, originally the homestead of a white Kenyan settler family, was founded in the 1950s by a group of people including the late William

Holden, and is now one of the most exclusive in the country. The views up to Mt Kenya are excellent, and facilities include golf, tennis, croquet, snooker, swimming (heated pool), fishing and bowls.

The tariff for all this luxury starts at US$239/310 with full board in a standard room, going up to US$579 for a presidential suite, plus there are more expensive cottages and villas. Children aged from two to 12 years sharing with their parents are charged US$48. The turn-off for the hotel is a couple of km from Nanyuki along the Naro Moru road, and from there it's nine km along a dirt road which becomes treacherous in the wet.

More luxury options exist on the *Ol Pejeta Ranch* (☎ (02) 216940 in Nairobi), west of Nanyuki along the Nyahururu road. This 9000 hectare ranch has been converted into a private rhino sanctuary and is accessible only to those who can afford the accommodation. The Ol Pejeta homestead, also belonging to the Lonrho group, was the former vacation getaway of the now bankrupt international financier Adnan Kashoggi. As he was not one to spare any expense, the hotel is lavishly decorated, and still features Kashoggi's four-metre-wide bed! Full-board rates are US$78/130 in the low season (April to June, and November to mid-December) and US$163/208 the rest of the year. More expensive suites are also available. Children under 16 years are *personae non gratae* here.

Also on the Ol Pejeta Ranch is the *Sweetwaters Tented Camp*, where a number of luxury permanent tents (though they are tents in name only) have been constructed beside a water hole (floodlit at night). The dining room, bar and reception are inside the quaint, original farmhouse. With the water hole as a focus, game-viewing is the main activity and there's a choice of day and night game drives in 4WD vehicles, walking safaris and camel safaris. Full-board accommodation is US$64/120 in the low season, and US$141/187 in the high season. Children aged from two to 12 years are charged US$44. Bookings should be made through Lonrho in Nairobi (☎ (02) 216940; fax 216796).

Yet another option, and a much more affordable one, is the *El Karama Ranch* (☎ (02) 340331; fax 336890 in Nairobi), 42 km north-west of Nanyuki on the Ewaso Nyiro River. Billed as a 'self-service camp', El Karama is a family-run ranch with a number of bandas for guests. The accommodation is basic but comfortable and each banda is supplied with beds, mattresses, table and chairs, wash basin, bucket, shower, fireplace and firewood. Long-drop toilets are situated close to the bandas. Prices are very reasonable at KSh 400 per person per night (KSh 200 for children between the ages of two and 12 years). You should bring along everything you need, including food, though you can rent bedding (KSh 80), cooking utensils (KSh 80) and kerosene lamps (KSh 80). Meals are not available. Activities here include wildlife walks (KSh 50 per person) starting daily at 7 am and 4 pm and horse riding (KSh 500 per person). During the rainy seasons (April, May and November) you preferably need a 4WD vehicle to get here. Let's Go Travel in Nairobi can provide you with a map of how to get here, and is also the booking agent.

ISIOLO

Isiolo, where the tarmac ends, is the frontier town for north-eastern Kenya – a vast area of both forested and barren mountains, deserts, scrub, Lake Turkana and home to the Samburu, Rendille, Boran and Turkana peoples. It's a lively town with a good market and all the usual facilities including petrol stations, a bank, a post office and a good choice of hotels and restaurants. There are also bus connections to places north, east and south of Isiolo.

The resident population of Isiolo is largely Somali in origin as a result of the resettlement of Somali ex-soldiers following WWI. It ought, in addition, to be famous for the number of formidable speed bumps which force traffic to a snail's pace on the way into town from the south. There are no less than 21 of these and more still at the northern edge of town!

Information

Isiolo is the last place going north which has a bank (Barclays) until you get to either Maralal or Marsabit. There are no banks on the way to or at Lake Turkana (assuming you bypass Maralal).

Likewise, there are no petrol stations north of here until you reach Maralal or Marsabit except at the Samburu Lodge (in Samburu National Park). This doesn't mean that petrol or diesel is totally unobtainable since you can buy it in Baragoi (with ease) and possibly at Christian mission stations elsewhere (with difficulty or not at all if they're low on stock) but you will pay well over the odds for it due to transport costs and irregularity of supply. Stock up in Isiolo.

Travellers about to go to the national parks north of here or to Lake Turkana, and who intend to do their own cooking, should stock up on food and drink in Isiolo as there's very little available beyond here except at Maralal, Marsabit and (less so) Wamba. There's a very good market in Isiolo adjacent to the mosque for fresh fruit, vegetables and meat. The general stores, too, have a good range of canned food and other items.

Places to Stay – bottom end

There are a number of fairly basic lodging houses available for those tight on funds. These include the *Maendeleo Hotel, Farmers Boarding & Lodging, Savannah Inn, Frontier Lodge, Coffee Tree Hotel* and the *National Hotel*, all offering rooms with shared bathroom facilities (cold water only) from KSh 180/250 a single/double. The downstairs area of the Frontier Lodge is taken up by a lively bar which sometimes hosts live bands.

The best place to stay, however, is the *Jamhuri Guest House* which is excellent value and has been popular with travellers for a number of years. The rooms are very clean and pleasant, mosquito nets are provided and the communal showers have hot water in the mornings. Rooms cost KSh 200/260 a single/double. Belongings left in the rooms are quite safe. Next door to it and similar in price and quality is the *Silent Inn*.

Isiolo

0   50   100 m

PLACES TO STAY
3 Talent Lodge
4 Maendeleo Hotel &
   Akamba Bus Office
6 Desert Trails Lodge
9 Bomen Hotel
10 Savannah Inn
11 Farmers Boarding
    & Lodging
12 National Hotel
14 Silent Inn
15 Jamhuri Guest House
16 Frontier Lodge
18 Pasoda Lodge
19 Coffee Tree Hotel

OTHER
1 Police Checkpoint
2 Post Office
5 Petrol Station
7 Petrol Station
8 Mwingi Bus Office
13 Barclays Bank
17 Silver Bells Hotel
20 Mosque
21 Market

Another possibility is the *Talent Lodge*, near the post office. It offers rooms with shared bath for KSh 150/200 a single/double. There is supposedly hot water all day in the showers but this is wishful thinking. The centre of the hotel and the terrace overlooking the street are taken up by a bar so it's not as quiet as the Jamhuri Guest House.

Going up in price, there is the *Pasoda Lodge* which is clean and quiet and offers doubles with bath for KSh 350. There are no singles. The hotel has its own restaurant and bar. At the top of the budget category is the *Desert Trails Lodge*, clearly visible behind the BP station on the main street. The design of this place is perhaps a little claustrophobic given all the wide open spaces close by, but it does mean the security is good. Rooms are good value at KSh 250/450 with a bathroom shared between two rooms.

Places to Stay – middle

There's only one mid-range hotel in Isiolo and that is the *Bomen Hotel* (☎ (0165) 2225). This three storey hotel has a total of 40 spacious rooms, tastefully decorated and furnished. Rates are KSh 900/1300 for singles/doubles with shower (hot water) and toilet, and prices include breakfast, taxes and service charges. The hotel has its own bar and restaurant which serves excellent food at very reasonable prices. Guarded parking is available in the hotel compound. This is an excellent place to stay if you want to visit the nearby reserves of Samburu or Buffalo Springs but can't afford the charges at the lodges inside the parks or don't want to camp.

Places to Eat

Most of the simple boarding houses also have restaurants where you can eat typical African-style meals for less than KSh 150. The *Frontier Lodge* has a good cafe, the restaurant at the *Pasoda Lodge* is one of the better ones, and the *Silver Bells Hotel* does excellent chicken curry.

For a minor splurge, go for lunch or dinner at the *Bomen Hotel*.

Things to Buy

A good proportion of the young men who hang around on the main street of Isiolo are salespeople for the brass, copper and aluminium/steel bracelets which you'll already have come across elsewhere except that the craft here is particularly fine. If you're one of those people who like decking out your forearms with as many of these bracelets as you can, then this is the place to buy them. They're much cheaper here than anywhere else though haggling is, of course, obligatory. The same people also sell daggers in leather scabbards but the craftsmanship in these is generally unremarkable.

If you're simply walking around Isiolo then these salespeople will hardly ever bother you but if you're driving around and especially if you're filling up with petrol at a station then expect a real hassle. Their wares will be thrust in front of your face from both sides and you'll be hard-pressed to drive away.

Getting There & Away

Akamba operates three buses daily to Nairobi at 7.30 and 9 am and 8 pm. The journey takes about seven hours and costs KSh 280. The buses travel via Nanyuki, Naro Moru and Thika, and it's not a bad idea to book one day in advance. If you'd prefer the more comfortable Nissan minibuses, the fare is KSh 330. Peugeot share-taxis cost KSh 380.

Mwingi Buses operates buses to Marsabit (KSh 350) supposedly a couple of times a week, but this is very flexible. It also operates less frequent buses to Moyale on the Ethiopian border (KSh 350 from Marsabit). For either of these services it's just a matter of enquiring at the office several times to try and pin down a departure time or day. There's no alternative except to simply hang around and wait, negotiate a ride on a truck (relatively easy and usually somewhat less than the bus fare) or walk out to the police checkpoint north of town where the tarmac ends and hitch a ride with tourists (not so easy). The Mwingi office is an anonymous shopfront at the rear of the Bomen Hotel; just look for the derelict buses out the front.

Mwingi also operates buses to Maralal a few times a week (depending on demand) which cost KSh 300. Again, the departure times are uncertain.

For Moyale there are regular convoys, and it's easy enough to hitch a ride on a truck. The journey takes two days, so stock up with provisions. The cost is KSh 100 to KSh 600, depending on the driver. If there has been any rain the road turns to mud and becomes impassable.

There's no scheduled transport to Wajir and Mandera, north-east of Isiolo, and besides, this area is the domain of the *shifta*

(Somali bandits, usually armed) and only those people with a specific reason (or a suicide wish) should contemplate travelling there. Every morning at 8 am a convoy of vehicles headed for Wajir, Mandera or Garissa leaves the police checkpost. They are mostly trucks and many will take passengers for a fee. If you are heading for Garissa a stop is made overnight in the beautiful little village of **Mado Gashi**. Here the *New Mount Kenya Lodge* is good value at KSh 200 for a large double room.

AROUND ISIOLO
Lewa Downs

Lewa Downs is a privately owned ranch of some 16,000 hectares which has been turned into a rhino and wildlife sanctuary, although ranching activities are still maintained. The entire area is enclosed by a solar-powered electric fence to keep out stock from neighbouring properties.

Black rhinos from other parts of the

Giraffes are a protected species in Kenya and are numerous; see them at Lewa Downs.

country have been relocated here and are now breeding. The ranch also has a small group of the more placid white rhino, and these are a big attraction, especially since those in Meru National Park were slaughtered a few years ago. Other wildlife abounds, and visitors can expect to see elephant, giraffe, eland, oryx, buffalo, lion and leopard.

The Craig family runs the *Wilderness Trails Lodge* on the ranch, and this is a small, superbly sited stone and makuti thatch set-up with stunning views across to Isiolo and the northern plains. It's a top-end place, so you can expect to part with about US$260 per person per day for full board, but the level of service is excellent and the setting perfect. The lodge is closed during April and May, and from 1 November to 15 December. Bookings must be made in advance through Chris Flatt in Nairobi (☎ (02) 502491; fax 502739).

MERU

Up at the north-eastern end of the ring road around the southern side of Mt Kenya, Meru is an important town which services the intensively cultivated and forested highlands in this part of Central province. It's quite a climb up to Meru from either Isiolo or Embu and, in the rainy season, you'll find yourself in the clouds up here along with dense forest which frequently reaches right down to the roadside. When the weather is clear there are superb views for miles over the surrounding lowlands. Views of the peaks of Mt Kenya, on the other hand, are hard to come by due mostly to the forest cover.

Although there's a small centre of sorts, Meru is essentially just a built-up area along the main road and, as far as travellers' interests go, there's precious little reason to stay the night there. It's certainly much too far away from any of the route heads leading to the peaks of Mt Kenya to be a suitable base to take off from. The nearest of these begins at Chogoria, about halfway between Meru and Embu.

Meru's main claim to fame is the quality of its miraa. These are the bundles of leafy

To Isiolo
& Nanyuki

B6

To Meru
National Park

C91

1 Market
2 Milimani Hotel
3 Stansted Hotel
4 Post Office
5 County Hotel
6 Meru National Museum
7 Castella Bar & Hotel
8 Akamba Booking Office
9 Matatu Stand for Embu
10 Standard Bank
11 Bus & Matatu Stand
12 Kenya Commercial Bank
13 Barclays Bank
14 Continental Hotel
15 Mosque
16 Miraa Market
17 Market

Meru

0   300   600 m

B6

To Embu
& Nairobi

twigs and shoots which you'll see people all over Kenya (and particularly Somalia and Ethiopia) chewing for its stimulant and appetite-suppressant properties. While it still grows wild here, much of it is now cultivated and it's become a major source of (legal) income for the cultivators and harvesters who supply both the internal market and also export it to neighbouring countries. No doubt the marijuana growers are green with envy!

For more information about the Meru people see the Tribal Groups & Cultures section which starts on page 78.

Meru National Museum

This small museum just off the main road is worth visiting if you're staying here or passing through. It has the usual display detailing the progress of evolution, along with exhibits of stuffed birds, animals and mounted insects, but there's also a small and informative section concerning the agricultural and initiation practices of the Meru people and their clothing and weapons. Out at the back of the building are a number of appallingly small and sordid cages containing obviously neurotic and pathetically bored specimens of baboon, vervet monkeys and a caracal cat which someone ought to liberate immediately as an act of sheer pity if not humaneness. There's also a reptile pit with a notice advising visitors that 'Trespassers will be bitten'.

The museum is open daily from 9.30 am to 6 pm except on Sunday and holidays when it's open from 11 am to 6 pm and 1 to 6 pm respectively. Entry costs KSh 50.

Places to Stay

Two of the cheapest places to stay in Meru are the *Castella Bar & Hotel* and the *Continental Hotel* in the town 'centre'. They're basic and neither is particularly special. The Castella has a noisy bar downstairs, and a curious sign at reception warns that 'Combing of the hair in the room is not allowed'. Somewhat better value is the *Stansted Hotel* (☎ (0164) 20360) on the main road past the post office. It is clean, quiet and offers rooms with attached bathrooms at KSh 200 per person including breakfast. The hotel has its own bar and restaurant.

Also good value is the *Milimani Hotel*, further up the hill from the Stansted. It offers good, rooms with attached bathrooms with hot water for KSh 400/550 a single/double. Vehicles can be parked safely in the hotel compound and at weekends there's a disco. If you don't have transport, this hotel is probably too far from the centre – it's about two km uphill.

The best mid-range hotel is probably the *County Hotel*, again on the main road and close to the turn-off for the museum. It's clean, comfortable, has its own restaurant and lively bar, and secure parking. Rooms with attached bathrooms cost KSh 1200/1750 a single/double with breakfast.

Those with their own transport might like to check out the *Rocky Hill Inn*, about eight km out of town to the north, which is essentially a barbecue and bar but has basic chalets for rent, or the *Forest Lodge*, even further out, which has a swimming pool and pretensions to being a sort of country club with expensive chalets.

Places to Eat

For a good, cheap meal of curried fish or chicken try the *Copper Coin* restaurant near the bus stand. Another good bet is the snack bar at the *County Hotel*. A la carte meals cost from around KSh 200 or there's a three course set meal which is great value at KSh 180. The food is unexciting, but it's filling and you can have a beer with your meal. The hotel also has a more up-market restaurant.

Getting There & Away

Meru is served by Akamba buses to and from Nairobi (KSh 240) with departures from Meru at 7.30 and 9 am, and 8 pm. The buses travel via Chogoria, Embu and Thika. The buses can be booked in advance, and the office is in the town centre, just off the main road.

From the matatu park there are regular departures for Isiolo, Embu and Nairobi. Nissan minibuses to Nairobi cost KSh 200.

CHOGORIA

The only reason to come to this small town on the lower eastern slopes of Mt Kenya is that it is the access point for one of the most scenic routes up the mountain – the Chogoria route. Guides and porters can be engaged through the Chogoria Guides Club, which is based at the Transit Motel.

Places to Stay & Eat

The choices here are limited. The *Transit Motel* (☎ 96 in Chogoria) is about half an hour's walk up from Chogoria, and has cheap and clean singles/doubles. Camping is also possible for KSh 100 per person. The other alternative is the *Forest Station*, at the barrier across the track about five km up the route from Chogoria. The 15 cabins here are fully equipped with kitchens, fireplaces, hot showers and three beds.

The *Lenana Restaurant*, just inside the gates of the hospital, is a good place for cheap, substantial meals.

Getting There & Away

The Akamba buses running between Nairobi and Meru pass through Chogoria, or there are regular matatus to Embu and Meru. The bus trip between Nairobi and Chogoria costs KSh 100 and takes about 3½ hours. Nissan minibuses are KSh 130.

EMBU

On the south-eastern slopes of Mt Kenya, Embu is an important provincial centre but is spread out over many km along the main road. It has a famous school and hotel and is set in a very hilly area which is intensively cultivated. It's also the provincial headquarters of the Eastern province though it's on the extreme eastern edge of this and can only have been chosen because of its agreeable climate. Not many travellers stay here overnight, and with good reason since there's nothing much to see or do and it's a long way from the Chogoria route up Mt Kenya.

Places to Stay

There are quite a few cheap hotels spread out along the main road but most of them are very basic and can't be recommended. Behind a row of shops almost opposite the bus and matatu park is the *Eden Guest House*. While hardly paradise, it offers clean, quiet rooms with shared facilities for KSh 180/280.

The *Al-Aswad Hotel*, just a little further up the road, has no single rooms, but the doubles are quite good value at KSh 350. The hotel also has a good restaurant where you can eat for just KSh 120. The *Kubukubu Lodge*, further down the hill from the Eden Guest House, is another reasonable choice.

The *Valley View Hotel* (☎ (0161) 20147), also in this range, has rooms with attached bathrooms with hot water for KSh 400/675 with breakfast. It's clean and tidy and soap and towel are provided, plus the staff are friendly and helpful. The hotel has its own bar and restaurant, and it's much quieter than the hotels around the bus stand.

If you'd like to splurge then consider a night at the *Izaak Walton Inn* (☎ (0161) 20128), about two km up the main road towards Meru from the town centre. It is right out of the colonial era and set in extensive lawns and gardens with a good restaurant and cosy bar – both with log-burning fireplaces. Rates are KSh 1200/1500

To Meru &
Izaak Walton
Inn (1.5 km)

1 Post Office
2 Library
3 Valley View Hotel
4 Matatus to Nyeri
5 Arkland Café
6 Barclays Bank
7 Al-Aswad Hotel
8 Eden Guest House
9 Bus & Matatu Stand
10 Kubukubu Lodge

Embu

0   75   150 m

To Kitui

To Thika &
Nairobi

for singles/doubles including breakfast, with suites and triples at KSh 2200. The staff are friendly and helpful and it's definitely *the* place to stay if you have the money. Even if you don't stay here it's worth turning up for a beer or a meal.

Places to Eat
The *Arkland Cafe* near the main roundabout in the centre of town, is a good place for a meal or snack at lunch time. If you want the full treatment, head for the restaurant at the Izaak Walton.

Getting There & Away
There are daily Akamba buses between Nairobi and Embu and this is the safest way to travel between the two places. The fare is KSh 120 and the booking office is on the top side of the bus and matatu stand.

Matatus also offer the same service but they are invariably overcrowded, often dangerously so, and the drivers really drive like maniacs. The fare to Nairobi on the matatus varies between KSh 100 and KSh 130 and they terminate on Accra Rd (if you're fortunate enough to get that far).

The alternative to a bus or matatu is a Peugeot share-taxi, although, if anything, these are more dangerous because they travel faster. The fare is KSh 150 to KSh 200 depending on the driver and the time of day.

The matatus to Meru are not quite the same hair-raising and dangerous prospect since there's not the same pressure on the drivers, but they're no joy ride either. Take the Akamba bus or a Peugeot taxi in preference.

The Akamba Country

The land of the Akamba people (Ukambani) lies to the south-east of Nairobi and encompasses a broad swathe of wooded hill country east of the Athi River through Machakos (the main town) all the way down onto the semi-arid plains around Kitui. It's a pleasant area and people here are very friendly but very few travellers get out this way. Most of the foreigners you see here work for NGOs or Christian missionary groups. There's not a great deal to do or see in this part of Kenya, but the hills around Machakos offer excellent walking opportunities and superb views down onto the plains to the east. For more details about the Akamba, see the Tribal Groups & Cultures section on page 78.

MACHAKOS
A decade or so before Nairobi was even established, Machakos was the site chosen by the Imperial British East Africa company as an upcountry trading post on account of the Akamba's reputation as middlemen between the Swahili of the coast and the Maasai and Kikuyu to the west and north.

It's a small town hemmed in on two sides between wooded hills and steep valleys and has a very laid-back feeling to it – though you wouldn't guess that judging by the number of buses and matatus which ply between here and Nairobi daily. Clearly, a lot of business must be being transacted as the goods for sale in the open market demonstrate but, basically, it's a place to come for a few days of recreation and rest from the urban madness of Nairobi.

Places to Stay – bottom end

One of the cheapest places to stay is the *Songa Guest House*, round the corner from the KAFOCA Club. It's clean and friendly and has singles/doubles with attached bathrooms for KSh 200/300.

The *Medium Lodge Boarding & Lodging* close to the market is also OK and has quite a few rooms for about the same price, but you wouldn't want to stay there on Saturday nights as the rooms sit above a large bar and disco area and would be very noisy. Not just that, but during the day it's almost impossible to find anyone to open up a room for you. The *T-Ten Lodge* on the road in from Nairobi is similar to the above but a little more down-at-heel, though it does have its own restaurant and bar.

Better is the *Ikuuni Hotel* (☎ (0145) 21166) which is very friendly and has rooms circling a central courtyard. All the sheets are washed and ironed (!) daily and it costs KSh 350/400 for singles/doubles with attached bathroom facilities (clean). The hotel has its own bar and restaurant out the front.

Places to Stay – middle

The only place to stay in this range – and it's superb value – is the *KAFOCA Club* which has singles/doubles with shared bathroom facilities for KSh 350/450 as well as singles with attached bathrooms for KSh 800. Everything is spotlessly clean, the staff are very friendly and there's a bar, beer garden, restaurant and guarded parking.

Places to Stay – top end

The best hotel in town is the *Garden Hotel* (☎ (0145) 30037) which is a huge place with its own restaurant, bar and beer garden and a range of room prices depending on what you take. Standard singles/doubles with attached bathrooms cost KSh 1700/3110 including breakfast, plus there are suites for KSh 3230/4370 for singles/doubles including breakfast. There's a live band in the bar most nights of the week. A lot of people use this place for seminars and conferences so this place for seminars and conferences so

don't be surprised if the place is humming with activity when you arrive. There's draught beer in the beer garden and the food is good.

Places to Eat

Other than the restaurants at the above hotels, there's not much choice. Quite a few of the hotels on the road adjacent to the open-air market and around the bus/matatu stand do standard African fare, but otherwise the most popular place to eat is *The Boiling Pot/Masaku Lodge* which features an upstairs bar/restaurant with a verandah overlooking the street. It's a very popular place to eat.

Getting There & Away

The best way to get here is to a take a Nissan minibus from the country bus station on Landhies Rd in Nairobi to Machakos. The fare is KSh 100 and the journey takes about one hour. There are also ordinary buses for KSh 80. Quite a few of the Nissans continue on to Kitui. The fare to Kitui from Nairobi is KSh 150. Ordinary buses cost KSh 100.

Western Kenya

Western Kenya is an area with many attractions, but is often overlooked by travellers, and you won't find a single safari minibus out this way either. For this reason alone it's worth spending a bit of time exploring here, just to get the feel of Kenya without the tourists.

The countryside is, for the most part, beautiful rolling hills, often covered with the bright green bushes of vast tea plantations. Further west you have Lake Victoria and the regional capital of Kisumu on its shore, and from here there are plenty of possibilities. Just a short distance to the north lies the Kakamega Forest with its lush vegetation and abundant wildlife. Further north still, close to the regional town of Kitale, are the national parks of Mt Elgon (well worth exploring) and Saiwa Swamp, where the only way of getting around is on foot and the attraction is the rare sitatunga or marshbuck deer. (See the National Parks & Reserves chapter for details.)

If you have your sights set on more distant horizons, head west for Busia or Malaba and Uganda, or south to Isebania and across the border into Tanzania.

This western part of the country is the home of Kenya's Luo people. Numbering around two million they make up the third largest ethnic group in the country. Marginalised politically, they are nevertheless a friendly people. (See the Tribal Groups & Cultures section starting at page 78 for more information.)

Getting Around

This is the most densely populated part of the country, so the road system is good and there are hundreds of matatus of varying shapes and sizes plying the routes. Accidents are unnervingly common, but they usually seem to involve the very small matatus, which are usually dangerously overloaded. The small-truck sized matatus are a lot safer as they generally travel more slowly and can carry loads with greater ease.

One annoying factor of matatu travel in this region is the way the destination changes suddenly depending on the number of passengers. So if your matatu is supposedly going from, say, Kakamega to Kitale and it gets to Webuye and everyone gets out, it's a fairly safe bet that you will have to as well. When this happens, and you have paid the fare to the final destination, the driver will find you a seat in another vehicle and fix things with its driver. You will get there in the end, but it may take longer than you think.

Lake Victoria

With an area approaching 70,000 sq km, Lake Victoria is obviously the major geographical feature in this part of the continent. Unlike the lakes further west, Victoria is not part of the Rift Valley system, and so is wide and shallow (only 100m deep) compared with, say, Lake Tanganyika which is nearly 1500m deep.

Lake Victoria touches on three countries – Uganda, Tanzania and Kenya – and it's possible to take a boat between Kenya (Kisumu) and Tanzania (Mwanza), and Uganda (Port Bell) and Tanzania (Mwanza), but not between Kenya and Uganda. The only possibility for lake excursions within Kenya is the ferry which runs from Kisumu to Kenyan ports further south.

Bilharzia is prevalent in Lake Victoria so don't swim in the water or walk in the grass along its shores – this is the hide-out of the snails which are the host for the parasitic flukes which invade your body. (See the Health section in the Facts for the Visitor chapter for more information.) Admittedly, you face only a very small risk of contracting bilharzia if you spend only a short time here.

KISUMU

Although it hardly feels like it, Kisumu is Kenya's third largest town. It has a very easy going, almost decaying, atmosphere. Kisumu was a busy port from early this century right up until the East African Community split up in 1977, but it seems that from this point on the town has just been marking time. With the recent increase in cooperation between the former partners in the community, however, Kisumu's fortunes may once again be on the rise. Already it is a major transhipment point for petroleum products: a recently completed pipeline brings the raw fuel from

Mombasa, and it is then refined and separated into the various individual products and shipped by truck to Uganda, Rwanda, Burundi and eastern Zaïre. The resumption of the international ferry route to Mwanza in Tanzania is another positive sign, although the sinking of the MV *Bukoba* in 1996, with the loss of at least 600 lives, won't do anything for the confidence of potential passengers.

Despite its relative isolation, Kisumu is the ideal place to head for from the east of the country as the travel connections are excellent, especially by rail. There's also enough to do in the town itself to make it an interesting place to stop for a few days.

If you've arrived from the higher country further east the first thing that you will notice is the heat and humidity. Kisumu is always a good few degrees hotter than, say, Nairobi and the steamy conditions only add to the general torporific air.

Orientation

Kisumu is sited on the gently sloping shore of Lake Victoria. Although it's a fairly sprawling town, everything you are likely to need is in walking distance. The main drag is Oginga Odinga Rd and along it are almost all the shops, the banks and the post office.

The railway station and ferry jetty are about a five minute walk from Oginga Odinga Rd, while the noisy bus and matatu station is behind the market on Jomo Kenyatta Highway, about a 10 minute walk from the centre.

Most of the cheap hotels are in the area between Oginga Odinga Rd and Otiena Oyoo St. The mid-range and top-end hotels are mostly to be found along Jomo Kenyatta Highway. The best access to the lake itself is at Dunga, a small village about three km south of town along Nzola Rd.

Information

The post office is in the centre of town on Oginga Odinga Rd. It's open Monday to Friday from 8 am to 5 pm, Saturday from 9 am to noon. If you need to make international calls there is a cardphone outside and you can call direct. Phonecards are sold at the post office.

The British Council, also on Oginga Odinga Rd, has newspapers and magazines and quite a good library. It's open from 9.30 am to 1 pm and 2 to 5 pm Monday to Friday, and 8.30 am to 12.45 pm on Saturday.

Immigration is on the 1st floor, Reinsurance Plaza (behind Deacons department store), on the corner of Oginga Odinga Rd and Jomo Kenyatta Highway. The officials here are friendly and helpful.

The best bookshop in town is the well-stocked Sarit Bookshop on Oginga Odinga Rd, diagonally opposite the post office.

Markets

Kisumu's main market is one of the most animated in the country, and certainly one of the largest. Whether you're after a bag of potatoes or are just curious, it's worth a stroll around.

If you're in town on a Sunday don't miss the Kibuye Market, a huge outdoor affair which draws people from all around the district. You can buy anything here, from second-hand clothes to furniture and food. It is held on Jomo Kenyatta Highway, about one km north of the main intersection with Nairobi Rd. Share-taxis from the intersection cost KSh 5.

Kisumu Museum

It comes as something of a surprise to find this excellent museum here – it's among the best in the country and is well worth a visit. The museum is on Nairobi Rd, within easy walking distance of the centre, and is open daily from 8.30 am to 6 pm; entry is KSh 200.

The displays are well presented and wide-ranging. There's a very good collection of everyday items from the various peoples of the area, including agricultural implements, bird and insect traps (including a white-ant trap!), food utensils, clothing, furniture, weapons, musical instruments and a fairly motley collection of stuffed birds and animals, including an amazing centrepiece of a lion riding on a wildebeest.

Outside there is a traditional Luo homestead consisting of the husband's mud and thatch house, and separate houses for each wife. There's usually a man near the homestead who will show you around for a few shillings and point out the salient features. Also outside are the inevitable crocodile and tortoise enclosures, which are small and a bit depressing. ■

Hippo Point

Hippo Point is at Dunga, about three km south of town, and the cafe on the point is a good place to head for. There are usually no hippos in evidence but it's a pleasant spot all the same. Known as Dunga Refreshments, the cafe is well signposted once you get out of town along Nzola Rd. This place also has the only camp site in Kisumu (see Places to Stay). If you want to get out on the lake there are a number of young boys hanging around who will oblige – for a reasonable fee.

Places to Stay – bottom end

Camping Campers should head for *Dunga Refreshments* (☎ (035) 42529) at Hippo Point, right on the shores of Lake Victoria, three km south of town. It takes nearly an hour to walk there, or you can take a taxi for KSh 250. It's a well-run place with good facilities but there's little shade. Camping here costs KSh 100 per person plus there's also a dormitory block which costs KSh 250 per bed with shared facilities. It's a relaxing place to stay and highly recommended. The complex includes a very pleasant restaurant with reasonably priced meals. It caters for vegetarians, and fruit juices and cold beers are available. The restaurant is open weekdays (closed Monday) from 10 am to 3 pm and 5 to 8 pm, and on weekends from 10 am to 9 pm.

Hotels One of the cheapest options for accommodation is the *YWCA* (☎ (035) 43192) on the corner of Omolo Agar and Nairobi Rds. It has dorm beds (three people per room) for KSh 150 with shared facilities, and also has double rooms with attached bathrooms which vary from KSh 250 to KSh 350 per person. The Y takes both men and women and there's a canteen where you can get basic meals.

A good budget option is the *Razbi Guest House* (☎ (035) 44771), upstairs on the corner of Oginga Odinga Rd and Kendu Lane. It's very secure (there's a locked grille at the top of the stairs), the rooms are clean and a towel and soap are provided. The rates

are KSh 150/200 for singles/doubles with shared cold-water bath.

Two streets south-east of Ogada St is Apindi St, where you'll find the basic *Mirukas Lodge* with OK rooms at KSh 120/200 – they don't come any cheaper than this.

Back on Oginga Odinga Rd, the *Mona Lisa Guest House* (behind the restaurant of the same name) has singles/doubles with attached bathrooms for KSh 200/300. This is probably the best value in Kisumu, and there's hot water supposedly 24 hours a day.

Places to Stay – middle

The *Black & Black Boarding & Lodging*, in the centre of town, has singles/doubles for KSh 340/560, all including breakfast. Bathrooms are shared by three rooms and there is hot water.

Close by is the very pleasant *New Victoria Hotel* (☎ (035) 21067), on the corner of Kendu Lane and Gor Mahia Rd. It's good value, especially if you get one of the front rooms with a balcony and views of Lake Victoria. The singles, at KSh 450, are probably overpriced; the doubles, at KSh 750, are about right. All rates include breakfast. The hotel also has a good restaurant and a popular TV lounge.

Closer to the lake, but without the views, is the *Western Lodge* (☎ (035) 42586) which only has single rooms with attached bathrooms at KSh 400.

Just off Jomo Kenyatta Highway, close to the Imperial Hotel, is the *Hotel Inca* (☎ (035) 40158) which is also good value. It's a large place and offers well-furnished, very clean, rooms with fan and attached bathroom with hot water for KSh 500/850. There's a bar and restaurant and the staff are friendly.

Places to Stay – top end

The best hotel in this range is the charming *Hotel Royale* (☎ (035) 21079) on Jomo Kenyatta Highway. It's an old hotel with a gleaming white façade, open-air terrace bar and polished wooden floorboards. If you have the money, and can get one of the rooms

PLACES TO STAY
2   Mirukas Lodge
6   New Victoria Hotel
7   Black & Black
    Boarding & Lodging
9   Razbi Guest House
10 Western Lodge
16 Mona Lisa Guest
    House & Restaurant
21 Hotel Royale
27 Imperial Hotel
29 Hotel Inca
31 YWCA

PLACES TO EAT
5   Kimwa Cafe
8   New Farmers Bar
    & Octopus Restaurant
    & Night Club
14 Kimwa Cafe
    Annexe & Bar
15 Cafe Natasha
28 Chicken Palace
30 Wimpy

OTHER
1   Kibuye Market
    (Sundays)
3   Hospital
4   Mosque
11 Standard Chartered
    Bank
12 Clock Tower
13 Barclays Bank
17 Akamba Bus Office
18 Train Station
19 Port Office
20 Craft Stalls
22 Kenya Commercial
    Bank
23 Immigration
24 Kenya Airways
25 Post Office
26 British Council
32 Market
33 Bus & Matatu Stand
34 Kisumu Museum

Kisumu

0   125   250 m

on the 1st floor, it's excellent value at KSh 1080/1600 for singles/doubles with attached bathrooms including breakfast. Some of the rooms on the ground floor are gloomy, so ask to see a room first before booking in. The hotel has its own very good restaurant, and credit cards are accepted.

The *Imperial Hotel* (☎ (035) 41485), also on Jomo Kenyatta Highway, is a much newer place with better facilities, which come at a price. The cheapest rooms with all the facilities you would expect cost KSh 3290/3900 a single/double, plus there are more expensive deluxe rooms. There's a rooftop bar, two restaurants (breakfast KSh 250, lunch/dinner KSh 400) and a swimming pool, but the pool is tiny and hemmed in by the building.

On the southern edge of town, the *Sunset Hotel* (☎ (035) 41100/4), in Impala Lane (off Jomo Kenyatta Highway), does indeed have views of the sunset, and of the lake, from each room. There's also a swimming pool and a good, if expensive, restaurant (KSh 500/750 for lunch/dinner). Bed and breakfast costs US$50/60 for singles/doubles throughout the year. All credit cards are accepted. The hotel is part of the African Tours & Hotels group so reservations are also possible in Nairobi (☎ (02) 336858).

There's also the *Gulfstream Hotel* (☎ (035) 43927), off to the east of town, which is very well appointed but inconvenient if you don't have your own transport. Standard singles/doubles cost KSh 1000/1200, plus there are more expensive luxury suites. The hotel has two bars and a restaurant.

Places to Eat

A popular place to eat is the *Cafe Natasha* just off Oginga Odinga Rd. It has a wide variety of good cheap meals and is a popular place for breakfast, though it's open all day. Similar is the *Mona Lisa Restaurant*, on Oginga Odinga Rd. Across the road from the Natasha is the *Kimwa Cafe Annexe*, a 24 hour cafe with a popular bar upstairs.

The *New Victoria Hotel* does an excellent breakfast of juice, papaya, eggs, toast, butter and tea or coffee for KSh 100. It's open for breakfast from 7 to 9 am and also serves standard dishes such as steak, chicken and chips. As this is a Muslim-run place, it doesn't serve alcohol. Just around the corner is the *Kimwa Cafe*, which has cheap local dishes such as matoke and irio.

For stand-up-and-eat or take-away greasy-spoon food there's the *Chicken Palace*, the *Wimpy* or *Rafiq Refreshments & Fast Burgers* – all on Jomo Kenyatta Highway.

For a splurge, go for lunch or dinner (especially the latter) at the *Hotel Royale* and soak in the atmosphere; both the service and the food are excellent. Food at the *Imperial Hotel* is equally good. A meal at either will cost you about KSh 600 per person. The open-air *Victoria Terrace* at the Imperial has nyama choma throughout the day from noon to 10 pm for KSh 160, but unfortunately the concrete surroundings do little for the ambience.

If you're out at Hippo Point don't forget *Dunga Refreshments*, which has good food at budget prices, plus you can eat outside right on the water's edge.

Entertainment

Everyone in search of action goes to the excellent disco/bar/restaurant complex called *Octopus Night Club* on Ogada St. It's a weird and wonderful place, and includes the Bottoms Up disco (entry KSh 90). Beers are sold at normal prices and the disco is a good rage on weekends. You haven't seen Kisumu until you've been here.

Things to Buy

Kisumu is about the best place to buy Kisii soapstone carvings and there are pavement stalls set up near the Hotel Royale on Jomo Kenyatta Highway.

Getting There & Away

Air Kenya Airways has 12 flights weekly to Nairobi. The trip takes one hour and costs US$44. You can pay in local currency, which makes the flight a good deal cheaper. Kenya Airways (☎ (035) 44055) is in the Alpha building on Oginga Odinga Rd.

Bus & Matatu Buses, matatus and Peugeots leave from the large bus station just north of the market.

The best buses for Nairobi are the double-decker KBS buses, which leave from the northern edge of the bus station. The fare is KSh 350 and the journey takes six hours. Akamba has its own depot in the centre of town and has departures for Nairobi at 10 am and 8.30 pm, also for KSh 350. There's also the deluxe Akamba Royal service to Nairobi daily at 10.30 am and 10.30 pm for KSh 600.

There are plenty of Nissan matatus to Nairobi (KSh 300), Busia (KSh 120), Eldoret (KSh 150), Kakamega (KSh 100) and Kisii (KSh 140). There are very few direct services to Kitale; take a vehicle to Kakamega and change there.

Peugeot share-taxis go to Nairobi (KSh 500), Nakuru (KSh 450), Kakamega (KSh 100) and Busia (KSh 100).

Uganda Akamba has a daily direct bus to Kampala at noon; the fare is KSh 600.

Train There are trains to Nairobi daily at 6 pm, arriving at 7 am the next day. Fares to Nairobi are KSh 1930/1320 in 1st/2nd class. It's advisable to book in advance. The booking office at the station is open daily from 8 am to noon and 2 to 4 pm.

There's also a daily 3rd class passenger train to Butere at 9 am, about 50 km north-west of Kisumu. It's strictly for the dedicated.

Car For car rental see Lake Travels (☎ (035) 42204) in the Reinsurance Plaza, corner of Jomo Kenyatta Highway and Oginga Odinga Rd. Avoid Mara Mbose Tours & Travels.

Boat Lake ferries ply between Kisumu and the small Kenyan ports to the south, as well as to Mwanza in Tanzania.

Kenyan Ports The MV *Alestes* plies the route to Homa Bay, departing on Tuesday at 9.30 am, arriving in Homa Bay at 2.30 pm. The fare is KSh 84/41 in 2nd/3rd class. It leaves Homa Bay at midnight on Saturday, returning to Kisumu late on Sunday night.

For the rest of the week it operates between Homa Bay and Mfangano Island.

Tanzania There is a weekly service between Kisumu and Mwanza. Although this was operated by the now-defunct MV *Bukoba*, the service should have now resumed with the MV *Victoria*. The vessel departs Kisumu at 6 pm on Friday, arriving at Mwanza around 10 am the following day. From Mwanza it sails for Kisumu on Thursday at 6 pm, arriving in Kisumu the following morning. The fare is KSh 1200/ 950/600 in 1st/2nd/3rd class, although 3rd class is not recommended as it is just seating space, not a berth. Advance bookings can be made at the port office on weekdays from 8 am to noon and 2 to 4 pm.

AROUND LAKE VICTORIA
Kendu Bay
This small lakeside village has little to offer apart from a somewhat strange volcanic lake a couple of km from town. There's basic accommodation in the town, and the ferry jetty is about one km away.

Homa Bay
This is a very nondescript yet surprisingly busy town on a small bay in Lake Victoria. Most of the action involves transporting agricultural products from the area to Kisumu. Nearby is the intriguing volcano-shaped **Mt Homa** and the small **Ruma National Park**.

Places to Stay & Eat There are several budget hotels along the main road from the ferry, but none are anything to rave about. The best is probably *Asego Stores*, up behind the main road. The sign just announces Bed & Breakfast (although the breakfast doesn't seem to exist). Doubles here cost KSh 200. Next door is the *Nyanza Lodge*, which costs the same but is not as good.

If, on the other hand, you have money to spare, there's the very pleasant *Homa Bay Hotel* (☎ (0385) 22070), set in its own grounds on the shore of the lake. It's part of the Msafiri Inns group so you can book in Nairobi (☎ (02) 330820; fax 227815). A good room here facing the lake costs KSh 1750/2250, and meals are reasonably priced. It's a mellow place to relax if you want to get away from it all for a few days.

Getting There & Away There are frequent matatus to Kisii (KSh 100), Kisumu (three hours, KSh 90) and Rusinga (KSh 40).

From Wednesday to Saturday the MV *Alestes* operates a daily service to Mfangano Island. On Saturday at around midnight it sails for Kisumu.

Rusinga Island

Mbita is the town on Rusinga Island which is connected by a causeway to the mainland. The only remarkable thing about the island is the mausoleum of Tom Mboya on the northern side of the island – he was born here in 1930 and was shot dead by police in 1969 during political unrest. (See the History section in the Facts about the Country chapter for more details.)

There are matatus to Homa Bay, as well as ferry services to Kisumu, Mfangano Island and Homa Bay.

Places to Stay & Eat There's one small lodge in Mbita, which is cheap, clean and friendly. The *Viking Hoteli* is a great little local eatery serving fish fresh from the lake.

On the northern side of the island is the exclusive *Rusinga Island Fishing Club*. As the name suggests, this place is for those whose primary concern is hooking things out of the water on the end of a bit of nylon, but the bird life is also prolific. Accommodation is in individual thatched huts, each with a fine lake view. For bookings contact Nairobi (☎ (02) 447267).

Mfangano Island

There's little to see here and very little in the way of facilities. The small fishing community is about as far off the beaten track as you can get in Kenya.

There is one cheap hotel, and the island is connected to the mainland by ferry (see Homa Bay, Getting There & Away). On other days you can catch a local boat from Mbita (at the causeway for Rusinga Island).

Places to Stay While there are no hotels on Mfangano, it should be possible to arrange accommodation with the local inhabitants. Failing that, the only possibility is the up-market *Mfangano Island Camp* on the northern side of the island, where accommodation costs US$125 per person for full board. This is primarily a fishing resort, and fishing trips are available at US$100 per day. For bookings contact Mutiara Ltd in Nairobi on ☎ (02) 331871.

On the tiny island of Takawira nearby, there's a similar lodge, the *Takawira Island Resort*. For bookings contact Kisumu (☎ (035) 43141; fax 44644).

Western Highlands

The western highlands make up the agricultural heartland of Kenya, and separate Kisumu and Lake Victoria from the rest of the country. In the south around Kisii and Kericho lie vast tea plantations, while further north around Kitale and Eldoret it's all fertile farming land.

The towns of the highlands are really just small agricultural service towns, much the same as you'd find in similar areas in Australia or the USA – and they're about as interesting. For visitors, the attractions of the area lie outside these towns – the tea plantations around Kericho, Kakamega Forest near Kakamega, Mt Elgon and Saiwa Swamp national parks (both near Kitale), and the Cherangani Hills which lie north-east of Kitale and Eldoret. See the National Parks & Reserves chapter for details.

KISII

As you might expect, this is where Kisii soapstone comes from but it's not on sale here at all, the simple reason being that Kisii sees very few tourists and those that do come this way tend to just keep moving. You can, however, visit the quarries if you like. Not much happens in Kisii, and even the locals will tell you that it's 'a remote place'. But the people are friendly and as so few tourists come here, you'll be regarded with curiosity.

Kisii is the main centre of the region known as the **Gusii Highlands**, home of the Gusii people. The Gusii, numbering around one million, are a Bantu-speaking people in the middle of a non-Bantu area; the Maasai to the south, Luo to the west and north and Kipsigis to the east all speak unrelated languages. (See the Tribal Groups & Cultures section on page 78 for more information.)

The town centre is compact and, as usual, the market is the liveliest place in the town during the day.

While you're here, it's worth making the four-hour round trip to the top of nearby **Manga Ridge** from which the views, especially over Lake Victoria, are magnificent. You can also see Kisumu in the distance and the tea plantations of Kericho behind you.

Places to Stay – bottom end
The best value budget place is the *Sabrina Lodge*, just around the corner from the Tabaka matatu stand. It's a very friendly place and has rooms with shared facilities for KSh 200/300 a single/double, and security is good. The hotel also has a bar and restaurant.

Somewhat more expensive, and not as good, is the *Safe Lodge* (☎ (0381) 202950), which has friendly staff but small and gloomy rooms. It costs KSh 200/300 for singles/doubles with hot-water bath. Soap and towels are provided, and breakfast is included in the price. The single rooms have double beds so a couple could get away with a single. It also has a rough and ready bar which can be noisy in the late afternoons when people come in for a drink after work.

On the Kisumu road out of town are two other budget hotels, the *Kianbu Lodge* and the *Highway Lodge*, right next door to each other. Both offer singles/doubles with attached bathrooms for KSh 250/400. There's a bar and restaurant upstairs at the Kianbu.

Places to Stay – middle
The modern high-rise building on the north-eastern side of the market is the *Sakawa Towers Hotel* (☎ (0381) 21218). Rooms with attached bathrooms, with balcony (some with good views) and hot water in the mornings cost KSh 450/600 including breakfast.

PLACES TO STAY
2 Kisii Hotel
3 Highway Lodge & Kianbu Lodge
4 Ngau Guest House
7 Sabrina Lodge
9 Capital Hotel
11 Sakawa Towers Hotel
14 Safe Lodge
21 Mwalimu Hotel

OTHER
1 Mosque
5 BP Station
6 Hospital
8 Matatus to Tabaka
10 Standard Chartered Bank

12 Market
13 Matatus to Kisumu, Homa Bay & Kericho
15 Police
16 Matatus to Nairobi & Nakuru
17 Gusii Express Buses
18 Akamba Buses
19 Post Office
20 Barclays Bank

Kisii

0   75   150 m

To Kisumu & Homa Bay

To Kericho

The staff are friendly and it's a clean place to stay. Towels are provided and there's a bar and restaurant on the 1st floor.

At the eastern end of town is the modern *Mwalimu Hotel* (☎ (0381) 20933) in its own compound. Singles/doubles with attached bathrooms cost KSh 420/620 including breakfast. The hotel has a popular bar, terrace, beer garden and restaurant. There's also guarded parking.

The most pleasant place to stay is the *Kisii Hotel* (☎ (0381) 30134) which is set in its own large gardens (complete with turkeys) on the western side of town. It's a single storey building with a popular bar and restaurant and has singles/doubles with attached bathrooms for KSh 420/600 including breakfast.

Places to Eat

There's not a lot of choice when it comes to eating. One good place is the tiny restaurant inside the *Sabrina Lodge*. It doesn't look all that flash, but it serves good honest local food at sensible prices, and you can have a cold beer with your meal.

For something a bit more sophisticated, head for the *Kisii Hotel* or the *Mwalimu Hotel*.

Getting There & Away

Most matatus leave from in front of the market on the main drag. There are regular departures to Kisumu (three hours, KSh 140), Kericho (KSh 120) and Homa Bay (one hour, KSh 60).

For Tabaka, Migori and the Tanzanian border, matatus leave from the stand behind the Standard Chartered Bank.

Akamba has two direct buses daily to Nairobi (KSh 360) at 9 am and 9 pm via Kericho (KSh 100) and Nakuru (KSh 200). Tickets should be booked one day in advance. Gusii Express Buses, across the road, also has daily departures for Nairobi (KSh 250). The trip to Nairobi takes around 8½ hours.

Akamba and Gusii Express both have daily departures to Homa Bay (KSh 100).

TABAKA

This is the village where the soapstone is quarried and carved, and on arrival it's easy enough to locate someone who can show you one of the workshops. It's basically just a cottage industry and there are few people who actually work the stone for a living – to most people it's just a handy way to supplement the meagre income made from agriculture.

To get there, take one of the fairly infrequent matatus from Kisii.

KERICHO

Tea – it's everywhere! This is the heart of western Kenya's tea plantation area and the rolling hills are a uniform bright green. Kericho's climate is perfect for growing tea, mainly because of the afternoon showers which fall every day of the year. Yes, Kericho is a wet place, but the showers are generally only brief and, apart from benefiting the tea bushes, they also make the area green and pleasant.

The town takes its name from the Maasai chief, Ole Kericho, who was killed by the Gusii in the 18th century in a battle over land – the Maasai had been in the area for years and didn't appreciate the Gusii moving in, though the Gusii themselves were being pushed out by the advancing Luo. The area today is the home of the Kipsigis people, who are part of the greater Kalenjin group. The name 'Kalenjin' (literally 'I tell you') was given in the 1950s to the group of Nandi-speaking tribes, including the Pokot, Nandi, Kipsigis and Marakwet. For more information about the Kalenjin see the Tribal Groups & Cultures section which starts on page 78.

There's not a great deal to the town itself but it's not a bad place to stop for the night.

Information

The post office and the two main banks are all on Moi Highway. The banks are open Monday to Friday from 8 am to 1 pm and on Saturday from 8.30 to 11 am.

Tea Plantations

The closest plantation to town is behind the Tea Hotel, itself once owned by the Brooke Bond company. If you walk through the hotel grounds behind what was the service station and out through the back gate, the path leads through the tea bushes to the hotel workers' huts. If you're lucky there may be picking in progress.

It may be possible to organise a tour of a plantation and processing plant through the Tea Hotel.

Places to Stay – bottom end

Campers should head for the *Kericho Garden Lodge* (☎ (0361) 20878), where you can camp in the pleasant grounds for around KSh 100 per person per night. The rooms here are reasonable value at KSh 240/330 with attached bath. With breakfast the price jumps to KSh 300/450.

Cheaper accommodation is not all that flash. At the *Njekimi Lodging* on John

Kericho Rd you can get a basic single/double with common bath for KSh 200/250.

A better bet is probably the *Fairview Tas Hotel*, which is pretty rough and ready, and has small rooms at KSh 150/250.

Places to Stay – middle

In the centre of town there's the reasonably modern *Mwalimu Hotel* (☎ (0361) 30039) which has a popular bar and restaurant. Singles/doubles with private bath cost KSh 400/520 including breakfast.

Places to Stay – top end

The cheapest of the top-range hotels is the *Mid-West Hotel* (☎ (0361) 20611) which has standard singles/doubles with private bath for KSh 875/1150, and more expensive deluxe rooms and suites. Prices include a substantial breakfast and all taxes. The hotel has its own bar and restaurant.

At the top of the line is the grand old *Tea Hotel* (☎ (0361) 30004; fax 20576), which

PLACES TO STAY
1 Cheap Hotels
4 Tea Hotel
5 Kericho Garden Lodge
7 Mid-West Hotel
10 Mwalimu Hotel
11 Njekimi Lodging
12 Fairview Tas Hotel
16 Sunshine Hotel
17 Sugutek Inn 89

OTHER
2 Bus & Matatu Stand
3 Market
6 Kobil Petrol Station
8 Shell Petrol Station
9 Police
13 Law Courts
14 Post Office
15 Standard Chartered Bank
18 Barclays Bank
19 Town Hall
20 Caltex Petrol Station
21 Hindu Temple
22 Hospital

Kericho

To Nakuru

To Kisii & Kisumu

0   100   200 m

Picking Tea

Kenya is the world's third largest producer of tea, and it accounts for about 20 to 30% of the country's export income. Tea picking is obviously one of the main jobs in the Kericho area. A top tea picker can pick up to 100 kg per day, and they are paid at the rate of KSh 0.80 per kg. The bushes are picked every 17 days, and the same picker picks the same patches of the plantations each time. If you look closely at one of the fields of bushes you can see how one stalk of a bush is left to grow here and there; these are the markers by which workers identify their patch. The bushes are cut right back to about 50 cm high in January to March every four years, and after 90 days are ready for picking again. ■

was originally built by the Brooke Bond company in the 1950s for its managers. It's set in its own well-tended grounds and exudes an atmosphere of days gone by. The rooms are spacious in the extreme, especially the two suites at the back overlooking the tea plantations. All the rooms have attached bathrooms with hot-water showers. Rates (including breakfast) are KSh 1725/2100 for singles/doubles, or KSh 2700 for triples, plus there are suites with two double beds for KSh 3190. Other meals cost KSh 650 (lunch) and KSh 750 (dinner). There's a popular bar/lounge area which sprawls over much of the ground floor and out onto the terrace. The staff are friendly and there's guarded parking.

Places to Eat

For a cheap breakfast head for the 1st floor balcony restaurant at the *Fairview Tas*, where eggs, sausage, toast and tea will set you back KSh 45.

The restaurant in the *Mwalimu Hotel* is a little more sophisticated, while the set lunch/dinner in the *Mid-West Hotel* is good value. The buffet lunches and dinners at the *Tea Hotel* are also good but somewhat more expensive. On the other hand, there is a grand piano which you are welcome to use if you feel like playing some Mozart or Elton John.

Getting There & Away

The matatu station is fairly well organised, with matatus on the upper level and minibuses and buses on the lower level.

As is the case throughout the west, there is plenty of transport in any direction. Nissan minibuses and matatus leave regularly for Kisumu (KSh 100), Kisii (KSh 100) and Nairobi (KSh 270). There are also Peugeots to Eldoret (KSh 180), Kitale (KSh 250), Nairobi (KSh 350), Kisii (KSh 120) and Kisumu (KSh 120).

If you are hitching, the turn-off to Kisumu is about two km south of town along the Kisii road, so you need to get there first, either on foot or by matatu.

KAKAMEGA

The town of Kakamega is on the A1 route, 50 km north of Kisumu and 115 km south of Kitale. About the only reason to stay here is if you are heading for the Kakamega Forest Reserve and arrive too late in the day to walk or get a vehicle. It's also the last place to stock up with supplies if you're heading for a forest sojourn.

The town has the usual facilities – a couple of banks, a post office, market and the ubiquitous boardings and lodgings. For information about Kakamega Forest Reserve see the National Parks & Reserves chapter.

Places to Stay & Eat

There's a limited range of hotels here. At the bottom end of the scale is the *New Garden View Lodge*, which is conveniently close to the matatu station and offers singles/doubles with shared facilities for KSh 150/250. It's basically a brothel. Much better is the *Franca Hotel*, which has two-bed rooms with hot-water bath for KSh 300 a room. The beds are larger than a single, but not quite a double.

At the opposite end of the scale is the *Golf Hotel* (☎ (0331) 20125; fax 30155), set in its own grounds with very comfortable rooms, with bathrooms, for KSh 1750/2250 a single/double, or KSh 2925 a triple, including breakfast. It has a bar, restaurant (lunch/dinner is KSh 400/500) and barbecue area. It's also a great place to relax with a cold beer even if you're not staying here.

Getting There & Away

The matatu station is at the Total station on the northern edge of town. There are buses and matatus to Kisumu (KSh 100), Webuye, Kitale (two hours, KSh 110), Nairobi and Busia. Hitching is not too difficult.

ELDORET

There is little to see or do in Eldoret but it may make a convenient stop for the night in your peregrinations around the western highlands, particularly if you are heading to or from the Cherangani Hills which lie to the north of Eldoret.

The town has benefited hugely from the university here, leading to a lot of new development. Eldoret has also been at the centre of some controversy recently, as the government has built a munitions factory in the area, and a brand-new international airport! Theories abound as to why Eldoret might need such an airport, one of them being that the western part of the country would secede if Moi lost the 1997 election. At this stage, both events seem unlikely.

Information

The post office is on the main street, Uganda Rd, and is open Monday to Friday from 8 am to 5 pm and Saturday from 9 am to noon. Also on the main street are branches of Barclays and Standard Chartered banks.

For car rental, check out the Eldoret Travel Agency (☎ (0321) 33351) on Kenyatta St.

Dorinyo Lessos Creameries Cheese Factory

Perhaps the main attraction here is the local cheese factory, where you can buy any of 20 locally made cheeses at very reasonable prices. Here they produce everything from Stilton to Gruyère and cheddar, all priced at around KSh 360 per kg. You can taste as many as you like, and there is a minimum purchase of 250 gm. They also make about a dozen different ice-cream flavours, and

you can buy these in dinky little buckets for KSh 12.50.

The factory is close to the centre of town, at the end of a very grubby lane which is the home of engineering workshops and car wreckers.

Places to Stay – bottom end

For cheap accommodation the best bet is the *Mahindi Hotel* (☎ (0321) 31520), which is close to the bus and matatu station and is good value at KSh 200 a single with shared bath or KSh 300/400 for singles/doubles with private bath. The hotel has a restaurant, and the noise from the hopefully named Silent Night Bar downstairs can sometimes be distracting. Very similar and also close to the bus station is the *New Miyako Hotel* (☎ (0321) 62757) which charges KSh 200 a single with shared bathroom facilities and KSh 250/400 for singles/doubles with attached bathrooms. There's hot water in the showers and the hotel has an upstairs bar.

Also in this same area is the *Sosani View Hotel* which offers singles/doubles with hot-water bath for KSh 300/400. The hotel has its own bar and restaurant.

One option for campers is the *Naiberi River Campsite*, some 22 km south-east of town on the C54 road to Kaptagat. It's a beautiful spot right on the Naiberi River, and is very popular with overland trucks. This is an utterly eccentric rabbit warren of a place, with two bars (one with waterfall) which stay open until the last person falls over, and meals are available. Solo females might find the comments in the visitors' book enlightening. As well as camping (KSh 150, there is a dormitory (KSh 250) and a few very comfortable double cabins with private bathrooms at KSh 1200. Getting there by local transport is a pain, but the owner, Raj Shah, works in Eldoret during the day, so if you ring before 5 pm on weekdays he can give you a lift out to the site. The contact number for Raj is ☎ (0321) 32644.

Places to Stay – middle

A popular place to stay in this range, and one of the cheapest, is the *New Lincoln Hotel*

PLACES TO STAY
1 Eldoret Wagon Hotel
2 Sirikwa Hotel
4 New Miyako Hotel
5 Sosani View Hotel
7 Mahindi Hotel
8 White Castle Motel
17 New Paradise Bar
& Lodging
23 New Lincoln Hotel

PLACES TO EAT
11 Otto Cafe
18 Wananchi Butchery
19 Murenju Restaurant
22 Sizzlers Cafe
24 Elcove Restaurant

OTHER
3 Post Office
6 Bus & Matatu Stand
9 Police
10 National Bank
of Kenya
12 Barclays Bank
13 Town Hall
14 Standard Chartered
Bank
15 Library
16 Church
20 Akamba Bus Office
21 Eldoret Travel Agency
25 Dorinyo Lessos
Creameries Cheese
Factory

Eldoret

0   150   300 m

(☎ (0321) 22093), which is quiet and has guarded parking. Rooms with attached bathrooms are good value at KSh 500/700 including breakfast. The staff are friendly, there's hot water in the showers and the hotel has its own bar and restaurant.

More expensive and somewhat characterless is the *White Castle Motel* (☎ (0321) 33095) on Uganda Rd, which offers bed and breakfast for KSh 900/1400 a single/double. There's a bar and restaurant on the ground floor.

The pick of the hotels in this range is the *Eldoret Wagon Hotel* (☎ (0321) 62270) on Oloo Rd. This hotel was built years ago in the colonial era and was once a watering hole for white settlers. It still exudes a certain charm but the open verandah where you used to be able to sit and drink a cold beer has been entirely enclosed. The bar memorabilia, however, is still intact. Singles/doubles with attached bathrooms including breakfast cost KSh 1000/1500. Credit cards are accepted.

The bar keeps 'English' hours: 11 am to 2 pm and 5 to 11 pm.

Places to Stay – top end
The only top-end hotel here is the modern *Sirikwa Hotel* (☎ (0321) 63433; fax 61018), which has rooms for KSh 3500/4300 a single/double including breakfast. All major credit cards are accepted and the hotel has the only swimming pool in Eldoret. Meals in the restaurant here cost KSh 300 (lunch) and KSh 500 (dinner).

Places to Eat
A popular lunch-time spot is *Otto Cafe* on Uganda Rd. It offers good, cheap westernstyle meals such as steak, chicken, sausages, eggs, chips and other snacks.

For a slightly more up-market meal or snack try the popular *Sizzlers Cafe* on Kenyatta St, near the Eldoret Travel Agency. Here you'll find a whole range of burgers, curries, steaks and sandwiches.

For nyama choma there are a couple of lively places. The *Wananchi Butchery* on Oginga Odinga St will hack you off a half kg and barbecue it for KSh 85. Slightly more salubrious is the *Murenju Restaurant* further down the same street, which has a nyama choma bar out the back.

The *Elcove Restaurant*, on Oloo Rd opposite the New Lincoln Hotel, is also good. For a splurge, eat at either the *Eldoret Wagon* or *Sirikwa* hotels.

Getting There & Away
Bus & Matatu The bus and matatu station is in the centre of town, just off Uganda Rd. For some strange reason *mzungu* males wandering around here all get called 'Mr John' by the locals. Just who John is/was remains a mystery for the moment.

Matatus/Peugeots depart throughout the day for Kisumu (KSh 150/180), Nakuru (KSh 150/200), Nairobi (KSh 300/400), Kericho (KSh 130/180) and Kitale (KSh 90/100). There are also buses on all these routes.

Akamba buses leave from the company's office/depot on Oginga Odinga St. Executive services to Nairobi (KSh 320) leave at 10.30 am and 9 pm, and there are daily Royal services to Nairobi at 1 pm (KSh 700) and Kampala (KSh 1800) at 11 am.

Train There are services three times a week to Nairobi (KSh 2340/1840 in 1st/2nd class) – on Saturday and Sunday at 9.35 pm, arriving the next day at 9.30 am, and on Thursday at 8.35 am. Trains to the Ugandan border at Malaba (KSh 1260/1030) depart on Saturday and Sunday at 2.40 am, and the train to Kampala (KSh 2250/1710) comes through at 9.45 pm on Tuesday.

CHERANGANI HILLS
The beautiful Cherangani Hills are part of the rift valley system and extend for about 60 km from the north-east of Eldoret. They form the western wall of the spectacular **Elgeyo Escarpment**. You could easily spend weeks exploring here, and never come across another mzungu.

The area is best explored on foot as the roads are rough and some of those which scale the Elgeyo Escarpment are incredibly steep. In wet conditions the roads in this area become treacherous. For serious exploration you would need copies of the relevant Survey of Kenya maps to the area, which are almost impossible to get (see the Maps section in the Facts for the Visitor chapter). Otherwise contact Jane or Julia Barnley of Sirikwa Safaris, PO Box 332, Kitale, who can organise ornithological tours of the hills along with a guide at a very reasonable price. Jane and Julia also run an excellent guest house and camp site 23 km north of Kitale (see the Kitale section for details).

The hills are dotted with small towns and although none of them have any recognised accommodation, it should be possible to arrange something with the local people (ask the village chief or ask in the bars). If you have a tent it's just a matter of finding a good spot and asking permission.

From Eldoret it should be possible to hitch, or find a matatu, as far as Kapsowar, 70 km to the north-east in the Kerio Valley and right in the heart of the hills. Coming from the north there is a road which starts from Sigor at the Marich Pass and finds its way to Kapsowar via Tot and the impossibly steep escarpment road, but don't expect much in the way of transport along it.

The hills are the home of the Marakwet or Markweta people (part of the greater Kalenjin grouping) who migrated here from the north. The area was secure, and the streams were ideal for agriculture as the rainfall was low. To this end they have made good use of, and extended, the water distribution channels which were already in existence when the Marakwet first migrated to the area. The channels distribute the water to all the small *shambas* in the hills.

For further details on these hills, see the Marich Pass section in the Northern Kenya chapter.

KABARNET
Kabarnet is a shabby little town with a spec-

tacular location in the Tugen Hills on the eastern edge of the Kerio Valley. It is the chief town of the Baringo district and boasts a post office, cinema and supermarket.

Places to Stay
The unmarked *lodge* in front of the market has good double rooms with attached bathrooms for KSh 170. You'll have to ask for directions.

Otherwise there's the *Mombasa Hotel* with double rooms with bucket shower at KSh 200. The video room here is a popular place (KSh 10 to see a movie!).

KITALE
Kitale is another in the string of agricultural service towns which dot the western highlands. It does have an interesting museum but its main function for travellers is as a base for explorations further afield – Mt Elgon, Saiwa Swamp National Park – and a take-off point for the trip up to the western side of

Lake Turkana. The Nationa Parks chapter has more details about these places. As such Kitale is a pleasant enough town and can make an enjoyable stopover for a couple of days.

Information
The post office is on Post Office Rd (surprise, surprise) and is open the usual hours. It's possible to make international calls but, as there's no cardphone, these have to be made through the operator in Nairobi, and this takes time. Kitale has the usual banks and a busy market.

Kitale Museum
The museum has a variety of indoor exhibits, including good ethnographic displays of the Turkana people. The outdoor exhibits include traditional homesteads of a number of different tribal groups, the inevitable tortoise enclosure and an interesting biogas display.

Kitale

PLACES TO STAY
3 Rock Hotel
9 Alakara Hotel
10 Executive Lodge
16 Bongo Hotel
18 Hotel Mamboleo &
   New Kitale House
19 Kahuroko Boarding
   & Lodging
21 Star Lodge

OTHER
1 Covered Market
2 Open-air Market
4 Police
5 Barclays Bank
6 Standard Chartered Bank
7 Post Office
8 Mwalimu Co-op Bookshop
11 Kitale Museum
12 Olaf Palme
   Agroforestry Centre
13 Law Courts
14 Akamba Bus Office
15 Town Hall
17 Kenya Commercial Bank
20 Bank (Bureau de Change)

To Kapenguria, Lodwar, Saiwa Swamp & Sirikwa Safaris (23 km)

Train Station

To Mt Elgon & Endebess

Bus & Matatu Park

To Budget Hotels

Post Office Road

To Eldoret & Kisumu

Kenyatta Street

Moi Avenue

0 100 200 m

Probably the most interesting feature is the small **nature trail** which leads through some virgin forest at the back of the museum. There are numbered points along the way; the small guidebook available from the craft shop in the museum explains the points of interest.

The museum is open daily from 8 am to 6 pm; entry is KSh 200.

Agroforestry Project
Next to the museum along the highway is the Olaf Palme Agroforestry Centre. It's a Swedish-funded program aimed at educating the local people about protection and rehabilitation of the environment. The project includes a small demonstration farm and agroforestry plot, and an information centre. It's open daily and entrance is free.

Places to Stay – bottom end
Best of the usual bunch of cheapies/brothels is the *New Kitale House*, which offers singles with clean sheets and shared bath for just KSh 150. Next door is the *Hotel Mamboleo* (☎ (0325) 20172), which is also not bad though the rooms are somewhat gloomy. Singles/doubles with attached bathrooms cost KSh 200/300, plus there's hot-water showers.

Up the scale somewhat is the *Executive Lodge* (☎ (0325) 30689), on Kenyatta St, which has singles with common bath at KSh 350 and doubles with attached bathrooms at KSh 650.

If you want to camp, the only place in the area is *Sirikwa Safaris*, 23 km north of Kitale on the Kapenguria road. It's run by Jane and Julia Barnley at their farmhouse and is a beautiful place to stay. Jane and Julia are very friendly and know the western highlands like the back of their hand, plus they're great conversationalists. Stay here and feel right at home! You won't regret the little effort it takes to get here. Camping with your own tent costs KSh 300 per person including the use of firewood, hot-water showers, flush toilets and electricity. If you don't have your own tent, that's no problem as there are also very comfortable 'permanent' furnished tents for KSh 900/1200, plus taxes (35%). To

find Sirikwa Safaris, look for the sign on the right-hand side one km after the small village of Kesagen. Kapenguria matatus from Kitale go right by Sirikwa (KSh 40), and the drivers all know it.

Places to Stay – middle
The most popular place to stay in this range is the *Bongo Hotel* (☎ (0325) 20593) on Moi Ave, with singles/doubles with shared bath for KSh 300/500, or KSh 550/700 with private bath, all including an excellent breakfast. There's hot water in the showers, clean sheets, and towel, soap and toilet paper are provided.

Also good value is the *Alakara Hotel* (☎ (0325) 20395) on Kenyatta St, offering spacious singles/doubles with shared bath for KSh 400/600. Rooms with private bath cost KSh 600/900. Prices include breakfast. Facilities include a good bar/restaurant, a car park and a residents' video room. The staff are friendly and helpful.

Outside of town, Sirikwa Safaris is the place to head for (see Places to Stay – bottom end for directions). Apart from tents there are two very comfortable rooms with double beds for KSh 1800/2700 a single/double plus tax (35%) and including breakfast. Half-board and full-board rates are also available. Children are half-price and babies stay free of charge. It's a very quiet and homely place and Jane and Julia are the perfect hosts. For advance bookings write to PO Box 332, Kitale.

Places to Eat
The *Executive Restaurant*, at the lodge of the same name, is a very popular lunch-time spot. The menu is extensive and the food good and reasonably priced.

The *Suncourt Cafe* has a nice terrace with views of the surrounding hills. It is behind the town hall, and has good cheap food.

The *Bongo Hotel*, on the corner of Moi Ave and Bank St, has a slightly more up-market restaurant which is a good place for an evening meal. It also serves alcohol. Right next door is the lively Bongo Bar and there's also a take-away food section.

Even better, though slightly more expensive, are the meals at the *Alakara Hotel* on Kenyatta St. You can either eat in the restaurant section or have meals brought to you in the popular bar.

Getting There & Away

The bus and matatu park is fairly chaotic – it's just a matter of wandering around and finding a vehicle going your way. Competition for passengers is usually keen and you'll soon be spotted and pointed in the right direction.

For Lodwar and Kalekol in the Turkana district, there is usually one minibus per day for KSh 350; you'll just have to ask around. The Nissan matatus are more reliable and leave about five times daily (five hours, KSh 400).

On the Nairobi route there is a variety of transport – bus, matatu, Peugeot – so it's a matter of finding which suits you. Akamba runs daily buses to Nairobi at 9 am and 9 pm (seven hours, KSh 400). There's also the Eldoret Express which runs a number of times daily and costs KSh 350. The bus companies have their offices mainly around the bus station area; the exception is Akamba which has its office on Moi Ave.

Matatus/Peugeots also run to Nairobi (KSh 400/500), Eldoret (KSh 90/120) and Nakuru (KSh 240/320). There are also matatus to Kisii (KSh 180) and Kakamega (KSh 110), and Peugeots to Nyeri (KSh 580) and Nyahururu (KSh 600).

For the village of Endebess (the nearest place to Mt Elgon National Park), Nissan matatus cost KSh 60. (See the National Parks & Reserves chapter for more details on getting to this national park.)

Northern Kenya

This vast area, covering thousands of sq km to the borders with Sudan, Ethiopia and Somalia, is an explorer's paradise hardly touched by the 20th century. The tribes which live here – the Samburu, Turkana, Rendille, Boran, Gabra, Merille and El-Molo – are some of the most fascinating people in the world. Like the Maasai, most of them have little contact with the modern world, preferring their own centuries-old traditional lifestyles and customs which bind members of a tribe together and ensure that each individual has a part to play. Many have strong warrior traditions and, in the past, it was the balance of power between the tribes which defined their respective areas.

As late as 1980 there was a clash between the Samburu and the Turkana over grazing land near South Horr which required army intervention. Since most of the tribes are nomadic pastoralists these sort of conflicts have a long history. Nevertheless, the settlement of disputes between the tribes is based on compensation rather than retribution so wholesale violence is a rare occurrence.

Change has been slowly happening to these people as a result of missionary activity (there is an incredible number of different Christian missions, schools and aid agencies, many of them in very remote areas), their employment as rangers and anti-poaching patrollers in national parks and game reserves, the construction of dams and roads, and the tourist trade. You may well be surprised, for example, to see a young man dressed smartly in Western-style clothes doing some business in a small town and then later on the same day meet him again out in the bush dressed in traditional regalia. It might even turn out that he's a college student in Nairobi for much of the year. Pride in their heritage is one thing these people are very unlikely to lose. For more information see Tribal Groups & Cultures on page 78.

Not only are the people another world away from Nairobi and the more developed areas of the country but the landscapes are tremendous with an incredible diversity.

Geography

Much of northern Kenya is scrub desert dissected by *luggas* (dry river beds which burst into a brief but violent life whenever there is a cloud burst) and peppered with acacia thorn trees which are often festooned with weaver birds' nests. But there are also extinct and dormant volcanoes; barren, shattered lava beds; canyons through which cool, clear streams flow; oases of lush vegetation hemmed in by craggy mountains and huge islands of forested mountains surrounded by sand deserts. And, of course, the legendary 'Jade Sea' (Lake Turkana) – Kenya's largest lake and, as a result of the Leakeys' archaeological digs, regarded by many as the birthplace of humanity.

A long narrow body of water, Lake Turkana stretches south from the Ethiopian border for some 250 km, yet is never more than 50 km wide. While it looks fairly placid most of the time, it is notorious for the vicious squalls which whip up seemingly out of nowhere and are largely responsible for fatalities among the local Turkana and El-Molo people who live along the lake shores.

The lake was first reached by Europeans in the late 19th century in the form of two Austrian explorers, von Hehnel and Teleki, who named it Lake Rudolf; it wasn't until the early 1970s that the name was changed to Turkana. The fossil hominid skulls discovered here by the Leakeys in the 1960s are thought to be around 2½ million years old. At that time it is believed that the lake was far more extensive than it is today and supported a richer plant and animal life. Around 10,000 years ago the water level was high enough for the lake to be one of the sources of the Nile, which accounts for the presence of the huge Nile perch still found in the lake.

Climate

The contrasts are incredible in this part of Kenya and the climate mirrors this. By noon on the plains the temperature can reach 50°C without a breath of wind to relieve the sweat pouring from your brow. Mirages shimmer in the distance on all sides. Nothing moves. Yet in the evening, the calm can suddenly be shattered as a violent thunderstorm tears through the place taking all before it. And, just as suddenly, it can all be over leaving you with clear, star-studded skies. It's adventure country *par excellence*.

National Parks & Reserves

There are several national parks and game sanctuaries in the area, three of them along the Ewaso Nyiro River just north of Isiolo (Samburu, Buffalo Springs and Shaba). Further north are the national reserves of Maralal, Losai and Marsabit, and right up near the Ethiopian border, on the eastern shores of Lake Turkana, is the Sibiloi National Park. For further information see the National Parks & Reserves chapter.

The national parks and game reserves of Marsabit, Maralal, Samburu, Buffalo Springs, Shaba and Meru on the eastern side of the lake, and Saiwa Swamp on the western side,

are all accessible by a combination of public transport and hitching, but that won't guarantee you access to the actual parks and game reserves. Think seriously instead about going on an organised safari or getting a small group together and renting a 4WD vehicle. See the Safari section of the Getting Around chapter for details of companies which offer safaris to Samburu, Buffalo Springs, Shaba and Marsabit game reserves and national parks.

Getting There & Around

Bus & Matatu There is regular public transport on the west side of Lake Turkana as far as Kalekol. On the east side of the lake you are pretty much on your own.

Car & 4WD For most travellers who want freedom of movement and to see a lot of places it comes down to hiring a vehicle or going on an organised safari. If you're taking your own vehicle remember to bring a high-rise jack, sand ladders, a shovel, a long, strong rope or chain (that you can hitch up to camels or other vehicles) plus enough fuel and water. The only regular petrol pumps you will find are at Isiolo, Maralal and Marsabit. Elsewhere there's usually nothing except missions, which will reluctantly sell you limited amounts of fuel for up to three times the price in Nairobi. You can't blame them – they have to transport it in barrels in the back of their Land Rovers or pay for someone else to do it in a truck. A 4WD vehicle is obligatory and, except for Samburu National Game Reserve and Buffalo Springs National Reserve, you'd be extremely foolhardy to attempt such a journey in anything else.

Hitching Apart from four routes (Kitale to Lodwar; Nyahururu to Baragoi via Rumuruti and Maralal, Isiolo to Moyale via Marsabit; and Isiolo to Maralal, there is no public transport in this area of Kenya). You can certainly hitch as far as Maralal or Marsabit (from Nyahururu or Isiolo) on the eastern side of Lake Turkana, and to Lodwar (from Kitale) on the western side, but that's about

---

Life In The Wild

A remote region like this with such diverse geographical and climatic features naturally supports varied fauna. Two species you will see a lot of here (but not elsewhere) are Grevy's zebra, with their much denser pattern of stripes and saucer-like ears, and the reticulated giraffe. Herds of domestic camel are commonplace in the area and often miraculously emerge from a mirage, along with their owner, when you are bogged down to the axles in soft sand or mud in the middle of the desert. A rope is all you need, although it's a seller's market of course. Lake Turkana also supports the largest population of Nile crocodiles in Kenya. They feed mainly on the lake fish but will quite happily dine on incautious humans swimming there. The giant eland finds sanctuary in the forested hills around Marsabit. ■

HUGH FINLAY

HUGH FINLAY

HUGH FINLAY

HUGH FINLAY

estern Kenya is fringed by Lake Victoria, the second largest freshwater lake in the world op). Kibuye Market draws a huge crowd from all over the district (middle right). Kericho is e tea-growing capital of Western Kenya (bottom & middle left).

DEBRA TAN

HUGH FINLAY

GEOFF CROWTHER

HUGH FINLAY

Lake Turkana is home to the El Molo people (top) who derive an income from fishing and tourism. It is also home to the Turkana tribe who make their living from fishing and mustering cattle (middle photos). The lushness of Eliye Springs at Lake Turkana (bottom) belies the barren land surrounding it.

the limit of reliable hitching possibilities. There is *very* little traffic on any other routes though travellers regularly report that hitching to Loyangalani is possible, although it does take time.

The mission stations/schools invariably have their own Land Rovers (and some have their own light aircraft) but they usually only go in to regional centres once a week or once a fortnight. Although most will try to help you out if you're stuck, you cannot be guaranteed a lift. The vehicle might be full of people who need urgent medical assistance or (on the return journey) full of supplies.

Hitching is possible, of course, but you must have no deadlines to meet and you must be the sort of person who is quite happy to wait around for days for a ride. In some ways, this could be a very interesting way of getting around and you'd certainly meet a lot of local people.

You could, of course, buy a camel and do a John Hillaby but this isn't something to approach lightly. It is, however, a distinct possibility especially if you are part of a small group. You'd have the adventure of your life!

Safaris There are no organised safaris which go to the west of Lake Turkana. All of them go to the east side of the lake and most of them last from seven to 10 days, though there are others which last 14 days, and they all seem to follow much the same route. Other options include camel and donkey safaris.

See the Safaris section in the Getting Around chapter for a full run-down of the options.

West of Turkana

From Kitale the road north winds through fertile highlands, passing the turn-off for the tiny Saiwa Swamp National Park (well worth a visit; see the National Parks & Reserves chapter) before reaching Kapengu-

ria, the town most famous for being the place where Jomo Kenyatta and five associates were held and tried in 1953 for their alleged part in the Mau Mau Rebellion.

The road then snakes its way up along a forested ridge and through the narrow northern gorges of the Cherangani Hills, emerging on to the desert plains through the Marich Pass. The change in scenery is dramatic and there are some fantastic views of the plains. The only town in this part of the hills is **Ortum**, just off the road. If you want to stop and explore the area, there is basic accommodation in the town but the best place to stay is the Marich Pass Field Studies Centre further north (see the following Marich Pass section).

Shortly after Marich Pass is a turn-off to the left (west) to the **Turkwel Gorge**. It's here that you'll find the huge hydroelectric project which was built to supply electricity to a large area of the densely populated highlands – the northern areas still have to rely on generators.

After km of endless plains and dry creek beds the town of **Lokichar** is little more than a collection of dismal *dukas* by the side of the road. The heat here is oppressive and the settlement seems to be gripped by a permanent torpor. The one redeeming feature of the place is that it is possible to buy basketware and other Turkana trinkets cheaper than you'll find them further north.

MARICH PASS AREA

The main reason for visiting this area is to stay at the Marich Pass Field Studies Centre (see Places to Stay & Eat) and use this as a base for a number of excursions in the area.

Those with their own vehicles should bring sufficient supplies of petrol as there are no service stations between Kapenguria and Lodwar. If you intend walking in the vicinity then you need to be adequately prepared for a variety of weather conditions.

A few km to the north-west, **Mt Sekerr** (3326m) can be climbed comfortably in a three-day, round trip via the agricultural plots of the Pokot tribe, passing through forest and open moors. The views from the top are magnificent in clear weather.

To the south are the **Cherangani Hills**, which offer some of the best hill walks anywhere in Kenya ranging from half-day excursions to week-long safaris by vehicle and on foot. Possibilities include a half-day walk along the old road perched high on the eastern side of the Marich Pass to a local Pokot trading centre; a hard day's slog up the dome of Koh which soars some 1524m above the adjacent plains; a safari of several days duration along the verdant Weiwei Valley to Tamkal and then up to Lelan Forest and the main peaks of the Cherangani.

The **Elgeyo Escarpment** rises to more than 1830m in places above the Kerio Valley and offers spectacular views and waterfalls. It's only 1½ hours away from the field studies centre along a road that passes through several local market centres and intensively farmed garden plots.

The **South Turkana National Reserve** in dry and rugged hills north-east of the field studies centre is the domain of Turkana herders and rarely visited by outsiders. The 50-km drive to get there traverses grazing lands of the pastoral Pokot.

Lastly, the **Turkwel Gorge** hydroelectric station is only 30 km away along a fine tarmac road. Much of the gorge, with its towering rock walls, has not been affected by the construction, while the dam itself (the highest of its type in Africa) is spectacular.

Places to Stay & Eat

The best place to stay in this area is the *Marich Pass Field Studies Centre* (☎ (0321) 31541), PO Box 2454, Eldoret. This is essentially a residential facility for groups pursuing field courses in geography, botany, zoology, ecology, conservation, geology and rural development, but it's also open to independent travellers who want to spend a day, a week or a month in a little-known corner of Kenya.

The centre occupies a beautiful site alongside the Weiwei River and is surrounded by dense bush and woodland. The bird life here is prolific, monkeys and baboons are 'in

residence', while wart hog, buffalo, antelope and elephant are regular visitors. Facilities include a secure camp site (KSh 200 per person per night) with drinking water, toilets, showers and firewood, as well as dorm beds for KSh 250 and simple but comfortable *bandas* for KSh 400 (two people) and KSh 700 (three people).

English-speaking Pokot and Turkana guides are available on request. There's also a restaurant where you can get reasonably priced meals, which should ideally be ordered in advance since the very friendly manager often has to walk into the nearest village to buy the food. You can, of course, bring your own food with you and cook it at the centre. There's little available in the villages of this area.

Getting There & Away

To reach the field studies centre, take the main Kitale to Lodwar road and watch out for the centre's signpost, two km north of the Sigor to Tot road junction (signposted), at Marich Pass. The centre is about one km down a clearly marked track.

There are three approaches to Marich Pass. The first and easiest is through Kitale and Kapenguria and then a further 67 km down a tarmac road (described as 'possibly Kenya's most spectacular tarmac road'). There are daily bus services from Nairobi to Kapenguria, and matatus (KSh 70 in a Nissan) from Kitale to Kapenguria. There are also a few daily matatus which cover the stretch from Kitale to Lokichar via Marich Pass.

The second approach is through Iten, either from Eldoret or via Kabarnet using the scenic road across the upper Kerio Valley from Kabarnet. The all-weather Cherangani Highway can be picked up from Iten to cross the main pass of the Cherangani Hills and join up with the Kitale to Lodwar road near Kapenguria.

The roughest of the three approaches is the road from Lake Baringo through the Kito Pass and across the Kerio Valley to Tot, but its main advantage is that it gives you the chance to visit the hot waterfalls at **Kapedo**.

From Tot, the track skirts the northern face of the Cherangani Hills and may be impassable after heavy rain.

LODWAR

The hot and dusty administrative town of Lodwar is the only town of any significance in the north-west. With a bitumen road connecting it with the highlands it is no longer the isolated outpost of the Northern Frontier District, as the area was known during colonial days, but is certainly lagging a few steps behind the rest of the country.

Lodwar is also the base for any excursions to the lake from the western side and you will probably find it convenient to stay here for a night at least. There's little to do in the town itself but it has an outback atmosphere which is not altogether unpleasant and just watching the garrulous locals is entertainment in itself. The Turkana have found that tourists are a good touch when it comes to selling trinkets and they approach with alarming audacity and don't conceal their disgust when you don't want to buy. They are also remarkably persistent. The small market is a good place to watch women weaving the baskets.

Information

The town has a post office and a branch of the Kenya Commercial Bank.

Places to Stay – bottom end

Lodwar is one place where it's worth spending a bit more on accommodation – mainly to get a room with a fan. The rooms in the cheaper places are all hellishly hot and, as the mosquitoes are fierce, you need to cover up or burn coils if you don't have a net.

Probably the best of the cheapies is the *Mombasa Hotel*. The friendly Muslim owners charge KSh 200/300 for singles/doubles. The singles are cooler (it's all relative though) as they have high ceilings. If you have a mosquito net you can sleep in the courtyard.

The *Marira Boarding & Lodging* is a small place which offers single/double rooms at KSh 250/350.

Another good option, and the only one for campers, is the *Nawoitorong Guest House* (☎ (0393) 21208). The turn-off is signposted one km south of Lodwar on the main road, and from there it's a further two km. This place was built entirely out of local materials and is run by a local women's group. Camping costs KSh 100, and meals are available. There's also one banda, which can accommodate up to six people, which costs KSh 300/400 for a single/double including breakfast.

Places to Stay – middle

The *Turkwel Hotel* (☎ (0393) 21201) is the town's social focus and also has the best accommodation. Single rooms with fan and shared bath go for KSh 300, while singles/doubles with fan and bath cost KSh 350/450. There are also a few spacious cottages which are very pleasant and cost KSh 650 for two, including breakfast.

Places to Eat

The restaurant at the *Mombasa Hotel* does reasonable local food. The *Marira Boarding & Lodging* has little variety but its chips are excellent and freshly cooked to order. For something a bit more sophisticated the *Turkwel Hotel* restaurant does standard Western fare such as steak, chips etc. Breakfast here consists of a couple of eggs and a sausage, and non-guests are not served until all the hotel guests have finished. The bar here is also a popular place.

Getting There & Away

There is one daily minibus from Kitale to Lodwar which generally leaves around 10 am, but sometimes it doesn't don't run at all. The Nissan matatus are more reliable and there are usually five per day which leave when full. The trip takes around seven hours and costs KSh 400.

Matatus also run from Lodwar to Kalekol near the lake if demand warrants, but you can't count on them. The trip takes one hour. If you want to hitch to Kalekol the place where the locals wait is under the tree about 200m north of the Kobil station. To give an indication of how long you can expect to wait, there is a chai (tea) stall here which also sells mandazis.

KALEKOL

Most visitors to the area head on from Lodwar to Kalekol, a fairly dismal little town a few km from the lake shore. The main building in this one-street town is the fish-processing factory built with Scandinavian money and expertise and, although not that old is currently not operating. There is also an Italian-sponsored plant closer to the lake shore.

Places to Stay & Eat

The main problem with a visit here is lack of accommodation options. Two basic budget places have closed down in recent years, leaving only the *Safari Hotel* which has a reasonable restaurant.

Getting There & Away

Irregular matatus do the run to Kitale.

To get out to the lake it's a hot 1½-hour walk. Local people will point you in the right direction, or just walk to the Italian fishing project and cut across the lake bed from there.

FERGUSON'S GULF

This is the most accessible part of the lake shore and although it's not particularly attractive, the sense of achievement in just getting there usually compensates. The water has receded greatly over the last decade or so, mainly due to water use in Ethiopia, so you have to walk a long way over the lake bed to actually get to the water. The birdlife along the shore is prolific. There are also hippos and crocodiles, so seek local advice before having a refreshing dip.

There's a small fishing village of grass huts on the far side of the defunct Turkana Fishing Lodge and that's about the limit of development.

In the middle of the lake is the **Central Island National Park**, a barren yet scenic volcanic island, but unless you're on an organised trip there is no way of getting to it

from here. Talk to the fishers and they *might* take you out but make sure their craft is sound – the danger posed by the lake's squalls is not to be taken lightly.

Places to Stay

If you don't mind really roughing it, the local villagers will put you up for a small fee, otherwise you'll have to come here just for a day trip from Kalekol.

The *Lake Turkana Fishing Lodge* closed some years ago, supposedly just for renovations, but it's doubtful it will reopen in the foreseeable future. It is supposedly on an island but the level of the lake has fallen so far in recent years that it's now possible to drive to the lodge. It takes around 1½ very hot hours to walk out there from Kalekol – follow the track to the Italian fishing project then head across the lake bed from there. There are children with canoes who will

Look for herons at Ferguson's Gulf, where they may be seen wading in shallow waters.

paddle you across the 20m or so of channel. By car you just follow the main road through Kalekol and it takes a circuitous route to the far side of the lodge. Although the water once used to lap at the edge of the bar terrace, it is now more than 100m away across a blinding expanse of sand.

ELIYE SPRINGS

This is a far more attractive place than Ferguson's Gulf but is inaccessible without a 4WD. The small village here has an army post, a couple of dozen grass huts, and a lodge which is of marginal status to say the least. The springs however do provide moisture enough for a curious variety of palm tree (the doum palm) to grow here which gives the place a very misplaced tropical island feel. This particular variety of palm tree has an unusually shaped fruit which the locals eat.

If you do make it here you will be greeted by a number of Turkana girls and young women selling trinkets at absurdly cheap prices. With an average of just a few vehicles a week, it's a real buyer's market. Items you might find for sale might include fossilised hippo teeth and fish backbones threaded into necklaces!

Places to Stay & Eat

The camp site at the lodge here is very pretty, with doum palms and views of the lake. The *Eliye Springs Lodge* itself has seen better days and is in fact something of an on-again, off-again set-up. You're best to make enquiries in Lodwar before relying on this place being open.

Getting There & Away

The turn-off for Eliye Springs is signposted about halfway along the road from Lodwar to Kalekol. There are a few patches of heavy sand so a 4WD is advisable, although you'd probably get through in a conventional vehicle. As there are so few vehicles, hitching is not an option and it's 35 long, hot km if you plan to walk it.

LOKICHOKIO

This frontier town is the last on the Pan African Highway before the Sudan border. The road is sealed all the way here and is in excellent condition but you can't get beyond Lokichokio without a police permit. Even if this was forthcoming, the area is not safe to visit as long as the civil war in southern Sudan continues.

Places to Stay

There's a hotel of sorts here with a couple of mud huts out the back, and there's a bar in town. On the other hand, if you get this far, you'll probably find yourself staying with aid/famine relief workers who take care of the refugee camps around here.

East of Turkana

There are two main routes here. The first is the A2 highway from Nairobi to Marsabit, via Isiolo and Laisamis, and north from there to Moyale on the Ethiopian border. The other is from Nairobi to Maralal, via Gilgil, Nyahururu and Rumuruti or via Nakuru and Lake Baringo, and north from there to Loyangalani on Lake Turkana, via Maralal, Baragoi and South Horr. It's also possible to cross from Isiolo to Maralal. From Loyangalani you can make a loop all the way round the top of the Chalbi Desert to Marsabit via North Horr and Maikona.

Getting There & Around

Bus & Matatu Mwingi buses run from Isiolo to Marsabit but there is no real schedule so you could be stuck in either place for a few days. The fare is KSh 350. There's no alternative except to simply hang around and wait or either negotiate a ride on a truck (relatively easy and usually somewhat less than the bus fare) or walk out to the police checkpoint north of Isiolo town where the tarmac ends and hitch a ride with tourists (not so easy). A convoy system is in operation in order to deter *shiftas* (bandits) from stopping and robbing trucks, buses and cars.

Mwingi also operates regular buses from Isiolo to Wamba where you can change onto another bus or matatu for Maralal. The cost from Isiolo to Wamba is KSh 100 and the journey takes about one hour. From Wamba to Maralal the buses cost KSh 150 and the matatus KSh 200, and the journey takes about 3½ hours.

North of Maralal, the only public transport is a matatu which plies between Maralal and Baragoi once daily if demand warrants it.

Car & 4WD None of the roads in this region are surfaced and the main A2 route is corrugated *murram* which will shake the guts out of both you and your vehicle depending on your speed.

The road connecting Isiolo with Maralal (which branches off the A2 north of Archer's Post) is similarly corrugated but otherwise in good shape. The road from Lake Baringo to Maralal and from Maralal to Loyangalani, however, is surprisingly smooth, though there are bad patches here and there including a diabolical section of several km from the plateau down to Lake Turkana.

There's also a minor cross route between Isiolo and Baragoi which bypasses Maralal and goes via Wamba and Parsaloi (though you don't actually go through Wamba itself). This route leaves the Archer's Post-Maralal road about 20 km north-west of Archer's Post and joins the Maralal to Loyangalani road about 15 km south of Baragoi. Though a minor route, this road is very smooth most of the way with the occasional rough patch. Its main drawback is the steep-sided luggas, none of which are bridged. In the dry season you won't have any problems with a 4WD (impossible with a 2WD) but you can forget about it in the wet season.

The worst of these luggas is just outside Wamba – there's a way around it by taking the Maralal road from Wamba and turning first right along a dirt road once you've crossed an obvious bridge. You'll probably only use it if you want to visit the Matthews Range and the Ndoto Mountains.

Forget about the Maralal to Parsaloi road

marked on the Survey of Kenya maps. It's all washed out and you won't even make it in 4WD.

WAMBA

Wamba is a small, essentially one-street town off the Isiolo to Maralal road north of Samburu National Game Reserve and a sort of provincial headquarters for the surrounding area. There's precious little here for the traveller and its only claim to fame is that it was from here that John Hillaby organised his camel trek to Lake Turkana which resulted in his book, *Journey to the Jade Sea*.

It has quite a few well-stocked dukas, a butchery, a hospital, schools and a large police station but no bank and no electricity despite its proximity to Isiolo.

Places to Stay & Eat

There's only one lodge in the village and that is the *Saudia Lodge* which is at the back of the main street off to the right-hand side coming into town (signposted). You get a pleasant, clean room here (mosquito nets, soap, towel and toilet paper are provided) for just KSh 250/325 a single/double. Bathroom facilities are communal. A wholesome breakfast can be provided for you if you order it in advance.

There's a lively bar on the main street, on the right-hand side as you enter the main part of town, where you can drink your fill though there's no refrigeration. You can't miss it – just listen for the cassette player blaring away!

MARALAL

Maralal is high up in the hills above the Lerochi Plateau (essentially a continuation of the central highlands), north of Nyahururu and Nanyuki and north-west of Isiolo, and connected to all these towns by gravel roads. Surrounding it is the Maralal National Sanctuary which is home to zebra, impala, eland, buffalo, hyena and wart hog, all of which you can see from the road leading into Maralal from the south or at the Maralal Safari Lodge which has the only permanent water hole in the area.

It's an attractive area of grassy undulating plains and coniferous forests which was coveted by white settlers in the colonial era. However, the settler's designs for taking it over were scotched by the colonial authorities due to anticipated violent opposition from the Samburu for whom it holds a special significance.

The town itself, while a regional headquarters, retains a decidedly frontier atmosphere. There's a sense of excitement blowing in the wind that frequently sweeps the plains and whips up the dust in this somewhat ramshackle, but very lively, township with its wide streets and wild-west-type verandahs.

It's also the preferred route and overnight centre for the safari companies which take people up to Lake Turkana. People here are very friendly and it's a great place to buy Samburu handicrafts.

There's a post office (with telephones), petrol stations, mechanics, the only bank north of Isiolo other than in Marsabit, shops with a good range of stock, hotels, bars, one of the best camp sites in Kenya, a surprising number of butchers' shops and regular bus transport to Isiolo. There are also matatus to Baragoi which leave from the Shell station. If you are not travelling with a safari company you may well consider spending a few days here. It's a bizarre but captivating place.

Information
Money The Kenya Commercial Bank is open during normal banking hours. This is the last bank going north, apart from those in Marsabit, so stock up on cash. Changing cash or travellers' cheques is fast and efficient here. Outside of banking hours, try Yare Safaris Club.

Post & Communications The post office is open normal hours and the staff are very helpful should you want to make national or international calls.

Fuel There are two petrol stations (Shell and Total) in the centre of town where you can be assured of getting what you need at regular prices. However, north of here you will only find petrol at Baragoi and Loyangalani, and if there is some petrol there you will find it is always at a much higher price.

PLACES TO STAY
5 New Garden Hotel
9 Mid Point Hotel
10 Wananchi Hotel
12 Buffalo Lodge
16 Kimaniki Boarding & Lodging
17 Corner Bar Boarding & Lodging
18 Maralal Safari Hotel
19 Jamhuri Boarding & Lodging

PLACES TO EAT
8 New Dynamic Starlight Bar & Restaurant
11 Paradise Bar & Restaurant
14 Hard Rock Cafe

OTHER
1 Council Offices
2 Police
3 Kenya Commercial Bank
4 Market
6 Bus Stand (for Buses to Isiolo)
7 Post Office
13 Shell Petrol Station & Matatus to Baragoi
15 Total Petrol Station

Maralal

To Baragoi & Maralal Safari Lodge

To Nyahururu, Isiolo & Yare Club & Campsite

Safaris

Regular camel safaris, and Lake Turkana safaris by truck depart from Yare Safaris' Yare Club & Campsite (see the Other Safaris section in the Getting Around chapter and earlier on in this chapter for details).

Places to Stay – bottom end

The best place to stay here, and one which is very popular with travellers is *Yare Club & Campsite*, three km south of town on the Isiolo/Nyahururu road, and signposted. Here you have a choice of camping or renting a self-contained banda. It's been thoughtfully constructed with local materials and the facilities include a well-stocked bar/lounge, games room, and self-service restaurant serving local dishes. There's also guarded parking (not that you need it around here). The camp site has its own showers (cold water only) and toilets. Camping costs KSh 200 per person per night.

The bandas have private bathrooms and are clean, comfortable and provide excellent value at KSh 820/1100 for singles/doubles

and KSh 1485 a triple including breakfast. Kenyan residents pay KSh 640/830 and KSh 1045, respectively. Soap and towels are provided and a bucket of hot water is available in the morning at no extra cost.

Advance booking is absolutely essential for any sort of accommodation here during the week of the camel derby (last week of October). For bookings, contact Yare Safaris (☎/fax (02) 214099), 1st floor, Union Towers, Mama Ngina St, PO Box 63006, Nairobi, or ☎/fax (0368) 2295, Maralal.

In Maralal itself the most popular place to stay is the *Buffalo Lodge* (☎ (0368) 2228) which is a fairly modern structure offering rooms with clean sheets, towels and hot water in the mornings for KSh 375 a single or double. It's a lively place and there's a bar/video room at the back. Sammy, the barman here, is a real live wire and very friendly. This place may be changing hands soon because, very sadly, Kamau, the owner died recently, however it probably won't change too much.

Cheaper, and excellent value, is the

Maralal International Camel Derby

Inaugurated by Yare Safaris in 1990, this annual event takes place on the Saturday of the third week of October. It's a great time to be here and the three races which are held (amateurs, semi-professional, and professional) are open to everyone. It attracts riders and spectators from the four corners of the earth, there's substantial prize money to be won (over US$5000), the media is there in force, you can make excellent contacts which will stand you in good stead for the rest of your trip, it's good fun, and, last but not least, it's one hell of a binge!

The races start and finish at Yare Safari's Club & Campsite, a few km south of town on the road to Nyahururu/Isiolo, and there's no chance of missing it as the road will be festooned with flags and bunting and choked with activity. Entry fees up until 15 October for the various categories are US$30 (KSh 300 for residents) in the amateur competition; US$50 (KSh 500 for residents) in the semi-professional and US$100 (KSh 500 for residents) on the professional races. Thereafter, entries are accepted up until the start of the race at a premium of 50%. Applications for entry should be made to either the Maralal International Camel Derby (MICD) Secretariat, PO Box 47874, Nairobi, or Yare Safaris, PO Box 63006, Nairobi. Camels with saddle and/or handler can be hired locally for US$125 (KSh 5000 for residents). The amateur class requires you to use a handler but the semi-professional and professional classes are not allowed to use them. If you need a handler, it will cost extra.

A substantial amount of the money made on these events goes towards the provision of medical facilities for the Samburu people.

And just in case you're thinking this is a good laugh for the humans but a lousy deal for the animals, International Camel Races Association rules apply so the camels are checked daily by a vet and monitored by a KSPCA officer. Any rider beating an animal unnecessarily is disqualified.

Get yourself up there! This is one of the major events on the Kenyan calendar and the social event after the races at Yare Safaris Lodge is unbelievable and goes on all night. For transport from Nairobi to Maralal, contact Yare Safaris, Payless Car Hire, Safari Camp Services or the Mountain Rock Lodge. ■

Kimaniki Boarding & Lodging which is a two-storey wooden building offering good rooms for KSh 100/150 a single/double. Clean sheets are provided as well as hot showers (if requested) and vehicles can be parked safely in the hotel compound. There's also the *Mid Point Hotel* (☎ (0368) 2221), which offers good lodging for single people at the same price plus there's hot water in the mornings.

Also good is the *Silence Hotel*, with 24-hour hot water and mosquito nets. Double rooms cost KSh 150.

Other possibilities include the *Corner Bar Boarding & Lodging, Jamhuri Boarding & Lodging, Maralal Safari Hotel, New Garden Hotel* and *Wananchi Hotel* – all rather basic.

Places to Stay – top end

The only top-range hotel in Maralal is the *Maralal Safari Lodge* (☎ (0368) 2060 in Maralal; (02) 211124 in Nairobi), PO Box 70, Maralal and PO Box 45155, Nairobi. It consists of a main building housing a restaurant, bar and souvenir shop, and a series of cottages. It costs US$120/150 for singles/doubles with full board. Extra beds are US$60. Half-board rates are also available but amount to only a small reduction per person on the full-board rates so it's hardly worth it. Meals are available to non-guests for KSh 250 (breakfast) and KSh 500 (lunch or dinner). There's a watering hole, which attracts a varied selection of game, right in front of the bar's verandah so you can watch the animals while sipping a cold beer. Facilities include a golf course and swimming pool – certainly the only ones for some km in any direction! – both of which are open to the public. The lodge is about three km away from the centre of Maralal, off the road to Baragoi (signposted).

Places to Eat & Entertainment

The best place to eat here is the *Hard Rock Cafe* opposite the Shell station. The food is good and the staff are friendly and eager to please. As a result, it's the most popular place in town. The Buffalo Lodge can also come up with a very tasty and filling meal.

The liveliest bar – and one where you can get good, tasty, cheap food – is the improbably named *New Dynamic Starlight Bar & Restaurant* which, nevertheless, does live up to its name. The inside rooms are painted with the most bizarre and florid representations of African flora and fauna. Unfortunately, there's no refrigeration so the beers are warm but the company makes up for it, and some of the characters who come in here have walked straight out of a Breugel canvas.

The Buffalo Lodge is equally popular and has two good bars but the one out at the back, although the best, is essentially a video lounge. The front bar is where the real drinkers come and it gets very lively here in the early afternoon. It's also where the 'Elastic Boys' come – local young entrepreneurs who sell handicrafts and can act as guides if you'd like to do some walking around the area. The Buffalo Lodge usually has a disco on Friday and Saturday nights.

Getting There & Away

There are Nissan minibuses which ply between Maralal and Nyahururu via Rumuruti on a daily basis, usually in the mornings. They cost KSh 200 to KSh 250 depending on the time of day and take four to five hours.

Between Maralal and Isiolo there are no direct buses or matatus. To get between the two towns you must first take a bus or matatu to Wamba and then change there. The cost between Maralal and Wamba is KSh 150 by bus and KSh 200 by matatu, and the journey takes about 3½ hours. Between Wamba and Isiolo there are many matatus and regular buses every day. The cost is KSh 100 and the journey takes about one hour.

The only other public transport out of Maralal is north to Baragoi by Land Rover. There's usually one each day or two – it depends on demand. The cost varies but, on average, it is KSh 300 and the journey takes about three hours. You need to make enquiries about this Land Rover in advance and, preferably, meet the driver. No-one ever seems to know when they're leaving.

All the buses and matatus leave from the dirt patch opposite the Shell station.

MATHEWS RANGE

North of Wamba, off the link road between Wamba and Baragoi via Parsaloi is the Mathews Range. Much of this area is thickly forested and supports rhino, elephant, lion, buffalo as well as many other animal species. The highest peak here rises to 2285m.

The whole area is very undeveloped and populated by Samburu tribespeople but the government is in the process of making it into a game sanctuary especially for the rhino. Some of the tribespeople are already employed to protect the rhino from poachers, and there's a game warden's centre.

A few km from this centre (where you have to report to on the way in to the sanctuary, though there are no charges as yet) is a camp site with no facilities other than river water and firewood. At one time it was a well set-up research centre, as the derelict huts indicate. It's a superb site and a genuine African bush experience. You are miles from the nearest village and elephant are quite likely to trundle through your camp in the middle of the night – lions too. During the day, traditionally dressed Samburu warriors will probably visit you to see if you need a guide (which you will if you want to see game or climb to the top of the range). Agree on a reasonable price beforehand, and remember you'll also have to pay for the one who stays behind to guard your vehicle.

Also, don't forget that the rules of hospitality will oblige you to provide them with a beer, soft drink or cup of tea, a few cigarettes and perhaps a snack when you get back to camp. They're extremely friendly people. One or two will be able to speak English (the nearest school is in Wamba) but most can converse in Swahili as well as Samburu.

Another accommodation possibility is the *Kitich Camp* (☎ (0176) 22053), on the banks of the Ngeng River, off the Wamba to Parsaloi road, about 40 km from Wamba. It's mainly set up as a luxury tented camp with all the facilities, and it costs KSh 3000 per person with full board. Children are half price. It's also possible to camp for KSh 200 per person, but the facilities for independent campers are minimal. You can also make bookings for this camp through Let's Go Travel (☎ (02) 340331) in Nairobi.

Getting There & Away

Getting to the camp site in the Matthews Range is not at all easy, even with 4WD. There are many different tracks going all over the place and you are going to have to stop many times to ask the way. Perhaps the best approach is from the Wamba to Parsaloi road. Just before Wamba you will get to a T-junction. Instead of going into Wamba, continue north and take the first obvious main track off to the right, several km after the junction. If there are tyre tracks in the sand – follow them. There are two missions down this track and both have vehicles. You will be able to ask the way at either one of them.

One of the mission stations is right next to a large river course which generally has some water flowing through it and which you have to ford. If you get lost, ask a local tribesman to come along and guide you but remember that you will have to drive him back to his *manyatta* after you have found the place. No-one in their right mind walks around in the bush after dark except if they are in large groups – the buffalo and elephant make it too dangerous. It might sound like a *tour de force* getting to this place but it's well worth it!

PARSALOI

Further north, Parsaloi (sometimes spelt Barsaloi) is a small scattered settlement with a few very basic shops but no petrol station. It has a large Catholic Mission which may or may not offer to accommodate you or allow you to camp. There are no lodges. The EC recently funded the construction of quite a large school.

There are two very rugged and steep-sided luggas at this point on the road, one on either side of the village, and you'll definitely need 4WD to negotiate them.

BARAGOI

Next up the road towards Loyangalani is Baragoi, a more substantial settlement full of tribespeople, a couple of very basic lodges, a new and better appointed hotel, and a few shops. There's also a derelict petrol station, but petrol can usually be bought here from a barrel – the local people will show you where to find it. If you're white, you'll probably be the only one in town and therefore an object of considerable curiosity. Quite a few people speak English around here. The town seems to get rain when everywhere else is dry so the surroundings are quite green.

Be careful not to take photographs in the town as it's supposedly forbidden and the local police are keen to enforce the rule and are not at all pleasant about it.

Places to Stay & Eat

If you ask at any of the restaurants in town they'll usually come up with accommodation, but it will be very basic – just a bed in a bare room with no toilet facilities. Some will also allow you to camp in their back yards.

If you have camping equipment, the best place to stay is the camp site at the water-pumping station about four km to the north of town. To get there, take the road north towards South Horr. After a while you'll go through a small gully and then, a little further on, across a usually dry river bed. Take the next track on the right-hand side and follow this for about one km. It will bring you to a concrete house and a fairly open patch of ground. This is the camp site and there's always someone around. Facilities include toilets and showers and your tent will be guarded by Samburu moran. It costs KSh 200 per person per night. Trips can be arranged to nearby manyattas for a small fee and you'll be allowed to take photographs.

There's a large hotel in town which costs KSh 350/650 for a clean single/double with shared bathroom. It's the first building you come to when arriving in Baragoi from the south.

For food in the town itself, the best is the *Wid-Wid Inn* run by Mrs Fatuma. It's on the top side of the main street and you'll know you've got the right place because all the staff wear garishly pink pinafores! She'll cook you up an absolutely delicious meat stew and chapatis for dinner as well as pancakes, omelettes and tea for breakfast. Prices are very reasonable.

There are also two bars in the town but only one of them – the *Sam Celia Joy Bar*, at the end of the main street going north – usually has beers. The other, on the back street, usually only has *konyagi* (local firewater) and other spirits.

SOUTH HORR

The next village is South Horr which is set in a beautiful lush canyon between the craggy peaks of Mt Nyiro (2752m) and Mt Porale (1990m) and Mt Supuko (2066m). It's a lively little place with a huge Catholic Mission, you'll find the missionaries won't sell you petrol.

Places to Stay & Eat

There are two small and very basic hotels on the main street – the *Mt Nyiro Hotel* and the *Good Tourist Hotel* – where you can find accommodation of sorts as well as a reasonably tasty meal of meat stew, mandazi and tea for around KSh 100 per person. The hotels will generally need up to two hours notice if you want to eat, but tea is usually immediately available. The price of accommodation is entirely negotiable.

For campers, the camp site which most people stay at is the Forestry HQ, off to the left as you enter town coming from the south (signposted). There's a river which runs past the site but, otherwise, it's completely undeveloped and there are no facilities but it costs just KSh 10 per person.

Other than this, there's Dick Hedges' (of Safari Camp Services, Nairobi) camp site some 15 km north of South Horr (the signpost reads 'Camping' but it's easy to miss) on the right-hand side as you head north. It's a pleasant site and facilities include showers and toilets. There's also plenty of firewood. The charge is KSh 150 per person per night.

Guards can be arranged to watch your tent if you want to eat in town.

South Horr also sports a very lively bar – the *Serima Bar* – on the main road heading north out of town. It's only open in the evening and seems to have a plentiful supply of beer, though there is no refrigeration.

LAKE TURKANA (THE JADE SEA)

Further north, the lushness of the Horr Valley gradually peters out until, finally, you reach the totally barren, shattered lava beds at the southern end of Lake Turkana. Top the ridge here and there it is in front of you – the Jade Sea. It's a breathtaking sight – vast and yet apparently totally barren. You'll see nothing living here except a few brave, stunted thorn trees. When you reach the lake shore, you'll know why – it's a soda lake and, at this end, highly saline. The northern end of the lake isn't anywhere near as saline because it's fed by the Omo River from Ethiopia (is that where the name of the washing powder came from!?). At this point, most people abandon whatever vehicle they're in and plunge into the lake. If you do this, watch out for crocodiles. They're quite partial to a meal of red meat as a change from Nile perch.

LOYANGALANI

A little further up the lake shore and you are in Loyangalani – Turkana 'city'. There is an airstrip, post office, fishing station, luxury lodge, two camp sites, a Catholic Mission (which may reluctantly sell petrol at up to three times the price in Nairobi) and all of it surrounded by the yurt-like, stick and doum-palm dwellings of the Turkana tribespeople. Taking photographs of people or their houses here will attract 'fees'.

If you're an independent traveller and want to visit the village where the El-Molo tribe live ask the safari-truck drivers at the camp sites if they have room for you and agree on a price. Organised safaris to this part of Kenya usually include a trip to the El-Molo village. They're one of the smallest tribes in Africa and quite different from the Turkana, though it seems their days are numbered as a distinct tribe. Tourism has

also wrought inevitable changes in their lifestyle and you may feel that the whole thing has been thoroughly commercialised. You'll also pay handsomely for taking photographs.

Trips to **Mt Kulal** and **Mt Porr** can be arranged at the Oasis Lodge but they're expensive. The Mt Kulal trip is a part-drive, part-walking trip up to the forest there, and Mt Porr is a well-known fossicking spot. A better thing to do would be to get in touch with Francis Langachar who is a very friendly young Turkana man and ask him to organise something similar for you. He speaks fluent English, and his father accompanied John Hillaby on his trek to Lake Turkana, recounted in *Journey to the Jade Sea*. If you do this trip by yourself in your own 4WD then allow two days and stay overnight. You can not do it in one day there and back from Loyangalani.

Places to Stay & Eat

Of the two camp sites, it's hard to favour one over the other, though only one has a restaurant and bar. Both are staffed by friendly people and theft doesn't appear to be a problem at either of them. The first you come to is *El-Molo Camp* (☎ (02) 724384), PO Box 34710, Nairobi. It has excellent facilities including good showers and toilets, a swimming pool (KSh 200 for day use), a large dining hall and bar (with cold beer at KSh 601) and electricity up to 9.30 pm at night (kerosene lanterns after that). Camping costs KSh 100 per person per night. There are also 20 self-contained bandas for rent which cost KSh 2000. Meals can be ordered at short notice in the dining room, whether you are staying on the site or not, but they take a long time to arrive: 1½ hours is normal. The food, on the other hand, is very good.

The other camp site adjacent to El-Molo is *Sunset Strip Camp*, which is run by Safari Camp Services in Nairobi. It costs KSh 100 per person per night. Facilities include showers and toilets and covered dining areas, but you cannot buy food and drink here and there's no electricity or swimming

Skull 1470

In the early 1970s, palaeontologist Richard Leakey made a significant fossil find on the shores of Lake Turkana. It was the discovery of a fossilised skull, which came to be known somewhat prosaically as 1470 (its Kenya Museum index number).

The almost complete, but fragmented, skull was thought to be from an early hominid. It was hoped that it would back up earlier fossil discoveries made by the Leakey Family in the Olduvai Gorge in Tanzania in the 1960s which suggested that the direct human ancestral line went back further than the 1½ million years that most people thought at the time.

The pieces of the skull were painstakingly fitted together – a demanding task in itself which kept two people fully occupied for over six weeks. The completed jigsaw confirmed what they had suspected: here was an evolutionary sophisticated hominid, named *Homo habilis*, which was a direct ancestor of *Homo sapiens*. It was 2½ million years old.

Since then *homo* fossil finds have been made which push the date back even further, but at the time the 1470 was a very important person! ■

pool. It's also dusty when the wind blows, which in this part of the world is most of the time.

Neither camp site has firewood so you will have to bring your own from further south.

Whichever place you camp at, beware of sudden storms which can descend from Mt Kulal. If there is a storm, stay with your tent otherwise it may not be there when you get back because of the wind, and neither will anything else.

Other than the camp sites there is the luxury *Oasis Lodge* (☎ (02) 751190; PO Box 34464, Nairobi) which has 25 double bungalows with private bathrooms and electricity (own generator) at US$100 per person with full board. It's a beautiful place with two spring-fed swimming pools, and ice-cold beer and meals are available. The only trouble is that if you are not staying there but you want to use the facilities (bar and swimming pools), it's going to cost you a KSh 600 entrance fee, and there are times when you won't even be allowed in.

For places to eat other than the El-Molo Camp, there are a couple of basic tea houses on the main street of Loyangalani and, if you ask around, you'll meet villagers who will cook up a meal of Nile perch for you in their homes.

Getting There & Away

There is no scheduled transport of any sort in or out of Loyangalani, so you need to be completely independent.

For the rich and/or famous, the Oasis Lodge can arrange a light plane to the local airstrip.

Going north or north-east from here involves crossing the Chalbi Desert towards North Horr. It's fine in the dry season but can be treacherous after rain.

You also need to stop at every village you come across and ask for directions otherwise it's very easy to go off on the wrong track and not even realise it until an hour or two later. Don't just assume that tyre tracks in the sand will lead you in the right direction, they won't necessarily.

NORTH HORR

North of Loyangalani the road loops over the lava beds to North Horr. There is a short cut across the desert through the village of Gus.

There are no lodges here and no petrol available but the people at the Catholic Mission are very friendly and may offer you somewhere to stay for the night if you are stuck. It's staffed by German and Dutch people.

MAIKONA

Next down the line is Maikona where there is a large village with basic shops (but no lodges) and a very friendly Catholic Mission and school, staffed by Italian people, where you will undoubtedly be offered a place to stay for the night. Please leave a donation before you go if you stay here. The mission usually has electricity and the Father goes into Marsabit once a fortnight in his Land Rover.

MARSABIT

South of Maikona is Marsabit, where you are back in relative civilisation. Here there are three petrol stations, a bank, post office, dry cleaners, shops, bars and lodges, buses and an airport. The main attraction here though is the Marsabit National Park & Reserve centred around Mt Marsabit (1702m).

The hills here are thickly forested and in stark contrast to the desert on all sides. Mist often envelopes them in the early morning and mosses hang from tree branches. The views from the telecommunications tower on the summit above town are magnificent in all directions. In fact, they're probably as spectacular as any of the views from Mt Kenya or Kilimanjaro.

The whole area is peppered with extinct volcanoes and volcanic craters (called *gofs*), some of which have a lake on the floor of the crater.

For information on Marsabit National Park & Reserve see the National Parks & Reserves chapter.

Places to Stay & Eat

If you have no camping equipment there's a good choice of lodges available in the town of Marsabit. One of the best is the *Marsabit Highway Hotel* which costs KSh 250 for a double with shower and toilet. It's a large place and very clean. The hotel has its own bar/restaurant which is open from 11 am to 2 pm and 5 pm to midnight. There is a disco on Friday and Saturday nights.

The cheapest place, though not such good value, is the *Hotel Al-Jazeera* which costs KSh 150 per person with communal showers. There's a bar and restaurant at the front.

For something vaguely mid-range, try the *Badassa Hotel*.

The best place for tea, mandazi and snacks is the *Bismillah Tea House* in front of the Catholic Technical School.

Marsabit Tribespeople

One of the most memorable sights in Marsabit is the tribespeople thronging the streets and roads into town. Most noticeable are the Rendille, dressed in skins with elaborate braided hairstyles and fantastic multicoloured beaded necklaces and bracelets. These people graze camels and, like the Samburu and Maasai, show little interest in adopting a more sedentary lifestyle, preferring to roam the deserts and only visiting the towns when necessary for trade. They are the major non-Muslim people in what is otherwise a largely Muslim area.

The other major tribes are the Boran and the Gabra, both pastoralists who graze cattle rather than camels. They're allied to the Galla peoples of Ethiopia from where they originated several hundred years ago. Many have abandoned their former transient life style and settled down to more sedentary activities. In the process, many have adopted Islam and the modes of dress of the Somalis with whom they trade and who have also migrated into the area. There are also quite a few Ethiopians in town as a result of that country's tragic and turbulent recent past. ■

Marsabit

To Maikona
& North Horr

To Moyale

To Isiolo
& Nairobi

0   250   500 m
Approximate Scale

To Karantin Summit
& Communications Tower

To Prison,
Park Gate (500m), &
Park Headquarters

To Lake Paradise
& Marsabit Lodge

Park Gate

1 Airstrip
2 Esso Petrol Station
3 Kenya Lodge
4 Marsabit Highway Hotel
5 Badassa Hotel
6 Bus Stand & Shell Petrol Station
7 Hotel Al-Jazeera
8 Post Office
9 Kenya Commercial Bank
10 Catholic Mission
11 District Commissioner's Office
12 Hospital
13 Camp Site

MOYALE

Straddling the Kenyan-Ethiopian border, Moyale lies some 250 km north of Marsabit across the Dida Galgalu Desert. It's a small town of sandy streets with bars, a post office, police station, several shops selling a reasonable selection of commodities, and a small market area. Unlike Marsabit, however, where most of the roofs these days are of corrugated iron, there are still a large number of traditionally built houses here. They have sturdy pole frames supporting mud and stick roofs which can be up to half a metre thick thus ensuring that the interiors stay cool even when the outside temperature is 30°C and more. There is a bank in Moyale which is open during normal banking hours.

The Ethiopian side of the town is somewhat larger and the facilities are much better, with sealed roads, electricity, a number of bars and small restaurants, a hotel, and a lively market area.

Places to Stay & Eat

There are only three places to stay on the Kenyan side of Moyale and they're all pretty basic but the best of the bunch is the *Hotel Medina* which costs KSh 100/160 a single/double. It's clean but, like the other hotels, there's no running water. The *Barissah Hotel*, which also has the town's only bar, is nowhere near as good but it does offer reasonable food, the usual fare being meat stew and chapatis.

If the above two are full, head for the *Bismillahi Boarding & Lodging* across from the Barissah and up behind the derelict Esso station. It's a family-run place and you'll find yourself sharing the same roof as the family. A bed here costs KSh 100 and facilities are absolutely minimal.

On the Ethiopian side of Moyale, a good place to stay is the *Hotel Awasha* near the checkpoint, which costs Birr 14 for a single room with running water and shower. The bank is nearby where you can change money legally – travellers' cheques are no problem but they may refuse to change cash. Another hotel recommended in the past is the *Bekele Molla Hotel* which is government owned and

Getting There & Away

Mwingi buses run from Marsabit south to Isiolo. They supposedly run a couple of times a week depending on demand and breakdowns – be prepared for a wait. The cost is KSh 350 and the trip takes six hours. If, for any reason, Mwingi buses are not running then you'll have to arrange a lift with a truck. Lifts on a truck are a standard US$10 (Marsabit to Isiolo).

All vehicles, including buses travelling between Marsabit and Isiolo or Marsabit and Moyale, must travel in convoy to minimise the danger of attack from shiftas.

about two km from the border. It has a very lively bar, especially in the evenings, and the rooms are clean and they have private bathrooms.

For somewhere to eat closer to the border, try the *Negussie Hotel*, which is up on the hill to the left after you have crossed the border. It offers the standard Ethiopian fare of wat (a fierce hot sauce) and injera (bread made of millet flour), and there's also a bar here.

Kenyan shillings are acceptable when paying for meals and drinks.

Getting There & Away

Trucks between Isiolo and Moyale take two days and cost KSh 600 to KSh 1000. See the Isiolo section in the Central Highlands chapter for details.

There are buses going north from the Ethiopian side of Moyale but they start early at around the break of dawn. See the Ethiopia information in the Land section of Getting There & Away.

A word of warning: When it's 1997 in Kenya, it's 1987 in Ethiopia, and when it's noon in Kenya, it's 6 am in Ethiopia (because, in Ethiopia, the day starts at 6 am, not midnight). This is very important when you're catching a bus otherwise you'll find yourself six hours out of kilter.

CROSSING TO ETHIOPIA

The border between the two countries is open, though you'll still need an Ethiopian visa to enter. After first clearing Kenyan immigration and customs you will arrive at the Ethiopian customs post where they will ask how much money (cash and travellers' cheques) you are bringing with you. This will be entered into your passport alongside your visa stamp. If you intend to use the street market for changing money inside the country (there's a 10% difference between the bank and street rates) then you'll have to declare less than you actually have. After customs, there's a two-km walk into town where you have to go to immigration for an entry stamp. It's a good idea to find a hotel along the way so you don't have to carry all your gear with you.

The North-East

Like the north of Kenya, the north-east up to the border with Somalia covers a vast area of desert and semidesert with very few centres of population and limited public transport possibilities. The main towns are Garissa and Wajir. Most of the area is relatively flat, yet it's through here that one of Kenya's major rivers, the Tana, flows. The river enters the ocean about halfway between Malindi and Lamu and is the territory of the Orma, Pokomo and Bajun tribes. Straddling this river just north of Garsen is the Tana River Primate Sanctuary which is included on a few safari companies' itineraries but otherwise difficult to get to.

The reserve was set up to protect the red colobus and the crested mangabey monkey both of which are endangered species. The other main river, the Ewaso Nyiro which flows through Samburu and Buffalo Springs National Reserves, eventually peters out into the Lorian Swamp, never quite reaching the ocean.

Few travellers come this way except those looking for trouble or a dangerous adventure. The area north and east of Garissa is now the domain of gun-toting shiftas from Somalia, so, if you come here, it helps if you speak Somali. When the UN/American troops went into Somalia in late 1992 to help in the distribution of food aid, many of those with guns sought shelter in Kenya where they could rustle cattle and create havoc with relative impunity. They're still doing it even though the UN has pulled out. It's not a safe area to venture into even if you're with one of the aid agencies. Although the Somali border is still open, the country itself is pretty much a no-go area for the average traveller.

Other than a visit to Meru National Park (see the National Parks & Reserves chapter), which would be worth it if security could be guaranteed, and the Tana River area, the north-east isn't a particularly interesting region even for desert fans, though Wajir, with its predominantly Somali population,

Beau Geste fort and market, would definitely have the edge over Garissa, itself quite a nondescript town hardly worth stopping for.

GARISSA

The only reason to come to Garissa is if you are taking the back route to Lamu direct from Nairobi via Garsen. There's nothing much to see or do here and the heat and humidity are unrelenting. However there is a bank (open normal hours), petrol stations, bars and a fair choice of places to stay. The only trouble with going via Garissa is getting there. As on the Malindi-Lamu run, most of the bus companies which used to service the town have pulled out because of the danger of shifta and the state of the road.

Places to Stay & Eat

Perhaps the best place to stay for the night is the *Safari Hotel* which offers relatively cheap, clean rooms with running water and reasonable food in the attached restaurant.

The *Garissa Government Guest House*, a short distance out of town, is somewhat more expensive for rooms with bathroom and breakfast, but is worth the extra money. If both are full then there's also the more basic *Nile Lodging* or the *Kenya Hotel & Lodging*, to check out.

Getting There & Away

Garissa Express operates a bus from the KBS depot Eastleigh, Nairobi, to Garissa on Monday, Wednesday, Friday and Sunday at 8 am. The depot is a 10-minute matatu ride from Ronald Ngala St (route No 9). The fare is KSh 350 and the journey takes about eight hours. It's a rough journey once you're off the tarmac so be prepared for discomfort.

LIBOI

Liboi, right on the Kenya-Somalia border, is a staging post in the *qat* (miraa) trade to Somalia. It has also become a major refugee centre following the civil war and famine in Somalia. It has only one place to stay, the *Cairo Hotel*, though depending on who you get a lift with (there are no buses) you might find accommodation in an NGO compound.

1 Safari Hotel
2 Barclays Bank
3 Post Office
4 Petrol Station
5 Nile Lodging
6 Mosque
7 Kenya Hotel & Lodging
8 Garissa Guest House

To Liboi & Wajir

Tana River

To Garsen & Nairobi

Garissa

0   100   200 m

NORTHERN KENYA

On the other hand, why you would come here unless you're into disaster tourism, a dangerous adventure, or work for an NGO, is anybody's guess. Basically no-one in their right mind attempts to enter Somalia overland any longer. Those who must go there fly from either Nairobi or Mombasa to either Kismayu or Mogadishu. As this edition was being researched, there was still no discernible central government in Somalia and fighting between the various factions had broken out yet again. Despite all this, Somalis must have their *qat* so there must be some intrepid characters to risk their lives coming through overland.

GARSEN

This is another nondescript town near Lamu. There's absolutely no reason to stay here if you're on the only remaining bus line between Malindi and Lamu (the Faza Express) but, if you're hitching between Garissa and Lamu (there are no longer any buses between the two), it may be necessary. There are several basic hotels to choose from. The best is the *3-in-1 Lodging & Restaurant* which is fairly clean and has its own restaurant.

National Parks & Reserves

Kenya's national parks and reserves rate among the best in Africa. Obviously the tremendous variety of birds and mammals is the main attraction, and the more popular parks such as Masai Mara Game Reserve and Amboseli National Park see huge numbers of visitors – from the budget campers to the hundreds-of-dollars-a-day Hilton hoppers. In the peak season (from January to February) on a game drive, you can observe at close quarters the daily habits of the prolific Nissan Urvan. Other smaller parks, such as Saiwa Swamp National Park, near Kitale in the country's western highlands, would be lucky to see a handful of visitors a day at any time of year.

In addition to the protection of wildlife, some parks have been created to preserve the landscape itself, and these too can be exciting and rewarding places to visit – places

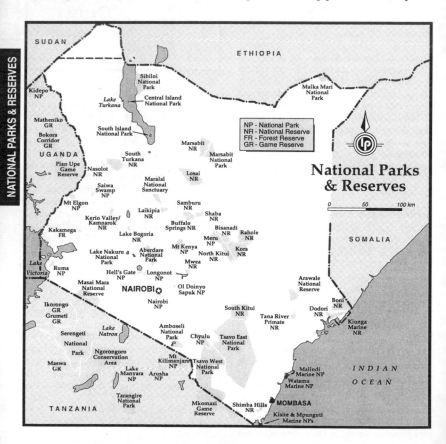

National Parks & Reserves

NP - National Park
NR - National Reserve
FR - Forest Reserve
GR - Game Reserve

REGION	FEATURES
Nairobi	
Nairobi National Park	Gazelle, oryx, lion, zebra, giraffe, buffalo, cheetah and leopard abound; great chance to spot a rhino.
The Rift Valley	
Hell's Gate National Park	Zebra, Thomson's gazelle, antelope, baboon, the occasional cheetah and leopard, ostriches and lammergeyer.
Lake Bogoria National Park	Thomson's gazelle, greater kudu and klipspringer; flamingos abound at the lakes southern end; hot springs and geysers.
Lake Nakuru National Park	'The world's greatest ornithological spectacle' is home to flamingos and pelicans; also waterbuck and black rhino.
Longonot National Park	The dormant volcano Longonot (2886m) offers much for hill climbers and view seekers.
The Central Highlands	
Aberdare National Park	A variety of fauna and flora and diverse scenery punctuated by the dramatic Gura Falls; best visited during the dry season.
Meru National Park	A luxuriant jungle of forest, swamp and tall grasses with a wide variety of herbivores and their predators.
Mt Kenya National Park	Africa's second highest mountain (5199m) offers great trekking; best visited January to late February or late August to September.
Western Kenya	
Kakamega Forest Reserve	This virgin tropical rainforest boasts the red-tailed monkey and black-and-white colobus monkey as well as over 330 bird species.
Masai Mara National Reserve	Annual wildebeest migration from July to October; spectacular Esoit Olooloo Escarpment and an astonishing amount of game.
Mt Elgon National Park	Elephants, bizarre giant groundsel and giant lobelia plants and Suam hot springs; best visited from December to January.
Saiwa Swamp National Park	Swamp area is the habitat of the sitatunga antelope and also home to the black-and-white colobus monkey.
Northern Kenya	
Marsabit National Park & Reserve	Wide variety of larger mammals including lion, leopard, cheetah, elephant, rhino, wart hog, Grevy's zebra and reticulated giraffe.
Samburu & Buffalo Springs National Reserves	Guaranteed close-up sightings of elephants, reticulated giraffe and various species of smaller gazelle.
Shaba National Reserve	Wide variety of wildlife including elephant, buffalo, cheetah, leopard, lion, dik-dik, wart hog, Grevy's zebra and crocodile.
Tana River Primate National Reserve	Reserve for a number of endangered monkey species, including the red colobus and crested mangabey monkeys.
The Coast & Southern Kenya	
Amboseli National Park	Spectacular backdrop of Mt Kilimanjaro; great chance to spot black rhino; large elephant herds.
Shimba Hills National Reserve	Beautiful forest setting; the rare sable antelope is seen only in this reserve; also leopard and elephant.
Tsavo National Park	Kenya's largest, split into west and east; west features Mzima Springs, Chaimu Crater and Ngulia Rhino Sanctuary; east features Kanderi Swamp, Aruba Dam and large elephant herds.

NATIONAL PARKS & RESERVES

such as Mt Kenya, Mt Elgon, Hell's Gate, Mt Longonot and the Kakamega Forest are all worth investigating.

Marine life is also in abundance and the marine national parks of Malindi and Watamu off the central coast both offer excellent diving possibilities. Shimoni and Wasini islands in the extreme south offer even better opportunities but are much less accessible and developed.

What probably helps to make Kenyan parks such a draw card for the budget traveller is that the competition among safari companies for the traveller's dollar is so fierce that a safari of at least a few days is within the reach of the vast majority of travellers. For those at the other end of the scale the competition is equally brisk and there are lodges and tented camps within the major parks which have superb facilities and are a real experience – if you can afford them.

Information

Entry Fees Entry fees to national parks are controlled by the Kenya Wildlife Services, while national reserves, such as Masai Mara, are administered by the local council.

Kenya Wildlife Services recently introduced a differential pricing structure for the various national parks which, it is hoped, will encourage visitation to less popular parks and take some of the strain off the major parks. The fees cover visitors for a 24-hour period, so if you enter a park at 3 pm, you have until 3 pm the following day before having to leave or pay again.

The parks now come into one of four categories, and you are charged accordingly.

The entry fee to Masai Mara Game Reserve is the same as for the Category A parks.

Books & Maps If you are driving your own vehicle it's a good idea to equip yourself with maps of the parks before you set out. The best are all published by the Survey of Kenya and obtainable either from the Public Map Office or bookshops in Nairobi. The ones you will need are SK 87 *Amboseli National Park*, SK 86 *Masai Mara Game Reserve*, SK 82 *Tsavo East National Park*, and SK 78 *Tsavo West National Park*.

Macmillan also publishes some pretty decent maps to a number of parks, including Masai Mara, Amboseli and Tsavo.

If you're interested in walking in the national parks of Mt Kenya, Mt Elgon and Aberdare, Lonely Planet's *Trekking in East Africa* has details.

Accommodation

Camping out in the bush is, of course, the authentic way of experiencing an African safari. There's nothing quite like having just a sheet of canvas between you and what you would normally see only on the residents' side of a zoo. Full-on contact with the bush along with its potential dangers and rewards is surely what you are looking for. Anything more luxurious than this is going to dilute the experience and remove the immediacy of it all.

There are some beautifully conceived and constructed game lodges and, if you have the

Park Entry Prices			
Category	Parks	Nonresident Adults/children	Resident Adults/children
A	Aberdares, Amboseli, Lake Nakuru	US$27/10	KSh 250/50
B	Tsavo East & West	US$23/8	KSh 200/50
C	Nairobi, Shimba Hills, Meru	US$20/5	KSh 150/50
D	All other parks	US$15/5	KSh 100/50
Others	Marine Parks	US$5/2	KSh 100/50
	Mountaineering	US$10/5	KSh 100/50

NATIONAL PARKS & RESERVES

Animal Spotting

When you visit Kenya's parks and reserves, you'll be spending a lot of time craning necks and keeping watchful eyes out for the animals and birds you've come so far to see. There are a few telltale signs to note, as well as a few things you can do, to maximise your chances. Most of them are just common sense, but it's amazing the number of people who go belting around noisily expecting everything to come to them:

- Drive slowly and, wherever possible, quietly, keeping eyes trained not only on the ground ahead but also to the side and in the branches above.
- Go in search in the early morning or the late afternoon. In the more popular parks, such as Amboseli and Masai Mara, the animals are actually changing their normal hunting habits to fit in with the tourists, so at midday, when most people are safely back in their lodges stuffing their faces, the carnivores are out hunting in the hope that they may be able to do the same thing – in peace.
- Vultures circling are not necessarily an indication of a kill below, but if they are gathering in trees and seem to be waiting you can reasonably assume they are waiting their turn for a go at the carcass.
- In wooded country, agitated and noisy monkeys or baboons are often a sign that there's a big cat (probably a leopard) around.

money, it's worth spending a night or two at one or another of them, though it's probably true to say they are mainly for those who prefer to keep the bush at arm's length and a glass of ice-cold beer within arm's reach.

Certainly the way in which some game lodges attract wildlife to their door is somewhat contrived. Hanging up shanks of meat in a tree which a 'resident' leopard comes to feed off 10 minutes later – despite the spotlights – is hardly the essence of Africa. It's only fair to add, however, that not all game lodges go in for this sort of circus.

The Parks

Kenya's national parks and reserves are listed in this chapter in alphabetical order.

ABERDARE NATIONAL PARK

This park essentially encloses the moorland and high forest of the 60-km-long Kinangop plateau along with an eastern salient reaching down to the lower slopes in the vicinity of Nyeri. Only rarely does this park feature in the itineraries of safari companies and it's even less visited by individual travellers. There are various reasons for this. The main one is perhaps the weather. As on Mt Kenya, rain can be expected at any time and when it arrives, it's heavy. Roads turn into mud slides and 4WD is absolutely essential. The park is often closed during the wet season as a result.

Another drawback (though the wild game would no doubt describe it as a plus) is the difficulty of seeing animals because of the dense forest. This is not savanna like Amboseli and Masai Mara so you have to take your time and stay a few nights, which brings us to the third drawback – finding a place to stay. Though there are three camp sites within the park, facilities are minimal and you're going to need a good tent and warm sleeping gear. Add to this the fact that there's no public transport whatsoever, hitching is virtually impossible and that, as elsewhere, walking isn't permitted without special permission. That essentially puts the Aberdares

Aberdare
National Park

out of reach of anyone without their own transport. And, lastly, unless you're camping, the only other accommodation possibilities are two very expensive lodges, The Ark and Treetops, which you are not allowed to drive to in your own vehicle. You must make advance reservations for both and be driven there in the lodges' transport.

In the dry season it may be possible to walk over the high moorland between the four main peaks if the weather is favourable but you can't do this without permission from the officials at the park headquarters at Mweiga, north of Nyeri (☎ (0171) 55024).

They will provide an armed ranger (obligatory) to guide you. If this is what you want to do then it might be best to first contact the Kenya Mountain Club in Nairobi before setting out, as they may be planning such a trip.

These sorts of difficulties and/or the expense involved put off most independent travellers but if you're determined to go then the rewards can well justify the effort.

The park does offer a variety of fauna, flora and scenery which you won't find elsewhere except, perhaps, on Mt Kenya. There are also the dramatic **Gura Falls** which drop a full 300m, thick forest, alpine moorland

and a slim chance of seeing a bongo, black leopard, elephant or rhino. There are also hundreds of species of birds. The major plus about this park is that you'll never feel part of the safari-bus gravy train as you can often do in Masai Mara, Amboseli or Nairobi national parks.

Currently there is a major fund-raising effort going on among the local community to raise enough cash to build an electric fence around the park perimeter. Such a fence is needed for two reasons: to keep the game within the park; and to stop the encroachment on the forest by local villagers. In countries with high populations and growth rates, demand for land is high. For this reason national parks and reserves are always a contentious issue among local people, and this is no exception.

Entry to the park costs US$27 per day (US$10 for children).

Game Drives

If you can't afford the overnight charges at the lodges there is a somewhat cheaper way of visiting the park and that is to go on a game drive organised by the Outspan Hotel in Nyeri. You can do this into the eastern park area for US$35 per person (minimum two people) for the day excluding park entry fees. You can also rent self-drive vehicles from the Outspan to explore the whole park for US$10 per day plus vehicle entry fee.

Game drives organised by the Aberdare Country Club are yet another option, although these aren't particularly cheap either. A game drive in the salient costs US$138 for the whole vehicle for half a day, or US$264 for a full day shared between however many there are of you. A surcharge of 20% is made if you're not staying at either the Country Club or The Ark. The Country Club also offers a half-day walking safari in its own private 500-hectare wildlife sanctuary for US$46 per person including brunch (plus 20% surcharge if you are not a guest). The sanctuary abounds with Thompson's and Grant's gazelle, zebra and giraffe and you may even catch sight of a leopard.

Places to Stay

If you wish to camp in the park, reservations have to be made at the park headquarters at Mweiga (☎ 24 in Mweiga), about 12 km north of Nyeri. The charges are US$8 per person (US$2 for children).

Both of the lodges in this park are built beside water holes, and animals – especially elephant and buffalo – are lured to them by salt which is spread below the viewing platforms each day. This is obviously a contrived way of getting the animals to turn up but it pulls in the well-heeled punters and they, in turn, keep Lonrho, Block Hotels, Kodak and Nikon in business. What it doesn't do is anything positive to the immediate environment. Elephants eat a prodigious amount of herbage each day and trample down even more. Buffalo aren't exactly light on the hoof either. The two combined make sure that the area in front of the viewing platforms resembles a matatu stand which, in turn, makes the smaller and more timid animals reluctant to approach because of the lack of cover.

On the other hand, *Treetops* isn't exactly a 'luxury' lodge with its trestle tables, creaking floorboards, shoe-box sized rooms and shared bathroom facilities, though it does have that yuppie appeal of knowing that you've stayed under the same roof as various crowned heads of Europe and presidents of state – there are even faded mug-shots of the *nomenclatura* on the walls.

Full board (including transfer from Nyeri but excluding park entry fees) at Treetops depends on the time of year you stay there. In the high season (16 December to 3 January and 1 April to 8 April) it costs US$124/248 for singles/doubles whereas in the low season (9 April to 30 June) it costs US$62/ 124 for the same thing. During the rest of the year, the prices are in-between the two. Kenyan residents are entitled to substantial discounts on the above prices. Children under seven years old are not admitted and those over seven years old are charged at full adult rates. You must book in advance through Block Hotels (☎ (02) 540780; fax 543810) in

Nairobi. Having booked, you then turn up at the Outspan Hotel in Nyeri by 12.30 pm for transfer to the park.

The Ark is somewhat better appointed than Treetops and is further into the park but it costs much more. Full board here, including transfer from Mweiga but excluding park entry fees, costs US$270/321 for singles/doubles in the high seasons and US$147/173 in the low seasons. As at Treetops, children under seven years old are not admitted and those over seven years pay the full adult rate. You must book in advance through Lonrho Hotels Kenya (☎ (02) 216940; fax 216796) in Nairobi. Having booked you must turn up at the Aberdare Country Club at Mweiga, 12 km north of Nyeri, on the appointed day and you'll be driven to the lodge.

AMBOSELI NATIONAL PARK

Amboseli is the next most popular park after Masai Mara, mainly because of the spectacular backdrop of Africa's highest peak, Mt Kilimanjaro, which broods on the southern boundary of the park.

At 392 sq km Amboseli is not a large park, and it certainly doesn't have the profusion of game which you find in Masai Mara but the game here is easy to spot. The western section of the park is the dry bed of Lake Amboseli, and although it is occasionally flooded in the wet season, for the majority of the time it is a dry, dusty, shimmering expanse.

Probably the best reason for visiting Amboseli is that you stand the best chance of spotting a black rhino. Amboseli also has huge herds of elephant, and to see a herd of them making their way sedately across the grassy plains, with Kilimanjaro in the background, may be a real African cliche but is an experience which certainly leaves a lasting impression.

Other animals which you are likely to see here include buffalo, lion, gazelle, cheetah, wildebeest, hyena, jackal, wart hog, Masai giraffe, zebra and baboon.

Amboseli more than any other park has suffered greatly from the number of minibuses which drive through each day. It has a much drier climate than Masai Mara and so

for much of the year is a real dust bowl. If you are driving through the park, stick to the defined tracks, and hopefully others will follow suit.

Most visitors approach Amboseli through **Namanga**, the main border post between Kenya and Tanzania. If you're stuck, there's accommodation at the *Namanga Hotel* among others. The petrol station is a good place to ask around for lifts.

Outside the town's petrol station there are a couple of shops selling Maasai crafts. The first prices asked are totally ridiculous, so bargain fiercely.

Entry to the park costs US$27 per person (US$10 children) per day.

Activities

Microlight Flights For an aerial view of the mountain and the plains, take a microlight flight from the Kilimanjaro Buffalo Lodge, east of the park (see Places to Stay). Flights are made on demand, and cost KSh 3500 per person.

Places to Stay – bottom end

Once again the only budget option is a *camp site*. This one is right on the southern boundary of the park. The only facilities are a couple of long-drop toilets, and a kiosk where you can buy warm beer and sodas and pay the camping fees (US$8 per person). The water supply here is extremely unreliable so bring some water with you. Elephants are a real problem in this camp site at night and practically everyone who has stayed here has an elephant story to relate – there are some hilarious (and not so hilarious) ones doing the rounds. At night make sure all food is locked away inside your vehicle. *Don't* keep food in your tent as elephants have a habit of investigating, as do baboons during the day when you're out on a game drive.

Places to Stay – top end

There are a number of options within the park, and also outside the park to the east, on the road to Tsavo. These latter places provide a good alternative to those within the park,

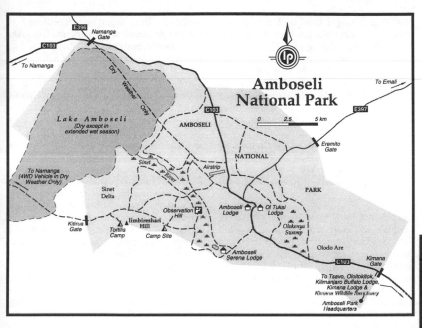

Amboseli
National Park

NATIONAL PARKS & RESERVES

as you don't have to pay the daily park entry fees.

In the Park The two lodges in the centre of the park are strategically situated for views of Kilimanjaro. The *Amboseli Lodge* is run by the Kilimanjaro Safari Club in Nairobi (☎ (02) 227136; fax 219982). The lodge consists of a number of comfortable cottages dotted around an expansive lawn and garden, with sweeping views of Kilimanjaro (weather permitting, of course). Facilities include a swimming pool, and airy central building with dining room and bar. Rooms cost US$70 per person for full board during the low season. High-season rates are US$168/210.

Close by is the new *Ol Tukai Lodge*, belonging to Block Hotels (☎ (02) 540780; fax 540821). This brand new lodge has a beautiful central building with polished floors and lots of timber. Like the Amboseli Lodge, the guest cottages are spread around

a lawn, and two of them have wheelchair access. This is a very comfortable hotel, complete with swimming pool. Rooms cost US$107/165 in the high season.

Close to the southern perimeter of the park is the *Amboseli Serena Lodge* (☎ (02) 711077; fax 725184 in Nairobi), a sensitively designed and constructed lodge which blends in well with the landscape. The nearby Enkongo Narok Swamp ensures constant bird and animal activity. Room charges are US$55/110 with full board during the low season, rising to US$128/166 in the high season.

Also on the southern edge of the park, at the western end, is the secluded *Tortilis Camp* (☎ (0154) 22551; fax 22553), beautifully situated with views across the plains to Kilimanjaro, which looms very large from here. The open-air, makuti-roofed lounge and dining areas are in an elevated position to make the most of the views, while the permanent tents, each with verandah, makuti shelter and wood-panelled bathroom, are nestled in among a stand of *Acacia tortilis* trees. The whole place has been designed to be eco-friendly, making use of solar power for water heating, and ensuring that no wood is used for fires. The food is excellent, and reflects the Kenyan owners' Italian background. As this place is actually on the national park boundary, they can offer activities such as guided nature walks, which are not possible within the park. There is no access to the camp from outside the national park. Accommodation rates are US$100/200 for full board in the low season, rising to US$170/264 in the high season. This price includes taxes.

Outside the Park Some 30 or so km east of the park, and close to the Kimana Wildlife Sanctuary (see next section) is the *Kilimanjaro Buffalo Lodge*, operated by the Kilimanjaro Safari Club in Nairobi (☎ (02) 227136; fax 219982). Although showing its age somewhat, this lodge is still a good prospect, and it's likely that the rooms will have been renovated by now. There are excellent views of the mountain, and the Hemingway Bar gives good views back towards the Chyulu Hills. Room rates are US$70/140 in the low season, up to US$160/ 200 in the high season. There's a swimming pool, and a demonstration of Maasai dance every evening.

Close by, and on the road which connects Emali on the Nairobi–Mombasa road with Oloitokitok on the Tanzanian border, is the *Kimana Lodge*, also owned by the Kilimanjaro Safari Club. The lodge has little in the way of views, although most evenings a leopard comes up to a bait out the front. Rates are US$50/100 in the low season, US$152/190 in the high.

Very close to the settlement of Oloitokitok, and accessible by matatu from Emali, is *Kibo Slope Cottages* (☎ (0302) 22091; fax 22427). The rates here are US$20/35 for bed and breakfast, dropping to KSh 600/1000 in the low season.

Getting There & Away
Air Air Kenya Aviation has daily flights between Wilson airport (Nairobi) and Amboseli. These depart from Nairobi at 7.30 am and Amboseli at 8.15 am; the trip takes about an hour and costs US$70 one way. The return flight leaves Amboseli at 8.30 am.

Car & 4WD The usual approach to Amboseli is through Namanga, 165 km south of Nairobi on the A104, and the last fuel stop before the park. The road is in excellent condition from Nairobi to Namanga, however, the 75-km dirt road from Namanga to the Namanga Gate is fiercely corrugated at times if the grader hasn't been over it for a while. The whole trip from Nairobi takes around four hours.

It's also possible to enter Amboseli from the east via Tsavo. This road is not in bad condition, but there have been bandit attacks in the past, so all vehicles must travel in a convoy, accompanied by armed policemen. The convoys leave the Kimana Gate of Amboseli at 8.30 and 10.30 am, and 2.30 pm. Most of the vehicles are tourist minibuses, and as the drivers belt along at great speed, the 'convoy' gets so spread out that any protection which might be offered by the police (who travel in the front and rear vehicle) is negligible. Fortunately, incidents are very rare (just one in the last five years). The trip to Chyulu Gate and Kilaguni Lodge in Tsavo East takes about three hours.

AROUND AMBOSELI
Kimana Wildlife Sanctuary
About 30 km east of Amboseli, close to the road which connects Amboseli to Tsavo, is this 40-hectare wildlife sanctuary. It is owned and run by the local Maasai people, and is an important project in giving them some control over their own land. Any communities living on the fringes of the national parks tend to get a pretty rough deal, not only because valuable land is set aside for wild animals, but also that these wild animals then come and encroach upon the land outside the park, often in a destructive manner. The Maasai here decided that a tourism venture was the best way to make the best of things, and so with the help of USAID and the Kenya Wildlife Service, the sanctuary was established, and opened in 1996. While it is

still in its early stages, and the rangers are still learning their craft, they are very enthusiastic and helpful, and it's well worth a visit – projects like this which empower the local people are all too rare.

There are graded tracks through the sanctuary, and wildlife viewing is probably as good – if not better – than within Amboseli itself. There's also a hippo pool.

Entry to the sanctuary cost US$10 per person, plus KSh 100 per vehicle.

Places to Stay There are three guarded *camp sites* within the sanctuary, where you can camp for KSh 150.

HELL'S GATE NATIONAL PARK

This park is one of only two lowland parks in the country which you can walk through without a ranger/guide (the other is Saiwa Swamp near Kitale). The looming cliffs and the Hell's Gate gorge itself are spectacular, and are home to a wide variety of bird and animal life. On a walk through the park it is possible to see zebra, Thomson's gazelle, antelope, baboon and even the occasional cheetah or leopard. Ostriches and the rare lammergeyer are also sighted on occasion.

The usual access point is through the main **Elsa Gate**, two km from Moi South Lake Rd. From here the road takes you past **Fischer's Tower**, a 25m-high column of volcanic rock named after Gustav Fischer, a German explorer who reached here in 1883. He had been commissioned by the Hamburg Geographical Society to find a route from Mombasa to Lake Victoria but this was about as far as he got, largely because he was unable to get on good terms with hostile Maasai.

The road then continues through the steep-sided gorge and emerges at the **Ol Karia Geothermal Station** – a power project which utilises one of the hottest sources in the world. You can see the plumes of steam rising into the air from many of the viewpoints in the park. South-east of here, you'll see Central Tower, another column of volcanic rock similar to Fischer's Tower but much larger. From the geothermal plant the track heads back to the lake shore via the Ol Karia Gate, and emerges in the vicinity of Oserian farm (now a large supplier of cut flowers, fruit and vegetables to the European market) and Elsamere.

The entire walk from the lake road turn-off via Elsa Gate and Ol Karia Gate to the lake shore is 22 km. The distance between the two

NATIONAL PARKS & RESERVES

Hell's Gate National Park

gates via the lake road is nine km. If you intend walking the whole way through the park, allow a full day, and take along some drinking water and something to eat. The only drinking water available in the park is at the camp sites.

Entry to the park costs US$15 (US$5 for children), and camping costs US$6 per person.

If you don't want to walk through the park it may be possible to arrange a trip by car if you ask around at Fisherman's Camp.

KAKAMEGA FOREST RESERVE

The Kakamega Forest Reserve is a superb slab of virgin tropical rainforest in the heart of an intensively cultivated agricultural area. It is home to a huge variety of birds and animals and is well worth the minimal effort required to get to it.

The Forest Department maintains a beautiful four-room rest house in the south of the reserve at Isecheno, as well as a large nursery for propagating trees and shrubs used for ceremonial occasions around the country and for planting in the area. The workers are very friendly and it's no problem to get shown around. In the northern part of the

reserve at Buyangu the Kenya Wildlife Services maintains a camp site and bandas.

For the visitor the choice is which area to visit – the Buyangu (northern) area is the more easily accessible by public transport and only involves a walk of two km; to Isecheno you may have to walk a lot further.

The forest itself comprises a number of habitats, but is generally very dense and is the home of a number of primate species, such as the red-tailed monkey, black and white colobus monkey and the blue monkey; and more than 330 species of birds have been recorded.

Information

As this is not a national park, there are no entry fees. The Kenya Indigenous Forest Conservation Program (KIFCON) publishes an excellent little guide to the forest (KSh 400), and this is available from the East African Wildlife Society Gift Shop in the Hilton Hotel Arcade in Nairobi.

Walking Trails

The best way to appreciate the forest here is to walk, and there are two trail systems which radiate out from the two forest stations. The trails are signposted and marked with coloured flashes at main junctions, so getting lost is not a major problem. To enhance your appreciation of the forest, it's not a bad idea to hire a guide. Staff at either of the forest stations should be able to arrange for somebody to accompany you.

The trails vary in length from one to seven km, the longest being the Isiukhu Trail up to the insignificant Isiukhu Falls.

Places to Stay & Eat

Isecheno The *Forest Rest House* is a superb place to put your feet up for a few days. It's an elevated wooden building with a verandah which looks directly on to the seemingly impenetrable Kakamega Forest. There are only four double rooms but they all have a bathroom and toilet. Blankets are supplied but you need to have your own sleeping bag or sheet. The rooms cost KSh 100 per person plus you can also camp for KSh 50. If the rest house is full when you arrive, and you have your own sleeping gear, it is usually possible to sleep on the verandah for next to nothing. If you want to be sure of a room, book in advance through the Forest Ranger, PO Box 88, Kakamega.

The only problem here is food. Basically you need to bring your own and preferably something to cook it on, although it is possible to cook on a fire. There's a small kiosk which sells beer, tea and soft drinks (sodas) and also cooks basic meals at lunch time. Evening meals are cooked on request (beans or corn and rice is about the limit), but you need to make sure they know you are coming as the kiosk closes at 6.30 pm. You can get basic meals and supplies from a small group of dukas about two km back towards Shinyalu.

Three km further along the road from Isecheno is the *Rondo Retreat*, a former sawmiller's residence built in the 1920s. It is owned by the church group and offers very comfortable top-end accommodation either in the main house or in bungalows with their own bathrooms. The charges are KSh 2500 per person for room only, or KSh 4400 for full board. Advance bookings can be made during business hours (☎ (0331) 41345, 30268).

Buyangu The KWS operates the *Udo's Bandas & Campsite*, named after Udo Savalli, a well-known ornithologist. There are seven bandas here each with two beds, a communal cooking and dining shelter, pit toilets and basic showers. While you need to bring your own food, it should be possible to find someone to cook it for you if need be. The bandas are a bargain at KSh 250 per person, and this is also the charge for camping. Advance booking can be made through the District Warden, KWS, PO Box 879, Kakamega (☎ (0331) 20425).

Getting There & Away
Isecheno The Forest Rest House lies about 12 km east of the A1 Kisumu–Kitale road, about 30 km north of Kisumu. Access is possible either from Kakamega village on the main road when coming from the north, or from Khayaga also on the main road when coming from the south. From both places dirt roads lead east to the small market village of Shinyalu, from where it's a further five km to the rest house, signposted to the left. There are matatus from Kakamega to Shinyalu, and even the occasional one from Khayaga to Shinyalu.

If you want to walk – and it is beautiful walking country – it's about seven km from Khayaga to Shinyalu, or about 10 km from Kakamega to Shinyalu. These roads become extremely treacherous after rain and you may prefer to walk when you see how the vehicles slip all over the road. There's very little traffic along either of the roads but you may get a lift with the occasional tractor or Forest Department vehicle. Whatever means you employ to get there, allow half a day from Kitale or Kisumu. From the turn-off to the rest house the dirt road continues on to Kapsabet, so you could also come from that direction but it is a long walk if you can't get a lift.

Buyangu It's somewhat easier to reach the northern part of the reserve as local matatus from Kakamega town run along the access road. The turn-off is well signposted about eight km north of Kakamega town on the Kitale road, and from there it's about 10 km to the forest turn-off, and this is where the matatus drop you, leaving a two-km walk.

LAKE BOGORIA NATIONAL RESERVE
Since Lake Nakuru dried up considerably in 1995 and continued to do so during 1996, most of the flamingos were forced to migrate to other lakes. Many of them came to Bogoria where the estimated population is currently around one million, most of them at the southern end of the lake. This situation could, however, change over as little as one year if Lake Nakuru fills up again. Should that happen, many of the flamingos will probably return there.

The other attractions of Lake Bogoria are the **hot springs** and **geysers** about three-quarters of the way along the lake going south. They're not comparable with those at Rotorua in New Zealand but if you've never seen geysers before then this is the place. The springs are boiling hot so don't put your bare foot or hand into them unless you want to nurse scalds for the next week.

The land to the west of the lake is a hot and relatively barren wilderness of rocks and scrub, and animals are few and far between though you'll almost always catch sight of small herds of Thomson's gazelle and you may be lucky to see a greater kudu, impala or klipspringer. The eastern side of the lake is dominated by the sheer face of the north-eastern extremities of the Aberdares.

Lake Bogoria is a very peaceful place not much visited by tourists so you'll probably have the park to yourself – though this may change if the flamingos stay on. As Bogoria is a national park there's an entry fee of US$15 per person (US$5 for children and students) plus KSh 200 per vehicle.

Places to Stay

There are two camp sites at the southern end of the lake – *Acacia* and *Riverside* – but there are no facilities and the lake water is totally unpalatable. Bring all water and food with you if you are intending to stay at either site. Otherwise, the camp sites are shady and very pleasant though the road to them deteriorates rapidly beyond the hot springs. Camping charges are the usual US$8 per person for nonresidents or KSh 150 for residents. Children and students pay US$2 and KSh 50, respectively.

If you don't want to camp there's an excellent cheap place to stay right outside the northern entry gate (the Loboi gate). This is the new *Papyrus Inn* (☎ 1 Loboi through the operator) which offers bed and breakfast at KSh 400/600 for singles/doubles with shared bathroom facilities. For large groups these prices are negotiable and there's a special student rate of KSh 200 per bed. It's well run and the staff are very friendly, plus there's a restaurant and bar.

Two km before the same entry gate is the huge *Lake Bogoria Hotel* (☎ (037) 42696). This top-end place is very pleasant and set in well-tended gardens, but few people seem to stay here. Rooms cost the equivalent of US$105/130 a single/double with half board and US$120/160 with full board. There's a swimming pool and the place is open to nonresidents for lunch (KSh 380) and dinner (KSh 420).

The only other feasible place to stay in this area is at the *Marigat Inn* in Marigat town. It's signposted on the main road but to get to it you have to walk or drive about 1.5 km through the town and turn left after the mosque just where the tarmac ends. You'll find it behind a row of small shops. It's a pleasant place with friendly staff and the rooms are arranged around a shady court-yard. Singles with shared bathroom facilities cost KSh 250 and doubles/triples with attached bathrooms are KSh 400/600. The hotel has its own bar and restaurant.

Getting There & Away

There are two entrance gates to Lake Bogoria – one from the south (Mogotio) and another from the north (Loboi). You'll see the sign-post for the Mogotio gate on the B4 about 38 km past Nakuru heading north but, if you take it, you'll probably regret it! Most of this road is good smooth dust or gravel but there is about five km of it leading down to the southern park entrance which will certainly rip apart any tyres and destroy any vehicle driven at more than a few km/h. Without 4WD you'd be wasting your time. These razor-sharp lava beds don't end once you reach the park gate but continue for at least as far on the other side. In addition, signpost-ing along the route from the turn-off is almost nonexistent.

A far better entry to the park is from the Loboi gate just a few km before you reach Marigat on the B4. It's also signposted. From the turn-off, it's 20 km to the actual park entry gate along a good, sealed road.

Whichever gate you use, you're going to need your own vehicle since hitching is well-nigh impossible. Very few people visit Bogoria and those who do are usually in tourist minibuses which won't pick you up unless you're booked with them. It *may* be

Rhino Rescue

Many of Africa's animals are threatened by the loss of their habitat due to human overpopulation or by poachers, and it's the poor rhino which is in the greatest danger. The rhino's horn, its trademark, causes the problem – plenty of people covet it and this only serves to push the price up as it becomes increasingly rare.

The stark statistics are horrific. In 1970, it is estimated that Kenya had about 20,000 black rhinos. By 1985, that number had dwindled to just 425, and rhinos were so few and so scattered that it was becoming increasingly difficult for a lady rhino to meet a compatible gentleman rhino, with the object of creating baby rhinos. With this huge fall in numbers, the price of rhino horns on the black market had soared from US$35 per kg to over US$30,000 per kg – and is still rising. Elsewhere in Africa, the fall in rhino numbers has been equally dramatic.

Rhino horn is a popular ingredient in many Chinese traditional medicines and we have all heard of the supposed effects of rhino horn on the libido. But the major market for rhino horn is the Yemen, where Djambia daggers with rhino horn handles are worth over US$15,000. These fantastic prices are inspiring ruthless tactics from poachers who tote modern weapons and are as likely to shoot as run when confronted by rangers. In 1990, their brazenness reached new heights when they shot not only Kenya's only five white rhinos (in Meru National Park) but first shot the armed guards in order to do so.

The only solution is felt to be the creation of small parks where rhinos can be carefully watched and protected. Funded by Rhino Rescue, an organisation set up in 1986 specifically to save the rhinos, the Nakuru National Park was selected as the first manageable rhino sanctuary. The park is now protected by a 74 km electric fence with guard posts at 15-km intervals. The construction involved over 11,000 fence posts and 880 km of high-tensile wire. An initial group of 19 rhinos was established and there are plans to increase this number, possibly to as many as 60.

Additional sanctuaries are planned but saving the rhino isn't going to come cheap. Donations can be sent to Rhino Rescue, PO Box 1, Saxmundham, Suffolk, IP17 3JT, UK. ∎

NATIONAL PARKS & RESERVES

possible to walk into the park since there are no large predators living here (with the possible exception of the occasional leopard) but don't count on it. Officially, you're supposed to tour the park in a vehicle.

If you're driving your own vehicle, there's an Esso petrol station on the main road at Marigat.

LAKE NAKURU NATIONAL PARK

Created in 1961, the park has since been considerably increased in size and now covers an area of some 200 sq km. Like most of the other rift valley lakes, it is a shallow soda lake. Some years ago the level of the lake rose and this resulted in a mass migration of the flamingos to other rift valley lakes, principally Bogoria, Magadi and Natron. What had been dubbed 'the world's greatest ornithological spectacle' suddenly wasn't anywhere near as spectacular. Since then the level of the lake has been decreasing steadily, and has now reached the point where it is almost dry during the dry season, and the flamingos have once again sought happy hunting grounds – mainly Lake Bogoria. While the situation does change from year to year, it seems that Lake Nakuru is no longer the ornithologists' paradise it once was. Hopefully the situation will change.

The lake is very shallow and the level fluctuates by up to four metres annually. When the water is low the soda crystallises out along the shoreline as a blinding white band of powder which is going to severely test your skills as a photographer. Lake Nakuru last dried up in the late 1950s and, at that time, soda dust storms and dust devils whipped up by high winds made life unbearable for people in the town and surrounding area. In the dry season you'll see these dust devils (like tiny tornadoes) whipping soda up into the air as they course along the shoreline.

Since the park also has areas of grassland, bush, forest and rocky cliffs there are many other animals to be seen apart from birds. One species you'll see plenty of are wart hogs with their amusing way of running with their tails erect. Right by the water you'll come across waterbuck and buffalo, while further into the bush are Thomson's gazelle and reedbuck – there's even the occasional leopard. Around the cliffs you may catch sight of hyrax and birds of prey. There's even a small herd of hippo which generally lives along the northern shore of the lake.

The park is also surrounded by a high electric fence, which keeps in a number of black rhino which were introduced some years ago.

The national park entrance is about six km from the centre of Nakuru. Entry costs US$27 per person (US$10 for children) plus KSh 200 per vehicle. As in most national parks, you must be in a vehicle. Walking is not permitted so you will either have to hitch a ride with other tourists, rent your own vehicle or go on a tour. You can, however, get out of your vehicle on the lake shore and at certain viewpoints.

Warning Don't drive too close to the water's edge, the mud is very soft! Take your cue from the tracks of other vehicles.

Places to Stay – bottom end

There is a good camp site, known as the *Backpackers' Camp Site* just inside the park gate. Fresh water is available and there are a couple of pit toilets, but you need to bring all your own food. Make sure tents are securely zipped up when you're away from them otherwise the vervet monkeys or baboons will steal everything inside them. If you are backpacking and trying to hitch a ride, the rangers at the gate will let you camp here without paying the park entry until you are successful. Camping here costs US$15 per person (US$2 for children).

A km or so further into the park is the *Njoro Camp Site* and this is the one to head for if you have a vehicle. It's a beautiful grassy site under acacia trees and there's firewood, water on tap and the usual pit toilets. The charge here is also US$15 per person.

If you have no camping equipment there's the very basic *Florida Day & Night Club* about half a km before the entrance gate.

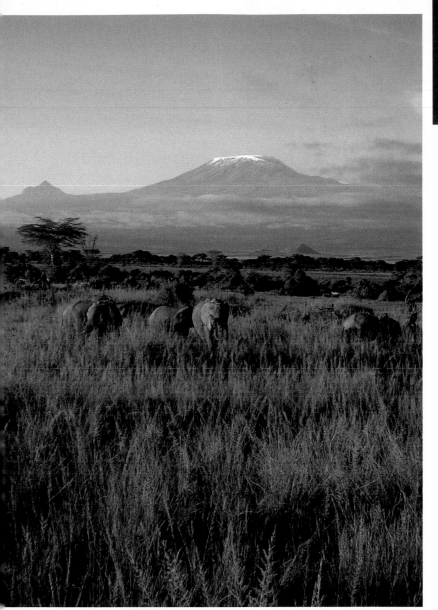

DAVID ELSE

Amboseli is one of Kenya's most popular national parks, mainly because of the spectacular backdrop of Africa's highest peak, Mt Kilimanjaro, which broods on the southern boundary of the park.

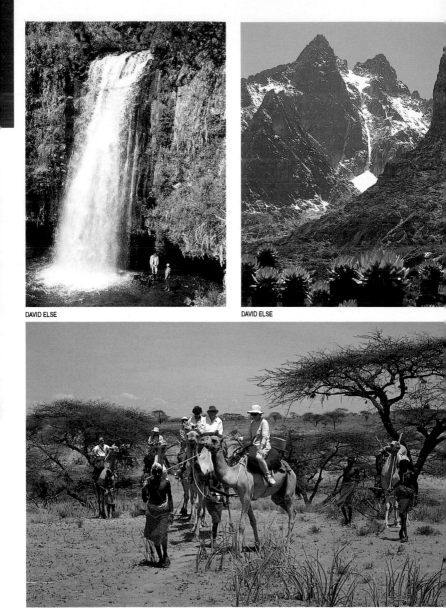

DAVID ELSE

DAVID ELSE

DAVID ELSE

They're both hard to get to but worth the effort: the dramatic Gura Falls in Aberdare National Park and the gleaming, snow-capped peaks of Mt Kenya. Camel safaris also rate as an unforgettable experience.

Lake Nakuru
National Park

NATIONAL PARKS & RESERVES

Places to Stay – top end

The first place you come to down the eastern access road of the park is Sarova Hotels' *Sarova Lion Hill Lodge* (☎ (02) 333248; fax 211472). It has all the usual facilities including a swimming pool and open-air bar/restaurant area. High-season prices with full board are US$135/165 for singles/doubles. In the low season, prices drop to US$55/110. There are also more expensive suites. It's a well thought-out site but there are only occasional views of the lake through the thorn trees.

Almost three km beyond the southern end of the lake is the *Lake Nakuru Lodge* (☎ (02) 224998; fax 230962). Like the Sarova Lion Hill, it has all the usual facilities and consists of a series of shingle-roofed cottages. Low season prices for full board are US$50/100; in the high season it's US$135/160. Children aged three to 12 are charged 50%.

Bear in mind that if you are staying at either of these lodges you must also add the US$27 per day park entry fee.

Actually outside the park, between Nakuru town and the national park, is the *Sundowner Lodge* (☎ (02) 226778; fax 230962), which may be more convenient if you have your own transport. Rooms here cost KSh 800/1500 for bed and breakfast.

Getting There & Away

If you don't have your own vehicle, the only way into the park from Nakuru is by taxi (unless you can persuade a tourist with a car to take you in). A taxi costs around KSh 1000 for three hours, though you'll have to bargain hard for this. Alternatively, contact Birds Paradise Tours (☎ (037) 211143), upstairs behind the Bethany Bookshop on Kenyatta Ave. They organise two-hour trips to the lake for KSh 1000 per person, plus park entry fees.

If you're driving, there's access from three points: the main gate; Lanet, just a few km along the Nairobi road; and Ndarit Gate near the southern end of Lake Nakuru.

LONGONOT NATIONAL PARK

Hill climbers and view seekers should not miss the opportunity of climbing to the rim of dormant Longonot (2886m), a fairly young volcano which still retains the typical shape of these mountains, although it's far from being a perfect conical shape.

As this is a national park there is an entrance fee of US$15. The scramble up to the rim takes about 45 minutes from the parking area, and to do the circuit of the rim a further 2½ to three hours is needed. If you're feeling game there's a track leading down inside the crater to the bottom, though it's worth hiring a local guide before you set off.

Places to Stay

There's no accommodation in the park or immediate vicinity, but it is possible to camp at the ranger station at the foot of the mountain. If you are just on a day trip you can leave your gear at the Longonot railway station or the police station.

Getting There & Away

If you don't have your own transport it's a long walk from Longonot railway station just off the old road to Naivasha. It's about seven km to the trail head, and even if you have your own car it's wise to pay someone to keep an eye on it, or leave it at the Longonot railway station.

MARSABIT NATIONAL PARK & RESERVE

The Marsabit National Park & Reserve is home to a wide variety of the larger mammals including lion, leopard, cheetah, elephant, rhino, buffalo, wart hog, Grevy's zebra, the reticulated giraffe, hyena, Grant's gazelle, oryx, dik-dik and greater kudu among others. Because the area is thickly forested, however, you won't see too much game unless you spend quite some time here and, preferably, camp at **Lake Paradise**. The lake, which occupies much of the crater floor of Gof Sokorte Guda, is appropriately named. It's an enchanting place and right out in the bush. Entry to the park, which is open from 6 am to 7.15 pm, costs US$15 per person (US$5 for students and children) plus KSh 200 for a vehicle (less than six seats) or KSh 500 (six to 12 seats).

The Survey of Kenya's map, *Marsabit*

National Park & Reserve (SK 84) is worth buying if you are touring this park.

Places to Stay & Eat

Few camp sites in Kenya would rival the one at Lake Paradise. There are no facilities (except lake water and firewood) so bring everything with you. A ranger has to be present when you camp here so it costs more than an ordinary site (US$10 per person for non-residents or KSh 200 per person for residents and only one group at a time is allowed to camp here) but you can arrange all this at the park entrance gate. There's also another good camp site next to the entrance gate (water and plenty of firewood) but the so-called showers are a joke. You could die of thirst waiting for enough water to wet the back of your ears here. Camping at this site costs US$8 per person.

There's also the *Marsabit Lodge* (☎ (0183) 2044), a luxury safari lodge overlooking a lake in another gof, Sokorte Dika. This costs

US$94/120 for a single/double with full board in the high season with triples at US$140. In the low season, the full-board rates are US$54/70 for singles/doubles and KSh 80 for triples. Bookings should be made with Msafiri Inns (☎ (02) 229751; fax 227815) in Nairobi.

For information on getting there and away see the Marsabit section in the Northern Kenya chapter.

MASAI MARA NATIONAL RESERVE

The Mara (as it's often abbreviated to) is the most popular game park in Kenya. Virtually every person who visits Kenya goes to Masai Mara, and with good reason as this is the Kenyan section of the wildly evocative Serengeti Plains and the wildlife abounds. This is also traditionally the land of the Maasai, but these people have been displaced in favour of the animals.

The Mara is a 320-sq-km slab of open grassland dotted with the distinctive flat-topped acacia trees tucked away in the south-west corner of the country. It is watered by the tree-lined Mara River and its tributary the Talek River. The western border of the park is the spectacular Esoit Oloololo (Siria) Escarpment and it's at this edge of the park that the concentrations of game are the highest. It must also be said that it's the most difficult area of the park to get around in as the swampy ground becomes impassable after heavy rain. Conversely, the concentrations of tourist and minibuses are highest at the eastern end of the park around the Oloolaimutiek Gate and Talek Gate as it's these areas which are the most accessible by road from Nairobi.

Fauna

Wherever you go in the Mara, however, the one certain thing is that you'll see an astonishing amount of game, often in the one place at the one time. Of the big cats, lion are found in large prides everywhere and it's not at all uncommon to see them hunting. Cheetah and leopard are harder to spot but are still fairly common. Elephant, buffalo, zebra and hippo also exist in large numbers within the

NATIONAL PARKS & RESERVES

Masai Mara
National Reserve

reserve. Of the antelopes, the black-striped Thomson's gazelle (Tommys) and the larger Grant's gazelle are found in huge numbers, while the impala, topi and Coke's hartebeest and of course the wildebeest are also profuse. Rhino do exist in the park but are rarely seen. Other common animals include the Masai giraffe, baboon (especially around the lodges), wart hog, spotted hyena and grey (or side-striped) jackal.

The highlight of the Mara is no doubt the annual wildebeest migration when literally millions of these ungainly beasts move north from the Serengeti in July and August in search of the lush grass, before turning south again around October. It is truly a staggering experience to be in the reserve at that time – and one which is likely to have a profound effect on your own feeling of insignificance.

Information

Entry to the reserve is US$27 per person per day (US$10 for children). Vehicle entry is KSh 200, or KSh 500 if there are more than six seats.

Maasai Village

Just outside the Oloolaimutiek Gate there's a Maasai village which has opened itself up as a tourist attraction. For around KSh 350 per person you can walk around and take as many pictures as you like. As you might imagine, it's a real zoo when you have a couple of dozen tourists poking their video cameras and long lenses everywhere. If you can manage to visit when there are no other tourists it's not too bad and you can at least talk to the villagers. At other times you'll have the crap hassled out of you to buy trinkets and bead work.

Ballooning

If you can afford the US$360 price tag, balloon safaris are definitely the way to go. It's a superb experience. For more details see the Safaris section in the Getting Around chapter.

Narok

Narok is the main access point to the Mara and is a small provincial town a few hours drive west of Nairobi. As most vehicles stop to refuel here (it's the last place to do so before the park itself) the town is chock-full with souvenir shops and hawkers. There are branches of Barclays and the Kenya Commercial banks, a post office, and a range of budget and mid-range hotels. For accommodation, try the *Spear Hotel* which has reasonable rooms with attached bathrooms at KSh 250/350.

A very popular place to grab a snack here is *Kim's Dishes* diagonally opposite the Agip station. It offers cheap fast-food items such as chips, sausages etc. There are also several basic but busy bars on the main street as well as *Pussy's Bar* across the river from the main street about one km from the centre.

There are frequent buses and matatus buzzing between Nairobi and Narok which park outside Kim's Dishes. The road, although bitumen, is currently in a diabolical state,

NATIONAL PARKS & RESERVES

National Reserve Status

Masai Mara doesn't have national park status. The fundamental difference between a national park and a national reserve is that in a national reserve people (in this case the Maasai) can graze their animals and can also shoot animals if they are attacked. In a national park, however, the entire area is set aside exclusively for the wildlife and the natural environment. Where it also differs from a national park is that it is administered by the local council – in this case, Narok – rather than by Kenya Wildlife Services. Unfortunately the Narok council seems unwilling to reinvest in the park, despite the enormous revenues it receives from the gate takings. Consequently the tracks within the park are in a shocking condition, and there is very little policing of vehicles straying from the defined trails, and so you find minibuses driving over the grasslands at will, with informal tracks crisscrossing all over the place. If this situation is allowed to continue the Mara is going to become seriously degraded. ∎

although in 1996 the contract was awarded for its resurfacing, so things should be better.

Places to Stay – bottom end

There is no budget accommodation within the reserve, so it's camp or pay high prices at the lodges and tented camps. It's possible to camp just outside the park at any of the gates for KSh 150 per person. There are no facilities but you can usually get water from the rangers.

The Maasai run the *Oloolaimutiek Campsite* between the gate of the same name and the Mara Sopa Lodge at the eastern extremity of the park. This place is very popular with the budget safari outfits and is usually pretty lively. For KSh 200 per person the Maasai provide firewood and an askari at night. The water supply here is very limited and if you need any water you'll have to buy it from the Maasai. The staff canteen of the nearby Mara Sopa Lodge is usually a lively place and you can get cheap meals and warm beer.

There are official camp sites within the reserve along the Talek River by the Talek Gate on the north-eastern border of the park, and just outside the reserve on the banks of the Mara River near the Oloololo Gate. The only problem with using these sites is that they are none too secure – baboons and thieves can both take their toll on your gear. The cost at the sites is a hefty US$15 per person.

Places to Stay – top end

The lodges and tented camps are all pitched at the top end of the market and should all be booked in advance. There's been a wild proliferation of these places over the years, and you now have the choice of a dozen or more.

Prices for accommodation with full board vary between about US$50 and US$250 per person per night. The lodges generally consist of separate bandas with their own bathrooms, while the tented camps are often almost identical, the difference being that the 'rooms' have canvas walls protected from the elements by an open-sided makuti-roofed structure. It's certainly stretching things to call them tents but it seems to satisfy the desire for a

token of authenticity among those with money to burn.

The *Mara Sopa Lodge* (☎ (02) 336088) by Oloolaimutiek Gate is a fairly modern place and has a commanding view. It's been attractively designed and built. The rates for singles/doubles with full board are US$78/120 in the low season, rising to US$162/216 in the high season.

The *Keekorok Lodge* is one of the Block Hotels (☎ (02) 540780; fax 543810) and is an older but well-maintained lodge on a grassy plain. Singles/doubles with full board cost US$47/94 in the low season, US$119/183 in the high season. Keekorok is one of the two lodges which operates balloon flights.

The *Mara Sarova Lodge* is part of the Sarova Hotels chain (☎ (02) 333248; fax 211472) and is not far from the Sekenani Gate and has the works, including a swimming pool. The room rates here with full board are US$55/110 a single/double in the low season, US$150/185 in the high season.

Along the northern banks of the Talek River are the *Fig Tree Camp* (☎ (02) 221439; fax 332170), and the *Mara Intrepids Club* (☎ (02) 338084; fax 217278). The Fig Tree Camp is attractively designed, has a swimming pool, and is approached across a wooden bridge from the car park on the opposite bank. It's a tented camp and has singles/doubles for US$125/170 with full board in the high season, US$50/100 in the low season. This is the other lodge from which you can take a balloon safari. It's wise to book them in advance at the Nairobi office though you can also do this at the camp. Game drives are available for US$35, game walks cost US$15, or you can take a horse safari for US$30. The Mara Intrepids Club has 30 tents and is considerably more expensive at US$223/304 for singles/doubles with full board but the price does include game drives. Low season prices of US$100/160 are a relative bargain. The views over the river from the bar are excellent, as are the sunset views over the plains.

In the centre of the reserve is the *Mara Serena Lodge* (☎ (02) 711077; fax 718103; e-mail 62578620@eln.attmail.com) on a superb site overlooking the Mara River. It blends in beautifully with the surrounding countryside and was built to resemble a modern Maasai village. Singles/doubles with full board cost US$120/160, dropping to US$50/100 in the low season.

More expensive again is the *Mara Safari Club* (☎ (02) 216940; fax 216796), part of the Lonrho chain of hotels. It is actually outside the reserve, so you don't pay the high park entry fees for just staying here. The camp is built on a bend in the Mara River, and the main building is cantilevered right out over the bank. Singles/doubles with full board cost US$275/372 in the high season and US$198/263 in the low season, and all prices include three game drives per day.

In the northern section of the park is another group of tented camps including the *Governor's Camp* (☎ (02) 331871; fax 726427) and *Little Governor's Camp* (owned by the same people). These are both beautiful little places where service is very personalised and excellent. Singles/doubles with full board plus game drives at either place costs US$260/390.

In this same area, and just outside the northern boundary, is the *Kichwa Tembo Camp* (☎ (02) 750298; fax 746826), which has spectacular savanna views. Rates are US$140/190 in the high season, dropping to US$60/120 in the low season.

Other accommodation outside the park north of Oloololo Gate includes the *Mara River Camp* (☎ (02) 331191) at US$60/104 in the low season, US$125/175 in the high season, including game drives and walks.

About 15 km from Sekenani Gate is another tented lodge, *Siana Springs* (☎ (02) 750298; fax 746826). The 'cottages' are dotted around a beautiful green clearing with shady trees, sweeping lawns and flowers. There's an open bar and dining room and a roaring log fire at night. Although it's not actually in the reserve there's a lot of game around the camp itself. There is a baited hide nearby and you have a good chance of seeing leopards. Dawn walks and night-time spotlight game drives are also organised from the

camp. The cost is US$140/190 in the low season, rising to US$205/280.

Also on the north-eastern boundary of the reserve is the *Sekenani Camp* (☎ (02) 333285; fax 228875). This is a small place, with just 15 tents, and is well placed to make the most of the views. The cost is US$58/116 in the low season, and US$167/225 in the high season, for full board including game drives.

The *Oseur Tented Camp* (☎ (02) 545648; fax 545649) is another in this area, and costs US$120/170 in the low season, rising to US$196/280 in the high season.

Even if you can't afford to stay in one of these camps, they are usually great places to drop in for a cleansing ale and perhaps a snack although, not surprisingly, prices are relatively high.

The Mara Sarova Camp, Keekorok Lodge and Mara Serena Lodge all sell petrol and will usually part with it to non-guests, though prices are higher than in Narok or Nairobi.

Getting There & Away

Air Air Kenya Aviation has twice-daily flights between Nairobi's Wilson airport and Masai Mara, departing from Nairobi at 10 am and 3 pm, and from the Mara at 11 am and 4 pm. The one-way fare is US$87, but if you are not on a package and being met by your hosts, to these you have to add the cost of chartering a vehicle in the park to collect you from the airstrip.

Car & 4WD The Mara is not a place you come to without transport. There is no public transport to or within the park, and even if there was there's certainly no way you could do a game drive in a matatu. If you are patient and persistent you should be able to hitch a ride with other tourists, in the high season at least, but get yourself to Narok first.

From Narok onwards the bitumen runs out and public transport dries up. It's almost 100 km from here to any of the park gates.

It's also possible to approach the reserve from Kisii and the west along reasonably well-maintained dirt roads. You can get closer to the park by public transport but there are far fewer tourist vehicles to hitch a ride with. Matatus run as far as Kilgoris directly south of Kisii, or Suna on the main A1 route close to Isebania on the Tanzanian border.

MERU NATIONAL PARK

On the lowland plains east of the town of Meru, the Meru National Park is a complete contrast to the more northerly reserves of Samburu, Buffalo Springs and Shaba where open bush is the norm. In Meru, abundant rainfall and numerous permanent streams flowing down from the Mt Kenya massif support a luxuriant jungle of forest, swamp and tall grasses which, in turn, provide fodder and shelter to a wide variety of herbivores and their predators. As in other parks, such as Marsabit, where the vegetation is dense, the wildlife is not so easily sighted so you need to spend a few days here if you're to fully appreciate what the park has to offer.

Unfortunately this area was one of the worst hit by poachers and shifta, and so there is not the abundance of wildlife that you find in other parks. With some difficulty, elephant, lion and cheetah can all be seen. Buffalo and giraffe are more common, and eland and oryx are the main antelope to be seen. Monkeys, crocodiles and a plethora of bird species are common in the dense vegetation alongside the watercourses.

Meru National Park was also the home of Kenya's only herd of white rhinos which were imported from the Umfolozi Game Reserve in South Africa. Jealously guarded 24 hours a day by rangers to protect them from poachers, these huge animals were quite unlike their more cantankerous cousins, the black rhino, in being remarkably docile and willing to allow their keepers to herd them around the camp sites and park headquarters area during the day and pen them up at night. Sadly, that's all gone now. Heavily armed poachers shot the lot of them and, for good measure, killed their keepers too.

The park is also famous for being Joy and George Adamson's former base where they raised orphaned lion and leopard cubs until they were old enough to be returned to the wild. Both paid for their efforts with their

lives – Joy many years ago when she was murdered in Meru park by poachers, and George in 1989 when he too met the same fate along with two of his assistants in the nearby Kora National Reserve.

Security in the park has been beefed up since George Adamson was murdered but there is still a small risk of encountering poachers and bandits here so you need to bear this in mind, especially if you're driving your own vehicle. It's true to say, however, that the chances of running into bandits is just as great in Masai Mara or Tsavo as it is in Meru. The one major plus about Meru National Park is that you're unlikely to come across another safari vehicle anywhere in the park except at the lodges.

The tracks through the park are well maintained and signposted though it's a good idea to have a copy of the Survey of Kenya's *Meru National Park* map with you.

Entry to the park costs US$20 (US$10 for students and US$5 for children) plus KSh 150 for a vehicle (less than six seats) and KSh 500 (six to 10 seats). Camping is the standard US$80.

Places to Stay

There are several public camp sites in the park, but the one at junction 12 is the only one operating. There's running water and an askari in attendance.

The only functioning lodge is the *Meru Mulika Lodge* (☎ (0164) 20000) which has all the usual facilities of a luxury lodge including a swimming pool and where singles/doubles with full board cost US$94/120 with triples at US$140, except from 1 April to 30 June when it drops to US$54/70 with triples at US$80. Bookings should be made through Msafiri Inns (☎ (02) 229751; fax 227815) in Nairobi.

Getting There & Away

Getting to Meru National Park by public transport is a problem. There are no buses or matatus which will take you either to the lodges or the camp sites and park headquarters. Likewise, attempting to hitchhike is basically a waste of time as so few vehicles

Meru National Park

To Garba Tula

To Meru, Nanyuki
& Nairobi

Murera Gate

Kinna Plains

Bisanadi Plains

Bisanadi Gate

Murera Plains

Leopard Rock Lodge

Meru Mulika Lodge

Mulika Plains

Kindani Plains

Rojewero Plains

Park Headquarters

Rhino Plains

Bwatherongi Plains

Kiolu Plains

Mughwango Plains

Pippa's Camp

Punguru Plains

MERU   NATIONAL   PARK

Ura Gate

Kampi ya Game

Kampi ya Kiko

Kampi ya Elsa

To Meru, Embu
& Nairobi

Kampi ya Teziwa

0   5   10 km

come into the park and those that do are mainly tour groups so they won't pick you up. Quite a few safari companies include Meru National Park on their itineraries but they are all liable to cancel visits at short notice if there has been any trouble with shiftas in the park.

MT ELGON NATIONAL PARK

Mt Elgon sits astride the Kenya-Uganda border and, while it offers similar trekking possibilities to Mt Kenya, its location makes it a far less popular goal. The lower altitude also means that conditions are not so cold,

although rain can be more frequent here than on Mt Kenya.

The mountain is an extinct volcano and the national park extends from the lower slopes right up to the border. The highest peak is Wagagai (4321m) which is actually on the far side of the crater in Uganda. The highest peak on the Kenyan side is Koito-boss. The Mt Elgon range is the fourth-highest in East Africa after Mt Kilimanjaro Mt Kenya and the Ruwenzoris. There are warm springs in the crater itself, the floor of which is around 3500m above sea level.

The mountain's biggest attraction is the

The African elephant is the world's largest living land mammal.

forests are the habitat of the impressive black-and-white colobus monkey along with many other species of birds and animals. Those most commonly sighted include buffalo, bushbuck, giant forest hog and Sykes monkey.

Elgon can be a wet place at any time of the year, but the driest months seem to be December, January and February. As well as waterproof gear you are going to need warm clothes as it gets cold up here at night.

Access to the 170-sq-km national park is now permitted without a vehicle. Entry costs US$10 per person per day. A ranger will escort you to the camp site (which is one km inside the park) and on any walks you may want to do on the lower forested slopes – such as to the caves – for which a small fee may be payable.

elephants, renowned the world over for their predilection for salt, the major source of which is in the caves on the mountain slopes. The elephants are such keen excavators that some have gone so far as to claim that the elephants are totally responsible for the caves! Sadly, the numbers of these saline-loving creatures has declined over the years, mainly due to incursions by poachers from the Ugandan side. There are three caves open to visitors – Kitum, Chepnyali and Mackingeny. Kitum is the one which you are most likely to see elephants in, while Mackingeny is the most spectacular. Obviously a good torch (flashlight) is essential if you want to explore the caves.

Kitum Cave has been associated with the fatal Ebola virus, following the deaths of two people who visited the cave. However, other people have safely visited the cave since. Research about Ebola is inconclusive, but there may be some risk of contracting it in Kitum Cave so the cave is probably best avoided at this point.

A less obvious attraction is the range of vegetation found on the mountain. Starting with rainforest at the base, the vegetation changes as you ascend to bamboo jungle and finally alpine moorland with the bizarre giant groundsel and giant lobelia plants. The lower

Walks

If you want to walk on the mountains, the most popular route is from **Kimilili**, a small village 36 km south of Kitale on the main A1 road to Webuye and Kisumu. There's basic accommodation here, and matatus run the 12 km to **Kapsakwany**, from where it's a five km walk to Kaberua Forest Station. There's a Department of Forestry office and a Kenya Wildlife Services office at Kaberua. From there it's a further 20 km to the now abandoned Chepkitale Forest Station, and another seven km past this station to a tumbledown mountain hut. You will need a tent and all your own gear for camping.

At the time of writing, the Kimili route was closed to hikers and trekkers, due to an outbreak of cross-border cattle-rustling and general banditry in the area. It was also because the Mt Elgon park authorities are trying to encourage hikers inside the park, rather than outside it. This is expected to change in 1997 and hikers should be allowed in again. For the latest situation phone the Kenyan Wildlife Services headquarters in Nairobi or Mt Elgon National Park (ask for the assistant warden, or chief tourism officer).

From the hut it takes around four hours to reach the lake known as Lower Elgon Tarn, and from here it's a further one-hour walk up a faintly marked trail (occasional cairns and white blazes) to Lower Elgon peak.

The pass at the foot of Koitoboss peak and the **Suam hot springs** are several hours of tough walking around the crater rim to the right (north-east) and once here you are in the national park. The options are to return the same way, or via the third route, known as the Masara route, which goes to the small village of **Masara** on the northern slopes of the mountain, a trek of about 25 km.

As park authorities are now trying to promote walks, hikes and treks in the park, those without vehicles may be allowed to trek from the park entrance, Chorlim Gate, to Koitoboss Peak (requiring one or two overnight camps on the way), or may even be able to arrange a lift part way in a park patrol vehicle.

Places to Stay

There are no lodges in the park itself but there is a beautiful camp site with good facilities close to the Chorlim Gate which you'll be allowed to walk to. You will need to bring all your own food, camping and cooking equipment with you as there's none for hire and there is only one small shop (called the canteen) which sells beer and a few basics for the park staff and their families.

About one km before the Chorlim Gate is the *Mt Elgon Lodge* (PO Box 7 Enderbess, Kitale), one of the Msafiri Inns chain of hotels (☎ (02) 330820; fax 227815). Comfortable rooms with full board cost KSh 2750/4250 a single/double. The hotel has a bar and restaurant.

Getting There & Away

To get to the village of Enderbess (the nearest place to Mt Elgon National Park), there are normal matatus for KSh 40 or Nissan matatus for KSh 60 from Kitale. Part of this road is good tarmac but there are also some horrific sections with huge potholes. The turn-off for Mt Elgon National Park (Chorlim Gate) is several km before Enderbess on the left-hand side (clearly signposted). If you're hitching, you'll need to get to the turn-off but it's still a long way into the park from there and

there's very little transport. Rangers' vehicles and support trucks do come along the road at least once a day but you could be waiting half the day. Although the road into the park is a good gravel road, in the wet season the only way in is to have your own 4WD.

MT KENYA NATIONAL PARK

Although a distinctly separate massif from the Aberdares, Mt Kenya also forms part of the central highlands. Africa's second-highest mountain at 5199m, its gleaming and eroded snow-covered peaks can be seen for miles until the late-morning clouds obscure the view. Its lower slopes, like those of the Aberdares, are intensively cultivated by the Kikuyu and the closely related Embu and Meru peoples, along with the descendants of the white settlers who grow mainly wheat on the grassy and largely treeless plains on the northern side.

So vast is this mountain that it's not hard to understand why the Kikuyu deified it, why their houses are built with the doors facing the peak and why it was probably never scaled until the arrival of European explorers. It's the seat of *Ghai*, the Kikuyu god. And Ghai is still very much alive despite the fact that it's every traveller's dream to get to the top and take home with them a memory which money cannot buy. You *must* climb to the top of this mountain. It's a superb experience. But take it steady otherwise Ghai will teach you a lesson.

Mt Kenya's highest peaks, Batian and Nelion, can only be reached by mountaineers with technical skills. However, Point Lenana, the third-highest peak, can be reached by trekkers and this is the usual goal for most people. As you might imagine, there are superb views over the surrounding country from Point Lenana and other high points around the main peaks, though the summit is often clothed in mist from late morning until late afternoon.

Safety

It's not surprising that trekking on this mountain is high on many travellers' priority list. However, because Mt Kenya is so easy to

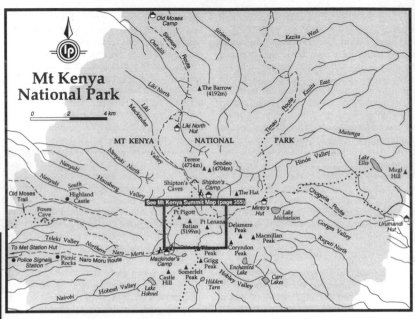

Mt Kenya National Park

0   2   4 km

Old Moses Camp

Sirimon Route

Ontulili

Kazita West

The Barrow (4192m)

Kazita East

Liki North

Mackinder

Liki

Liki North Hut

MT KENYA   NATIONAL   PARK

Mutonga

Tana Route

Namyuki

Namyuki North

Hausberg

Terere (4714m)

Sendeo (4704m)

Hinde Valley

Lake Ellis

Mugi Hill

Namyuki

South

Valley

Shipton's Caves

Shipton's Camp

The Hat

Chogoria Route

Old Moses Trail

Highland Castle

See Mt Kenya Summit Map (page 355)

Minto's Hut

Lake Michaelson

Gorges Valley

Urumandi Hut

Foxes Cave

Pt Pigott

Pt Lenana

Delamere Peak

Macmillan Peak

Ruguti North

Teleki Valley

Batian (5199m)

To Met Station Hut

Northern

Naro – Moru

Tilman Peak

Corydon Peak

Police Signals Station

Picnic Rocks

Naro Moru Route

Mackinder's Camp

Grigg Peak

Enchanted Lake

Hobley Valley

Carr Lakes

Castle Hill

Somerfelt Peak

Hidden Tarn

Nairobi

Hohnel Valley

Lake Hohnel

reach, and because Point Lenana is not technically difficult, this can create its own set of problems. Many people do the ascent much too quickly and end up suffering from headaches, nausea and other (sometimes more serious) effects of altitude sickness (see the Health section in the introductory Facts for the Visitor chapter for more details). Another problem can be the weather; even though they end up seeing the glaciers on the summits, many visitors go up the mountain without proper gear and completely unprepared for the cold and wet conditions often encountered.

This situation is made worse by some tour companies (and some guidebooks) billing the trek to Point Lenana as an easy hike. It's not unknown for ill-prepared independent trekkers to get hopelessly lost on Mt Kenya, sometimes with fatal results. Most years there are reports of people simply disappearing on the mountain.

So, when planning your trek up Mt Kenya,

it is important to realise that this is no small mountain: Point Lenana is just under 5000m – not much lower than the Everest Base Camp in Nepal. If you spend at least three nights on the ascent before going to the summit of Lenana, you stand a much better chance of enjoying yourself, and with proper clothes and equipment, you stand a much better chance of surviving too.

If you're not a regular mountain walker, and don't know how to use a map and compass, going up and down anything other than the Naro Moru or Sirimon routes, without a competent companion or a local guide, is simply asking for trouble. A guide is not compulsory but a very good idea.

The best times to go, as far as fair weather is concerned, is from mid-January to late February or from late August to September.

Books & Maps

Before you leave Nairobi we strongly recommend that you buy a copy of *Mt Kenya*

1:50,000 Map & Guide (1993) by Mark Savage & Andrew Wielochowski. It has a detailed topographical map on one side and a full description of the various routes, mountain medicine, flora & fauna, accommodation, etc on the reverse. This is money well spent and contains everything which most trekkers will need to know. It's stocked by all the main bookshops.

For keen trekkers looking for more information, or for details on wilder routes and some of the more esoteric variations that are possible on Mt Kenya, get hold of Lonely Planet's *Trekking in East Africa* by David Else. This book covers not only Mt Kenya but also covers a selection of treks and long-distance walks in Kenya, Tanzania, Uganda and Malawi.

Those who intend to do some technical climbing or mountaineering (as opposed to walking) should think seriously about getting a copy of the Mountain Club of Kenya's *Guide to Mt Kenya & Kilimanjaro*, edited by Iain Allan. This is a much more substantial and comprehensive guide, and is also available in all the main bookshops, or contact the

Mt Kenya – Geology, Flora & Fauna

Africa's second-highest mountain at 5199m, Mt Kenya was formed between 2½ and three million years ago as a result of successive eruptions of the volcano. Its base diameter is about 120 km, and it is probable that when first formed it was over 6000m in height and had a summit crater much like that on Kilimanjaro. Intensive erosion, however, principally by glacial ice, has worn away the cone and left a series of jagged peaks, U-shaped valleys and depressions containing glacial lakes, or tarns.

In many of these valleys you will come across terminal moraines (curved ridges of boulders and stones carried down by the glaciers) whose position – some as low as 3000m – indicates that during the Ice Ages the glaciers must have been far more extensive than they are today. They began retreating rapidly about 150,000 years ago as the climate changed and the process is still going on today. Since records were first kept back in 1893, seven of the glaciers have already disappeared leaving only the current 11, yet even these are getting quite thin. It's estimated that if the present trend continues, there might be no permanent ice left on the mountain in 25 years.

The volcanic soil and the many rivers which radiate out from the central cone have created a very fertile environment, especially on the southern and eastern sides which receive the most rain. Human agricultural activity currently extends up to around 1900m in what used to be rainforest, yet which today is still well wooded in many parts. Above this zone – except where logging takes place – stretches the untouched rainforest, characterised by an abundance of different species, particularly the giant camphors, along with vines, ferns, orchids and other epiphytes. This forest zone is not quite so dense on the northern and eastern sides, since the climate here is drier and the predominant tree species are conifers. Vines, likewise, are absent here.

The forest supports a rich variety of wildlife and it's quite common to come across elephant, buffalo and various species of monkey on the forest tracks. Rhino, numerous varieties of antelope, giant forest hog, and lion also live here but are usually only seen in the clearings around lodges.

On the southern and western slopes the forest gradually merges into a belt of dense bamboo which often grows to 12m or more. This eventually gives way to more open woodland consisting of hagena and hypericum trees along with an undergrowth of flowering shrubs and herbs.

Further up still is a belt of giant heather which forms dense clumps up to four metres high interspersed with tall grasses. Open moorland forms the next zone and can often be very colourful because of the profusion of small flowering plants which thrive there. The only large plants to be found in this region – and then only in the drier, sandier parts such as the valley sides and the ridges – are those bizarre specimens of the plant kingdom, the giant lobelias and senecios. This moorland zone stretches right up to the snow line at between 4500m and 4700m though the vegetation gets more and more sparse the higher you go. Beyond the snow line, the only plants you will find are mosses and lichens.

The open woodland and moorland support various species of antelope, such as the duiker and eland, as well as zebra, but the most common mammal is the rock hyrax. Leopard also live in this region and have occasionally been observed as high as 4500m! The larger birds you'll undoubtedly see up here include the verreaux eagle (which preys on hyrax), auger buzzard and the lammergeier (or bearded vulture). Smaller birds include the scarlet-tufted malachite sunbird, which feeds on nectar and small flies, and the friendly cliff chat which often appears in search of scraps. ■

Mountain Club of Kenya, PO Box 45741, Nairobi.

Clothing & Equipment

The summits of Mt Kenya are covered in glaciers and snow, and the temperature at night often drops to below -10°C so you are going to need a good sleeping bag. A closed-cell foam mat is also advisable if you are going to sleep on the ground as it provides the necessary insulation under your body and is far more comfortable than sleeping without one. A good set of warm clothes is equally important and that should include some sort of headgear and gloves. As it can rain at any time of year – and heavily – you will also need waterproof clothing. A decent pair of boots is an advantage but not strictly necessary. A pair of joggers is quite adequate most of the time though it's a good idea to have a pair of thongs, sandals or canvas tennis shoes to wear in the evening if your main shoes get wet. The one thing you will be very glad you brought with you is a pair of sunglasses. When the sun hits those snow-beds and glaciers on the summits, your eyes will hurt unless they're protected.

Remember that it's not a good idea to sleep in clothes which you have worn during the day because the sweat which your day clothes absorb from your skin keep them moist at night and therefore reduce their heat-retention capabilities.

If you don't intend to stay in the huts along the way you'll need a tent and associated equipment.

Unless you intend to eat only canned and dried food along the way (not recommended) then you'll also need a stove, basic cooking equipment and eating utensils and a water container with a capacity of at least two litres per person as well as water-purifying tablets for use on the lower levels of the mountain. Stove fuel in the form of petrol and kerosene (paraffin) is fairly easily found in towns, and methylated spirits is available in Nairobi, as are gas cartridges although the supply of these is not guaranteed. Except in an emergency, using wood gathered from the vicinity of camp sites to light open fires is prohibited within the confines of the national park and for good reason. In any case, there's no wood available once you get beyond the tree line. If you intend to engage porters then you'll also have to supply each of them with a rucksack to carry your gear and theirs.

Equipment Hire All the gear you need for the trek can be hired in Nairobi at Atul's (☎ (02) 225935), Biashara St, PO Box 43202, which is open Monday to Friday from 9 am to noon and 2 to 5 pm and on Saturday from 9 am to noon and 2.30 to 4 pm or from the Natural Action Mountain Centre (☎ (02) 740214), PO Box 12516. Atul's also sells some second-hand and locally made trekking and camping equipment. Examples of the sort of daily hire charges and deposits which you'll have to pay at Atul's are indicated on the equipment hire table.

These rates apply for the first 10 days of hire; longer term rentals are quite a bit cheaper. Rates at the Naro Moru River Lodge are consistently higher than those at Atul's.

Natural Action claims to be the only specialist outdoor shop on the African continent

Equipment Hire Price List

Item	Hire Cost (KSh)	Deposit (KSh)
sleeping bag	70 to 220	1300 to 3000
air mattress	80 to 150	600 to 1200
air-mattress pump	40	800
dome tent		
(two-person)	320 to 620	3000 to 4000
(three-person)	420	4000 to 5000
gas stove	110 to 170	1000 to 2000
kerosene stove	75	600
water container		
(one litre)	10	40
(10 litre)	25	60
mess kit	10	300
cooking pot	15 to 60	120 to 500
gas lamp	100 to 160	2000
kerosene lamp	30	400
rucksack	150 to 300	2000 to 4000
woollen socks	40	300
woollen gloves	40	300
rain poncho	70	800
rain pants	60	800

(outside South Africa) and also has a good range of equipment. The guys who run the shop are off-duty guides from Mt Kenya and are helpful with information and advice. Advance booking of gear (from Atul's) is a good idea if you want to be absolutely sure, but is not normally necessary except in the case of boots – an ill-fitting pair will make the trip a misery.

Rental gear is also available at the Naro Moru River Lodge (☎ (0176) 22018), PO Box 18, Naro Moru, and is mostly in good condition and well maintained, although it cannot be booked in advance. Both places carry plenty of stock. The Mountain Rock Hotel near Naro Moru also has equipment for hire, but the range is less extensive.

Food
In an attempt to cut down on baggage, quite a few people forgo taking a stove and cooking equipment and exist entirely on canned and dried foods. You can certainly do it so long as you keep up your fluid intake but it's not a good idea. That cup of hot soup in the evening and pot of tea or coffee in the morning can make all the difference between enjoying the trek and hating it or, at least, feeling irritable.

There are, however, a few things to bear in mind about cooking at high altitudes. The major consideration is that the boiling point of water is considerably reduced. At 4500m, for example, water boils at 85°C. This is too low to sufficiently cook rice or lentils (pasta is better) and you won't be able to brew a good cup of tea from it either (instant coffee is the answer). Cooking times are also considerably increased as a result (with consequent increased use of fuel).

The best range of suitable foods for the mountain is, of course, to be found in the supermarkets of Nairobi. If you're going straight to the mountain from Nairobi by bus or share-taxi, it's no problem to bring all your supplies from there. The best supermarkets in Nairobi are the Nakumatt and Uchumi chains.

Otherwise there's a good range of food in the towns around the mountain (Nyeri, Nanyuki, Embu and Meru) although precious little at Naro Moru. Remember when you're buying dehydrated foods to buy the pre-cooked variety to cut down on cooking time – two-minute noodles are the answer here. Fresh fruit and vegetables are available in all reasonably sized towns and villages.

Take plenty of citrus fruits and/or citrus drinks with you as well as chocolate, sweets or dried fruit to keep your blood sugar levels high on the trek.

One last thing – and this is important to avoid severe headaches caused by dehydration – is to drink at least three litres of fluid per day. It may also help to avoid altitude sickness.

Park Fees
Entry fees to the national park are US$10 per day (US$5 if you have an international student card and US$5 for children). If you take a guide and/or porters then you'll have to pay their entry fees too, and these are KSh 150 per person per night. Camping fees are an additional US$8 per person.

Guides, Cooks & Porters
The charges for guides, porters and cooks vary according to the route taken but as a general guide assume KSh 450 per day for a senior guide, KSh 300 for an ordinary guide, KSh 350 per day for a cook and KSh 250 per day for a porter excluding all park entry fees (KSh 150 per person per day) and tips at the end of the trek. If you assume KSh 500 per trip for guides and cooks and KSh 250 per trip for porters as a tip you won't be too far off the mark.

Porters will carry up to 18 kg for a three-day trip or 16 kg for a longer trip, excluding the weight of their own food and equipment. If you want them to carry more then you'll have to negotiate a price for the extra weight. A normal day's work is regarded as one stage of the journey – from the Met Station to Mackinder's Camp on the Naro Moru route or from the Chogoria road head to Minto's Hut on the Chogoria route, for example. If you want to go further than this then you'll have to pay them two days wages even if they don't do anything the following day.

One important thing you must remember regarding guides and porters is that, if you ascend the mountain along one route and descend along a different one, you will be responsible for arranging and paying for their transport back to where they started from. It would be a good idea to sort this out before you set off and agree on a price for return transport plus any additional wages, food and hotel costs along the way. If, for instance, you ascend via the Naro Moru or Sirimon routes and descend via the Chogoria route then, depending on what time you arrive in Chogoria village, the guide and porters may have to stay the night at a hotel before returning and they'll be entitled to another day's wages as well.

Guides, porters and cooks can be engaged at the Naro Moru River Lodge, the Mountain Rock Lodge, the Mt Kenya Hostel and the Mountain Stop Motel on the northern side of the mountain. You can also find them at the Naro Moru entry gate but this isn't as reliable so it's better to contact the Naro Moru Porters & Guides Association (☎ (0176) 6205), PO Naro Moru, in advance.

On the southern side they can be booked through one of the hotels in Chogoria village or at the Chogoria Forest Station or in advance through Mr Nabae, PO Box 449, Chogoria. If you book through Mr Nabae there's a booking fee of KSh 40 for each guide, cook or porter. You can also book them at the Meru Mt Kenya Lodge but, in this case, you'll have to pay for them to be transported to the lodge (KSh 1500) or the road head (KSh 1750). Don't assume you can engage guides and porters at the Chogoria Gate. You might be lucky but you might not. Better still, contact the Chogoria Porters (☎ 88 in Chogoria), PO Box 96, Chogoria, who are based at the Transit Hotel in the village.

Everyone likes to think they're super-fit and capable of scaling this mountain without a worry. If you are – no problem. Most people are not and even fewer are acclimatised to heights of 4000m and more. Even British Army squaddies sometimes have to be rescued on account of altitude sickness and it's unlikely your training regime matches theirs. That being so, think seriously about whether you want to enjoy this climb or flunk out on the last leg to the summit. Having someone carry your heavy gear up this mountain is like the difference between a matatu and a Mercedes Benz. The difference in enjoyment is immeasurable. In other words, think seriously about taking on a guide and porters. It will enhance your appreciation of this mountain a hundred fold and at the wages (and even tips) which they charge, it's a bargain.

Accommodation

There are quite a lot of huts on the mountain but not all of them are available to the general public. Several are owned by the Mountain Club of Kenya (MCK). A few of these huts are reserved exclusively for use by members, others can be used by the public, although these are all basic and most are in very bad condition.

There are also some larger bunkhouses with more facilities on the mountain. These are owned by lodges outside the park and are mainly for people going on treks organised by these lodges, but they can also be used by independent trekkers. Beds in the large bunkhouses have to be booked and paid for, but there is no reservation system.

On the Naro Moru route, the bunkhouses are at the meteorological station (always called the Met Station), and Teleki Lodge (more usually called Mackinder's Camp), and both can be booked through the Naro Moru River Lodge, or Let's Go Travel in Nairobi. The Met Station costs US$8 per bed and Mackinder's costs US$11 per bed.

On the Sirimon route, the bunkhouses are at Old Moses Camp and Shipton's Camp, and both can be booked through the Mountain Rock Hotel. They cost US$8 and US$9, respectively, if you pay at the Mountain Rock but otherwise KSh 600 and KSh 800 if you pay on arrival. Make sure you get a receipt otherwise, when you leave the park, the rangers will assume you've been camping and will charge you US$8 per night.

On the Chogoria route, there are 12 comfortable bandas at the *Meru Mt Kenya Lodge*, near the park gate, each containing a lounge/dining area with fireplace, bedroom with two single beds and a small extra bed, and a bathroom with shower (hot water) and toilet. Electricity (at an additional charge) is provided by generator in the evenings until 11 pm and in the early mornings. Cooking is on single ring electric cookers and primus stoves. All crockery, cutlery, cooking utensils and bed linen are provided. There's also a central lounge/dining area with a kitchen and toilets. The bandas cost KSh 625 per person per day (KSh 105 for children between the ages of two and 15 years). Electricity costs KSh 10 per day. Reservations are not always necessary but probably best and can be made through Let's Go Travel (☎ (02) 340331) in Nairobi.

The small MCK huts can be booked and paid for in Nairobi at the MCK clubhouse, at Let's Go Travel or at the Naro Moru River Lodge. They cost around US$3, but are generally in such bad condition that very few trekkers use them. If you are going independently and not planning to use the bunkhouses, it's much better to camp than to use these MCK huts.

You don't have to worry about any of these hut bookings if you're going on an organised climb because all this will be taken care of.

Officially you can camp anywhere on the mountain but it is usual to camp near one of the huts or bunkhouses as there is often a water supply nearby.

Getting to the Trekking Routes

There are at least seven different routes up the mountain, but only the three main routes are covered here – Naro Moru, Sirimon and Chogoria. The other routes are much harder to follow and there's a real chance you can get lost without decent maps and the ability to read them, and if you have no experience with a compass.

If you intend to do the trek independently then public transport (bus or matatu) along the Mt Kenya ring road is the first step towards getting to the mountain. For the Naro Moru route it's Naro Moru village where there's a prominent signpost on the right-hand side just outside the village on the way to Nanyuki. For the Sirimon route, first go to Nanyuki and then take another matatu about 13 km up the main road towards Isiolo where the route is signposted off to the right. For the Chogoria route all matatus and buses between Embu and Meru stop at Chogoria village, just off the main road. From where the buses or matatus drop you it's quite a walk to any of the park entry gates but it's possible to find private (though relatively expensive) transport from the main roads to the park entry gates. See the individual routes for details.

If you have your own transport, you can get up to the Naro Moru and Sirimon national park entry gates in 2WD but you will not get up to the Chogoria park entry gate in anything other than 4WD. Likewise, you'll probably make it up to the road head (Old Moses Camp) on the Sirimon route in 2WD but you certainly won't make it up to the Met Station on the Naro Moru route or the road head on the Chogoria route in 2WD. There are times, too, when you won't even make it to the Met Station or the park entry gate on the Chogoria route in a small Suzuki 4WD after rain. The road from Chogoria village to the park entry gate is diabolical and the top section of the 'road' through the bamboo forest is totally impassable in wet weather even for 4WDs fitted with snow chains.

Mt Kenya Routes

The normal weather pattern is for clear mornings with the mist closing in from 10 am, though this sometimes clears again in the early evening. This means that if you want to make the most of the trek you should set off early every morning and, for the final assault on Point Lenana (the highest point that can be reached by trekkers), you need to make an early start if you want to see the sunrise from the top.

Naro Moru Route

This is the most straightforward and popular of the routes. It's also the least scenic, although it's still a spectacular and very enjoyable trail. You should allow a minimum of four days for the trek up and down this route, or three if you have transport between Naro Moru and the meteorological station, although doing it this quickly if you're not acclimatised is asking for altitude sickness.

Naro Moru to the Met Station Your starting point here is the village of Naro Moru. The first part of the route takes you along a relatively good gravel road through farmlands for some 12 km (all the junctions are signposted) to the start of the forest where there's a wooden bridge across a small river. A further five km brings you to the park entry gate at 2400m. Having paid your fees, you continue on another eight km to the road head and Met Station Hut (3000m) where you stay for the night.

If your time is limited you can cut out this part of the trek by taking the Naro Moru River Lodge's Land Rover or the Mt Kenya Hostel's 4WD all the way to the meteorological station but remember that this is an expensive way of getting there unless you're sharing the cost with a full complement of other climbers. Hitching is also possible but the chances of a lift *up* the mountain are limited – it's easier to get a ride on the way down.

Met Station to Mackinder's Camp On the second day you set off up the Teleki Valley along a well-marked path past the police signals station and up to the edge of the forest at around 3200m. From here you scale the so-called Vertical Bog and up onto a ridge from where you can see Mackinder's Camp. The route divides into two here and you have the choice of taking the higher path, which gives the best views but is often wet, or the lower path which crosses the Naro Moru River and continues gently up to Mackinder's Camp (4160m). This part of the trek should take around 4½ hours. Here you can stay the night (bunkhouse or camping). The stone

cabins at Mackinder's are quite comfortable with two large dorms. The bunk beds have mattresses, there are toilets, and drinking water is available. The caretaker here checks your bunkhouse booking receipts.

Mackinder's Camp to Point Lenana On the third day you can either rest at Mackinder's Camp (to help acclimatise) or aim for Point Lenana. From Mackinder's to Point Lenana takes about four to five hours, so it's usual to leave around 2 am (you'll need a torch or flashlight) to reach the summit of Lenana in time for sunrise. From the bunkhouse, continue up the valley past the ranger station to a fork in the path. Keep right, and go across a swampy area, followed by a moraine and then up a very long scree slope – this is a long, hard slog. You reach Austrian Hut about three to four hours from Mackinder's. This is about one hour below the summit of Lenana, so it's a good place to rest before the final push for the summit. This section of the trek, from Austrian Hut up to Point Lenana, takes you up a steep ridge and then across the edge of a snow-covered glacier. In good weather the going is fairly straightforward, but in bad weather you should not attempt to reach the summit unless you are experienced in trekking in mountain conditions, or have a guide. Plenty of inexperienced trekkers have come to grief on this section, falling off icy cliffs or even disappearing into crevasses.

To avoid the long slog in the dark, it is also possible to walk from Mackinder's to the Austrian Hut on the third day, stay there, then go for the summit of Lenana on the morning of the fourth day. However, conditions at Austrian Hut are very basic, so you need to be well equipped.

Those who are camping and not staying at either Mackinder's Camp or the Austrian Hut have a third choice of where to spend the night. This is the so-called American Camp, which you get to by branching off left along a minor track just before the swampy area and above the ranger station. It's an excellent camp site on a grassy meadow.

Mt Kenya Summit

0   250   500 m

Contour Interval 50 m

Return Routes From Point Lenana most people return to the Met Station back down the same route. Assuming you get to Point Lenana early in the day, you can reach the Met Station on the same day.

Alternatively, you can return to Austrian Hut then walk north and north-west around the base of the main peaks to reach the top of either the Sirimon or Chogoria routes, and go down one of those routes. This is on the Summit Circuit path (described briefly in the Sirimon Route section), which is reckoned to be one of the most exciting trekking routes in East Africa. Completely circling the mountain, you cross several major cols, and get great views of the peaks and glaciers from all angles. The Summit Circuit path can also be demanding and potentially dangerous. Many people have got lost on this trail and you should not attempt it unless you have plenty of time, proper equipment, and a map and compass that you know how to use.

Sirimon Route

This is the least used of the three main routes but the driest and one of the most scenic. It is also the longest approach to Point Lenana but, once you reach the Mackinder Valley, it's plain sailing all the way to Shipton's Camp and there's beautiful alpine vegetation the whole way. You should allow a minimum of four days to undertake this trek.

Probably the best way to climb the mountain along this route is to first head for the Mountain Rock Hotel between Naro Moru and Nanyuki. Here you stay for the night, book the mountain lodges – Old Moses Camp and Shipton's Camp – and arrange transport the next day to the park entry gate.

If that's not in your budget then take transport from Nairobi to Nanyuki, stay the night there and then take one of the frequent Nissan minibuses going to Timau on the main road towards Isiolo and tell the driver you want to be dropped off at the start of the Sirimon trail (signposted). It's about 13 km north of Nanyuki. If you go over a fairly large river (the Sirimon River), you've gone too far.

Turn-Off to Old Moses Camp On the first day you walk from the main road to the park entrance gate (about 10 km) and on from there to the road head at 3150m (a further nine km). The going is straightforward to this point. At the road head there's a good camp site and the Old Moses Camp bunkhouse. This bunkhouse is well maintained, clean, and the bunks are provided with mattresses but you need your own cooking equipment and food. There's also plenty of water for washing and cooking and toilets on site.

Old Moses Camp to Shipton's Camp On the second day you leave Old Moses Camp, aiming uphill on a gradually deteriorating track. After about one hour you reach a fork – the left branch goes to the Liki North Hut, although this route is not used much. Take the right branch, which leads to a path over two ridges into the Mackinder Valley. Look out for red and white marker posts. When you get to the top of the last ridge you'll be presented with breathtaking views of the snow-covered peaks and others, to the north, of the Aberdares. It's even possible to see the Mt Kenya Safari Club way down below. From here, the path leads down the east side of the valley, eventually crossing the Liki North Stream and passing Shipton's Caves (in an obvious cliff on the left side of the path) before reaching Shipton's Camp bunkhouse and camp site, directly below the peaks of Batian and Point Lenana. From the road head at Old Moses Camp to Shipton's Camp takes about seven hours. Shipton's Camp is a good place to spend two nights and have a rest day to help acclimatise. However, if you're feeling OK, one night here is sufficient. The bunkhouse is well maintained, clean and the bunks have mattresses. There are toilets on site and a clean stream which goes directly past the bunkhouse.

Shipton's Camp to Point Lenana There are various ways you can approach Point Lenana from Shipton's Camp.

Via the North Face This is the shortest route, which means you can go from Shipton's up to Lenana then down to a high camp or hut on one of the other routes in one day. However, the option is very difficult, and impassable after snow. There are no tracks and it should only be tackled by experienced trekkers, or by groups with competent local guides. It's basically straight uphill, and very steep, so if it's the one you take, go easy! You reach Harris Tarn, then aim for the summit of Lenana up the North Face. It takes 3½ to five hours to reach the summit this way.

Once you get to the top, you have a choice of descending back the same way you came (two to four hours back to Shipton's), or descend part of the way, then branch off down the Chogoria route. If you choose the Chogoria route you're looking at a strenuous descent over an enormous scree bed which will take you the best part of two hours followed by another one to 1½ hours down to Minto's Hut. Your other option is descending to Austrian hut, where you join the Summit Circuit path, and then dropping down to the Naro Maru route (about three to four hours to Mackinder's Camp).

Via American Camp This option requires an extra day. From Shipton's Camp on the third day you can follow the Summit Circuit path west of the main peaks. Go straight up the valley side from Shipton's, keeping the main peaks to your left, to reach Kami Hut (which is in very bad condition) and then continue up a long scree slope to reach the Hausberg Col. From here you drop down into the next valley to reach Hausberg Tarn and Oblong Tarn. Follow the path between the tarns, then go up again to the col between the summit of Arthur's Seat and the Western Terminal. Aim south from here, passing Nanyuki Tarn to your right, to reach Two Tarn Hut, from where you drop down to American Camp at the head of the Teleki Valley. You can camp here or go down to the nearby Mackinder's Camp bunkhouse. From Shipton's Camp to American Camp by this route takes about four to five hours. On the fourth day you can reach Point Lenana (as described in the Naro Moru Route section).

Via Austrian Hut Your other choice from Shipton's is to go east of the main peaks. This option also requires an extra day. Head up the steep-sided valley to Simba Col, or go up the large scree slopes to Harris Tarn. From both of these points you can reach Simba Tarn, then Square Tarn. From Square Tarn you aim south, through Tooth Col (next to a large, jagged pinnacle) and then gradually up to reach Austrian Hut. From Shipton's Camp to Austrian Hut by this route takes about six hours. On the fourth day you can reach Point Lenana (as described in the Naro Moru Route section). If you are going east of the main peaks and don't feel like going for the summit of Lenana, from Simba Col you can join the Chogoria route and drop down to Minto's Hut.

Chogoria Route

This route, from the eastern side of the mountain, is undoubtedly the most beautiful of the access routes to the summit and certainly one of the easiest as far as gradients go. This is a good route if you've got a tent and some trekking experience. From Minto's Hut there are breathtaking views of the head of the Gorges Valley and the glaciers beyond.

To get started on this route, take an Akamba bus from Nairobi direct to Chogoria village, or one first to Embu and then a matatu to Chogoria. Unless you get to Chogoria village early in the day, you will probably have to spend the night in Chogoria before setting off up the mountain, as the first day's hike is a long slog. It's about 30 km from the village to the park entry gate up the forest track with nowhere to stay en route.

Chogoria to Park Entry Gate The first day is spent walking up to the park entry gate at 2990m through superb rainforest and on into the bamboo zone. You have the choice here of staying at the Meru Mt Kenya Lodge, near the park entry gate, or continuing on a further three km to the small MCK's Urumandi Hut. At the road head itself (3200m), six km from the park entry gate, there's also an excellent camp site but there are no facilities whatsoever except water (from the adjacent river).

It's possible to hitch all the way to the park entry gate from Chogoria as at least one official vehicle does the run most days between the village and the Meru Mt Kenya Lodge, though there's no set timetable. There may also be people staying at the lodge who can help out with lifts. Alternatively, if you want guaranteed transport, this can be arranged at one of the hotels in Chogoria village for around KSh 1500 per person. Natural Action (see the earlier Equipment Hire section for details) also has a base and transport here.

Park Entry Gate to Minto's Hut The second day is spent walking from either the Meru Mt Kenya Lodge, the Urumandi Hut or the road head camp site to Minto's Hut with spectacular views all the way. The route is well defined and first crosses a stream then climbs to a ridge which it follows all the way to Minto's Hut. You need to bring water with you as there are no sources en route. From the road head to Minto's Hut should take you about 4½ to five hours. Minto's Hut is in a disgusting state and you wouldn't keep pigs in there but that's hardly the point because the guides and porters will have taken over the place long before you get there. The only realistic option here is to camp in the field next to the tarn – which is also your source of water. It's a good site and there may still be a few small sheets of corrugated iron to shield your stove from the wind (there were in 1996). There's also a long-drop toilet adjacent to the hut. Take time out here to peer over the precipice of the gorge. It's spectacular!

Minto's Hut to Austrian Hut On the third day you continue to the head of the Gorges Valley, a steep climb eventually across scree slopes, aiming south-west to reach Square Tarn. The last section of this leg of the route is very steep.

From the tarn the route becomes the Summit Circuit path, continuing south through Tooth Col (to the east of Point Lenana), after which it descends briefly and then goes up across a scree slope to the right to reach Austrian Hut.

The route is marked with cairns in some places but it is still easy to get lost, especially in mist or snow. The section between Tooth Col and Austrian Hut is where most trekkers get lost. It is essential to realise that there is another huge valley (called Hobley Valley) in-between the Gorges and Teleki valleys. The route goes *around* the head of the Hobley, not down into it. From Minto's to Austrian Hut should take about four hours.

Austrian Hut to Point Lenana From Austrian Hut you can scale Point Lenana (allow another one to two hours) the same day or stay there for the night and make the ascent the following morning, as described in the Naro Moru section.

Return Routes From Point Lenana you can retrace the route back down to Minto's Hut which should take about three to four hours after which it's a further four to five hours back down to the Meru Mt Kenya Lodge. Alternatively, from Austrian Hut you can descend to Mackinder's Camp, and then return via the Naro Moru route.

Organised Treks
If your time is limited or you'd prefer someone else to make all the arrangements for a trek on Mt Kenya, there are several possibilities.

The Mountain Rock Lodge (☎ (0176) 62625), or Mountain Rock Tours & Adventure Safaris (☎ (02) 210051; fax 333448), PO Box 40270, Jubilee Insurance House, Wabera St, Nairobi, are the real specialists in Mt Kenya climbs, though not exclusively. They offer a two-tier pricing structure: a 'Standard' (budget) package for those who are willing to be flexible but want to keep costs down, and an 'Executive' package for those who don't want to share facilities, guides and porters with other climbers. The cost of one of their organised climbs, whether it be 'Standard' or 'Executive' depends very much on how many are in your group. It's cheapest with eight or more people rising to about double this amount if there's only one of you.

There's a whole range of options to choose from starting with quick two-day treks all the way through to seven-day treks. A three-day trek up and back down the Sirimon route, costs US$316 to US$174 (one to eight people, respectively). An alternative which takes the same time is to ascend along the Sirimon route and descend via the Naro Moru route. This is slightly more expensive at US$346 to US$190. Four-day treks up and back down the Sirimon route cost US$398 to US$236. An alternative which takes the same amount of time is to ascend via the Sirimon route and descend via the Chogoria route. This costs US$480 to US$320.

Their longest trek is a seven-day package which takes in the Sirimon route as well as the Summit Circuit path and costs US$572 to US$403.

The above prices are for 'Standard' treks; 'Executive' packages are somewhat more expensive. If you're a student or a Kenyan resident there are substantial discounts on these prices because of the reductions available on park entry and camping fees. All prices include park entry and camping fees, food, hut accommodation, a guide, cook and porters and transfer to the Mountain Rock Hotel before and after a climb. Some packages also include transfer to and from Nairobi and one or two nights at the hotel. Write, ring or fax for a copy of their brochure before you set off.

The Naro Moru River Lodge (☎ (0176) 22018), PO Box 18, Naro Moru, also does a range of trips, all of which include a guide/cook, porters, all meals, park entry fees, camping fees, and transport to and from the road heads. Their prices are similar to those of the Mountain Rock Hotel but the normal route up the mountain from here is via the Naro Moru route. Write or ring for their brochure before you set off. If you take one of their treks, you're entitled to a special half-board deal at the hotel.

There are several safari companies in Nairobi which offer Mt Kenya treks, but most of these companies just sell the treks operated by Naro Moru and Mountain Rock lodges, charging you an extra commission in the process. However, some companies are running their own treks, and these include:

Kenya Hiking & Cycling
Arrow House, Koinange St, PO Box 39439, Nairobi (☎ (02) 218336)
This company's Mt Kenya trek goes up the Sirimon route and down the Naro Moru in five days, staying at bunkhouses. The cost is US$520 including transport to and from Nairobi.

Natural Action Ltd
PO Box 12516, Nairobi (☎ /fax (02) 763927)
This is a specialist, high quality trekking outfit, favouring remote routes. A standard five-day Mt Kenya trek goes up the Chogoria route and down the Naro Moru, following more unusual paths for some of the way. The cost is around US$754 per person, including park fees, transport to/from Nairobi, and hotel accommodation after the trek.

Bike Treks
PO Box 14237, Nairobi (☎ (02) 446371; fax 44237)
This company offers a range of possibilities from three days/two nights Naro Moru route for US$300, four days/three nights Sirimon/Naro Moru routes for US$400, and seven days/six nights Sirimon/Chogoria routes for US$560. The prices include transfer to and from Nairobi, park entry and camping fees, guide, cook and porters, food and tents. It excludes rucksacks, clothing and boots and tips.

Executive Wilderness Programmes
PO Box 15014, Nairobi (☎ (02) 884068; fax 882723)
This company specialises in mountain trekking all over East Africa including Mt Kenya, Kilimanjaro, Mt Elgon, Mt Kulal, the Chyulu Hills and the Ruwenzori.

NAIROBI NATIONAL PARK

This park is the most accessible of all Kenya's game parks, being only a few km from the city centre. You should set aside a morning or an afternoon to see it. As in all the game parks, you must visit it in a vehicle; walking is prohibited. This means you will either have to arrange a lift at the entrance gate with other tourists, go on a tour, or hire a car.

Nairobi National Park is the oldest park in the country, having been created in 1946. For a park so close to the city centre you can see an amazing variety of animals – with a backdrop of jumbo jets coming in to land at Jomo Kenyatta International airport which is adjacent to the park. Gazelle, oryx, lion, zebra, giraffe, buffalo, cheetah and leopard are all seen regularly. Elephants are not to be found in this park as the habitat is not suitable.

NATIONAL PARKS & RESERVES

NATIONAL PARKS & RESERVES

Nairobi National Park

However, it's in this park that you have one of the best chances of spotting a rhino – they are doing quite well here because poachers prefer more remote areas.

The concentrations of game are higher in the dry season when water sources outside the park have dried up. Water is more plentiful inside the park as small dams have been built on the Mbagathi River which forms the southern boundary of the park.

The **Animal Orphanage** by the main gate has a sign inside the gate which reads 'this is not a zoo' – it is. From time to time there are young abandoned animals which are nursed through to good health and then released, but basically it is just a zoo; entry is US$5, and US$2 for children.

Entry to the park costs US$20 (KSh 150 for residents) and US$5 for children (KSh 50 for residents) plus KSh 200 for a vehicle with less than six seats and KSh 500 for a vehicle with six to 12 seats.

Getting There & Away
If you want to hitch a ride through the park from the main gate, city bus No 24 from Moi Ave will get you there.

There are many companies offering tours of Nairobi National Park and there's probably not much between them. The four-hour tours usually depart twice a day at 9.30 am and 2 pm and cost around US$50. If you hang around in front of the Hilton Hotel at around 2 pm it is often possible to get a discounted seat on a tour at the last minute as the operators try to fill the van.

Most of the tour companies also offer a day-long combined tour of the national park with a visit to the Bomas of Kenya (or the Karen Blixen Museum) and including a gargantuan lunch at the Carnivore, but it's an expensive day out at US$130 per person (see the Nairobi Organised Tours section for details).

SAIWA SWAMP NATIONAL PARK
This small park north of Kitale is a real delight. The swamp area is the habitat of the sitatunga antelope, known in Swahili as the *nzohe*, and this park has been set aside to protect it. Sadly the park has seen better days, and there are very few sitatunga left, although it is possible that some may be translocated from elsewhere.

What makes this park unique is that it is only accessible on foot. There are marked walking trails which skirt the swamp, duckboards right across the swamp in places, and some extremely rickety observation towers.

The park is also home to the impressive black-and-white colobus monkey. It inhabits the higher levels of the trees and, not having the gregarious nature of many primates, is easy to miss as it sits quietly in the heights. When they do move, however, the flowing 'cape' of white hair is very distinctive. Bird life within the park is also prolific.

With all this on offer it's surprising how few people visit Saiwa Swamp.

Entry to the national park costs US$15 per person per day.

Places to Stay
It is possible to camp at the ranger station inside the park but there is nothing in the way of facilities. Camping fees are US$10 per person.

A much better option is to camp or stay at the *Sirikwa Safaris* farmhouse about five km

---

Sitatunga Antelope
The sitatunga is fairly elusive and really the only way to spot one is to sit atop one of the observation towers armed with a pair of binoculars and a hefty dose of patience. As is the case in most of the parks, the best time for animal-spotting is in the early morning or late afternoon.

This shy antelope is not unlike a bushbuck in appearance, although larger, and has elongated hooves which are supposed to make it easier for it to get around in swampy conditions – it's hard to see how, but no doubt nature has it all worked out. The colouring is basically grey-brown, with more red noticeable in the females, and both sexes have white spots or stripes on the upper body. The males have long twisted horns which grow up to a metre in length. ■

further north along the Kapenguria road from the Saiwa Swamp turn-off. For the cost of camping or staying in a room here see the Kitale section. The owners can also arrange a field guide who is well versed in the bird life of the park for KSh 300 (half day) or KSh 600 (full day) as well as transport to the park entrance.

Getting There & Away
Saiwa Swamp National Park lies five km east of the main A1 road, 18 km north of Kitale. Any of the matatus running between Kitale and Kapenguria will let you off at the signposted turn-off, from where you'll probably have to walk to the park as there is little traffic along the dirt road.

SAMBURU, BUFFALO SPRINGS & SHABA NATIONAL RESERVES
Just north of Isiolo are three national reserves, Samburu, Buffalo Springs and Shaba, all of them along the banks of the Ewaso Nyiro River and covering an area of some 300 sq km. They are mainly scrub desert and open savanna plain, broken here and there by small rugged hills. The river, however, which is permanent, supports a wide variety of game and you may see elephant, buffalo, cheetah, leopard and lion as well as dik-dik, wart hog, Grevy's zebra and the reticulated giraffe. Crocodiles can also be seen on certain sandy stretches of the riverbank.

You are guaranteed close-up sightings of elephants, reticulated giraffe and various species of smaller gazelle in both Samburu and Buffalo Springs but other game is remarkably thin on the ground, particularly on the route into Samburu from Archer's Post. The rhino were wiped out years ago by poachers.

If you are driving around these parks in your own vehicle it's useful to have a copy of the Survey of Kenya map, *Samburu & Buffalo Springs Game Reserves* (SK 85).

The roads inside Buffalo Springs and Samburu are well maintained and it's easy to get around, even in 2WD, though you might need a 4WD on some of the minor tracks.

Entry to each of the three parks or game reserves costs US$27 per person (US$10 for students and children) plus KSh 200 per vehicle per day (less than six seats) or KSh 500 per day (six to 12 seats). Even though they're continuous, if you drive from Buffalo Springs to Samburu (or vice versa) in one day then you'll have to pay two lots of park entry fees. However, if it's very late in the afternoon when you cross the boundary, the guards will generally postdate your ticket for the following day.

These parks are much less touristed than Amboseli or Masai Mara so, once you're out of the immediate vicinity of the lodges and camp sites, you'll frequently have the place to yourself.

Places to Stay
Buffalo Springs In Buffalo Springs National Reserve there are four *public camp sites* close to the Gare Mara entrance gate (the nearest to Isiolo and accessible from the main Isiolo–Marsabit road). However, none of them are particularly safe as far as robberies go so stick with a group and make sure your tent is guarded when you're out on game drives or pack it up and take it with you. There's also a *special camp site* further west. Camping costs US$2.50 per person per night.

For those with adequate finances, there's the *Buffalo Springs Tented Lodge* (☎ (0165) 2234) up at the north-eastern end of the reserve just south of the Ewaso Nyiro River. The lodge consists of 30 tents shielded from the sun by makuti roofs and each with its own bathroom. There are also eight cottages which sleep two to four people. The lodge has a swimming pool and a bar/restaurant overlooking a natural spring where you can sit and observe the wildlife. In the high season, tents or cottages cost US$120/160 for singles/doubles with full board. In the low season the prices are US$50/90. The price includes a game drive. Advance bookings can be made through African Tours & Hotels Ltd (☎ (02) 223285; fax 218109), PO Box 30471, Nairobi. The best access to the lodge is either from the Gare Mara Gate or the Buffalo Springs Gate just south of Archer's Post.

Samburu & Buffalo Springs
National Reserves

Samburu In Samburu National Reserve, the most convenient places to stay are the *public camp sites* close to the Samburu Lodge and close to the wooden bridge which connects the western extremity of Buffalo Springs to Samburu across the Ewaso Nyiro River. The sites themselves are fairly pleasant and adjacent to the river but the facilities are minimal and the 'toilets' are nothing short of pigsties. If you don't want to cook for yourself the only advantage is that they're very close to the lodge with its restaurant and bar. There are also two *special camp sites* which are further west. Camping costs US$2.50 per person per night.

For those with money, there's a choice of four top-range lodges/tented camps. The most popular is perhaps the *Samburu Lodge* which is part of the Block Hotels chain (☎ (02) 540780; fax 543810), PO Box 40075, Block House, Lusaka Rd, Nairobi. It's built right alongside the river and consists of a main building (stone and makuti roof) which houses the restaurant, bar and reception area, and a series of cottages with their own bathrooms strung out along the riverbank. The tariff depends on the season. In the high season it's US$100/153 with half-board for singles/doubles, whereas in the low season it's US$39/78 with half board for singles/doubles. Rates in the two shoulder seasons are intermediate. Kenyan residents pay KSh

3185/4730 with half board for singles/doubles. The lodge is the only place in the two parks where petrol can be bought. Game drives through the park can be organised at the lodge.

Further east and also alongside the river is *Larsens* which is a luxury tented camp also owned by the Block Hotels chain. The rates depend on the season. In the high season (16 December to 3 January and 1 April to 8 April) half board costs US$142/219 in a tent and US$165/255 for a suite, whereas in the low season (9 April to 30 June) the corresponding rates are US$57/114 and US$67/134. All these rates include two game drives. Children under seven years old are not allowed at Larsens and those over this age are charged the full adult rate.

The *Samburu Intrepids Club* (☎ (02) 335208; fax 217278 in Nairobi), further upstream on the northern side of the river, is another luxury tented lodge and more like a beach resort in many ways. A night here costs US$121/183 with full board.

The *Samburu Serena Lodge* charges US$110/150 for singles/doubles with full board in the high seasons and US$50/100 with full board in the low season (9 April to 30 June). These prices are subject to 10% service charge, 2% training levy and 15% VAT. For bookings contact Serena Lodges & Hotels (☎ (02) 711077; fax 718103), PO Box 48690, Nairobi.

You can take any of the park access gates to get to these lodges but remember that if you drive through Buffalo Springs and into Samburu on the same day then you'll be up for two lots of park entry fees. You can avoid this by entering through the Archer's Post Gate.

Shaba The spectacular *Shaba Sarova Lodge* in Shaba National Game Reserve has single/double rooms with full board for US$55/110 in the low season, rising to US$130/165 for high season. Bookings should be made through Sarova Hotels (☎ (02) 333248; fax 211742), PO Box 30680, New Stanley Hotel, Kenyatta Ave, Nairobi. For those with lots of money to spend but little time at their

---

Night Show

The supposed 'highlights' of any evening here are the appearance of a leopard across the other side of the river and the crocodiles which crawl up onto a sandy bank adjacent to the bar. The leopard, which is lured by a hunk of meat strung up from a tree by two very blasé employees just before dusk, is extremely contrived but Kodak make a fortune supplying film to fools who think they can get anything but a picture of midnight in the bush with an Instamatic from about 100m. The crocodile 'show' is equally contrived but at least it takes place right in front of you even if pieces of dead meat in the sand don't encourage dynamism. ∎

disposal, there's a weekend package (Saturday and Sunday) available which costs KSh 18,100 per person and includes a return flight from Nairobi to Shaba (twin-engine light aircraft), full-board accommodation at the lodge, three game drives, park fees, and transfers from the airports at both ends.

For campers there's a beautiful *camp site* about 20 minutes drive away. There's abundant firewood here but you need to bring water from the lodge.

SHIMBA HILLS NATIONAL RESERVE

This national reserve is in the hills behind the coast south of Mombasa, directly inland from Diani Beach. The forest setting is beautiful but the game is not prolific. There is a baited water hole at the Shimba Hills Lodge, and so it's possible you'll see leopards and plenty of elephants but not much else. Other animals which frequent the reserve include the rare sable antelope – a tall and compact animal with beautifully curved horns on both the male and female. The adult bull is a dark brown on the upper body and white below, while the female is a lighter brown. The animals are, unfortunately, often killed by poachers for meat, and this is the only reserve where they are found.

Entry to the reserve costs US$20 (US$5 for children) for nonresidents.

Places to Stay

The camp site has a superb location on the edge of the range with views right down to Diani Beach. It's about three km from the main gate, which itself is about three km from the village of Kwale. Camping charges are KSh 200 per person.

The only alternative to camping is Block Hotels' *Shimba Hills Lodge* (☎ (02) 540780 in Nairobi) where singles/doubles with half board cost US$44/88 in the low season (9 April to 30 June) and US$71/142 in the high season. Note that children under seven years old are not admitted to this lodge, and that children over seven pay full rates. The water hole here is baited to attract a few animals and is floodlit at night.

Getting There & Away

There are KBS buses to Kwale, from where it shouldn't be too difficult to hitch to the park entrance. Once there, however, you may have a long wait for a vehicle back. The road from Kwale to Kinango, the next inland town, actually passes through the northern part of the park and there's a chance of seeing animals from the KBS buses. The No 34 bus runs from Likoni to Kwale.

TANA RIVER PRIMATE NATIONAL RESERVE

Well south of Garissa and not too far north of Garsen is the Tana River Primate National Reserve which, as its name suggests, is a reserve for a number of endangered monkey species. It's possible to get close to the sanctuary by public transport but there's still a lot of walking involved and the facilities have long fallen into disrepair so you need to take everything with you. Very few safari companies include the reserve on their itineraries. Check with Let's Go Travel (☎ (02) 340331) to see if they still provide for a visit to this sanctuary on one of its safaris.

TSAVO NATIONAL PARK

At just over 20,000 sq km, Tsavo is the largest national park in Kenya, and for administrative purposes it has been split into Tsavo West National Park, with an area of 8500 sq km, and Tsavo East National Park, which covers 11,000 sq km.

The northern area of Tsavo West, west of the Nairobi–Mombasa A109 road, is the most developed and has some excellent scenery. It is particularly beautiful at the end of the wet season when things are green; at other times of the year it tends to get very dusty in Tsavo. Tsavo East consists of vast rolling plains with scrubby vegetation. Almost the entire area north of the Galana River (and this constitutes the bulk of the park) is off limits to the general public. This is due to the ongoing campaign against poachers, who still find the relative remoteness of Tsavo a good prospect. Happily it seems the authorities are winning the battle, but in the meantime the rhino population has been absolutely decimated – from around 8000 in 1970 to less than 200 today.

By Kenyan standards, Tsavo sees relatively few visitors, which means for those that do visit there is none of the congestion found in other parks and reserves.

Information

Entry to the park is US$23 per person per day. Note that the two parks are administered separately, and to visit both parks you'll need to pay separate entrance fees.

All track junctions in Tsavo West have a numbered and signposted cairn, which in theory makes navigation fairly simple. In practice, however, the cairns are not all there (especially in the little-visited southern reaches of the park), and those which are there don't always give comprehensive directions. It's also difficult to find a map which marks these numbered intersections and therefore gives you some clue as to where you are. The Macmillan map is about the best. To their credit, the Kenya Wildlife Services are in the process of redoing all these cairns, and, once completed, navigation with a reliable map will be easy.

Don't attempt this park without 4WD if you intend to get off the main routes. You can certainly get to Kilaguni Lodge and Ngulia Lodge on the main service road from Mtito Andei in a 2WD but you'll get into strife and possibly get hopelessly stuck on the minor tracks. You will not make it to the above lodges in a 2WD if you enter through the Tsavo Gate further south unless you're a rally driver and/or willing to risk damaging the car. There are some diabolical sections on this access road; the lava flows along here will rip the underside of any normal car apart.

Fuel is available at Kilaguni and Ngulia lodges in Tsavo West.

Tsavo West National Park

The focus here is the watering holes by the Kilaguni and Ngulia lodges. The one at Kilaguni is the better of the two and attracts huge varieties of animals and birds, particularly during the dry season when water may be scarce elsewhere.

The **Mzima Springs** are not far from Kilaguni Lodge and the pools here are favourite haunts of both the hippo and crocodile. The much vaunted underwater viewing chamber was designed to give you a view of the hippos' submarine activities, but the hippos have retreated to the far end of the pool. There are, however, plenty of fish to be observed. The springs are the source of the bulk of Mombasa's fresh water and there is a direct pipeline from here to the coast.

Also in the area of the lodges is the spectacular **Shetani lava flow** and **caves**. Both are worth investigating, though for the caves you'll need to exercise caution and carry a torch (flashlight). The black lava flow is very spectacular and is actually outside the Chyulu Gate on the track which leads to Amboseli.

The **Chaimu Crater** just south of Kilaguni Lodge can also be climbed. It's worth remembering while walking on any of these nature trails that the park animals are far from tame, and while there's little danger, you do need to keep your eyes on what's happening around you. These nature trails are also the only places where you are permitted to get out of the vehicle.

Another attraction in Tsavo West is the **Ngulia Rhino Sanctuary**, at the base of Ngulia Hills, not far from the Ngulia Lodge. Here 70 sq km has been surrounded by a metre-high electric fence, and 30 black rhinos now live here in relative security. There are tracks within the enclosed area and there's a good chance of seeing one of these elusive creatures.

Places to Stay – bottom end Tsavo West has a number of basic camp sites, namely at each of the three main gates (Tsavo, Mtito Andei and Chyulu). The fees to use these are KSh 150 per person.

The self-service accommodation at the *Ngulia Safari Camp* and the *Kitani Safari Camp* is, by park standards, quite cheap at KSh 500 per person (minimum charge of KSh 2000 per banda) in the fully equipped bandas but you must bring all your own food

Note: Most of Tsavo East National Park north of Galana River is closed to the general public

Tsavo East & West National Parks

0   15   30 km

and drink with you or eat at one of the lodges. The Kitani Camp is in the north-western part of the park, and while it's not the best location, is well set up. The Ngulia camp is perched on the edge of the Ngulia Hills, and with its elevation has some fine views. Both camps consist of one-bedroom bandas with bedding, towels, mosquito nets, bathroom, a fully equipped kitchen, and kerosene lanterns. Take with you toilet paper, washing-up liquid, soap, matches, drinking water and an ice box. For reservations at either camp, contact Let's Go Travel (☎ (02) 340331; fax 336890 in Nairobi).

Places to Stay – top end The *Ngulia Lodge* is part of the African Tours & Hotels group (☎ (02) 336858; fax 218109). It's not the most attractive of lodges but it is comfortable and the views are excellent. Singles/doubles with full board cost US$120/150 in the high season and US$60/120 in the low season. The water hole here is small but there's a leopard which visits each evening to pick up

NATIONAL PARKS & RESERVES

Kilaguni Lodge

The lodge is beautifully situated looking out over the rolling hills. The large water hole, floodlit at night, is right in front of the lodge and you can sit in the bar or restaurant, or on the verandah in front of your room, and watch the wildlife. You can even lie in bed with your binoculars to hand – every room faces a water hole. All this luxury, including a swimming pool and lush garden, doesn't come cheap, but where else do you need a pair of binoculars and a field guide at hand while you eat?

We arrive in time for lunch and watch the comings and goings at the water hole. To the left there are impala and a couple of waterbuck; back from the water there's a small group of ostrich, and off to the right there's a herd of oryx. Marabou storks lounge around in the foreground while right in front of the restaurant are groups of smaller birds and mongoose. There's so much activity it's hard to concentrate on lunch – and this is just after the wet season when the game are less concentrated at the water holes!

The scene is only spoilt by the idiots who persist, in spite of numerous posted warnings, in throwing bread out to the animals. This has already taught some of the storks (notoriously efficient scavengers) to line up in front of the restaurant wall. It would be all too easy to turn this wonderful scene into a cheap zoo with animals begging for hand-outs. This is the same Africa of Ethiopia and Mozambique and there's something obscene about dumb tourists hurling whole bread rolls just for amusement and a better shot with the Instamatic.

After lunch we watch from the verandah of our room – some zebra and two more ostriches appear but all the storks have left and gradually the animals wander off as the afternoon wears on. By 4.30 pm there's only the solitary waterbuck left; even the ostriches finally troop off in a stately line.

Down at the northern end of the lodge grounds is a tree full of weaver-bird nests with twittering hordes of these bright yellow birds furiously at work. Some of their nests, mainly older ones, have fallen out of the tree, and on close examination they are amazingly intricate and neatly woven; coconut-sized with a funnel-like entrance underneath. Right in front of our room a small squad of mongoose appears, cavorts around for a few minutes, then wanders away. By 5 pm it's baboon time again and the tribe wanders down to the water hole again for their evening visit. A few of them come up to our room to hassle us but soon give up. Rock hyrax scamper around, one even coming right into our room, and the mongoose come and go. Gradually the impala reappear.

Dinner time, unhappily, is the one blot on the perfect experience. Once again there are the idiotic food hurlers at work and a hyena trots up and waits expectantly for hand-outs, joined by a slender mongoose-like genet. With much shouting, loud conversation and cameras flashing madly there's a distinct theatre-restaurant feel to the whole meal and we're glad to get back to the quiet of our rooms.

The baboons leave soon after dark and by bedtime it's basically the impala and zebra. I get up several times in the night to check what's out but, apart from bats swooping around, the scene seems static until dawn. The impala keep watch all night long.

At dawn the zebra wander off, the oryx reappear, the whole baboon tribe wanders back and immediately start carousing merrily. A couple of pairs of impala bucks square off for a morning duel and the whole cycle starts again.

Although we didn't see elephants or lions we still enjoyed every minute of it. Now if only they could put those 'don't feed the animals signs' on every table…

Tony Wheeler

meat strung up on a dead tree outside the patio. Elephants are also regular evening visitors to the lodge's waterhole.

The *Kilaguni Lodge* is owned by the same hotel group and costs exactly the same, and the main attraction here is also the water hole which attracts a wide variety of game. It's a more attractive lodge than the Ngulia and there are extensive views of the Chyulu Hills out to the north-west. See the separate boxed story.

In a fairly isolated spot on the western boundary of the park and almost on the Tanzanian border, the *Lake Jipe Lodge* (☎ (02) 227623; fax 218376) is one of the cheaper places but it's a long way from anywhere else. Once again, the views are excellent; this time it's the Pare Mountains just across the border in Tanzania. As well as game drives, it's also possible to take a dhow ride on nearby Lake Jipe for KSh 750 per person. Accommodation costs US$100/160 for full board.

Also tucked away is *Ziwani*, a permanent tented camp on the bank of the Tsavo River and just outside the boundaries of the national park.

If you don't have the money to stay at one of the lodges in the park but don't want to camp or go to the trouble of organising your own food, etc for one of the self-catering camps, then you have options though they involve staying just outside the park boundaries at Mtito Andei on the main Nairobi to Mombasa road.

Right opposite the Mtito Andei Gate is the *Tsavo Inn* (☎ (014) 30217) which is fairly pleasant but otherwise unremarkable. Singles/doubles with breakfast cost KSh 2080/2600, but there seems little reason to stay.

Mtito Andei also has plenty of cheap and basic 'boardings & lodgings' if you need them.

Better is the *Hunter's Lodge* (☎ (0302) 22469) at Kiboko, 85 km from Mtito Andei on the main Nairobi to Mombasa road. The lodge's outdoor *Tilapia Springs Restaurant* is a popular lunch stop for tour groups, and the food is priced accordingly. Room rates are KSh 990/1670 including tax. Breakfast costs KSh 320, lunch or dinner KSh 415.

Getting There & Away The main access to Tsavo West is through the Mtito Andei Gate on the Mombasa–Nairobi road near the northern end of the park. The park headquarters is here and there's a camp site. From the gate it's 31 km to the Kilaguni Lodge.

A further 48 km along the main road away from Nairobi is the Tsavo Gate, where there's another camp site. This gate is 75 km from the Kilaguni area, so if you're hitching the Mtito Andei Gate is much closer and far busier. It's also worth taking into consideration the diabolical state of certain sections of the road between the Tsavo Gate and the lodges.

From Voi there is access past the Hilton-owned Taita Hills and Salt Lick lodges via the Maktau Gate. This road cuts clear across the park, exiting at the Mbuyuni Gate, to Taveta from where it's possible to cross into Tanzania and the town of Moshi at the foot of Kilimanjaro.

There's also a road running west from the Chyulu Gate which connects Tsavo West with Amboseli. This is a popular route with groups from Mombasa, but because of problems with bandits, all vehicles must travel in convoy, and an armed policeman rides in the first and last vehicles. However, within minutes of setting off the safari bus drivers have bolted at a million miles an hour and the convoy is spread out over many km. The convoys leave daily from the Chyulu Gate at 8.30 and 10.30 am, and at 2.30 pm. The trip to Amboseli takes a couple of hours.

Tsavo East National Park

The southern third of this park is open to the public and the rolling scrub-covered hills are home to large herds of elephants, usually covered in red dust.

The **Kanderi Swamp**, not far into the park from the main Voi Gate and park headquarters, is home to a profusion of wildlife and there's a camp site here. Further into the park, 30 km from the gate, is the main attraction in this part of the park, the **Aruba Dam** built across the Voi River. Here too you'll encounter a wide variety of game without the

NATIONAL PARKS & RESERVES

usual hordes of tourists – very few people visit Tsavo East.

Places to Stay – bottom end There are camp sites at the Voi Gate, Kanderi Swamp *(Ndololo Campsite)*, Aruba Lodge and the *Mukwaju Campsite* on the Voi River 50 km in from the main gate.

Places to Stay – top end The *Voi Safari Lodge* (clearly signposted in the town of Voi) is part of the African Tours & Hotels group (☎ (02) 336858; fax 218109) and is five km inside the park from the Voi Gate. As you might imagine, things are a good deal more peaceful here than at the lodges in Tsavo West. Singles/doubles with full board cost US$150/200 in the high season. In the low season they are US$60/120.

The nicest place to stay is the *Tsavo Safari Camp*, run by the Kilimanjaro Safari Club (☎ (02) 338888; fax 219982), in a beautifully shady spot on the banks of the Athi River. Vehicles are left on the west bank of the river (guarded parking), and guests are shuttled across in rubber rafts. The camp is very peaceful and is a great place to chill out for a few days. There's a swimming pool, and game drives can be arranged for the energetic. Access to the lodge, which lies 27 km off the main Nairobi–Mombasa road, is from Mtito Andei; the turn-off is well signposted, one km out of town towards Mombasa. To stay in the well set-up permanent tents costs US$50/100 for full board in the low season, rising to US$152/190 in the high season.

Getting There & Away The main access point and the park headquarters is Voi Gate near Voi off the Nairobi–Mombasa road. Further north near the Tsavo Gate entrance of Tsavo West is the Manyani Gate. The murram (dirt) road from here cuts straight across to the Galana River and follows the river clear across the park, exiting at Sala Gate on the eastern side, a distance of 100 km. From Sala Gate it's a further 110 km to Malindi.

AROUND TSAVO
Taita Hills

The Taita Hills to the west of the main Nairobi–Mombasa road cover a vast area and are scenically spectacular. They have the status of a game reserve despite the fact that the main Voi–Taveta road and railway line pass through it on the southern side. Game is prolific in this area and you can even see plenty of it along the road to Taveta. There are also two up-market Hilton lodges on the south-western side – the Taita Hills Lodge and the Salt Lick Lodge.

Places to Stay The *Taita Hills Lodge* and the *Salt Lick Lodge*, are both owned by the Hilton Hotel in Nairobi (☎ (02) 334000; fax 339462), and the charge is US$193/225 in the low season; US$236/268 in the high season.

Getting There & Away There are matatus from Voi to Wundanyi (in the heart of the Taita Hills) for KSh 60, and both trains (five hours) and matatus (2½ hours) from Voi to Taveta for KSh 150. The trains and matatus from Voi to Taveta will get you close to the lodges but, if you can afford to stay there, you'll probably be in your own vehicle anyway.

Voi

The town of Voi was once described by a Peace Corps volunteer who worked there as, 'an attractive spaghetti western-like setting surrounded by hills that are good for hiking and catching expansive views of the surrounding plains'. That's close to the truth but it's not Maralal and a lot of development is going on. Nevertheless, it's a pleasant, small town and worth considering as a base for exploring the Taita Hills and Tsavo National Park or even as an overnight stop between Mombasa and Nairobi.

The cheapest place to stay with decent facilities is *Johari's Guest House* (☎ (0147) 2079) where singles/doubles go for KSh 200/350 with shared bath. They also show videos here each evening starting at 7.30 pm.

The *Voi Restpoint Hotel* (☎ (0147) 2079)

Voi

Scale Unknown

1 Caltex Petrol Station
2 Town Hall
3 Vuria's Bar & Lodging
4 KCB
5 Kahn Silent Guest House
6 Johari's Guest House
7 Market
8 BP Petrol Station
9 Bus & Matatu Stand
10 Voi Restpoint Hotel
11 Tsavo Chips & Chicken
12 Post Office
13 Total Petrol Station
14 Train Station

is the only budget hotel with rooms with attached bathrooms including fan and telephone. Singles/doubles with breakfast cost KSh 350/500. There are three restaurants in the hotel, including one on the rooftop.

Slightly more expensive is the *Kahn Silent Guest House* (☎ (0147) 2058), on Moi Hospital Rd opposite the Kenya Commercial Bank. It has singles/doubles for KSh 250/ 350.

Up in price is *Vuria's Bar & Lodging*, opposite the town hall, which offers rooms with attached bathrooms for KSh 300/400 including breakfast.

All the guesthouses have reasonable restaurants plus there's *Tsavo Chips & Chicken* at the matatu stand. The *Bird's Cafe* next to the bus and matatu stand is also worth a try.

Out on the main Nairobi–Mombasa road at the roundabout is the Caltex petrol station which has a whole complex of shops, fast-food outlets and a bar. The food here is OK and very reasonably priced, plus beers in the bar are ice-cold.

Getting There & Away There are plenty of buses and matatus to both Nairobi (five hours) and Mombasa (two hours). They also run regularly to Taveta, on the Tanzanian border.

There is also a weekly (Saturday) train which connects Voi with Moshi in Tanzania. The journey takes five hours, and the train returns the same day. See the Getting There & Away chapter for full details.

Glossary

The following are words you are likely to come across when in Kenya. For a glossary of food terms see page 75.

askari – security guard, watchman

banda – thatched hut with wooden or earthen walls
boma – village
bui-bui – black cover-all garment worn by Islamic women outside the home

chai – tea, but also a bribe
chakula – food
choo – toilet (pronounced as 'cho')

duka – small shop or kiosk selling household basics

fundi – repair man/woman (eg clothing, building trades, cars etc)

hakuna matata – no problem. (Watch out – there often is!)
Harambee – the concept of community self-help – voluntary fund-raising; a cornerstone of Kenyatta's ideology

jinga! – crazy! (Also used as an adjective.)
jua kali – literally, 'hot sun'; usually an outdoor vehicle repair shop or market

kanga – printed cotton wrap-around incorporating a Swahili proverb; worn by many women both inside and outside the home. A *kikoi* is similar.
kiondas – woven baskets
kitu kidogo – 'a little something': a bribe

lugga – dry river bed, mainly in northern Kenya

makonde – wood carving
makuti – roof made of palm leaves, mainly on the coast
malaya – prostitute
manamba – matatu tout, often a veritable Daddy Cool
mandazi – semisweet, flat doughnut
manyatta – Maasai or Samburu livestock camp often surrounded by a circle of thorn bushes
matatu – minibus with mega-decibel sound system, seemingly unlimited carrying capacity and two speeds – stationary and flat out
moran – Maasai or Samburu warrior (pl *morani)*
murram – dirt or part-gravelled road
mwananchi – worker of any kind but usually agricultural (pl *wananchi*, which is also used to refer to 'the people')
mzee kipara – 'mosquito airport' (bald man)
mzungu – white person (pl *wazungu)*

Nyayo – 'footsteps'. One of the cornerstones of Moi's political ideology; in other words, to follow in the footsteps of Kenyatta.

panga – machete, carried by most people in the countryside and, often, by thieves in the cities
parking boys – unemployed youths/young men who offer various services
pesa – money

safari – journey
shamba – small farm or plot of land
shifta – bandit
shilingi – money

taka taka – rubbish

Uhuru – freedom or independence

Index

MAPS

BOXED STORIES

TEXT

LONELY PLANET JOURNEYS

JOURNEYS is a unique collection of travel writing – published by the company that understands travel better than anyone else. It is a series for anyone who has ever experienced – or dreamed of – the magical moment when they encountered a strange culture or saw a place for the first time. They are tales to read while you're planning a trip, while you're on the road or while you're in an armchair, in front of a fire.

JOURNEYS books catch the spirit of a place, illuminate a culture, recount a crazy adventure, or introduce a fascinating way of life. They always entertain, and always enrich the experience of travel.

THE RAINBIRD
A Central African Journey
Jan Brokken
translated by Sam Garrett

The Rainbird is a classic travel story. Following in the footsteps of famous Europeans such as Albert Schweitzer and H.M. Stanley, Jan Brokken journeyed to Gabon in central Africa. A kaleidoscope of adventures and anecdotes, *The Rainbird* brilliantly chronicles the encounter between Africa and Europe as it was acted out on a side-street of history. It is also the compelling, immensely readable account of the author's own travels in one of the most remote and mysterious regions of Africa.

Jan Brokken is one of Holland's best known writers. In addition to travel narratives and literary journalism, he has published several novels and short stories. Many of his works are set in Africa, where he has travelled widely.

SONGS TO AN AFRICAN SUNSET
A Zimbabwean Story
Sekai Nzenza-Shand

Songs to an African Sunset braids vividly personal stories into an intimate picture of contemporary Zimbabwe. Returning to her family's village after many years in the West, Sekai Nzenza-Shand discovers a world where ancestor worship, polygamy and witchcraft still govern the rhythms of daily life – and where drought, deforestation and AIDS have wrought devastating changes. With insight and affection, she explores a culture torn between respect for the old ways and the irresistible pull of the new.

Sekai Nzenza-Shand was born in Zimbabwe and has lived in England and Australia. Her first novel, *Zimbabwean Woman: My Own Story*, was published in London in 1988 and her fiction has been included in the short story collections *Daughters of Africa* and *Images of the West*. Sekai currently lives in Zimbabwe.

LONELY PLANET PHRASEBOOKS

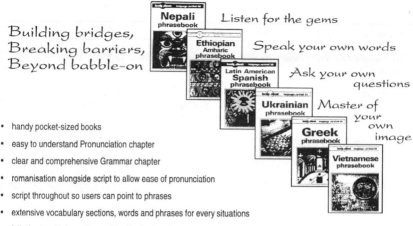

Building bridges,
Breaking barriers,
Beyond babble-on

Listen for the gems

Speak your own words

Ask your own questions

Master of your own image

- handy pocket-sized books
- easy to understand Pronunciation chapter
- clear and comprehensive Grammar chapter
- romanisation alongside script to allow ease of pronunciation
- script throughout so users can point to phrases
- extensive vocabulary sections, words and phrases for every situations
- full of cultural information and tips for the traveller

'...vital for a real DIY spirit and attitude in language learning' – Backpacker

'the phrasebooks have good cultural backgrounders and offer solid advice for challenging situations in remote locations' – San Francisco Examiner

'...they are unbeatable for their coverage of the world's more obscure languages' – The Geographical Magazine

---

Arabic (Egyptian)
Arabic (Moroccan)
Australia
  Australian English, Aboriginal and Torres Strait languages
Baltic States
  Estonian, Latvian, Lithuanian
Bengali
Burmese
Brazilian
Cantonese
Central Europe
  Czech, French, German, Hungarian, Italian and Slovak
Eastern Europe
  Bulgarian, Czech, Hungarian, Polish, Romanian and Slovak
Egyptian Arabic
Ethiopian (Amharic)
Fijian
French
German
Greek

Hindi/Urdu
Indonesian
Italian
Japanese
Korean
Lao
Latin American Spanish
Malay
Mandarin
Mediterranean Europe
  Albanian, Croatian, Greek, Italian, Macedonian, Maltese, Serbian, Slovene
Mongolian
Moroccan Arabic
Nepali
Papua New Guinea
Pilipino (Tagalog)
Quechua
Russian
Scandinavian Europe
  Danish, Finnish, Icelandic, Norwegian and Swedish

South-East Asia
  Burmese, Indonesian, Khmer, Lao, Malay, Tagalog (Pilipino), Thai and Vietnamese
Spanish
Sri Lanka
Swahili
Thai
Thai Hill Tribes
Tibetan
Turkish
Ukrainian
USA
  US English, Vernacular Talk, Native American languages and Hawaiian
Vietnamese
Western Europe
  Basque, Catalan, Dutch, French, German, Irish, Italian, Portuguese, Scottish Gaelic, Spanish (Castilian) and Welsh

---

LONELY PLANET TRAVEL ATLASES

Lonely Planet has long been famous for the number and quality of its guidebook maps. Now we've gone one step further and in conjunction with Steinhart Katzir Publishers produced a handy companion series: Lonely Planet travel atlases – maps of a country produced in book form.

Unlike other maps, which look good but lead travellers astray, our travel atlases have been researched on the road by Lonely Planet's experienced team of writers. All details are carefully checked to ensure the atlas corresponds with the equivalent Lonely Planet guidebook.

The handy atlas format means no holes, wrinkles, torn sections or constant folding and unfolding. These atlases can survive long periods on the road, unlike cumbersome fold-out maps. The comprehensive index ensures easy reference.

- full-colour throughout
- maps researched and checked by Lonely Planet authors
- place names correspond with Lonely Planet guidebooks
  – no confusing spelling differences
- legend and travelling information in English, French, German, Japanese and Spanish
- size: 230 x 160 mm

Available now:
Chile & Easter Island • Egypt • India & Bangladesh • Israel & the Palestinian Territories •Jordan, Syria & Lebanon • Kenya • Laos • Portugal • South Africa, Lesotho & Swaziland • Thailand • Turkey • Vietnam • Zimbabwe, Botswana & Namibia

---

LONELY PLANET TV SERIES & VIDEOS

Lonely Planet travel guides have been brought to life on television screens around the world. Like our guides, the programmes are based on the joy of independent travel, and look honestly at some of the most exciting, picturesque and frustrating places in the world. Each show is presented by one of three travellers from Australia, England or the USA and combines an innovative mixture of video, Super-8 film, atmospheric soundscapes and original music.

Videos of each episode – containing additional footage not shown on television – are available from good book and video shops, but the availability of individual videos varies with regional screening schedules.

Video destinations include: Alaska • American Rockies • Australia – The South-East • Baja California & the Copper Canyon • Brazil • Central Asia • Chile & Easter Island • Corsica, Sicily & Sardinia – The Mediterranean Islands • East Africa (Tanzania & Zanzibar) • Ecuador & the Galapagos Islands • Greenland & Iceland • Indonesia • Israel & the Sinai Desert • Jamaica • Japan • La Ruta Maya • Morocco • New York • North India • Pacific Islands (Fiji, Solomon Islands & Vanuatu) • South India • South West China • Turkey • Vietnam • West Africa • Zimbabwe, Botswana & Namibia

The Lonely Planet TV series is produced by:
Pilot Productions
The Old Studio
18 Middle Row
London W10 5AT UK

For video availability and ordering information contact your nearest Lonely Planet office.

Music from the TV series is available on CD & cassette.

PLANET TALK

Lonely Planet's FREE quarterly newsletter

We love hearing from you and think you'd like to hear from us.

When...is the right time to see reindeer in Finland?
Where...can you hear the best palm-wine music in Ghana?
How...do you get from Asunción to Areguá by steam train?
What...is the best way to see India?

For the answer to these and many other questions read PLANET TALK.

Every issue is packed with up-to-date travel news and advice including:

* a letter from Lonely Planet co-founders Tony and Maureen Wheeler
* go behind the scenes on the road with a Lonely Planet author
* feature article on an important and topical travel issue
* a selection of recent letters from travellers
* details on forthcoming Lonely Planet promotions
* complete list of Lonely Planet products

To join our mailing list contact any Lonely Planet office.

Also available: Lonely Planet T-shirts. 100% heavyweight cotton.

LONELY PLANET ONLINE

Get the latest travel information before you leave or while you're on the road

Whether you've just begun planning your next trip, or you're chasing down specific info on currency regulations or visa requirements, check out Lonely Planet Online for up-to-the-minute travel information.

As well as travel profiles of your favourite destinations (including maps and photos), you'll find current reports from our researchers and other travellers, updates on health and visas, travel advisories, and discussion of the ecological and political issues you need to be aware of as you travel.

There's also an online travellers' forum where you can share your experience of life on the road, meet travel companions and ask other travellers for their recommendations and advice. We also have plenty of links to other online sites useful to independent travellers.

And of course we have a complete and up-to-date list of all Lonely Planet travel products including guides, phrasebooks, atlases, Journeys and videos and a simple online ordering facility if you can't find the book you want elsewhere.

www.lonelyplanet.com
or
AOL keyword: lp

LONELY PLANET PRODUCTS

Lonely Planet is known worldwide for publishing practical, reliable and no-nonsense travel information in our guides and on our web site. The Lonely Planet list covers just about every accessible part of the world. Currently there are nine series: *travel guides, shoestring guides, walking guides, city guides, phrasebooks, audio packs, travel atlases, Journeys – a unique collection of travel writing and Pisces Books - diving and snorkeling guides.*

EUROPE

Amsterdam • Austria • Baltic States phrasebook • Berlin • Britain • Canary Islands• Central Europe on a shoestring • Central Europe phrasebook • Czech & Slovak Republics • Denmark • Dublin • Eastern Europe on a shoestring • Eastern Europe phrasebook • Estonia, Latvia & Lithuania • Finland • France • French phrasebook • Germany • German phrasebook • Greece • Greek phrasebook • Hungary • Iceland, Greenland & the Faroe Islands • Ireland • Italian phrasebook • Italy • Lisbon • London • Mediterranean Europe on a shoestring • Mediterranean Europe phrasebook • Paris • Poland • Portugal • Portugal travel atlas • Prague • Romania & Moldova • Russia, Ukraine & Belarus • Russian phrasebook • Scandinavian & Baltic Europe on a shoestring • Scandinavian Europe phrasebook • Slovenia • Spain • Spanish phrasebook • St Petersburg • Switzerland •Trekking in Spain • Ukrainian phrasebook • Vienna • Walking in Britain • Walking in Italy • Walking in Switzerland • Western Europe on a shoestring • Western Europe phrasebook

Travel Literature: The Olive Grove: Travels in Greece

NORTH AMERICA

Alaska • Backpacking in Alaska • Baja California • California & Nevada • Canada • Chicago • Deep South• Florida • Hawaii • Honolulu • Los Angeles • Mexico • Mexico City • Miami • New England • New Orleans • New York City • New York, New Jersey & Pennsylvania • Pacific Northwest USA • Rocky Mountain States • San Francisco • Southwest USA • USA phrasebook • Washington, DC & the Capital Region

Travel Literature: Drive thru America

CENTRAL AMERICA & THE CARIBBEAN

•Bahamas and Turks & Caicos •Bermuda •Central America on a shoestring • Costa Rica • Cuba •Eastern Caribbean •Guatemala, Belize & Yucatán: La Ruta Maya • Jamaica

SOUTH AMERICA

Argentina, Uruguay & Paraguay • Bolivia • Brazil • Brazilian phrasebook • Buenos Aires • Chile & Easter Island • Chile & Easter Island travel atlas • Colombia Ecuador & the Galápagos Islands • Latin American Spanish phrasebook • Peru • Quechua phrasebook • Rio de Janeiro • South America on a shoestring • Trekking in the Patagonian Andes • Venezuela

Travel Literature: Full Circle: A South American Journey

ISLANDS OF THE INDIAN OCEAN

Madagascar & Comoros • Maldives• Mauritius, Réunion & Seychelles

AFRICA

Africa - the South • Africa on a shoestring • Arabic (Moroccan) phrasebook • Cairo • Cape Town • Central Africa • East Africa • Egypt • Egypt travel atlas• Ethiopian (Amharic) phrasebook • Kenya • Kenya travel atlas • Malawi, Mozambique & Zambia • Morocco • North Africa • South Africa, Lesotho & Swaziland • South Africa, Lesotho & Swaziland travel atlas • Swahili phrasebook • Tunisia • Trekking in East Africa • West Africa • Zimbabwe, Botswana & Namibia • Zimbabwe, Botswana & Namibia travel atlas

Travel Literature: The Rainbird: A Central African Journey • Songs to an African Sunset: A Zimbabwean Story